"Not only does Harley Hahn know more about the Internet than should be allowed by law, he actually makes learning fun. If the original yellow pages were this entertaining, I'd spend my spare time reading the phone book."

— *Alan Colmes*
National radio talk show host

"*The Internet Yellow Pages* is an excellent guide to the Internet for Net users of any level. With this book, you will be able to find whatever information you need, quickly and easily. A terrific reference to have sitting beside your desk late at night. The completeness of this book will surprise even the most seasoned Net user."

— *Bill Schwartz*
System Manager, Auggie BBS and BBSLIST
Network Manager, 3M Corporation

"The Internet is the world's largest information appliance, and *The Internet Yellow Pages* is your handbook for the 1990s. Welcome to the largest resource of human knowledge ever accumulated: just be sure to keep the *Yellow Pages* handy."

— *Iain Lea*
Creator of the tin Usenet newsreader
Engineer and programmer, Siemens AG

"Harley Hahn's *The Internet Yellow Pages* promises indeed to be the book that gets used. It's the best reference list of Internet services we've ever seen."

— *Jack Rickard*
Publisher, Boardwatch *Magazine*

"In the hotel rooms of the near future — in between the Gideon Bible and the modem jack — there will be a copy of *The Internet Yellow Pages*. What a fun book! Harley Hahn is the wizard of the Internet."

— *Jean Armour Polly*
Author of Surfing the Internet, *Director of User Services, NYSERNet*

"It's amazing how much information is freely available on the Internet. But to make use of it, you have to know where to find what you want. *The Internet Yellow Pages* is just the book to help you. Well organized, comprehensive, and fun to browse — this book will show you how to find everything from obscure song lyrics to Woody Allen jokes to the first million digits of PI."

— *Joe Halpern*
Research Staff Member, IBM Almaden Research Center
Consulting Professor, Stanford University, Computer Science Department

"This book has replaced all the scraps of paper with my notes about the tons of important things I have found around the Net. Now whenever anyone asks me where something is, I just look it up in *The Internet Yellow Pages* (which is always next to my terminal). My advice is to sit down with this book — and about 10 hours of spare time — and start exploring."

— *Lee Brintle*
System Manager, University of Iowa Campus-Wide Information System
Director of Project Panda

"As an information specialist, I pride myself on keeping up with the Internet's vast resources. *The Internet Yellow Pages* contains everything I expected and a whole lot more. This book is unique, comprehensive, indispensable — and funny. I lug it around with me wherever I go, and so will you."

— Mary A. Axford, MLS
Reference Librarian, Georgia Institute of Technology

"Imagine what it would be like if we didn't have the telephone Yellow Pages and you couldn't find a plumber on Christmas Eve. Having this book is like being handed a wrench when you are knee deep in water. *The Internet Yellow Pages* is a *must-have* for anyone attempting to use the Internet."

— Maureen O'Gara
Publisher, Unigram•X *and* Client Server NEWS

"Once again Harley Hahn has shown himself to be a member of that rare breed: a writer who is at once informative and entertaining. *The Internet Yellow Pages* contains an astonishing amount of Net-related information in a style that is both clear and enjoyable. I recommend this massive directory of resources to anyone who is interested in exploring the Internet in all its curious charm."

— Michael Tucker
Executive Editor, Sun Expert *Magazine*

"This is a great book to skim through while you're downloading files from the Internet, and then you'll find other files you have to download, and faster than you can double grains of wheat on the squares of a checker board you'll have no life, and soon after that you'll have no time to read the stuff you downloaded before you had this goddamn book."

— Penn "informationsuperhighwayhangin'" Jillette
Magician and humorist (the big one of Penn and Teller)

"This trailblazing work has been sorely needed. A truly inspired solution to the vast tangle of information the Internet is becoming. What a COOL book to add to anyone's library!"

— Simona Nass
President, The Society for Electronic Access

I have introduced countless people to the Internet, and the first thing they ask me is: Where's the cool stuff? I tell them: My personal favorite Net resource is *The Internet Yellow Pages*. This is the place *I* go to when I need to find out where I can talk to people about Spam.

— Stacy Horn
Founder and President of Echo (East Coast Hang Out)
Professor, New York University, Interactive Telecommunications Program

"This book is essential for every Internet user. You need it. Buy it.

—Sara Rushniek
Professor of Computer Information, University of Miami

THE INTERNET YELLOW PAGES

Harley Hahn
and
Rick Stout

Osborne McGraw-Hill

Berkeley New York St. Louis San Francisco Auckland Bogotá Hamburg London
Madrid Mexico City Milan Montreal New Delhi Panama City Paris São Paulo
Singapore Sydney Tokyo Toronto

THE INTERNET YELLOW PAGES

OSBORNE McGRAW-HILL
2600 TENTH STREET
BERKELEY
CALIFORNIA 94710
U.S.A.

For information on translations or book distributors outside of the U.S.A., please write to Osborne **McGraw-Hill** at the above address.

Copyright © 1994 by Harley Hahn. All rights reserved. Printed in the United States of America. Except as permitted under the Copyright Act of 1976, no part of this publication may be reproduced or distributed in any form or by any means, or stored in a database or retrieval system, without the prior written permission of the publisher, with the exception that the program listings may be entered, stored, and executed in a computer system, but they may not be reproduced for publication.

234567890 DOC 9987654

ISBN 0-07-882023-5

Information has been obtained by Osborne **McGraw-Hill** from sources believed to be reliable. However, because of the possibility of human or mechanical error by our sources, Osborne **McGraw-Hill**, or others, Osborne **McGraw-Hill** does not guarantee the accuracy, adequacy, or completeness of any information and is not responsible for any errors or omissions or the results obtained from the use of such information.

To my wonderful wife and best friend, Kimberlyn.

—Harley Hahn

To the two beautiful women in my life: My wife Dawn and my daughter Jenna.

—Rick Stout

Table of Contents

Introduction

This book will change the way that you think about the world.

Even more important, this book will change the way that you think about people and how we exist as a species.

How can this be? After all, this book is really just a large catalog, and what could be so important about a catalog?

Well, take a look at the list of categories on the back cover, and you will see that virtually every important type of human activity is represented. Indeed, this book contains descriptions of thousands of separate items, grouped into over 150 different categories.

The importance of all this is not so much in the details, but in the fact that it even exists at all. Not long ago, most of what you see in this book had not yet been created. A few years ago, none of it existed. But what does it all mean to *you*?...

Imagine yourself exploring. You walk for days through hot steamy jungles, you climb over rocky hills and through canyons; you drag yourself across an endless arid plain until, one day, you look at the horizon and see what looks like a city. As you approach, you see that it is not really a city but — whatever it is — it is vast beyond description: more buildings, vehicles, works of art, and so on, than you have ever seen or even imagined.

You spend many hours exploring, always finding something new, something challenging, and something delightful. Being a stranger, you feel confused and, much of the time you find yourself wandering haphazardly. Once in a while you see a bit of a pattern and, for an instant, you make some sense out of the immediate neighborhood. But for the most part, you wander from place to place in a cloud of distraction and fascination. What makes it all so frustrating is that you get the feeling that everything you see is part of something very large that you just can't understand.

One day, you happen upon a stranger who looks like he knows his way around; at least he seems familiar with the surroundings.

You ask him, how do you find your way?.

He shrugs. You'll get used to it.

But, you ask, why is this all here?

I don't know, he says, and he starts to wander away.

Wait, you call after him, where can I get a map?

No such thing, he answers over his shoulder.

But can't you help me at all?

He turns around and looks at you with a gleam in his eye and a funny half smile on his face. Clearly, he knows something that you don't. Something important.

This place, he gestures widely, is only a few years old. In fact, you could travel for days and almost everything you'd see would be less than a year old. You will see new places almost everywhere you look and, every so often, you will notice that old ones have disappeared. You turn around, and when you turn back it's changed — larger, more complicated, more... well, it's hard to explain. Like I said, you'll get used to it.

But don't be confused, he continues, the meaning in what you see is not about the structures or the vehicles. It's not about the art or the beauty; or pleasure or truth or good or bad. It's about people and what they have created. People working together and by themselves.

You will notice that wherever you go, you will never see another person (I know this to be a fact, and I have been here as long as anyone). However, you can talk to other people whenever you want, so you will never be lonely. No matter who you are, no matter how individual your desires and your preferences, there are people just like you here, somewhere.

So where are you? Nobody really knows. The important thing is that we are all here together. We are all connected. We all share. We all belong, especially those of us who have nowhere else to go. And the best thing is that you can come here whenever you want. No one is ever turned away.

Personally, I don't really understand why this place is so important. Most of us just move around from place to place, doing whatever we feel like. Still, just be glad that you are here at all. As I say, most of this is only a few years old and you are among the first.

But wait, you say. You told me that I would never actually see anyone. What about you? I can see you.

He looks at you for a long moment.

You only *think* you see me. I don't really exist. Anyway, for what it's worth, there is a map of sorts. Don't lose it and you can take it with you wherever you go.

He points behind you to a single piece of paper lying on the ground. You turn around to pick it up, and by the time you turn back he is gone. You look down. In the center of an otherwise blank piece of paper, is a big "X" and the words "You are here".

You stuff the paper into your pocket and start walking. After a few minutes, you turn around and gasp. Behind you is a large sign. It must have been there all the time, how could you have missed it? Okay, you say to yourself, I may not know where I am, or why I am here, or what anyone is really doing, but now at least, I know the name of this place. For the sign says:

Welcome to the Internet.

The Internet and This Book

In order to make sure that you enjoy this book as much as possible, I want to take a few moments to explain some basic concepts.

WHAT DO YOU NEED TO KNOW TO USE THIS BOOK?

To use this book, you need to have access to the Internet and you need to know how to use the Internet. Both these topics are fully explained in another one of our books, *The Internet Complete Reference* (Osborne McGraw-Hill).

If you do not as yet have Internet access, start with that book. Read Chapter 3 ("How to Connect to the Internet") for basic concepts, and then use Appendix A ("Public Access to the Internet") for advice on how to find and choose an Internet provider. The book contains a long list of such providers, as well as a special offer to new users that lets you arrange for one month's free access.

Once you have Internet access, you need to master the skills necessary to use the Internet. In practice, this means learning how to use the various Internet resources, all of which are different. The following table shows the various resources that are in this book. The chapter numbers show which part of *The Internet Complete Reference* explains that resource. For a quick introduction to all the resources, see Chapter 2.

Resource	Chapters
Quick tour of the Internet	2
Anonymous FTP	16
Archie	17
Finger	8
Gopher	21
Internet Mailing Lists	25
Listserv Mailing Lists	25
Mail	5, 6
Telnet	7
Usenet: in general	9, 10, 11
Usenet: newsreaders	12, 13, 14, 15
Wais	23

People often ask, how much do I really need to learn? There are two answers — one bad and one good — to that question. The bad answer is:

You do not need to know how to use everything. You only need to learn how to use the resources that you are interested in.

The good answer is a lot more realistic:

You will likely become interested in all the resources, so you really do have to know how to use everything.

IS IT HARD TO LEARN HOW TO USE THE INTERNET?

No, it is not hard at all. It just takes practice.

Don't be put off by people who say that the Internet is hard to use or is not "user friendly". You must be realistic. The Internet is one of the most important and complex inventions of mankind. "Using the Internet" really means learning some basic concepts and then teaching yourself how to use a variety of different programs.

Once you become an experienced user, you will see that — considering all that it offers — the Internet and its programs are remarkably user friendly. The problem is that some people confuse the idea of "easy to use" with "easy to learn". The only way you can make a complex system so easy to learn that you can use it on the first day, is by removing (or hiding) most of its power. But then, once you become experienced, you find that the system is too simple and awkward.

Millions of people around the world already use the Internet. You don't need to be a computer expert. To put this in perspective, using the Internet is a lot easier than many things that we all do every day, such as driving a car or shopping for groceries. All you need is some practice and some patience.

Our best advice? Open this book to any page and find something interesting. Then, use *The Internet Complete Reference* to teach yourself what you need to know. Experiment. Have fun. Go slow. Enjoy.

CENSORSHIP: OR, WHAT SHOULD I DO WHEN I AM OFFENDED?

I promise you that, sooner or later, something on the Internet will offend you. Indeed, something in this catalog may offend you. Please don't let this bother you.

The Internet is the largest gathering of human beings ever assembled and one of the ground rules is that there is No-One-In-Charge, which means that there is no censorship. This freedom is the prime reason that the Internet has become so important and why there are so many diverse resources.

Still, some people have a little trouble getting used to such license. Eventually, we all come to realize that if we don't like something, we can ignore it. For example, if you are reading the articles in a Usenet newsgroup, and you encounter one that you find particularly offensive, you can skip it. However, for some new users, the temptation to complain is too strong.

So someone complains... "Yes, I do believe in freedom of expression, but comparing the President of the United States to a retarded Nazi feminist minority member with AIDS is just too much and should not be allowed. After all, we must remember that using the Internet is a privilege and not a right, and that if people like you continue to pollute the network with ignorant, racist, dangerous opinions, the

Internet will be taken away and... blah, blah, blah..."

Well now. All that such a diatribe means is that, as an Internet user, the writer is still immature. I assure you that no one, anywhere, will pay the least bit of attention to a self-righteous pronouncement of what is right or wrong. So, should you ever run into such a person, remind them gently that the best part of the Internet is its diversity, and that tolerance of other people's opinions and ways of thinking is a virtue.

Indeed, if there is one Internet Golden Rule, it is:

Censor yourself, not others.

Realistically, we all come to learn that we can't do anything about how other people use the Internet, so there is no point even trying. The idea is to share and enjoy. If you don't like something, forget about it.

HOW TO CONTACT US

This catalog contains thousands of items, but still only a small fraction of what the Internet has to offer. If you would like to add something to the next edition of the catalog, just let us know. The address is **catalog@rain.org**.

Similarly, if you have any comments, don't bother the publisher. Send them to us directly (at **catalog@rain.org**), and Rick and I will be glad to listen.

Acknowledgments

A great many people helped Rick and me with the production of this book and, if you don't mind, we'd like to take a few minutes to thank these people by name and acknowledge their help. Of course, you don't really need to read all of this. No one is watching and you could probably just skip this section without being caught. Remember though, the real mark of a person is how he or she behaves when no one is watching.

I don't want to scare you, but we did receive a letter from one person who refused to read the acknowledgments in our last book. Actually, it was pitiful to even hear about it. This poor soul thought no one would ever notice, but he forgot that when you neglect to do what you know is right, you are only fooling yourself. So, throwing caution to the wind, he completely ignored the acknowledgments and within three days, his entire life was exposed as a shallow, meaningless sham.

Still with me? Okay.

To start, Rick and I would like to thank Michael Peirce (of Trinity College in Ireland), our principal research assistant. I suppose that it is possible to write a best-selling computer book without Michael's help but, personally, I can't imagine doing so. This guy is just amazing. In fact, I bet that you could walk into any Unix conference and throw a brick and not have to worry about hitting someone who knew more about Internet resources than Mike. (Although it might be interesting to try.)

Next, we have Wendy Murdock, a multi-talented artist and writer whose skill, patience and hard work contributed greatly to the quality of this book. Just between us, Wendy never stops amazing me; I still can't figure out how someone can be so talented and accomplished.

To continue. There are three other researchers who also made important contributions: Scott Yanoff (from the University of Wisconsin at Milwaukee), John Navarra (from Northwestern University in Illinois), and Paola Kathuria (from London, England). Closer to home, both Jim Hall and Brooke Jarrett (of San Diego) provided valuable assistance to Rick.

Moving right along, we have Lunaea Hougland (our favorite copy editor), Peter ten Kley (our favorite correspondent from the Netherlands), Rick Broadhead (our favorite Freenet executive from Canada), and Jane Melkonian (our favorite Unitarian).

Now, aside from all these individuals, there are a number of people at various companies who helped us. At Netsys, Len Rose gave me access to the most comprehensive Usenet facility on the planet. At

Rain (Santa Barbara's Regional Access Information Network), Marcy Montgomery and Timothy Tyndall provided me with Internet access, while John Detch, the system manager, did an excellent job maintaining the system. At Netcom, Desiree Madison-Biggs provided Rick and his assistants with Internet access. At Telebit, Greg Dumas helped out with telecommunications equipment. Finally, at Borland, Karen Giles and Nan Borreson supplied us with database software (Paradox for Windows).

At this point you might be wondering, does this mean that Harley and Rick are recommending these companies? Are they telling me that I should buy Internet service from Netsys, Rain or Netcom, modems from Telebit, or software from Borland? The answer is that we did think about suggesting that these are good people for you to do business with, but we decided not to, as we felt that we should not make any endorsements.

Next we have our publisher, Osborne McGraw-Hill. By far, the person to whom we owe the most is Scott Rogers, our editor. Technically, Scott's title is "Acquisitions Editor", because his job is to find authors and plan new books. However, he does much more than that: Scott was involved with many aspects of this book — including content, production, marketing and sales — often on a day to day basis. So much so, that at one point we even considered sharing the royalties with him. Fortunately, it took but a moment for cooler heads to prevail and reason to return to her throne. Still, Scott worked hard and he certainly deserves as much credit as is safe to give an editor. (You have to be careful though. Once you let

editors get above themselves, they let it go to their heads; and the publishing industry is full of editors who just love to throw their weight around like Donald Duck.)

After Scott, the people who worked the most with us (and have the gray hair to prove it) are Kelly Barr, the Project Editor, who oversaw the preparation and processing of the book; and Emily Rader, the Associate Editor, who formatted the raw text.

On the production side of the fence, Rick and I would like to thank Marla Shelasky, Helena Charm, Kristin Peterson and Lance Ravella, the artists who created the wonderful drawings that you see throughout this book. As you can see for yourself, these people have real talent and their contribution to this book was an important one. I, for one, am especially grateful, as I had despaired of ever finding artists who had just the right mixture of skill and whimsy to illustrate my jokes. If I had only had Marla to illustrate my essays in high school, who knows where I might be today.

The last two production miracle workers are Peter Hancik, who designed and laid out the entire book (not an easy job); and Kendal Anderson, who produced the front and back cover, as well as the entry in the Osborne book catalog.

Of course, these nine people do not run the whole publishing company by themselves. From time to time, they receive small bits of help from a few other people who deserve a mention: Sherith Pankratz (Editorial Assistant); Lisa Kissinger (Head of Marketing); Heather Wood (Special Sales); Larry Levitsky (Publisher, the big cheese); Jeff Pepper (Editor-in-Chief, the medium-sized cheese); Alexa Maddox (also an Editorial Assistant); Kimberly Kradel (receptionist); and Ann Pharr (also a receptionist).

Special thanks must also go to Linda Poon of the McGraw-Hill legal department in New York, for showing us just how much fun it can be to ask a lawyer for permission to include questionable material in a book.

For extra special delivery service (more important than you might think), I would like to thank the folks at the DHL office in Santa Barbara: Terry Chlentzos-Keramaris, Christine Abate, Kraig Williamson, Danielle Ritchko, Sheila Burrows, Kelan Raph, Marc Rossi and the manager, Bob Kubitza.

And finally, for her constant encouragement and support, I would like to thank my wife, Kimberlyn Hahn, without whose help this book would have been finished in half the time.

— Harley Hahn

AGRICULTURE

Advanced Technology Information Network

Agricultural news, daily reports, an event calendar, California Agriculture Teacher's Project, agricultural degrees at California State Universities, job listings, weather, labor and safety information, as well as other items of interest.

Telnet:
Address: **caticsuf.csufresno.edu**
Login: **super**

Agricultural Mailing List

Grassland husbandry, crop science, ecological simulation, crop production, tropical forestry, plant physiology, water management, irrigation and anything else to do with agriculture that you want to discuss.

Listserv mailing list:
List Address: **agric-l@uga.bitnet**
Subscription Address: **listserv@uga.bitnet**

Agricultural Software Search

Search for all types of agricultural software.

Gopher:
Name: Johns Hopkins University
Address: **merlot.welch.jhu.edu**
Choose: **Search and Retrieve Software | Search for Agricultural Software**

Agricultural, Flood, and Food Supply Information

A Gopher interface for all kinds of useful information on floods, food supplies and food safety, agricultural market news, and other topics, including vegetable crops and landscaping.

Telnet:
Address: **idea.ag.uiuc.edu**
Login: **flood**

Animal Science

A mailing list for undergraduates, graduate students, and teaching faculty in animal science, dairy, and poultry science curriculums.

Listserv mailing list:
List Address: **ansstds@msu.bitnet**
Subscription Address: **listserv@msu.bitnet**

Bee Biology

Mailing list information, details on honey bees and bumblebees, pollination, honey, and related material.

Anonymous FTP:
Address: **sunsite.unc.edu**
Path: **/pub/academic/agriculture/ sustainable_agriculture/beekeeping/***

Listserv mailing list:
List Address: **bee-l@albnyvm1.bitnet**
Subscription Address: **listserv@albnyvm1.bitnet**

To Bee, or Not To Bee?

What could be more inviting than sitting on your front porch, relaxing on your rocking chair, and listening to the steady, comforting drone of your pet bees making you honey? Join the **bee-l** mailing list and keep up with the latest in apiarist circles. Bee there or bee square.

Chinchilla Farming

The cultivation and breeding of chinchillas.

Usenet:
Newsgroup: **alt.chinchilla**

Clemson University Forestry and Agriculture Network

Information on weather, agri-economics, plants, animals, engineering, food, home, health, family and youth, as well as other items of interest.

Telnet:
Address: **eureka.clemson.edu**
Login: **public**

A B C D E F G H I J K L M N O P Q R S T U V W X Y Z

Commodity Market Reports

This server contains the agricultural commodity market reports compiled by the Agricultural Market News Service of the United States Department of Agriculture. There are over a thousand reports from all over the United States. Most of these reports are updated daily. Try searching for "portland grain".

Wais:
> Database: **agricultural-market-news**

Cornell Extension NETwork

CENET is a service provided by Cornell University and offers information on various agricultural topics, including crops and agronomy, food and nutrition, fruit and vegetable information, horticultural, floriculture, and other similar topics.

Telnet:
> Address: **empire.cce.cornell.edu**
> Login: **guest**

Farming and Agriculture

All aspects of farming and agriculture.

Usenet:
> Newsgroup: **alt.agriculture.misc**

Excerpt from the Net...

```
Newsgroup: alt.agriculture.misc
Subject: Sugar Production

Can anyone tell me where to find sugar
production by country?

Look in the yearbooks issued by United
Nations organizations, including the
Food and Agriculture Organization's
"Production Yearbook".

Top sugar producers are usually India,
Brazil, China (rising), Russia, Cuba
(falling), USA, Mexico, Pakistan,
France, Colombia and Australia, in that
order.
```

Fruit Farming

All aspects of fruit farming.

Usenet:
> Newsgroup: **alt.agriculture.fruit**

Iowa State University SCHOLAR System

A publication database that contains documents on many topics including agriculture, applied sciences and technology, biology, and other agriculture-related subjects.

Comment: At the DIAL: prompt, login with the userid **scholar**, press ENTER when prompted for a vt100 terminal or enter another terminal type, then type **scholar** again at the Command: prompt. Type **stop** to leave the SCHOLAR system.

Telnet:
> Address: **isn.iastate.edu**
> Login: **scholar**

Not Just Cows

A guide to agricultural resources on the Net. Written by Wilfred Drew, this text directs the reader to many different agricultural resources, including BBSs, mailing lists, and other important services.

Anonymous FTP:
> Address: **ftp.sura.net**
> Path: **/pub/nic/agricultural.list**

Man Does Not Live By Cows Alone

There is a lot more to life than cows. True, they can be a lot of fun at birthday parties, and your pet cow does come in handy when you need a fourth for bridge. Still, the needs of the farming community stretch far beyond the bovine.

CHECK OUT **Not Just Cows**

...a comprehensive guide to the Internet's agricultural resources, and make your life happy and complete.

PENpages

International Food & Nutrition Database, National Family Database, The 4-H Youth Development Database, agricultural and weather statistics, market news, newsletters, and drought information. This resource is provided by the Penn State College of Agricultural Sciences.

Comment: Login with the two-letter abreviation for your state (e.g., PA).

Telnet:
Address: **psupen.psu.edu**

Sustainable Agriculture

The politics and technology of ecologically sound agriculture.

Usenet:
Newsgroup: **alt.sustainable.agriculture**

ARCHAEOLOGY

Archaeological Computing

A bibliography of archaeological computing in BibTeX format.

Wais:
Database: **archaeological_computing**

Archaeology Mailing List

Discussion of archaeological problems, news on conferences, job announcements, calls for papers, publications, bibliographies and software related to archaeological studies.

Listserv mailing list:
List Address: **arch-l@dgogwdg1.bitnet**
Subscription Address: **listserv@dgogwdg1.bitnet**

Classics and Mediterranean Archaeology

Dedicated to information and other resources of interest to classicists and Mediterranean archaeologists. Offers access to journals, texts, and spatially referenced data, as well as information on museum and library exhibits.

Gopher:
Name: Classics and Mediterranean Archaeology
Address: **rome.classics.lsa.umich.edu**

Dead Sea Scrolls

"Scrolls from the Dead Sea: the Ancient Library of Qumran and Modern Scholarship" is a Library of Congress exhibit. It describes the historical context of the scrolls and the Qumran community where they may have originated.

Anonymous FTP:
Address: **ftp.tex.ac.uk**
Path: **/archaeology/gopher/deadsea/***

Address: **seq1.loc.gov**
Path: **/pub/deadsea.scrolls.exhibit/***

Gopher:
Name: UK Tex Archive
Address: **ftp.tex.ac.uk**
Choose: **Archaeology**
 | Dead Sea Scrolls Exhibit Online

National Archaeological Database

A database of over 100,000 reports of archaeological investigations. Search by keyword, location, author, and publication date.

Telnet:
Address: **cast.uark.edu**
Login: **nadb**

**Need a laugh?
Check out Humor**

**Lonely?
Try the Personals.**

A B C D E F G H I J K L M N O P Q R S T U V W X Y Z

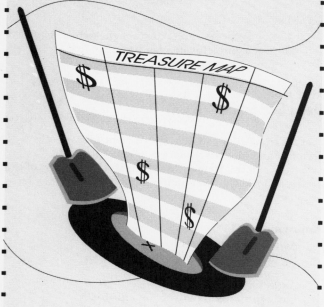

Treasure In Your Back Yard?

How many people are unaware of important --and perhaps valuable--archaeological treasures right in their own back yard? This need never happen to you.

The National Archaeological Database

contains information on more investigations than you can shake a 500-year-old stick at. Telnet to this bountiful resource and get the lowdown on what's low down.

ARCHITECTURE

Alternative Architecture

Discuss non-traditional building designs and techniques. Swap tips and techniques about solar energy, innovative designs, new materials, and much more.

Usenet:
> Newsgroup: **alt.architecture.alternative**

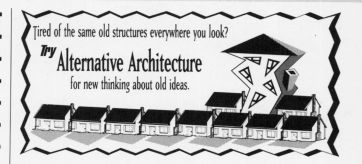

Tired of the same old structures everywhere you look? *Try* **Alternative Architecture** for new thinking about old ideas.

ArchiGopher

A Gopher at the University of Michigan that is dedicated to the dissemination of architectural knowledge. ArchiGopher resources include samples of five Kandinsky paintings, a sample of Andrea Palladio's architectural projects, computer images from the CAD group, and scenes and images from other projects and settings.

Gopher:
> Name: University of Michigan
> Address: **libra.arch.umich.edu**

Architronic

An electronic journal dedicated to the profession and issues of architecture. For the FTP site, log in with a user name of **architecture** and a password of **archives.**

Anonymous FTP:
> Address: **ksuvxa.kent.edu**
> Path: **ksu1:[architecture]/***

Gopher:
> Name: North Carolina State University
> Address: **dewey.lib.ncsu.edu**
> Choose: **NCSU's Library Without Walls**
> | **Electronic Journals and Books**
> | **Architronic**

Listserv mailing list:
> List Address: **arcitron@kentvm.bitnet**
> Subscription Address: **listserv@kentvm.bitnet**

General Discussion

Talk about architecture-oriented topics: building design, construction, architecture schools, materials, and so on.

Usenet:
> Newsgroup: **alt.architecture**

ART

Art Criticism Forum

A mailing list billed as open to anyone interested in the visual arts. Topics are often political.

Listserv mailing list:
List Address: **artcrit@yorkvm1.bitnet**
Subscription Address: **listserv@yorkvm1.bitnet**

Art News

The real story on the art scene. Get news on drama, music, and the fine arts.

Usenet:
Newsgroup: **clari.news.arts**

Art Papers

A collection of art-related papers and documents, including aesthetic perspectives, bibliography of arts, and catalog reviews.

Gopher:
Name: English Server
Address: **english-server.hss.cmu.edu**
Choose: **Art and Architecture | Text**

Artistic Community

What is happening in the art community? Artists increase their sense of community by sharing ideas, reviewing shows, announcing workshops, and being available for advice. See the creative process in action; participate by joining round-robin projects.

Usenet:
Newsgroup: **alt.artcom**

Artistic Melange

Find out about music, opera, plays. Read reviews and interviews. If you've been looking for art in all the wrong places, you will definitely be able to find it here.

Usenet:
Newsgroup: **rec.arts.misc**

Spare time?
Take a look at Games

Arts and Entertainment Reviews

Reviews films, books, and the arts. Reviews are updated regularly.

Gopher:
Name: The Electronic Newsstand
Address: **gopher.internet.com 2100**
Choose:
Arts & Entertainment - Selected Reviews

Arts Online

A bibliography of arts-related resources available on the Internet and other networks.

Anonymous FTP:
Address: **nic.funet.fi**
Path: **/pub/doc/library/artbase.txt.Z**

ASCII Cartoons

A selection of ASCII art, including *The Simpsons*, cows, smileys, spaceships, dragons, and Slimer.

Gopher:
Name: Universitaet des Saarlandes
Address: **pfsparc02.phil15.uni-sb.de**
Choose: **INFO-SYSTEM BENUTZEN**
| Fun
| Cartoons

Cadence Design Systems

A mailing list for users, and potential users, of the software tools from Cadence Design Systems.

Internet mailing list:
List Address: **artist-users@uicc.com**
Subscription Address:
artist-users-request@uicc.com

Ceramic Arts Discussion List

A mailing list of interest to folks into ceramic arts and pottery. Discuss any related subject you like, including aesthetic issues, grant information, and exhibition opportunities.

Listserv mailing list:
List Address: **clayart@ukcc.bitnet**
Subscription Address: **listserv@ukcc.bitnet**

A B C D E F G H I J K L M N O P Q R S T U V W X Y Z

Ceramic City

Yes it's true: in Ceramic City there are two pots for every guy (and gal).

Join the **clayart** mailing list and have your mailbox filled with information and discussion that will bring fire to your life and make your eyes glaze over in happiness.

Ceramics Gopher

An experimental database of glazes, clay recipes, and other items of interest concerning the ceramic arts.

Gopher:
> Name: San Diego State University
> Address: **athena.sdsu.edu**
> Choose: **SDSU Campus Topics**
> | **Departmental Information**
> | **Art Department**
> | **The Ceramics Gopher**

Fine Art Forum

Delve into the mystery and meaning of art. Artists come together for lively exploration of the meaning, impact, responsibility, and history of art. This forum is scholarly, but not intimidating, and can provide answers to the most obscure technical or theoretical questions. Because artists are always in the studio, this is a great way to finally get them all in one place.

Usenet:
> Newsgroup: **rec.arts.fine**

Fine Art Pictures

The modern age means art for everyone. Digitized fine art pictures are available here for downloading. The **.d** list is exclusively for discussion of the posting of pictures. Both groups are moderated.

Usenet:
> Newsgroup: **alt.binaries.pictures.fine-art.d**
> Newsgroup:
>   **alt.binaries.pictures.fine-art.digitized**

Art, Art, Art (and more Art)

Fine art is yours for the asking... on the Internet

FineArt Forum's Directory of On-line Resources

An excellent directory of Internet resources relating to the arts.

Anonymous FTP:
> Address: **ra.msstate.edu**
> Path: **/pub/archives/fineart_online/**
>   **Online_Directory**

Graphics

Graphics is on the rise as an art form. Capture some of your favorites. This group is moderated.

Usenet:
> Newsgroup:
>   **alt.binaries.pictures.fine-art.graphics**

Japanese Animation

Immerse yourself in the magical world of Japanese animation (anime). Devotees of animation provide information not only on the art form, but also movie reviews, schedules of showings, announcements of new releases, conventions, and club meetings.

Usenet:
> Newsgroup: **rec.arts.anime.info**

Monalisa

DaVinci's famous painting in electronic format.

Gopher:
Name: English Server
Address: **english-server.hss.cmu.edu**
Choose: **Art and Architecture | Images | monalisa**

Images of original art, such as the Mona Lisa, are widely available on the Net. This version of monalisa.gif was downloaded from Washington University at St. Louis (**ftp.wustl.edu**). Use Archie to find the current directory or other sites. (Search for **monalisa**.)

OTIS Project

OTIS (Operative Term Is Stimulate) distributes original artwork and photographs over the network for public perusal, scrutiny, and distribution. OTIS also offers a forum for critique and exhibition of your works. A virtual art gallery that never closes and exists in an information dimension where your submissions will hang on thousands of glowing monitors.

Anonymous FTP:
Address: **sunsite.unc.edu**
Path: **/pub/multimedia/pictures/OTIS/***

Reviews

Reviews of new and soon-to-come books, CDs, and videos.

Listserv mailing list:
List Address: **booknews@columbia.ilc.com**
Subscription Address: **listserv@columbia.ilc.com**

Rome Reborn

An electronic exhibition of the Vatican library and Renaissance culture in the form of texts, image captions, and JPEG images.

Anonymous FTP:
Address: **orion.lib.virginia.edu**
Path: **/pub/alpha/vat/***

Gopher:
Name: University of Virginia
Address: **gopher.virginia.edu**

ASTRONOMY

Amateur Radio Transmissions

Technical details and considerations relating to radio transmissions and telemetry data to and from space (for amateurs).

Usenet:
Newsgroup: **rec.radio.amateur.space**

Astro FTP List

A list with descriptions of FTP sites that contain astronomy and space research material.

Anonymous FTP:
Address: **ftp.funet.fi**
Path: **/pub/astro/general/astroftp.txt**

Too much spare time? Explore a MUD

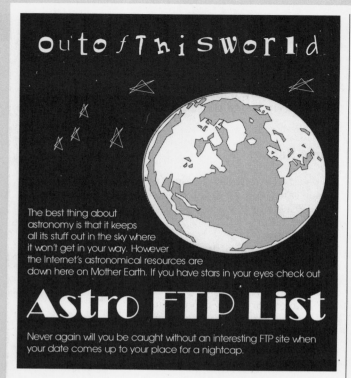

out of This world

The best thing about astronomy is that it keeps all its stuff out in the sky where it won't get in your way. However the Internet's astronomical resources are down here on Mother Earth. If you have stars in your eyes check out

Astro FTP List

Never again will you be caught without an interesting FTP site when your date comes up to your place for a nightcap.

Astronomy Program

Programs for all popular systems, texts, documents, pictures, news, and equipment information about astronomy and stargazing.

Anonymous FTP:
Address: **nic.funet.fi**
Path: **/pub/astro/***

FITS

Technical discussion about FITS (Flexible Image Transport System), a computer data format used to exchange astronomical data. FITS is designed to facilitate convenient data transfer between different types of computer systems.

Usenet:
Newsgroup: **sci.astro.fits**

General Discussion

Stars, planets, telescopes, cosmology, and all aspects of astronomy and astrophysics. Talk with people who really do understand black holes.

Usenet:
Newsgroup: **sci.astro**

Hubble Telescope

Mull over data and observations from the Hubble Space Telescope. This moderated newsgroup contains technical information released as part of the Hubble project.

Usenet:
Newsgroup: **sci.astro.hubble**

Planetariums

Do you think that planetariums can be used for more than laser light shows to Pink Floyd music? If so, you can discuss issues with people who plan and implement planetarium programs.

Usenet:
Newsgroup: **sci.astro.planetarium**

Planets and the Solar System

The planets, asteroids, and other bodies that make up our solar system. Discuss astronomical details as well as the space missions sent to explore these places.

Usenet:
Newsgroup: **alt.sci.planetary**

PLANETS ARE COOL

Yes, there is no doubt about it, planets are high up on just about everybody's list of favorite astronomical objects.
Join the folks on
alt.sci.planetary
and talk about the large, significant objects that comprise our solar system, and our efforts to visit them before prices go up.

AUTOMOBILES

Antiques

Wash it, buff it, tuck your baby in at night. Antique automobiles hold a special place in everyone's heart. Care and feeding of all older automobiles is covered in **alt.autos.antique**. Automobiles over 25 years old are parked in **rec.autos.antique**.

Usenet:
Newsgroup: **alt.autos.antique**
Newsgroup: **rec.autos.antique**

Automobile Discussion Groups

Everything to do with automobiles, including design, construction, service, tires, karting, competitions, driving, manufacturers, and antique cars.

Usenet:
Newsgroup: **alt.autos.karting**
Newsgroup: **alt.autos.rod-n-custom**
Newsgroup: **alt.hotrod**
Newsgroup: **rec.audio.car**
Newsgroup: **rec.autos**
Newsgroup: **rec.autos.antique**
Newsgroup: **rec.autos.driving**
Newsgroup: **rec.autos.sport**
Newsgroup: **rec.autos.tech**
Newsgroup: **rec.autos.vw**

Automotive Archives

Mailing lists, archive and new user guides, consumer automotive FAQs, and other material about automobiles, automotive products, and laws.

Anonymous FTP:
Address: **rtfm.mit.edu**
Path: **/pub/usenet/rec.autos.tech**

Automobile Archives are gassed up and ready to go! ....Drive in and download..........

Beemer List

A mailing list for owners, or anyone else interested in cars made by BMW.

Internet mailing list:
List Address: **bmw@balltown.cma.com**
Subscription Address:
bmw-request@balltown.cma.com

Why be normal? Read Bizarre.

British Cars

Of owning, repairing, racing, cursing, and loving British cars, especially sports cars. Some Land Rover topics as well.

Internet mailing list:
List Address: **british-cars@autox.team.net**
Subscription Address:
british-cars-request@autox.team.net

Car Audio

"My woofer is bigger than your woofer!" Make the most of your automobile's audio system by learning about installation, trouble shooting, and consumer information.

Usenet:
Newsgroup: **rec.audio.car**

California Driving

Material concerning driving, parking tickets, traffic laws, insurance, highway patrol, and other aspects of driving in California.

Anonymous FTP:
Address: **rtfm.mit.edu**
Path: **/pub/usenet/news.answers/ca-driving-faq**

Driving

Slide into your car, start her up, see the road race beneath you. Make your driving experience exquisite. Stay informed about driving laws and learn how to better handle your car.

Usenet:
Newsgroup: **rec.autos.driving**

General Automobiles

Cars need love, too. Learn to feed, wash, and care for your automobile so you can see a good return on your investment. A wide variety of topics are covered including repairs, recalls, new products, leasing, security, laws, and consumer advice.

Usenet:
Newsgroup: **rec.autos**

A
B
C
D
E
F
G
H
I
J
K
L
M
N
O
P
Q
R
S
T
U
V
W
X
Y
Z

High Performance

Don't just drive your car, experience it. Which cars perform the best? How can you increase your auto's performance? Learn about safety, technical aspects, and techniques.

Usenet:
> Newsgroup: **alt.autos.rod-n-custom**
> Newsgroup: **rec.autos.rod-n-custom**

Life in the Fast Lane

We all know that fast, high-performance cars are just a substitute for you-know-what. (Well we do know, but we aren't allowed to talk about stuff like that in a family-oriented book.) Join the boys in the **rod-n-custom** Usenet groups and fin out how to soup-up your performance and enhance your experience with high speed and quick starts.

Hotrods

Rev your engine and burn rubber. Learn the dos and don'ts of working with high-speed automobiles. Hotrod enthusiasts know the nuts and bolts. This group is moderated.

This image was downloaded from Northern Arizona University (**ftp.nau.edu**). The file is **/graphics/gif/digi/ferrarigto.gif** and was originally located with an Archie substring search for **ferrari**.

Usenet:
> Newsgroup: **alt.hotrod**

Motorcycle Archive

FAQs, photo images in gif format, and "Denizens of Doom" (DoD) information.

Anonymous FTP:
> Address: **cerritos.edu**
> Path: **/DOD/***

Motorcycle Discussion List

Talk about anything having to do with motorcycles.

Internet mailing list:
> List Address: **bparker@rigel.uark.edu**
> Subscription Address:
> **bparker-request@rigel.uark.edu**

Motorcycle Reviews

A large collection of motorcycle and accessory reviews written by readers of the Usenet **rec.motorcycles** newsgroups and based on their own experiences. New reviews are always welcome. Includes some motorcycle pictures.

Anonymous FTP:
> Address: **ftp.cecm.sfu.ca**
> Path: **/pub/RMR/***

Racing

Put the pedal to the metal and aim for the checkered flag. Discover the thrill of all aspects of organized automobile racing.

Usenet:
> Newsgroup: **rec.autos.sport**

Technical

Points, carbs, blocks, calibration; what's it all mean? A wide variety of topics are discussed. If you absorb only half the information offered by these enthusiasts, you will be highly informed.

Usenet:
> Newsgroup: **rec.autos.tech**

Volkswagen

Volkswagens have a unique following. Learn the ins and outs of your VW. Share your experiences or benefit from the experience of others.

Usenet:
Newsgroup: **rec.autos.vw**

Volkswagen Names

A list of names people have given to their Volkswagen cars, and why.

Anonymous FTP:
Address: **ftp.spies.com**
Path: **/Library/Document/names.vw**

Gopher:
Name: Internet Wiretap
Address: **wiretap.spies.com**
Choose: **Wiretap Online Library**
    | Assorted Documents
    | The Grand VW Car Name List

AVIATION

Aerospace Engineering

A mailing list dedicated to the theoretical side of aerospace engineering. Includes discussion on aerospace technology, calls for papers, seminar announcements, and other related topics.

Internet mailing list:
List Address: **aviation-theory@mc.lcs.mit.edu**
Subscription Address:
    aviation-theory-request@mc.lcs.mit.edu

Aircraft Discussion Forum

A mailing list forum for people interested in aircraft and helicopters, both new and old. The list also includes information about air-shows and similar events.

Listserv mailing list:
List Address: **aircraft@grearn.bitnet**
Subscription Address: **listserv@grearn.bitnet**

Aircraft Group Ownership

Ever wonder how you could afford to own an airplane? Group ownership may be one way you can. This mailing list will fill you in on all you need to know.

Internet mailing list:
List Address: **airplane-clubs@dg-rtp.dg.com**
Subscription Address:
    airplane-clubs-request@dgrtp.dg.com

Sharing an Airplane

For years you have been dreaming of your own airplane...

...unfortunately, your two feet are firmly planted on the ground while your bank account grows slower than a dead Christmas tree. It's all too true that an airplane is just a hole in the sky into which you throw money.

Join the **airplane-clubs** mailing list and meet the people who form clubs to share the only hobby more expensive than running for Congress.

Airline and Airliner Discussion List

A mailing list featuring airlines, airliners, and other civil aircraft and related topics. Modelers are welcome too.

Listserv mailing list:
List Address: **airline@cunyvm.bitnet**
Subscription Address: **listserv@cunyvm.bitnet**

Airline Travel

Solve travel problems before they happen. If you are traveling, scope out trials that may occur between your departure and destination: ticket purchases, layovers, connecting flights, luggage dramas, and airline strikes. Information is available for the entire planet. Next stop: The Rest of the Universe.

Usenet:
Newsgroup: **rec.travel.air**

"I see you have a copy of The Internet Yellow Pages. We will be glad to upgrade you to first class."

Airport Codes

The three-letter identification codes for nearly every airport in the world.

Anonymous FTP:
    Address: **ftp.spies.com**
    Path: **/Library/Article/Aero/airport.lis**

Gopher:
    Name: Internet Wiretap
    Address: **wiretap.spies.com**
    Choose: **Wiretap Online Library | Articles**
      | Aeronautics and Space
      | Airport 3 Letter Abbreviations

Aviation Archives

In-flight cockpit visits, aviation humor, trivia, and so on.

Anonymous FTP:
    Address: **rascal.ics.utexas.edu**
    Path: **/misc/av/***

Aviation Gopher

This Gopher has bundles of information about aviation and contains most of the items that appear on or are covered in the Usenet newsgroup **rec.aviation**. It offers numerous articles, pictures, stories, and also has weather and fly-in information.

Gopher:
    Name: Northwestern University
    Address: **av.eecs.nwu.edu**

is no fly-by-night operation. Just the place to be when you're fogged in.

DUATS

Aviation weather, PIREPS, and flight plans.

Telnet:
    Address: **duat.contel.com** *(for pilots only)*

    Address: **duats.contel.com** *(for non-pilots)*

Flight Planning

Public domain flight-planning software and data, written in C and complete with source.

Anonymous FTP:
    Address: **eecs.nwu.edu**
    Path: **/pub/aviation/***

    Address: **lifshitz.ph.utexas.edu**
    Path: **/pub/aviation/***

Want some fun?
Read the Fun section

Flight Simulators

Flight simulation theory, products, reviews, scenery for specific software, and other material related to air and spacecraft simulators.

Anonymous FTP:
Address: **ftp.iup.edu**
Path: **/flight-sim/***

Address: **ftp.ulowell.edu**
Path: **/msdos/Games/FltSim/***

Address: **kth.se**
Path: **/kth/misc/fltsim.tar.Z**

Address: **nic.funet.fi**
Path: **/pub/X11/contrib/acm4.0.tar.Z**

Address: **onion.rain.com**
Path: **/pub/falcon3/***

Address: **rtfm.mit.edu**
Path: **/pub/usenet/news.answers/aviation/
    flight-simulators**

Wais:
Database: **flight_sim**

See also:
Video Games

Crash and Burn

The great thing about flight simulators is that you can do anything you want and not get into real trouble. (The only drawbacks are that you have to bring your own salted peanuts and you don't get any frequent flyer miles.) The Internet has a gaggle of FTP sites with information about flight and space simulators. Never again will you have to settle for the real thing.

Flying

Material about learning how to fly, technical information, ownership costs, equipment guides, aviation policies, and many more related FAQs.

Anonymous FTP:
Address: **rtfm.mit.edu**
Path: **/pub/usenet/news.answers/aviation/***

Flying and Aviation

Topics of interest to pilots, including training systems, laws, airports, planes, procedures, characteristics of aircraft and avionic products, as well as comments on commercial aviation and much more.

Internet mailing list:
List Address: **aviation@mc.lcs.mit.edu**
Subscription Address:
    aviation-request@mc.lcs.mit.edu

General Aviation Discussion

You'll go into a flat spin when you see all the information you can find in this group. If you're not sure where to start in one of the specific aviation groups, try this group. There are often cross-postings from other groups to **.misc**, so you'll see a wide variety of topics, including comparisons of different types of planes, what to do about engine fires, pros and cons of leasing, and what happens when an instrument malfunctions. There's something for everyone.

Usenet:
Newsgroup: **rec.aviation.misc**

This image was downloaded from Northern Arizona University (**ftp.nau.edu**). The file is **/graphics/gif/misc/x29.gif**. This file also exists on many other sites around the world.

A
B
C
D
E
F
G
H
I
J
K
L
M
N
O
P
Q
R
S
T
U
V
W
X
Y
Z

Gliding

Follow the example of the eagle and experience the powerful magic of gliding. Piloting sailplanes and hang-gliders has its own unique set of considerations. Learn about glide ratios, wind, flying in the rain, good places to glide, safety, gliding championships, and more.

Usenet:
Newsgroup: **rec.aviation.soaring**

IFR Flight Simulator

A demo of a PC program that simulates IFR (Instrument Flight Rules) flight training.

Anonymous FTP:
Address: **ftp.iup.edu**
Path: **xevious:/ift5demo.zip**

Instrument Flight Rules

Find out the concerns of flying under Instrument Flight Rules. Alternative mnemonics and IFR tasks just scratch the surface of the topics covered.

Usenet:
Newsgroup: **rec.aviation.ifr**

Jumbo Jets

Archives and information about airliners from the Usenet newsgroup **sci.aeronautics.airliners**. Includes airliner specifications and Boeing codes.

Anonymous FTP:
Address: **ftp.eff.org**
Path: **/pub/airliners/***

Learning to Fly

Learning to fly—what a wonderful experience. It's nice to know you have a place to ask questions or share your experiences with people who enjoy the same hobby or way of life. Find out all the questions new students are asking and learn about instructors, lessons, equipment, PPL qualifications, and airspace.

Usenet:
Newsgroup: **rec.aviation.student**

Excerpt from the Net...

```
Newsgroup: rec.aviation.student
Subject: Nausea and Learning to Fly

> I'm at about 15 hours now, and the
> nausea has pretty much entirely sub-
> sided. Anyone else have stress-
> related nausea while flying?

You're most definitely not alone there.
As a student I don't think that I know
of anyone as stressed out as I was in
my learning days. All I can say to oth-
ers as unfortunate is stick it out, it
WILL go away if you want.
```

Military Aircraft

From the Sopwith Camel to the F-117A Stealth Fighter and beyond, experience the thrill of military aircraft. See the past, present, and even the future, as aviation devotees share their ideas on what are the best aircraft, who are the most notorious pilots in history, and how military aircraft of various countries compare with one another.

Usenet:
Newsgroup: **rec.aviation.military**

News About the Industry

What's going on in the aviation and aerospace industries? Read the real news and get the facts.

Usenet:
Newsgroup: **clari.news.aviation**
Newsgroup: **clari.tw.aerospace**

Owning Airplanes

Don't you wish owning an airplane was as simple as installing a bigger garage door on your house? Learn the joys and travails of being the owner of a powerful flying machine. If you are interested in building or restoring aircraft, check out **.homebuilt** to indulge in your aviation obsession. A word of warning: one of the questions in the Homebuilt FAQ list is, "Will my marriage survive?"

Usenet:
Newsgroup: **rec.aviation.homebuilt**
Newsgroup: **rec.aviation.owning**

YOUR OWN AIRPLANE

Oh, how these three simple words invoke deep feelings in all of us.

Wouldn't it be great to be able to fly to the market or the dry cleaners instead of having to wait in rush hour traffic?

Join the discussion on Usenet (rec.aviation.homebuilt and rec.aviation.owning) and share ideas about what might well be the personal transportation vehicle of the 20th century.

Piloting

The tower says you're clear for takeoff into the wide world of piloting. You'll discover handy tips on priming cold engines, how to deal with rough weather, safety hints, and announcements on flying seminars.

Usenet:
> Newsgroup: **rec.aviation.piloting**

Products

Squidgets, widgets and do-hickeys—find out what's new and useful for pilots.

Usenet:
> Newsgroup: **rec.aviation.products**

Q & A

Looking for thorough, well-researched information on aviation? Willing to pass on your knowledge through concise, streamlined postings? This is the place for you. This group is moderated and it would be in your best interest to read the FAQ list before posting.

Usenet:
> Newsgroup: **rec.aviation.answers**

Stories

How does it feel to be so high above the Earth? What was it like the first time you went solo? What excites you about flying? Read anecdotes of flight experiences and share your own. Even if you don't fly, you can experience the thrill of the moment in the stories of others.

Usenet:
> Newsgroup: **rec.aviation.stories**

Technology

Don't just be content to fly, dig deep into what makes aeronautics work. See the latest NASA press releases and learn about the physics of flight, pitch moment damping, aircraft stability, boarding design, and technical safety.

Usenet:
> Newsgroup: **sci.aeronautics**
> Newsgroup: **sci.aeronautics.airliners**

Upcoming Events

What's going on? Do you have an open weekend you want to fill? Are you going to be traveling to a new city and want to catch some aviation action? Find out what's happening on the aviation scene.

Usenet:
> Newsgroup: **rec.aviation.announce**

All revved up and nowhere to go? Check out Aviation UPCOMING EVENTS

Xpilot Game

Xpilot, a game for X Window, is one you really have to try if you like games and flying. Enthusiasts provide tips on sensors and cloaking devices, suggestions for saving disk space, special options to add to your game, ideas for team playing, and even homemade programs to enhance Xpilot.

Usenet:
> Newsgroup: **alt.games.xpilot**

A B C D E F G H I J K L M N O P Q R S T U V W X Y Z

BBSs (BULLETIN BOARD SYSTEMS)

AfterFive

Both a BBS and a MUD chat-like system in one. The BBS has lots of active topics while the chat is based on the colorful adults-only Bourbon Street in New Orleans. Open 5 P.M. until 8 A.M. CST weekdays, and 24 hours on weekends.

Telnet:
Address: **af.itd.com 9999**

Auggie BBS

A varied BBS with a wide spread of discussion boards, public files, and chat and talk facilities. Friendly people are always ready to chat, day or night, through the numerous online communication programs.

Telnet:
Address: **bbs.augsburg.edu**
Login: **bbs**

BBS Acronyms

A list of commonly used acronyms on BBS systems.

Anonymous FTP:
Address: **ftp.spies.com**
Path: **/Library/Cyber/acronyms.bbs**

Gopher:
Name: Internet Wiretap
Address: **wiretap.spies.com**
Choose: **Wiretap Online Library | Cyberspace | Common BBS Acronyms**

BBS Lists

Lists of BBSs compiled from a number of sources, including Internet BBSs, government lists, law BBSs, and so on.

Anonymous FTP:
Address: **oak.oakland.edu**
Path: **/pub/misc/bbslists**

BBSs Around the World

Information and advertisements describing various BBSs to which you can connect.

Usenet:
Newsgroup: **alt.bbs.ads**
Newsgroup: **alt.bbs.internet**
Newsgroup: **alt.bbs.lists**
Newsgroup: **alt.bbs.lists.d**

Bulletin Boards Around the World

There was a time when computerized bulletin board systems (BBSs) were accessible only by their very own phone number. Not any more. As an Internet user, you can telnet to many different BBSs without making the slightest dent in your phone bill. Even government agencies have BBSs, putting the "bull" back in "bulletin" and the "bored" back in "board".

Cat Talk Network

A BBS with conferences and technical special interest groups not to be found elsewhere. This site also stores many files and programs for PCs, Macs, Amigas, and Atari-STs.

Telnet:
Address: **tygra.michigan.com**
Login: **new**

Cetys-BBS

A Mexican BBS with many Spanish discussion groups. Interesting place to talk and practice your Spanish, but English speakers are welcome also.

Telnet:
Address: **infux.mxl.cetys.mx**
Login: **bbs**

Citadel (Unix BBS software)

A Unix BBS package with add-ons, complete with source code and editor.

Anonymous FTP:
Address: **quartz.rutgers.edu**
Path: **/pub/citadel/***

Gopher:
Name: Rutgers Quartz Text Archive
Address: **quartz.rutgers.edu**
Choose: **Citadel/UX BBS Software and Add-ons**

Csb/Sju BBS

This easy-to-use menu-driven BBS, with its simple and unique message navigating commands and use of graphics, allows for quick scanning of all the different topics it has to offer.

Telnet:
Address: **tiny.computing.csbsju.edu**
Login: **bbs**

CueCosy

A conferencing system in Canada allowing posting and reading of messages on many topics. There is a special education section called TIX, the Teachers Information Exchange.

Telnet:
Address: **cue.bc.ca**
Login: **cosy**

Cybernet

Offers many interesting and varied resources, including Internet mail, limited Usenet, hytelnet, finger, talk, multiuser chat, file downloading, games and even a match-making program for lonely hearts.

Telnet:
Address: **cybernet.cse.fau.edu**
Login: **bbs**

Doors

External programs (doors) that are integrated into a BBS in order to provide access to special services.

Usenet:
Newsgroup: **alt.bbs.doors**

DUBBS

A quiet little BBS in The Netherlands, offering message and bulletin systems, and lots of downloadable computer files. If you have a flair for Dutch, check it out.

Telnet:
Address: **tudrwa.tudelft.nl**
Login: **bbs**

Need a laugh?
Check out Humor

Eagles' Nest BBS

Offers lots of variety in its discussion groups, including two public chat rooms.

Comment: After you log in, you'll be asked for a userid and a password. Use **guest** for both.

Telnet:
Address: **seabass.st.usm.edu**
Login: **bbs**

Endless Forest BBS

Some say alternate space/time continuums exist for the known reality. The Endless Forest is one such continuum. Here the Forest dwellers roam, purely for the exchange of technical information, controversial debate, inane babble, and general fun.

Telnet:
Address: **forest.unomaha.edu**
Login: **ef**

European Southern Observatory Bulletin Board

A bulletin board system for people involved in, or interested in, the European Southern Observatory. Discussion and information regarding astronomy and telescopes.

Telnet:
Address: **bbhost.hq.eso.org**
Login: **esobb**

FedWorld

FedWorld BBS is sponsored by the National Technical Information Service (NTIS) and is tasked by Congress to help disseminate vast amounts of scientific and technical information along with other, non-technical information. As a central point of connectivity, NTIS FedWorld offers access to thousands of files across a wide range of subject areas. You can find information ranging from environmental protection to small business.

Telnet:
Address: **fedworld.gov**

A
B
C
D
E
F
G
H
I
J
K
L
M
N
O
P
Q
R
S
T
U
V
W
X
Y
Z

Foothills Multiuser Chat

A popular chat system and a great place to relax and talk. Foothills provides a secure environment in which you can converse, with many features that make life easier.

Telnet:
> Address: **marble.bu.edu 2010**

Frequently Asked Questions re: Internet BBSs

Frequently asked questions (FAQs) and answers about Internet bulletin boards.

Anonymous FTP:
> Address: **nigel.msen.com**
> Path: **/pub/gopher/stuff/stuff.old/inet-bbs-faq**

Archie:
> Pattern: **inet-bbs-faq**

Usenet:
> Newsgroup: **alt.bbs.internet**

General BBS Information

General information on using and understanding BBSs.

Usenet:
> Newsgroup: **comp.bbs.misc**

Government Sponsored Bulletin Boards

A list of U.S. government bulletin boards. This list is compiled by the Department of Commerce, Economics and Statistics Administration and lists many BBSs by government agency.

Gopher:
> Name: Library of Congress
> Address: **marvel.loc.gov**
> Choose: **Fed. Govt. Info.**
>   **| Fed. Info. Resources | Info. by Agency**
>   **| General Info. | Federal Bulletin Boards**

Need help understanding BBSs?

Read
comp.bbs.misc

Internet BBS Access via Gopher

Access more BBSs through Gopher than you can imagine. Just choose the BBS you wish to use from the large list available and you will be connected. Get rid of those long cumbersome BBS lists.

Gopher:
> Name: Texas A&M University
> Address: **gopher.tamu.edu**
> Choose: **Hot Topics: A&M's Most Popular Items**
>   **| Bulletin Boards**

> Name: University of Texas at Austin
> Address: **actlab.rtf.utexas.edu**
> Choose: **Networks**
>   **| The Internet**
>   **| Bulletin Board Systems**

Internet BBS Lists

Together, Mathew (CC) May's NAL list and Scott Yanoff's Internet Services List form the most complete updated source of all the Internet BBS addresses and like-minded services that you will ever need. Endless hours of roaming the Net await you.

Excerpt from the Net...

(from "Government Sponsored Bulletin Boards")

NATIONAL INSTITUTE FOR STANDARDS AND TECHNOLOGY

```
Microcomputer Electronic Information Exchange
     Voice Number:   301-975-3359
     Data Number:    301-948-5717 (2400 bps)
                     301-948-5718 (9600 bps)
```

Describes software, systems, and techniques that combat unauthorized access to your computer, and contains files that describe computer viruses and how to prevent them.

Anonymous FTP:

Address: **aug3.augsburg.edu**
Path: **/files/bbs_lists/***

Address: **/pds.nchu.edu.tw**
Path: **/pub/bbs-list/***

ISCA BBS

The largest and most popular BBS on the Internet (and the largest non-profit BBS in the world). There are discussion groups to satisfy all tastes, especially groups of a more esoteric nature that seem to be lacking on Usenet. ISCA is often full, with users from all over the globe busily rambling away.

Telnet:

Address: **bbs.isca.uiowa.edu**
Login: **guest**

Address: **whip.isca.uiowa.edu**
Login: **guest**

Launchpad BBS

Much more than a BBS, this Internet Service Mediator welcomes all new users with open arms. Offering complete network news, local mail, Wais, Gopher, and access to many other information systems, it is well worth investigating.

Telnet:

Address: **launchpad.unc.edu**
Login: **launch**

The Launchpad Spoonfeeder

We know that you are a cool dude who has memorized all the commands that you need to use the Internet. But we are sure you have a friend (probably a Mac user) who always expects things to be "easy". Send him to Launchpad: a BBS that allows you to access Internet services by choosing items from a menu. If you know how to order food in a restaurant, you can use Launchpad.

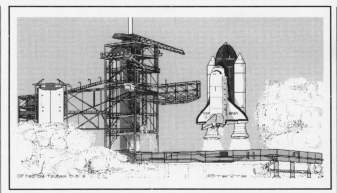

Drawings created with computers are available on the Internet as well as scanned photographs. This image is commonly named **blastoff.gif** and is available at many image archive sites including Washington University at St. Louis (**ftp.wustl.edu**).

Monochrome

Monochrome is a sophisticated multiuser messaging system. It includes local messages, multitudes of files, a multiuser talker, and a unique presentation capability which takes full advantage of your terminal type, throwing delightful quotes and scrolling messages at you constantly.

Telnet:

Address: **mono.city.ac.uk**
Login: **mono**
Password: **mono**

NSYSU BBS

A friendly BBS located in the heart of Taiwan. It offers an amazing selection of resources, including local discussion boards, games, Usenet news, Gopher, and great chat facilities. It can display everything in Chinese (if you download the necessary client), which is an interesting touch.

Telnet:

Address: **cc.nsysu.edu.tw**
Login: **bbs**

OuluBox

A small BBS located in Finland offering bulletins, a selection of discussion conferences, and downloadable files. A great place to practice your Finnish.

Telnet:

Address: **tolsun.oulu.fi**
Login: **box**

A B C D E F G H I J K L M N O P Q R S T U V W X Y Z

Prism Hotel BBS

The Prism Hotel is divided into multiple floors, each with its own subject area. On each floor there are numerous rooms that can be entered where you can view the discussion posts within. All this makes for interesting BBS navigation.

Telnet:
    Address: **bbs.fdu.edu**
    Login: **bbs**

Quartz BBS

One of the oldest BBSs on the Internet, though age has not withered it. There are many interesting discussion topics here, as well as a useful Internet information system.

Telnet:
    Address: **quartz.rutgers.edu**
    Login: **bbs**

Radford University CS BBS

Offers an amazing number of services, including general discussion groups, IRC, public files, local mail, access to libraries, and games.

Telnet:
    Address: **muselab-gw.runet.edu**
    Login: **bbs**

Skynet BBS

A friendly BBS, based in Norway, with many varied and interesting discussion groups. The policy of no censorship has led to many diverse and informative topics covering a wide spectrum of life's mysteries.

Telnet:
    Address: **hpx6.aid.no**
    Login: **skynet**

Softwords COSY

A friendly conferencing system with a variety of discussion groups, including many technical and business issues. Also offers Internet mail.

Telnet:
    Address: **softwords.bc.ca**
    Login: **cosy**

Specific BBS Programs

Discussion groups devoted to particular BBS software.

Usenet:
    Newsgroup: **alt.bbs.first-class**
    Newsgroup: **alt.bbs.majorbbs**
    Newsgroup: **alt.bbs.metal**
    Newsgroup: **alt.bbs.pcboard**
    Newsgroup: **alt.bbs.searchlight**
    Newsgroup: **alt.bbs.waffle**
    Newsgroup: **alt.bbs.wildcat**
    Newsgroup: **comp.bbs.waffle**

Sunset BBS

Lots of varied discussion groups, local mail, and a scenic login screen.

Telnet:
    Address: **paladine.hacks.arizona.edu**
    Login: **bbs**

Sysop Information

A forum for BBS system operators (sysops).

Usenet:
    Newsgroup: **alt.bbs.allsysop**

Unix and BBSs

BBS software for Unix systems and the UUCP mail facility.

Usenet:
    Newsgroup: **alt.bbs.pcbuucp**
    Newsgroup: **alt.bbs.unixbbs**

UTBBS

Based in Holland but featuring both English and Dutch-speaking users, UTBBS offers public and personal messaging, online chat, and a large file selection covering many areas of computing and more.

Telnet:
    Address: **utbbs.civ.utwente.nl**
    Login: **bbs**

**Spare time?
Take a look at Games**

BIOLOGY

Aging

There's more to aging than getting old. Despite what skin cream commercials say, you age from the inside out and no amount of Oil of Olay will cure that. Learn about cellular and organismal aging and begin your quest for the fountain of youth.

Usenet:
> Newsgroup: **bionet.molbio.ageing**

THE WORST PART OF AGEING IS GETTING OLD (THE REST ISN'T SO BAD). Still, AT LEAST YOU CAN BE WELL-INFORMED ABOUT WHAT YOUR CELLS ARE DOING BY READING **bionet.molbio.ageing**.

American Type Culture Collection

A natural language database. Compose your queries in plain English and the system will provide documents relating to your queries.

Telnet:
> Address: **atcc.nih.gov**
> Login: **search**
> Password: **common**

Lonely?
Try the Personals.

Announcements

This newsgroup is the loudspeaker of Bionet, Usenet's hierarchy of biology-oriented newsgroups. Find out what's going on in the wide world of biology: new electronic journals, conference announcements, calls for research papers, and new databases are a few of the things that people are shouting about. This group is moderated.

Usenet:
> Newsgroup: **bionet.announce**

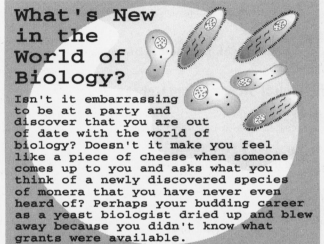

What's New in the World of Biology?

Isn't it embarrassing to be at a party and discover that you are out of date with the world of biology? Doesn't it make you feel like a piece of cheese when someone comes up to you and asks what you think of a newly discovered species of monera that you have never even heard of? Perhaps your budding career as a yeast biologist dried up and blew away because you didn't know what grants were available.

Well, no need to worry: just read **bionet.announce** and become biologically correct.

The Arabidopsis Project

Imagine how carefree you would feel running through a huge field of Arabidopsis, your lab coat flapping behind you. Capture that experience, or at least the next best thing, by discussing the Arabidopsis project with others who share your interest in these little herbs.

Usenet:
> Newsgroup: **bionet.genome.arabidopsis**

Bioinformatics Resource Gopher

This resource develops and operates DNA sequence analysis software.

Gopher:
> Name: University of Florida
> Address: **dna.cedb.uwf.edu**

A
B
C
D
E
F
G
H
I
J
K
L
M
N
O
P
Q
R
S
T
U
V
W
X
Y
Z

Biological Culture Collections

The World Directory of Culture Collections of Microorganisms, serving to support activities of culture collections and their users. Contains details of over 500 culture collections from 60 countries.

Anonymous FTP:
   Address: **fragrans.riken.go.jp**

Biological Databases

For seemingly endless amounts of information, check out these biological databases. Find computer applications to suit your biological needs, so to speak.

Usenet:
   Newsgroup: **bionet.molbio.bio-matrix**

Biological Sciences Conferences

A large list of mailing lists related to the biological sciences; divided into subject areas.

Anonymous FTP:
   Address: **ksuvxa.kent.edu**
   Path: **/library/acadlist.file5**

Gopher:
   Name: NYSERNet
   Address: **nysernet.org**
   Choose: **Special Collections: Higher Education | Scholarly Electronic Conferences [Kovacs], 7th rev. | Biological Sciences**

Biological Scientist's Network Guide

Useful FAQs, papers, press releases, announcements, and project information for biological scientists who work on a variety of computer networks.

Gopher:
   Name: World Data Center on Microorganisms
   Address: **fragrans.riken.go.jp**
   Choose: **About bioinfo... | Useful articles..**

Biologist's Guide to Internet Resources

This document explains how to find everything of use to a biologist on the Internet.

Gopher:
   Name: Center for Scientific Computing
   Address: **finsun.csc.fi**
   Choose: **Information in English | Scientific Topics | Finnish EMBnet BioBox | FAQ Files | A Biologist's Guide..**

Biology Journals

Periodical references to various biology journals.

Wais:
   Database: **biology-journal-contents**

Biology Newsletter

Selection of newsletters about agriculture, botany, ecosystems, genetics, and general biology, including publications such as *Starnet*, *Tiempo*, and *Flora* online.

Anonymous FTP:
   Address: **nigel.msen.com**
   Path: **/pub/newsletters/Bio/***

Biology Resources

Explore the many biology-related resources available on the Internet via the Gopher. Contains FAQs, FTP sites, book lists, and access to many biology servers around the globe.

Gopher:
   Name: Center for Scientific Computing
   Address: **finsun.csc.fi**
   Choose: **Information in English | Scientific Topics | Finnish EMBnet BioBox**

Biology Software and Archives

An extensive collection of more than 70 biology resources available via the Internet. Includes a gene server, molecular graphics, software, project information, and access to many more biological tools and programs.

Anonymous FTP:
   Address: **ftp.bio.indiana.edu**
   Path: **/archive.doc**

Gopher:
   Name: Computational Biology
   Address: **gopher.gdb.org**
   Choose: **FTP Sites, Software and Data Archives for Biology**

Biology Software Search

Search and retrieve biology-related software for all the popular computers.

Gopher:
   Name: Johns Hopkins University
   Address: **merlot.welch.jhu.edu**
   Choose: **Search and Retrieve Software | Search and Retrieve Software for Biology**

Biomechanics

A mailing list intended for members of the International, European, American, Canadian and other Societies of Biomechanics, and anyone else interested in this field.

Internet mailing list:
List Address: **biomch-l@nic.surfnet.nl**
Subscription Address:
biomch-l-request@nic.surfnet.nl

Biosphere and Ecology

Life does not exist in a vacuum. Ecology cannot exist strictly in a lab. For you rugged, active types, try studying the relations between living organisms and their environment.

Usenet:
Newsgroup: **bit.listserv.biosph-l**
Newsgroup: **sci.bio.ecolog**

Biotechnology

Biotechnology is not simply the clicking of switches and the turning of dials. It's the graceful application of science and technology to all aspects of biology, but especially to molecular and cellular biology and genetics. Catch technology hot off the presses.

Usenet:
Newsgroup: **sci.bio.technology**

Brazilian Tropical Databases

Brazilian biological information, including tropical plants and animals, census of animals in Brazilian zoos, antimicrobials, and discussions of biodiversity.

Gopher:
Name: Base de Dados Tropical
Address: **bdt.ftpt.br**
Choose: **BDTNet - Tropical Data Base Network**

Cell Biology

This is where life happens, in tiny units of protoplasm. Unless you are a robot, cell biology concerns you. Cell scholars from all over the world dissect studies, research and experiments that relate to cell biology.

Usenet:
Newsgroup: **bionet.cellbiol**

Chromosome 22

Play the Chromatin Lotto, the game of human chance. If 22 is your lucky number, you've hit the jackpot. Get all sorts of information on Chromosome 22 and its function in the larger scheme of things.

Usenet:
Newsgroup: **bionet.genome.chrom22**

Computers and Mathematics

There's more to life than just cells and DNA. Not much more, but nevertheless, it's true. Feeding in data, spitting out numbers, running this, programming that—it's all part of computer and mathematical biology. This group is moderated.

Usenet:
Newsgroup: **bionet.biology.computational**

Counting on your genes to pull you through?

Read
bionet.biology.computational

Excerpt from the Net...

Newsgroup: sci.bio.ecology
Subject: Why are foxes the main carrier of rabies in the wild?

In Ontario [Canada], foxes are definitely one of the main vectors (skunks are good vectors too). I think that the reason for this is as simple as the fact that there is a specific rabies strain which attacks foxes but doesn't kill them very quickly. This would allow the number of foxes with rabies to build up due to contact with others before its death. I think that the primary vector depends on which strain of rabies predominates in a particular area.

A
B
C
D
E
F
G
H
I
J
K
L
M
N
O
P
Q
R
S
T
U
V
W
X
Y
Z

Drosophila

The media is always reporting recent exploits of the pesky, globe-trotting fruit fly. More amazing is the fact that there are people who study these critters for long periods of time. If you are one of those special people, find kinship with your peers as they discuss the biology of Drosophila.

Usenet:
    Newsgroup: **bionet.drosophila**

EMBL Nucleic Acid Database

If you're searching for information on EMBL nucleic acids, this is the place for you. People from all over the world feed this database with information.

Usenet:
    Newsgroup: **bionet.molbio.embldatabank**

Evolution of Genes and Proteins

You won't see it happen right before your eyes, unless you're watching a bad science fiction movie, but nevertheless evolution is happening all around us all the time. Study ideas and research on the evolution of genes and proteins.

Usenet:
    Newsgroup: **bionet.molbio.evolution**

Funding and Grants

Don't wait for your million dollar sweepstakes check to come in. Where are some of the funding agencies in biology? Who's giving out research grants? Find out who has got the money and how you can get some, too.

Usenet:
    Newsgroup: **bionet.sci-resources**

Too much spare time?
Explore a MUD

Funding and Grants in Biology

So you've got this great idea for developing wheat that grows in thin rows, just perfect for making sliced bread. But what can you do for seed money?

Participate in the bionet.sci-resources discussion group and perhaps, just perhaps, you will find the financial source that will send you on your way to becoming the next Internet Nobel prize winner.

Fungi

It's fair to say that fungi are just about everbody's favorite biological kingdom (although some people do prefer monera). Find out what makes these multicelled, eukaryotic heterotrophs so much fun to work with. Whether saprobic or parasitic, these cool organisms will well repay a lifetime of study. Join the crowd.

Usenet:
    Newsgroup: **bionet.mycology**

GenBank Database

It's not just a database, it's a way of life. Not only is the GenBank nucleic acid database available, but there is a **.updates** group that gives the most recent news about GenBank. The **.gdb** group holds messages to and from the GDB database staff.

Usenet:
    Newsgroup: **bionet.molbio.gdb**
    Newsgroup: **bionet.molbio.genbank**
    Newsgroup: **bionet.molbio.genbank.updates**

General Biology

This forum covers all the biological sciences. Catch glimpses of a little bit of everything that makes up the world around us. Discover what makes your body tick, what's in that yeast bread you've been eating, and how everything you touch teems with life. Life will never be the same.

Usenet:
    Newsgroup: **bionet.general**

Genetic Linkage

How many genes does it take to organize a chromosome? It's not a joke, it's genetic linkage trivia. Read linkage analyses on **.gene-linkage**. On **.gene-org**, experience how genes are organized on chromosomes. They would put any board of directors to shame.

Usenet:
  Newsgroup: **bionet.molbio.gene-linkage**
  Newsgroup: **bionet.molbio.gene-org**

The Human Genome Project

Join the discussion about the Human Genome Project, the massive, ambitious scheme to ferret out and document all of the genes in human chromosomes. Maybe one day they will isolate the gene for TV watching and we will all be saved.

Usenet:
  Newsgroup: **bionet.molbio.genome-program**

Immunology

Bigger, stronger people mean quicker and faster viral mutations. Why do you get sick, but your co-worker doesn't? Immunology reveals the magic of our ability to withstand the effects of disease and sickness.

Usenet:
  Newsgroup: **bionet.immunology**

Information Theory

Speculation, brainstorming, and sharing of ideas is what happens when you get everyone together to talk about biological information theory.

Usenet:
  Newsgroup: **bionet.info-theory**

Job Opportunities

Why be a telemarketer when you can have a job in the exciting field of biology? See cells reproduce right before your eyes, cut up small, unsuspecting micro-organisms with lightning speed, and create new life forms seemingly from scratch. Opportunities abound for pre- or post-docs, undergraduates looking for something to keep them out of trouble for the summer, assistant professors who don't mind grading papers, and upwardly mobile tenure-track seekers.

Usenet:
  Newsgroup: **bionet.jobs**

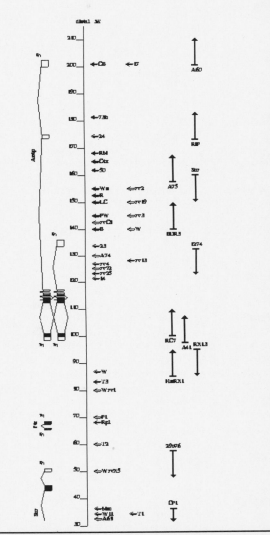

Computer pictures aren't only for fun. This image is the genome of a drysophila melanogaster (whatever that is). Many university science departments store image files on their systems that could be of interest to you. This image is from the Biology Department of the University of Indiana (**ftp.bio.indiana.edu**).

Journals

If you like biological journals, or even if you don't and have to read them anyway, check the **.contents** group for a brief outline of what's in the latest journals. Look at the **.note** group for advice on dealing with biology journals.

Usenet:
  Newsgroup: **bionet.journals.contents**
  Newsgroup: **bionet.journals.note**

Kinetics and Thermodynamics

Kinetics and thermodynamics are fitness programs for cells, except that cells don't wear little spandex suits. Discuss the dynamics of chain reactions at the cellular level.

Usenet:
    Newsgroup: **bionet.metabolic-reg**

Mapping Chromosomes

Much like the quest of Indiana Jones, only on a smaller scale (much smaller), mapping and sequencing eucaryote chromosomes can be mysterious and revealing. Join the discussion and find out the why and how.

Usenet:
    Newsgroup: **bionet.genome.chromosome**

Methods and Reagents

Develop some flair when experimenting. Show a little imagination when you stain your DNA or measure your plasma renin activity. See your peers use PCR to introduce silent mutations—the genetic ninjas of biology. Learn the methods and reagents that work and run quickly away from the ones that don't.

Usenet:
    Newsgroup: **bionet.molbio.methds-reagnts**

Molecular Biology of HIV

There is so much information going around about the family of HIV viruses. Everyday it seems there are new studies and new research. See it broken down to a molecular level and learn how HIV operates.

Usenet:
    Newsgroup: **bionet.molbio.hiv**

Neuroscience

When you tell someone you are a bundle of nerves, you are telling more of the truth than you probably realize. Neuroscience involves the study of the nervous system, its structure and diseases. Join the discussion and meet the pros.

Usenet:
    Newsgroup: **bionet.neuroscience**

Nitrogen Fixation

Most people don't think of bacteria as a handy and useful thing to have around. You clean them, spray them, call them bad names. Just hope they don't go on strike and stop carrying ammonia-bound nitrogen to their designated delivery areas, causing the collapse of the food chain right at the weakest link (you). See such nitrogen fixing in action and discover how this process keeps us in pizza and Chinese food.

Usenet:
    Newsgroup: **bionet.n2-fixation**

Population Biology

The biology of populations used to be as simple as counting the legs and dividing by two. Modern methods are a lot more complex and require considerable biological, mathematical and computational expertise. Visit this newsgroup when you need to swap stories with the experts.

Usenet:
    Newsgroup: **bionet.population-bio**

Primates

A Gopher dedicated to primate biology, including discussions, directory of primatology, newsletters, behavioral patterns, animal welfare legislation, and other items of interest.

Gopher:
    Name: Primate Info Net
    Address: **saimiri.primate.wisc.edu**

Protein Crystallography

Discover the latest thoughts on the form, structure, and properties of crystallized protein. It's not recommended for trail mix, but it certainly has its merits.

Usenet:
    Newsgroup: **bionet.xtallography**

Protein Data Bank

An experimental Gopher server at the Protein Data Bank. Provides convenient and useful search methods, sparkling graphics, and some analysis information.

Gopher:
Name: Protein Data Bank
Address: **pdb.pdb.bnl.gov**

Protein Databases

Immerse yourself in the mystery and intrigue of proteins. Why would a peptide with prolyl residue spontaneously cleave during synthesis, but refuse to do it at a proline? Find out what happens when the talk turns to protein, the most important nitrogenous organic substance on planet Earth.

Usenet:
Newsgroup: **bionet.molbio.proteins**

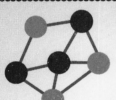

PROTEINS PROTEINS PROTEINS

It's hard not to like proteins: those cute molecules with a primary, secondary, tertiary and even quaternary structure. It's been said that if there were no proteins, there would be no life as we know it (or at least no daytime television). When you are stuck in a protein quandry, read **bionet.molbio.proteins** and join the folks who really understand the difference between "cysteine" and "cystine". (Of course, what's a disulfide bridge between friends?)

Randomly Amplified Polymorphic DNA

It's late in the day. You have optimized your PCR reaction conditions with a pair of specific primer sets. You then switch to random primers from UBC to do RAPD (not forgetting to lower the annealing temperature to 35 degrees C). However, you try 30 random primers and still do not get any good results. Isn't it good to know you have a place to turn for help?

Usenet:
Newsgroup: **bionet.molbio.rapd**

Related Sciences

Unbutton your top button and roll up your sleeves in preparation for some lively biological bantering. While informative and educational, subjects are never strictly hard-core science. Debate is sparked by such topics as evolution, the ethics of cloning, and the instinctual mating habits of animals and humans.

Usenet:
Newsgroup: **sci.bio**

Software

Computers lighten your workload, if you have the right tools. The right tools are available, if you know where to look. There are many software sources for general biology or for more specific needs.

Usenet:
Newsgroup: **bionet.software**
Newsgroup: **bionet.software.acedb**
Newsgroup: **bionet.software.gcg**
Newsgroup: **bionet.software.sources**
Newsgroup: **bit.listserv.info-gcg**

Taxacom FTP Server

Technical information, software, and information on standards and workshops in the field of systematic biology.

Anonymous FTP:
Address: **huh.harvard.edu**
Path: **/pub/README.TAX**

Taxacom Listserv Lists

Taxacom bitnet Listserv mailing lists focus on systematic biology and accept mail messages from any network source and then distribute those messages to list subscribers. The Listserv is capable of delivering mail to users on bitnet, the Internet, or to any mail service on a gatewayed network. There are no restrictions on participation and there is no cost.

Anonymous FTP:
Address: **huh.harvard.edu**
Path: **/pub/taxacom/taxacom.txt**

Want some fun?
Read the Fun section

A
B
C
D
E
F
G
H
I
J
K
L
M
N
O
P
Q
R
S
T
U
V
W
X
Y
Z

Tropical Biology

Imagine being on the beach, the wind whispering through your hair, sand between your toes—a scalpel in one hand, a mollusk in the other. What could be more beautiful? Experience the exotic essence of tropical biology with other people who think Life is one long Spring Break. The only thing that could make it more interesting would be a drink with a little umbrella in it.

Usenet:

Newsgroup: **bionet.biology.tropical**

Virology

Nobody likes to invite a virus to the party, but biologists have a knack for making virology appealing. Talk often turns speculative, as topics include such debatable issues as destroying the last remaining specimens of the smallpox virus or whether certain vires are capable of cross-species infection.

Usenet:

Newsgroup: **bionet.virology**

Who's Who in Biology

Who was that guy that wrote the article on yeast vector shuttles? If you are looking for someone particular in the field of biology, check here. While the bionet is a small world, it covers a huge area. It has been said that you are only six people away from any person in the world. Try out this newsgroup and skip the five missing links.

Usenet:

Newsgroup: **bionet.users.addresses**

Women in Biology

Women discuss why the field of biology is important to them. Discover gender-related issues and other concerns that are specifically tied to women in biology. This group is not just about science; it has that added touch of something special that only women can give.

Usenet:

Newsgroup: **bionet.women-in-bio**

Yeast

Yeast is good for more than bread and beer. It's a fascinating, multi-useful mass of minute fungi. Find out what the molecular biology and genetics of yeast is all about. Maybe you'll even get some good recipes for bread and beer.

Usenet:

Newsgroup: **bionet.molbio.yeast**

BIZARRE

Aleister Crowley

Documents and texts by Aleister Crowley, including *Book 4*, *Magick Without Tears*, *Book of the Law*, *Magick in Theory and Practice*, and *Equinox*.

Anonymous FTP:

Address: **slopoke.mlb.semi.harris.com**
Path: **/pub/magick/magick/Crowley/***

Anonymity

Greta Garbo used to participate in this discussion group, but under a pseudonym. Want to be alone with other people? This is the place to be or not to be.

Usenet:

Newsgroup: **alt.anonymous**

Arcana Arcanorum

Arcana Arcanorum, the Playing-Card Oracle, is a method of fortune telling using an ordinary deck of playing cards.

Anonymous FTP:

Address: **ftp.spies.com**
Path: **/Library/Document/arcana.doc**

Gopher:

Name: Internet Wiretap
Address: **wiretap.spies.com**
Choose: **Wiretap Online Library**
  ❘ Assorted Documents
  ❘ Arcana Arcanorum (Playing-Card Oracle)

Bigfoot

I saw Bigfoot, the animal/man/monster, in K-Mart reading *The Internet Complete Reference*. Immediately, I ran to share my experience with the people in this, my favorite Usenet newsgroup. Honest, it's true, I really saw him. (He was looking up Archie servers.)

Usenet:

Newsgroup: **alt.bigfoot**

Bizarre Literature

A mailing list devoted to bizarre, disturbing, and offensive short stories and ramblings.

Listserv mailing list:
List Address: **weird-l@brownvm.brown.edu**
Subscription Address:
listserv@brownvm.brown.edu

Callahan's Bar

A home away from home: meet the regular patrons of Callahan's Bar, a virtual bar for real people. Friends, fellowship, good will, and bad puns.

Usenet:
Newsgroup: **alt.callahans**

Life can be tough.
Take a break at

Callahan's
Bar

Cesium

How much can you say about the element cesium? You would be surprised—you *will* be suprised—when you join this discussion group. This is the group that proves Usenet has something for everyone.

Usenet:
Newsgroup: **alt.cesium**

The Bizarre section has some cool stuff

Excerpt from the Net...

Newsgroup: alt.cesium
Subject: Cesium in water

> What would happen if Cesium were to
> be thrown into water?
> Would it cause an explosion?

No. In fact, it would not. It would just sit there like a lump of cesium thrown into water...which would then, of course, explode with the force of a billion suns. Don't try this at home, kids (unless your home happens to be in Jersey).

Church of the SubGenius

Experience the weirdness of the Church of the SubGenius, their Everyman Messiah Bob (Dobbs), and the SubGenius Foundation. As Louis Armstrong once said, "If you gotta ask, you'll never know."

Usenet:
Newsgroup: **alt.slack**

Excerpt from the Net...

Newsgroup: alt.slack
Subject: There are hookers in my town

I just found out yesterday from my Scuba Instructor that there are hookers here in our town. I am shocked. I have never actually seen a real hooker. I kind of want to see one or maybe even talk to one and I was wondering if there are any prostitutes on the Internet? Please post here so we can begin email correspondence. Only real hookers need apply, because I'm certainly not going to waste my time with some impersonator. I'm gonna know if you're not a hooker, too, because I have a sure-fire test.

Thank you very much.

If you like trouble, take a look at Mischief

A
B
C
D
E
F
G
H
I
J
K
L
M
N
O
P
Q
R
S
T
U
V
W
X
Y
Z

Complaining

Welcome to the Usenet complaint department. Complain about anything you want and read other people's pet peeves. Just the thing to get you back in a good mood after reading **alt.good.morning**.

Usenet:
    Newsgroup: **alt.peeves**

THE USENET COMPLAINT DEPARTMENT

We all need to complain. The trouble is, most of our complaints are heard only by people in our immediate vicinity. Much better to send your complaints to **alt.peeves**.
That way, anyone on the Internet will have a chance to find out what you think of parents who can't keep their kids quiet in public, or talk show hosts who swank around like they own the place.

Cryonics

We all have to go sometime, but maybe a lucky few will actually get to come back. Is it possible to have yourself frozen today in preparation for the time when unspecified future technology will be ready to bring you back to the future? If you are deadly serious about an encore, this is a newsgroup you will not want to miss. To start, read the frequently asked question list (available from the FTP site). Next, decide whether you should have your whole body frozen or just your head (neuropreservation). Why let yourself get carried away when you can chill out?

Anonymous FTP:
    Address: **rtfm.mit.edu**
    Path: **/pub/usenet/news.answers/cryonics-faq/***

Usenet:
    Newsgroup: **sci.cryonics**

Excerpt from the Net...

Newsgroup: sci.cryonics
Subject: Expiring minds want to know...

Neuropreservation is a form of cryonic suspension in which only the patient's head or brain is preserved. It clearly is less expensive than whole-body cryonic suspension. Being more compact, the patient (normally) is more portable, too, enabling faster escape from disaster. Furthermore, neuropatients arguably can get better perfused brains than whole-body patients, since the perfusion protocol can focus only on their brains rather than all their other organs, too. The most obvious disadvantage of neuropreservation, however, is the lack of a body.

At first glance, lacking a body sounds like a fatal flaw in the plan...

Question sent to sci.cryonics:

> Do you have to be DEAD to have this
> done? Is there any way that I could
> have them do it to me when I'm 90 or
> so? And then specify to warm me back
> up in another 75 years?

Dark Side of the Net

A list of Gothic, vampire, occult, and various other dark resources; including IRC channels, mailing lists, FTP sites, Usenet newsgroups and e-zines. To subscribe, send mail to the address below. In addition, this list is posted regularly to the **alt.gothic** and **news.lists** newsgroups.

Mail:
    Address: **carriec@eskimo.com**
    Body: **subscribe dark side of the net** *your name and address*

Devilbunnies

What are these devilbunnies? Tiny little creatures that seem to pop up everywhere and make the best laid plans of mice and men gang aft agley. Are they real, or figments of warped imaginations that have been too long glued to the computer? Tune in for the latest update on the spiritual descendants of the gremlins of World War II.

Usenet:
    Newsgroup: **alt.devilbunnies**

Discord and Destruction

Serious talk about serious talk. Destroy the earth or just our way of life: it's up to you. Remember, life is stern and earnest and nobody gets out of here alive.

Usenet:
    Newsgroup: **alt.destroy.the.earth**
    Newsgroup: **alt.discordia**

Excerpt from the Net...

Newsgroup: alt.destroy.the.earth
Subject: Earth is cool

I am new to this discussion group, but I think I can figure it out, at least more so than the "Earth is cool" person. Couldn't you think of a better word to use than cool? I mean, idiots like Beavis and Butthead can say "Yeah, that was cool" so maybe you are on the same level as them. I wouldn't be surprised.

Anyway, the "Earth is cool" person is without a clue. I don't think that anyone here wants to really destroy the earth, but we just like talking about the possibilities of it. We aren't losers who think that we've been wronged by society. We don't hate society. In fact (at least as far as I'm concerned) society is, to use your vocabulary, "cool." It's just that we're a bunch of cynics who like to express our senses of humor. Before you post another note here, maybe you should check if you ever received a sense of humor in the first place.

Explosions and Blowing Things Up

Okay, we know it sounds weird, but we all have a primal urge to blow things up. Well, guys do, anyway. Well, some guys. Okay, so we like things that go boom in the night. Check out Usenet's answer to the big bang. (Kibo, of course, is just along for the ride.)

Usenet:
    Newsgroup: **alt.exploding.kibo**

Furry Animals

Whether live or stuffed, there's something about small furry animals that brings out the latent anthropomorphism in us all. They are just too cute for words, so we won't even try. Be there or be square.

Usenet:
    Newsgroup: **alt.fan.furry**

Future Culture Digest Archives

Collection of archives for the Future Culture mailing list (which brings you tomorrow's reality today), including the Future Culture and **alt.cyberpunk** FAQs.

Anonymous FTP:
    Address: **ftp.rahul.net**
    Path: **/pub/atman/**
        UTLCD-preview/future-culture/*

Listserv mailing list:
    List Address: **uafsysb@uark.edu**
    Subscription Address: **listserv@uark.edu**

Geeks and Nerds

Remember, if it wasn't for geeks and nerds there wouldn't be an Internet (and you wouldn't be able to read this totally cool Internet book). Pay tribute to these unsung heros of the Star Trek generation. Join Usenet's own mutual admiration society: take a nerd to lunch today.

Usenet:
    Newsgroup: **alt.geek**

General Bizarre Discussion

The unusual, curious, and often stupid: here is Usenet's newsgroup for canonical strangeness. Just don't make the mistake of sending in an article that is not bizarre enough.

Usenet:
    Newsgroup: **talk.bizarre**

Gopher problems?
Read "The Internet Complete Reference"

A B C D E F G H I J K L M N O P Q R S T U V W X Y Z

Gross and Disgusting

Tales to make you cringe, poems to offend you, and bets you wouldn't believe, all utterly tasteless.

Anonymous FTP:
>Address: **ftp.spies.com**
>Path: **/Library/Fringe/Gross/***

Gopher:
>Name: Internet Wiretap
>Address: **wiretap.spies.com**
>Choose: **Wiretap Online Library**
>| **Fringes of Reason**
>| **Gross and Disgusting**

Happy Birthday

Wish yourself a happy birthday and see if anyone cares. Gather round for birthday greetings from all over the world in this once a year newsgroup for everybody. In case you are wondering: Harley's birthday is December 21 and Rick's is October 9. (And money is always in good taste.)

Usenet:
>Newsgroup: **alt.happy.birthday.to.me**

High Weirdness

Incredible collection of information and lists detailing where and how to locate the more esoteric and weird resources on the Internet.

Anonymous FTP:
>Address: **slopoke.mlb.semi.harris.com**
>Path: **/pub/weirdness/weird2_1.doc**

>Address: **slopoke.mlb.semi.harris.com**
>Path: **/pub/weirdness/weird2_1.sup**

Lemurs

What is it that makes these monkey-like mammals from Madagascar so adorably desirable? Serious lemur-lovers hang out in the **.lemurs** group. Those who prefer their lemurs broiled with a touch of paprika will be more at home in **.lemurs.cooked**.

Usenet:
>Newsgroup: **alt.fan.lemurs**
>Newsgroup: **alt.fan.lemurs.cooked**

Naked Guy

Andy Martinez is a man of conviction. In order to make a point, he started going to class at U.C. Berkeley dressed only in a small loincloth and, eventually, completely naked. Well, Martinez—now affectionately known as The

Excerpt from the Net...

```
Newsgroup: alt.geek
Subject: What the well-dressed geek is wearing
```

While we are discussing various facets of geek paraphernalia, I just wanted to mention something which *seems* to be becoming extinct: horned-rim glasses.

As I mentioned before, I'm only 14; but I have a NIFTY pair of horned-rim glasses straight out of any high school picture from 1964. I don't know about you, but I think extra-thick horned-rims are a classic geek symbol. Maybe I'm wrong. However, they look pretty good with tape.

My grandpa bestowed me his leather slide-rule case. I don't wear it much anymore because I tend to use my graphics calculator and my palmtop a bit more. I don't have a holster for my calc, but I do have a clip (which I'm sure is not as good). My palmtop, on the other hand, is a different story. I can't find anything with which I can attach it to my belt.

Regarding pocket-protectors. I agree with what someone said earlier: you should only wear them to suit a cause. Any other reason would be stupid and (dare I say it) rather superficial. If you like to have your pens and screwdrivers at hand like I do, then a protector is a good idea. I have a day-glo neon yellow protector that says "Kiss me, I'm a Physicist". Of course, I'm not a physicist, but a friend of mine who works at a research lab gave it to me.

Naked Guy—got thrown out of school, but he did make his point (at least in the summer). Read this newsgroup and follow the career of one whom, arguably, can be described as the best man.

Usenet:
    Newsgroup: **alt.fan.naked-guy**

Necromicon

FAQ and material about this near-legendary text written in Damascus in 730 A.D. Includes documents about the Voymich Manuscript.

Anonymous FTP:
    Address: **nic.funet.fi**
    Path: **/pub/doc/occult/necronomicon/***

Negative Emotions

Angst, bitterness, misanthropy, fear, disgust, anxiety and just plain being in a bad mood. Join the folks down at the not-OK corral for some roll-up-your-sleeves-and-get-down-to-it homestyle bitchin'. As John Milton put it (when they took away his Internet account), "So little is our loss. So little is our gain."

Usenet:
    Newsgroup: **alt.angst**
    Newsgroup: **alt.bitterness**
    Newsgroup: **alt.misanthropy**

Why be normal? Read Bizarre.

Excerpt from the Net...

```
Newsgroups: alt.angst.xibo.sex
Subject: Angst and sex
```

> What is this angst thing?

> And what does it have to do with sex?

[*A woman responds...*]

What does angst have to do with sex? It has everything to do with sex.

What is sex without angst? The sweaty palms, the racing heart, the little doubts. Or if you're more like me, it's the raging desire when there is no chance of reciprocation and the frigid response when someone is there. The inability to give in all the way yet the fierce desire to experience everything all at once. The beauty of unrequited passionate expectations, dashed by a harsh word or unthinking distance of a lover. The pain of wanting to be a single person, if only for a few hours (or minutes) and yet always being separate.

[*Another person—a man—responds to the previous answer...*]

Is sex without angst possible? Sure, but usually only via monstrous self-deception, shutting out all those nagging doubts, untruths, outside desires, wandering attentions, etc. I've always wanted to be completely honest in and about sex, but that's hard for a sex junkie to do under the expectations of monogamy. The resulting tensions produce ever-mounting layers of angst, but then so do the deceptions. I sometimes want to lose myself in completely anonymous sex where I don't even have to know the other person's name, but alas that is also ultimately unsatisfying.

> How's your love life?

> Have you been reading Sartre?

[*To which the woman responds...*]

Love life? You must be jesting. I didn't know such a thing existed. I've heard of 'sex life' and even had one for a little while recently. But alas and alak, totting myself off to school has taken care of that. My lover is now my platonic lover and I am left strung-out and voiceless...

Sorry, but I'm completely unfamiliar with Sartre. He was a French philosopher, no?

A
B
C
D
E
F
G
H
I
J
K
L
M
N
O
P
Q
R
S
T
U
V
W
X
Y
Z

Excerpt from the Net...

```
Newsgroup: alt.bitterness
Subject: Too much happiness

> People only want you happy.

> Everything else is a drag because
> we're all too wrapped up in ourselves.
```

I actually do enjoy sharing others' misery—why else are we all reading this group?

Even if you are normally happy, it's a good sign that you can have these bouts of "down", as constantly joyous people are incredibly nauseating and—as the other postings have pointed out—usually stupid. Intelligence gives birth to thought, and thought breeds introspection and analysis, and in this world, analysis usually leads to depression.

People don't only want you to be always happy. Incredibly stupid, shallow people want you to be always happy. They don't want to think that someone is more thoughtful than they are, and they don't want you to derail them from their incredibly stupid, shallow, happy lives. Put a log on their tracks. Then they'll have time to stop and think.

Occult

Collection of occult material and pictures, covering such subjects as astrology, druidism, herbs, magic, rituals, tarot, and wicca.

Anonymous FTP:
    Address: **etext.archive.umich.edu**
    Path: **/pub/Quartz/occult/***

    Address: **ftp.funet.fi**
    Path: **/pub/doc/occult/***

    Address: **slopoke.mlb.semi.harris.com**
    Path: **/pub/magick/***

Real life is so boring. Why mess with reality and common sense when you can immerse yourself in the SUPERNATURAL?? join the occult and make up your own rules.

Occult and Paranormal

A collection of articles on the occult and paranormal, including the "Eight Sabbats of Witchcraft", "The Runes", and "The Chalice of Ecstasy".

Excerpt from the Net...

```
Newsgroup: alt.misanthropy
Subject: Humans are scum

> I've come to the conclusion (a long time ago) that
> the human race is the most ignorant, selfish,
> terrified, unpredictable bunch of animals that will
> ever walk this planet.
```

You left out 'nasty', 'brutish', and 'arrogant'. Good thing we misanthropes are so damned enlightened, huh?

```
> Why does the evening news show murder and
> rape statistics as though they were football scores?

> Why does the evening news show the football scores as if they were murder and rape
> statistics?

> For that matter, what other species has an evening news?
```

Anonymous FTP:
>Address: **ftp.spies.com**
>Path: **/Library/Fringe/Occult/***

Gopher:
>Name: Internet Wiretap
>Address: **wiretap.spies.com**
>Choose: **Wiretap Online Library**
>   **| Fringes of Reason | Occult and Paranormal**

Occultist Temple of Set

Material, guides, and rituals relating to the Occultist Temple of Set.

Anonymous FTP:
>Address: **etext.archive.umich.edu**
>Path: **/pub/Quartz/occult/set/***

Pagan Yule Customs

An Asatru viewpoint of Yule customs and traditions.

Anonymous FTP:
>Address: **ftp.spies.com**
>Path: **/Library/Fringe/Occult/pagan.yul**

Gopher:
>Name: Internet Wiretap
>Address: **wiretap.spies.com**
>Choose: **Wiretap Online Library**
>   **| Fringes of Reason | Occult and Paranormal**
>   **| Pagan Yule Customs**

Pantyhose

We know a newsgroup devoted to pantyhose sounds a little strange but, after all, you have to admit that there is something about long, sensuous legs wrapped in sheer black stockings that will turn even the most dignified gentleman into a wild jungle cat with the morals of a U.S. senator. For appropriate pictures to download, check out the FTP site.

Anonymous FTP:
>Address: **alycia.andrew.cmu.edu**
>Path: **/pub/graphics/over_age_18_only/hosiery/***

Usenet:
>Newsgroup: **alt.pantyhose**

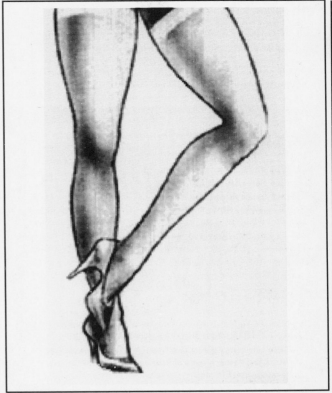
The Internet is famous for some interesting art collections.

Paranormal Phenomena

Freewheeling discussion of things that have to be believed to be seen. The **.skeptic** newsgroup is for people who believe that it is more fun to have both feet on the ground at the same time.

Usenet:
>Newsgroup: **alt.dreams**
>Newsgroup: **alt.out-of-body**
>Newsgroup: **alt.paranormal**
>Newsgroup: **sci.skeptic**

Want to know
what makes the Internet run?

Read Internet: RFCs

A
B
C
D
E
F
G
H
I
J
K
L
M
N
O
P
Q
R
S
T
U
V
W
X
Y
Z

Parties

Party till you drop. Share info on upcoming debauchery with people who are looking for love in all the right places.

Usenet:
> Newsgroup: **alt.party**

Paving the Earth

Have you ever wondered what it would be like to pave the Earth? No more grass to stain your white pants, no more insects to eat your picnic food, no more dirt on your new sneakers. Just imagine everything nice and smooth and hard. Seriously. (Do you think we make this stuff up?)

Usenet:
> Newsgroup: **alt.pave.the.earth**

Planet Yip Junk Mail List

Random dribblings and brain drippings.

Internet mailing list:
> List Address: **awerling@nmsu.edu**
> Subscription Address:
> **awerling-request@nmsu.edu**

Porter List

High Weirdness by e-mail.

Anonymous FTP:
> Address: **nexus.yorku.ca**
> Path: **/pub/Internet-info/high-weirdness**

Positive Emotions

As if there isn't enough to deal with already, here are newsgroups devoted to good feelings and happiness. Bah, humbug. If God had wanted us to hear good news, he wouldn't have given us television and newscasters with bad toupees. Most sickening of all has to be the **.good.morning** group: people from all over the world wishing each other a good morning. As Butt-head says, "I don't like stuff that sucks."

Usenet:
> Newsgroup: **alt.good.morning**
> Newsgroup: **alt.good.news**
> Newsgroup: **clari.news.goodnews**

Raves

FAQs, archives, drug information, flyer pictures, media articles, techno music reviews, and other information about energy-pounding techno parties.

Anonymous FTP:
> Address: **techno.stanford.edu**
> Path: **/pub/raves/***

Revelations of Awareness

The *New Age Cosmic Newsletter* is aimed at introducing people to cosmic awareness.

Anonymous FTP:
> Address: **etext.archive.umich.edu**
> Path: **/pub/Politics/Conspiracy/**
> **Cosmic.Awareness/***

Roommates from Hell

Next time your roommate borrows your girlfriend without asking, count yourself lucky. Tune in to the roommate version of "Can You Top This?" and it won't be long before you realize that some people have real trouble.

Usenet:
> Newsgroup: **alt.flame.roommate**

Rumors

Check out all the new rumors, both serious (Elvis and aliens) and less serious (the FBI and CIA). Did you hear that readers of this book are entitled to free admission to Disney World?

Usenet:
> Newsgroup: **talk.rumors**

Santa Claus

Ho! Ho! Ho! Santa is real. Search your hearts for the truth; celebrate the magic of the Christmas season by joining in with other devout Santa believers. Just don't forget to be good for goodness sake.

Usenet:
>Newsgroup: **alt.religion.santaism**

Sex and Magick

An essay on sex and sex magic entitled "Liber Conjunctus", by Fr. Nigris.

Anonymous FTP:
>Address: **ftp.spies.com**
>Path: **/Library/Fringe/Occult/magick.sex**

Gopher:
>Name: Internet Wiretap
>Address: **wiretap.spies.com**
>Choose: **Wiretap Online Library**
>> **| Fringes of Reason | Occult and Paranormal | Liber Conjunctus - Essay on Sex & Magick**

Strange Tales

A collection of weird articles; subjects include hedgehog songs, recursive storytelling, the Kloo Gnomes, and other strange tales.

Anonymous FTP:
>Address: **ftp.spies.com**
>Path: **/Library/Fringe/Weird/***

Gopher:
>Name: Internet Wiretap
>Address: **wiretap.spies.com**
>Choose: **Wiretap Online Library**
>> **| Fringes of Reason | Very Strange**

SubGenius

Find out about the Church of the SubGenius, Bob and his pipe, and slack. The Church of the SubGenius is a cult parody that sharply satirizes what's wrong with religion and society in general.

Anonymous FTP:
>Address: **quartz.rutgers.edu**
>Path: **/pub/subgenius/***

Gopher:
>Name: Rutgers Quartz Text Archive
>Address: **quartz.rutgers.edu**
>Choose:
>> **SubGenius-The Church of the SubGenius**

Swedish Chef

Remember that lovable Swedish Chef on the Muppets? The one who would chase little chickens with a meat cleaver, talk with a Swedish accent, and say "Bork, bork, bork"? Well, he is alive and well on the Internet. Read this newsgroup and find out how to get the encheferizer program: software to turn regular English text into a speech from the Swedish chef. Und noo, buys und gurls, ve-a veell leern hoo tu cuuk cheeckees. Bork bork bork!

Usenet:
>Newsgroup: **alt.swedish.chef.bork.bork.bork**

Tasteless Tales

Dozens of the best tales from the Usenet group **alt.tasteless**, divided into anecdote, prank, tasteless fact, and art sections.

Anonymous FTP:
>Address: **ftp.spies.com**
>Path: **/Library/Fringe/Gross/tasteles.92**

Gopher:
>Name: Internet Wiretap
>Address: **wiretap.spies.com**
>Choose: **Wiretap Online Library**
>> **| Fringes of Reason | Gross and Disgusting | Alt.Tasteless 26 Best of 1992**

Tasteless Topics

All that is tasteless. Say whatever you want: just make sure it is disgusting. This is not the place to bring your grandmother for her birthday.

Usenet:
>Newsgroup: **alt.tasteless**

Three-Letter Acronyms

Join the only worldwide discussion group devoted to three-letter acronyms and extended three-letter acronyms. FYI, IMHO, you will love TLAs and ETLAs. (Don't forget to RTFM in order to CYA.)

Usenet:
>   Newsgroup: **alt.tla**

UFO Digests

Digests about UFOs, from the Paranet Information Service.

Anonymous FTP:
>   Address: **grind.isca.uiowa.edu**
>   Path: **/info/paranet/***

Telnet:
>   Address: **grind.isca.uiowa.edu**
>   Login: **iscabbs**

UFOs

A cool, rational, scientific, intellectual, well-reasoned, and plausible discussion about aliens visiting Earth and swanking around like they own the place. Investigate, in person, the theory that humans are really Nature's last word. Just the place to spend your time when the TV is on the fritz.

Usenet:
>   Newsgroup: **alt.alien.visitors**

Excerpt from the Net...

```
Newsgroups: alt.alien.visitors
Subject: You idiots!

This is the first time I ever read this
group, but this still made me mad. What
gives this person the right to say "You
are such idiots", just because someone
believes he had an alien encounter. I
guess that's why a lot of people never
mention their experiences with aliens.

Actually I had a roommate from
Mars...but then again hasn't everybody?
```

UFOs and Mysterious Abductions

A collection of articles and FAQs about visitors from outer space, crop circles, Project Blue Book, UFO conspiracies, and other items of interest.

Anonymous FTP:
>   Address: **ftp.spies.com**
>   Path: **/Library/Fringe/Ufo/***

Gopher:
>   Name: Internet Wiretap
>   Address: **wiretap.spies.com**
>   Choose: **Wiretap Online Library**
> | **Fringes of Reason**
> | **UFOs and Mysterious Abductions**

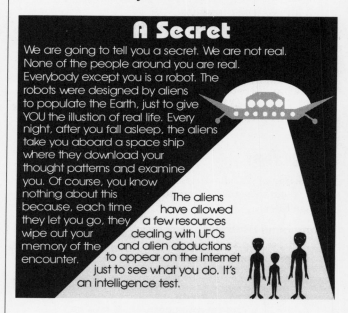

A Secret

We are going to tell you a secret. We are not real. None of the people around you are real. Everybody except you is a robot. The robots were designed by aliens to populate the Earth, just to give YOU the illusion of real life. Every night, after you fall asleep, the aliens take you aboard a space ship where they download your thought patterns and examine you. Of course, you know nothing about this because, each time they let you go, they wipe out your memory of the encounter. The aliens have allowed a few resources dealing with UFOs and alien abductions to appear on the Internet just to see what you do. It's an intelligence test.

Unplastic News

An electronic magazine devoted to the aberrant, bizarre, and preposterous, containing weird and humorous quotes from the computer underground.

Anonymous FTP:
>   Address: **etext.archive.umich.edu**
>   Path: **/pub/Zines/Unplastic_News**

If you're feeling risque, take a look at X-Rated Resources

BOOKS

Book and Publishing News

Find out the real news on books and the publishing industry, what's hot off the press, and which Internet book by Hahn and Stout is on the bestseller list.

Usenet:
Newsgroup: **clari.news.books**

Book FAQs and Info

FAQs about books, list of bookstores, bibliography of quotation compilations, list of recommended Unix books, book reviews, and reading lists.

Anonymous FTP:
Address: **quartz.rutgers.edu**
Path: **/pub/books/***

Gopher:
Name: Rutgers Quartz Text Archive
Address: **quartz.rutgers.edu**
Choose: **Book FAQs and Info**

Book Reviews

Why waste your time and money on an unrewarding book? Read the reviews in this newsgroup and find out the real scoop before you make a serious commitment. Save your excess time and money for unrewarding people. The Usenet newsgroup is for ongoing discussion and current reviews. To take a look at previous reviews, use the Gopher reference, or download reviews by Anonymous FTP.

Anonymous FTP:
Address: **csn.org**
Path: **/pub/alt.books.reviews/***

Gopher:
Name: Whole Earth Lectronic Link
Address: **gopher.well.sf.ca.us**
Choose: **Whole Earth Review, the Magazine | Book Reviews**

Usenet:
Newsgroup: **alt.books.reviews**

Book Stacks Unlimited (Online Bookstore)

An online bookstore and reader's conference system that allows you to search for books by author or title, or just browse by subject.

Telnet:
Address: **books.com**
Login: Just press RETURN

Book Talk Mailing List

A discussion list for soon-to-be published books, CDs, and videos.

Listserv mailing list:
List Address: **book-talk@columbia.ilc.com**
Subscription Address: **listserv@columbia.ilc.com**

Bookstore Reviews

Reviews and information about bookstores, from the motif of the store to ratings of the salespeople. These reviews are written by book buffs and are compiled and categorized by region and city on this Gopher server.

Anonymous FTP:
Address: **rtfm.mit.edu**
Path: **/pub/usenet/news.answers/books/stores/***

Gopher:
Name: University of Minnesota
Address: **gopher.micro.umn.edu**
Choose: **Fun & Games | Games | Bookstores**

Buying and Selling Books

Get a piece of the buying and selling action. See what's hot and what's not. Book reviews and business news make up the bulk of the traffic in this newsgroup.

Usenet:
Newsgroup: **biz.books.technical**

Computer Books

Offers news, book descriptions, lists, and ordering information for publications from O'Reilly & Associates.

Gopher:
Name: O'Reilly & Associates
Address: **ora.com**

Cucumber Information Services

Cucumber Information Service, run by Martha Anderson, is the world's leading vendor of books on the Internet, Unix, C, C++ and X Window. Send them a message by e-mail and ask for their free catalog. Be sure to include your name and postal address. Once you decide what you want, you can also order by e-mail.

Mail:
Address: **orders@cucumber.com**

A B C D E F G H I J K L M N O P Q R S T U V W X Y Z

Electronic Books at Wiretap

A huge index of full-length electronic books on the Internet Wiretap Gopher and FTP site.

Anonymous FTP:
Address: **ftp.spies.com**
Path: **/Books/***

Gopher:
Name: Internet Wiretap
Address: **wiretap.spies.com**
Choose: **Electronic Books at Wiretap**

Etext Resources

Access to many Gophers and archives around the world offering various electronic books and online texts.

Gopher:
Name: Internet Wiretap
Address: **wiretap.spies.com**
Choose:
    Various ETEXT Resources on the Internet

General Book Discussion

A good place to find a variety of information about books. This newsgroup covers books of all genres, including reviews and discussion of reviews. This is a fairly free forum, provided you know something about your topic. Moreover, talk is not limited to books: there is much discussion of the publishing industry, as well as requests for information on interesting bookstores and hard-to-find bargains.

Usenet:
Newsgroup: **rec.arts.books**

Need a good book?
"The Internet Complete Reference"
is the best.
Need another book?
Try the **NYSERNet** gopher.

If you would like to send us a comment, mail to: catalog@rain.org

Internet Books List

An Internet RFC (1432), containing a list of books related to using the Internet, divided into category types.

Anonymous FTP:
Address: **athos.rutgers.edu**
Path: **/rfc/rfc1432.txt**

Address: **ftp.denet.dk**
Path: **/pub/rfc/rfc1432.txt**

Address: **sunsite.unc.edu**
Path: **/pub/docs/rfc/rfc1432.txt**

Archie:
Pattern: **rfc1432.txt**

Gopher:
Name: NYSERNet
Address: **nysernet.org**
Choose: **Special Collections: Internet Help**
    | Internet Books

Internet Surfer Books

A list of recommended Internet books with a short comment, ISBN number, and price for each.

Anonymous FTP:
Address: **nysernet.org**
Path: **/pub/guides/surfing.2.0.2.txt**

Gopher:
Name: NYSERNet
Address: **nysernet.org**
Choose: **Special Collections: Internet Help**
    | Good Internet Books

Microsoft Windows 3.1 Book List

A list of books about Microsoft Windows 3.1.

Anonymous FTP:
Address: **sunsite.unc.edu**
Path: **/pub/UNC-info/IAT/guides/ug-09.txt**

Gopher:
Name: University of North Carolina at Chapel Hill
Address: **sunsite.unc.edu**
Choose: **UNC-CH Information and Facilities**
    | Institute for Academic Technology
    Documents for browsing | guides | irg-09.txt

The Internet will set you free.

O'Reilly & Associates

News, book descriptions and information, a complete listing of book titles, online indexes, instructions on obtaining book samples and archives.

Anonymous FTP:
    Address: **ftp.ora.com**
    Path: **/pub**

Gopher:
    Name: O'Reilly & Associates
    Address: **ora.com**
    Choose: **Book Descriptions and Information**

O'Reilly Book Samples

Samples from many of the computer books published by O'Reilly & Associates.

Anonymous FTP:
    Address: **ftp.uu.net**
    Path: **/published/oreilly**

Online Book Initiative

The Online Book Initiative offers freely redistributable collections of information such as books, journals, catalogs, magazines, manuals, and maps.

Gopher:
    Name: The World
    Address: **world.std.com**
    Choose: **OBI The Online Book Initiative**

Internet mailing list:
    List Address: **obi@world.std.com**
    Subscription Address: **obi-request@world.std.com**

Online Bookstore

An online bookstore with computer and non-computer books. Mail for more information. Order extra copies of this book for all your friends.

Mail:
    Address: **obs@tic.com**

Free Books

There is a lot to read on the Internet. Many well-known (and not so well-known) books are available to you to download from the Online Book Initiative.

Snarf a couple for yourself and spend tonight cuddled up with a warm display screen. Moreover, since the text is stored electronically, you can make changes. . .

Think what you can do with Albert Hoffman's story of how he discovered LSD, or Conan Doyle's Sherlock Holmes tales. This time, you can let Moriarty win.

Pulp Fiction

Pulp magazines existed in America from the turn of the century to the early 1950s. They offered an impressive array of stories about crime, mystery, detectives, war, love, romance, science fiction, horror, sports, westerns, and adventure. The spirit of pulp fiction is alive today in modern paperback adventure series and in this Usenet newsgroup. Did you know that the Shadow was really Kent Allard, a World War I ace and spy? Lamont Cranston was merely a disguise. If you listen to the radio show, you will be misinformed, but if you read this newsgroup, you will know the truth.

Usenet:
    Newsgroup: **alt.pulp**

Rare Book Dealers Mailing List

A mailing list expressly for rare book dealers to exchange information and books and to meet with individuals and institutions looking for specific books.

Internet mailing list:
    List Address: **antiquaria@aol.com**
    Subscription Address: **antiquaria-request@aol.com**

A B C D E F G H I J K L M N O P Q R S T U V W X Y Z

Reviews of New Titles

Booknews is a moderated information list with reviews of upcoming books, CDs, and videos. Members of this mailing list are encouraged to submit articles for publication regarding upcoming or new titles, but submissions may be edited.

Internet mailing list:
List Address: **booknews@columbia.ilc.com**
Subscription Address:
booknews-request@columbia.ilc.com

Roswell Electronic Computer Bookstore

An online computer bookstore devoted exclusively to computer books, with a database listing over 7000 titles. Browse the list by subject or search by author, title, or ISBN.

Gopher:
Name: Nova Scotia Technology Network
Address: **nstn.ns.ca**
Choose: **NSTN Electronic Shopping Mall | Roswell Electronic Computer Bookstore**

Science Fiction Reviews

This is the place to find reviews of your favorite (or not so favorite) books, magazines, movies, and videos. Although the name implies science fiction only, you will also find speculative fiction, fantasy, horror, and even (sometimes) comics. This group is moderated.

Usenet:
Newsgroup: **rec.arts.sf.reviews**

Technical Books

If you have a squeak in your clicker or you can't get slot A to line up with tab B, check in to this newsgroup to see if there is a technical book that can help. Just the place to look when you need to decide which Unix book to give your grandmother for her birthday.

Usenet:
Newsgroup: **alt.books.technical**
Newsgroup: **misc.books.technical**

Unix Book Bibliography

A bibliography of some of the best books and documentation on Unix and related areas, based on sales figures and recommendations from netnews readers.

Anonymous FTP:
Address: **rtfm.mit.edu**
Path: **/pub/usenet/news.answers/books**

Gopher:
Name: O'Reilly & Associates
Address: **ora.com**
Choose: **Unix Bibliography**

Unix Book List

A compilation of titles and other pertinent information on books about the Unix operating system and the C programming language. This list was organized and is maintained by Mitch Wright.

Anonymous FTP:
Address: **ftp.rahul.net**
Path: **/pub/mitch/YABL/**

Address: **ucselx.sdsu.edu**
Path: **/pub/doc/general/Unix-C-Booklist**

BOTANY

Agroforestry

As the population grows, the need for better crops and soil increases. Agroforestry studies plant growth and nutrition in an effort to find crops and soil that are compatible with each other and with the rest of the surrounding environment.

Usenet:
Newsgroup: **bionet.agroforestry**

Botany Database

A database of nearly 100,000 records in the Type Specimen Register for the U.S. National Herbarium.

Gopher:
Name: Smithsonian Institution
Address: **smithson.si.edu**
Choose: **Department of Botany**

Chlamydomonas

Chlamydomonas reproduces faster than that blue fuzzy stuff in the refrigerator. Learn about this happy little algae as it works its way through life making a pest of itself with neighboring filtration plants.

Usenet:
Newsgroup: **bionet.chlamydomonas**

Endangered Australian Flora and Fauna

A guide to endangered Australian plants and animals. The lists include other vulnerable and already extinct species.

Gopher:
Name: Australian Environmental Resources Information Network
Address: **kaos.erin.gov.au**
Choose: **Biodiversity**

General Plant Biology

How does your garden grow? Discover the myth and mystery of plant growth and reproduction. Discussion of all aspects of plant biology are encouraged. You'll never have a guilt-free salad again.

Usenet:
Newsgroup: **bionet.plants**

Mammal Database

A database of all the known mammals of the world, with a variety of information, including the scientific names for each species.

Gopher:
Name: Smithsonian Institution
Address: **smithson.si.edu**
Choose: **Vertebrate Zoology**

Missouri Botanical Garden

Volumes of botanical information, including the flora of North America, plants of Costa Rica, types of moss, journals, and other items of interest.

Gopher:
Name: Missouri Botanical Garden
Address: **gopher.mobot.org**

Photosynthesis

Plants kissed by the sun get their own version of a tan. See green plant cells become little organic factories as their chlorophyl explodes into action. Read about the ins and outs of photosynthesis, the original food processor.

Usenet:
Newsgroup: **bionet.photosynthesis**

Smithsonian Botany Gopher

This Gopher contains information resources that are compiled and maintained by Smithsonian staff and includes newsletters and projects, as well as pointers to other network resources that may be of interest to botanical researchers.

Gopher:
Name: Smithsonian Institution
Address: **nmnhgoph.si.edu**
Choose: **Department of Botany at the Smithsonian Institution**

Name: United States Military Academy
Address: **euler.math.usma.edu**
Choose: **Reference_Section | Smithsonian Institution's Natural History Gopher | Department of Botany**

Smithsonian Vertebrate Zoology Gopher

A database of the thousands of currently recognized species of mammals, in a taxonomic hierarchy that includes Order, Family, Subfamily, and Genus.

Gopher:
Name: Smithsonian Institution
Address: **nmnhgoph.si.edu**
Choose: **Vertebrate Zoology**

Name: United States Military Academy
Address: **euler.math.usma.edu**
Choose: **Reference_Section | Smithsonian Institution's Natural History Gopher | Vertebrate Zoology**

There's no getting around it: plants are cool.
And the Missouri Botanical Garden is farm out.

Lots and lots of music on the Internet: check out the Music category

A B C D E F G H I J K L M N O P Q R S T U V W X Y Z

BUSINESS AND FINANCE

Amway Distributor's Mailing List

A mailing list for Amway distributors interested in positive discussion.

Mail:
Address: **spp@cis.ufl.edu**

Your Way is My Way is Amway

We once dropped in to an Amway convention and it was impressive. After all, what's wrong with a world in which we all take in each other's laundry? As Rich De Vos once asked so poignantly, "Why not sell soap?". We couldn't have put it better ourselves. So, as you work your way from Direct Distributor to Double Diamond and all the way to Crown Ambassador, see what those Amway distributors smart enough to be on the Internet have to say.

Asia Pacific Business and Marketing Resources

Articles about business and management in China, Asia, Japan and Korea.

Gopher:
Name: Simon Fraser University
Address: **hoshi.cic.sfu.ca**
Choose: **David See-Chai Lam Centre for International Communications | Asia Pacific Business & Marketing Resources**

Banks and Financial Industries News

Learn why lending rates fluctuate and how it affects you. News on banks and financial industries will keep you up to date.

Usenet:
Newsgroup: **clari.biz.finance.services**

Business and Commerce

I'll give you one bag of flour and two chickens for three bags of grain. While business and commerce are not quite this simple, it still doesn't have to be over your head. Read about business and commerce of all kinds.

Usenet:
Newsgroup: **alt.business.misc**

Business and Industry

Newsbytes offer insights into the real stories in business and industry news. Don't settle for less than the facts.

Usenet:
Newsgroup: **clari.nb.business**

Business Conferences

A list of mailing list discussion groups related to the business world.

Anonymous FTP:
Address: **ksuvxa.kent.edu**
Path: **/library/acadlist.file7**

Gopher:
Name: NYSERNet
Address: **nysernet.org**
Choose: **Special Collections: Higher Education | Scholarly Electronic Conferences | Business, Miscellaneous Academia, & News**

Business E-mail Addresses

A large list of business e-mail addresses, including names and descriptions.

Gopher:
Name: NYSERNet
Address: **nysernet.org**
Choose: **Special Collections: Business and Economic Development | Business and Academic Related Email Addresses**

Do you have a favorite item that is not in the catalog? Let us know by sending mail to catalog@rain.org

Business Statistics

General business indicators, commodity prices, construction and real estate stats, and many more indicators and statistics. Also includes statistics for (among others) the food, leather, lumber, metals, and manufacturing industries.

Gopher:
Name: University of California San Diego
Address: **infopath.ucsd.edu**
Choose: **News & Services | Economic.. | Current Business..**

Canadian Business

An American magazine once referred to Canada as "the retarded giant on our doorstep". Read this newsgroup and get the real scoop. You will find that Canadian news is about as exciting as. . .well. . .Canadian news.

Usenet:
Newsgroup: **clari.canada.biz**

Canadian Investment

If you're looking to spread your money around a little, try investing in Canada. Learn about Canadian money markets, investment clubs, financial publications, and government. (And, if you have a little extra money, we have a snow farm you might want to invest in.)

Usenet:
Newsgroup: **misc.invest.canada**

Cogeneration

Tired of paying the electric company? Join this list and learn how to generate your own power—even how to sell your excess power to the utility company at their rates!

Listserv mailing list:
List Address: **cogeneration@iup.bitnet**
Subscription Address: **listserv@iup.bitnet**

Commerce Business Daily

A daily publication that announces invitations to bid on proposals requested by the U.S. government.

Gopher:
Name: CNS, Inc.
Address: **cscns.com**
Choose: **Commerce Business Daily**

Commodities

Trading commodities is a great way to snatch financial defeat from the jaws of victory. Why wait for the newspaper to check on how Arkansas pork bellies are doing? Check this newsgroup for up-to-the-minute news and price reports.

Usenet:
Newsgroup: **clari.biz.commodity**

Corporate Finance News

Exchange rates, percentages, the value of the ruble. Get real news on finance and currency.

Usenet:
Newsgroup: **clari.biz.finance**

E-mail Addresses of Ukrainian Businesses

This file contains the e-mail addresses of nearly 200 businesses in the Ukraine.

Anonymous FTP:
Address: **kekule.osc.edu**
Path: **/pub/russian/business/ ukraine/commercial.directory**

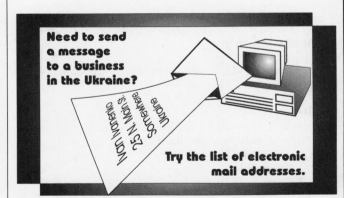

Need to send a message to a business in the Ukraine?

Ivon Ivanenko
25 N. Main St.
Somewhere
Ukraine

Try the list of electronic mail addresses.

Earnings and Dividend Reports

Track your earnings and dividends by staying informed. See the latest news on earnings and dividend reports and make the most of your money.

Usenet:
Newsgroup: **clari.biz.finance.earnings**

A B C D E F G H I J K L M N O P Q R S T U V W X Y Z

Eastern Europe Trade Leads

A repository of requests from entrepreneurs in Eastern European countries seeking business partners and trade leads in the U.S.

Gopher:
Name: University of California San Diego
Address: **infopath.ucsd.edu**
Choose: **News & Services**
 | **Economic..**
 | **Eastern Europe trade..**

EBB and Agency Information

The Economic Bulletin Board (EBB) is a bulletin board run by the U.S. Department of Commerce, Office of Business Analysis and provides a one-stop source of current economic information. The EBB contains press releases and statistical information from the Bureau of Economic Analysis, the Bureau of the Census, the Federal Reserve Board, the Bureau of Labor Statistics, the Department of Treasury, and several other federal agencies. A menu-driven system.

Gopher:
Name: University of California San Diego
Address: **infopath.ucsd.edu**
Choose: **News & Services**
 | **Economic..**
 | **EBB and Agency Info..**

Economic Indicators

The raw data for the leading (and lesser) economic indicators in the U.S.

Gopher:
Name: University of California San Diego
Address: **infopath.ucsd.edu**
Choose: **News & Services**
 | **Economic..**
 | **Economic Indicators**

The Economy

If you're like us, the economy is one of your favorite parts of the social infrastructure. Get the latest poop on what money and labor are doing in the U.S. and worldwide.

Usenet:
Newsgroup: **clari.biz.economy**
Newsgroup: **clari.biz.economy.world**

Entrepreneurs

Tired of being manacled to that creaking metal desk with the file drawer that always sticks shut? Take charge of your life— own your own business. Learn about the pitfalls and glories that await you, the entrepreneur.

Usenet:
Newsgroup: **misc.entrepreneurs**

Your Own Business

What could be more fun than running your own business?

Why let someone else worry about health care, liability insurance, meeting the payroll, and making a profit, when you can do so yourself?

(Of course, there are drawbacks as well.)

If you are starting your own business, make sure to read **misc.entrepreneur**. There are a lot of people just like you.

European Commission Host Organization

ECHO offers scientific, language, business, and research databases in any of 8 languages.

Telnet:
Address: **echo.lu**
Login: **echo**

Feature Stories

Read real news stories on the movers and shakers of the business world. Stories relate to all aspects of business.

Usenet:
Newsgroup: **clari.biz.features**

Federal Information Exchange

Federal Information Exchange, Inc., is a company that provides database services, software development, and technical support to the government, private sector, and academic communities.

Gopher:
Name: Federal Information Exchange
Address: **fedix.fie.com**

Financial Ratios for Manufacturing Corporations

Supporting data and computation of FRMCs.

Gopher:
> Name: University of California San Diego
> Address: **infopath.ucsd.edu**
> Choose: **News & Services**
> | **Economic..**
> | **Special Studies and Reports**

General News

Survey what's going on around you in the business world. There is a little of everything here to provide you with a healthy overview of business, even if it's just to decide that you want someone else to handle it for you.

Usenet:
> Newsgroup: **clari.biz.misc**

Hot News

Get the latest news in business and get it fast. When the market has a wild swing, it might pay to know the minute it happens.

Usenet:
> Newsgroup: **clari.biz.urgent**

Industry Statistics

Benchmark and periodic statistics for a number of industry segments. Includes quarterly financial reports and technical documents.

Gopher:
> Name: University of California San Diego
> Address: **infopath.ucsd.edu**
> Choose: **News & Services**
> | **Economic..**
> | **Industry Statistics**

International Market Insight (IMI) Reports

Market briefs on opportunities and news in international markets.

Gopher:
> Name: University of California San Diego
> Address: **infopath.ucsd.edu**
> Choose: **News & Services**
> | **Economic..**
> | **International Market...**

Internet Company

The Internet Company provides a commercial presence on the Internet for companies that lack the technical expertise to get connected themselves. This Gopher also includes information on current projects and how to access them, publication guides, and news.

Gopher:
> Name: The Internet Company
> Address: **gopher.internet.com 2000**

Investments

Mutual funds, IRAs, discount brokerages, margin terms—do you sometimes feel like your head is going to spin right off? Learn everything you need to know about investments and handling money. Make your money work for you.

Usenet:
> Newsgroup: **clari.biz.invest**
> Newsgroup: **misc.invest**

Labor

Even more fun than actually working is reading about other people who do (or don't as the case may be). Read this group for the latest news on strikes, unions, and labor relations.

Usenet:
> Newsgroup: **clari.biz.labor**

Legal News

Who's suing who? Find out the latest news on America's favorite pastime: litigation. News items cover any business-related legal matter.

Usenet:
> Newsgroup: **clari.biz.courts**

**Make sure you are prepared:
Read
Emergency and Disaster.**

A
B
C
D
E
F
G
H
I
J
K
L
M
N
O
P
Q
R
S
T
U
V
W
X
Y
Z

Libraries

If you are interested in more than saving loose bills in a sock in a coffee can buried under Aunt Grace's gladioli, then pull up a chair and do some research. If you can't find the information you need in business libraries, you just don't need to know it. Or you can ask Aunt Grace.

Usenet:
Newsgroup: **bit.listserv.buslib-l**

Management Science Archives

Working papers and preprints in the management sciences, recent paper calls, teaching materials, conference announcements, discussion lists, and other resources related to research, education, and practice of management.

Gopher:
Name: The Management Archive
Address: **chimera.sph.umn.edu**

Mergers and Acquisitions

Stay on top of the turbulent world of business mergers and acquisitions. This group has the lowdown on everything that is going on.

Usenet:
Newsgroup: **clari.biz.mergers**

Multilevel Marketing

The great pyramids are not just in Egypt. Learn all about the "trickle-up theory" and hear stories of why multilevel marketing is the greatest money making scheme, er... plan, ever. Don't settle for a rattling car and a rental home. Sell Amway so you can drive a Rolls Royce and own a yacht. These folks can show you how.

Usenet:
Newsgroup: **alt.business.multi-level**

**Did you know there are many different books
that you can download to
your own computer?
See Literature for the details**

Multilevel Marketing Strategies

A Usenet group and related FAQ list exploring aspects of multilevel marketing.

Anonymous FTP:
Address: **rtfm.mit.edu**
Path: **/pub/usenet-by-group/alt.answers/mlm-faq**

Usenet:
Newsgroup: **alt.business.multi-level**

Question List
Need the scoop on serious multi-level marketing?
Download the frequently asked question list, then tell five friends, who will tell five friends, who will. . .

New Products and Services

Think what an advantage you would have over the rest of the world if you were the first to find out about all kinds of cool, new stuff. Here is a quick update on innovative products and services while they are still hot off the economic griddle.

Usenet:
Newsgroup: **clari.biz.products**

Office Automation

A paper discussing the methods necessary for an office to thrive: you need to have a hierarchy of well-defined realms which are controlled by and support the needs of each group.

Gopher:
Name: Whole Earth Lectronic Link
Address: **gopher.well.sf.ca.us**
Choose: **Whole Systems**
  | **Good Office Patterns**

Penn World Trade Tables

An expanded set of International Economic and Business comparisons and statistics from 1950-1988, including population and GDP data.

Anonymous FTP:
>   Address: **nber.harvard.edu**
>   Path: **/pub/pwt55/***

Gopher:
>   Name: National Bureau of Economic Research
>   Address: **nber.harvard.edu**
>   Choose: **Penn-World Tables v. 5.5**

Personal Investing and Finance News

It's hard to decide the best place to put your money. Take the mystery out of investing by keeping up on the latest investing and finance news.

Usenet:
>   Newsgroup: **clari.biz.finance.personal**

Real Estate

It's just like a Monopoly game, except you use real money and the bail is higher if you end up in jail. Learn tips on acquiring real estate: how to choose a good agent, perks for first-time homebuyers, and how to avoid the rental property blues. Invest in something tangible.

Usenet:
>   Newsgroup: **misc.invest.real-estate**

**Look around.
Is anyone watching?
Good.
Take a look at the X-Rated section.
(But remember, you didn't read it here.)**

REAL ESTATE REALITY

Isn't it great? All you have to do is spend some money and you can own your very own piece of an actual planet (Earth).

We love real estate because it brings out the best in people; and some of the best real estate people hang out in **misc.invest.real-estate**.

Remember, though, talking on the Net is no substitute for experience: the smart way is to "walk the dirt, smell the dirt and feel the dirt". (Fortunately, there's no shortage of dirt.)

Stock Market

View stock market closing quotes and comments for specific recent dates.

Gopher:
>   Name: Colorado State University
>   Address: **lobo.rmhs.colorado.edu**
>   Choose: **Other Information Services
> | Stock Market Closing Quotes**

Stock Market News

Whether you are the portfolio manager of a multimillion dollar mutual fund, or simply the CEO of a large, international corporation, stock market news is important to you. Check these newsgroups for the latest numbers and reports.

Usenet:
>   Newsgroup: **clari.biz.market**
>   Newsgroup: **clari.biz.market.amex**
>   Newsgroup: **clari.biz.market.dow**
>   Newsgroup: **clari.biz.market.ny**
>   Newsgroup: **clari.biz.market.otc**
>   Newsgroup: **clari.biz.market.report**

This is the first book of the rest of your life.

A B C D E F G H I J K L M N O P Q R S T U V W X Y Z

Stock Market Report

Daily stock market summary report. Provided as a free service of a2i.

Telnet:
Address: **a2i.rahul.net**
Login: **guest**

Technical Aspects

This is where money and math collide. Flying formulas, staggering statistics, and profitable predictions abound to provide the basis for economic decision-making. How do you know when to buy a mutual fund? What good is a regression analysis? Take part in the discussion and learn how to buy and sell by the numbers.

Usenet:
Newsgroup: **misc.invest.technical**

Top News

Find out the big news events. If you don't have time to wade through all the news, at least get the top stories.

Usenet:
Newsgroup: **clari.biz.top**

Vienna Stock Exchange

If you can read German, take a look at this telnet site and let us know how to describe it.

Telnet:
Address: **fiivs01.tu-graz.ac.at**
Login: **boerse**

World of Coca-Cola

An article about the Coca-Cola Company in Atlanta, Georgia. A tribute to a unique product and the consumers who have made it the world's favorite soft drink.

Gopher:
Name: English Server
Address: **english-server.hss.cmu.edu**
Choose: **Cultural Theory**
 | **Friedman - World of Coca Cola**

BUYING AND SELLING

Anime

Buy and cell—sorry, sell—all types of items related to anime (Japanese animation).

Usenet:
Newsgroup: **rec.arts.anime.marketplace**

Bicycles

Drop in to the bicycle marketplace: buying, selling, and reviews. Soon you'll be bopping around town on your very own bicycle built for one. How totally cool.

Usenet:
Newsgroup: **rec.bicycles.marketplace**

Comics

What do you do when it's 2 A.M. and you just have to lay your hands on the Superman comic in which Lois Lane pretends to marry Peewee Herman, but it turns out to be a hoax? Fire up the old computer and visit the Usenet comics marketplace.

Usenet:
Newsgroup: **rec.arts.comics.marketplace**

There are a lot of books that you can download for free on the Internet.
See the Literature sections for details.

Computers

Buying a computer? Check out the **clari** newsgroup for the latest prices. For buying and selling particular machines, see the specialized groups. The **.d** group is for discussion of the computer buy-and-sell groups. Here is our hint for the day: it is difficult to buy too much speed, too much memory, or too much video resolution.

Usenet:
Newsgroup: **clari.streetprice**
Newsgroup: **comp.sys.amiga.marketplace**
Newsgroup: **comp.sys.apple2.marketplace**
Newsgroup: **comp.sys.next.marketplace**
Newsgroup: **misc.forsale.computers.d**
Newsgroup: **misc.forsale.computers.mac**
Newsgroup: **misc.forsale.computers.other**
Newsgroup: **misc.forsale.computers.pc-clone**
Newsgroup: **misc.forsale.computers.workstation**

General Buy and Sell

Here is the main Usenet marketplace: buy, sell, or trade anything. If you need it and someone has it, this is the place to find it.

Usenet:
Newsgroup: **misc.forsale**

MarketBase Online Catalog

The MarketBase Online Catalog of Goods and Services is a unique online service dedicated to providing a forum where buyers and sellers meet to exchange electronically the attributes of products and services.

Gopher:
Name: University of North Carolina
Address: **gopher.ncsu.edu**
Choose: **Entertainment | Online Mall**

Role-Playing Games

Materials to buy and sell relating to role-playing and fantasy games. (Does not include "Clinton in '92" campaign buttons.)

Usenet:
Newsgroup: **rec.games.frp.marketplace**

Reality is for people who aren't smart enough for role playing games.

San Francisco

Would you like to buy the Golden Gate Bridge? Too bad, we could have given you a great deal. Anyway, check out this group about things for sale in the Bay Area. If you find a bargain, you will have an excuse to visit San Francisco to pick it up.

Usenet:
Newsgroup: **rec.arts.sf.marketplace**

Satellite TV Equipment

All manner of home satellite equipment to buy, sell, and talk about. Just the place to pick up an extra Ku LNB. (By the way, for information about economical Usenet feeds using a personal satellite dish, send mail to **pagesat@pagesat.com**.)

Usenet:
Newsgroup: **alt.satellite.tv.forsale**

Travel

Upgrades, frequent flyer plans, hotel discounts, travel guides—the longest journey begins with but a single step into Usenet's one-stop travel marketplace. Buy, sell, beg, borrow, steal—then go!

Usenet:
Newsgroup: **rec.travel.marketplace**

Video Games

When you are not playing a video game, you are wasting your time (unless you are talking about video games). If God didn't want us to spend all our time staring at the screen and manipulating a surrogate being, why did he give us this newsgroup?

Usenet:
Newsgroup: **rec.games.video.marketplace**

A
B
C
D
E
F
G
H
I
J
K
L
M
N
O
P
Q
R
S
T
U
V
W
X
Y
Z

CANADA

Canadian Documents

The Canada Constitution Act, Canada Meech Lake Accord, Charlottetown Constitutional Agreement, excerpts from the Canada Constitution Act and proposals for shaping the future of Canada (in both French and English).

Anonymous FTP:
> Address: **ftp.spies.com**
> Path: **/Gov/Canada/***

Gopher:
> Name: Internet Wiretap
> Address: **wiretap.spies.com**
> Choose: **Government Docs (US & World)**
> | **Canadian Documents**

Canadian Investment

If you're looking to spread your money around a little, try investing in Canada. Learn about Canadian money markets, investment clubs, financial publications and the government. (And, if you have a little extra money, we have a snow farm you might want to invest in.)

Usenet:
> Newsgroup: **misc.invest.canada**

Canadian Issues Forum

A mailing list discussion forum for political, social, cultural and economic issues in Canada.

Listserv mailing list:
> List Address: **canada-l@mcgill1.bitnet**
> Subscription Address: **listserv@mcgill1.bitnet**

Canadian Music

After more than 25 years of federal "Canadian content" rules, Canadian music is alive and well and living in...ahem...Canada. Join the discussion of your favorite musicians from the land where a rich musical tradition resonates from sea to shining sea. (Bagpipes and accordians are optional.)

Usenet:
> Newsgroup: **alt.music.canada**

WANT TO HEAR SOME REALLY "COOL" SOUNDS? TRY *CANADIAN MUSIC*

Canadian News

An American magazine once referred to Canada as "the retarded giant on our doorstep". Read the Clarinet Canadian newsgroups and get the real scoop. You will find that Canadian news is about as exciting as... well... Canadian news.

Usenet:
> Newsgroup: **clari.canada.biz**
> Newsgroup: **clari.canada.briefs**
> Newsgroup: **clari.canada.briefs.ont**
> Newsgroup: **clari.canada.briefs.west**
> Newsgroup: **clari.canada.features**
> Newsgroup: **clari.canada.general**
> Newsgroup: **clari.canada.gov**
> Newsgroup: **clari.canada.law**
> Newsgroup: **clari.canada.newscast**
> Newsgroup: **clari.canada.politics**
> Newsgroup: **clari.canada.trouble**
> Newsgroup: **clari.news.canada**

Charlottetown Agreement

Consensus Report of the Canadian Charlottetown Constitutional Agreement of August 28th, 1992, including highlights, fact sheets, legal text and the report itself.

Gopher:
> Name: Nova Scotia Technology Network
> Address: **nstn.ns.ca**
> Choose: **Other Information | Constitutional Kit**

Culture

There is an old riddle: What is Canadian culture? The answer is, "mostly American". Some people feel that "Canadian culture" is an oxymoron. What do they know? Haven't they ever heard of the Blue Jays? William Shatner? Rick Moranis? (who Harley went to summer camp with). After all, if Canadian culture is good enough for Wayne Gretzky, it should be good enough for Doug and Bob.

Usenet:
> Newsgroup: **soc.culture.canada**

CANADIAN (?) CULTURE

It's amazing how many people know nothing about Canadian Culture. If you are one of those unfortunate individuals, do not dismay. All you need to do is drop in to the **soc.culture.canada** forum where you can discuss recipes for Eskimo pies, the demise of the Oopik, and secret ways to sneak into Ontario Place.

Statistics Canada Daily Reports

Reports on international transactions, agriculture and other key Canadian economic statistics.

Telnet:
Address: **info.carleton.ca**

CHEMISTRY

Chemical Engineering

Various aspects of chemical engineering.

Usenet:
Newsgroup: **sci.engr.chem**

Chemical Engineering List

A mailing list forum focused on the role of chemical engineering in a changing world economy and new research trends in industry and academia.

Listserv mailing list:
List Address: **cheme-l@psuvm.bitnet**
Subscription Address: **listserv@psuvm.bitnet**

Chemistry in Israel List

A mailing list as a forum for discussion of chemistry in Israel.

Listserv mailing list:
List Address: **chemic-l@taunivm.bitnet**
Subscription Address: **listserv@taunivm.bitnet**

Chemistry Information

An electronic reference source that uses library resources to answer to frequently asked chemistry questions. It covers nomenclature, compound identification, properties, structure determination, toxicity, synthesis and registry numbers. For each component it lists the most appropriate reference resources (online catalog, indexes, journals, etc.).

Anonymous FTP:
Address: **ucssun1.sdsu.edu**
Path: **pub/chemras/***

Chemistry Talk

All about chemistry and related sciences.

Usenet:
Newsgroup: **sci.chem**

Chemistry Telementoring

A mailing list fostering the exchange of ideas and information between chemistry teachers and students from the high school to university level.

Internet mailing list:
List Address: **chemistrytm@dhvx20.csudh.edu**
Subscription Address: **chemistrytm-request@dhvx20.csudh.edu**

Computational Chemistry List

A mailing list for the discussion of quantum chemistry, molecular mechanics and dynamics, and other fields related to computational chemistry.

Internet mailing list:
List Address: **chemistry@osc.edu**
Subscription Address: **chemistry-request@osc.edu**

Organometallic Chemistry

Chemistry and techniques used in working with organometallic compounds.

Usenet:
Newsgroup: **sci.chem.organomet**

Periodic Table of the Elements

Download a text or graphic version of the periodic table of the elements.

Telnet:
>   Address: **camms2.caos.kun.nl 2034**

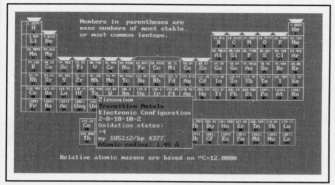

On the Internet, software programs are available by the tens of thousands for just about anything you can think of. This program shows the Periodic Table of the Elements. You move a cursor around to choose an element, then press ENTER, and the program will give you more detailed information about that element. This program is available on most University systems. This copy was obtained from **freebsd.cdrom.com** in the file **/.1/games/msdos/educate/periodic.zip**.

COMPUTERS: CULTURE

Art of Technology Digest

Journals dedicated to sharing information among computerists and to the presentation and debate of diverse views.

Anonymous FTP:
>   Address: **wuarchive.wustl.edu**
>   Path: **/doc/misc/aot/***

Byte Bandit

"The Baudy World of the Byte Bandit" is a postmodernist interpretation of the computer underground.

Anonymous FTP:
>   Address: **ftp.spies.com**
>   Path: **/Library/Cyber/meyer.cu**

Gopher:
>   Name: Internet Wiretap
>   Address: **wiretap.spies.com**
>   Choose: **Wiretap Online Library**
> | **Cyberspace**
> | **Computer Underground (Meyer & Thomas)**

Computer Underground Digest

The complete collection of the *Computer Underground Digest*, the weekly electronic publication covering matters concerning the computer underground.

Anonymous FTP:
>   Address: **ftp.eff.org**
>   Path: **/pub/cud/cud/***

Computers and Academic Freedom (CAF)

Discussion about everything to do with computers and academic freedom, and how it all applies to university computers and networks.

Anonymous FTP:
>   Address: **ftp.eff.org**
>   Path: **/pub/academic/***

Gopher:
>   Name: Electronic Frontier Foundation
>   Address: **gopher.eff.org**
>   Choose: **Computers & Academic Freedom**
>   **mailing list archives & info**

Usenet:
>   Newsgroup: **alt.comp.acad-freedom.news**
>   Newsgroup: **alt.comp.acad-freedom.talk**

Concerning Hackers...

"Concerning Hackers Who Break into Computer Systems" is a paper which addresses hackers and the hacker community.

Anonymous FTP:
>   Address: **ftp.spies.com**
>   Path: **/Library/Cyber/denning.txt**

Gopher:
>   Name: Internet Wirenet
>   Address: **wiretap.spies.com**
>   Choose: **Wiretap Online Library**
> | **Cyberspace**
> | **Concerning Hackers who Break into Systems**

Cyberspace

Articles about cyberspace and the cyberspace culture, including papers on hackers, the computer underground, MUDs and IRC.

Anonymous FTP:
    Address: **ftp.spies.com**
    Path: **/Library/Cyber/***

Gopher:
    Name: Internet Wiretap
    Address: **wiretap.spies.com**
    Choose: **Wiretap Online Library | Cyberspace**

Disabled Computing

Articles and information about computing for those with physical disabilities.

Gopher:
    Name: CODI
    Address: **val-dor.cc.buffalo.edu**
    Choose: **Computing**

Ethics

Dissertations on the computer ethics policies of many universities and organizations.

Anonymous FTP:
    Address: **ariel.unm.edu**
    Path: **/ethics/**

Social Organization of the Computer Underground

A thesis paper examining the social organization of computer hackers, phone phreaks and software pirates.

Anonymous FTP:
    Address: **ftp.spies.com**
    Path: **/Library/Cyber/hacker.ths**

Gopher:
    Name: Internet Wiretap
    Address: **wiretap.spies.com**
    Choose: **Wiretap Online Library | Cyberspace**
    | Soc Organiz of Comp Underground (thesis)

If you like studying ants or bees...
take a look at
Social Organization of the Computer Underground

COMPUTERS: GRAPHICS

Acid Warp

A much sought-after graphics program with a wonderful psychedelic graphics display.

Anonymous FTP:
    Address: **ftp.rahul.net**
    Path: **/pub/atman/UTLCD-preview/**
        mind-candy/acidwarp.arj

Animations Mailing List

A list for the distribution of animation files, discussion of how animation files are created, as well as Regis Graphics and Regis Animations files.

Internet mailing list:
    List Address: **anmi-l@rmcs.cranfield.ac.uk**
    Subscription Address:
        anmi-l-request@rmcs.cranfield.ac.uk

Excerpt from the Net...

(from the article "Concerning Hackers Who Break into Computer Systems")

A diffuse group of people, often called "hackers," has been characterized as unethical, irresponsible and a serious danger to society, for actions related to breaking into computer systems. This paper attempts to construct a picture of hackers, their concerns and the discourse in which hacking takes place. My initial findings suggest that hackers are learners and explorers who want to help rather than cause damage, and who often have very high standards of behavior... Based on my findings, I recommend that we work closely with hackers, and suggest several actions that might be taken...

A B C D E F G H I J K L M N O P Q R S T U V W X Y Z

Computer Graphics Bibliography

A database of computer graphics bibliographic references covering a wide span of the field. Organized by year and formatted in the BibTeX bibliography format.

Gopher:
> Name: ACM SIGGRAPH
> Address: **siggraph.org**
> Choose: **Publications | Bibliography**

Telnet:
> Address: **siggraph.org**
> Login: **biblio**

Computer Graphics Gopher

Information on computer graphics techniques, online bibliographies, conference news, utilities and other items of interest.

Gopher:
> Name: ACM SIGGRAPH
> Address: **siggraph.org**

COMPUTER GRAPHICS

Computer graphics is a lot more than just using the Internet to trade erotic pictures.

For detailed information and discussion, try the *Computer Graphics Gopher*

Fract Int

A popular freeware fractal generator for DOS, Windows, OS/2 and Unix X Window. Available in source or executable form.

Anonymous FTP:
> Address: **ftp-os2.nmsu.edu**
> Path: **/os2/2_x/graphics/pmfra2.zip**

> Address: **ftp.uni-koeln.de**
> Path: **/windows/xcontrib/xfract***

> Address: **ftp.wustl.edu**
> Path: **/mirrors/msdos/graphics/frain***

> Address: **ftp.wustl.edu**
> Path: **/mirrors/msdos/graphics/frasr***

> Address: **ftp.wustl.edu**
> Path: **/mirrors/msdos/windows3/winfr***

> Address: **ftp.wustl.edu**
> Path: **/mirrors/msdos/windows3/winsr***

Fractal Images

A collection of fractal images in gif format, fractal documents, formulas and programs.

Anonymous FTP:
> Address: **csus.edu**
> Path: **/pub/alt.fractals.pictures/***

> Address: **spanky.triumf.ca**
> Path: **/fractals/***

Fractals

All you ever wanted to know about fractals, including reading and resource lists, FAQs about chaos, the Mandelbrot set, Julia set, quaternion arithmetic, plasma clouds and other related subjects.

Anonymous FTP:
> Address: **rtfm.mit.edu**
> Path: **/pub/usenet/news.answers/fractal-faq**

Archie:
> Pattern: **fractal-faq**

Usenet:
> Newsgroup: **sci.fractals**

Graphix

A mailing list that covers everything to do with graphics, including file format, new boards, drivers, interfaces, scanners, databases, FTP sites and other items of interest.

Listserv mailing list:
> List Address: **graphix@utfsm.bitnet**
> Subscription Address: **listserv@utfsm.bitnet**

Professionally created images are yours for the taking. This image is one of many similar images based on the floating metallic ball concept. This one is called **balls2.gif**. Others have similar names.

Image and Audio File Formats

Documents and descriptions of image and sound data file formats.

Anonymous FTP:
Address: **rtfm.mit.edu**
Path: **/pub/usenet-by-group/
comp.answers/audio-fmts**

Address: **wuarchive.wustl.edu**
Path: **/doc/graphic-formats/***

Archie:
Pattern: **audio-fmts**

JPEG File Viewer for Macintosh

A program for viewing JPEG format graphics files. Do an Archie search for JPEG-view for other locations and newer versions.

Anonymous FTP:
Address: **ipc1.rvs.uni-hannover.de**
Path: **/pub/mac/app/jpeg-view-20.hqx**

Address: **world.std.com**
Path: **/pub/jpeg-view-20.hqx**

Lonely? Try the Personals.

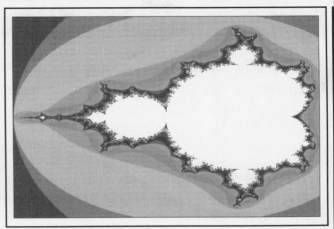

To view the graphics files you download from the Internet, you need software capable of displaying graphics. This software is just as free and just as available as all of the images themselves. Once you've got software that can display graphic images, you can download and display images of images being displayed! This picture is **mandelbr.gif** (for Mandelbrot [the fractal guy]).

JPEG File Viewer for Windows

A Windows 3.x-based JPEG file viewer. This type of file gets moved around alot. Do an Archie substring search for **winecj** for the most current locations.

Anonymous FTP:
Address: **ftp.cica.indiana.edu**
Path: **/pub/pc/win3/desktop/winecj.zip**

Address: **wcarchive.cdrom.com**
Path: **/.2/simtel/msdos/windows3/winecj12.zip**

Text-based Animation

Files that produce interesting animation sequences when routed to a VT100 terminal.

Anonymous FTP:
Address: **quartz.rutgers.edu**
Path: **/pub/computer/vt100/***

Gopher:
Name: Rutgers Quartz Text Archive
Address: **quartz.rutgers.edu**
Choose: **Computer-Sources, Documentation, Comp.Sci | vt100**

A B C D E F G H I J K L M N O P Q R S T U V W X Y Z

COMPUTERS: HARDWARE

386BSD Unix Supplements for Compaq Computers

The original 386BSD 0.1 file systems with bootstrap programs modified to boot on Compaq hardware.

Anonymous FTP:
> Address: **ftp.compaq.com**
> Path: **/pub/386bsd/***

Compaq Fixes and Patches

All the available fixes and patches for Compaq hardware in SoftPaq form. Read the file **patches.1st** for more information.

Anonymous FTP:
> Address: **ftp.compaq.com**
> Path: **/pub/softpaq**

Computer Information

Information on various computer architectures and software, including IBM, Apple/Mac and NeXT, and information on new releases, prices and future events.

Gopher:
> Name: University of Minnesota
> Address: **ashpool.micro.umn.edu**
> Choose: **Computing**

CPUs and Assembly Language

Tutorials, opcode listings, compatibility issues and reports on a variety of CPUs.

Anonymous FTP:
> Address: **ftp.spies.com**
> Path: **/Library/Techdoc/Cpu/***

Gopher:
> Name: Internet Wiretap
> Address: **wiretap.spies.com**
> Choose: **Wiretap Online Library**
> **| Technical Information**
> **| CPU's and Assembly Language**

Hard Disk Guide

Comprehensive dictionary of hard drives, floppy drives, optical drives, drive controllers and host adapters. Designed to help the novice and pro alike with integration problems and system setups.

Anonymous FTP:
> Address: **ftp.uwasa.fi**
> Path: **/pc/doc-hard/harddisk.zip**

> Address: **ftp.wustl.edu**
> Path: **/systems/ibmpc/garbo/**
> **doc-hard/harddisk.zip**

Hardware Architectures

Technical information and tutorials about some of the large IBM systems, including the ES/9000, RS600 and the Scalable Powerparallel systems.

Gopher:
> Name: Cornell University
> Address: **gopher.tc.cornell.edu**
> Choose: **Hardware Platforms**

Hardware Technical Material

Details on various hardware including S100 bus pins, Multimedia PC specification, hard disk interleave factors and Multibus II.

Anonymous FTP:
> Address: **ftp.spies.com**
> Path: **/Library/Techdoc/Hardware/***

Gopher:
> Name: Internet Wiretap
> Address: **wiretap.spies.com**
> Choose: **Wiretap Online Library**
> **| Technical Information | Hardware**

How Computers Work

A list of articles on the basic workings of the computer. Includes sections on ASCII, bits and bytes, memory, operating systems, files and directories and software programs.

Gopher:
> Name: La Trobe University
> Address: **gopher.latrobe.edu.au**
> Choose: **Computing Services | 1993 Handbook**
> **| Introduction to Computing Services**

What is the magic inside the box?

Take a look at **HOW COMPUTERS WORK**

MODEMS and FUN

Modems are now an indispensible accoutrement of modern life. However, anyone who has ever tried to get a recalcitrant modem to cooperate understands just how much fun these delightful little devices can be. When your modem gets its back up, turn to the modem information site for help and enlightenment.

List of EPROM Models and Manufacturers

A list of manufacturers, models and statistics for many EPROM (Erasable/Programmable Read Only Memory) chips.

Anonymous FTP:
Address: **oak.oakland.edu**
Path: **/pub/misc/eprom/eprom-types.list**

Macintosh Usergroup

Der Austrian Mac group.

Telnet:
Address: **amdalinz.edvz.uni-linz.ac.at**

Modem News

Recent editions of the online *Modem News* publication.

Anonymous FTP:
Address: **wuarchive.wustl.edu**
Path: **/pub/modemnews/***

Modems

Discussion, reviews, comparative statistics, program source code and much more for and about modems.

Anonymous FTP:
Address: **oak.oakland.edu**
Path: **/pub/misc/modems**

PC and Macintosh Guides

Information sheets, articles, hints and tricks for people with PCs and Macintosh computers.

Anonymous FTP:
Address: **ftp.spies.com**
Path: **/Library/Techdoc/Micro/***

Gopher:
Name: **Internet Wiretap**
Address: **wiretap.spies.com**
Choose: **Wiretap Online Library**
  | Technical Information
  | PC's and Macintoshes

Powerful Computer List

A list of the world's most powerful computing sites.

Mail:
Address: **gunter@yarrow.wt.uwa.edu.au**

RS232 Pinouts

Detailed technical information about the connections of the RS232 terminal lead.

Gopher:
Name: **University of Surrey**
Address: **gopher.cpe.surrey.ac.uk**
Choose: **Misc Info | RS232 pinouts**

A B C D E F G H I J K L M N O P Q R S T U V W X Y Z

SCO Unix Files for Compaq Computers

Patches for SCO Unix on Compaq computers. Download these files, make them executable by **root**, then just execute them as **root**.

Anonymous FTP:
    Address: **ftp.compaq.com**
    Path: **/pub/SCO/patches**

SCO Unix Supplements for Compaq Computers

Enhanced function supplements for running SCO Unix specifically on Compaq computers.

Anonymous FTP:
    Address: **ftp.compaq.com**
    Path: **/pub/SCO/releases/***

Supercomputer Documentation

Collection of information about applications packages, graphics software, languages and compilers and scientific libraries available for supercomputers.

Gopher:
    Name: Texas A&M University
    Address: **gopher.tamu.edu**
    Choose: **Texas A&M Gophers**
      | **Supercomputer Center Gopher**
      | **Available Applications & Software**

Troubleshooting your PC

Guide to the built-in diagnostic procedures to help identify computer component problems.

Anonymous FTP:
    Address: **ftp.spies.com**
    Path: **/Library/Techdoc/Micro/diagnose.txt**

Gopher:
    Name: Internet Wiretap
    Address: **wiretap.spies.com**
    Choose: **Wiretap Online Library**
      | **Technical Information**
      | **PC's and Macintoshes**
      | **Troubleshooting your IBM PC**

Ultrasound

An area devoted to information and utilities supporting the Gravis Ultrasound card for ISA-based computers, including IBM-PCs. Includes demos, digests, games, bulletins, sounds and utilities.

Anonymous FTP:
    Address: **wuarchive.wustl.edu**
    Path: **/systems/ibmpc/ultrasound/***

Vaxbook

A guide made by users for users of VAX/VMS, available in postscript and TeX formats.

Anonymous FTP:
    Address: **nic.funet.fi**
    Path: **/pub/vms/VaxBook**

COMPUTERS: LITERATURE

Amateur Computerist

Complete run of the *Amateur Computerist* newsletter and archives from the **alt.amateur-comp** Usenet group, dedicated to informing people of developments in an effort to advance computer education.

Anonymous FTP:
    Address: **wuarchive.wustl.edu**
    Path: **/doc/misc/acn/***

Artificial Intelligence Journal

Back issues of the *Artificial Intelligence Journal* in PC file formats.

Anonymous FTP:
    Address: **ftp.univie.ac.at**
    Path: **/pc/dos/aijournal/***

    Address: **ftp.wustl.edu**
    Path: **/systems/ibmpc/msdos/aijournal/***

    Address: **plaza.aarnet.edu.au**
    Path: **/micros/pc/oak/aijournal/***

Archie:
    Pattern: **aijournal**

Gopher:
    Name: The World
    Address: **world.std.com**
    Choose: **Periodicals, Magazines, and Journals**
      | **Artificial Intelligence Journal**

BBS Issues

Items of interest to BBS operators, including the text and analysis of law suits, FCC regulations, opinions and more.

Anonymous FTP:
 Address: **oak.oakland.edu**
 Path: **/pub/misc/bbs**

Big Dummy's Guide to the Internet

An entertaining guide to surviving on the Net. This guide covers everything from electronic mail to Usenet and MUDs.

Anonymous FTP:
 Address: **ftp.eff.org**
 Path: **/pub/EFF/papers/big-dummys/***

 Address: **ftp.germany.eu.net**
 Path: **/pub/books/big-dummys-guide/***

 Address: **ftp.vifp.monash.edu.au**
 Path: **/pub/userdocs/bdgtti/***

Archie:
 Pattern: **big-dummys**

Gopher:
 Name: Nippon Telegraph and Telephone Corporation
 Address: **gopher.ntt.jp**
 Choose: **Other Information
  | Big Dummy's Guide to the Internet**

Okay, you're a smart guy who knows everything. However, you probably have at least one friend who might be helped by the **BIG DUMMY'S GUIDE TO THE INTERNET**

Bits and Bytes

A weekly computer and technology summary compiled from various sources, including *Newsweek*, *Information Week* and *American Press*.

Mail:
 Address: **jmachada@pacs.pha.pa.us**
 Subject: **subscribe**
 Body: *your e-mail address*

 Address: **slakmaster@aol.com**
 Subject: **subscribe**
 Body: *your e-mail address*

Computer Emergency Response Team (CERT)

Lots of technical and advisory documents about specific computer security problems and bugs from the Computer Emergency Response Team (CERT).

Anonymous FTP:
 Address: **cert.org**
 Path: **/pub/***

 Address: **ftp.uu.net**
 Path: **/doc/security/cert_advisories**

Computer Science Technical Reports

Large archive of technical computer science reports, arranged by institution.

Anonymous FTP:
 Address: **fas.sfu.ca**
 Path: **/projects/EPiCS/CS-TechReports/***

Gopher:
 Name: Simon Fraser University
 Address: **fas.sfu.ca**
 Choose: **Internet Resouce Projects | EPiCS
  | Technical Report Archives in
  Computer Science**

Computer Underground

Largest collection of hacker, phreaker, anarchist, cyberpunk and underground material to be found anywhere on the Internet. Includes such fabled publications as *Phrack*, *Magik*, *Phantasy* and *The Legion of Doom Technical Journals*.

Anonymous FTP:
 Address: **ftp.eff.org**
 Path: **/pub/cud/***

HACKING for FUN and PROFIT
The hacker community is a lot more convoluted and sophisticated than you might think. If you are a teenager looking for something exciting that your parents and teachers will never understand, take a look at the literature of the *Computer Underground.*

A B C D E F G H I J K L M N O P Q R S T U V W X Y Z

Computer Virus Technical Information

Detailed technical information about many of the known viruses, their detection and eradication, and the damage they cause. Includes entries for MS-DOS, Amiga and Macintosh viruses.

Anonymous FTP:
Address: **oak.oakland.edu**
Path: **/pub/misc/virus**

Computing Across America

Tales of adventure from Nomad and his electronic cottage, as he travelled across America on a techno-gizmo encumbered recumbent bicycle.

Gopher:
Name: Mount Holyoke College
Address: **orixa.mtholyoke.edu**
Choose: **Document Library | Misc & Fun Stuff | The NOMAD Papers**

Computing Newsletters

Selection of newsletters and articles about operating systems, software and other technical computer topics.

Anonymous FTP:
Address: **nigel.msen.com**
Path: **/pub/newsletters/Computing/***

Desktop Publishing

FAQs, current job opportunities, accounting database and cashbook programs for Pagemaker users and desktop publishers in general.

Anonymous FTP:
Address: **wuarchive.wustl.edu**
Path: **/doc/misc/pagemaker/***

Guide to PC Downloading

A guide to downloading Internet files to a PC, using the Procomm or Kermit communications programs and protocols.

Anonymous FTP:
Address: **nic.funet.fi**
Path: **/pub/doc/library/download.txt**

The Hacker's Dictionary

A comprehensive compendium of hacker slang illuminating the many aspects of hackish tradition, folklore and humor. Also known as the "jargon file".

Gopher:
Name: Mount Holyoke College
Address: **orixa.mtholyoke.edu**
Choose: **Document Library | The Hackers Dictionary**

How to Steal Code

Also known as "Inventing the Wheel Only Once". A guide by Henry Spencer on the merits of using the wealth of existing software and libraries instead of rewriting programs from scratch.

Anonymous FTP:
Address: **ucselx.sdsu.edu**
Path: **/pub/doc/general/steal.doc**

HPCwire

HPCwire publishes a weekly news bulletin on high-performance computing that is distributed to thousands of users on the Internet. Topics range from workstations to supercomputers, with news briefs, feature stories and in-depth, exclusive interviews.

Telnet:
Address: **hpcwire.ans.net**
Login: **hpcwire**

Internet Bibliography

An extensive list of Internet-related books, compiled by the Institute for Academic Technology at the University of North Carolina.

Anonymous FTP:
Address: **sunsite.unc.edu**
Path: **/pub/UNC-info/IAT/guides/ug-14.txt**

Gopher:
Name: University of North Carolina at Chapel Hill
Address: **sunsite.unc.edu**
Choose: **UNC-CH Information and Facilities | Institute for Academic Technology Documents for browsing | guides | irg-14.txt**

Internet Overview

An interesting history and overview of the Internet, written by cyberpunk author Bruce Sterling.

Gopher:
Name: University of Texas at Austin
Address: **actlab.rtf.utexas.edu**
Choose: **Networks | The Internet
| An Article on the Internet...**

IRC Thesis

An honors thesis entitled "Electropolis: Communication and Community on IRC", by E.M. Reid, detailing the culture and ways of Internet Relay Chat.

Anonymous FTP:
Address: **ftp.spies.com**
Path: **/Library/Cyber/electrop.txt**

Kermit Manual

Sixth edition of the manual for the Kermit file transfer protocol, often used by communications programs to transfer files using a modem.

Anonymous FTP:
Address: **nic.funet.fi**
Path: **/pub/kermit/docs/***

Logintaka

An entertaining guide to becoming a Unix wizard.

Gopher:
Name: Oregon State University
Address: **gopher.fsl.orst.edu**
Choose: **Other Sources of Information
| Hugo's Lore-House
| Where the Sun Doesn't Shine &
Other Bottomless Pits | The Logintaka**

Network Bibliography

A list of many computer networks.

Mail:
Address: **comserve@rpiecs.bitnet**
Body: **send compunet biblio**

Excerpt from the Net...

(from "An Article on the Internet" by Bruce Sterling)

Some thirty years ago, the Rand Corporation, America's foremost Cold War think-tank, faced a strange strategic problem. How could the U.S. authorities successfully communicate after a nuclear war?...

Rand mulled over this grim puzzle in deep military secrecy, and arrived at a daring solution. The Rand proposal (the brainchild of Rand staffer Paul Baran) was made public in 1964. In the first place, the network would have no central authority. Furthermore, it would be designed from the beginning to operate while in tatters...

In fall 1969, the first such node was installed in UCLA. By December 1969, there were four nodes on the infant network, which was named ARPANET, after its Pentagon sponsor...

It wasn't long before the invention of the mailing-list, an ARPANET broadcasting technique in which an identical message could be sent automatically to large numbers of network subscribers. Interestingly, one of the first really big mailing-lists was "SF-LOVERS," for science fiction fans. Discussing science fiction on the network was not work-related and was frowned upon by many ARPANET computer administrators, but this didn't stop it from happening...

ARPA's network, designed to assure control of a ravaged society after a nuclear holocaust, has been superceded by its mutant child the Internet, which is thoroughly out of control, and spreading exponentially through the post-Cold War electronic global village...

A B C D E F G H I J K L M N O P Q R S T U V W X Y Z

Network Newsletters

Selection of newsletters related to networks, including their social aspect and impact.

Anonymous FTP:
Address: **nigel.msen.com**
Path: **/pub/newsletters/Networker/***

Networking Computers

Lots of information on computer networking, school computing, hardware for networking, Unix networking and programming languages.

Gopher:
Name: Pacific Systems Group
Address: **gopher.psg.com**
Choose: **Networking...**

PC/MS-DOS: The Essentials

A brief guide for beginners with MS-DOS/PC-DOS computers. Written by George Campbell, this guide starts at the very beginning and takes it one step at a time.

Anonymous FTP:
Address: **ucselx.sdsu.edu**
Path: **/pub/doc/general/msdos.txt**

> *If you weren't lucky enough to buy one of the older Peter Norton DOS books (when Harley was working on them), you may need some help with your PC.*
>
> *Try PC/MS-DOS: The Essentials*

Tao of Programming

A complete text.

Anonymous FTP:
Address: **ucselx.sdsu.edu**
Path: **/pub/doc/etext/tao-of-programming**

**Need a laugh?
Check out Humor**

Tipsheet

A computer help and tip exchange where people can discuss a project or ask questions and get answers.

Listserv mailing list:
List Address: **tipsheet@wsuvm1.csc.wsu.edu**
Subscription Address:
listserv@wsuvm1.csc.wsu.edu

Unix Today

Binary programs, source code and other files of interest from *Unix Today* magazine.

Anonymous FTP:
Address: **ftp.uu.net**
Path: **/published/unix-today/***

Gopher:
Name: The World
Address: **world.std.com**
Choose: **Periodicals, Magazines, and Journals | UNIX Today**

FREE UNIX SOFTWARE

UNIX TODAY is one of the most important Unix magazines (today). If you are a Unix fan, you will certainly appreciate their Gopher and FTP site. Remember the Unix philosophy: why write your own shell scripts when you can use someone else's, and why even type them in if you can download them for free?

Unix World

Program listings, articles and other files of interest from *Unix World* magazine.

Anonymous FTP:
Address: **ftp.uu.net**
Path: **/published/unix-world/***

Gopher:
Name: The World
Address: **world.std.com**
Choose: **Periodicals, Magazines, and Journals | UNIX World**

Zen and the Art of the Internet

The first edition of the booklet by Brendan Kehoe, which covers all the basics of the Internet, including e-mail, FTP, Usenet, Telnet and other tools.

Anonymous FTP:
Address: **csn.org**
Path: **/pub/net/zen**

Address: **ftp.cs.widener.edu**
Path: **/pub/zen/***

COMPUTERS: MACINTOSH

Announcements

This moderated newsgroup contains announcements related to the Macintosh and Apple. Covers hardware and software problems and solutions.

Usenet:
Newsgroup: **comp.sys.mac.announce**

Buying and Selling

Here is the Usenet swap meet for Macs. The **.wanted** newsgroup is the place to send a request for Macintosh-related hardware or software. The **.computers** group is more for buying and selling systems and components.

Usenet:
Newsgroup: **comp.sys.mac.wanted**
Newsgroup: **misc.forsale.computers.mac**

Hardware

General discussion about Macintosh hardware of all types. The **.portable** newsgroup is for anything small and easy to move: laptops, notebooks and so on.

Usenet:
Newsgroup: **comp.sys.mac.hardware**
Newsgroup: **comp.sys.mac.portables**

Why be normal?
Read Bizarre.

Macintosh General Discussion

Discussion and commentary on every topic under the Macintosh sun. The **.advocacy** newsgroup is for debate and opinion. The **.digest** is a moderated magazine that contains articles of interest to Mac people. The **.misc** group is a forum for general discussion.

Usenet:
Newsgroup: **comp.sys.mac.advocacy**
Newsgroup: **comp.sys.mac.digest**
Newsgroup: **comp.sys.mac.misc**

News

News stories that involve Apple and the Macintosh.

Usenet:
Newsgroup: **clari.nb.apple**

Science and Technology

Discussion using the Macintosh for scientific and technological work. Just the place, for example, to ask if anyone knows of a catalog for organic chemistry substances to use with a Mac.

Usenet:
Newsgroup: **comp.sys.mac.scitech**

COMPUTERS: NETWORKS

Bibliography of Internetworking Information

Technical information about connecting computer networks. This document is RFC-1175.

Anonymous FTP:
Address: **ds.internic.net**
Path: **rfc/rfc1175.txt**

Bitnet Network

Information on the Bitnet network, including a node list and introductory guide.

Anonymous FTP:
Address: **quartz.rutgers.edu**
Path: **/pub/internet/bitnet/***

Gopher:
Name: Rutgers Quartz Text Archive
Address: **quartz.rutgers.edu**
Choose:
Internet Information and Documentation
| bitnet

A B C D E F G H I J K L M N O P Q R S T U V W X Y Z

Computer and Networking Column

Converse with Fred about computers and networking in his electronic newspaper column.

Gopher:
> Name: The World
> Address: **world.std.com**
> Choose: **Periodicals, Magazines, and Journals**
> **| Middlesex News | Columns | Fred**

Cyberspace Communications

A collection of articles covering communications in cyberspace and the Internet and what we have to gain or lose with these new technologies.

Gopher:
> Name: Whole Earth Lectronic Link
> Address: **gopher.well.sf.ca.us**
> Choose: **Communications**

High Performance Computing and Communications Gopher

This Gopher provides information on the Federal High Performance Computing and Communications Program and on the burgeoning National Information Infrastructure. There are also links to other government, public interest and private sector Gopher servers related to HPCC and the Internet.

Gopher:
> Name: National Coordination Office for HPCC
> Address: **gopher.hpcc.gov**

Inter-Network Mail Guide

A publication by John Chew and Scott Yanoff that documents methods for sending mail from one network to another. If you're not sure how to e-mail someone on CompuServe, America Online or any of many different networks, or how to e-mail someone on CompuServe from Prodigy, this document has information and detailed instructions.

Anonymous FTP:
> Address: **csd4.csd.uwm.edu**
> Path: **/pub/internetwork-mail-guide**

Finger:
> Address: **yanoff@csd4.csd.uwm.edu**

Usenet:
> Newsgroup: **alt.internet.services**

Does your postman never even ring once?

Try the
Inter-Network Mail Guide

Mail Gateway Guide

Jeremy Smith's "Getting Through the Matrix", a guide to sending mail from one network to another through gateway computers.

Gopher:
> Name: Oregon State University
> Address: **gopher.fsl.orst.edu**
> Choose: **Other Sources of Info**
> **| Hugo's Lore-House**
> **| Dr.Fegg's Big House o'Fun..**
> **| Jeremy Smith's Guide to Gateways**

Managing Networked Information

A compendium of papers on network information management from the "Drinking from a Firehose" VALA Conference.

Gopher:
> Name: La Trobe University
> Address: **gopher.latrobe.edu.au**
> Choose: **Library Services**
> **| VALA Conference Papers**
> **| Index of VALA Papers**

Matrix News

Samples and information about Matrix News, a newsletter about cross-network issues.

Anonymous FTP:
> Address: **tic.com**
> Path: **/matrix/news/***

Gopher:
> Name: Texas Internet Consulting
> Address: **tic.com**
> Choose: **Matrix Information...**
> **| About Matrix News, the..**

National Information Infrastructure Agenda

The text of the executive order dated September 15, 1993 that creates an advisory council of 25 appointed members to advise the Secretary of Commerce on ways to integrate hardware, software and skills to facilitate interaction between people. (No doubt, they will begin by reading *The Internet Complete Reference*.)

Gopher:
    Name: U.S. Department of Agriculture
    Address: **ace.esusda.gov**
    Choose: **Americans Communicating Electronically**
      | **National Information Infrastructure documents**

Network Maps

A color geographical map of the world showing the main global networks in the matrix of computer networks that exchange electronic mail.

Anonymous FTP:
    Address: **tic.com**
    Path: **/matrix/maps/***

Gopher:
    Name: Texas Internet Consulting
    Address: **tic.com**
    Choose: **Matrix Information..**
      | **Maps of Networks**

Networking Articles

Articles on all aspects of networking, including TCP/IP LAN, ethernet, Internet protocols and the Wiretap Algorithm.

Anonymous FTP:
    Address: **ftp.spies.com**
    Path: **/Library/Techdoc/Network/***

Gopher:
    Name: Internet Wiretap
    Address: **wiretap.spies.com**
    Choose: **Wiretap Online Library**
      | **Technical Information | Networking**

TCP/IP Introduction

An introduction to the TCP/IP set of networking protocols and advice on what to read for more information.

Anonymous FTP:
    Address: **ftp.spies.com**
    Path: **/Library/Techdoc/Network/intro.tcp**

Gopher:
    Name: Internet Wiretap
    Address: **wiretap.spies.com**
    Choose: **Wiretap Online Library**
      | **Technical Information | Networking**
      | **TCP/IP Introduction**

Excerpt from the Net...

(from the "Information Infrastructure Executive Order 9/15/93")

                    THE WHITE HOUSE
              Office of the Press Secretary

_____

For Immediate Release   September 15, 1993

                    EXECUTIVE ORDER
                    - - - - - - -

            UNITED STATES ADVISORY COUNCIL
        ON THE NATIONAL INFORMATION INFRASTRUCTURE

By the authority vested in me as President by the Constitution and the laws of the United States of America, including the Federal Advisory Committee Act, as amended (5 U.S.C. App. 2) ("Act"), and section 301 of title 3, United States Code, it is hereby ordered as follows:

Section 1. Establishment. (a) There is established in the Commerce Department the "United States Advisory Council on the National Information Infrastructure"...

COMPUTERS: PC

Hardware

General discussion of all types of PC hardware. The **.pc** newsgroup is for any type of PC hardware from any vendor; the **.ps2** group is for PS/2 and Microchannel hardware. The **.gateway2000** group is devoted to products from the Gateway 2000 company. The **.pcmcia** group is for discussion of PCMCIA add-in cards for portable computers.

Usenet:
>   Newsgroup: **alt.periphs.pcmcia**
>   Newsgroup: **alt.sys.pc-clone.gateway2000**
>   Newsgroup: **comp.sys.ibm.pc.hardware**
>   Newsgroup: **comp.sys.ibm.ps2.hardware**

PC Hardware

Ah, those halcyon days of our youth when--screwdrivers and chip pullers in hand--we spent so many wonderful hours working on the innards of our PCs. What could be more fun on a summer's afternoon than discussing PC hardware when everybody else is wasting their time at the beach?

(Tip for the guys: women really go for men who know their hardware.)

Magazine

This moderated newsgroup contains an electronic magazine devoted to PCs.

Usenet:
>   Newsgroup: **alt.znet.pc**

News about IBM

News stories about IBM and its products.

Usenet:
>   Newsgroup: **clari.nb.ibm**

PC General Discussion

General discussion about PCs and related topics. The **.digest** newsgroup is moderated. The **.misc** group is an open forum.

Usenet:
>   Newsgroup: **comp.sys.ibm.pc.digest**
>   Newsgroup: **comp.sys.ibm.pc.misc**

Soundcards

Discussion covering all aspects of PC soundcards. The **.soundcard** group is for general discussion about any aspect of any soundcard and its related software. The **sb** group is for Sound Blaster cards. The **.GUS** group is for the Gravis Ultrasound card.

Usenet:
>   Newsgroup: **alt.sb.programmer**
>   Newsgroup: **comp.sys.ibm.pc.soundcard**
>   Newsgroup: **comp.sys.ibm.pc.soundcard.GUS**

COMPUTERS: PICTURES

Amiga Pictures

Pictures and related material for those wonderfully-equipped Amiga computers.

Usenet:
>   Newsgroup: **comp.sys.amiga.graphics**

Cartoon Pictures

Pictures of your favorite cartoon characters—Chip 'n' Dale Rescue Rangers, Snow White, Ren and Stimpy, Bill and Hillary—here they are, waiting for you to download.

Usenet:
>   Newsgroup: **alt.toon-pics**

Chinese GIF Collection

A collection of over 50 GIF image files which you can view through Gopher (if you have the appropriate software).

Anonymous FTP:
>   Address: **National Chung Cheng University**
>   Path: **gopher.ccu.edu.tw**

Fine Art

As Tennyson said when he first started using the Internet, "the fact that picture newsgroups exist for more than just erotica proves that man can rise on the stepping stones of his dead self to better things". Participate and download fine art suitable for framing. The **.d** newsgroup is for discussion. The other groups are for pictures only. The rules (if you care to follow them) are that **.digitized** is for original, digitized artwork and **.graphics** is for original pictures created with a computer.

Usenet:
Newsgroup: **alt.binaries.pictures.fine-art.d**
Newsgroup: **alt.binaries.pictures.fine-art.digitized**
Newsgroup: **alt.binaries.pictures.fine-art.graphics**

Fractals

Ah fractals, those wonderful fractional dimensional thingies that nobody understands but that lend themselves to such totally cool pictures that really blow you away for the first five minutes. Get some for yourself.

Usenet:
Newsgroup: **alt.binaries.pictures.fractals**

GIF Image Files

A collection of interesting GIF files, including Pepsi, Reagan and Bush images.

Anonymous FTP:
Address: **aug3.augsburg.edu**
Path: **/files/other_gifs/***

Girls, Girls, Girls

Pictures, mostly in JPEG format, of many top models, including Stephanie Seymour, Niki Taylor, Claudia Schiffer, Cindy Crawford and many more.

Gopher:
Name: University of Pisa
Address: **gopher.unipi.it**
Choose: **Top Models**

The resolution, colors, and overall quality of the graphic images on the Internet will astound you. Of course, nobody uses the Internet just to look at pictures. (At least, no one seems to admit to it.) This image was derived from **swim85.gif**, which is available from Washington University, St. Louis (**wuarchive.wustl.edu**).

Japanese Animation Images

A large collection of Japanese Anime images in JPG format.

Anonymous FTP:
Address: **ftp.tcp.com**
Path: **/pub/anime/Images/***

Gopher:
Name: National Chung Cheng University
Address: **gopher.ccu.edu.tw**
Choose: **miscellanies | Japanese Anim Picture**

JPEG Files

Graphic image files in the JPEG format. Selections include **aliens**, **punisher**, **wolverine** and **saddog**.

Anonymous FTP:
Address: **aug3.augsburg.edu**
Path: **/files/jpeg/***

Kandinsky Image Archive

GIF images of paintings by Wassily Kandinsky, abstract artist.

Gopher:
Name: University of Michigan
Address: **libra.arch.umich.edu**
Choose: **The Kandinsky Image Archive**

A B C D E F G H I J K L M N O P Q R S T U V W X Y Z

Need a quick artistic fix?

Try the Kandinsky Image Archive

Mandelbrot Images

A collection of Mandelbrot images in GIF format.

Anonymous FTP:
Address: **ftp.ira.uka.de**
Path: **/pub/graphic/fractals/***

Miscellaneous Pictures

General Usenet groups devoted to the sharing of pictures. The **.d** newsgroup is for discussion about pictures. The other groups are for pictures only.

Usenet:
Newsgroup: **alt.binaries.pictures**
Newsgroup: **alt.binaries.pictures.d**
Newsgroup: **alt.binaries.pictures.misc**

A Thousand Pictures are Worth a Single Word

There are so many fabulous pictures waiting to be downloaded that we sometimes wonder why anyone would use a computer for anything else.

All you need is an Internet connection, a few utility programs and a lot of time, and you too can turn your personal computer into a sophisticated photo album.

MPEG Animation Shows

Dozens of MPEG binary animation files containing a dizzying array of clips from waterskiing feats to space aliens.

Gopher:
Name: National Chung Cheng University
Address: **gopher.ccu.edu.tw**
Choose: **miscellanies | mpeg**

Nude Pictures

Explicit scanned photos.

Usenet:
Newsgroup: **alt.sex.pictures**

Picture Viewing Software

Before you can view pictures on your own computer, you need the appropriate software. Read this newsgroup to get info on what programs are available and how to use them.

Usenet:
Newsgroup: **alt.binaries.pictures.utilities**

Picture-Related Files Anonymous FTP Site List

Large list of Anonymous FTP sites that contain files related to viewing, extracting, encoding, compressing, archiving, converting and anything else you can do to pictures of all format types.

Anonymous FTP:
Address: **bongo.cc.utexas.edu**
Path: **/gifstuff/ftpsites**

Satellite Images of Europe

Europe, as seen by the Meteosat weather satellite, in GIF and JPG formats.

Anonymous FTP:
Address: **cumulus.met.ed.ac.uk**
Path: **/images/***

Address: **liasun3.epfl.ch**
Path: **/pub/weather/***

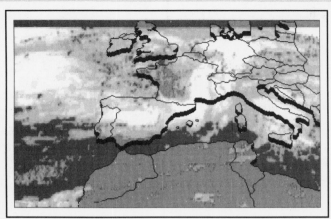

Weather satellite images available on the Internet are updated daily, if not more often. These images are almost always in standard GIF or JPG formats.

Sex Pictures

Let's take a minute to stop and appreciate the vast resources of the Internet: All those computers, communications lines, satellites. Not to mention the tens of thousands of people working day and night to ensure that it all hangs together. All of this, just so you can download sexy...er...erotic pictures to display on your own computer. Usenet, mirroring the world, has a large selection of newsgroups devoted to various aspects of visual gratification. The **.d** newsgroups are for discussions. All the other groups are for pictures only. (Note: If you want to learn how to download pictures and what software you need, read *The Internet Complete Reference*".)

Usenet:
>Newsgroup: **alt.binaries.pictures.erotica**
>Newsgroup: **alt.binaries.pictures.erotica.blondes**
>Newsgroup: **alt.binaries.pictures.erotica.d**
>Newsgroup: **alt.binaries.pictures.erotica.female**
>Newsgroup: **alt.binaries.pictures.erotica.male**
>Newsgroup: **alt.binaries.pictures.erotica.orientals**
>Newsgroup: **alt.sex.pictures**
>Newsgroup: **alt.sex.pictures.d**
>Newsgroup: **alt.sex.pictures.female**
>Newsgroup: **alt.sex.pictures.male**

Shuttle and Satellite Images

Photographs in electronic formats of spacecraft and spectacular views from Earth and space.

Anonymous FTP:
>Address: **iris1.ucis.dal.ca**
>Path: **/pub/GIF**

>Address: **pioneer.unm.edu**
>Path: **/pub/info**

>Address: **sseop.jsc.nasa.gov**
>Path: **/***

Gopher:
>Name: NASA Goddard Space Flight Center
>Address: **gopher.gsfc.nasa.gov**
>Choose: **Nasa information**
> | **Space images and information**

Mail:
>Address: **kelley@sanddunes.scd.ucar.edu**

Telnet:
>Address: **sanddunes.scd.ucar.edu**

Smithsonian Photographs

Photographs of gems, jungles, stars and artifacts taken by the Smithsonian Institution. Available with viewing software in JPEG and JFIF formats.

Gopher:
>Name: The Pipeline Gopher
>Address: **pipeline.com**
>Choose: **Arts and Leisure**
> | **Smithsonian photographs and viewing software**

Supermodels

The next best thing to living next door to a supermodel is being able to download one whenever you want. Just the thing to look at when you get tired of fractals.

Usenet:
>Newsgroup: **alt.binaries.pictures.supermodels**

You never need to be without the image of your favorite model. Supermodels are plentyful on the Internet, as Cindy Crawford will attest. This file is **c-crwfrd.gif** and you should be able to find it easily with Archie. The Mona Lisa came from **ftp.wustl.edu**. Use Archie to search for **monalisa**.

A B C D E F G H I J K L M N O P Q R S T U V W X Y Z

Tasteless Pictures

Here is a newsgroup for the posting of tasteless, bizarre
and grotesque pictures only. For the truly demented: get
your fill of car wrecks, mangled bodies, freaks, and so on.
What is tasteless? Well, all we can say is that this
newsgroup is not for the faint of heart. You will see
pictures of things we can't even mention in a family book.
Suffice to say that if you are the type of person who likes
to look at things that make other people cringe, then this
group is for you. And don't say we didn't warn you.

Usenet:
Newsgroup: **alt.binaries.pictures.tasteless**

COMPUTERS: SECURITY

Computer Security Gopher

The DFN-Cert Gopher in Germany offers lots of
information about computer security through their
archives, including information on firewalls, worm
attacks and Unix security.

Anonymous FTP:
Address: **ftp.informatik.uni-hamburg.de**
Path: **/pub/security/***

Gopher:
Name: University of Hamburg
Address: **gopher.informatik.uni-hamburg.de**

PGP Keyservers

Public PGP keyservers which allow you to exchange
public PGP encryption keys running through the Internet
and UUCP mail systems.

Mail:
Address: **pgp-public-keys@cs.tamu.edu**
Subject: **help**

Address: **pgp-public-keys@demon.co.uk**
Subject: **help**

Address: **pgp-public-keys@pgp.iastate.edu**
Subject: **help**

Address: **pgp-public-keys@pgp.mit.edu**
Subject: **help**

Address: **pgp-public-keys@phil.utmb.edu**
Subject: **help**

Privacy and Anonymity Issues

Details on encryption, e-mail and account privacy,
anonymous mailing and posting and other Internet and
global network privacy issues.

Anonymous FTP:
Address: **rtfm.mit.edu**
Path: **/pub/usenet/news.answers/net-anonymity/***

Address: **rtfm.mit.edu**
Path: **/pub/usenet/news.answers/net-privacy/***

Gopher:
Name: Oregon State University
Address: **gopher.fsl.orst.edu**
Choose: **Other Sources of Info**
 | **Hugo's Lore-House**
 | **Where the Sun Doesn't Shine..**
 | **Identify, Privacy and Anonymity on the
 Internet**

Privacy Forum Digest

A moderated digest for the discussion and analysis of the
legal aspects of privacy in the information age.

Anonymous FTP:
Address: **ftp.vortex.com**
Path: **/privacy/***

Gopher:
Name: Vortex Technology
Address: **cv.vortex.com**
Choose: **Privacy Forum**

Unix Security Tutorial

A detailed guide to improving the security of your Unix
system.

Anonymous FTP:
Address: **quartz.rutgers.edu**
Path: **/pub/computer/security/
 unix-security-tutorial**

Gopher:
Name: Rutgers Quartz Text Archive
Address: **quartz.rutgers.edu**
Choose: **Computer-Sources, Documentation,
 Comp.Sci | security | unix-security-tutorial**

COMPUTERS: SOUNDS

Amiga Sounds

Sounds and related material for Amiga computers.

Usenet:
> Newsgroup: **comp.sys.amiga.audio**

Barney Meets his Maker

Ever wish Barney would just go away? Well, in this sound file he meets his maker in a most convincing way.

Comment: Sound file is a .VOC format.

Anonymous FTP:
> Address: **wuarchive.wustl.edu**
> Path: **/pub/MSDOS_UPLOADS/games/barney.zip**

Miscellaneous Sounds

Aren't sounds great? Without them there would be nothing to listen to. Join the Usenet group devoted to sharing sounds of all types. Music, people, things and lots of what-have-you. The **.misc** groups is for sounds only. The **.d** group is for discussion about sounds and the requisite hardware and software, especially audio formats.

Usenet:
> Newsgroup: **alt.binaries.sounds.d**
> Newsgroup: **alt.binaries.sounds.misc**

Music

All types of music, especially classical music. Endow your computer with the charms it needs to tame the savage beast within you.

Usenet:
> Newsgroup: **alt.binaries.sounds.music**

NeXT Sounds

Hundreds of megabytes of sounds for the NeXT machine, including lots of theme songs and samples from well-known artists.

Anonymous FTP:
> Address: **wuarchive.wustl.edu**
> Path: **/pub/NeXT-Music/***

Rplay

A Sun software package that allows you to play multiple sounds at once on the same machine (and on different machines). Also supports sound broadcasting. Make your office sound like the bridge of the starship Enterprise.

Anonymous FTP:
> Address: **athena.sdsu.edu**
> Path: **/pub/rplay/***

Gopher:
> Name: San Diego State University
> Address: **athena.sdsu.edu 71**
> Choose: **pub | rplay**

SDSU Sound Archives

Located at San Diego State University, this is one of the largest sound archive sites around. This archive has sound clips from movies, as well as a huge selection of sayings, screams, mechanical sounds and even whale conversations. One favorite: Arnold's "I'll be back".

Comment: Most sounds are in Sun format, but conversion programs are available on the system.

Anonymous FTP:
> Address: **athena.sdsu.edu**
> Path: **/sounds/***

Gopher:
> Name: San Diego State University
> Address: **athena.sdsu.edu 71**

Sound Advice

Shhhhh...

The trouble with a regular library is that there is no talking. And, even if you hear something interesting, you can't take it home with you. However, the SDSU Sound Archives fill that important human need: to be able to collect a multitude of sounds that you can play over and over. For your next party, don't depend on your guests to fill the air with interesting talk. Download some sounds and leave nothing to chance.

A B C D E F G H I J K L M N O P Q R S T U V W X Y Z

Sex Sounds

Simon and Garfunkel used to wax eloquent about the sounds of silence. Come on, who are we fooling? Check out this newsgroup and download some sounds of you-know-what. Of course, in order to really enjoy the experience, you will need the proper hardware (as if you didn't know).

Usenet:
    Newsgroup: **alt.sex.sounds**

Sound Cards

For a PC to play any sounds worth listening to, it needs a sound card. Join these discussion groups and swap hints and tips about PC sound cards. The **.soundcard** newsgroup is for all hardware and software aspects of such cards. The **.sb** group is for the Sound Blaster card. The **.GUS** group is for the Gravis Ultrasound.

Usenet:
    Newsgroup: **alt.sb.programmer**
    Newsgroup: **comp.sys.ibm.pc.soundcard**
    Newsgroup: **comp.sys.ibm.pc.soundcard.GUS**

Sound File Converter

A C program for converting sound files between many different platforms, including PCs, Unix systems, Macs and even Commodores.

Anonymous FTP:
    Address: **athena.sdsu.edu**
    Path: **/pub/SoundConversion/***

Sounds Wanted

A place where you can request a particular song or sound in machine readable format, or fulfill the requests of others.

Anonymous FTP:
    Address: **athena.sdsu.edu**
    Path: **/sound_requests/***

Gopher:
    Name: San Diego State University
    Address: **athena.sdsu.edu 71**
    Choose: **sound_requests**

SOX

A multiformat sound converter, with source code, for Amiga, PC, Unix and Macintosh machines. SOX converts audio files to other formats.

Anonymous FTP:
    Address: **athena.sdsu.edu**
    Path: **/pub/SoundConversion/***

Gopher:
    Name: San Diego State University
    Address: **athena.sdsu.edu 71**
    Choose: **pub | SoundConversion**

Sun Sound Files

Large collections of songs, roosters, cackles, gongs, dialtones and other miscellaneous sounds to play on your Sun Sparcstation. Includes the Sparctracker software.

Anonymous FTP:
    Address: **toybox.gsfc.nasa.gov**
    Path: **/pub/sounds/***

Gopher:
    Name: National Chung Cheng University
    Address: **gopher.ccu.edu.tw**
    Choose: **miscellanies | Funny Sounds**

COMPUTERS: TECHNOLOGY

Chinese Computing and Word Processing

A mailing list discussion group on technology relating to the use of Chinese on computers. A forum for both experts and regular users that reaches from North America to the Far East.

Listserv mailing list:
    List Address: **ccnet-l@uga.bitnet**
    Subscription Address: **listserv@uga.bitnet**

Computer Lore

Famous computer bugs, unofficial Unix horror stories, Old Iron at Home stories and much more computer folklore.

Anonymous FTP:
    Address: **ftp.spies.com**
    Path: **/Library/Techdoc/Lore/***

Gopher:
    Name: Internet Wiretap
    Address: **wiretap.spies.com**
    Choose: **Wiretap Online Library**
      | Technical Information
      | Computer Lore

Computer Products, Services and Publications

Mailing lists dedicated to computer products, service and publication announcements, and general information about computers.

Mail:
Address: **maillist@internet.com**
Body: **subscribe computer.products** *your name*

Address: **maillist@internet.com**
Body: **subscribe computer.info** *your name*

Computer Science Conferences

A large list of mailing lists related to computer science, the social, cultural and political aspects of computers, and academic computing support.

Anonymous FTP:
Address: **ksuvxa.kent.edu**
Path: **/library/acadlist.file8**

Gopher:
Name: NYSERNet
Address: **nysernet.org**
Choose: **Special Collections: Higher Education**
  | Scholarly Electronic Conferences [Kovacs]
  | Computer Science

Computer Speech

Archives and information about computer speech technology and speech science.

Anonymous FTP:
Address: **svr-ftp.eng.cam.ac.uk**
Path: **/comp.speech/***

Computer Standards

Technical documents on many standards including GIF, ymodem, zmodem, rich text format and binhex.

Anonymous FTP:
Address: **ftp.spies.com**
Path: **/Library/Techdoc/Standard/***

Gopher:
Name: Internet Wiretap
Address: **wiretap.spies.com**
Choose: **Wiretap Online Library**
  | Technical Information | Computer Standards

Computer Viruses

FAQs and articles on viruses, including Bulgarian and Soviet Virus Factories, boot sector viruses, Bitnet and Internet viruses and virus protection.

Anonymous FTP:
Address: **ftp.spies.com**
Path: **/Library/Techdoc/Virus/***

Gopher:
Name: Internet Wiretap
Address: **wiretap.spies.com**
Choose: **Wiretap Online Library**
  | Technical Information | Viruses

SFI BBS

A research BBS devoted to Complex Systems.

Telnet:
Address: **bbs.santafe.edu**
Login: **bbs**

Technology Magazines

Sample articles and subscription information for computer technology and network related magazines.

Gopher:
Name: The Electronic Newsstand
Address: **gopher.internet.com 2100**
Choose: **Titles Arranged By Category**
  | Technology - Computers, Networks

Virtual Reality

This menu contains items relevant to the concept of a single-user virtual reality. It includes some interesting articles and access to the Interactive Fiction archive.

Anonymous FTP:
Address: **ftp.u.washington.edu**
Path: **/public/VirtualReality/***

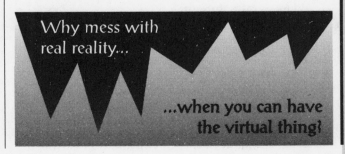

Why mess with real reality...

...when you can have the virtual thing?

A B C D E F G H I J K L M N O P Q R S T U V W X Y Z

Wombat Dictionaries

A glossary of programming languages, architectures, networks, domain theory, mathematics and, in fact, anything to do with computing.

Gopher:
Name: Imperial College, London
Address: **wombat.doc.ic.ac.uk**

CONSUMER SERVICES

Consumer News

Real news about real products bought by real consumers (you). Find out what is happening before the Joneses do.

Usenet:
Newsgroup: **clari.news.consumer**

Consumer Products, Services and Publications

Mailing lists dedicated to consumer products, services, publication announcements and general information about consumer products and services.

Mail:
Address: **maillist@internet.com**
Body: **subscribe consumer.products** *your name*

Address: **maillist@internet.com**
Body: **subscribe consumer.info** *your name*

Credit Information

FAQ list detailing everything you need to know about consumer credit.

Anonymous FTP:
Address: **rtfm.mit.edu**
Path: **/pub/usenet/news.answers/
  consumer-credit-faq/***

Gopher:
Name: Oregon State University
Address: **gopher.fsl.orst.edu**
Choose: **Other Sources of Info
  | Hugo's Lore-House
  | Where the Sun Doesn't Shine & Other
    Bottomless Pits | All you should ever need..**

Fair Credit Reporting Act

The full text of this Congressional act.

Gopher:
Name: Internet Wiretap
Address: **wiretap.spies.com**
Choose: **Government Docs
  | Fair Credit Reporting Act**

FaxLinq

FaxLinq allows e-mail users worldwide to receive facsimile messages without owning a fax machine. For more information on FaxLinq and subscription forms, mail the addresses below.

Comment: This is a commercial service for which a fee is charged.

Mail:
Address: **faxlinq-faq@antigone.com**
Address: **info@antigone.com**

FAXNET

Send and receive faxes to and from anywhere in the world from your computer or terminal. All you need is the ability to send mail on the Internet. Send a mail message to the address below for a FAQ list about this service.

Comment: This is a service of AnyWare Associates and they do charge fees.

Mail:
Address: **info@awa.com**

Just the Fax, Ma'am

Now that we have the Internet, are faxes obsolete? Not really, because there are times when you will need to send material to someone not smart enough to have e-mail access. Not to worry, use the FAXNET service and send your fax from the comfort of your Internet account. It does cost money, but when you figure it out in dollars/dot, it's really quite reasonable.

General Consumer Information

Here is Usenet's general consumer forum. And, since we are all consumers, there is something for everyone. Send in your questions, share your answers, read the reviews, opinions and general bad-mouthing of the bad guys. Before you spend your next dime, check with the world at large.

Usenet:
Newsgroup: **misc.consumers**

Houses

What did you ever do with your weekends before you bought a house? Don't you feel sorry for all those people who have nothing better to do than go out and have fun? Share your experiences with hardwood floors, mortgages, roofing repairs, plumbing, carpeting, contractors, real estate agents, painting, ventilation systems and other great ways to spend your short, all-too-brief time on planet Earth.

Usenet:
Newsgroup: **misc.consumers.house**

Infinity Link Corporation Consumer Access Services

Bookstores, music CDs, Unix software and movies on VHS video cassettes and laserdiscs. This service provides you with a window into a wide variety of unique and hard to find products. Some sections of ILC/CAS provide you with information on these products and some sections allow you to actually purchase these products online with only a few keystrokes.

Telnet:
Address: **columbia.ilc.com**
Login: **cas**

Excerpt from the Net...

```
Newsgroup: misc.consumers.house
Subject: Too much house?

> Has anyone bought or rented a house
> and discovered that there was
> too much space for you?

I don't know if you're going to get
much sympathy for your problems.
It is far easier to make a house
smaller than to make it larger...
```

Internet Marketing Service

Information and subscription instructions for mailing lists that inform readers about new commercial products and services. Lists currently exist for computer, the Internet, and consumer products, services and publications.

Gopher:
Name: The Internet Company
Address: **gopher.internet.com 2000**
Choose: **User Services**
  | **The Internet Marketing Service**

MarketBase

The MarketBase Online Catalog of Goods and Services is a unique online service dedicated to providing a forum where buyers and sellers meet to exchange information on products and services.

Gopher:
Name: MarketBase
Address: **mb.com**

Telnet:
Address: **mb.com**
Login: **mb**

Online Bookstore

An online bookstore with computer and non-computer books. Mail for more information. Order extra copies of this book for all your friends.

Mail:
Address: **obs@tic.com**

Trade Names Material Safety Data Sheets

A database of information on hundreds of chemicals and compounds. Includes scientific data such as molecular formulas and atomic weights, as well as health hazards and fire-fighting procedures.

Gopher:
Name: Iowa State University
Address: **isumvs.iastate.edu**
Choose: **ISU Research Information | MSDS**

A B C D E F G H I J K L M N O P Q R S T U V W X Y Z

Your Complete Guide to Credit

A consumer guide by Mark J. Allen.

Anonymous FTP:
Address: **oak.oakland.edu**
Path: **/pub/misc/consumers/credit.txt**

CRYPTOGRAPHY

All About Cryptography

Articles about aspects of cryptography, including DES, Clipper, wiretaps and other security issues.

Anonymous FTP:
Address: **ftp.spies.com**
Path: **/Liberty/Article/Crypto/***

Gopher:
Name: Internet Wiretap
Address: **wiretap.spies.com**
Choose: **Wiretap Online Library | Articles | Cryptography**

Crypto Glossary

Glossary of cryptography-related terms, from the Cypherpunks mailing list.

Anonymous FTP:
Address: **ftp.spies.com**
Path: **/Library/Document/crypto.dic**

Gopher:
Name: Internet Wiretap
Address: **wiretap.spies.com**
Choose: **Wiretap Online Library | Assorted Documents | Crypto Glossary (cyberpunks)**

Spare time? Take a look at Games

General Discussion

A general discussion of all aspects of data encryption and decryption.

Usenet:
Newsgroup: **sci.crypt**

Government

How the government is involved in cryptography. Do they want to protect us all, or snoop on our private lives?

Usenet:
Newsgroup: **talk.politics.crypto**

PGP Encryption/Decryption Program

Where to get and how to use the ubiquitous PGP (Pretty Good Privacy) encryption package. Use it to send secret messages to your friends.

Usenet:
Newsgroup: **alt.security.pgp**

Public Key Exchange

Share your public key with everyone else so you can send and receive secret encoded messages.

Usenet:
Newsgroup: **alt.security.keydist**

Want to trade secrets? I'll show you my public key if you show me yours.

CYBERPUNK

Agrippa: A Book of the Dead

The complete text of this cyberpunk tale by William Gibson.

Anonymous FTP:
> Address: **ftp.rahul.net**
> Path: **/pub/atman/UTLCD-preview/**
> **assorted-text/agrippa.arj**

Bruce Sterling Articles

A selection of essays and articles by Bruce Sterling, the renowned cyberpunk author, covering a variety of topics about cyberspace and its surrounding culture.

Anonymous FTP:
> Address: **ftp.eff.org**
> Path: **/pub/agitprop/***

Gopher:
> Name: Whole Earth Lectronic Link
> Address: **gopher.well.sf.ca.us**
> Choose: **Cyberpunk and Postmodern Culture**
> **| Bruce Sterling**

Cyberspace City

Fans of Bruce Sterling (Mr. Cyberspace) can rejoice. Selected articles are available by Anonymous FTP or via a Gopher. Why go all the way to the library or bookstore just to read something on...ugh... paper. Read Sterling the way God meant you to read him: on your computer screen.

Cyberculture

A collection of articles, papers and FAQs, pertaining to cyberspace and the electronic culture.

Anonymous FTP:
> Address: **quartz.rutgers.edu**
> Path: **/pub/cyberculture/***

Gopher:
> Name: Rutgers Quartz Text Archive
> Address: **quartz.rutgers.edu**
> Choose: **Cyberculture Papers and Info**

Cyberpunk News

Collection of cyberpunk-related material, including *Locus* magazine, Bruce Sterling articles and the latest information about cyberpunk conventions, those mind-blowing meetings of the computer underground.

Gopher:
> Name: Whole Earth Lectronic Link
> Address: **gopher.well.sf.ca.us**
> Choose: **Cyberpunk and Postmodern Culture**

Cyberpunk Reading List

A long list of cyberpunk-related books, novels and material, arranged by author.

Anonymous FTP:
> Address: **ftp.spies.com**
> Path: **/Library/Media/Sci-Fi/cyber.lis**

Gopher:
> Name: Internet Wiretap
> Address: **wiretap.spies.com**
> Choose: **Wiretap Online Library | Mass Media**
> **| Science Fiction and Fantasy**
> **| Cyberpunk Reading List**

Cypherpunks

Clipper documents, cryptanalysis tools, crypt FTP site list, FAQs, PGP and other cryptography-related material can be found at this Cypherpunk mailing list archive.

Anonymous FTP:
> Address: **nic.funet.fi**
> Path: **/pub/doc/cypherpunks/***

> Address: **soda.berkeley.edu**
> Path: **/pub/cypherpunks/***

Future Culture and Cyberpunks Mailing List

Discussion and news about tomorrow's reality today. Become a dreamer of the dreams.

Internet mailing list:
> List Address: **uafsysb@uark.edu**
> Subscription Address: **uafsysb-request@uark.edu**

Too much spare time?
Explore a MUD

A B C D E F G H I J K L M N O P Q R S T U V W X Y Z

DANCE

Dance Archives and Discussion

Discussion and materials of interest to fans of dance, including swing, ballroom, rock and roll, and others. Materials include information on places to dance, events, new CDs, and steps.

Anonymous FTP:
Address: **ftp.cs.dal.ca**
Path: **/comp.archives/rec.arts.dance/***

Address: **ftp.cs.dal.ca**
Path: **/comp.archives/rec.folk-dancing/***

Address: **fuzzy.ucsc.edu**
Path: **/pub/bds93.Z**

Internet mailing list:
List Address: **ballroom@athena.mit.edu**
Subscription Address:
ballroom-request@athena.mit.edu

Usenet:
Newsgroup: **rec.arts.dance**
Newsgroup: **rec.folk-dancing**

Folk and Traditional Dance Mailing List

A global forum for information exchange for those interested in folk dance and traditional dance.

Listserv mailing list:
List Address: **dance-l@hearn.nic.surfnet.nl**
Subscription Address:
listserv@hearn.nic.surfnet.nl

Folk Dancing

There aren't too many ways to have fun, get exercise, listen to music, enjoy your friends, and act like a jerk, all at the same time. Whether you are into folk, dance, or folk dance, this is the place to meet the kind of people who like lining up and stepping out.

Usenet:
Newsgroup: **rec.folk-dancing**

General Discussion

Are you wondering what is the theme of this year's Winter Biannual Formal Dance at the University of Wisconsin, Madison? Perhaps you have a less esoteric question about choreography, dance videos, stretching exercises or how to learn the tango. Step along with dance folk of all types in this general bop-till-you-drop discussion group.

Usenet:
Newsgroup: **rec.arts.dance**

DRAMA

Play Scripts

Numerous play scripts and other drama-related materials, including reviews, and Shakespeare information and works.

Gopher:
Name: English Server
Address: **english-server.hss.cmu.edu**
Choose: **Drama**

Shakespeare Discussion

A global discussion open to all persons interested in Shakespeare, offering announcements, scholarly papers, and informal discussion.

Listserv mailing list:
List Address: **shaksper@utoronto.bitnet**
Subscription Address: **listserv@utoronto.bitnet**

Shakespeare Glossary

A glossary of Shakespearean terms.

Gopher:
Name: English Server
Address: **english-server.hss.cmu.edu**
Choose: **Drama | Shakespeare-Glossary**

Need a laugh?
Check out Humor

Spare time?
Take a look at Games

Excerpt from the Net...

Newsgroup: rec.folk-dancing
Subject: Perpetually awkward dancers

There's a guy at the group I dance with who is -- how can I put this? -- not the most incredibly coordinated person in the world. For some reason this fascinates me, and every now and then I try to figure out exactly what it is that he is or isn't doing. *Why* does he look so awkward? He's been dancing a lot in the past year and has actually improved a whole lot, and he knows some pretty complex Balkan dances now. So he can learn the patterns of footwork. But he still looks awkward. Why??

It seems that he somehow never bends at the hip, or resists hopping clear of the ground, or puts his feet down very flat-footed. He seems very earthbound. What fascinates me is, is he EVER going to improve? I know this may sound kind of crass but I'm curious (being a new dancer myself). I know that for a lot of slow learners, they are just that, *slow* learners, not *non*-learners, and given enough time they DO learn and are eventually as good as the fast learners. (Thank god, or there are lots of things I'd've never learned.)

But does he KNOW what he looks like? There's a sort of grisly fascination.

I was horrified to realize that I was deliberately avoiding dancing near him (and near a couple other similar people) because of his dancing ability. What a snobby thing to do. If people had done that to me when I was just starting, I probably wouldn't have enjoyed it very much and certainly would not have gotten any better. So now I just join the line and dance next to him. (And actually it isn't bad at all.)

One thing I have started to do when I'm next to a truly rotten dancer is to make my cues a little stronger. I haul him around more. I don't know if this is helpful or not. At least it keeps the rest of the line moving normally.

(Sigh) So what do you all do about the Stupendously Awkward Among Us? Do you just dance with them resignedly, or do you attempt to gently show them how to improve, or subtly model for them or guide them in some way? And do they eventually get better, or not?

On the reverse note, since I started dancing I have noticed that it is now a REAL turn-on when I see a guy who really dances well. Zipping around out there with flashy, crisp leg-lifts and neat, smooth movements and boots flying. (Sigh, drool...)

A
B
C
D
E
F
G
H
I
J
K
L
M
N
O
P
Q
R
S
T
U
V
W
X
Y
Z

Want some fun?
Read the Fun section

Too much spare time?
Explore a MUD

Theater, Plays, and Musicals

Theater FAQs, lyrics to musicals, reviews, guides, and other material relating to the theater.

Anonymous FTP:
> Address: **quartz.rutgers.edu**
> Path: **/pub/theater/***

Gopher:
> Name: Rutgers Quartz Text Archive
> Address: **quartz.rutgers.edu**
> Choose: **Theater-Plays and Musicals**

DRUGS

Anti War-on-Drugs Activist List

A list of organizations that are active in drug law reform.

Anonymous FTP:
> Address: **rtfm.mit.edu**
> Path: **/pub/usenet-by-group/alt.answers/
>   law-reformers**

Caffeine

Start reading this newsgroup and find out everything you always wanted to know about the world's most overused stimulant. Do you know how to make really sludgy, sweet espresso? Are you wondering how much caffeine is in Jello Pudding Pops? Don't let it keep you up at night.

Usenet:
> Newsgroup: **alt.drugs.caffeine**

Drug Use History

A brief history of drug use and prohibition since 5000 B.C.

Anonymous FTP:
> Address: **ftp.spies.com**
> Path: **/Library/Fringe/Pharm/drug.use**

Gopher:
> Name: Internet Wiretap
> Address: **wiretap.spies.com**
> Choose: **Wiretap Online Library**
>   **| Fringes of Reason**
>   **| Pharmacological Cornucopia**
>   **| A brief history of drug use**

Illegal Recreational Drug Information

Lots of information about drugs, including drug tests, FAQs, statistics, growing methods, chemical notes, marijuana brownie recipes, and much more.

Anonymous FTP:
> Address: **ftp.u.washington.edu**
> Path: **/public/alt.drugs/***

LSD—My Problem Child

The father of LSD, Albert Hofmann, discusses his discovery and career as a research chemist in this book translated by Jonathan Ott.

Anonymous FTP:
> Address: **world.std.com**
> Path: **/obi/A.Hofmann/probchild.Z**

Gopher:
> Name: The World
> Address: **world.std.com**
> Choose: **OBI The Online Book Initiative**
>   **| The Online Books**
>   **| A.Hofmann**

The Bizarre section has some cool stuff

News About Drugs

All the news about drug-related crimes and newsworthy events. Tonight, read your kids something relevant instead of letting them watch Barney the Dinosaur.

Usenet:
    Newsgroup: **clari.news.law.drugs**

Pharmacological Cornucopia

A collection of drug information, including a brief history of drug use, and articles and FAQs on absinthe, ecstasy, hemp, LSD, mushrooms, marijuana, opium and psychedelic drugs.

Anonymous FTP:
    Address: **ftp.spies.com**
    Path: **/Library/Fringe/Pharm/***

Gopher:
    Name: Internet Wiretap
    Address: **wiretap.spies.com**
    Choose: **Wiretap Online Library**
        | Fringes of Reason
        | Pharmacological Cornucopia

JUST SAY "NO"

That's right, just say "no" to computer networks that do not offer you enough information to make intelligent decisions about drugs. Fortunately, that's not a problem on the Internet. All you have to do is read the information in *Pharmacological Cornucopia* and your brain cells will never be the same again.

Politics and Drugs

Politicians, reporters, professors, doctors, and Ann Landers all have it wrong. Read what the people who really understand drugs and politics have to say.

Usenet:
    Newsgroup: **talk.politics.drugs**

Psychoactive Drugs

The Internet is just a crutch for people who can't cope with drugs. But if you happen to be one of those lucky few who can handle both at the same time, join the discussion about psychoactive drugs, legal and illegal. Just don't let it go to your head.

Usenet:
    Newsgroup: **alt.psychoactives**

Recreational Drugs

Drugs for fun and not for profit. Where else can you go for advice on what to do with a pot of leftover phenyl acetic acid? How do you tell the difference between *Aminita Muscaria*, *Psilocybe Cubensis*, and Chinese take-out? Turn on, tune out and drop into the only Usenet newsgroup where "Better Living Through Modern Chemistry" is more than just a slogan.

Usenet:
    Newsgroup: **alt.drugs**

If you like trouble, take a look at Mischief

Did you know there are many different books that you can download to your own computer? See Literature for the details

A B C D E F G H I J K L M N O P Q R S T U V W X Y Z

EARTH SCIENCE

Earth Science Data Directory

The Earth Science Data Directory (ESDD) is being developed by the U.S. Geological Survey as a system for readily determining the availability of specific earth-science and natural-resource data. It offers access to a USGS computer repository of information about earth-science and natural-resource databases.

Gopher:
Name: University of California, Santa Cruz
Address: **scilibx.ucsc.edu**
Choose: **The Researcher**
l Science and Engineering
l Earth and Marine Sciences
l USGS Earth Science Data Directory

Oceanplanet.gif is available from Northern Arizona University (**ftp.nau.edu**) in the directory **/graphics/gif/digi**.

Earth Sciences Resources

A list of earth-science-related Internet resources.

Anonymous FTP:
Address: **csn.org**
Path: **/COGS/internet.resources.earth.sci**

Gopher:
Name: Oregon State University
Address: **gopher.fsl.orst.edu**
Choose: **Other Sources of Info**
l Hugo's Lore-House
l Where the Sun Doesn't Shine..
l Internet Resources for the Earth Sciences

Smithsonian Natural History Gopher

This Gopher contains information resources that are compiled and maintained by Smithsonian staff and includes newsletters and projects as well as pointers to other network resources of interest to researchers in natural history.

Gopher:
Name: Smithsonian Institution
Address: **nmnhgoph.si.edu**

Name: United States Military Academy
Address: **euler.math.usma.edu**

Choose: **Reference_Section**
l Smithsonian Institution's Natural History Gopher

ECONOMICS

British Economics Research

View and search hundreds of the latest economic research papers and statistics on the British economy.

Anonymous FTP:
Address: **netec.mcc.ac.uk**
Path: **/pub/NetEc/***

Gopher:
Name: University of Manchester
Address: **netec.mcc.ac.uk**
Choose: **Economics**

Telnet:
Address: **netec.mcc.ac.uk**
Login: **netec**

Computational Economics

Working papers, handbooks, conferences, software and more related to computational economics.

Gopher:
Name: SARA (Stichting Academisch Rekencentrum Amsterdam)
Address: **gopher.sara.nl**
Choose: **Computational Economics**

Directory of Economists

A large alphabetical list of economists on the Internet, including their e-mail addresses and other contact and research information.

Gopher:
Name: SARA (Stichting Academisch Rekencentrum Amsterdam)
Address: **gopher.sara.nl**
Choose: **Computational Economics | Directory of Economists (by name)**

Economic Bulletin Board

The Economic Bulletin Board is operated by the U.S. Department of Commerce. It has 20 separate file areas that contain current economic and trade information, such as economic indicators, U.S. Treasury auction results and employment statistics.

Gopher:
Name: University of Michigan
Address: **gopher.lib.umich.edu**
Choose: **Social Sciences Research | Economics**

Telnet:
Address: **ebb.stat-usa.gov**
Login: **guest**

Economics Discussion

A mailing list forum for discussion of issues relevant to economics and distribution of new research papers.

Listserv mailing list:
List Address: **corryfee@hasara11.bitnet**
Subscription Address: **listserv@hasara11.bitnet**

Economics Gopher

Wide array of economics-related information, including discussion list archives, census summaries, budget reports, directory of economists and access to other economic resources.

Gopher:
Name: Sam Houston State University
Address: **niord.shsu.edu**
Choose: **Economics (SHSU Network Access Initiative Project)**

Economies of the Caribbean Basin

Articles, information and opinions concerning the economies of countries in the Caribbean Basin, as well as the overall economic health of the entire region.

Internet mailing list:
List Address:
caribbean-economy@vela.acs.oakland.edu
Subscription Address:
caribbean-economy-request@vela.acs.oakland.edu

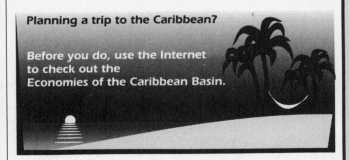

**Spare time?
Take a look at Games**

A B C D E F G H I J K L M N O P Q R S T U V W X Y Z

Economist Resources

A list of resources for economists on the Net, covering archives, Gophers, library catalogs, Usenet newsgroups and mailing lists.

Gopher:
Name: NYSERNet
Address: **nysernet.org**
Choose: **Special Collections: Business and Economic Development I Resources for Economists on the Internet**

Excerpt from the Net...

(from "Resources for Economists on the Internet")

While relatively few economists use the Internet, there is a surprising amount of very useful information on it. For instance, there are two very extensive sets of macro data, a bibliography of some 20,000 working papers in economics, household surveys from 21 countries, two interactive electronic markets, 24 mailing lists and two Usenet newsgroups.

Employment Statistics

Civilian and government labor force statistics and unemployment information by state.

Gopher:
Name: University of California San Diego
Address: **infopath.ucsd.edu**
Choose: **News & Services I Economic.. I Employment Statistics**

Energy Statistics

Compilations of statistics on energy consumption, requirements and reserves in the U.S., including specific information on coal, crude oil, natural gas and other sources.

Gopher:
Name: University of California San Diego
Address: **infopath.ucsd.edu**
Choose: **News & Services I Economic.. I Energy Statistics**

Foreign Trade

Statistics and data on U.S. foreign trade of merchandise and textiles. Includes import and export data, as well as foreign spending, capital expenditures and summaries.

Gopher:
Name: University of California San Diego
Address: **infopath.ucsd.edu**
Choose: **News & Services I Economic.. I Foreign Trade**

Gross State Product Tables

The gross state product data tables estimate the value of goods and services produced for 61 industries in 50 states, eight regions, and the nation as a whole. The value is the sum of four components: compensation of employees; proprietors' income with inventory valuation adjustment and capital consumption allowances; indirect business tax and nontax liability; and other, mainly capital-related, charges.

Gopher:
Name: University of Michigan
Address: **gopher.lib.umich.edu**
Choose: **Social Sciences Research I Economics I Gross State Product Tables from US Bureau of Econ. Analysis**

Monetary Statistics

Foreign exchange rates, aggregate reserves, daily bond rates, consumer credit, flow of funds, savings bond rates, treasury yields and much more.

Gopher:
Name: University of California San Diego
Address: **infopath.ucsd.edu**
Choose: **News & Services I Economic.. I Monetary Statistics**

National Income and Products Accounts

Annual income statistics for past years, estimates, gross domestic product tables, quarterly and annual NIPA reports and source statistics used to calculate GDP.

Gopher:
Name: University of California San Diego
Address: **infopath.ucsd.edu**
Choose: **News & Services I Economic.. I National Income..**

NetEc

A bibliography and electronic collection of working papers in economics.

Gopher:
   Name: University of Manchester
   Address: **uts.mcc.ac.uk Economics | NetEc**

Press Releases from the U.S. Trade Representative

A collection of the press releases from the U.S. Trade Representative. Releases are named by subject.

Gopher:
   Name: University of California San Diego
   Address: **infopath.ucsd.edu**
   Choose: **News & Services | Economic..**
      | Press releases...

Price and Productivity Statistics

Supporting data and statistics used in computation of the Consumer Price Index, import and export price indexes, the producer price index, and productivity and cost statistics.

Gopher:
   Name: University of California San Diego
   Address: **infopath.ucsd.edu**
   Choose: **News & Services | Economic..**
      | Price and Productivity...

Regional Economic Statistics

Supporting data and computations of disposable per capita income by state, total personal incomes, metropolitan, state and regional incomes. Also includes wage and salary by industry data by state, region and U.S. total.

Gopher:
   Name: University of California San Diego
   Address: **infopath.ucsd.edu**
   Choose: **News & Services | Economic..**
      | Regional Economic Stat...

Summaries of Current Economic Conditions

Government and industry statistical summaries on trade, the balance of payments, the consumer price index, retail sales, inventories, construction, durable goods, employment cost index, housing starts, production and capacity, plant and equipment spending, and much more.

Gopher:
   Name: University of California San Diego
   Address: **infopath.ucsd.edu**
   Choose: **News & Services | Economic...**
      | Summaries of current...

Thoughts on Economics

A collection of articles relating to economics, business, and finance, including a Christmas price index, investment guide and the lawnmower strategy.

Anonymous FTP:
   Address: **quartz.rutgers.edu**
   Path: **/pub/economics/***

Gopher:
   Name: Rutgers Quartz Text Archive
   Address: **quartz.rutgers.edu**
   Choose: **Economics, Business, Finance**

Working Paper Archive

An archive of working papers on economics, grouped in 21 subject areas with abstracts.

Anonymous FTP:
   Address: **econwpa.wustl.edu**
   Path: **/econ-wp/***

Gopher:
   Name: Washington University, St. Louis
   Address: **gopher.wustl.edu**
   Choose: **Departmental Information Servers**
      | Economics Department
      | Economics Working Paper Archive

Too much spare time? Explore a MUD

The Bizarre section has some cool stuff

A
B
C
D
E
F
G
H
I
J
K
L
M
N
O
P
Q
R
S
T
U
V
W
X
Y
Z

EDUCATION

Apple Computer Higher Education Gopher

Offers product information, news, publications and support from Apple. You can post information to this Gopher using e-mail.

Gopher:
Name: Apple Computer
Address: **info.hed.apple.com**

Armadillo

The Texas Studies Gopher, Armadillo, has been designed with the middle-school teacher and student in mind, and presents information about Texas natural and cultural history.

Gopher:
Name: Rice University
Address: **chico.rice.edu 1170**

Brown University Alumni

A mailing list for friends and alumni of Brown University. Discussions involve issues affecting the university and its students, faculty, staff and alumni.

Listserv mailing list:
List Address: **brunonia@brownvm.bitnet**
Subscription Address: **listserv@brownvm.bitnet**

Educational Listserv Lists

A guide to mailing lists relating to all aspects of education, arranged by subject area.

Anonymous FTP:
Address: **nic.umass.edu**
Path: **/pub/ednet/educatrs.lst**

Gopher:
Name: NYSERNet
Address: **nysernet.org**
Choose: **Special Collections: Internet Help
| Guide to Educational Listservs**

If you like trouble, take a look at Mischief

Educational Newsgroups

A guide to education-related Usenet groups, cataloged by subject area.

Anonymous FTP:
Address: **nic.umass.edu**
Path: **/pub/ednet/edusenet.gde**

Gopher:
Name: NYSERNet
Address: **nysernet.org**
Choose: **Special Collections: Internet Help
| Guide to Educational Newsgroups**

Education and Usenet

Usenet has many newsgroups related to teaching, schools and education in general. You could spend time in all of them - what a learning experience that would be! - but it would take the rest of your life.

Better to use the guide in **Educational Newsgroups**

and narrow your focus. That way, you can spend more time reading jokes.

EDUPAGE

An education-related news service provided by EDUCOM, a consortium of leading colleges and universities seeking to transform education through the use of information technology. The vehicle for news delivery is periodical mail messages with summary news briefs.

Mail:
Address: **edupage@educom.edu**

Health Sciences Libraries Consortium

The Health Sciences Libraries Consortium (HSLC) Computer Based Learning Software Database contains listings of PC-compatible and Macintosh programs used in health sciences education.

Telnet:
Address: **shrsys.hslc.org**
Login: **cbl**

Higher Education Resources and Opportunities (HERO)

A 24-hour, online database service that provides access to valuable information from colleges and universities on scholarships, grants, fellowships, conferences, faculty and student development, research opportunities, partnership initiatives, and other opportunities for minorities and women.

Telnet:
Address: **fedix.fie.com**
Login: **new**

College students!!

Need a scholoarship, grant, fellowship or just plain money to buy some books?

Telnet to the *HERO* database for info.

The IBM Kiosk for Education (IKE)

A Gopher-based server offering IBM information, application software, and a bulletin board for IBM users in the higher education community. The system is funded by IBM and developed and operated by the Center for Information Systems Optimization at the University of Washington.

Gopher:
Name: University of Washington
Address: **ike.engr.washington.edu**

Telnet:
Address: **isaac.engr.washington.edu**
Login: **register**

Incomplete Guide to the Internet

The Incomplete Guide to the Internet and Other Telecommunications Opportunities Especially for Teachers and Students, K-12 is a resource guide and how-to manual for beginning and intermediate Internet users as well as an excellent reference for advanced users.

Anonymous FTP:
Address: **ftp.ncsa.uiuc.edu**
Path: **Education/Education_Resources/ Incomplete_Guide/***

Institutional Communications Network (INet)

The U.S. Department of Education's first Internet node, INet is designed to facilitate communication and information sharing among major education institutions. INet also provides access to databases and files with both statistical data and research and development information aimed at improving teaching and learning.

Gopher:
Name: U.S. Department of Education
Address: **gopher.ed.gov**

JANET Network

Long- and short-term information on the JANET network, the UK's joint academic network.

Gopher:
Name: Joint Academic Network
Address: **news.janet.ac.uk**

MicroMUSE

An educational multiuser simulated environment.

Telnet:
Address: **michael.ai.mit.edu**
Login: **guest**

Minority College & University Capability Information

This resource provides comprehensive information on minority colleges and universities, such as institutional capabilities, student and faculty profiles, educational programs, research centers, scholarships, and other points of interest.

Telnet:
Address: **fedix.fie.com**

A B C D E F G H I J K L M N O P Q R S T U V W X Y Z

National Education BBS

A system sponsored by the National Education Supercomputing Program (NESP). Full access is only available to NESP members, but limited access is granted to guests. Includes files, news, talk and chat.

Telnet:
>   Address: **nebbs.nersc.gov**
>   Login: **guest**

National Referral Center Master File

The National Referral Center Resources File (NRCM) provides thousands of descriptions of organizations qualified and willing to answer questions and provide information on many topics in science, technology and the social sciences. The file is updated weekly, and each entry in the file lists the name of the organization, mailing address and other information.

Telnet:
>   Address: **locis.loc.gov**
>   Password: **Organizations**

Newton

A BBS for anyone teaching or studying science, math or computer science.

Telnet:
>   Address: **newton.dep.anl.gov**
>   Login: **bbs**

Project Kaleidoscope

Weekly seminars over the Internet to exchange ideas and information about reforming American undergraduate science and mathematics educational programs.

Anonymous FTP:
>   Address: **aug3.augsburg.edu**
>   Path: **/files/pkal**

QUERRI

Questions on University Extension Regional Resource Information (QUERRI) is a database maintained by the North Central Region Educational Materials Project. QUERRI offers online access to bibliographic information and thousands of North Central Region Extensions resources.

Telnet:
>   Address: **isn.rdns.iastate.edu**
>   Login: **querri**

Reading Disabilities

A scientific paper discussing reading disabilities.

Anonymous FTP:
>   Address: **ftp.spies.com**
>   Path: **/Library/Article/Misc/disable.rd**

Gopher:
>   Name: Internet Wiretap
>   Address: **wiretap.spies.com**
>   Choose: **Wiretap Online Library | Articles | Misc | Reading Disabilities**

Scholarly Conferences

Descriptions of mailing lists, Internet interest groups, Usenet newsgroups, electronic journals, FTP sites and more of interest to students and scholars.

Anonymous FTP:
>   Address: **ksuvxa.kent.edu**
>   Path: **/library/acad***

Gopher:
>   Name: NYSERNet
>   Address: **nysernet.org**
>   Choose: **Special Collections: Higher Education | Scholarly Electronic Conferences**

Academic Excellence on the
Internet

Do you like to tell other people what to think? Do you love to pontificate using sentences that start with "It turns out that. . ."?

Do you want to work for an organization that never makes a profit?

If so, academia may be for you.

The only trouble is that you may have to do research, which can really eat into your spare time.

Not to worry. Use the

Scholarly Conferences

resource and find out what's already there for the taking.

Schoolnet

An educational networking initiative of Industry and Science Canada. It provides educational information, discussion areas and learning tools. Eventually, every school in Canada will be hooked up to Schoolnet.

Anonymous FTP:
Address: **ernest.ccs.carleton.ca**
Path: **/pub/schoolnet/***

Gopher:
Name: Schoolnet Gopher
Address: **ernest.ccs.carleton.ca**

Schoolnet Resource Manual

Details of more than one hundred science, engineering and technology resources available on the Internet and of special interest to schools. Available in Word for Windows and ASCII formats.

Anonymous FTP:
Address: **alfred.carleton.ca**
Path: **/pub/schoolnet/manuals/Resource.txt**

Address: **alfred.carleton.ca**
Path: **/pub/schoolnet/manuals/Resource.wfw**

Gopher:
Name: Schoolnet Gopher
Address: **ernest.ccs.carleton.ca**
Choose: **Resources and References...**
| Access to SchoolNet FTP site | manuals
| Resource.txt

Schoolnet's News Flash

Contains information on current events in the real world, on the Internet and in Canada's Schoolnet.

Gopher:
Name: Schoolnet Gopher
Address: **ernest.ccs.carleton.ca**
Choose: **Newsflash...**

Shadowy Science Projects

A collection of articles, discussions and projects about shadows, the sun, solar noon, Earth's rotation and related topics.

Gopher:
Name: Ralph Bunche School
Address: **ralphbunche.rbs.edu**
Choose: **Shadows Science Project**

Abstract earthscapes and architecture are the norm in cyberspace. This image is called **building.gif** and is widely available. One location is the University of North Carolina (**sunsite.unc.edu**) where it's located in the directory **/pub/multimedia/pictures/OTIS/raytraces**.

Simultaneous Projects

Information and details about school projects that make use of the Internet.

Gopher:
Name: Schoolnet Gopher
Address: **ernest.ccs.carleton.ca**
Choose: **Projects...**

Spacenet BBS

A bulletin board with databases and documents for use by schools interested in science, computers and engineering.

Telnet:
Address: **spacemet.phast.umass.edu**
Login: Press RETURN

Don't space out.
Use the
Spacenet BBS
to keep your school connected to the world of science and computers.

TECHNET

Technical Support for Education and Research (TECHNET) is an open, unmoderated discussion list for technical support staff at universities and other non-profit educational/research institutions worldwide. Discussions may cover such topics as electronic and software design, interfacing of laboratory equipment to computers, construction of unique laboratory equipment, data collection methods, etc.

Listserv mailing list:
List Address: **technet@acadvm1.uottawa.ca**
Subscription Address:
listserv@acadvm1.uottawa.ca

Technical Reports and Publication Archives

Numerous technical reports covering a large variety of academic fields, collected from hundreds of institutions, companies and universities.

Gopher:
Name: University of Nottingham
Address: **trellis.cs.nott.ac.uk**
Choose: **Technical Reports and Publications Archives**

Technology and Information Education Services

TIES provides leadership in the application of technology to education by means of support services and training. Their Gopher provides access to many K-12 educational resources.

Gopher:
Name: TIESnet Internet Gopher
Address: **tiesnet.ties.k12.mn.us**

U.S. National K12 Gopher

The National K12 Gopher is a national research and development resource in which schools, school districts and community organizations can experiment with applications that bring significant new educational benefits to teachers and students.

Gopher:
Name: US National K12 Gopher
Address: **copernicus.bbn.com**

Gopher problems? read "The Internet Complete Reference"

Usenet University

FAQs, history, ideas, papers and newsgroup lists for the Usenet University, a society of people interested in learning, teaching and tutoring.

Anonymous FTP:
Address: **nic.funet.fi**
Path: **/pub/doc/uu/***

Virginia Public Education Network

An education-oriented Freenet with many education resources, including specific math, science and physics areas.

Telnet:
Address: **vdoe386.vak12ed.edu**
Login: **guest**
Password: **guest**

EDUCATION: INSTITUTIONS

Academic E-mail Addresses

A large list of e-mail addresses of academic institutions, including names and descriptions of the organizations.

Gopher:
Name: NYSERNet
Address: **nysernet.org**
Choose: **Special Collections: Business and Economic Development | Business and Academic Related Email Addresses.**

Campus-Wide Information Systems

A large list of many campus-wide information systems, providing local and regional information from many academic institutions worldwide.

Anonymous FTP:
Address: **ftp.oit.unc.edu**
Path: **/pub/docs/about-the-net/cwis/cwis-l**

Gopher:
Name: National Chung Cheng University
Address: **gopher.ccu.edu.tw**
Choose: **Internet Resources | Information Servers via Telnet | CWIS**

Daily Report Card

Presents up-to-date information on the state of educational concerns in the U.S.

Gopher:
>Name: University of Maryland
>Address: **info.umd.edu**
>Choose: **Educational Resources**
> **| The Reading Room | Newletters**
> **| DailyReportCard**

Jackson Community College

Jackson Community College in Jackson, Michigan, has offered full-credit sociology courses over the Internet.

Mail:
>Address: **adamsr@umcc.umich.edu**

Research and Advanced Study: Canada and Italy

The Canadian Academic Centre in Italy sponsors this forum for the research communities in Canada and Italy. Researchers in all fields and disciplines are invited to subscribe.

Listserv mailing list:
>List Address: **caci-l@ualtavm.bitnet**
>Subscription Address: **listserv@ualtavm.bitnet**

EDUCATION: STUDENTS

Academic Advice

Sound suggestions for attacking poor study habits, relieving stress, and making it happily through college—and life.

Gopher:
>Name: Healthline Gopher Service
>Address: **selway.umt.edu 700**
>Choose: **General Health Information**
> **| Academic Help**

Telnet:
>Address: **selway.umt.edu**
>Login: **health**

Academic Magazines

Sample articles and subscription information for scholarly, academic and university-related magazines.

Gopher:
>Name: The Electronic Newsstand
>Address: **gopher.internet.com 2100**
>Choose: **Titles Arranged by Category**
> **| Scholarship - Culture, Politics, History, Ethics, Medicine**

Scavenger Hunt

Learn to use the Internet in a fun and entertaining way by following these scavenger hunts for school kids. Elementary school and secondary school editions are available, as well as a special hunt focusing on space resources.

Gopher:
>Name: Schoolnet Gopher
>Address: **ernest.ccs.carleton.ca**
>Choose: **Scavenger Hunts**

Looking for Stuff

Students: Learn how to use the Internet by looking for stuff. Yes, there is a lot of stuff out there, and it is your job to find to find it. Check out

Scavenger Hunt

for some cool stuff to look for. Stuff, stuff . . . find more stuff . . .

Want to know what makes the Internet run? Read Internet: RFCs

A B C D E F G H I J K L M N O P Q R S T U V W X Y Z

School Humor

Humor related to school, including fifty ways to confuse a roommate, fun things to do in a final, and math professor quotes.

Anonymous FTP:
Address: **quartz.rutgers.edu**
Path: **/pub/humor/School/***

Gopher:
Name: Rutgers Quartz Text Archive
Address: **quartz.rutgers.edu**
Choose: **Humor | School**

EDUCATION: TEACHERS

Academic Dialogs

Offers articles and comments on several academic disciplines that use computers; readers respond by using the unique posting capability of this Gopher.

Gopher:
Name: Apple Computer, Inc.
Address: **info.hed.apple.com**
Choose: **Computing in Higher Ed Academics**

AskERIC

ERIC (Educational Resources Information Center) is a taxpayer-funded information system that provides access to education-related literature for teachers, library media specialists, administrators and others.

Gopher:
Name: Syracuse University
Address: **ericir.syr.edu**
Choose: **Departmental & Other S.U. Servers | AskERIC**

Mail:
Address: **askeric@ericir.syr.edu**

The Best of K-12

A large selection of educational resources for grades K-12 and their teachers, including news, guides, books, exchange information and access to other Gophers and BBSs.

Gopher:
Name: TIESnet Internet Gopher
Address: **tiesnet.ties.k12.mn.us**
Choose: **Best of the K-12 Internet Resources**

TEACHERS!
The Internet has a lot for you.
Check out
The Best of K-12

Excerpt from the Net...

(from "School Humor")

Fun things to do during a final exam:

-- When you get a copy of the exam, run out screaming "Andre, Andre, I've got the secret documents!!"

-- Walk in, get the exam, sit down. About five minutes into it, loudly say to the instructor, "I don't understand ANY of this. I've been to every lecture all semester long! What's the deal? And who the hell are you? Where's the regular guy?"

-- Find a new, interesting way to refuse to answer every question. For example: I refuse to answer this question on the grounds that it conflicts with my religious beliefs.

-- Run into the exam room looking about frantically. Breathe a sigh of relief. Go to the instructor, say "They've found me, I have to leave the country" and run off.

Business School Faculty

A mailing list to allow business school faculty all over the world to share problems, discuss solutions and research ideas.

Listserv mailing list:
List Address: **busfac-l@cmuvm.bitnet**
Subscription Address: **listserv@cmuvm.bitnet**

Chronicle of Higher Education

Offers information about job openings, best-selling books on campuses, and news articles from the Chronicle of Higher Education in its free online service "Academe This Week".

Gopher:
Name: Merit Computer Network
Address: **chronicle.merit.edu**

Dead Teacher's Society

A mailing list for broad discussions of teaching and learning.

Listserv mailing list:
List Address: **dts-l@iubvm.bitnet**
Subscription Address: **listserv@iubvm.bitnet**

Education Net

Ednet is for those interested in exploring the educational potential of the Internet. Discussions range from K-12 through postsecondary education.

Listserv mailing list:
List Address: **ednet@nic.umass.edu**
Subscription Address: **listserv@nic.umass.edu**

Globe and Mail

Classroom and teacher editions of the *Toronto Globe and Mail's* monthly Infoglobe, a service aimed at bringing news and events into the classroom.

Gopher:
Name: Schoolnet Gopher
Address: **ernest.ccs.carleton.ca**
Choose: **Newsflash... | Globe and Mail Newsfeed**

KIDSPHERE

A mailing list for teachers (grades K-12), school administrators, scientists and others around the world. Send a mail message to join the list.

Internet mailing list:
List Address: **kidsphere@vms.cis.pitt.edu**
Subscription Address:
kidsphere-request@vms.cis.pitt.edu

Kindergarten to Grade 6 Corner

Learn about interesting facts, neat tricks, things to try and penpals to meet in this educational forum for kids.

Gopher:
Name: Schoolnet Gopher
Address: **ernest.ccs.carleton.ca**
Choose: **Kindergarten to Grade 6 Corner**

Lesson Plans

This Gopher is being used to test ways of making a database of lesson plans available. It contains sample school lessons that can be searched and viewed.

Gopher:
Name: US National K12 Gopher
Address: **copernicus.bbn.com**
Choose: **National School Network Testbed | Lessons Plans from UCSD (test area)**

Free Lesson Plans

IF YOU ARE A TEACHER YOU KNOW HOW EMBARRASSING IT CAN BE TO TEACH SOMETHING UNEXPECTED BY ACCIDENT. USE THE

Lesson Plan Gopher

AND YOU CAN SYNCHRONIZE YOUR PLANS WITH TEACHERS ALL OVER THE INTERNET. JUST THE THING WHEN YOUR LESSON BOOK IS EMPTY AND THE INSPECTOR IS DUE FOR A VISIT.

A
B
C
D
E
F
G
H
I
J
K
L
M
N
O
P
Q
R
S
T
U
V
W
X
Y
Z

Neat Educational Tricks

A collection of teaching tricks—including how to see a hole in your hand, how to make your arms float, and how to move things with your mind—aimed at teaching basic human biology to younger users.

Gopher:
    Name: Schoolnet Gopher
    Address: **ernest.ccs.carleton.ca**
    Choose: **Kindergarten to Grade 6 Corner**
      | Neat tricks you can do...

Network Nuggets

A mailing list to help you locate Internet educational resources and to encourage the use of telecommunications as part of the teaching and learning processes.

Listserv mailing list:
    List Address: **network_nuggets-l@cln.etc.bc.ca**
    Subscription Address: **listserv@cln.etc.bc.ca**

Reading Room

A large collection of journals, newsletters and texts (as well as access to other subject-related Gophers) at the University of Maryland.

Gopher:
    Name: University of Maryland
    Address: **info.umd.edu**
    Choose: **Educational Resources**
      | The Reading Room

If you're feeling risque, take a look at X-Rated Resources

ELECTRONICS

Circuit Analysis Discussion List

A mailing list for anyone interested in the discussion of circuit analysis and design.

Internet mailing list:
    List Address: **circuits-l@uwplatt.edu**
    Subscription Address:
      circuits-l-request@uwplatt.edu

English-Chinese Electronics Terms

An English-Chinese, Chinese-English dictionary of electronic and electrical terms.

Comment: Requires Chinese viewing software.

Gopher:
    Name: National Chung Cheng University
    Address: **gopher.ccu.edu.tw**
    Choose: **micscellanies**
      | English <-> Chinese Electric Term

HP Calculator BBS

A BBS just for users of HP calculators. Chat or message with other users and enthusiasts of HP scientific and business calculators. The HP Calculator Bulletin Board is a free service designed for the exchange of software and information between HP calculator users, software developers and distributors.

Telnet:
    Address: **hpcvbbs.cv.hp.com**

IEEE Gopher

The IEEE Computer Society is a world-renowned source of information relating to all aspects of computer science, electronics and engineering, including the publication of periodicals and newsletters, sponsoring conferences, workshops and symposiums, and the development of standards. Computer Society Online now offers an electronic source of this information—in many cases before the information is published in hard copy form.

Gopher:
    Name: IEEE Computer Society
    Address: **info.computer.org**

EMERGENCY AND DISASTER

Disaster Management

Selection of resources related to disasters and how to deal with them, including access to the Australian Disaster Management Information Network, earthquake information, Emergency Preparedness Information Exchange and more.

Gopher:
    Name: Monash University
    Address: **gopher.vifp.monash.edu.au**
    Choose: **Disaster Management**

EPIX

The Emergency Preparedness Information eXchange (EPIX) is dedicated to the promotion of networking in support of disaster mitigation research and practice. Offers information on emergency/disaster management organizations, topics, conferences and access to other emergency management resources.

Gopher:
    Name: EPIX
    Address: **hoshi.cic.sfu.ca 5555**

The Newcastle Earthquake

A well-written and horrific account of the deadly Newcastle, Australia, earthquake of December 1989, the first known Australian quake to result in fatalities.

Gopher:
    Name: Monash University
    Address: **brain.vifp.monash.edu.au**
    Choose: **Disaster Management**
      | Aust. Disaster Management Information Network | What If - The Newcastle Earthquake

ENGINEERING AND DESIGN

Advanced Nuclear Reactor Technology

A mailing list to facilitate substantive discussion on the worldwide advocacy, design and deployment of advanced nuclear reactor technology.

Listserv mailing list:
    List Address: **anurt-l@doevm.bitnet**
    Subscription Address: **listserv@doevm.bitnet**

Build a Flying Saucer

An essay in speculative engineering on how to build a flying saucer.

Anonymous FTP:
    Address: **ftp.spies.com**
    Path: **/Library/Fringe/Ufo/build.ufo**

Gopher:
    Name: Internet Wiretap
    Address: **wiretap.spies.com**
    Choose: **Wiretap Online Library**
      | Fringes of Reason
      | UFOs and Mysterious Abductions
      | How to Build a Flying Saucer

No need to put up with rush hour traffic. Build your own flying saucer.

The plans are free for the downloading on **Build a Flying Saucer.**

CAD Mailing Lists

Mailing lists devoted to Computer Aided Design (CAD) interests and subjects.

Listserv mailing list:
    List Address: **cadam-l@suvm.syr.edu**
    Subscription Address: **listserv@suvm.syr.edu**

    List Address: **cadlist@suvm.syr.edu**
    Subscription Address: **listserv@suvm.syr.edu**

    List Address: **caeds-l@suvm.syr.edu**
    Subscription Address: **listserv@suvm.syr.edu**

    List Address: **vtcad-l@vtvm1.cc.vt.edu**
    Subscription Address: **listserv@vtvm1.cc.vt.edu**

Chemical Engineering

An electronic newsletter covering many aspects of the field of chemical engineering.

Internet mailing list:
    List Address: **chem-eng@cc.curtin.edu.au**
    Subscription Address:
        chem-eng-request@cc.curtin.edu.au

A
B
C
D
E
F
G
H
I
J
K
L
M
N
O
P
Q
R
S
T
U
V
W
X
Y
Z

Congress of Canadian Engineering Students

A mailing list forum for the Canadian Federation of Engineering Students to discuss current topics and exchange information.

Listserv mailing list:
List Address: **cces-l@unbvm1.bitnet**
Subscription Address: **listserv@unbvm1.bitnet**

Fluid Mechanics

A mailing list for Ph.D. students attached to the J.M. Burgers Centre for fluid mechanics; used for discussing all aspects of fluid mechanics and the J.M. Burgers Centre.

Listserv mailing list:
List Address: **burg-cen@hearn.bitnet**
Subscription Address: **listserv@hearn.bitnet**

Robotics

Archives, software and FAQs related to robotics and any preprogrammable, electro-mechanical devices that perform useful functions.

Anonymous FTP:
Address: **ftp.cs.yale.edu**
Path: **/pub/nisp/***

Address: **kame.media.mit.edu**
Path: **/pub/el-memos/***

Address: **rtfm.mit.edu**
Path: **/pub/usenet/news.answers/robotics-faq/***

Address: **wilma.cs.brown.edu**
Path: **/pub/comp.robotics/***

Archie:
Pattern: **robotics**

ENVIRONMENT

Air Pollution BBS

A BBS devoted to the collection and dissemination of pollution and pollution control information.

Telnet:
Address: **ttnbbs.rtpnc.epa.gov**

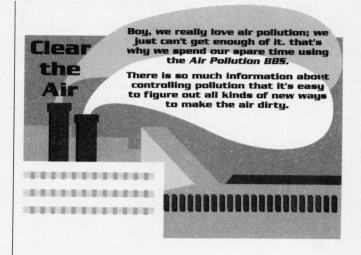

Clear the Air

Boy, we really love air pollution; we just can't get enough of it. that's why we spend our spare time using the *Air Pollution BBS*.

There is so much information about controlling pollution that it's easy to figure out all kinds of new ways to make the air dirty.

Biosphere Mailing List

Discussions related to the environment and the biosphere, including such topics as wind power, whaling, wildlife conservation and fossil fuels.

Listserv mailing list:
List Address: **biosph-l@ubvm.bitnet**
Subscription Address: **listserv@ubvm.bitnet**

Usenet:
Newsgroup: **bit.listserv.biosph-l**

Biosphere Newsletter

Back issues of this newsletter discussing environmental topics with both scientific and reader-friendly articles.

Comment: Hours are 6 P.M. to 10 A.M. EST

Anonymous FTP:
Address: **mthvax.cs.miami.edu**
Path: **/pub/biosph/***

Chemical Substance Factsheets

Information from the EPA on hundreds of chemicals, elements and compounds. Factsheets include data on toxicity, identification, reason for citation, how to determine if you've been exposed, OSHA safety limits, ways to reduce exposure, and more relevant information.

Gopher:
Name: University of Virginia
Address: **ecosys.drdr.virginia.edu**
Choose: **Education | Environmental Fact Sheets | EPA Chemical Substance Factsheets**

Earth Day Bibliography

A bibliography of environment-related books, including books about global warming, environmental ethics, nuclear waste, ecology, energy and other topics.

Anonymous FTP:
Address: **mthvax.cs.miami.edu**
Path: **/pub/biosph/earthday.bib.Z**

EnviroGopher

A large resource of environmental information from the EnviroLink Network. It covers all aspects of the environment, including environmental action, issues, media, networks, organization and politics, and gives easy access to other environmental Gopher servers.

Gopher:
Name: Carnegie Mellon University
Address: **envirolink.hss.cmu.edu**

EnviroNet

A menu-driven, user-friendly resource with environmental data in textual, graphic and tabular form.

Telnet:
Address: **envnet.gsfc.nasa.gov**
Login: **envnet**
Password: **henniker**

Environmental Factsheets

Articles and facts about automobiles, climate, energy, meat, ozone depletion, chemical substances and other environmental issues.

Gopher:
Name: EcoGopher at the University of Virginia
Address: **ecosys.drdr.virginia.edu**
Choose: **Education: The EcoGopher Environmental Library | Environmental Factsheets**

Environmental Issues

A variety of stories, essays and book reviews covering various environmental issues and ideas.

Gopher:
Name: Whole Earth Lectronic Link
Address: **gopher.well.sf.ca.us**
Choose: **Environmental Issues and Ideas**

Environmental Services Data Directory

A large database that provides detailed and diverse information on Earth's environment.

Telnet:
Address: **esdim1.nodc.noaa.gov**
Login: **noaadir**

EPA Online Library System

Search the EPA's online system by author, title, keywords, year of publication and so on.

Telnet:
Address: **epaibm.rtpnc.epa.gov**

FireNet

An information service for everyone interested in any aspect of rural and landscape fires. The information concerns all aspects of fire science and management —including fire behavior, fire weather, fire prevention, mitigation and suppression, plant and animal responses to fire, and all aspects of fire effects.

Anonymous FTP:
Address: **life.anu.edu.au**
Path: **pub/landscape_ecology/firenet**

Gopher:
Name: Australian National University
Address: **life.anu.edu.au**
Choose: **Landscape Ecology, Fire,.. | firenet**

Listserv mailing list:
List Address: **firenet@life.anu.edu.au**
Subscription Address: **listserv@life.anu.edu.au**

If you would like to send us a comment, mail to: catalog@rain.org

Lots and lots of music on the Internet: check out the Music category

A
B
C
D
E
F
G
H
I
J
K
L
M
N
O
P
Q
R
S
T
U
V
W
X
Y
Z

Forests

Reference materials relating to forest environments, forest-related industries and other documents of interest regarding forests.

Gopher:
>Name: The Community Learning Network
>Address: **cln.etc.bc.ca**
>Choose: **The Community Learning Network (BC)**
>| **Special Projects for the CLN (CLN.ETC)**
>| **The Forest (Online Reference Materials)**

Great Lakes Information Network

A network to store and disseminate binational data and information regarding environmental issues, resource management, transportation, demographic and development data and other information and resources in the Great Lakes region of the U.S. and Canada.

Gopher:
>Name: CICnet
>Address: **gopher.cic.net**

GreenDisk Environmental Information

GreenDisk is a forum for the publication of research reports, press releases, action alerts, and news summaries from the world's environmental groups and governmental agencies.

Gopher:
>Name: University of Maryland
>Address: **info.umd.edu**
>Choose: **Educational Resources**
>| **The Reading Room | Environment**
>| **GreenDisk**

National Environmental Data Referral Service

This NOAA-sponsored database documents environmental data from the sun, the atmosphere, the Earth and the oceans. Solar and upper atmosphere physics, satellite remote sensing, oceanography, climatology, meteorology, pollution, toxic substances, geophysics and geology, geochemistry, and freshwater and marine fisheries are some of the disciplines included.

Gopher:
>Name: University of California, Santa Cruz
>Address: **scilibx.ucsc.edu**
>Choose: **The Researcher**
>| **Science and Engineering**
>| **Environmental Science**
>| **NOAA Nat. Env. Referral Service**

Ozone Depletion

FAQs discussing the depletion of the ozone layer, including the Antarctic ozone hole and ultraviolet radiation.

Anonymous FTP:
>Address: **rtfm.mit.edu**
>Path:
>/pub/usenet/news.answers/ozone-depletion/*

Usenet:
>Newsgroup: **sci.environment**

ISN'T OZONE GREAT?

If there's too much you die, and if there's not enough you get skin cancer.
If you want more details, look under
Ozone Depletion
(a great way to spend a Saturday night).

Pollution and Groundwater Recharge

A mailing list discussing the vulnerability of aquifers to pollution, and what can be done about it.

Listserv mailing list:
>List Address: **aquifer@ibacsata.bitnet**
>Subscription Address: **listserv@ibacsata.bitnet**

U.S. Environmental Protection Agency

A menu-driven system that provides information on the EPA and what they're up to.

Telnet:
>Address: **epaibm.rtpnc.epa.gov**

Need help reading the Usenet news? Try "The Internet Complete Reference."

FOOD AND DRINK

Assorted Recipes

Numerous food and drink recipes, including beef jerky, fajitas, vegan recipes, the ultimate mixed drink list, and instructions for a medieval pig feast.

Anonymous FTP:
Address: **ftp.spies.com**
Path: **/Library/Article/Food/***

Address: **ftp.uu.net**
Path: **/doc/literary/obi/HM.recipes/TheRecipes**

Address: **ftp.uu.net**
Path: **/doc/literary/obi/Recipes**

Address: **ftp.uu.net**
Path: **/doc/literary/obi/Usenet.Cookbook**

Gopher:
Name: Internet Wiretap
Address: **wiretap.spies.com**
Choose: **Wiretap Online Library | Articles | Food and Drink**

Beer

Making, choosing and imbibing: These discussion groups will help you find out everything you want to know about beer and related beverages. Read the regular posting about which beers are best, based on the votes of Usenet participants. (Anyone can vote, although you do have to supply your own beer.) For specialists, the **.zima** group discusses this odd, beer-like drink.

Usenet:
Newsgroup: **alt.beer**
Newsgroup: **alt.zima**
Newsgroup: **rec.crafts.brewing**

Beer Archive

Offers a beer FAQ from the Usenet **alt.beer** newsgroup, lists of beer magazines, and information about CAMRA, the Campaign for Real Ale.

Anonymous FTP:
Address: **ftp.cwru.edu**
Path: **/pub/alt.beer/***

Big Drink List

Mixing hints, tips, and recipes for hundreds of mixed drinks.

Anonymous FTP:
Address: **ocf.berkeley.edu**
Path: **/pub/Library/Recreation/big-drink-list**

Booze Cookbook

More drink recipes, including the Hemorrhaging Brain and the Vulcan Death Grip.

Anonymous FTP:
Address: **ocf.berkeley.edu**
Path: **/pub/Library/Recreation/Booze_Cookbook**

Creative Drinking

Has this ever happened to you?

It's your turn to mix the drinks, but you can't remember the recipes. So you end up putting in some Drano and nobody will ever speak to you again.

Next time, take a moment and check with the

Booze Cookbook

Coca-Cola

Talk to the fans of Coca-Cola, the most important beverage in the refrigerator of American hegemony.

Usenet:
Newsgroup: **alt.food.cocacola**

A B C D E F G H I J K L M N O P Q R S T U V W X Y Z

Novelty images abound on the Internet. Think of it as your world-spanning repertoire of color photographic clipart. Finding images is usually easy. We found this image by doing an Archie search for **pepsi**.

College Food

Ah, those good old college days. How nostalgic we will be when our hair turns silver and we wax eloquent about mystery meat burgers and the blue-green algae surprise. Come on in and discuss college dining halls, cafeterias, and pay-for-it-even-if-you-don't-want-it food plans.

Usenet:
    Newsgroup: **alt.college.food**

Cookie Recipes

Cookie recipes, including one that costs over $200 to obtain.

Anonymous FTP:
    Address: **quartz.rutgers.edu**
    Path: **/pub/food/cookie.recipes**

Gopher:
    Name: Rutgers Quartz Text Archive
    Address: **quartz.rutgers.edu**
    Choose: **Food, Recipes, and Nutrition
    | cookie.recipes**

Cooking

International conversion helper, food terms, liquid measures, ingredient guides, and other material related to cooking.

Anonymous FTP:
    Address: **rtfm.mit.edu**
    Path: **/pub/usenet/news.answers/cooking-faq**

Drinking Games

Magnificent collection of nearly one hundred beer drinking games, including such gems as Beat the Barman, Kings and Blood, and Viking.

Anonymous FTP:
    Address: **ocf.berkeley.edu**
    Path: **/pub/Library/Recreation/drinking.games**

    Address: **sauna.cs.hut.fi**
    Path: **/pub/drinking_games/***

Fat-free Food

Remember, just because it has no taste doesn't mean it's good for you. Immerse yourself in the world of fat-free fanatics and lower your cholesterol, blood pressure, and enjoyment quotient.

Usenet:
    Newsgroup: **alt.food.fat-free**

Food and Beverages

General discussion group for people who think that eating is more than just putting stuff into your mouth.

Usenet:
    Newsgroup: **rec.food.drink**

Good Food

Discussion of cooking techniques, equipment, recipes, vegetarianism, restaurants, and food and drink in general.

Usenet:
    Newsgroup: **alt.food**
    Newsgroup: **rec.food.cooking**
    Newsgroup: **rec.food.drink**
    Newsgroup: **rec.food.recipes**
    Newsgroup: **rec.food.restaurants**
    Newsgroup: **rec.food.veg**

Need a laugh?
Check out Humor

Have a Coke

Make your own cola with this recipe. It looks time-consuming, but could be worth the trouble for the true Coke connoisseur or the budding chemist.

Anonymous FTP:
    Address: **ftp.spies.com**
    Path: **/Library/Article/Food/newcoke.txt**

Gopher:
    Name: Internet Wiretap
    Address: **wiretap.spies.com**
    Choose: **Wiretap Online Library | Articles
    | Food and Drink
    | Laszlo Nibble: The New Coke**

Herbs

Do you wonder how your favorite chile would do on the Scoville Organoleptic Test? Do you have a cold and want to know whether to eat the zinc before or after the garlic? Get together with the Herbs-R-Us people and discuss all manner of herbal lore and treatments.

Usenet:
    Newsgroup: **alt.folklore.herbs**

Excerpt from the Net...

```
Newsgroup: alt.folklore.herbs
Subject: Food for thought

Gotu Kola and Ginkgo are both used in
Ayurvedic medicine as brain tonics.

One's supposed to help clear and focus
the mind, the other's supposed to give
your thoughts energy, but I forget
which is which.
```

History of Food

Where do you ask for information about what type of food the peasants ate during the French Revolution? What do you do when the in-laws are due any moment and you need the recipe for figgy pudding? Check out this newsgroup and move forward into the past.

Usenet:
    Newsgroup: **rec.food.historic**

Homebrew Mailing List

All about making and tasting beer, ale, and mead. This mailing list also covers related issues such as breweries, books, judging, commercial beers, and beer festivals.

Anonymous FTP:
    Address: **mthvax.cs.miami.edu**
    Path: **/pub/homebrew/***

Internet mailing list:
    List Address: **homebrew@hpfcmi.fc.hp.com**
    Subscription Address:
        homebrew-request@hpfcmi.fc.hp.com

Homebrewing

All kinds of material related to beer and homebrewing, including recipes, *Homebrew Digest* archives, color images of various beer labels and coasters, and much more.

Anonymous FTP:
    Address: **nic.funet.fi**
    Path: **/pub/culture/beer/***

How to Make Your Own Booze

A guide to making alcoholic beverages, including recipes for vodka, rum, moonshine, whiskey, beer, wine, and hard cider.

Anonymous FTP:
    Address: **ftp.spies.com**
    Path: **/Library/Untech/alcohol.mak**

Gopher:
    Name: Internet Wiretap
    Address: **wiretap.spies.com**
    Choose: **Wiretap Online Library | Questionables
    | How To Make Alcohol**

Why pay for the real thing when you can make your own? Check out *How to Make Your Own Booze*

Just be sure to watch out for revenooers.

A B C D E F G H I J K L M N O P Q R S T U V W X Y Z

Ketchup

A whole newsgroup devoted to this most wonderous of tomato foodstuffs. Ketchup, ketchup, ketchup...wowie, zowie...just keep it away from us.

Usenet:
> Newsgroup: **alt.ketchup**

Excerpt from the Net...

Newsgroup: alt.ketchup
Subject: Ketchup on Bee Stings?

> Can I put ketchup on bee stings?

Yes. It won't do any good for the bee
sting, but dousing oneself liberally
with ketchup is generally just a good
thing to do.

McDonalds

If your junk food is missing that *je ne sais quois* that makes all the difference, perhaps you should share the experience. Come on in and discuss McDonalds, everybody's favorite home away from home.

Usenet:
> Newsgroup: **alt.food.mcdonalds**
> Newsgroup: **alt.mcdonalds**

Mead Recipes

An assortment of recipes for making honey-sweet mead.

Anonymous FTP:
> Address: **ftp.spies.com**
> Path: **/Library/Article/Food/mead.rcp**

Gopher:
> Name: Internet Wiretap
> Address: **wiretap.spies.com**
> Choose: **Wiretap Online Library | Articles
> | Food and Drink | Mead Recipes**

Spare time? Take a look at Games

Recipe Archives

Search this large database of food recipes for that special something.

Anonymous FTP:
> Address: **ftp.cs.ubc.ca**
> Path: **/pub/local/RECIPES**
>
> Address: **ftp.neosoft.com**
> Path: **/pub/rec.food.recipes**
>
> Address: **gatekeeper.dec.com**
> Path: **/pub/recipes**
>
> Address: **mthvax.cs.miami.edu**
> Path: **/pub/recipes**
>
> Address: **wuarchive.wustl.edu**
> Path: **/usenet/rec.food.recipes/recipes**

Gopher:
> Name: Albert Einstein College of Medicine
> Address: **gopher.aecom.yu.edu**
> Choose: **Internet Resources | Miscellaneous
> | Search the Food Recipes Database**

Wais:
> Database: **recipes**
> Database: **usenet-cookbook**

Recipes

What do you do when your boss and his family are coming over for dinner and all you have is a couple of frozen armadillos? Connect to Usenet and check out the recipe groups. The **.gourmand** and **.recipes** groups are moderated. The **.cooking** group is open to all.

Usenet:
> Newsgroup: **alt.gourmand**
> Newsgroup: **rec.food.cooking**
> Newsgroup: **rec.food.recipes**

Recipes from Slovakia

For example, "Bryndzove pirohy" (dumplings filled with feta cheese).

Gopher:
> Name: Academy of Sciences, Bratislava
> Address: **savba.savba.sk**
> Choose: **Slovakia | Recipes of Grand Mother**

Restaurants

Tips on where to go for good eats, and complaints about the stinkers. This is the place to read about dining out.

Usenet:
  Newsgroup: **rec.food.restaurants**

Eating Out is Good

These days, more and more people who go to restaurants are going to restaurants. (Strange, but true.)

But where's the best place to go?

No need to guess.

Before you spend your hard-earned cash for stuff to put in your mouth, check with your friends on

rec.food.restaurants

Sourdough

The best thing in the world: sourdough bread as originally baked in San Francisco. Discuss the ins and outs of making this tricky, but addictively pleasing foodstuff.

Usenet:
  Newsgroup: **rec.food.sourdough**

Spam

To quote *The Encyclopedia of Bad Taste* by Jane and Michael Stern, "Spam is ground pork shoulder and ground ham combined with salt, sugar, water and sodium nitrite, stuffed into a can, sealed, cooked, dried, dated and shipped." It's hard to explain the world's love affair with this most versatile of foods. Join Spam enthusiasts as they debate the pros and cons of this twentieth-century culinary wonder. As the Sterns point out, "Next

to spit-roasted dog meat, Spam is just about Korea's favorite delicacy."

Usenet:
  Newsgroup: **alt.spam**

Sugar Cereals

Sweetness is what sweetness does. Start your day with a sugar-charged bang. Check out the latest scoop on sugar cereals and related issues of importance.

Usenet:
  Newsgroup: **alt.food.sugar-cereals**

Vegetarian Archives

General information on all aspects of vegetarianism, answers to common questions, vegetarian recipes, and a world guide to vegetarianism.

Anonymous FTP:
  Address: **flubber.cs.umd.edu**
  Path: **/other/tms/veg/***

  Address: **rtfm.mit.edu**
  Path: **/pub/usenet/rec.answers/vegetarian/faq**

Vegetarianism

Is it worth living forever if you can't have a hotdog? That seems to be the central issue of our time, and here is the place to talk about it. Share your thoughts, hopes, dreams, and vegetarian recipes.

Usenet:
  Newsgroup: **rec.food.veg**

Wine

Tired of the pedestrian charms of beer? Move up to the big time, where drinking is an art form and 1983 was a good year. Join the Bacchus society, wine lovers extraordinaire, maybe even make your own homegrown vino. Oenophiles of the world unite: You have nothing to lose but your grains.

Usenet:
  Newsgroup: **alt.bacchus**
  Newsgroup: **rec.crafts.winemaking**

A
B
C
D
E
F
G
H
I
J
K
L
M
N
O
P
Q
R
S
T
U
V
W
X
Y
Z

Need a refresher on using Archie to find files? You can find a picture of practically anything in less than a minute. *The Internet Complete Reference* (Chapter 17) shows you how. This picture is **jemerson.gif**.

FREEDOM

Banned Computer Material

A list of computer material that has been banned or challenged in academic institutions.

Anonymous FTP:
Address: **ftp.eff.org**
Path: **/pub/academic/banned***

Address: **ftp.spies.com**
Path: **/Liberty/Article/Rights/banned.91**

Gopher:
Name: Internet Wiretap
Address: **wiretap.spies.com**
Choose: **Wiretap Online Library | Articles | Civil Rights and Liberties | Banned Computer Material of 1991**

Censored Books

A list of over fifty books that were challenged, burned, or banned somewhere in the United States in the last fifteen years.

Anonymous FTP:
Address: **ftp.spies.com**
Path: **/Library/Article/Rights/censored.bk**

Gopher:
Name: Internet Wiretap
Address: **wiretap.spies.com**
Choose: **Wiretap Online Library | Articles | Civil Rights and Liberties | Censored Books (and Waldenbooks Promotion)**

Civil Rights and Liberties

Articles about instances of censorship, banned computer material, firearms, copyright laws, and legal information.

Anonymous FTP:
Address: **ftp.spies.com**
Path: **/Liberty/Article/Rights/***

Gopher:
Name: Internet Wiretap
Address: **wiretap.spies.com**
Choose: **Wiretap Online Library | Articles | Civil Rights and Liberties**

Guide to Using the Freedom of Information Act

A publication from the federal government that explains to citizens how to use the Freedom of Information Act and the Privacy Act of 1974.

Anonymous FTP:
Address: **ftp.spies.com**
Path: **/Gov/foia.cit**

Gopher:
Name: Internet Wiretap
Address: **wiretap.spies.com**
Choose: **Government Docs | Citizens Guide to Using the FOIA**

FREQUENTLY ASKED QUESTION LISTS

Newsgroups

The reason for frequently asked question lists is that newcomers to a Usenet discussion group often seem to ask the same questions. Veterans don't mind answering new questions, but nobody wants to explain, over and over and over, what "Unix" means.

Through the years, many newsgroups have developed a frequently asked question (FAQ) list that contains all of the common questions that have been answered repeatedly in that group. Some FAQ lists are so large as to be divided into several parts. Whenever you start reading a new group, look for a FAQ list to orient you. More important, before you post a question to the group, check the FAQ list to see if your question has already been answered.

The people who maintain FAQ lists post them regularly, not only to their own newsgroup, but to special newsgroups that have been created just to hold FAQ lists and related material. The **news.answers** group contains FAQ lists from every possible source. The other **.answers** groups contain FAQ lists for their respective hierarchies. For example, **comp.answers** contains computer FAQ lists.

When you have a spare moment, check out these groups, especially **alt.answers**. You will see a lot of interesting and strange stuff that you might never encounter otherwise. You will see that these groups contain not only FAQ lists, but important summaries of information that are not tied to specific newsgroups.

Usenet:
Newsgroup: **alt.answers**
Newsgroup: **comp.answers**
Newsgroup: **misc.answers**
Newsgroup: **news.answers**
Newsgroup: **rec.answers**
Newsgroup: **sci.answers**
Newsgroup: **soc.answers**
Newsgroup: **talk.answers**

Usenet FAQ List Archive

It's the middle of the night. An emergency arrises that requires you read one of the Usenet frequently asked question lists. So you fire up your favorite newsreader program only to find that the article you want has expired. Never you mind. Many of the Usenet FAQ lists are available from the Usenet archive maintained by Jonathan Kamens.

Anonymous FTP:
Address: **rtfm.mit.edu**
Path: **/pub/usenet/news.answers/***

FUN

Big Fun Lists

Big fun in the Internet. Lists fun resources on the Net, from Uncle Bert and Conan.

Anonymous FTP:
Address: **owl.nstn.ns.ca**
Path: **/pub/netinfo/bigfun.***

Address: **quartz.rutgers.edu**
Path: **/pub/internet/sites/internet-bigfunlist.gz**

Finger:
Address: **conan@access.digex.net**

Comic Books

Stimulating discussion of rare and exotic comic books.

Internet mailing list:
List Address: **comix@world.std.com**
Subscription Address:
comix-request@world.std.com

As you might imagine, pictures of superheroes are plentiful on the Internet. Most such image files are named in a straightforward manner to make them easy to find. For example, this collage was created from a number of such pictures. Try using Archie to search for **batman** or **roger** (Rabbit, that is).

Too much spare time?
Explore a MUD

Conversational Hypertext Access Technology

CHAT (Conversational Hypertext Access Technology) is a natural language database query engine. Take part in a simulated conversation with a dragon or a woman named Alice. They correctly understand just about anything you say to them. Be careful, though, it takes skill and cunning to talk the dragon out of flaming you on the spot.

Telnet:
Address: **debra.dgbt.doc.ca**
Login: **chat**

Crosswords

Dictionary, word-list books, technical paper guides, software pointers, solution tips, and other material about crosswords.

Anonymous FTP:
Address: **rtfm.mit.edu**
Path: **/pub/usenet/news.answers/crossword-faq/***

Disney

Interesting facts, animated feature film guides, character notes, event news, and more about Walt Disney and his magic kingdom.

Anonymous FTP:
Address: **rtfm.mit.edu**
Path: **/pub/usenet/news.answers/disney-faq/***

Disneyland

Prices, opening hours, entertainment guide, attraction information and ratings, and a list of things not to be missed, such as the Matterhorn bobsleds, Fantasmic, and Pirates of the Caribbean.

Anonymous FTP:
Address: **rtfm.mit.edu**
Path: **/pub/usenet/news.answers/disney-faq/ disneyland**

Want some fun?
Read the Fun section

Disneyland: The Real Poop

Going to Disneyland is such a Big Deal that it's silly not to be prepared. Don't even think about stepping into the Magic Kingdom without first reading the **Disneyland** frequently asked question list. (When you go there, see if you can find the secret Club 33, the only place in Disneyland where where liquor is served.)

Electronic Shopping Mall

Access to online stores, including a music CD store, bookstore, and product description forum.

Gopher:
Name: Nova Scotia Technology Network
Address: **nstn.ns.ca**
Choose: **NSTN Electronic Shopping Mall**

Historical Costuming

Pattern and supplier lists, bibliography, and information relevant to the Society for Creative Anachronism (SCA). The SCA recreates interesting historical costumes, including attire from the Middle Ages, Renaissance, and the Civil War.

Anonymous FTP:
Address: **grasp1.univ-lyon1.fr**
Path: **/pub/faq/crafts-historical-costuming**

Address: **rzsun2.informatik.uni-hamburg.de**
Path: **/pub/doc/news.answers/ crafts-historical-costuming**

Address: **svin02.info.win.tue.nl**
Path: **/pub/usenet/news.answers/crafts/ historical-costuming**

Internet Hunt

A monthly scavenger hunt for facts and trivia on and about the Net. Be the first to submit the correct answers to the questions and win fame and notoriety. Participate in the individual category, or work with friends in the team category. Look for the hunt questions on Usenet.

Anonymous FTP:
> Address: **ftp.cic.net**
> Path: **pub/internet-hunt/***

Gopher:
> Name: CICnet
> Address: **gopher.cic.net**
> Choose: **The Internet Hunt**

Usenet:
> Newsgroup: **alt.bbs.internet**
> Newsgroup: **alt.internet.services**

Juggling

Large collection of information, news, FAQs, animations, publications, help, programs and archives concerning juggling. Learn how to juggle the cascade, fountain, or shower patterns in no time.

Anonymous FTP:
> Address: **moocow.cogsci.indiana.edu**
> Path: **/pub/juggling/***

Nude Beaches

Lists of some magnificent beaches, hot springs, and parks around the world where clothing is optional.

Anonymous FTP:
> Address: **rtfm.mit.edu**
> Path: **/pub/usenet/rec-answers/nude-faq/***

Puzzles

Hundreds of puzzles to open your mind, complete with solutions. If one cat can kill one rat in one minute, how many rats can six cats kill in six minutes?

Anonymous FTP:
> Address: **rtfm.mit.edu**
> Path: **/pub/usenet/news.answers/puzzles/faq**

The Bizarre section has some cool stuff

Recreational Arts

A collection of fun and interesting recreational documents, articles and factsheets.

Gopher:
> Name: NYSERNet
> Address: **nysernet.org**
> Choose: **Reference Desk**
> | **700 - Arts and Recreation**
> | **790 - Recreational Arts**

Roller Coaster

All sorts of goodies about roller coasters, including images, a FAQ, and descriptions and reviews of parks and coasters.

Anonymous FTP:
> Address: **gboro.rowan.edu**
> Path: **/pub/Coasters/***

Up, Up, and Away!

A mailing list for discussing anything about the sport and preoccupation of ballooning.

Internet mailing list:
> List Address: **balloon@lut.ac.uk**
> Subscription Address:
> **balloon-request@lut.ac.uk**

This image, **balloons.gif**, was retrieved from Washington University in Saint Louis (**wuarchive.wustl.edu**). **wuarchive** is arranged in a hierarchical directory structure. Within the directory **/multimedia/images** are directories for each letter of the alphabet. Just **cd** into the **b** directory for "balloon", and have a look.

A B C D E F G H I J K L M N O P Q R S T U V W X Y Z

GAMES

Advanced Dungeons and Dragons

Lots of Advanced Dungeons and Dragons role-playing material, including spell and priest books, campaigns, modules, new monsters, new spells, rules, interactive games, comments, and anything else to do with AD&D.

Listserv mailing list:
List Address: **adnd-l@utarlvm1.bitnet**
Subscription Address: **listserv@utarlvm1.bitnet**

Anonymous FTP:
Address: **ccosun.caltech.edu**
Path: **/pub/adnd/***

Address: **ftp.cs.pdx.edu**
Path: **/pub/frp/***

Address: **greyhawk.stanford.edu**
Path: **D_D/***

All About Games

Articles, rules, tips, spoilers, reviews, and FAQs for popular games and video games.

Anonymous FTP:
Address: **ftp.spies.com**
Path: **/Library/Media/Games/***

Gopher:
Name: Internet Wiretap
Address: **wiretap.spies.com**
Choose: **Wiretap Online Library | Mass Media | Games and Video Games**

Backgammon Server

Play backgammon with others over the Internet.

Telnet:
Address: **ouzo.rog.rwth-aachen.de 8765**
Login: **guest**

Need a laugh?
Check out Humor

Backgammon with Strangers

These days you have to be careful who you mix with. Playing backgammon in person presents all kinds of potential problems. For example, someone might sneeze on you and give you pneumonia, or your opponent could get mad and stab you with an ice pick.

Much better to play it safe: telnet to the

Backgammon Server,

where you can depend on the kindness of strangers. Moreover, you can play in your underwear and no one will care.

Bizarre Board Game

Rules, instructions, and board diagrams for playing "T.B, the Board Game", a game that duplicates all the action of a typical month on the Usenet newsgroup **talk.bizarre**.

Anonymous FTP:
Address: **ftp.spies.com**
Path: **/Library/Fringe/Weird/bizarre.gam**

Gopher:
Name: Internet Wiretap
Address: **wiretap.spies.com**
Choose: **Wiretap Online Library | Fringes of Reason | Very Strange | The Talk.Bizarre Board Game**

Car Wars

A mailing list for the discussion of the Steve Jackson game, Car Wars. Topics of discussion include rules debates, tournament organization and computer versions.

Internet mailing list:
List Address: **carwar-l@ubvm.buffalo.edu**
Subscription Address:
carwar-l-request@ubvm.buffalo.edu

Chess Archives

Many freeware chess programs for different machines and operating systems, game scores, and other chess-related material.

Anonymous FTP:
Address: **chess.uoknor.edu**
Path: **/pub/chess/***

Chess Discussion List

A mailing list for the discussion of chess, specific interesting chess games, strategies, lore, and even programming chess logic.

Listserv mailing list:
List Address: **chess-l@grearn.bitnet**
Subscription Address: **listserv@grearn.bitnet**

Chess Gopher

Press articles, extensive game reports, chess columns, and FAQs about the game of chess.

Gopher:
Name: University of Missouri
Address: **kasey.umkc.edu**
Choose: **Chess**

Chess News

News, events, and up-to-date moves from the world of international chess.

Gopher:
Name: The World
Address: **world.std.com**
Choose: **Periodicals, Magazines, and Journals | Middlesex News | Columns | Your Move (chess)**

Chess Servers

Meet and play chess with other chess enthusiasts throughout the world. Watch others play or join in and play a game of your own. You can save a game and return to it later.

Comment: Mail addresses are for questions, telnet addresses are for playing.

Mail:
Address: **danke@daimi.aau.dk**
Address: **shaheen@eve.assumption.edu**
Address: **tange@daimi.aau.dk**

Telnet:
Address: **bentley.daimi.aau.dk 5000**
Login: *your name*

Address: **ics.uoknor.edu 5000**
Login: *your name*

Address: **testbed.access.net 5000**
Login: *your name*

Usenet:
Newsgroup: **alt.chess.ics**

Core War

Offers documents, tutorials, source code, and system information for a variety of formats for Core War, a system where programs battle against programs and try to destroy each other in cyberspace.

Anonymous FTP:
Address: **soda.berkeley.edu**
Path: **/pub/corewar/***

Diplomacy

A game you play by mail. The setting is pre-WWI Europe. Players send in their moves every week and results are distributed each week. Conspire with your neighbors to conquer the Old World.

Mail:
Address: **judge@dipvax.dsto.gov.au**
Address: **judge@morrolan.eff.org**
Address: **judge@shrike.und.ac.za**
Address: **judge@u.washington.edu**

Fantasy Role-Playing Games

This site has a number of role-playing games to choose from, such as Empire of the Petal Throne.

Gopher:
Name: University of Minnesota
Address: **gopher.micro.umn.edu**
Choose: **Fun & Games | Games | Fantasy Role-Playing Games**

Spare time? Take a look at Games

A
B
C
D
E
F
G
H
I
J
K
L
M
N
O
P
Q
R
S
T
U
V
W
X
Y
Z

Flame BBS Gopher

Offers lots of information from Flame BBS, including information boards and many documents. It even allows exploration of rooms and is a neat place to "flop around and zip and burble".

Gopher:
> Name: University of Western Australia
> Address: **mackerel.gu.uwa.edu.au 3452**

Gambling

Collection of gambling information including a FAQ list, blackjack card-counting information, poker statistics, and much more.

Anonymous FTP:
> Address: **soda.berkeley.edu**
> Path: **/pub/rec.gambling/***

Gambling and Oddsmaking

Guides on how to win at blackjack, optimal wagering, shuffle-tracking, lowball, and other games. Includes other gambling-related topics, such as how to test for loaded dice.

Anonymous FTP:
> Address: **ftp.spies.com**
> Path: **/Library/Article/Gaming/***

Gopher:
> Name: Internet Wiretap
> Address: **wiretap.spies.com**
> Choose: **Wiretap Online Library | Articles | Gambling and Oddsmaking**

Excerpt from the Net...

(from the "Gambling and Oddsmaking" directory on the Wiretap Gopher)

The Kelly Criterion [for Blackjack] is a betting heuristic that minimizes your chance of going broke while maximizing your long-run profits. To bet consistently with the Kelly Criterion, you should divide your bankroll into 300-400 units and normally bet 1-4 units on each hand. Your optimal bet on a hand is a percentage of your current bankroll equal to about $0.5*R/D + B$, where R is the running count, D is the number of remaining decks (so R/D is the true count), and B is the basic strategy expectation.

Game Bytes

Game reviews, interviews, reports and actual screen shots from games can be found in this free electronic gaming magazine.

Anonymous FTP:
> Address: **ftp.uml.edu**
> Path: **/msdos/Games/Game_Bytes/***

> Address: **wuarchive.wustl.edu**
> Path: **/pub/msdos_uploads/game_byte/***

Game Server

Choose from a multitude of exciting online games including Bucks, Moria, Tetris, Sokoban, Reversi, Nethack, and many adventure games, including MUDs.

Gopher:
> Name: University of Stuttgart
> Address: **rusinfo.rus.uni-stuttgart.de**

Telnet:
> Address: **castor.tat.physik.uni-tuebingen.de**
> Login: **games**

Game Solutions

Hints and solutions to more games than you will ever have time to play. Covers hundreds of popular adventure games.

Anonymous FTP:
> Address: **nic.funet.fi**
> Path: **/pub/doc/games/solutions/***

GNU Chess

A chess-playing program, complete with source. X Window, Suntools, curses, ASCII, and IBM PC character set displays are available.

Anonymous FTP:
> Address: **aeneas.mit.edu**
> Path: **/pub/gnu/gnuchess***

> Address: **sunsite.unc.edu**
> Path: **/pub/gnu/gnuchess***

Archie:
> Pattern: **gnuchess**

Lonely? Try the Personals.

GNU Go

The Japanese game Go, complete with source, for Unix systems.

Anonymous FTP:
Address: **aeneas.mit.edu**
Path: **/pub/gnu/gnugo***

Address: **sunsite.unc.edu**
Path: **/pub/gnu/gnugo***

Archie:
Pattern: **gnugo**

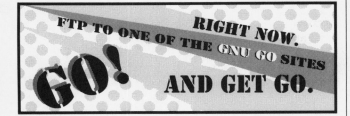

Go

Play Go with other admirers of this popular Japanese game. Watch others play, join in yourself, or discuss strategy with the masters. The FTP site contains information of interest to Go players.

Anonymous FTP:
Address: **bsdserver.ucsf.edu**
Path: **/Go/prog**

Telnet:
Address: **hellspark.wharton.upenn.edu 6969**

Interactive Fiction

Archive for interactive fiction games, development tools, game solutions, programming examples, and the interactive fiction Usenet newsgroups.

Anonymous FTP:
Address: **ftp.gmd.de**
Path: **/if-archive/***

Address: **wuarchive.wustl.edu**
Path: **/mirrors/if-archive/***

Nethack

The famous game of Nethack, for Unix systems, where avid adventurers travel deep into dungeons unknown.

Anonymous FTP:
Address: **aeneas.mit.edu**
Path: **/pub/gnu/nethack***

Address: **sunsite.unc.edu**
Path: **/pub/gnu/nethack***

Archie:
Pattern: **nethack**

PC Games FAQ

An invaluable document for PC gamers providing related Usenet newsgroups, FTP guide, acronym list, computer issues, software issues, and much more essential information.

Anonymous FTP:
Address: **rtfm.mit.edu**
Path: **/pub/usenet/comp.answers/PC-games-faq/***

Role-Playing

A large collection of information connected to role-playing, including convention reports, FTP site lists, list of games and companies, and game-system specifics.

Gopher:
Name: University of San Diego
Address: **teetot.acusd.edu**
Choose: **Everything.. | Entertainment and Food | Role-Playing**

Role-Playing Archives

Large archive of role-playing materials—pictures, programs, game sheets, stories, specific systems and texts on all aspects of role-playing. Includes AD&D, Traveller, Champions, Navero, Runequest, and others.

Anonymous FTP:
>Address: **ccosun.caltech.edu**
>Path: **/pub/adnd/***

>Address: **ftp.cs.pdx.edu**
>Path: **/pub/frp/***

>Address: **ftp.white.toronto.edu**
>Path: **/pub/frp/***

>Address: **greyhawk.stanford.edu**
>Path: **D_D/***

>Address: **ics.uci.edu**
>Path: **/usenet/rec.games.frp/***

>Address: **nic.funet.fi**
>Path: **/pub/doc/games/roleplay/***

>Address: **ocf.berkeley.edu**
>Path: **/pub/Traveller/***

>Address: **soda.berkeley.edu**
>Path: **pub/***

ScrabbleMOO

Play the popular Scrabble board game with other enthusiasts over the Internet.

Telnet:
>Address: **nextsrv.cas.muohio.edu 7777**

Shogi

Play the Japanese version of chess known as Shogi. Source code is available for Unix and X Window versions.

Anonymous FTP:
>Address: **nic.funet.fi**
>Path: **/pub/gnu/gnushogi***

>Address: **nic.funet.fi**
>Path: **/pub/gnu/xshogi***

>Address: **sunsite.unc.edu**
>Path: **/pub/gnu/gnushogi***

>Address: **sunsite.unc.edu**
>Path: **/pub/gnu/xshogi***

Archie:
>Pattern: **gnushogi**
>Pattern: **xshogi**

Source Code to OMEGA (a ROGUE-style game)

Complete C source code to OMEGA, a popular role-playing game. This source also exists in a number of other locations.

Anonymous FTP:
>Address: **sun.soe.clarkson.edu**
>Path: **/pub/src/games/omega/***

Archie:
>Pattern: **omega**

Tiddlywinks

Learn the rules, history, and terminology of this complex game of strategy and tactics.

Anonymous FTP:
>Address: **rtfm.mit.edu**
>Path: **/pub/usenet/alt.games.tiddlywinks/***

Top 100 PC Games

A weekly list of the top one hundred PC games, as voted by game players on the Internet.

Mail:
>Address: **appelo@dutiba.twi.tudelft.nl**

Usenet:
>Newsgroup: **comp.sys.ibm.pc.games.announce**

Trading Post

Requests and offers for arcade game boards; you can place your own "for sale" or "wanted" messages.

Anonymous FTP:
>Address: **ftp.spies.com**
>Path: **/game_archive/tradingPost/***

Gopher:
>Name: Internet Wiretap
>Address: **wiretap.spies.com**
>Choose: **Video Game Archive | tradingPost**

GARDENING

All About Trees

All you need to know about tree selection, planting, and care.

Gopher:
Name: University of Delaware
Address: **lobster.mis.udel.edu**
Choose: **UD Department & College Information Services AGINFO: College of Agricultural Sciences | Fact Sheets | Ornamental Horticulture**

Bonsai

Develop patience and an appreciation for long-term planning by practicing the fine art of bonsai. You will be rewarded with plants that are exquisite in form and grace. If you feel your skill or attention span are not up to the task, you can always try Zen rock gardening.

Usenet:
Newsgroup: **alt.bonsai**
Newsgroup: **rec.arts.bonsai**

Bonsai Mailing List

The art and craft of bonsai and related art forms. Bonsai is the Japanese art (craft?) of miniaturizing trees and plants into forms that mimic nature. Anyone interested, whether novice or professional, may join this mailing list.

Listserv mailing list:
List Address: **bonsai@waynest1.bitnet**
Subscription Address: **listserv@waynest1.bitnet**

Gardener's Assistant

A PC program to help aspiring gardeners choose plants according to growing conditions.

Anonymous FTP:
Address: **ftp.wustl.edu**
Path: **/systems/ibmpc/msdos/database/gardener.zip**

Address: **plaza.aarnet.edu.au**
Path: **/micros/pc/oak/database/gardener.zip**

Address: **rigel.acs.oakland.edu**
Path: **/pub/msdos/database/gardener.zip**

Archie:
Pattern: **gardener.zip**

Gardening Information

A large collection of material about fertilizers, herbs, peppers, ivy, poisonous plants, pruning, roses, seeds, fruit trees, turf grasses, and much more. If your thumb doesn't turn green with all this help, give it up.

Anonymous FTP:
Address: **sunsite.unc.edu**
Path: **/pub/academic/agriculture/ sustainable_agriculture/recgardens/***

Gopher:
Name: Texas Agricultural Extension Service
Address: **taex-gopher1.tamu.edu**
Choose: **Master Gardening Information**

Gardens and Plants

If things aren't going right in the garden, don't just raze everything with the Rototiller: Turn to your fellow Internet buddies for ideas. For the organically challenged, you have the opportunity to cry, scream, and beg for help. Bragging is also welcome; you can pass on the news that it was your 25-pound tomato that made the cover of *The National Enquirer*.

Usenet:
Newsgroup: **rec.gardens**

Excerpt from the Net...

```
Newsgroup: rec.gardens
Subject: Plants that attract birds?

> Has anyone had any particular success
  attracting birds to their yard
> with particular plants?  I've bought
  a book called "How to Attract
> House and Feed Birds" which contains
  a list of trees and shrubs that
> birds are attracted to, but it lists
  several dozen and I'm having a
> hard time choosing among them.

If I had room for just one bird-feeding
plant, it would be a serviceberrry (Ame-
lenchier species): either a shrub or
tree.  Robins and other birds love the
berries.  In addition, the plants have
beautiful spring blooms and great fall
color.
```

A B C D E F G H I J K L M N O P Q R S T U V W X Y Z

Growing Vegetables

A guide to planting and growing vegetables.

Gopher:
> Name: University of Delaware
> Address: **lobster.mis.udel.edu**
> Choose: **UD Department & College Information Services | AGINFO: College of Agricultural Sciences | Fact Sheets | Vegetables**

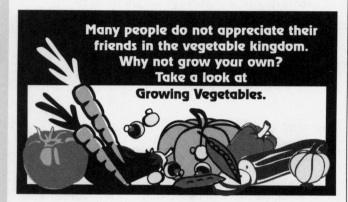

Many people do not appreciate their friends in the vegetable kingdom. Why not grow your own? Take a look at **Growing Vegetables.**

Home Gardening Mailing List

Gardens and Gardening mailing list promotes and exchanges information about home gardening. Topics include vegetable gardens, herbs, flowers, ornamental gardening and other topics. Both novice and experienced gardeners are welcome.

Listserv mailing list:
> List Address: **gardens@ukcc.uky.edu**
> Subscription Address: **listserv@ukcc.uky.edu**

GEOGRAPHY

Australian Postal Codes

Search a database for Australian postal codes by keywords, including state, city, and so on.

Gopher:
> Name: Austin Hospital
> Address: **austin.unimelb.edu.au**
> Choose: **General Information and Services | Look Up Australian Post Codes**

CARIS Geographic Information System Users

A mailing list designed to encourage CARIS software users on the Internet to get together and share information.

Internet mailing list:
> List Address: **carisuse@sun1.cogs.ns.ca**
> Subscription Address:
> **carisuse-request@sun1.cogs.ns.ca**

CIA World Factbook

The complete text. Detailed information about every country and territory in the world. Includes geographic, climate, economic, and political information.

Anonymous FTP:
> Address: **ucselx.sdsu.edu**
> Path: **/pub/doc/etext/world.text.Z**

Gopher:
> Name: Internet Wiretap
> Address: **wiretap.spies.com**
> Choose: **Electronic Books | CIA World Factbook**

> Name: University of Minnesota
> Address: **gopher.micro.umn.edu**
> Choose: **Libraries | Reference Works | CIA World Fact Book**

Wais:
> Database: **world-factbook**

CIA INFO FOR YOU

TOP SECRET

The U.S. Central Intelligence Agency is so secret that its budget is not even made public. (We don't even know if they have enough money to buy copies of our Internet books.)

What we do know is that they spend a lot of time and effort keeping track of all the countries of the world. And you can get it all (the non-secret stuff anyway) for free. The CIA World Factbook resource is invaluable for anyone who is planning to create their own military alliance.

Earth

A world fact book, world map, and topological relief database about Earth.

Anonymous FTP:
    Address: **nic.funet.fi**
    Path: **/pub/doc/world/***

European Postal Codes

List of examples of postal country codes used by most European and Mediterranean countries.

Anonymous FTP:
    Address: **nic.funet.fi**
    Path: **/pub/doc/mail/stamps/***

Geographic Information System

A large collection of geographic data. Search the database first, then request specific items via e-mail.

Gopher:
    Name: Oregon State University
    Address: **gopher.fsl.orst.edu**
    Choose: **Corvallis FSL GIS Data Catalog**

Geographische Informationssyteme

An Austrian list for discussion and other postings regarding geography and Geographic Information Processing.

Listserv mailing list:
    List Address: **acdgis-l@awiimc12.bitnet**
    Subscription Address: **listserv@awiimc12.bitnet**

Geography Server

Get information about cities, regions, countries, etc., including population, latitude and longitude, elevation, and so on.

Telnet:
    Address: **martini.eecs.umich.edu 3000**

Global Land Information System

Download land use and geological survey maps of the United States.

Telnet:
    Address: **glis.cr.usgs.gov**
    Login: **guest**

Local Times Around the World

Local times in many cities around the world. This Gopher menu connects to a computer in the city of interest, which reports the local time.

Gopher:
    Name: Austin Hospital
    Address: **austin.unimelb.edu.au**
    Choose: **General Information and Resources
      | Local Times**

New York State Statistics

Figures and data on New York state, including population, crime, education, industry and other vital information.

Gopher:
    Name: State University of New York
    Address: **gopher.acsu.buffalo.edu**
    Choose: **Miscellany | New_York_State_Facts**

U.S. Geographic Name Server

Obtain geographic position, population, elevation, state, and other statistics for a U.S. city or ZIP code.

Gopher:
    Name: NASA Goddard Space Flight Center
    Address: **gopher.gsfc.nasa.gov**
    Choose: **Other Resources
      | US geographic name server**

U.S. Snow Cover Maps

Images and snow cover maps for the U.S., updated regularly and available in GIF and other formats, from the National Weather Service.

Anonymous FTP:
    Address: **snow.nohrsc.nws.gov**
    Path: **/pub/bbs/***

U.S.A. Statistics

Facts, figures, statistics, and other information about the United States.

Gopher:
    Name: State University of New York
    Address: **gopher.acsu.buffalo.edu**
    Choose: **Miscellany | American_Facts**

A B C D E F G H I J K L M N O P Q R S T U V W X Y Z

ZIP Codes of the U.S.

The FTP site has a file with all the ZIP codes in the U.S. and the city and state of their location. The Gopher is a geographic name server. To use it, you type in the ZIP code and it displays information about the location for the ZIP code.

Anonymous FTP:
> Address: **oes.orst.edu**
> Path: **/pub/data/zipcode.p2**

Gopher:
> Name: Seymour
> Address: **seymour.md.gov**
> Choose: **Find a Fact | USA Zip Code database**

> Name: University of California San Diego
> Address: **infopath.ucsd.edu**
> Choose: **Reference Shelf**
> **| Search Geographic Name Server by City or ZIP code**

> Name: University of California Santa Cruz
> Address: **scilibx.ucsc.edu**
> Choose: **The Library**
> **| Electronic Reference Books**
> **| Zip Codes for US Cities**

GEOLOGY

Earthquake Information

Get up-to-date news about earthquakes around the world.

Finger:
> Address: **quake@geophys.washington.edu**

Gopher:
> Name: St. Olaf College
> Address: **gopher.stolaf.edu**
> Choose: **Internet Resources**
> **| Weather and Geography**

Telnet:
> Address: **geophys.washington.edu**
> Login: **quake**
> Password: **quake**

For **vasquez.jpg** and other interesting photographs, you can go to the University of North Carolina (**sunsite.unc.edu**). Look in the directory **/pub/multimedia/pictures/OTIS/photos**.

Geological Time Scale

A time scale charting the eras and events of the last 4 to 5 million years.

Anonymous FTP:
> Address: **ftp.spies.com**
> Path: **/Library/Document/geologic.tbl**

Gopher:
> Name: Internet Wiretap
> Address: **wiretap.spies.com**
> Choose: **Wiretap Online Library**
> **| Assorted Documents | Geologic time table**

Oklahoma Geological Survey Observatory

Near real-time continuous and event seismic and magnetic data, Oklahoma earthquake catalog, a catalog of known nuclear explosions, and the text of nuclear testing treaties.

Gopher:
> Name: Oklahoma Seismic Gopher
> Address: **wealaka.okgeosurvey1.gov**

U.C. Berkeley Museum of Paleontology

Museum collections information and paleontological database information.

Gopher:
> Name: University of California, Berkeley
> Address: **ucmp1.berkeley.edu**

U.S. Geological Survey Gopher

A Gopher sponsored by the United States Geological Survey. This system has geographic and geological information as well as links to other government Gophers, phone books, and publications.

Gopher:
Name: U.S. Geological Survey
Address: **info.er.usgs.gov**

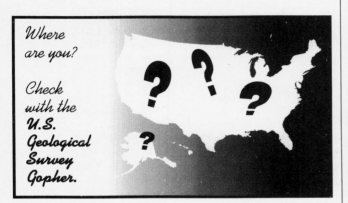

Where are you?

Check with the U.S. Geological Survey Gopher.

U.S.G.S. Seismology Reports

Weekly and historical seismic reports and data as well as programs and source code for crunching seismic data.

Gopher:
Name: Northwestern University
Address: **somalia.earth.nwu.edu**
Choose: **Seismology Resources | USGS Seismology and Tectonophysics Information**

World Paleomagnetic Database

This program allows remote users to search the Abase ASCII version of the World Paleomagnetic Database. The Search program is simple to use and will search the Soviet, non-Soviet, rock unit, and reference databases and create output files which can be downloaded back to a researcher's local system via Anonymous FTP.

Telnet:
Address: **earth.eps.pitt.edu**
Login: **Search**

GOVERNMENT

1990 USA Census Information

The full text from Project Gutenberg.

Gopher:
Name: University of Minnesota
Address: **gopher.micro.umn.edu**
Choose: **Libraries | Electronic Books | By Title**

Name: University of Missouri
Address: **bigcat.missouri.edu**
Choose: **Reference Center**

Americans with Disabilities Act

The full text of the 1990 act which was signed into law.

Gopher:
Name: University of California, Santa Cruz
Address: **scilibx.ucsc.edu**
Choose: **The Library | Electronic Books**

Americans with Disabilities Act Documents

Manuals and other documents regarding the Americans with Disabilities Act.

Gopher:
Name: University of Maryland
Address: **info.umd.edu**
Choose: **Educational Resource | United States | Government | ADA Regulation**

Bureau of Justice Statistics Documents

Statistics on a plethora of justice-related topics, including drug enforcement and treatment in prisons, prison inmates, drunk driving, police departments, felony sentences, prisoner statistics by year, women in prison, capital punishment, and other subjects.

Gopher:
Name: University at Albany
Address: **uacsc2.albany.edu**
Choose: **United Nations Justice Network | Bureau of Justice Statistics Documents**

A B C D E F G H I J K L M N O P Q R S T U V W X Y Z

Make Yourself Feel Bad

No need to walk around always feeling good. Use your Gopher and take a look at the crime statistics from the *Bureau of Justice Statistics Documents.*

Just the thing to take the edge off a beautiful spring day.

Code of the Federal Register

The Federal Register is responsible for the central filing of original acts enacted by Congress, original documents containing executive orders and proclamations of the President, and other official documents and regulations. This resource contains the full text of the law granting this authority and responsibility to the Federal Register.

Gopher:
Name: Netsys Communications Services
Address: **gopher.netsys.com**
Choose: **Counterpoint Publishing**
  | Code of Federal Regulations

Cooperative Extension System

A Gopher system sponsored by the United States Department of Agriculture's Children Youth Family Education Research Network (CYFER-net). CYFER-net provides access to information from the USDA Extension Service and the National Agriculture Library.

Gopher:
Name: U.S. Department of Agriculture
Address: **cyfer.esusda.gov**

Copyright Information

Works registered for copyright since 1978. These include books, films, music, maps, sound recordings, software, multimedia kits, drawings, posters, sculpture, etc.

Telnet:
Address: **locis.loc.gov**
Password: **Copyright Information**

Federal Information Exchange (FIE)

Federal Information Exchange, Inc. (FIE), is a diversified information services company providing a full range of database services, software development and technical support to the government, private sector and academic communities.

Gopher:
Name: University of California San Diego
Address: **infopath.ucsd.edu**
Choose: **The World | Misc Special..**
  | Federal Gov.. | FEDIX

Telnet:
Address: **fedix.fie.com 23**
Login: **new**

Federal Information Processing Standards

A publication of the U.S. Department of Commerce describing standards for information processing.

Anonymous FTP:
Address: **oak.oakland.edu**
Path: **/pub/misc/standards**

Federal Register

Documents from the Federal Register, and information on how to gain full access to the daily U.S. Federal Register via the Internet. Documents include proclamations, executive orders, and so on.

Gopher:
Name: Internet Wiretap
Address: **wiretap.spies.com**
Choose: **Government Docs**

Name: Netsys Communications Services
Address: **gopher.netsys.com**
Choose: **Counterpoint Publishing**
  | Federal Register

Name: Texas A&M University
Address: **gopher.tamu.edu**
Choose: **Hot Topics: What's New in Gopher**
  | Federal Register..

FedWorld

An enormous resource for scientific, technical, and other information provided by the federal government. FedWorld is taxpayer-supported through the National Technical Information Service (NTIS). It is an easy-to-use system that offers information on a wide variety of subjects.

Telnet:
Address: **fedworld.gov**

GAO (General Accounting Office) Reports

Reports from the GAO on budget issues, investment, government management, public services, health care, energy issues and virtually every other area of government on which the GAO reports.

Anonymous FTP:
Address: **ftp.cu.nih.gov**
Path: **/gao-reports**

Gopher:
Name: Internet Wiretap
Address: **wiretap.spies.com**
Choose: **GAO Transition Reports**

Government and Civics Archives

A large collection of laws, treaties and historical and legal documents.

Anonymous FTP:
Address: **ftp.spies.com**
Path: **/Gov/***

Gopher:
Name: Internet Wiretap
Address: **wiretap.spies.com**
Choose: **Government Docs (US & World)**

Internet Sources of Government Information

Sources of U.S. federal government information compiled by Blake Gumprecht.

Anonymous FTP:
Address: **ftp.nwnet.net**
Path: **/user-docs/government/**
gumprecht-guide.txt

Gopher:
Name: Nysernet
Address: **nysernet.org**
Choose: **Special Collections:**
New York State and Federal Info

Name: OARnet
Address: **gopher.oar.net**
Choose: **beginning unix and the internet**

Name: University of Michigan
Address: **gopher.lib.umich.edu**
Choose: **clearinghouse**

Name: University of Virginia
Address: **gopher.virginia.edu**
Choose: **library services**

National Archives and Records Administration

National archives for still pictures, motion pictures, sound and video recordings, World War II pictures, and electronic records.

Gopher:
Name: Library of Congress
Address: **gopher.loc.gov**
Choose: **Federal Government Information**
| National Libraries and National Archives

North American Free Trade Agreement (NAFTA)

The full text of the controversial proposal.

Gopher:
Name: Internet Wiretap
Address: **wiretap.spies.com**
Choose: **North American Free Trade Agreement**

Name: University of Michigan
Address: **gopher.lib.umich.edu**
Choose: **Social Sciences Resources**
| Government and Politics
| U.S. Government Resources:
Legislative Branch

Patent Office Reform Panel Report

The final report of a committee sponsored by the U.S. Patent Office considering a switch from a first-to-invent to a first-to-file patent policy.

Gopher:
Name: Internet Wiretap
Address: **wiretap.spies.com**
Choose: **Government Documents**
| Patent Office Reform Panel Final Report

A B C D E F G H I J K L M N O P Q R S T U V W X Y Z

Who has priority? The person who invents something or the person who is the first to patent it?

*Read the **Patent Office Reform Panel Report** and see what the pros think.*

Pennsylvania Census and Housing Information

Income and poverty statistics, housing information, population, race and sex mixes, and other statistical data.

Gopher:
Name: University of Pennsylvania
Address: **gopher.upenn.edu**
Choose: **Penninfo | Penninfo | Libraries
| Electronic Reference Desk
| US Census and Statistical Data
| Pennsylvania**

Social Security Administration

The Social Security Administration Office Support System Information Server (OSS-IS) offers data on monthly benefits, current operating statistics, history of benefits paid, and income data on the aged.

Anonymous FTP:
Address: **soaf1.ssa.gov**
Path: **/pub/***

Social Security Administration Information

Information about the Social Security Administration, Social Security numbers, and obtaining information on others for genealogical purposes.

Anonymous FTP:
Address: **oak.oakland.edu**
Path: **/pub/misc/ss-info**

U.S. Federal Government Information

Don't take the politicians' word. Look up government data yourself and make your own decisions. Information is categorized by source (e.g. Government Accounting Office). Choose a source, then a document.

Gopher:
Name: University of Minnesota
Address: **gopher.micro.umn.edu**
Choose: **Libraries
| Information from the US Federal Government**

U.S. Government BBS List

List of dial-up U.S. government department bulletin boards, including BBSs for the Commerce, Customs, Defense, Energy, and Justice Departments.

Gopher:
Name: Panix
Address: **gopher.panix.com**
Choose: **Society for Electronic Access
| List of U.S. Gov..**

Government BBSs

Did you know that the U.S. Government supports lots and lots of bulletin board systems? Don't feel bad. They probably don't know anything about what you are doing. Still, it's all there and it's free at *U.S. Government BBS List.* Why not take a few minutes and find out what government for the people and by the people is up to.

U.S. Government Gophers

An informal list of Gopher servers that are either operated or funded by the federal government. Gophers in this list are arranged by government agency.

Gopher:
Name: National Science Foundation
Address: **stis.nsf.gov**
Choose: **Other U.S. Government Gopher Servers**

U.S. Government Today

Current information about the U.S. government, including the House of Representatives and Senate memberships, Congressional phone and fax numbers, and the U.S. budget.

Anonymous FTP:
Address: **ftp.spies.com**
Path: **/Gov/US-Gov/***

Gopher:
Name: Internet Wiretap
Address: **wiretap.spies.com**
Choose: **Government Docs (US & World)
| US Government Today**

GOVERNMENT: CONGRESS

Bibliography of Senate Hearings

North Carolina State University produces monthly bibliographies of Senate hearings, prints, and publications from title page proofs received weekly from the Senate Library.

Anonymous FTP:
    Address: **ftp.ncsu.edu**
    Path: **/pub/ncsu/senate/***

Gopher:
    Name: North Carolina State University
    Address: **dewey.lib.ncsu.edu**
    Choose: **NCSU's Library without Walls**
    | Study Carrels | Government and Law
    | Bibliography of Senate Hearings

Budget of the United States Government

Past budgets and proposed budgets for the upcoming fiscal year, in total and broken down by sections.

Gopher:
    Name: University of North Carolina
    Address: **sunsite.unc.edu**
    Choose: **Sunsite Archives**
    | US and World Politics
    | Sunsite Political Science Archives
    | US-Budget...

Catalog of Federal Domestic Assistance

A search program interface to a catalog of the many federal assistance programs.

Gopher:
    Name: Library of Congress
    Address: **marvel.loc.gov**
    Choose: **Federal Government Information**
    | Fed. Info. Resources | Info. by Agency
    | General Info. | Catalog...

Congress Members

Search a database containing the names, addresses, and phone numbers of members of Congress for all 50 states.

Gopher:
    Name: Library of Congress
    Address: **marvel.loc.gov**
    Choose: **U.S Congress**
    | Congressional Directories

Congressional Committee Assignments

Committee assignments for Congressional, Senate, and joint committees and subcommittees.

Gopher:
    Name: University of Michigan
    Address: **gopher.lib.umich.edu**
    Choose: **Social Science Resources**
    | Govt and Politics
    | US Govt Resources: Legislative
    | US Congress : Committee Assignments

Congressional Firsts

A list of racial firsts in the 103rd Congress.

Gopher:
    Name: University of Maryland
    Address: **info.umd.edu**
    Choose: **Educational Resources**
    | United States
    | Government | Congress | 103rd-firsts

Congressional Legislation

These files track and describe legislation (bills and resolutions) introduced in the Congress, from 1973 (93rd Congress) to the current Congress (103rd). Each file covers a separate Congress.

Telnet:
    Address: **locis.loc.gov**
    Password: **Federal Legislation**

Want some fun?
Read the Fun section

Too much spare time?
Explore a MUD

A
B
C
D
E
F
G
H
I
J
K
L
M
N
O
P
Q
R
S
T
U
V
W
X
Y
Z

GOVERNMENT: EXECUTIVE BRANCH

Campaign '92 and Election Results

Details of the last presidential campaign and the election results.

Gopher:
Name: Texas A&M University
Address: **tamuts.tamu.edu**
Choose: **Browse Information by Subject**
 | Political Science
 | Campaign '92 and Election Results

Name: University of Missouri
Address: **bigcat.missouri.edu**
Choose: **Reference Center**
 | Speeches from the 1992 Presidential Campaign

Clinton's Cabinet

The resumes of President Clinton's cabinet members, including contact information for each.

Anonymous FTP:
Address: **nifty.andrew.cmu.edu**
Path: **/pub/QRD/qrd/info/GOVT/cabinet***

Address: **vector.intercon.com**
Path: **/pub/QRD/info/GOVT/cabinet***

Clinton's Inaugural Address

The full text from Project Gutenberg.

Gopher:
Name: University of Minnesota
Address: **gopher.micro.umn.edu**
Choose: **Libraries | Electronic Books | By Title**

The Bizarre section has some cool stuff

Daily Summary of White House Press Releases

Receive by mail daily summaries of the activities and goings on at the White House. To start the service, send a mail message to the address below.

Mail:
Address: **almanac@esusda.gov**
Body: **subscribe wh-summary**

Executive Branch Resources

Cabinet members' addresses and phone numbers, how to access White House e-mail, NAFTA, budget information, the Federal Register, and other items provided by the executive branch of the federal government.

Gopher:
Name: University of Michigan
Address: **gopher.lib.umich.edu**
Choose: **Social Sciences Resources**
 | Government and Politics
 | U.S. Government Resources: Executive Branch

National Performance Review

Clinton's "reinventing government" program—the full 180-page text.

Gopher:
Name: University of North Carolina
Address: **sunsite.unc.edu**

President's Daily Schedule

Ever wonder what the President of the United States is doing today? Examine the public schedule for the current month or previous months.

Gopher:
Name: Texas A&M University
Address: **gopher.tamu.edu**
Choose: **Hot Topics: A&M's Most Popular Items**
 | Information from the White House
 | President's Daily Schedule

There is absolutely no excuse for not knowing what the President of the United States is doing when all you have to do is check the *President's Daily Schedule Gopher*. Maybe you should take a moment now and do so.

Think how embarrassing it would be if Bill and the family were coming to your house for lunch and you didn't even know.

President's Economic Plan

The details of the President's economic plan.

Gopher:
Name: Internet Wiretap
Address: **wiretap.spies.com**
Choose: **Government Docs**
| Clinton's Economic Plan

Name: University of California San Diego
Address: **infopath.ucsd.edu**
Choose: **News & Services | Economic...**
| Summaries of current...
| President Clinton's Economic Plan

Presidential Documents

Lots of information from the White House, including domestic, international, business and economic affairs, and the President's daily schedule.

Gopher:
Name: Texas A&M University
Address: **gopher.tamu.edu**
Choose: **Hot Topics: A&M's Most Popular Items**
| Information from the White House

The White House

Information and details about the White House, including the electronic mail system, press conferences, information policy, and the federal budget.

Gopher:
Name: University of North Carolina
Address: **sunsite.unc.edu**
Choose: **Sunsite Archives**
| Sunsite Political Science Archives
| Whitehouse Papers

Name: Whole Earth Lectronic Link
Address: **gopher.well.sf.ca.us**
Choose: **Politics | The White House**

If you like trouble, take a look at Mischief

White House Electronic Publications

Sign up for daily distribution of electronic publications via e-mail, search for and retrieve White House documents, and get information on sending e-mail to the White House.

Mail:
Address: **clinton-hq@campaign92.org**
Address: **clinton-info@campaign92.org**

Keeping Up with the Clintons

Each day, the office of the President of the United States sends out a lot of documents, so there is no reason for you to do without. Send them a note and tell them to put you on the list.

At *White House Electronic Publications* you can find out, each day, just what is happening in Mr. Clinton's Dream House.

White House Papers

White House press briefings and other papers dealing with the President, Vice President, First Lady, the Cabinet, Socks (the First Cat), and other important White House personalities.

Wais:
Database: **White-House-Papers**

White House Press Releases

Press releases and other information about White House characters.

Anonymous FTP:
Address: **ftp.spies.com**
Path: **/Clinton/***

Gopher:
Name: Internet Wiretap
Address: **wiretap.spies.com**
Choose: **Clinton Press Releases**

A B C D E F G H I J K L M N O P Q R S T U V W X Y Z

GOVERNMENT: INTERNATIONAL

NATO (North Atlantic Treaty Organization)

Communiques, studies, factsheets, fellowships, handbook, military, scientific, and other papers and positions of NATO.

Gopher:
> Name: University of North Carolina
> Address: **sunsite.unc.edu**
> Choose: **Sunsite Archives**
>   **| US and World Politics**
>   **| Sunsite Political Science Archives | nato**

NATODATA

A mailing list that distributes public information about the North Atlantic Treaty Organization, including press releases, communiques, articles, factsheets, programs, speeches and the NATO handbook.

Listserv mailing list:
> List Address: **natodata@cc1.kuleuven.ac.be**
> Subscription Address: **listserv@cc1.kuleuven.ac.be**

Treaties

A number of treaties, including the Maastricht Treaty, Geneva Convention, North Atlantic Treaty of 1949, the Treaty on the Nonproliferation of Nuclear Weapons 1968, and other important agreements.

Gopher:
> Name: Internet Wiretap
> Address: **wiretap.spies.com**
> Choose: **Government Docs**
>   **| Treaties and International Covenants**

> Name: Swedish University Network
> Address: **sunic.sunet.se**
> Choose: **Subject Tree | Politics**

United Nations Gopher

Contains lots of information about the United Nations, including what it is and what it does, its organizations and resources, press releases, conference news and much more.

Gopher:
> Name: United Nations
> Address: **nywork1.undp.org**

United Nations Resolutions

The text of three of the U.N. resolutions on Iraq, as well as U.N. covenants on civil and political rights, economic, social and cultural rights, and the Universal Declaration of Human Rights.

Gopher:
> Name: Internet Wiretap
> Address: **wiretap.spies.com**
> Choose: **Government Docs**
>   **| United Nations Resolutions**

Look around. Is anyone watching? Good. Take a look at the X-Rated section. (But remember, you didn't read it here.)

There are a lot of books that you can download for free on the Internet. See the Literature sections for details.

HEALTH

Addictions

A mailing list for mature discussion of addictions, including food disorders, sex, co-dependency, nicotine, and other addictions.

Listserv mailing list:
    List Address: **addict-l@kentvm.kent.edu**
    Subscription Address: **listserv@kentvm.kent.edu**

AIDS Information

AIDS statistics, including daily summaries from newspaper articles, details of those at risk, and the full text of *AIDS Treatment News*.

Anonymous FTP:
    Address: **nifty.andrew.cmu.edu**
    Path: **/pub/QRD/qrd/aids/***

    Address: **vector.intercon.com**
    Path: **/pub/QRD/aids/***

Gopher:
    Name: Healthline Gopher Server
    Address: **selway.umt.edu 700**
    Choose: **Sexuality | Acquired Immune
        Deficiency Syndrome (AIDS)**

    Name: National Institute of Health
    Address: **odie.niaid.nih.gov**
    Choose: **AIDS Related Information**

Telnet:
    Address: **selway.umt.edu**
    Login: **health**

Cancer Mailing List

Discussion of any aspect of cancer, including diagnosis, treatments, self-examination, and living with cancer.

Listserv mailing list:
    List Address: **cancer-l@wvnvm.bitnet**
    Subscription Address: **listserv@wvnvm.bitnet**

Clinton's Health Care Package

Documents, reports, and the text of briefings and press releases regarding the Health Security Act of 1993. The documents here only support the proposal.

Anonymous FTP:
    Address: **sunsite.unc.edu**
    Path: **/pub/academic/political-science/
        Health-Security Act**

Gopher:
    Name: U.S. Department of Agriculture
    Address: **ace.esusda.gov**
    Choose: **Americans Communicating
        Electronically
        | National Health Security Act of 1993**

    Name: University of North Carolina
    Address: **gopher.unc.edu**
    Choose: **National Health Security Plan**

Telnet:
    Address: **fedworld.gov**

Clinton's Health Care Package

Personally, we wouldn't get sick if you paid us. The trouble is, no one will pay us, and sometimes we get sick anyway. So, if you're going to be sick, you might as well read all about the Clintons' plans for reforming the American health care system.

Computers and Health

Is your computer emitting gamma rays that are slowly eating out your brain? Read about computers and health and get up-to-date facts, opinions and fallacies about this and other timely topics.

Usenet:
    Newsgroup: **bit.listserv.c+health**

Cornucopia of Disability Information (CODI)

Provides disability information, including digests, computing information, legal issues, college guides, government documents, employment and other topics.

Gopher:
    Name: CODI
    Address: **val-dor.cc.buffalo.edu**

A B C D E F G H I J K L M N O P Q R S T U V W X Y Z

Dental Poisoning

A mailing list for the discussion and dissemination of information about dental amalgam and alleged mercury poisoning.

Listserv mailing list:
List Address: **amalgam@dearn.bitnet**
Subscription Address: **listserv@dearn.bitnet**

Diabetes

Need the latest info about diabetes? Will new immune-desensitizing therapies provide a much-needed preventative measure, or even a cure? Read all about the management, treatment and research of diabetes. Talk with other diabetics who share their experience, tips and opinions.

Usenet:
Newsgroup: **misc.health.diabetes**

Dietary Information

Diet goals, cholesterol statistics, fat and calorie information, and other guides to healthy eating.

Gopher:
Name: Healthline Gopher Service
Address: **selway.umt.edu 700**
Choose: **General Health Information**
| Dietary Information

Telnet:
Address: **selway.umt.edu**
Login: **health**

Dieting

Does your diet work? Or like the other 99.9 percent of humanity, do you have to suffer to lose excess weight?

Join ultra-nutrition-conscious people around the world who will thank you for sharing. Trade stories, scientific trivia, and leftover Weight Watchers' menus. Are you just about ready for your own zip code? Lonely no more.

Usenet:
Newsgroup: **alt.support.diet**

Drug and Alcohol Information

Detailed documents and guides about the risks involved in drug and alcohol use, blood alcohol concentration statistics, state laws and other related facts.

Gopher:
Name: Healthline Gopher Server
Address: **selway.umt.edu 700**
Choose: **Drug & Alcohol Information**

Listserv mailing list:
List Address: **alcohol@lmuacad.bitnet**
Subscription Address: **listserv@lmuacad.bitnet**

Telnet:
Address: **selway.umt.edu**
Login: **health**

Exercise

If you are not exercising right now, you should be feeling guilty. Still, the next best thing to exercising is reading about it. Check out the discussion and trade info with some of the best-conditioned fanatics on the Internet. Are you embarrassed that you still mix up "endomysium", "perimysium" and "epimysium"? All you have to do is read the regularly posted "Stretching and Flexibility" frequently asked question list.

Usenet:
Newsgroup: **misc.fitness**

Excerpt from the Net...

```
Newsgroup: alt.support.diet
Subject: Bodyfat Measurement

Hi all.  Since a lot of people have been asking me about various methods of bodyfat measure-
ment, I figured I ought to post something.

There are a variety of methods used to measure bodyfat, each with their own pros and cons.

The most accurate method is to have the body dissected, and then to separate and weigh the
fat cells.  This will give the most accurate value but is rather inconvenient as you have
to be dead for it to work...
```

Eye Care

An informational guide that explains how your eyes work and how you can prevent eye problems.

Gopher:
Name: Healthline Gopher Server
Address: **selway.umt.edu 700**
Choose: **General Health Information
| How Do Your Eyes Work?**

Telnet:
Address: **selway.umt.edu**
Login: **health**

Food and Drug Administration Bulletin Board System

Sponsored and operated by the FDA, this BBS offers drug and device product approval lists, reports from the Center for Devices and Radiological Health, AIDS information, FDA Consumer magazine index and selected articles, veterinary medicine news, import alerts, and other topics.

Telnet:
Address: **fdabbs.fda.gov**
Login: **bbs**

Food Labeling Information

Rulings on labeling requirements for ingredients, serving sizes, terms, fat and cancer, fruits and vegetables, nutritional claims, and other related topics.

Gopher:
Name: U.S. Department of Agriculture
Address: **esusda.gov**
Choose: **USDA and Other Federal
Agency Information
| Food Labeling Information**

General Health Information

Documents and guides on many health problems, including asthma, back pain, headaches and sleeping disorders.

Gopher:
Name: Healthline Gopher Service
Address: **selway.umt.edu 700**
Choose: **General Health Information**

Telnet:
Address: **selway.umt.edu**
Login: **health**

Handicap BBS Lists

Lists of more than eight hundred dial-up BBSs that offer disability-related information.

Anonymous FTP:
Address: **handicap.shel.isc-br.com**
Path: **/pub/bbslists/***

Health Info-Com Network Newsletter

A biweekly publication by medical professionals that addresses issues and concerns about medicine and health.

Gopher:
Name: University of Maryland
Address: **info.umd.edu**
Choose: **Educational Resources
| The Reading Room | Newletters
| HealthInfoCom**

Health Issue Discussion

Usenet and electronic mail discussion groups on health issues, including health-related archives.

Gopher:
Name: Healthline Gopher Server
Address: **selway.umt.edu 700**
Choose: **Internet Health-related Resources
| Usenet News & Electronic Mail Discussion
Groups on Health Issue**

Telnet:
Address: **selway.umt.edu**
Login: **health**

Health News

Read the news about health care and medicine. Find out if there is a cure for what ails ya.

Usenet:
Newsgroup: **clari.tw.health**

Health Newsletters

Selection of newsletters covering medicine, medical research, disease and therapy.

Anonymous FTP:
Address: **nigel.msen.com**
Path: **/pub/newsletter/Health/***

KEEP A HEALTHY INTEREST IN HEALTH.
SEE **HEALTH NEWSLETTERS**

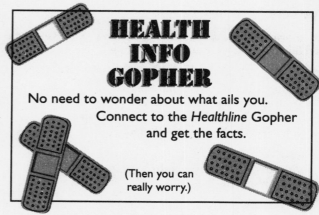

HEALTH INFO GOPHER

No need to wonder about what ails you. Connect to the *Healthline* Gopher and get the facts.

(Then you can really worry.)

Health Science Resources

A large list of Internet and Bitnet resources related to the health sciences.

Gopher:
>Name: NYSERNet
>Address: **nysernet.org**
>Choose: **Reference Desk**
>> | **600 - Applied Science and Technology**
>> | **Health Sciences Resource**

Health Sciences Libraries Consortium (HSLC)

The Health Sciences Libraries Consortium (HSLC) Computer Based Learning Software Database, begun in 1987, contains listings of PC compatible and Macintosh programs used in health sciences education. This project has been endorsed and funded by the American Medical Informatics Association's Education Working Group. Records have also been contributed by the University of Michigan's Software for Health Sciences Education.

Telnet:
>Address: **hslc.org**
>Login: **cbl**

Healthline

Documents and information on a wide range of topics from migraine headaches to health products.

Gopher:
>Name: Healthline Gopher Service
>Address: **selway.umt.edu 700**

Telnet:
>Address: **selway.umt.edu**
>Login: **health**

Migraine Headaches

Information about the symptoms of—and ways to cope with— migraine headaches.

Gopher:
>Name: Healthline Gopher Server
>Address: **selway.umt.edu 700**
>Choose: **General Health Information**
>> | **Migraine Headaches**

Telnet:
>Address: **selway.umt.edu**
>Login: **health**

Morbidity and Mortality Weekly Report

Current and back issues of the *Morbidity and Mortality Weekly Report*.

Gopher:
>Name: National Institute of Health
>Address: **odie.niaid.nih.gov**
>Choose: **AIDS Related Information**

National Institute of Allergy and Infectious Disease

The NIAID Gopher offers up-to-date information on a wide variety of health topics.

Gopher:
>Name: National Institute of Health
>Address: **gopher.niaid.nih.gov**

National Institute of Health

Announcements, information for researchers, a molecular biology database, library and literature resources, the NIH phone book and more.

Gopher:
Name: National Institute of Health
Address: **gopher.nih.gov**

Name: University of California San Diego
Address: **infopath.ucsd.edu**
Choose: **The World | Misc Special..
| Federal Gov.. | National...**

News about AIDS

News about AIDS: stories, research, new treatments and political issues.

Usenet:
Newsgroup: **clari.tw.health.aids**

Nutrition

Should you eat the Twinkie or opt for another seaweed sandwich? Join the conversation and talk about all aspects of diet and eating. Vitamins, carbohydrates, proteins, fats, minerals, fiber—the usual gang of suspects is waiting for you here.

Usenet:
Newsgroup: **sci.med.nutrition**

Physical Sciences Conferences

A large list of mailing lists related to the physical sciences, arranged by subject area.

Anonymous FTP:
Address: **ksuvxa.kent.edu**
Path: **/library/acadlist.file6**

Gopher:
Name: NYSERNet
Address: **nysernet.org**
Choose: **Special Collections: Higher Education
| Scholarly Electronic Conferences
| Physical Sciences**

Sexual Health Topics

Guides to many sex-related health topics, including contraception, STDs, AIDS, cervical cancer, and other health issues.

Gopher:
Name: Healthline Gopher Server
Address: **selway.umt.edu 700**
Choose: **Sexuality**

Telnet:
Address: **selway.umt.edu**
Login: **health**

Sleeping Problems

Antidepressant and sleep disorder guides and advice on how to get a good night's sleep.

Gopher:
Name: Healthline Gopher Server
Address: **selway.umt.edu 700**
Choose: **General Health Information
| Antidepressants and Sleep Disorders**

Name: Healthline Gopher Servers
Address: **selway.umt.edu 700**
Choose: **General Health Information
| Do's and Don'ts for Poor Sleepers**

Telnet:
Address: **selway.umt.edu**
Login: **health**

Snakebites

Learn how to prevent and treat bites by poisonous North American snakes. Also includes information on the effects of snakebites.

Anonymous FTP:
Address: **ftp.spies.com**
Path: **/Library/Article/Outdoors/snake.bc**

Gopher:
Name: Internet Wiretap
Address: **wiretap.spies.com**
Choose: **Wiretap Online Library | Articles
| Backcountry and Outdoors
| BC: Snakebite Distilled Wisdom**

Software and Information for the Handicapped

This FTP site has many directories of informational files of interest to the handicapped.

Anonymous FTP:
Address: **handicap.shel.isc-br.com**
Path: **/***

A B C D E F G H I J K L M N O P Q R S T U V W X Y Z

Surgeon General's Warning on AIDS

A message from the Surgeon General of the United States about AIDS.

Anonymous FTP:
> Address: **ftp.spies.com**
> Path: **/Library/Article/Sex/aids.sg**

Teaching Health and Physical Education

Talk to people who teach health and physical education. Trade ideas, tips, and stories. Find out if it is really true that "Those who can, do. Those who can't, teach. Those who can't teach, teach P.E."

Usenet:
> Newsgroup: **k12.ed.health-pe**

Trade Names Material Safety Data Sheets

A database of information on hundreds of chemicals and compounds. Includes scientific data, such as molecular formulas and atomic weights, as well as health hazards and fire fighting procedures.

Gopher:
> Name: Iowa State University
> Address: **isumvs.iastate.edu**

Typing Injuries

All the information about typing injuries and their treatments. Includes a long list of keyboard alternatives and some related GIF pictures.

Anonymous FTP:
> Address: **soda.berkeley.edu**
> Path: **/pub/typing-injury/***

World Health Organization

The objective of WHO (World Health Organization) is the attainment of the highest possible level of health for all people. Health, as defined in the WHO Constitution, is a state of complete physical, mental, and social well-being and not merely the absence of disease or infirmity.

Gopher:
> Name: World Health Organization
> Address: **gopher.who.ch**

HISTORICAL DOCUMENTS

American Historical Documents

Amendments to the Constitution, Annapolis Convention, Articles of Confederation, Bill of Rights, Charlottetown Resolves, the Constitution, Continental Congress Resolves, Japanese and German surrenders, Martin Luther King Jr.'s "I Have a Dream" speech, Inaugural addresses, the Monroe Doctrine, Rights of Man, treaties and more.

Anonymous FTP:
> Address: **ftp.spies.com**
> Path: **/Gov/US-History/***

Gopher:
> Name: Internet Wiretap
> Address: **wiretap.spies.com**
> Choose: **Government Docs**
> **| US Historical Documents**

> Name: University of Minnesota
> Address: **gopher.micro.umn.edu**
> Choose: **Libraries | Electronic Books**
> **| By Title | Historical**

Nothing to do?

Go to *American Historical Documents*, download a copy of the U.S. Constitution and change all the parts you don't like.

Constitution of the United States of America

The complete text of the U.S. Constitution.

Anonymous FTP:
> Address: **ocf.berkeley.edu**
> Path: **/pub/Library/Politics**

> Address: **ucselx.sdsu.edu**
> Path: **/pub/doc/etext/USConstitution.txt**

Gopher:
> Name: University of Maryland
> Address: **info.umd.edu**
> Choose: **Educational Resources | United States**
> **| Government | Constitution**

Declaration of Arms, 1775

The complete text of the Declaration of the Causes and Necessity of Taking Up Arms, July 6, 1775.

Anonymous FTP:
Address: **ftp.spies.com**
Path: **/Gov/US-History/arms1775.txt**

Gopher:
Name: Internet Wiretap
Address: **wiretap.spies.com**
Choose: **Government Docs (US & World)**
   I US Historical Documents
   I Declaration of Arms, 1775

Declaration of Independence

The complete text of the Declaration of Independence.

Anonymous FTP:
... .edu
...tics/
...pendence.gz

... lu
...eclaration.txt

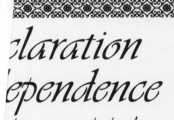

...claration

...ependence

...nts are as important and
...eclaration of Independence.
... one we can think of is
The ...... Complete Reference.)

Download a copy and take a few minutes to examine this crucial piece of history. After all, if it wasn't for the Declaration of Independence, America would still be British and the whole country would have to eat boiled food and worry about Charles and Diana.

Nicolet
INSTRUMENTS OF DISCOVERY

VFINT.386

Need a laugh?
Check out Humor

Emancipation Proclamation

Lincoln's Emancipation Proclamation of 1862, with comments and explanations.

Anonymous FTP:
Address: **tp.spies.com**
Path: **/Gov/US-History/emancip.txt**

Gopher:
Name: Internet Wiretap
Address: **wiretap.spies.com**
Choose: **Government Docs (US & World)**
   I US Historical Documents
   I Emancipation Proclamation

Federalist Papers

The full text from Project Gutenberg.

Gopher:
Name: University of Minnesota
Address: **gopher.micro.umn.edu**
Choose: **Libraries I Electronic Books I By Title**

HISTORY

Anglo-Saxon Mailing List

A mailing list for scholars and others interested in the culture and history of England in the later Middle Ages and early Medieval periods.

Internet mailing list:
List Address: **ansaxnet@wvnvm.wvnet.edu**
Subscription Address:
   ansaxnet-request@wvnvm.wvnet.edu

Camelot

Mythology and history concerning King Arthur, the Knights of the Round Table, and the Holy Grail, including reenactments, literature, linguistics, archaeology, and mysticism. This FTP site contains archives, GIFs of an Arthurian nature, FAQs, and other documents of interest.

Anonymous FTP:
Address: **sapphire.epcc.ed.ac.uk**
Path: **/pub/camelot/***

Internet mailing list:
List Address: **camelot@castle.ed.ac.uk**
Subscription Address:
   camelot-request@castle.ed.ac.uk

A B C D E F G H I J K L M N O P Q R S T U V W X Y Z

Civil War

Answers to dozens of interesting questions about the American Civil War. A good resource for historical information and trivia.

Anonymous FTP:
Address: **quartz.rutgers.edu**
Path: **/pub/history/civil-war-faq**

Gopher:
Name: Rutgers Quartz Text Archive
Address: **quartz.rutgers.edu**
Choose: **History | civil-war-faq**

Dinosaurs

An open discussion about dinosaurs of the Mesozoic Era. Discussion topics range from detailed theories to popular news items.

Internet mailing list:
List Address:
dinosaur@donald.wichitaks.ncr.com
Subscription Address:
dinosaur-request@donald.wichitaks.ncr.com

Feudal Terms

A dictionary of terms from feudal times, including such words as "abbey", "Black Monks", "fief", and "yoke".

Anonymous FTP:
Address: **ftp.spies.com**
Path: **/Library/Article/Socio/feudal.dic**

Gopher:
Name: Internet Wiretap
Address: **wiretap.spies.com**
Choose: **Wiretap Online Library | Articles | Sociological Issues | Feudal Terms Dictionary**

Historians Database and Information Server

HNSource is the central information server for historians and is located at the University of Kansas. This system allows users to browse through a wide variety of information resources related to the historical discipline.

Gopher:
Name: United States Military Academy
Address: **euler.math.usma.edu**
Choose: **Department of History | History Source at the University of Kansas**

Telnet:
Address: **ukanaix.cc.ukans.edu**
Login: **history**

Historians Newsletter

A newsletter for historians and anyone else interested in history.

Listserv mailing list:
List Address: **histnews@ukanvm.ccukans.edu**
Subscription Address:
listserv@ukanvm.ccukans.edu

Historic American Speeches

The text of many historic American speeches and addresses, including some of those given by Washington, Jefferson, Lincoln, Martin Luther King, Jr., Kennedy and Bush.

Anonymous FTP:
Address: **ftp.spies.com**
Path: **/Gov/US-Speech/***

Gopher:
Name: Internet Wiretap
Address: **wiretap.spies.com**
Choose: **Government Docs | US Speeches and Address**

History Archives

Archives of history material, including articles, bibliographies, databases, software, GIF images, papers, newsletters and diaries. Historical subjects include diplomacy, ethnicity, military, maritime, political, scientific, women and many more.

Anonymous FTP:
Address: **byrd.mu.wvnet.edu**
Path: **/pub/history/***

Address: **ra.msstate.edu**
Path: **/pub/docs/history/***

History Databases

A menu driven interface for databases, electronic texts, journals and other archive sites for American and European historical topics.

Telnet:
Address: **clus1.ulcc.ac.uk**
Login: **ihr-uk**

Address: **ukanaix.cc.ukans.edu**
Login: **history**

History Mailing Lists

Devoted to people interested in any aspect of history. Discussions range from trivial to very serious. Newcomers are welcome.

Listserv mailing list:
    List Address: **hist-l@ukanvm.bitnet**
    Subscription Address: **listserv@ukanvm.bitnet**

    List Address: **history@earn.cvut.cz**
    Subscription Address: **listserv@earn.cvut.cz**

    List Address: **history@irlearn.bitnet**
    Subscription Address: **listserv@irlearn.bitnet**

    List Address: **history@mcgill1.bitnet**
    Subscription Address: **listserv@mcgill1.bitnet**

    List Address: **history@psuvm.psu.edu**
    Subscription Address: **listserv@psuvm.psu.edu**

    List Address: **history@rutvm1.rutgers.edu**
    Subscription Address:
      listserv@rutvm1.rutgers.edu

    List Address: **history@ubvm.cc.buffalo.edu**
    Subscription Address:
      listserv@ubvm.cc.buffalo.edu

    List Address: **historya@uwavm.bitnet**
    Subscription Address: **listserv@uwavm.bitnet**

History of the Ancient Mediterranean

Debate, discussion and the exchange of information by students and scholars of the history of the Ancient Mediterranean.

Listserv mailing list:
    List Address: **ancien-l@ulkyvm.bitnet**
    Subscription Address: **listserv@ulkyvm.bitnet**

Holocaust Online Exhibit

This archive houses testimony, descriptions, informational files and first-hand accounts of the Holocaust.

Gopher:
    Name: University of Florida
    Address: **gaia.sci-ed.fit.edu**
    Choose: **Subject Area Resources**
      | Educational TV | Holocaust Online Exhibit

I Have a Dream

Martin Luther King, Jr.'s "I Have a Dream" speech.

Anonymous FTP:
    Address: **ocf.berkeley.edu**
    Path: **/pub/Library/Politics**

Lore

A broad-based mailing list that examines and discusses all aspects of folklore.

Listserv mailing list:
    List Address: **lore@vm1.nodak.edu**
    Subscription Address: **listserv@vm1.nodak.edu**

Everybody likes folklore. Join the lore mailing list and move forward, into the past.

Perseus Gopher

Contains manuals and materials for use with Perseus, the multimedia interactive database designed to facilitate the study of archaic and classical Greece. Also contains classics material and software.

Gopher:
    Name: Perseus Project Gopher Server
    Address: **perseus.harvard.edu**

Prehistoric Flying Creatures

An article discussing large flying creatures of the distant past and how they overcame gravity.

Anonymous FTP:
    Address: **ftp.spies.com**
    Path: **/Library/Article/Misc/dinosaur.fly**

Gopher:
    Name: Internet Wiretap
    Address: **wiretap.spies.com**
    Choose: **Wiretap Online Library | Articles**
      | Misc
      | Prehistoric Flying Creatures and Gravity

A B C D E F G H I J K L M N O P Q R S T U V W X Y Z

Vietnam War

Documents and reports about the Vietnam era, including the Senate Select POW-MIA Affairs Report.

Anonymous FTP:
Address: **ftp.spies.com**
Path: **/Gov/US-History/Vietnam/***

Gopher:
Name: Internet Wiretap
Address: **wiretap.spies.com**
Choose: **Government Docs (US & World)**
| **US Historical Documents**
| **Vietnam Era Documents**

World War II Documents

Historical documents relating to incidents leading up to, and during, the Second World War.

Anonymous FTP:
Address: **ftp.spies.com**
Path: **/Gov/US-History/WWII/***

Gopher:
Name: Internet Wiretap
Address: **wiretap.spies.com**
Choose: **Government Docs (US & World)**
| **US Historical Documents**
| **World War II Documents**

World War II Documents

There are so many interesting World War II documents, it's hard to know where to start:

Captain America comic books, scripts for Hogan's Heroes, notes from John Wayne's diary...

Yes, the war certainly left us with a great legacy of written material. If you would like to investigate for yourself, just try the Wiretap Gopher.

BLAMO

HOBBIES

Amateur Radio

We all have a need to communicate: some of us just like to do it over long distances. Usenet provides a large number of newsgroups devoted to the enjoyment of amateur radio. Tune in, turn on, and drop whatever you are doing: whether you are a novice or a pro, there is a discussion group for you.

Usenet:
Newsgroup: **rec.radio.amateur.antenna**
Newsgroup: **rec.radio.amateur.digital.misc**
Newsgroup: **rec.radio.amateur.equipment**
Newsgroup: **rec.radio.amateur.homebrew**
Newsgroup: **rec.radio.amateur.misc**
Newsgroup: **rec.radio.amateur.packet**
Newsgroup: **rec.radio.amateur.policy**
Newsgroup: **rec.radio.cb**
Newsgroup: **rec.radio.shortwave**
Newsgroup: **rec.radio.swap**

Amateur Radio Information by Mail

Interested in amateur radio? This site has all the information, including how to get started in this exciting hobby. ARRL offers information and files by e-mail.

Mail:
Address: **info@arrl.org**
Body: **help**

Antique Newspaper Column

An electronic newspaper column offering advice and information on a variety of antique gadgets and furniture.

Gopher:
Name: The World
Address: **world.std.com**
Choose: **Periodicals, Magazines, and Journals**
| **Middlesex News** | **Columns** | **Antiques**

Antiques

Capture a bit of the past by collecting antiques and vintage items. Learn to restore your old Victrola, music box, or clock. Find out where you can get issues of the Charlie Chaplin comics. Buy, sell, and trade.

Usenet:
Newsgroup: **rec.antiques**

Aquaria Mailing List

An open discussion about all things related to the hobby of keeping fish and other aquatic things in an aquarium.

Listserv mailing list:
List Address: **aquarium@emuvm1.bitnet**
Subscription Address: **listserv@emuvm1.bitnet**

Photographic images like this can make a good backdrop for your system running Microsoft Windows or X-Window. This image is **swim1a.gif** and was downloaded from Washington University, Saint Louis (**wuarchive.wustl.edu**).

Aquariums

What does it mean when your gourami is leaning thirty degrees to the right? He could be trying to steer, but that's probably not the case. Splash around with other ichthyophiles as you explore the true nature of tropical fish. Learn a wide variety of new things, like the best way to earthquake-proof your tanks, how to name your fish after famous Internet book writers, or what to feed your black piranha when all he really wants is you.

Usenet:
Newsgroup: **alt.aquaria**
Newsgroup: **rec.aquaria**

Archery

You don't have to wear a short top and tights to fit in here. You do have to have a passion for nocking an arrow onto a taut bowstring, pulling the string to its absolute limit, then letting go and seeing the arrow silently sink into your target. Archery is great for so many things—hunting, competition, relaxation—and they are all covered in this group.

Usenet:
Newsgroup: **alt.archery**

Astrology

You've discovered that Uranus is in conjunction with your ascendant ruler, Jupiter. And as if that's not enough, Uranus also squares Mercury, your tenth house ruler, and you have four yods that are creating frustration and dissatisfaction in your life. What's a person to do? Besides calling the psychic hotline, you can post queries or hints to stargazers across the globe, or even—depending on who they know—across the universe.

Usenet:
Newsgroup: **alt.astrology**

Audio

A real audio system will make the windows of your living room bulge. Take the squeak out of your tweeter and the growl out of your woofer with a few helpful hints from the folks who know audio. High-fidelity, high-end and professional audio are some of the topics covered.

Usenet:
Newsgroup: **rec.audio**
Newsgroup: **rec.audio.high-end**
Newsgroup: **rec.audio.pro**

Beads

Beads are not just for jewelry. You can make clothes, home decorations, toys and much more. If you like making beads from scratch, your material is nearly limitless. Paper, clay, glass and synthetics are a few of the things that you can learn how to use. Share your ideas and tips with like-minded bead people.

Usenet:
Newsgroup: **alt.beadworld**

Bird Watching

This is a hobby that can be as simple or as elaborate as you wish. Basic pieces of equipment are a lawn chair, a bird book, and a pair of binoculars—and some birds, of course. On the high end, you can use sophisticated camouflage, blinds and camera equipment. No matter what your aim is, bird watching is an endlessly fascinating pastime.

Usenet:
Newsgroup: **rec.birds**

A B C D E F G H I J K L M N O P Q R S T U V W X Y Z

Bird Watching Mailing Lists

The **birdband** and **birdchat** mailing lists are for anyone interested in wild birds, including endangered and extinct birds, as well as common birds.

Listserv mailing list:
    List Address: **birdband@arizvm1.bitnet**
    Subscription Address: **listserv@arizvm1.bitnet**

    List Address: **birdchat@arizvm1.bitnet**
    Subscription Address: **listserv@arizvm1.bitnet**

Boating

Moving on water, how basic a feeling it invokes within us. Join the boating crowd and discuss all aspects of things that float. The **.paddle** newsgroup is specifically for canoes, rowboats and other paddle-propelled vessels.

Usenet:
    Newsgroup: **rec.boats**
    Newsgroup: **rec.boats.paddle**

Bonsai

Dictionary of terms, soil information, FAQs, reading guides, supplier lists and other material relevant to this ancient art.

Anonymous FTP:
    Address: **bonsai.pass.wayne.edu**
    Path: **/pub/GIFS/***

    Address: **bonsai.pass.wayne.edu**
    Path: **/pub/Information/***

    Address: **rtfm.mit.edu**
    Path: **/pub/usenet/news.answers/bonsai-faq/***

Listserv mailing list:
    List Address: **bonsai@waynest1.bitnet**
    Subscription Address: **listserv@waynest1.bitnet**

Clocks and Watches

A mailing list for people interested in clock and watch collecting, timepiece repair, the history of timekeeping, antique timepieces and trading.

Listserv mailing list:
    List Address: **clocks@suvm.bitnet**
    Subscription Address: **listserv@suvm.bitnet**

Don't be late. Check out **clocks**, the Internet's most timely mailing list.

Coins and Money

All about coins, tokens, and paper money from the world over. Historic U.S. pieces as well as ancient European and Middle Eastern money.

Internet mailing list:
    List Address: **coins@iscsvax.uni.edu**
    Subscription Address:
        coins-request@iscsvax.uni.edu

    List Address: **coins@rocky.er.usgs.gov**
    Subscription Address:
        coins-request@rocky.er.usgs.gov

Collecting

Is there anyone who doesn't collect anything? (We, for example, collect Internet books.) Collecting seems to be part of our heritage as human beings. Thus, if you are human, there is a place in the discussion for you. Use your imagination: anything that can be quantified or categorized is fair game. The **.cards** newsgroup is for those who collect trading cards, both sport and non-sport.

Usenet:
    Newsgroup: **rec.collecting**
    Newsgroup: **rec.collecting.cards**

Comics

Zap! Biff! Pow! Action dialogue brings comics to life. Whether you are a collector or just a person who likes to read comics now and then, you'll love the variety of discussion you can find in Usenet.

Usenet:
    Newsgroup: **alt.comics.batman**
    Newsgroup: **alt.comics.buffalo-roam**
    Newsgroup: **alt.comics.elfquest**
    Newsgroup: **alt.comics.lnh**
    Newsgroup: **alt.comics.superman**
    Newsgroup: **rec.arts.comics.info**
    Newsgroup: **rec.arts.comics.misc**
    Newsgroup: **rec.arts.comics.strips**
    Newsgroup: **rec.arts.comics.xbooks**

Crafts

Relax and be creative with a craft. Anyone can make a craft out of anything. (Remember pop-top art?) Dried flowers, matting, calligraphy, basket-weaving—the list goes on and on, but we have to get to the next item.

Usenet:
> Newsgroup: **rec.crafts.misc**

Drums and Marching

You've seen those rowdy children who sit in the middle of the kitchen floor and beat pots and pans together. What you may not know is that these very same children grow up to become members of the drum corps, where they can make lots of noise and people praise them instead of sending them to their rooms. Join the high-spirited marching bands as they talk tech and tell the world why their group is better than yours.

Usenet:
> Newsgroup: **alt.drumcorps**
> Newsgroup: **rec.arts.marching.drumcorps**
> Newsgroup: **rec.arts.marching.misc**

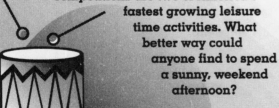

Drums and Marching

You may not know it, but there are a whole lot of people who march to someone else's drummer. Drum-corp groups and competitions are two of America's fastest growing leisure time activities. What better way could anyone find to spend a sunny, weekend afternoon?

Spare time? Take a look at Games

Entertainment Magic

FAQs and book reviews about performing entertainment magic, including close-up, sleight-of-hand, platform, stage and illusion magic.

Anonymous FTP:
> Address: **quartz.rutgers.edu**
> Path: **/pub/misc/magic-faq**
>
> Address: **rtfm.mit.edu**
> Path: **/pub/usenet/news.answers/magic-faq/***

Gopher:
> Name: Rutgers Quartz Text Archive
> Address: **quartz.rutgers.edu**
> Choose: **Miscellaneous | magic-faq**

Equestrian

Why do so many young women love to ride horses? Well, we know, but we can't tell. What we can tell you is that this newsgroup is the place to meet horse lovers of all types for a general discussion of horses, riding and all-round good, clean, equestrian fun.

Usenet:
> Newsgroup: **rec.equestrian**

Exploring Caves

A mailing list to serve as an information resource and forum for anyone interested in exploring caves.

Internet mailing list:
> List Address: **cavers@vlsi.vu.edu**
> Subscription Address: **cavers-request@vlsi.vu.edu**

Fiber Arts

Textiles are so, well, earthy. Sewing, weaving and knitting can be a lot of fun and certainly make for an enjoyable way to relax while creating something useful. Drop in to the ongoing discussion and mix with and meet the sort of people who can cross-stitch and latch-hook in their sleep.

Usenet:
> Newsgroup: **rec.crafts.textiles**

Firearms

This moderated group discusses all manner of firearms and related topics. Remember, if Usenet newsgroups about guns are outlawed, only outlaws will have Usenet newsgroups about guns.

Usenet:
> Newsgroup: **rec.guns**

A
B
C
D
E
F
G
H
I
J
K
L
M
N
O
P
Q
R
S
T
U
V
W
X
Y
Z

Guns

Discussions and material about shooting sports, reloading, training, personal defense, gun laws, weaponry and other topics related to firearms in general.

Anonymous FTP:
Address: **flubber.cs.umd.edu**
Path: **/rec/***

Address: **ftp.vmars.tuwien.ac.at**
Path: **/pub/misc/guns/***

Usenet:
Newsgroup: **rec.guns**

Ham Radio Archives

Archives of interest to ham radio buffs.

Anonymous FTP:
Address: **ftp.cs.buffalo.edu**
Path: **/pub/ham-radio/***

Address: **ftp.cs.tamu.edu**
Path: **/pub/hamradio/***

Address: **oak.oakland.edu**
Path: **/pub/misc/hamradio**

Gopher:
Name: Texas A&M University
Address: **gopher.cs.tamu.edu**
Choose:
   Access to TAMU CS Anonymous FTP Files
 | **hamradio**

Ham Radio Callbooks

The national ham radio call-sign book.

Telnet:
Address: **callsign.cs.buffalo.edu 2000**
Address: **ns.risc.net**
Login: **hamradio**

Juggling

Harley can juggle three oranges at the same time. Rick can juggle numbers. So, when we tell you that juggling is a great way to make friends and influence people, you know we are telling the truth. Join the group and learn how to keep none of your eggs in one basket.

Usenet:
Newsgroup: **rec.juggling**

Kites

Flight is fascinating no matter how rudimentary the form. Kite flying is a hobby that has an enormous following. Some people start from scratch and build their own kites; others work from kits. Then there are those who are perfectly happy with a plastic super-hero kite from the dime store. (Of course, they would never admit that.) Purist or just playful, you can learn a great deal about the skill of flying via a surrogate at the end of a string.

Usenet:
Newsgroup: **rec.kites**

Kiting Information

All the information you need to know about kites. Offers kite reviews, stories, tips on flying, general information, event guides and much more.

Gopher:
Name: University of Surrey
Address: **gopher.cpe.surrey.ac.uk**
Choose: **Kites**

Living History

History seems so exciting in retrospect; much more exciting than it probably was when it was happening. (How interesting is *your* life?) Relive history by joining others who find delight in reenacting historical periods or events. Remember, those who remember history are fated to repeat it.

Usenet:
Newsgroup: **alt.history.living**

Magic

Even after seeing the cut-up tie trick or the lady and the tiger a hundred times, you still can't figure it out. Brush up on your magic and learn some trade secrets. Learn how to make your little brother disappear or how to change that pesky tax auditor into a pen and pencil set. You don't have to sell your soul to the devil, you just have to be more clever than the rest of us.

Usenet:
Newsgroup: **alt.magic**

Massage

Just by using your fingers, you can turn someone into a noodle. Massage is a delicious and therapeutic way to alleviate the effects of tension and ill health. Discover new techniques and new methods of massage along with recommendations for oils and additional things that can take massage to a new level.

Usenet:
Newsgroup: **alt.backrubs**

Metalworking

Get the hammer, the acetylene torch, a pair of tongs, and the right side of your brain, and create wonderful new things made of metal. If you can't handle a scheme that elaborate, then get the box of paper clips from your desk and create a magnificent desk sculpture. Metalworkers find great variety in their metal and use it to their advantage.

Usenet:
Newsgroup: **rec.crafts.metalworking**

Metalworking. . .

doesn't the very idea just make you so. . .

malleable?

Model Railroads

Modeling techniques, railroading information sources, operation guides and notes on real railroads.

Anonymous FTP:
Address: **rtfm.mit.edu**
Path: **/pub/usenet/rec.models.railroad/***

Models

Model building can be a lot of fun. The **.rc** newsgroup is for discussion about radio-controlled models; **.rockets** is for model rockets; **.scale** is for the building of models; **.railroad** is for all types of model railroads; and **alt.models** is for modeling in general.

Usenet:
Newsgroup: **alt.models**
Newsgroup: **rec.models.railroad**
Newsgroup: **rec.models.rc**
Newsgroup: **rec.models.rockets**
Newsgroup: **rec.models.scale**

Motorcycles

Anything named "Harley" is bound to be sexy. No doubt that is why so many people just love their motorcycles. If you just can't live without something hard and powerful, this is the place to be.

Usenet:
Newsgroup: **alt.motorcycles.harley**
Newsgroup: **rec.motorcycles**
Newsgroup: **rec.motorcycles.dirt**
Newsgroup: **rec.motorcycles.harley**
Newsgroup: **rec.motorcycles.racing**

Nudity

Naturists are cool because they never have to iron their clothes. Sense the freedom and vitality of the human body unfettered by fabric. Nudists and naturists discuss the meaning, the legality, and the public's opinion of being naked. If you are looking for a hot game of strip poker, you are bound to be disappointed.

Usenet:
Newsgroup: **rec.nude**

Origami

Discussion of all facets of origami, the Japanese art of paper folding, including bibliographies, folding techniques, display ideas, materials, organizations, tips, tricks and pointers.

Anonymous FTP:
Address: **nstn.ns.ca**
Path: **/listserv/origami-l/***

Internet mailing list:
List Address: **origami-l@nstn.ns.ca**
Subscription Address:
origami-l-request@nstn.ns.ca

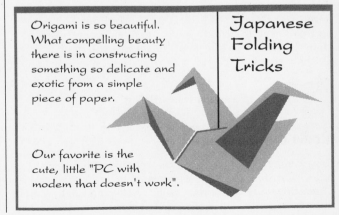

Origami is so beautiful. What compelling beauty there is in constructing something so delicate and exotic from a simple piece of paper.

Our favorite is the cute, little "PC with modem that doesn't work".

Japanese Folding Tricks

A B C D E F G **H** I J K L M N O P Q R S T U V W X Y Z

Outdoors

While the wilderness is not quite as scary as city life, it still has its potential for adventure. If you aren't already captivated with the outdoors, shame on you. It's natural, magical and pure. It also has snakes and poison ivy and, oh yeah, a bear or two. Any activity you can think of doing outdoors is discussed. (Well, almost any activity.) Learn about good camping and hiking equipment, survival training, sledding, safety and much more.

Usenet:
  Newsgroup: **rec.backcountry**

Photography

If you use a point and shoot camera, you might feel out of your league in this neighborhood. While you don't have to be a pro, you might feel lost without the basics on focusing, f-stops, bracketing, and shutter speeds. Photographers love to talk as much as they love to shoot, and they are always ready to give advice and brag about their equipment.

Usenet:
  Newsgroup: **rec.photo**

Puzzles

What's a six-letter word for the best place to read the news? Drive your friends wild with an endless supply of puzzles, quizzes and problems. Open yourself up for a little brain teasing or be merciless and create a mind bender that hardly anyone can solve. (!tenesU :rewsnA)

Usenet:
  Newsgroup: **rec.puzzles**
  Newsgroup: **rec.puzzles.crosswords**

Quilting

Do you like to take small, soft things and join them into large, soft things? Quilting is an old tradition kept alive in this Age of Information by Usenet-savvy enthusiasts. Join the folks who know how to get just the right tension in their hoops.

Usenet:
  Newsgroup: **rec.crafts.quilting**

Radio Broadcasting

Boy, radio has just got to be the best invention since television. Join the folks who love to listen. The **.broadcasting** newsgroup is for discussing local broadcast radio. The **.info** group is for informative postings about radio in general. Both of these groups are moderated. For those who hate advertising, **.noncomm** is for talking about noncommercial radio. Finally, the **.scanner** group is for utility broadcasting, above 30 MHz. (Just the place to learn how to eavesdrop on your neighbor's cordless phone.)

Usenet:
  Newsgroup: **rec.radio.broadcasting**
  Newsgroup: **rec.radio.info**
  Newsgroup: **rec.radio.noncomm**
  Newsgroup: **rec.radio.scanner**

Radio-Controlled Models

Lots of information for hobbyists about all types of radio-controlled models.

Anonymous FTP:
  Address: **rtfm.mit.edu**
  Path: **/pub/usenet/rec.models.rc/***

Railroad

Who's been working on the railroad, all the live-long day? And what has Dinah been doing in the kitchen? Join the railroad fanatics and discuss real and model trains.

Usenet:
  Newsgroup: **rec.railroad**

Roller Coasters

You are utterly terrified, screaming. Your heart is pounding and you think you might vomit. You love every minute of it and want more, more, more. You are addicted to roller coasters. It's okay, because you are not alone. Frenzied coaster fans review the best amusement parks and the top roller coasters in the country and discuss accidents and safety.

Usenet:
  Newsgroup: **rec.roller-coaster**

Sewing

Your bobbin is tangled and your darts are crooked. Needle little advice? Ask questions, get answers, give answers, learn new sewing shortcuts. Whether you're a pro or someone who can't stitch your way out of a paper bag, you'll be able to gain insight into the theory and practice of sewing. (And remember, sewing is not just for women; it just seems that way because men don't do it.)

Usenet:
  Newsgroup: **alt.sewing**

Sewing Archives

Supply information, antique sewing machine guide, trade tips, techniques and patterns with sewing buffs and professionals. Also pointers to historical costuming and textile-related books, and much more material about sewing, fitting and pattern drafting.

Anonymous FTP:
Address: **rtfm.mit.edu**
Path: **/pub/usenet-by-group/alt.sewing**

Address: **rtfm.mit.edu**
Path: **/pub/usenet/news.answers/crafts/
   textiles-books/***

Address: **rtfm.mit.edu**
Path: **/pub/usenet/news.answers/crafts/textiles/***

Siamese Fighting Fish

A mailing list for people interested in keeping and breeding *Betta splendens* (Siamese fighting fish).

Listserv mailing list:
List Address: **bettas@arizvm1.bitnet**
Subscription Address: **listserv@arizvm1.bitnet**

Skateboarding

If you can't skateboard there, why bother going? Maybe because your law firm doesn't like it when you jump the ramp into the office, sliding your briefcase into the receptionist's hands before doing the slalom between all the associates' desks. Beyond that, there's no sense in ever getting off your board. Discover all the clever things you can do with wheels under your feet.

Usenet:
Newsgroup: **alt.skate-board**

Skating

Some people look like they were born with wheels or blades on their feet. The rest of us are like pigs on ice. Hockey, figure skating and rollerblading are the mainstay of this group. Discuss trivia, learn new competition rules on routines and dance music, and discuss the physical rigors of being a skater.

Usenet:
Newsgroup: **alt.skate**

Snowmobiles

A snowmobile is one thing at which you won't have to yell, "Mush!" Feed it some gas, tell it you love it, then ride like a maniac across the frozen tundra (or whatever happens to be in front of you). Avid snowmobile fans tell how they keep their machines happy, safe and healthy.

Usenet:
Newsgroup: **alt.snowmobiles**

Society for Creative Anachronism

Step back in time to the Middle Ages where chivalry lives and everyone's lives are ordered by the rising and setting of the sun. Watch people dress up in metal and hit each other with sticks. Experience the grace and beauty of period costuming. Discover the festivity of a real medieval feast. Members and friends of the SCA discuss how it feels to live life in the modern Middle Ages.

Usenet:
Newsgroup: **alt.heraldry.sca**
Newsgroup: **rec.heraldry**
Newsgroup: **rec.org.sca**

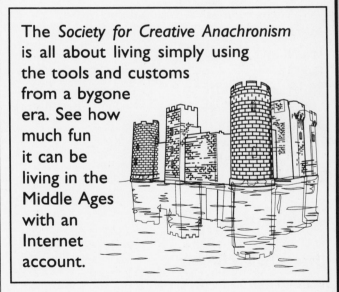

The *Society for Creative Anachronism* is all about living simply using the tools and customs from a bygone era. See how much fun it can be living in the Middle Ages with an Internet account.

Stamp Collecting

Collection of stamp pictures and related material.

Anonymous FTP:
Address: **nic.funet.fi**
Path: **/pub/doc/mail/stamps/***

A B C D E F G H I J K L M N O P Q R S T U V W X Y Z

Steam Engines

A list of over 1400 surviving steam engines in the United States, including location, line and technical information on each.

Anonymous FTP:
Address: **ftp.spies.com**
Path: **/Library/Document/steam.lis**

Gopher:
Name: Internet Wiretap
Address: **wiretap.spies.com**
Choose: **Wiretap Online Library**
| **Assorted Documents**
| **Steam Engines in the United States**

Trading Cards

A forum for people interested in collecting, speculating and investing in baseball, football, basketball, hockey and other trading cards or memorabilia. Discussion is open to anyone and "wanted" and "for sale" lists are welcome.

Internet mailing list:
List Address: **cards@tanstaafl.uchicago.edu**
Subscription Address:
cards-request@tanstaafl.uchicago.edu

Trains and Railways

Material relating to railways and trains, including the history of trains, a list of Amtrak and other trains, and an article on underground stations and wooden railways.

Anonymous FTP:
Address: **quartz.rutgers.edu**
Path: **/pub/railfan/***

Gopher:
Name: Rutgers Quartz Text Archive
Address: **quartz.rutgers.edu**
Choose: **Railfan Info**

Usenet Hobby Groups

Discussion of pastimes, hobbies, crafts and many other recreational activities.

Usenet:
Newsgroup: **rec.***

Woodworking

While it isn't the most forgiving medium, wood is rich in texture and color. Rev-up your chainsaw or sharpen your chisel. Whatever your approach, the wood will yield to your skilled handling of the blade. Your neighbors will probably prefer the chisel approach, but if you use a chainsaw, they probably won't complain. At least not to your face.

Usenet:
Newsgroup: **rec.woodworking**

Woodn't it Be Great?

Wood is so cool–and organic too. There is something about a nicely-shaped piece of wood that can turn on just about anybody. (We call it the Pinocchio factor.) Join the folks on **rec.woodworking** *and see what's happening wood-wise.*

Woodworking Archives

Discussions of tools, safety notes, FAQ, Woodsmith plans, electric woodworking motor information, and supplier addresses.

Anonymous FTP:
Address: **ftp.cs.purdue.edu**
Path: **/pub/sjc/woodworking/***

Address: **ftp.cs.rochester.edu**
Path: **/pub/rec.woodworking/***

Address: **rtfm.mit.edu**
Path: **/pub/usenet/news.answers/woodworking/***

HOME CARE AND IMPROVEMENT

Controlling Pests

Information and control guides to common pests found in the home, yard and garden, including fabric pests, house flies, Japanese beetles and millipedes.

Gopher:
Name: University of Delaware
Address: **lobster.mis.udel.edu**
Choose: **UD Department & College Information Services**
| **AGINFO: College of Agricultural Sciences**
| **Fact Sheets** | **Home, Yard and Garden**

HOMOSEXUALITY/ BISEXUALITY

Bisexuality

The Internet offers some important forums for bisexuals: people who are attracted to both men and women. The **biact-l** mailing list is for bisexual activists; **bifem-l** is for female bisexuals; **bisexu-l** is for general discussion.

Usenet:
　　Newsgroup: **soc.bi**

Listserv mailing list:
　　List Address: **biact-l@brownvm.brown.edu**
　　Subscription Address:
　　　　listserv@brownvm.brown.edu

　　List Address: **bifem-l@brownvm.brown.edu**
　　Subscription Address:
　　　　listserv@brownvm.brown.edu

　　List Address: **bisexu-l@brownvm.brown.edu**
　　Subscription Address:
　　　　listserv@brownvm.brown.edu

Homosexuality

Members of the same sex (MOTSS) discuss their thoughts, feelings and experiences about being gay. The general group on homosexuality covers a wide range of topics on how gays relate to the rest of the world, while the **.motss** groups discuss how gays relate to one another.

Usenet:
　　Newsgroup: **alt.homosexual**
　　Newsgroup: **alt.sex.motss**
　　Newsgroup: **soc.motss**

Homosexuality and Gay Rights

Don't be taken in by rumors and gossip. Read the real news on homosexuality and gay rights. Significant upcoming events and current events are highlighted.

Usenet:
　　Newsgroup: **clari.news.group.gays**

Politics and Homosexuality

Gays in the military and child custody battles put the politics of homosexuality on the front page. Discuss the latest civil rights cases, pending legislation, and who to boycott (or not). Keep informed so you can make a difference in your community.

Usenet:
　　Newsgroup: **alt.politics.homosexuality**

HUMANITIES

American Philosophical Association BBS

A BBS offering information about philosophical societies, grants, fellowships, seminars and institutes. Also a mail directory of the APA membership and bibliographical and journal information.

Gopher:
　　Name: Occidental College
　　Address: **apa.oxy.edu**

Cognition

Selection of publications about cognition, the mind, and related subjects from the Indiana-based Center for Research on Concepts and Cognition.

Anonymous FTP:
　　Address: **moocow.cogsci.indiana.edu**
　　Path: **/pub/***

Coombspapers Social Sciences Research Data Bank

Electronic repository of the social science and humanities papers, offprints, departmental publications, bibliographies, directories, abstracts of theses and other material.

Anonymous FTP:
　　Address: **wuarchive.wustl.edu**
　　Path: **/doc/coombspapers/***

Gopher:
　　Name: Australian National University
　　Address: **coombs.anu.edu.au**
　　Choose: **Coombspapers Soc.Sci.Research Data Bank**

Humanist Mailing List

A large international discussion group for humanists and for those who support the application of computers in the humanities.

Listserv mailing list:
　　List Address: **humanist@brownvm.brown.edu**
　　Subscription Address:
　　　　listserv@brownvm.brown.edu

A B C D E F G H I J K L M N O P Q R S T U V W X Y Z

Objectivism Mailing List

Students of Objectivism and Ayn Rand discuss ideas, concrete issues, and exchange news. Any issue of relevance to Objectivists is welcomed.

Internet mailing list:
> List Address: **objectivism@vix.com**
> Subscription Address:
> > **objectivism-request@vix.com**

Personal Ideologies Discussion List

"What is good?" "What happens after death?" These are topics the Personal Ideologies mailing list attempts to cover.

Internet mailing list:
> List Address: **belief-l@brownvm.brown.edu**
> Subscription Address:
> > **belief-l-request@brownvm.brown.edu**

Resource Guides

Internet resource guides for diversity, linguistics, mysticism, philosophy, psychology, religious studies and history.

Anonymous FTP:
> Address: **una.hh.lib.umich.edu**
> Path: **/inetdirs/humanities/***

Gopher:
> Name: University of Michigan
> Address: **una.hh.lib.umich.edu**
> Choose: **Inetdirs**
> > **| Guides on the Humanities (UMich)**

HUMOR

Amusing Tests and Quizzies

A collection of humorous tests, including a life quiz, a nerd test, creativity test and the feminist quiz.

Anonymous FTP:
> Address: **quartz.rutgers.edu**
> Path: **/pub/humor/Tests/***

Gopher:
> Name: Rutgers Quartz Text Archive
> Address: **quartz.rutgers.edu**
> Choose: **Humor | Tests**

Bastard Operator from Hell

A hilarious sequence of stories about a system operator you *don't* want running your system.

Anonymous FTP:
> Address: **rs3.hrz.th-darmstadt.de**
> Path: **/pub/docs/fun/bastard-operator.tar.Z**

> Address: **sunsite.unc.edu**
> Path: **/pub/docs/humor/bastard-operator**

Archie:
> Pattern: **bastard-op**

British Humor

England has a long tradition of world-famous comedians: Prince Charles, Margaret Thatcher, Neville Chamberlain, and on and on. If you are a fan of British humour, tune in to this newsgroup and discuss your favorite TV shows, performers, movies and personalities.

Usenet:
> Newsgroup: **alt.comedy.british**

Nothing is funnier than *British Humor*

(except maybe their food, or the weather, or the Royal Family, or. . .)

Canonical List of Steven Wright Jokes

The definitive collection of Steven Wright (and similar) jokes.

Mail:
> Address: **ajs@ajs.fc.hp.com**

Cathouse Archives

Hundreds of humorous and amusing files. Animal jokes, ASCII art, why a * is better than a *, British humour, holiday jokes, Dave Barry, geography, sex, jobs, life, politics, Murphy's laws, political correctness, quotes, religion, sports and much more.

Anonymous FTP:
> Address: **cathouse.org**
> Path: **/pub/cathouse**

Classic Practical Jokes

Read about some of the best practical jokes ever perpetrated and contribute your own experiences.

Anonymous FTP:
Address: **elf.tn.cornell.edu**
Path: **/shenanigans/***

Usenet:
Newsgroup: **alt.shenanigans**

College Humor

College humor has certainly come a long way since Max Shulman and Dobie Gillis (who?). Join the discussion and hear some real, honest-to-god stories, rumors and anecdotes—some of which might even be true.

Usenet:
Newsgroup: **alt.folklore.college**

Excerpt from the Net...

```
Newsgroup: alt.folklore.college
Subject: Early birds

> Someone here just did a poll on vir-
> ginity at The University of
> Pennsylvania.
>
> The Results:
>    Over 50% of incoming freshman are
> virgins.
>    Less than 20% of outgoing seniors
> are virgins.
>
> What does this mean?

It means that if you're into virgins,
come and get it fast during freshman
orientation.
```

Comics

Discussions about the comic *Watchmen*, and a bibliography, episode guide and glossary for the comic book *Cerebus*.

Anonymous FTP:
Address: **ftp.white.toronto.edu**
Path: **/pub/comics/***

Firesign Theater

Firesign Theater, an American comedy and satire group from the 1970s, has a cult following. Join this group to discuss what-ever-happened-to-so-and-so, as well as upcoming appearances by ex-FST members, and a host of trivia questions. Read the regularly posted FAQ list and find out if we really are all bozos on this bus.

Usenet:
Newsgroup: **alt.comedy.firesgn-thtre**
Newsgroup: **alt.fan.firesign-theatre**

Don't Crush That Gopher, Hand Me the Telnet

Firesign Theater is one of the highest achievements of modern American theater. However, you need to have just the right type of warped mind to appreciate it. Fortunately, we do; and so can you.

Tune in to the **Firesign Theater** Usenet groups and join George Tirebiter, Ralph Spoilsport and Nick Danger back on the Internet (which is already in progress...)

Funny News

Every now and then, something funny happens in the real world (the one that you don't need a computer to access). Read about such happenings here.

Usenet:
Newsgroup: **clari.news.interest.quirks**

Funny People

Usenet has a whole set of newsgroups devoted to the worship and discussion of various famous people and their work. Humor, of course, is well represented. Join the disciples and discuss your favorite humorists: Bill Gates, Dave Barry, Andrew Dice Clay, the Goons (from the old *Goon Show*), David Letterman, Monty Python, Terry Pratchett, P.G. Wodehouse (pronounced "Woodhouse", please) and Woody Allen.

Usenet:
Newsgroup: **alt.fan.bill-gates**
Newsgroup: **alt.fan.dave_barry**
Newsgroup: **alt.fan.dice-man**
Newsgroup: **alt.fan.goons**
Newsgroup: **alt.fan.letterman**
Newsgroup: **alt.fan.monty-python**
Newsgroup: **alt.fan.pratchett**
Newsgroup: **alt.fan.wodehouse**
Newsgroup: **alt.fan.woody-allen**

A B C D E F G H I J K L M N O P Q R S T U V W X Y Z

Funny Texts

A selection of humorous articles and stories.

Gopher:
Name: Universidade Nova de Lisboa
Address: **gopher.fct.unl.pt**
Choose: **Public info | Humor | Funny Texts**

Make sure you are prepared: Read Emergency and Disaster.

Hacker Test

Find out if you are a Computer Illiterate, nerd, hacker, guru or wizard with this set of questions.

Gopher:
Name: Universitaet des Saarlandes
Address: **pfsparc02.phil15.uni-sb.de**
Choose: **INFO-SYSTEM BENUTZEN | Fun | Hacker**

Humor Archives

Massive collections of jokes, anecdotes, humorous stories, one-liners, and riddles.

Anonymous FTP:
Address: **donau.et.tudelft.nl**
Path: **/pub/humor**

Excerpt from the Net...

```
Newsgroup: alt.fan.bill-gates
Subject: Top 10 ways a computer guy can impress his date

THE TOP TEN WAYS A COMPUTER GUY CAN IMPRESS HIS DATE

10. Flash the big wads of tens and twenties you created with your color laser printer
    and top-notch graphics program.

 9. Spend an evening playing floppy disks backward, listening for the secret messages
    about Satan.

 8. Invite her back to your place to show her the etchings on your Newton MessagePad.

 7. Let the lady go first when you reach the virtual reality escalator.

 6. Serenade her with your MIDI-compatible drum pads.

 5. Have your dinner illuminated by the soft glow of an active-matrix LCD panel.

 4. If you're getting serious, consider a set of "his 'n' her" system unit keys.

 3. Drive her crazy by murmuring tender love words with the help of a French-speaking
    voice synthesizer.

 2. Never type on your date's laptop computer without permission, particularly if the
    system is on her lap.

AND THE #1 WAY A COMPUTER GUY CAN IMPRESS HIS DATE:

 1. When things get tough, simply ask yourself, "What would Bill Gates do in a
    situation like this?"
```

Address: **ftp.cco.caltech.edu**
Path: **/pub/bjmccall/non-political/Funny**

Address: **ftp.cs.dal.ca**
Path: **/comp.archives/alt.humor.oracle**

Address: **ftp.cs.dal.ca**
Path: **/comp.archives/rec.humor**

Address: **ftp.cs.dal.ca**
Path: **/comp.archives/rec.humor.d**

Address: **ftp.spies.com**
Path: **/Library/Humor/***

Address: **ftp.uu.net**
Path: **/doc/literary/obi/DEC/humor**

Address: **gatekeeper.dec.com**
Path: **/pub/misc/humour**

Address: **jerico.usc.edu**
Path: **/pub/jamin/sciina**

Address: **mc.lcs.mit.edu**
Path: **/its/ai/humor**

Address: **nic.funet.fi**
Path: **/pub/doc/humour**

Address: **ocf.berkeley.edu**
Path: **/pub/Library/Humor**

Address: **quartz.rutgers.edu**
Path: **/pub/humor**

Address: **rascal.ics.utexas.edu**
Path: **/misc/funny**

Address: **shape.mps.ohio-state.edu**
Path: **/pub/jokes**

Address: **sifon.cc.mcgill.ca**
Path: **/pub/docs/misc/dave_barry**

Address: **slopoke.mlb.semi.harris.com**
Path: **/pub/doc/humor**

Address: **theta.iis.u-tokyo.ac.jp**
Path: **/JUNET-DB/jokes**

Address: **toklab.ics.osaka-u.ac.jp**
Path: **/JUNET-DB/jokes**

Address: **tolsun.oulu.fi**
Path: **/pub/humor**

Address: **trantor.ee.msstate.edu**
Path: **/files/Text**

Gopher:
Name: Internet Wiretap
Address: **wiretap.spies.com**
Choose: **Wiretap Online Library | Humor**

Jive Server

Send a mail message to this system and, within minutes, you'll receive your message translated into jive. Example: "Ask not, what your country can do for you, but what you can do for your country," becomes "Ask not, whut yo' country kin do fo' ya', but whut ya' kin do fo' yo' country. Slap mah fro!"

Mail:
Address: **jive@ifi.unizh.ch**

Joke Collections

Irish jokes, condom jokes, elephant jokes, lightbulb jokes, sorority girl jokes, Clinton jokes, offensive jokes, math jokes, nun jokes, religious jokes, lawyer jokes and blonde jokes—not necessarily in that order.

Anonymous FTP:
Address: **ftp.spies.com**
Path: **/Library/Humor/Jokes/***

Gopher:
Name: Internet Wiretap
Address: **wiretap.spies.com**
Choose: **Wiretap Online Library | Humor
| Jokes**

Joke Database

Find that perfect joke for every occasion by performing a keyword search of this extensive database.

Gopher:
Name: University of Manchester
Address: **uts.mcc.ac.uk**
Choose: **Gopher Services | The Joke File**

**Got too much stuff?
Need some more stuff?
Try
Buying and Selling.**

A
B
C
D
E
F
G
H
I
J
K
L
M
N
O
P
Q
R
S
T
U
V
W
X
Y
Z

Jokes

Here is the most important place on the entire Internet: the joke-telling newsgroup. Anyone may post a joke about anything (although truly tasteless jokes are best sent to **alt.tasteless.jokes**). Beginners note: The **.d** newsgroup is for the discussion of jokes or for requests (such as "Does anyone have the canonical list of Hillary and Beavis jokes?"). The **rec.humor** group is for jokes only.

Usenet:
    Newsgroup: **rec.humor**
    Newsgroup: **rec.humor.d**

Jokes, Moderated

This moderated group is to **rec.humor** what CompuServe is to the Internet: there is Someone in Charge. All jokes are submitted to a moderator who posts the ones she thinks are funny. What this means is that, unlike **rec.humor**, you don't have to wade through a whole lot of junk, silliness and bad jokes. It also means that you have to put up with irritating messages that are tacked onto the end of each joke, as well as regularly posted draconian ukases setting out rules and regulations. Still, this newsgroup is one of the most popular on the entire Usenet (in our estimation, coming between **rec.arts.erotica** and **alt.sex.bondage**).

Usenet:
    Newsgroup: **rec.humor.funny**

Jokes and Stories

A collection of popular jokes and humorous stories, such as, "A Role-player's Famous Last Words" and "The Vaxorcist".

Gopher:
    Name: Technische Universitaet Muenchen
    Address: **gopher.informatik.tu-muenchen.de**
    Choose: **ISAR Gopher | Vershiedenes
      | Satirische Texte und Witze (Englisch)**

The Internet will set you free

Manly Men's Ten Commandments

It is hoped that all men obey these sacred laws, for any breach of these written rules will be considered a sin against womanhood, and may result in the loss of manly privileges such as *Monday Night Football*.

Gopher:
    Name: Manchester Computing Centre
    Address: **uts.mcc.ac.uk**
    Choose: **Experimental..
      | Manly-Men's Ten Commandments**

Monty Python's Flying Circus

Collection of all the popular Monty Python sketches and screenplays, including *Holy Grail* and *Life of Brian*.

Anonymous FTP:
    Address: **nic.funet.fi**
    Path: **/pub/culture/tv+film/series/MontyPython**

    Address: **ocf.berkeley.edu**
    Path: **/pub/Library/Monty_Python**

Nothing to do? Download some Monty Python skits and put on a show for your friends.

More Comics

Graphics and album lists from a selection of comics, including *Tintin*, and *The French Valerian*.

Anonymous FTP:
    Address: **nic.funet.fi**
    Path: **/pub/culture/comics/***

Too much spare time?
Explore a MUD

ADVERTISEMENT

They Laughed When I Stood Up To Tell a Joke

A True Story by Albert Gendeau

Yes, it's true.

I'm not ashamed to admit it. I would stand up at a party to tell a joke and everyone would laugh—at me.

But that was before I discovered the Internet humor resources.

Now I am the life of more parties than an Italian parliamentary coalition. Beautiful women cross the room just to ask me if I've heard any good ones lately. Celebrities call my private phone number and leave fawning messages on my answering machine. Headwaiters at exclusive restaurants slip folded fifty dollar bills into my palm and ask me if I want a seat near the band.

And yet, only 2 years ago, my joke repertoire was so poor I couldn't afford to pay attention. I was lower than a centipede with flat feet.

My boss had fired me for telling light bulb jokes during business meetings. My best girl had dumped me for some clown who could imitate Bart Simpson singing Bob Dylan songs. Irate bill collectors were threatening to repossess my collection of Steve Martin albums.

Perhaps worst of all, I had lost my self-respect.

I knew that I had hit bottom when I found myself in bed, reading old Scrooge McDuck comics and watching reruns of *The Cosby Show*. I was so desperate that I considered ending it all. In fact, I had even written a suicide note reading "A-the-be-dibby-the-the-THAT'SALL FOLKS".

Fortunately, Fate stepped in and saved me.

It happened late one night when, in a fit of desperation, I had called the suicide hotline and was put on hold. As I was waiting, I heard a tiny voice say "Use the Internet, use the Internet". (Later, I found out it was the woman next door, entertaining her boyfriend.)

At the time, it was a sign from heaven. The very next day, I rushed out and bought a copy of *The Internet Complete Reference*. Later that day, I contacted a local Internet access provider and signed up.

Within a week, I was swaggering around cyberspace like a pro. In those early days, I virtually lived on Usenet. I spent hours in **rec.humor** and lapped up every morsel I could from **rec.humor.funny**. I even read the Submission Guidelines, marvelling at Brad Templeton's suave grasp of the obvious, and Maddi Hausmann's wry sense of humor.

Within days, I had graduated to **alt.tasteless.jokes**, revelling in blond jokes, the canonical list of ASCII nudes, and the 1001 question Purity Test.

Soon I had mastered FTP and the Catstyle Archives became my second home. I downloaded all the Monty Python sketches and, with the help of my stuffed bear, acted them out in my living room for my friends and neighbors.

Best of all, my love life improved beyond measure. All I had to do was hunt down the list of Steven Wright jokes, memorize them, and hang around the local bowling alley, casually tossing off one sardonic observation after another. My personal phone book is now so large that I need a wheelbarrow just to carry it from one room to another.

Okay, I know what you are saying to yourself: This could happen to Albert, but it could never happen to a goofball like me. But that's where you are wrong. The Internet is an equal access network—even goofballs like you can use it and laugh yourself silly. Just consider these actual testimonials from satisfied users:

> "The first time I read **rec.humor** I laughed so hard I thought I'd die."
> — J. Kevorkian

> "Even I am grossed out by **alt.tasteless.jokes**."
> — H. Stern

> "I love reading all those jokes about young women. (I only wish I could remember why.)"
> — G. Burns

Humor. Jokes. Funny stuff. Success. Money. Power. Romance.

It's all there on the Internet, waiting for you.

Yes, they used to laugh when I stood up to tell a joke. Now, they have to beg me to stop.

Nerd Humor

Computer humor of all sorts, including computer songs, smileys, Story of Creation, Turing Shroud, and Unix Wars.

Anonymous FTP:
Address: **ftp.spies.com**
Path: **/Library/Humor/Nerd/***

Gopher:
Name: Internet Wiretap
Address: **wiretap.spies.com**
Choose: **Wiretap Online Library | Humor | Nerd Humor**

Netwit Mailing List

Netwit is a mailing list of jokes and "net humor".

Mail:
Address: **help@netwit.cmhnet.org**
Body: **add** *your@own.address*

Address: **netwit@netwit.cmhnet.org**
Body: **add** *your@own.address*

Oracle

You send in any question you want to the Usenet Oracle. After a short wait, you receive your response. Great, you say, the wondrous powers of omnipotent wisdom are at my disposal whenever I want. Then you notice a catch: in return for answering your question, the Oracle sends YOU a question to answer. Why not, you say, maybe the Oracle is overworked this week, and it is really quite a compliment to be asked for my opinion. Then you notice that whenever you ask a question, you are sent one in return. Eventually you catch on, "Why, we are all just answering..." Well, we're sure you don't need our help to figure it out (especially if you have ever sold Amway products). The Usenet Oracle is a time-honored tradition. Read the best of the Oracle's answers in the moderated group **rec.humor.oracle**. The .d group is non-moderated and is for an open discussion of the Oracle's wisdom.

Usenet:
Newsgroup: **rec.humor.oracle**
Newsgroup: **rec.humor.oracle.d**

Oracle: Wisdom in Its Ultimate Form

No problem is too small, no quandry too big. Whatever you need, whenever you need it, the Usenet Oracle is there for you. Get in on the ground floor of what is sure to be the new computer-based religion of the Age of the Internet. Remember, even God started as a cult figure.

Parodies

Parodies of popular movies and TV shows.

Anonymous FTP:
Address: **ocf.berkeley.edu**
Path: **/pub/Library/Parodies**

Religious Humor

Humor related to a number of religions.

Anonymous FTP:
Address: **quartz.rutgers.edu**
Path: **/pub/humor/Religion/***

Gopher:
Name: Rutgers Quartz Text Archive
Address: **quartz.rutgers.edu**
Choose: **Humor | Religion**

This is the first book of the rest of your life

Streamlined Bill O' Rights

The new, streamlined Bill O' Rights, as amended by the recent federal and state decisions.

Gopher:
>Name: NASA Goddard Space Flight Center
>Address: **gopher.gsfc.nasa.gov**
>Choose: **Other Resources**
>> **| Bill O' Rights**

Tasteless (and Dirty) Jokes

Don't read this newsgroup unless you want to see sickening, tasteless, repulsive, humiliating, insulting jokes and stories (many of which are silly, but—like Congressmen—you get what you pay for). Don't you dare post anything that is not tasteless. And don't you dare complain that anything in this newsgroup offends you. You have been warned... now check it out.

Usenet:
>Newsgroup: **alt.tasteless.jokes**

Ten Commandments for C Programmers

Example: "Thou shalt check the array bounds of all strings (indeed, all arrays), for surely where thou typest *foo* someone someday shall type *supercalifragilisticexpialidocious*.

Anonymous FTP:
>Address: **ucselx.sdsu.edu**
>Path: **/pub/doc/general/ten-commandments**

Ten Commandments for C Programmers (Annotated)

The annotated edition of this humorous document for C programmers.

Anonymous FTP:
>Address: **ftp.spies.com**
>Path: **/Library/Techdoc/Language/c-command.10**

Gopher:
>Name: Internet Wiretap
>Address: **wiretap.spies.com**
>Choose: **Wiretap Online Library**
>> **| Technical Information | Languages**
>> **| Ten Commandments for C Programmers**

Tintin

Extensive list of *Tintin* comic albums and scanned images of album covers.

Anonymous FTP:
>Address: **nic.funet.fi**
>Path: **/pub/culture/comics/Tintin/***

Toxic Custard Workshop

Complete archives for this mildly warped and totally entertaining set of brain drippings from Australia.

Anonymous FTP:
>Address: **ftp.cs.widener.edu**
>Path: **/pub/tcwf/***

Toxic Custard Workshop Files

A dry, hilariously funny newsletter about everything and nothing. It's occasionally available through Usenet, but send mail to the address below for more information.

Mail:
>Address: **tcwf@gnu.ai.mit.edu**

Virus Jokes

A collection of amusing computer virus jokes.

Gopher:
>Name: North Dakota State University
>Address: **chiphead.cc.ndsu.nodak.edu**
>Choose: **Other Stuff | Fun Stuff | Virus Alert**

The Internet has lots of free software. Check out Computers, Software and Operating Systems.

The only place where Politics comes before Star Trek is in the Internet Yellow Pages.

A B C D E F G H I J K L M N O P Q R S T U V W X Y Z

INTERNET

Future of the Internet

Information and technical proposals for the future of the Internet.

Mail:
   Address: **Internet-drafts@nri.reston.va.us**
   Body: **help**

GopherMail

A guide to accessing Gopher resources via electronic mail. This is useful for people with no direct Internet access, but who have electronic mail.

Gopher:
   Name: National Institute for Physiological Sciences
   Address: **gopher.nips.ac.jp**
   Choose: **About GopherMail**

Internet Engineering

Charters, technical documents, service, and up-to-date activity information about the Internet Engineering Task Force (IETF).

Anonymous FTP:
   Address: **wuarchive.wustl.edu**
   Path: **/doc/ietf/***

Internet Growth Statistics

Figures and statistics showing the growth of the Internet, as well as discussion of other global networks, including the Bitnet, uucp and Fidonet.

Anonymous FTP:
   Address: **tic.com**
   Path: **/matrix/growth/internet/***

Gopher:
   Name: NYSERNet
   Address: **nysernet.org**
   Choose: **Special Collections: Internet Help**
    | Growth information about the Internet

Internet Society Gopher

Contains detailed information about the Internet Society, including conference news, charts and graphics, newsletters and other general information related to the technical side of the Internet.

Gopher:
   Name: Corporation for National Research Initiatives
   Address: **ietf.cnri.reston.va.us**

Internet Worm

Technical papers and reports about the Internet Worm, the program that crippled the Internet.

Anonymous FTP:
   Address: **nic.funet.fi**
   Path: **/pub/doc/security/worm/***

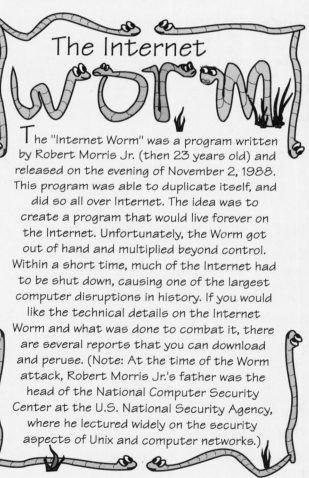

The Internet Worm

The "Internet Worm" was a program written by Robert Morris Jr. (then 23 years old) and released on the evening of November 2, 1988. This program was able to duplicate itself, and did so all over Internet. The idea was to create a program that would live forever on the Internet. Unfortunately, the Worm got out of hand and multiplied beyond control. Within a short time, much of the Internet had to be shut down, causing one of the largest computer disruptions in history. If you would like the technical details on the Internet Worm and what was done to combat it, there are several reports that you can download and peruse. (Note: At the time of the Worm attack, Robert Morris Jr.'s father was the head of the National Computer Security Center at the U.S. National Security Agency, where he lectured widely on the security aspects of Unix and computer networks.)

InterNIC Information Services

Find information about people, organizations and resources on the Internet. Also find and retrieve documents from all over the world with lookups by name or keyword.

Telnet:
   Address: **ds.internic.net**
   Address: **rs.internic.net**

Excerpt from the Net...

(from Internet Growth Statistics)

Here is a graph (in logarithmic scale), showing the growth of the Internet. The "@" characters show an estimate of the number of hosts (that is, computers connected to the Internet) at various times.

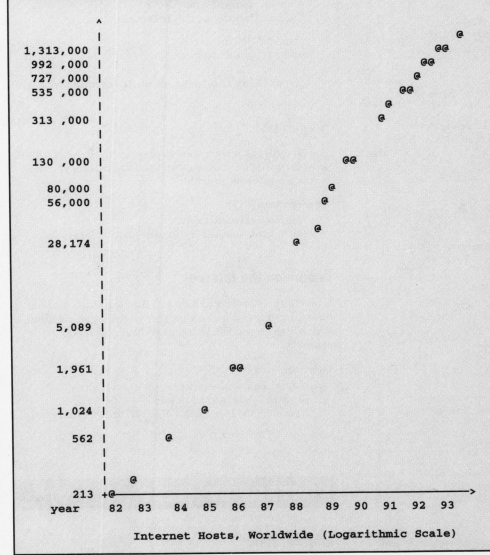

Internet Hosts, Worldwide (Logarithmic Scale)

**Lonely?
Try the Personals**

**Why be normal?
Read Bizarre**

A
B
C
D
E
F
G
H
I
J
K
L
M
N
O
P
Q
R
S
T
U
V
W
X
Y
Z

InterText Magazine

A network-distributed bi-monthly magazine covering a wide range of topics from science fiction to humor, fantasy and horror.

Gopher:
Name: University of Maryland
Address: **info.umd.edu**
Choose: **Educational Resources | The Reading Room | Miscellaneous | InterText**

IP Address Resolver

This resource will determine the IP address of an Internet site and send you a mail message with the address. Useful for people who don't have access to the **host** or **nslookup** command.

Mail:
Address: **dns@grasp.insa-lyon.fr**
Body: **site** *site name*

Address: **resolve@cs.widener.edu**
Body: **site** *site name*

Loopback Service

Use this Internet address and you'll bounce back to your own system.

Telnet:
Address: **127.0.0.1**

Net Happenings

A mailing list of everything interesting going on with the Net. Includes interesting events such as The Geek of the Week contest.

Listserv mailing list:
List Address: **net-happenings@is.internic.net**
Subscription Address: **listserv@is.internic.net**

Need a laugh?
Check out Humor

Network Information Services

Easy access to information about important networks and information services around the globe, including ASK, DDN, Hytelnet, Janet, MichNet and others.

Gopher:
Name: Yale University
Address: **yaleinfo.yale. edu**
Choose: **People on the Internet**

Name: Yale University
Address: **yaleinfo.yale.edu**
Choose:
Searching the Internet with various tools

Nixpub List

The Nixpub list is a comprehensive list of Internet providers. The list contains all the information you need to find an Internet provider.

Anonymous FTP:
Address: **rtfm.mit.edu**
Path: **/pub/usenet-by-group/alt.bbs/Nixpub***

People on the Internet

Collection of services to help you find that lost comrade on the Internet. It includes access to Knowbot, Netfind, PSI White Pages, UK searches, Whois and X.500 searches.

Gopher:
Name: Yale University
Address: **yaleinfo.yale.edu**
Choose: **The Internet | People on the Internet**

INTERNET: HELP

Internet Help

Collection of documents, guides, and publications to help you find your way around the vastness of the Internet. Includes a FAQ, *Hitchiker's Guide to the Internet, Zen and the Art of the Internet* and much more.

Gopher:
Name: Yale University
Address: **yaleinfo.yale.edu**
Choose: **The Internet | Help about the Internet**

Internet Information

Over fifty documents and resources detailing the Internet, its resources, its culture and its technical features.

Gopher:
Name: Swedish University Network
Address: **sunic.sunet.se**
Choose: **Internet Information**

Jargon File

Pronunciation, definitions and examples of computer and Internet terms, acronyms and abbreviations. Humorous, but informative. This file is available via Anonymous FTP from many sites, one of which is listed below. Search for **jargon** with Archie for other sites.

Anonymous FTP:
Address: **world.std.com**
Path: **/obi/Nerd.Humor/webster/jargon**

Wais:
Database: **jargon**

Let's Go Gopherin' Now

Everybody's learnin' how. Workshop tutorials to help the novice learn to surf the Net with a Gopher board.

Anonymous FTP:
Address: **ubmv.cc.buffalo.edu**
Path: **/gophern/***

Gopher:
Name: University of Saarbruecken, Gopher-Project
Address: **pfsparc02.phil15.uni-sb.de**
Choose: **INFO-SYSTEM BENUTZEN...**
 | GOPHER allgemain... | Kuerzlich...
 | Listen | gophern

Listserv mailing list:
List Address: **gophern@ubvm.cc.buffalo.edu**
Subscription Address:
 listserv@ubvm.cc.buffalo.edu

Usenet:
Newsgroup: **bit.listserv.gophern**

> # Spare time?
> # Take a look at Games

Merit Network Information Center

A Gopher operated by the Merit network that provides information on a variety of topics, including how to connect to the Internet, how to Anonymous FTP, the National Research Education Network, and links to the National Science Foundation Network.

Gopher:
Name: Merit Computer Network
Address: **nic.merit.edu**

FOR SOME QUICK INTERNET INFORMATION, TRY THE **MERIT NETWORK INFORMATION CENTER GOPHER.**

Mining the Internet

A tutorial on using the Internet from the University of California. Request this document by mailing Gee Lee.

Mail:
Address: **gblee@ucdavis.edu**

Real Life on the Internet

Examples of real uses of the Internet. Real people working through real problems.

Anonymous FTP:
Address: **wuarchive.wustl.edu**
Path: **/doc/internet-info/user.profiles**

Surfing the Internet

A short introduction to the Internet, by Jean Armour Polly. *Surfing the Internet* was originally written for librarians, but has proven popular with Internet users everywhere.

Anonymous FTP:
Address: **nysernet.org**
Path: **/pub/resources/guides/surfing.2.0.3.txt**

Gopher:
Name: NyserNet
Address: **nysernet.org**
Choose: **Special Collections: Internet Help**
 | Surfing the Internet

A B C D E F G H I J K L M N O P Q R S T U V W X Y Z

Tutorial for PC Users

A computer-based tutorial, written by Pat Suarez, in the form of a DOS program that you can download and run on your own PC. The tutorial describes all the basic Internet services and is a good way for beginners to start learning about the Internet.

Anonymous FTP:
> Address: **oak.oakland.edu**
> Path: **/pub/msdos/info/bgi12.zip**

**Tutorial for PC Users-
An Easy Way to Learn
About the Internet**

Are you new to the Internet?

**If you have a PC, download the tutorial by
Pat Suarez and start teaching yourself.
Then, rush out and buy a copy of**

The Internet Complete Reference

Why Are Internet Resources Free?

Article discussing why most of the resources on the Internet are provided at no cost.

Anonymous FTP:
> Address: **ftp.spies.com**
> Path: **/Library/Cyber/freeserv.net**

Gopher:
> Name: Internet Wiretap
> Address: **wiretap.spies.com**
> Choose: **Wiretap Online Library | Cyberspace
> | Why are Internet Resources Free?**

INTERNET: RESOURCES

Anonymous FTP Site List

A huge list of Anonymous FTP sites on the Internet.

Anonymous FTP:
> Address: **ftp.shsu.edu**
> Path: **/pub/ftp-list/sites.Z**

Data Explorer

Tutorials, news, examples, extensions and other information for the IBM Visualization Data Explorer software.

Anonymous FTP:
> Address: **info.tc.cornell.edu**
> Path: **/pub/Data.Explorer/***

Gopher:
> Name: Cornell University
> Address: **gopher.tc.cornell.edu**
> Choose: **Anonymous FTP
> | Data Explorer Repository**

Database via Finger

Several databases provided for public use by the University of Sydney, Australia. Finger for more information and instructions.

Finger:
> Address: **help@dir.su.oz.au**

Databases via Telnet

Access major commercial and free databases around the world, including Nicolas, Penpages, Dow Jones, Epic/Firstsearch and Orbit.

Gopher:
> Name: Swedish University Network
> Address: **sunic.sunet.se**
> Choose: **Library Services | Databases via Telnet**

> Name: Swedish University of Agricultural Sciences
> Address: **pinus.slu.se**
> Choose: **Databases via telnet**

December List

Information sources on the Internet.

Anonymous FTP:
> Address: **ftp.rpi.edu**
> Path: **/pub/communications/internet-cmc**

Discovering Internet Resources

A document describing various methods to retrieve information from the Internet. The document covers Archie, Gopher, Wais and World-Wide Web.

Gopher:
> Name: National Chung Cheng University
> Address: **gopher.ccu.edu.tw**
> Choose: **Information Resources
> | About Resource.. | Networked Info..
> | intdiscovery.doc**

Distance Learning Resources

Dr. E's Eclectic Compendium of electronic resources for adult distance learning consists of information on related mailing lists, electronic journals and other Internet resources.

Gopher:
Name: NYSERNet
Address: **nysernet.org**
Choose: **Special Collections: Higher Education | Distance Learning Resources**

Find an E-mail Address

To find someone's mail address when you only know their userid or real name, try this service.

Mail:
Address: **mail-server@rtfm.mit.edu**
Body: **send usenet-addresses/***name*

Freenets via Gopher

Access Freenets through a Gopher menu. Simply choose the Freenet you wish to reach from the menu and the Gopher will make the connection for you automatically.

Gopher:
Name: Texas A&M University
Address: **gopher.tamu.edu**
Choose: **Hot Topics: A&M's Most Popular Items | FreeNets**

FTP by E-mail

The Dutch Unix Users Groups (NLUUG) Mail Server provides access to the combined NLUUG and EU.NET archives.

Mail:
Address: **mail-server@nluug.nl**
Subject: **help**
Body: **help**

FTP Services for Non-FTP Users

A guide to FTP-by-mail and other FTP services for those without FTP.

Comment: European addresses are for requests from Europe only.

Mail:
Address: **bitftp@pucc.princeton.edu**

Address: **bitftp@vm.gmd.de**

Address: **ftpmail@decwrl.dec.com**
Body: **help**

Address: **ftpmail@grasp.insa-lyon.fr**
Body: **help**

Gopher Resources

A large list of Gopher sites, divided by category for easy access to specific topics and subject areas.

Anonymous FTP:
Address: **usc.edu**
Path: **/pub/gopher/gopher-jewels***

Gopher:
Name: University of Southern California
Address: **cwis.usc.edu**
Choose: **Other Gophers and Information Resources | Gopher Jewels**

IBM Whois Server

Use the IBM Whois server to find out if your favorite IBMer has an Internet mail address. Just send mail to the address below. You do not need a subject. In the body of the message, type **whois**, followed by the person's last name, a comma, and their first name or initial. For help, send a message that contains only the single word "help".

Mail:
Address: **nic@vnet.ibm.com**
Body: **whois** *last name, first name*

Internet Products, Services, and Publications

Mailing lists dedicated to Internet products, services and publication announcements, and general information about the Internet.

Mail:
Address: **maillist@internet. com**
Body: **subscribe internet.info** *your name*

Address: **maillist@internet.com**
Body: **subscribe internet.products** *your name*

Internet Resource Guide

A comprehensive document listing Internet resources and how to access them.

Mail:
Address: **info-server@nnsc.nsf.net**

A B C D E F G H I J K L M N O P Q R S T U V W X Y Z

Internet Services

A list of documents on how to find indexes to Internet services.

Mail:
> Address: **fileserv@shsu.edu**
> Body: **sendme MaasInfo.TopIndex***

Internet Services List

Also known as the Yanoff list, this is a comprehensive list of Internet resources.

Anonymous FTP:
> Address: **csd4.csd.uwm.edu**
> Path: **/pub/inet.services.txt**

HOORAY FOR SCOTT YANOFF

If there is any single person who is most responsible for helping Internet users become aware of just what is available, it would have to be Scott Yanoff, the creator of the Yanoff Internet Services List.

In fact, you could consider this book to be the spiritual descendent of the Yanoff list. So, let us all take a moment and thank Scott for all his hard work...

(Okay, that's enough. You can get back to your reading now.)

Internet Services and Resources

The LIBS system is a comprehensive collection of Internet resources presented in an easy-to-use menu-driven interface. The system operates like a bulletin board, but offers direct access to remote resources.

Telnet:
> Address: **garam.kreonet.re.kr**
> Login: **nic**
>
> Address: **info.anu.edu.au**
> Login: **library**
>
> Address: **nessie.cc.wwu.edu**
> Login: **libs**

> No need to be confused by the Internet. Take a look at **Internet Services and Resources** and try using the LIBS system, then choose whatever you want from the menus.

Internet Tools List

A brief and to-the-point summary of the tools available on the Internet for searching out files and information.

Anonymous FTP:
> Address: **ftp.rpi.edu**
> Path: **/pub/communcations/internet-tools**

Interpedia Mailing List

Discussions about an Internet Encyclopedia, or Interpedia, and using the Internet as an encyclopedia.

Internet mailing list:
> List Address: **interpedia@telerama.lm.com**
> Subscription Address:
> **interpedia-request@telerama.lm.com**

Knowbot Information Service

Knowbot, or netaddress, is an information service that provides a uniform user interface to the various Internet information services. By learning the Knowbot interface, you can query a variety of remote information services and see the results of your search in a uniform format.

Telnet:
> Address: **info.cnri.reston.va.us 185**

List of Internet Mailing Lists

A comprehensive list of mailing lists you can join on the Internet. An electronic version of the Prentice Hall book *Internet: Mailing Lists*. Nearly 500 pages of detailed descriptions and instructions. Topics range from children's rights and other political issues to beekeeping and yachting.

The Internet will set you free.

Anonymous FTP:
>Address: **ftp.nisc.sri.com**
>Path: **/netinfo/interest-groups**

Mail:
>Address: **mail-server@nisc.sri.com**
>Body: **send netinfo/interest-groups**

MaasInfo Files

A particularly comprehensive collection of information about what is available on the Net.

Anonymous FTP:
>Address: **niord.shsu.edu**
>Path: **maasinfo/***

Mailbase Gopher

Mailbase aims to provide groups of people with the ability to have focused discussions by using several lists, each with a specific topic. Mailbase provides access to hundreds of mailing lists, including descriptions, contact addresses and archive sites for each list.

Gopher:
>Name: UK Mailbase Gopher
>Address: **mailbase.ac.uk**

Telnet:
>Address: **mailbase.ac.uk**
>Login: **guest**
>Password: **mailbase**

Mailing List Search

Search and view the enormous selection of Listserv and Internet mailing lists through this easy-to-use Gopher interface. Includes lists of recent additions, deletions and updates.

Gopher:
>Name: Nova Scotia Technology Network
>Address: **nstn.ns.ca**
>Choose: **Internet Resources | Mail Lists**

New Gophers

Access the latest new Gopher sites from this menu.

Gopher:
>Name: Washington & Lee University
>Address: **liberty.uc.wlu.edu**
>Choose: **Explore Internet Resources**
> **| New Internet Sites | New Gopher Sites**

New Sites

A list of new Gopher, Telnet and Wais sites on the Internet. This list is updated on a regular basis.

Gopher:
>Name: Washington & Lee University Gopher
>Address: **liberty.uc.wlu.edu**
>Choose: **Explore Internet Resources**
> **| New Internet Sites**

New Telnet Sites

Explore the latest public access Telnet sites on the Internet from this menu.

Gopher:
>Name: Washington & Lee University
>Address: **liberty.uc.wlu.edu**
>Choose: **Explore Internet Resources**
> **| New Internet Sites**
> **| New Telnet Sites (Hytelnet)**

New Wais Sources

New Wais databases.

Gopher:
>Name: Washington & Lee University
>Address: **liberty.uc.wlu.edu**
>Choose: **Explore Internet Resources**
> **| New Internet Sites**
> **| New WAIS Server Databases**

NICOL

A Gopher that brings together some of the best sources of Internet network information via Wais, the World-Wide Web, Anonymous FTP and Gopher in a seamless, orderly manner.

Telnet:
>Address: **nicol.jvnc.net**
>Login: **nicol**

Popular FTP Archives

Browse some of the most popular FTP sites on the Internet from this menu. Just select the subject or system you wish to look at, and you'll be connected.

Gopher:
>Name: NASA Goddard Space Flight Center
>Address: **gopher.gsfc.nasa.gov**
>Choose: **FTP Archives**

A
B
C
D
E
F
G
H
I
J
K
L
M
N
O
P
Q
R
S
T
U
V
W
X
Y
Z

Resource Guides

A large collection of subject-oriented guides to Internet resources, provided by the Clearinghouse Project.

Anonymous FTP:
>Address: **una.hh.lib.umich.edu**
>Path: **/inetdirs/***

Gopher:
>Name: University of Michigan
>Address: **una.hh.lib.umich.edu**
>Choose: **Inetdirs**

Searching the Internet

A collection of all the most useful tools to search the Internet for that resource you need. It includes a FAQ about searches and archives, and describes all the important searching tools, including Archie, Hytelnet, Veronica, Wais and the World-Wide Web.

Gopher:
>Name: Yale University
>Address: **yaleinfo.yale.edu**
>Choose: **The Internet**
> | **Searching the Internet with...**

Subject Trees

A collection of different subject trees maintained all over the Internet. Each tree acts like a Gopher road map allowing you to find the subjects you want to investigate in the vastness of gopherspace.

Gopher:
>Name: Yale University
>Address: **yaleinfo.yale.edu**
>Choose: **The Internet | Subject Trees**

Know what you need, but not where it is? **Try the Subject Trees.**

This Week on the Internet

News about the Internet, as well as announcements of new resources and services. Updated regularly.

Gopher:
>Name: The Pipeline Gopher
>Address: **pipeline.com**
>Choose: **This Week on the Internet**

Traveler Memories

A set of specialized programs that travel regularly through gopherspace and FTP servers finding resources, omitting uninteresting items and compiling the information.

Gopher:
>Name: Universidade Nova de Lisbon (PT)
>Address: **gopher.fct.unl.pt 4320**
>Choose: **Traveler Memories**

Trickle Server Documentation

All about trickle servers. What they are, how to use them, technical information and user tips.

Anonymous FTP:
>Address: **ak.oakland.edu**
>Path: **/pub/misc/trickle**

INTERNET: RFCs

RFC 1118

Hitchhiker's Guide to the Internet. Detailed hints to allow new network participants to understand how the direction of the Internet is set, how to acquire online information, and how to be a good Internet neighbor.

Anonymous FTP:
>Address: **nic.ddn.mil**
>Path: **/rfc/rfc1118.txt**

>Address: **nis.nsf.net**
>Path: **/rfc/rfc1118.txt**

>Address: **wuarchive.wustl.edu**
>Path: **/doc/internet-info/hitchhikers.guide**

RFC 1173

Responsibilities of host and network managers.

Anonymous FTP:
>Address: **ds.internic.net**
>Path: **/rfc/rfc1173.txt**

RFC 1207

Topics of interest and answers for experienced Internet users.

Anonymous FTP:
    Address: **ds.internic.net**
    Path: **rfc/rfc1207.txt**

RFC 1208

A networking glossary of terms.

Anonymous FTP:
    Address: **ds.internic.net**
    Path: **rfc/rfc1208.txt**

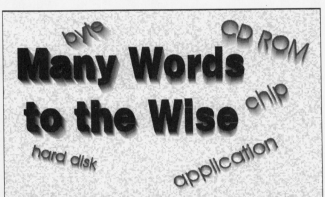

byte   CD ROM
chip
hard disk   application

It's true. People do judge you by the words you use. So, if you want computer people to take you seriously, you need to learn their words. Still, it won't be long before you *are* a computer person and then they will be *your* words! So, download *RFC 1208* and check out more networking terms than you ever knew existed.

bit   download   modem

RFC 1325

Topics of interest and answers for new Internet users.

Anonymous FTP:
    Address: **ds.internic.net**
    Path: **rfc/rfc1325.txt**

**Too much spare time?
Explore a MUD**

RFC 1359

Connecting to the Internet.

Anonymous FTP:
    Address: **ds.internic.net**
    Path: **rfc/rfc1359.txt**

RFC 1392

Internet Users' Glossary. A glossary for all the technical terms and phrases encountered on the Internet.

Anonymous FTP:
    Address: **ds.internic.net**
    Path: **rfc/rfc1392.txt**

Gopher:
    Name: Swedish University Network
    Address: **sunic.sunet.se**
    Choose: **Internet Users' Glossary**

RFC 1402

Gold in the Network.

Anonymous FTP:
    Address: **ds.internic.net**
    Path: **rfc/rfc1402.txt**

RFC—Repositories

A current list of repositories and instructions about how to obtain RFCs from each of the major U.S. sites.

Anonymous FTP:
    Address: **isi.edu**
    Path: **/in-notes/rfc-retrieval.txt**

RFC—RFC Lists

An index of all the RFCs. Lists each RFC, starting with the most recent, and for each RFC provides the number, title, author, issue date and number of hardcopy pages. In addition, it lists the online formats for each RFC and the number of bytes of each version online.

Anonymous FTP:
    Address: **isi.edu**
    Path: **/in-notes/rfc-retrieval.txt**

Wais:
    Database: **internet-rfcs**

A
B
C
D
E
F
G
H
I
J
K
L
M
N
O
P
Q
R
S
T
U
V
W
X
Y
Z

RFC Archives

Complete set of the Internet "Request for Comments" technical documents (RFCs).

Anonymous FTP:
Address: **wuarchive.wustl.edu**
Path: **/doc/rfc/***

Anonymous FTP:
Address: **ftp.uu.net**
Path: **/inet/rfc**

INTRIGUE

Conspiracies

Amazing conspiracies of all kinds, from AIDS being a government plot to Russia's operational Star Wars system.

Anonymous FTP:
Address: **ftp.spies.com**
Path: **/Library/Fringe/Conspiry/***

Gopher:
Name: Internet Wiretap
Address: **wiretap.spies.com**
Choose: **Wiretap Online Library**
| Fringes of Reason | Conspiracies

Want some fun?
Read the Fun section

J.F.K. Conspiracy

John F. Kennedy assassination conspiracy material, and archives from the **alt.conspiracy.jfk** Usenet newsgroup.

Anonymous FTP:
Address: **grind.isca.uiowa.edu**
Path: **/info/jfk/***

Telnet:
Address: **grind.isca.uiowa.edu**
Login: **iscabbs**

Taylorology

In 1922, one of Hollywood's top movie directors, William Desmond Taylor, was shot to death in his home. The murder was never solved and remains one of Hollywood's most fascinating mysteries. *Taylorology* is a lengthy newsletter devoted to analyzing and reprinting source material pertaining to the crime and its coverage in the press.

Anonymous FTP:
Address: **etext.archive.umich.edu**
Path: **/Zines/Taylorology**

Address: **ftp.uu.net**
Path: **/doc/literary/obi/Zines/Taylorology**

Usenet:
Newsgroup: **alt.true-crime**

This is the first book of the rest of your life.

Excerpt from the Net...

(From "Conspiracies", on the Wiretap gopher)

The following memorandum, written by J. Edgar Hoover [head of the FBI] immediately after his meeting with President Johnson, just seven days after the assassination of President Kennedy, is a remarkable document to say the least. There is much information imparted in the memo regarding just how fluid and unstable the cover story about who killed JFK still was shaping up to be at that time.

By analyzing the discrepancies between the story Hoover briefed Johnson about on November 29th, and what the final cover story handed down by the Warren Commission would claim almost a year later, we can better appreciate the degree to which the final "official report" was sculpted to fit the constraints the Commission was forced to adhere to, regardless of the actual facts of the assassination...

JOBS

Academic Jobs

The Academic Position Network is an online system for placing and reviewing open academic position announcements. Allows one to browse currently available positions, or place an advertisement for academic position openings.

Gopher:
Name: Academic Position Network
Address: **staff.tc.umn.edu 11111**

Career Books

Details, reviews and ordering information on a wide selection of career-oriented books and publications.

Gopher:
Name: Msen
Address: **garnet.msen.com 9062**
Choose: **Career Assistance**

Career Events

Details of upcoming career fairs and other employment-related events.

Gopher:
Name: Msen
Address: **garnet.msen.com 9062**
Choose: **Employment Events**

Contract Labor

More and more people are working from contract to contract. Aside from the cachet of getting to call yourself a "consultant", you will find that life is a lot more fun and challenging without fringe benefits. Here is the place to offer your services, look for a contract job, or swap experiences. (For hourly contracts, see **alt.sex.wanted**.)

Usenet:
Newsgroup: **misc.jobs.contract**

Education-Related Jobs

Detailed descriptions of education-related jobs. Information includes required education and experience, and compensation levels.

Gopher:
Name: Schoolnet Gopher
Address: **ernest.ccs.carleton.ca**
Choose: **Career Centre | Job Descriptions**

Employee Search

Search through thousands of resumes from every corner of the U.S. and Canada in the Online Career Center database. This resource is updated on a daily basis.

Gopher:
Name: Msen
Address: **garnet.msen.com 9062**
Choose: **Search Resumes**

Employer Profiles

Details and other information about many of the companies that participate in the Online Career Center.

Gopher:
Name: Msen
Address: **garnet.msen.com 9062**
Choose: **Company Sponsors and Profiles**

Need Work?

Are you. . . how shall we say it?. . . between jobs? The Internet can help you out. The Msen Gopher contains all kinds of information for the job seeker. Get the lowdown on many different companies, read helpful hints about the job market, take a peek at other people's resumes, and – best of all – upload your own resume to the data bank, where anyone on the Internet can look at it.

(Aww. . . on second thought forget it. What do you want to get a job for anyway? You'd only have to wake up early every day.)

Entry Level Jobs Offered

What does an Arts graduate say to a Computer Science graduate? "Would you like fries with your order?" If you are all ready for an entry-level job, this is the newsgroup for you. Check out the jobs that offer you no place to go but up.

Usenet:
Newsgroup: **misc.jobs.offered.entry**

Federal Jobs

Lists of federal job openings, including computer-related jobs and information for DOD employees in downsized agencies. Also includes information useful to federal job applicants.

Gopher:
Name: Dartmouth University
Address: **dartcms1.dartmouth.edu**
Choose:
Job Openings in the Federal Government

General Discussion

Before you send away for instructions on how to make money at home stuffing envelopes, maybe you should check it out with your friends on the Net. Just as important, don't start your job hunt without finding out which companies allow their employees to wear long hair and earrings. If you need a job, have a job or are offering a job, this newsgroup is the place to talk and trade tips about employment, the workplace and careers.

Usenet:
Newsgroup: **misc.jobs.misc**

Job Search

Browse and search through a database of thousands of job advertisements in all disciplines and from all over the U.S. and Canada. This resource is updated daily.

Gopher:
Name: Msen
Address: **garnet.msen.com 9062**
Choose: **Search Jobs**

Jobs Offered

Nothing to do all day? Perhaps you might like a job. Here are two general announcement forums for all types of employment.

Usenet:
Newsgroup: **biz.jobs.offered**
Newsgroup: **misc.jobs.offered**

Major Resource Kit

Entry-level job titles, job descriptions, and lists of the major employers for many of the common undergraduate degree programs.

Gopher:
Name: University of Delaware
Address: **lobster.mis.udel.edu**
Choose: **Student Information**
 | Career Planning and Placement
 | CPPO Major Resource Kit

Online Career Center

Career and employment-related information and advertisements, including huge job and resume databases, an event guide and company profiles.

Gopher:
Name: Msen
Address: **garnet.msen.com 9062**

Mail:
Address: **occ-info@mail.msen.com**

Professional Career Organizations

Details and contact addresses of professional career organizations and networks.

Gopher:
Name: Msen
Address: **garnet.msen.com 9062**
Choose: **Professional Organizations**

Need a laugh?
Check out Humor

Spare time? Take a look at
Games

Resume Database

Make your resume available to thousands of employers across the United States by entering it in the Online Career Center database.

Gopher:
Name: Msen
Address: **garnet.msen.com 9062**
Choose: **About Online Career Center | How to Enter Your Resume**

Mail:
Address: **occ-resumes@msen.com**
Subject: *resume title*
Body: *text of your resume*

Resumes

Here is the place to post your resumes (or look for ideas from other people's resumes to put on your own). Also the place to advertise for that specific job you're seeking.

Usenet:
Newsgroup: **misc.jobs.resumes**

VMS Jobs

Jobs offered and wanted for people knowledgeable in DEC computers and the VMS operating system and network.

Usenet:
Newsgroup: **vmsnet.employment**

Women in Science and Engineering

Woman to woman, share your experiences, tips and feelings about science and engineering, especially when it comes to jobs. For biologists, there is the **.women-in-bio** group. For science and engineering in general, there is **.wisenet**. (The Women In Science and Engineering Network. Get it? W.I.S.E.NET... Oh, never mind. Silly acronyms are for men, anyway.)

Usenet:
Newsgroup: **bionet.women-in-bio**
Newsgroup: **info.wisenet**

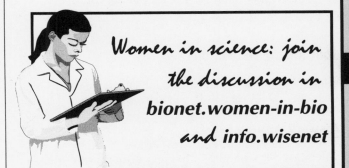

Women in science: join the discussion in bionet.women-in-bio and info.wisenet

Too much spare time? Explore a MUD

Excerpt from the Net...

```
Newsgroup: info.wisenet
Subject: Why men are the way they are

Sports metaphors in the workplace bother me a lot.

Not long ago, a male friend of mine was telling me about his high school football
days, and how part of training involved fighting on demand.  If the coach didn't like
a player's performance, he would pick another player and assign them to fight.  Liter-
ally.  Just beat the crap out of each other until someone couldn't fight anymore.  In
most cases, the boys involved were friends; certainly, they were teammates.

I listened and marveled at what VERY different youths we'd experienced, and how very
differently we might see the world, or life, as a result...
```

A B C D E F G H I J K L M N O P Q R S T U V W X Y Z

JOURNALISM AND MEDIA

Journalism

A mailing list to facilitate communication between working journalists of any media, journalism educators, and news librarians and researchers. The main focus is on the use of computers in journalism, rather than general journalism.

Listserv mailing list:
> List Address: **carr-l@ulkyvm.bitnet**
> Subscription Address: **listserv@ulkyvm.bitnet**

Journalism Discussions

Topics of interest to journalists and journalism educators, including issues related to magazine publishing.

Listserv mailing list:
> List Address: **journet@qucdn.queensu.ca**
> Subscription Address: **listserv@qucdn.queensu.ca**

> List Address: **magazine@rpitsvm.bitnet**
> Subscription Address: **listserv@rpitsvm.bitnet**

Mass Media

Articles about mass media, including sections on television, science fiction, video games, movies, comics and books.

Anonymous FTP:
> Address: **ftp.spies.com**
> Path: **/Library/Media/***

Gopher:
> Name: Internet Wiretap
> Address: **wiretap.spies.com**
> Choose: **Wiretap Online Library | Mass Media**

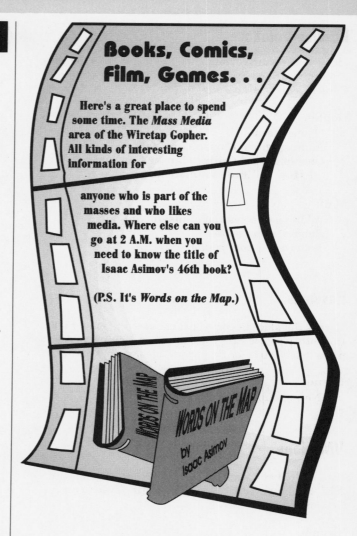

Books, Comics, Film, Games. . .

Here's a great place to spend some time. The *Mass Media* area of the Wiretap Gopher. All kinds of interesting information for anyone who is part of the masses and who likes media. Where else can you go at 2 A.M. when you need to know the title of Isaac Asimov's 46th book?

(P.S. It's *Words on the Map*.)

Media Magazines

Sample articles and subscription information for television and media-related magazines.

Gopher:
> Name: The Electronic Newsstand
> Address: **gopher.internet.com 2100**
> Choose: **Titles Arranged by Category | Media—Television**

Want some fun?
Read the Fun section

The Bizarre section has some
cool stuff

KEYS AND LOCKS

Lock Picking

Material covering lock pick sets, skeleton keys, Kryptonite locks, automatic pickers, related books, legal issues and more.

Anonymous FTP:
Address: **rtfm.mit.edu**
Path: **/pub/usenet/alt.locksmithing/***

THE KEY TO SUCCESS

One thing we have learned in life is that some of the most interesting things happen in places where people don't want us to be. All the more reason why the well-dressed man or woman should never be without a few lock picks and master keys. However, tools by themselves are useless, so before you even think about becoming a lock-and-key person, check out the Internet's *Lock Picking* archives.

(And remember, you should only use your lock picking skills to help friends who lose their keys. The last thing we want is for you to be sneaking into places just to see if anything interesting is happening.)

Lock Talk

Do you need the name of a book that will show you how to get into a locked, keyless automobile? How about a reference on safe-cracking? Or an electronic copy of *The MIT Guide to Lockpicking,* by Ted the Tool? Or are you an amateur locksmith with a picky problem? Check with

the lock and key set for all your needs. Just don't tell anyone where you found out about it.

Usenet:
Newsgroup: **alt.locksmithing**

Locksmithing Archives

Technical information and pictures related to locksmithing.

Anonymous FTP:
Address: **ftp.rahul.net**
Path:
/pub/atman/UTLCD-preview/locksmithing/*

Excerpt from the Net...

```
(from the Locksmithing frequently asked
question list)

-------------------------------------------
How can I make my own picks and tension
wrenches?

You can file or grind picks out of spring
steel.  It is best to use spring steel --
sources include hacksaw blades, piano
wire, clock springs...  In a pinch,
safety pin steel, or even a bobby pin can
be used...

-------------------------------------------
Where can I get the "MIT Guide to Picking
Locks"?

The author of the "MIT Guide to Picking
Locks", Ted the Tool, has posted a Post-
script version of the guide which can be
retrieved via Anonymous FTP...

-------------------------------------------
What are "pick guns" or "automatic pick-
ers" and do they work?

A "pick gun" is a manual or powered de-
vice that uses a vibrating pin to try to
bounce the pin tumblers so there are
spaces at the shear line so the the plug
can rotate.  They are not a panacea,
aren't always effective, and the Net
seems to feel that these are no substi-
tute for a little skill with a pick and
learning how locks work...

-------------------------------------------
```
(continued on next page)

A B C D E F G H I J K L M N O P Q R S T U V W X Y Z

(continued from previous page)

Can the Club be picked? Is the Club any good?

[Note: The "Club" is a widely-advertised automobile anti-theft device that you use to lock the steering wheel when you leave your car.]

"I used to have a Club, purchased on the recommendation of a coworker. The first time I tried picking it, it took me approximately 30 seconds, using the cap of a Papermate Flexgrip pen for tension, and a bent jumbo paperclip to rake the pins. With practice, I was able to reliably pick every "Club" I encountered in 5-30 seconds using these tools."

However, it doesn't really matter, no car thief is going to pick it, they are going to cut the soft plastic steering wheel with a hacksaw or bolt cutters and slip the Club off.

Here are some of the things collected about locations and availabilities (most are from alt.locksmithing). We do not endorse any of these, but feel that you can get information by reading.

PADLOCK SHIM PICKS. Open padlocks in seconds! Our new Padlock Shim pick's unique design makes them so successful that it is frightening! Simply slide the shim down between the shackle and the lock housing, twist and the lock is open. Works best on laminated type padlocks (the most popular type) but will open almost any type of padlock -- including the popular 3 number combination type...

PICK GUN. Picks locks FAST. Open locks in less than 5 seconds. Specifically designed for tumbler locks. Insert pick into key slot, then just pull trigger. Throws all pins into position at one time. Lock is then turned with tension bar. Used extensively by police and other government agencies...

PRO-LOK "CAR KILLER" KIT. Over the years we have had thousands of requests for a multi-vehicle opening kit. We are now able to offer the most complete kit that we have ever seen. This kit of tools will open over 135 automobiles, both domestic and foreign, on the road today. The opening procedure for each vehicle is diagrammed and explained in the instruction manual...

TUBULAR LOCK PICK. This tool is an easy and reliable method for picking tubular locks, as found on commercial vending machines, washers, dryers, etc...

HOW TO GET IN ANYWHERE, ANYTIME (video tape). Nearly two full hours of on-site techniques to get in any building, beat any lock, open any safe, enter any car...

TECHNIQUES OF BURGLAR ALARM BYPASSING.
Alarms covered include: Magnetic Switches, Window Foil, Sound and Heat Detectors, Photoelectric Devices, Guard Dogs, Central Station Systems, Closed-Circuit Television and more...

TECHNIQUES OF SAFECRACKING...

HIGH SPEED ENTRY: INSTANT OPENING TECHNIQUES (video tape)...

THE COMPLETE GUIDE TO LOCK PICKING by Eddie the Wire. The very best book ever written on how to pick locks...

CIA FIELD-EXPEDIENT KEY CASTING MANUAL. How to make a duplicate key when you can keep the original only a short time...

HOW I STEAL CARS: A REPO MAN'S GUIDE TO CAR THIEVES' SECRETS (video tape). How to open and enter practically any modern automobile and how to start them without the key...

LANGUAGE

Acronyms

Thousands of acronyms, defined.

Anonymous FTP:
Address: **ucselx.sdsu.edu**
Path: **/pub/doc/general/acronyms.txt**

Gopher:
Name: Manchester Computing Centre
Address: **info.mcc.ac.uk**
Choose: **Miscellaneous items**
  | Acronym dictionary

Wais:
Database: **acronyms**

American to British Translator

Translates words from American English to British English.

Gopher:
Name: University of Manchester
Address: **uts.mcc.ac.uk**
Choose: **Gopher Services**
  | US -> UK English Dictionary

American/British Dictionary

A dictionary containing both American and British words and meanings.

Gopher:
Name: University of Manchester
Address: **uts.mcc.ac.uk**
Choose: **Gopher Services**
  | American English Dictionary

Need a laugh?
Check out Humor

American/British Lexicon

A dictionary of American and British language usage. A fun and useful reference for American travelers in Great Britain, or British travelers in the U.S.

Gopher:
Name: Oregon State University
Address: **gopher.fsl.orst.edu**
Choose: **Other Sources of Info**
  | Hugo's Lore-House
  | Dr. Fegg's Big House o'Fun..
  | Jeremy Smith's American/British Lexicon

British to American Translator

Translates words from British English to American English.

Gopher:
Name: University of Manchester
Address: **uts.mcc.ac.uk**
Choose: **Gopher Services**
  | UK -> US English Dictionary

Chinese Text Viewers

Programs, documents and fonts for viewing Chinese text on IBM-PC and Unix systems.

Anonymous FTP:
Address: **nic.funet.fi**
Path: **/pub/culture/chinese/***

College Slang Dictionary

The official Usenet dictionary of college slang, as compiled by the readers of the Usenet **soc.college** newsgroup.

Anonymous FTP:
Address: **ftp.spies.com**
Path: **/Library/Article/Language/slang.col**

Gopher:
Name: Internet Wiretap
Address: **wiretap.spies.com**
Choose: **Wiretap Online Library | Articles**
  | Language | College Slang Dictionary

A B C D E F G H I J K L M N O P Q R S T U V W X Y Z

COLLEGE SLANG

At Princeton, when you "blow off", you are cutting a class. At Purdue, "blow off" has the more generic meaning of ignoring something important. However, at the University of Pittsburgh, "blowing off" refers to breaking off a relationship. (But you know what they say about Pittsburgh romances, anyway.)

Clearly, you can get yourself into a lot of trouble just by using the wrong word. For some definitive info on college slang, check out the Usenet **College Slang Dictionary** as compiled by Jennifer Doyle.

The Devil's Dictionary

A cynical, sarcastic, and hilarious lexicon of terms and phrases. This dictionary was completed in 1911 by Ambrose Bierce.

Anonymous FTP:
> Address: **world.std.com**
> Path: **/obi/Ambrose.Bierce/**
> **The.Devils.Dictionary.Z**

Gopher:
> Name: The World
> Address: **world.std.com**
> Choose: **OBI The Online Book Initiative**
> **| The Online Books | Ambrose.Bierce**
> **| The.Devils.Dictionary**

Spare time?
Take a look at Games

Excerpt from the Net...

(from the "College Slang Dictionary")

```
Geek Box/Nerd Box [Purdue University]:
-- a container, usually a tackle box, carried by electrical engineering students and
containing the millions of electronic components needed in the lab


Plasma [MIT]:
-- caffeine, in any of its forms


Random [MIT]:
-- a non-MIT person who hangs out at MIT anyway


Sexile [Swarthmore College]:
-- the state of banishment from one's room while one's roommate is with his/her
   significant other


Shooting the Shabookie [Carnegie-Mellon University]:
-- taking it all in the card game Hearts


Slort [Carnegie-Mellon University]:
-- to go to class with the express purpose of sleeping through it


Tool [Princeton University]:
-- someone with political or business ambitions


Wendy [Wellesley College]:
-- to be like the stereotypically WASP'y Wellesley woman
```

Dictionary of Computing Terms

Detailed glossary of programming languages, architectures, domain theory, mathematics, networking and many other computing areas.

Anonymous FTP:
    Address: **wombat.doc.ic.ac.uk**
    Path: **/pub/Dictionary.gz**

Gopher:
    Name: Imperial College
    Address: **wombat.doc.ic.ac.uk**
    Choose: **Dictionary of Computing**

Dictionary Word Lists

Word lists for many languages and topics, including Dutch, German, Italian, Norwegian, Swedish, Finnish, Japanese and Polish names. Also includes ZIP codes, and *Star Trek* terms.

Anonymous FTP:
    Address: **black.ox.ac.uk**
    Path: **/wordlists/***

Esperanto

A forum for people interested in any aspect of the international language Esperanto.

Internet mailing list:
    List Address: **esperanto@rand.org**
    Subscription Address:
        esperanto-request@rand.org

Listserv mailing list:
    List Address: **esper-l@trearn.bitnet**
    Subscription Address: **listserv@trearn.bitnet**

Esperanto-English Dictionary

A dictionary for translating Esperanto into English.

Anonymous FTP:
    Address: **ftp.spies.com**
    Path: **/Library/Article/Language/esperant.eng**

Gopher:
    Name: Internet Wiretap
    Address: **wiretap.spies.com**
    Choose: **Wiretap Online Library | Articles | Language | Esperanto English Dictionary**

Foreign Language Dictionaries

Dictionaries for a number of European languages, including Dutch, English, German, Italian, Norwegian and Swedish.

Anonymous FTP:
    Address: **ftp.uu.net**
    Path: **/doc/dictionaries/DEC-collection/***

Gaelic

Multidisciplinary discussion list for exchange of news, views and information between speakers of Scottish Gaelic, Irish and Manx. Provides tuition for people learning to speak Gaelic.

Listserv mailing list:
    List Address: **gaelic-l@irlearn.ucd.ie**
    Subscription Address: **listserv@irlearn.ucd.ie**

Language Articles

Many language-related resources, including unusual language dictionaries, lists of mnemonics, spoonerisms, palindromes and language guides.

Anonymous FTP:
    Address: **ftp.spies.com**
    Path: **/Library/Article/Language/***

Gopher:
    Name: Internet Wiretap
    Address: **wiretap.spies.com**
    Choose: **Wiretap Online Library | Articles | Language**

Latin Study Guides

Study guides to *Wheelock's Latin*, the most widely used introductory Latin textbook in American colleges and universities.

Anonymous FTP:
    Address: **ftp.spies.com**
    Path: **/Library/Article/Language/latin.stu**

Gopher:
    Name: Internet Wiretap
    Address: **wiretap.spies.com**
    Choose: **Wiretap Online Library | Articles | Language | Study Guide to Wheelock Latin**

A B C D E F G H I J K L M N O P Q R S T U V W X Y Z

Mnemonics

A selection of mnemonics for remembering everything from trigonometric equations to resistor color codes, pi and music scales.

Anonymous FTP:
Address: **ftp.spies.com**
Path: **/Library/Article/Language/mnemonic.txt**

Gopher:
Name: Internet Wiretap
Address: **wiretap.spies.com**
Choose: **Wiretap Online Library | Articles | Language | Mnemonics**

Name Guide

An interesting guide to naming conventions in many cultures around the world. This paper outlines differences between Mac and Mc, and many other cultural variations of names and naming conventions.

Gopher:
Name: World Data Center on Microorganisms
Address: **fragrans.riken.go.jp**
Choose: **Important note ...**

Palindromes

A large list of palindromes—words and phrases that read the same way backward as they do forward. For example, "A man, a plan, a canal, Panama!"

Anonymous FTP:
Address: **ftp.spies.com**
Path: **/Library/Article/Language/palindro.txt**

Gopher:
Name: Internet Wiretap
Address: **wiretap.spies.com**
Choose: **Wiretap Online Library | Articles | Language | Palindromes**

Pronunciation

An interesting poem about pronunciation in the English language, written to help students learning English.

Anonymous FTP:
Address: **quartz.rutgers.edu**
Path: **/pub/misc/pronunciation**

Gopher:
Name: Rutgers Quartz Text Archive
Address: **quartz.rutgers.edu**
Choose: **Miscellaneous | pronunciation**

Excerpt from the Net...

```
(from "Mnemonics", easy ways to remember sequences of words)

        To remember the hardness scale for minerals:

                1)  Talc
                2)  Gypsum
                3)  Calcite
                4)  Flurite
                5)  Appetite
                6)  Orthoclase
                7)  Quartz
                8)  Topaz
                9)  Corumdum
                10) Diamond


        All you have to do is memorize:

    "Toronto girls can flirt and only quit to chase dwarves."

[By the way, Harley was born in Toronto and he can assure you that the observation
about Toronto girls is perfectly true.]
```

Quick and Dirty Guide to Japanese

This useful information will help you learn to use Japanese in the shortest possible time. It places emphasis on communicating rather than complete correctness.

Anonymous FTP:
Address: **ftp.spies.com**
Path: **/Library/Article/Language/grammar.jap**

Gopher:
Name: Internet Wiretap
Address: **wiretap.spies.com**
Choose: **Wiretap Online Library**
  | Articles | Language
  | Quick & Dirty Guide to Japanese Grammar

Got a hot date at the sushi bar? Better take a moment to review the **Quick and Dirty Guide to Japanese.**

Roget's Thesaurus

The complete reference, provided by Project Gutenberg. Search and consult the original 1911 *Roget's Thesaurus*.

Gopher:
Name: University of Manchester Computing Centre
Address: **uts.mcc.ac.uk**
Choose: **Experimental & New Services**
  | Roget's 1911 Thesaurus

Name: University of Minnesota
Address: **gopher.micro.umn.edu**
Choose: **Libraries | Electronic Books | By Title**

Russian Swear Words

More Russian swear words than you could learn even if you were Russian.

Anonymous FTP:
Address: **kekule.osc.edu**
Path: **/pub/russian/obscenities/***

Shorter Oxford Dictionary

The complete shorter Oxford Dictionary word list, including parts of speech information.

Anonymous FTP:
Address: **ftp.white.toronto.edu**
Path: **/pub/words/sodict.gz**

Slang Dictionary

The definitive, and complete, reference to street and trash talk.

Anonymous FTP:
Address: **ftp.spies.com**
Path: **/Library/Misc/slang.txt**

Gopher:
Name: Internet Wiretap
Address: **wiretap.spies.com**
Choose: **Wiretap Online Library**
  | Miscellaneous
  | Slang Dictionary (Western PA, USA)

Spoonerisms

A collection of malapropisms, mixed metaphors, and spoonerisms, bringing new phrases to the English language.

Anonymous FTP:
Address: **ftp.spies.com**
Path: **/Library/Article/Language/spooner.lis**

Gopher:
Name: Internet Wiretap
Address: **wiretap.spies.com**
Choose: **Wiretap Online Library | Articles**
  | Language | Spoonerisms and Malapropisms

Urdu Dictionary

An Urdu-English Dictionary.

Anonymous FTP:
Address: **ftp.spies.com**
Path: **/Library/Article/Language/urdu.dic**

Gopher:
Name: Internet Wiretap
Address: **wiretap.spies.com**
Choose: **Wiretap Online Library | Articles**
  | Language | Small Urdu Dictionary

A
B
C
D
E
F
G
H
I
J
K
L
M
N
O
P
Q
R
S
T
U
V
W
X
Y
Z

Webster's Dictionary Servers

Online Webster's dictionary and spelling reference. This service repeatedly prompts you for a word. If you misspell a word, the system will prompt you to choose between a number of similar words. Gives spelling, pronunciation and definitions.

Gopher:
Name: University of California San Diego
Address: **infopath.ucsd.edu**
Choose: **Reference Shelf**
  | Webster's Online Dictionary

Telnet:
Address: **chem.ucsd.edu**
Login: **webster**

Address: **cs.indiana.edu 2627**
Login: **webster**

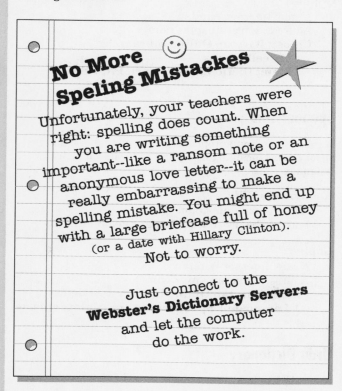

No More Speling Mistackes

Unfortunately, your teachers were right: spelling does count. When you are writing something important--like a ransom note or an anonymous love letter--it can be really embarrassing to make a spelling mistake. You might end up with a large briefcase full of honey (or a date with Hillary Clinton). Not to worry.

Just connect to the **Webster's Dictionary Servers** and let the computer do the work.

Too much spare time?
Explore a MUD

Word Lists

Word lists for several languages, including Dutch, English, German, Italian, Norwegian and Swedish. Useful for linguistic research and text-processing applications such as spell-checkers.

Anonymous FTP:
Address: **nic.funet.fi**
Path: **/pub/doc/dictionaries/***

LAW

Access Legislative Information Service

The Hawaii state legislature's information system offers access to legal documents, including the text of laws, pending bills, and a database of bills, as well as a keyword search.

Telnet:
Address: **access.uhcc.hawaii.edu**

Artificial Intelligence and the Law

A mailing list for the discussion of topics relating to artificial intelligence and law.

Internet mailing list:
List Address: **ail-l@austin.onu.edu**
Subscription Address:
  ail-l-request@austin.onu.edu

Australian Law

Australian legal documents, including the Australian Heritage Commission Act, Environmental Protection Act, and the Wildlife Protection Act.

Anonymous FTP:
Address: **ftp.spies.com**
Path: **/Gov/Aussie/***

Gopher:
Name: Internet Wiretap
Address: **wiretap.spies.com**
Choose: **Government Docs (US & World)**
  | Australian Law Documents

Computer Fraud and Abuse Act

The United States Computer Fraud and Abuse Statute (18 USC 1030).

Anonymous FTP:
Address: **ftp.spies.com**
Path: **/Gov/US-Docs/compfraud.act**

Gopher:
Name: Internet Wiretap
Address: **wiretap.spies.com**
Choose: **Government Docs (US & World)**
  | US Miscellaneous Documents
  | Computer Fraud and Abuse Act (18 USC 1030)

Computer Laws

Collection of information about laws involving computers, including computer crime laws for many states and countries.

Anonymous FTP:
Address: **ftp.eff.org**
Path: **/pub/cud/law/***

Criminal Justice Country Profiles

Information files on organizational structure and methods of criminal justice systems in many countries.

Gopher:
Name: University at Albany
Address: **uacsc2.albany.edu**
Choose: **United Nations Justice Network**
  | U.N. Criminal Justice Country Profiles

Criminal Justice Discussion Group

The Journal of Criminal Justice and Popular Culture is designed to serve the criminal justice community by providing film reviews and original essays on the intersection of popular culture with criminal justice.

Listserv mailing list:
List Address: **cjmovies@albany.bitnet**
Subscription Address: **listserv@albany.bitnet**

Want some fun?
Read the Fun section

CU-LawNet

Legal reference resource and information about Columbia University and the Columbia University Law School, provided by the Columbia Law School Public Information Service. Also offers Columbia University and Law School catalogs.

Telnet:
Address: **lawnet.law.columbia.edu**
Login: **lawnet**

European Law Students Association

A mailing list to improve the communication between ELSA members and other interested parties.

Internet mailing list:
List Address: **all-of-elsa@jus.uio.no**
Subscription Address:
  all-of-elsa-request@jus.uio.no

Indiana University School of Law WWW Server

An amazing, text-based, Hypertext information retrieval service with topics such as information about the Indiana University School of Law, career services, libraries, Internet radio shorts and other law-related resources on the Internet.

Telnet:
Address: **www.law.indiana.edu**
Login: **www**

Law Resources

A large list of Internet resources related to the law, including mailing lists, law library catalogs, FTP sites and Usenet newsgroups.

Gopher:
Name: NYSERNet
Address: **nysernet.org**
Choose: **Reference Desk | 300 - Social Science**
  | 340 - Law | Law resources on the Internet

The Bizarre section has some
cool stuff

A
B
C
D
E
F
G
H
I
J
K
L
M
N
O
P
Q
R
S
T
U
V
W
X
Y
Z

STAY OUT OF TROUBLE: USE THE INTERNET'S LAW RESOURCES.

Law Server

Legal discussions and reference material for United States, foreign and international law. Library resources, government agencies, periodicals and lists of other legal resources on the Internet.

Gopher:
    Name: Cleveland State University
    Address: **gopher.law.csuohio.edu**

    Name: Cornell University Law School
    Address: **fatty.law.cornell.edu**

League for Programming Freedom

The League for Programming Freedom is a grass-roots organization of professors, students, businessmen, programmers, and users dedicated to reversing the current trend toward copyright and patent laws covering software.

Anonymous FTP:
    Address: **ftp.cs.widener.edu**
    Path: **/pub/lpf/***

Legal and Criminal Articles

Documents about the law and law-breakers, including adoption laws by state, definition and jurisdiction, law heritage and more.

Anonymous FTP:
    Address: **ftp.spies.com**
    Path: **/Library/Article/Legal/***

Gopher:
    Name: Internet Wiretap
    Address: **wiretap.spies.com**
    Choose: **Wiretap Online Library | Articles**
      | Legal and Criminal

The League for Programming Freedom

Don't you just hate it when you develop your own operating system and then find out that you can't market it because it infringes on a copyright held by Microsoft? So do we (and, evidently, so does IBM). That's why we think that anyone who cares about software and the freedom that it brings to the emerging human species should find out about the League for Programming Freedom.

Net Law

Discussion of the various legal issues affecting the Internet community.

Gopher:
    Name: Electronic Frontier Foundation
    Address: **gopher.eff.org**
    Choose: **Electronic Frontier...**
      | Discussion of legal...

Steve Jackson Games

Collection of all the information surrounding the Secret Service raid on the Steve Jackson Games company, and the following court case.

Anonymous FTP:
    Address: **ftp.eff.org**
    Path: **/pub/SJG/***

Supreme Court Rulings

With Project Hermes, the United States Supreme Court makes its opinions and rulings available in electronic format within minutes of their release. Case Western Reserve University is one of the sites the Supreme Court supplies with this information. Get and read the files **info** and **readme.first**.

Anonymous FTP:
Address: **ftp.cwru.edu**
Path: **/hermes/***

Gopher:
Name: University of Maryland
Address: **info.umd.edu**
Choose: **Educational Resources | United States | Supreme Court**

Wais:
Database: **supreme-court**

Washington & Lee University Law Library

Gateway to an amazing volume of Internet law resources, including many universities in the United States and around the world. Use an easy menu interface to navigate through law libaries all over the nation. Search for keywords, read the case law, or search for books, articles and publications.

Telnet:
Address: **liberty.uc.wlu.edu**
Login: **lawlib**

LIBRARIES

Accessible Library Catalogs & Databases

A large document with detailed instructions on how to access the computerized library systems of many universities around the world.

Anonymous FTP:
Address: **ftp.unt.edu**
Path: **/library/libraries.txt**

Address: **nic.funet.fi**
Path: **/pub/doc/library/internet.libraries.Z**

Archives & Archivists list

Learn the finer points of being an archivist.

Listserv mailing list:
List Address: **archives@indycms.bitnet**
Subscription Address: **listserv@indycms.bitnet**

Billy Barron's Library List

Details of how to access hundreds of online bibliographic databases and libraries around the world.

Anonymous FTP:
Address: **ftp.utdallas.edu**
Path: **/pub/staff/billy/libguide/***

Gopher:
Name: Yale University
Address: **yaleinfo.yale.edu 7000**
Choose: **Libraries**

Carl System

A computerized network of library systems. Search for keywords from any of five databases (library catalogs, current articles, information databases, other library systems, library and system news).

Telnet:
Address: **pac.carl.org**

Current Cites

A monthly publication of the Library Technology Watch Program, which provides articles on modern technology and librarianship.

Anonymous FTP:
Address: **ftp.cni.org**
Path: **/pub/Current.Cites/***

Gopher:
Name: University of Virginia
Address: **gopher.virginia.edu**
Choose: **Library Services | University Library Resources (Alphabetic Organization) | Current Cites**

Listserv mailing list:
List Address: **pacs-l@uhupvm1.bitnet**
Subscription Address: **listserv@uhupvm1.bitnet**

A B C D E F G H I J K L M N O P Q R S T U V W X Y Z

Eureka

An easy-to-use search service. With Eureka, any individual or institution can search the online resources of the Research Libraries Group (RLG), including the RLIN bibliographic files and the CitaDel article-citation and document-delivery service. Eureka contains information about more than 20 million books, serials, sound recordings, musical scores, archival collections and other materials.

Telnet:
Address: **eureka-info.stanford.edu**

Hytelnet

This program assists people using library resources by automating the process. Hytelnet is a program that presents library resources on an easy-to-use menu interface. When you choose a resource, Hytelnet will show you how to access the resource, or even connect you to it automatically. Executables for various machines, as well as source, are available.

Anonymous FTP:
Address: **ftp.usask.ca**
Path: **/pub/hytelnet/pc/hyteln***

Address: **liberty.uc.wlu.edu**
Path: **/pub/lawlib.hyteln***

Archie:
Pattern: **hytelnet**

Telnet:
Address: **access.usask.ca**
Address: **info.ccit.arizona.edu**

Launchpad

This system provides access to many library systems across the country. You can perform searches, download files, find other users and even connect to the local Gopher client. Try the CIA World Fact Book in the experimental gopherspace section.

Telnet:
Address: **launchpad.unc.edu**
Login: **launch**

Library of Congress

The Library of Congress maintains records of millions of publications in the United States as well as legislative and copyright information.

Gopher:
Name: Library of Congress
Address: **marvel.loc.gov**

Telnet:
Address: **locis.loc.gov**

Need info on a book? Any book? Try the Library of Congress Gopher.

Library Newsletters

Selection of newsletters about cataloging, indexing, collecting and preserving books.

Anonymous FTP:
Address: **nigel.msen.com**
Path: **/pub/newsletters/Libraries/***

Library Policy Archive

A collection of library policy statements, including the American Library Association's Freedom to Read statement and the ALA Library Bill of Rights.

Anonymous FTP:
Address: **ftp.eff.org**
Path: **/pub/academic/library/***

Gopher:
Name: Electronic Frontier Foundation
Address: **gopher.eff.org**
Choose: **Computers & Academic Freedom
    mailing list archives & info
 | Library Policy Statements**

Library Resources

Access to many Internet library-related resources, including lists, articles, newsletters, archives, electronic journals and library catalogs.

Gopher:
Name: NYSERNet
Address: **nysernet.org**
Choose: **Special Collections: Libraries**

Library Resources on the Internet

This file contains strategies for selection and use of library resources on the Internet. A 40+ page document for download via FTP includes information on how to get started, road maps, travel guides, search strategies and information about other library resources.

Anonymous FTP:
Address: **dla.ucop.edu**
Path: **/pub/internet/libcat-guide**

Library Topic Lists

List of mailing lists and serials related to all aspects of libraries.

Gopher:
Name: NYSERNet
Address: **nysernet.org**
Choose: **Special Collections: Libraries
| Library conferences**

Public Access Catalogs

A list of online Internet public access library catalogs and databases and other related information.

Anonymous FTP:
Address: **world.std.com**
Path: **/obi/Access/***

Gopher:
Name: The World
Address: **world.std.com**
Choose: **OBI The Online Book Initiative
| The Online Books | Access**

University of Maryland Information Database

Information and documents on many subjects of interest.

Telnet:
Address: **info.umd.edu**

Using Internet Libraries

A multitude of software, documents and resource guides, including those for Archie, Wais, FTP, e-mail, listserv, and resource lists for librarians and library users on the Internet.

Anonymous FTP:
Address: **nic.funet.fi**
Path: **/pub/doc/library/***

The Internet, Librarian Style

Some of the most passionate users of the Internet are librarians. (Of course, this has nothing to do with the Internet: by their very nature, librarians are passionate people.) Indeed, there are so many resources on the Internet that only a librarian could really catalog and describe them all. Take a look at *Using Internet Libraries,* and see what the book people have to offer us civilians.

Washington University Services

Washington University in St. Louis provides an easy-to-use menu interface to university library systems and Internet resources all over the world.

Telnet:
Address: **library.wustl.edu**
Login: **services**

Wiretap Online Library

A collection of useful and entertaining information from Usenet and elsewhere.

Anonymous FTP:
Address: **ftp.spies.com**
Path: **/Library/***

Gopher:
Name: Internet Wiretap
Address: **wiretap.spies.com**
Choose: **Wiretap Online Library**

A B C D E F G H I J K L M N O P Q R S T U V W X Y Z

Excerpt from the Net...

(from the "Questionables" area of the "Wiretap Online Services" gopher)

Outlaw Labs Atomic Bomb:

...Plastic explosives work best in this situation since they can be manipulated to enable both a Uranium bomb and a Plutonium bomb to detonate. One very good explosive is Urea Nitrate. The directions on how to make Urea Nitrate are as follows...

LITERATURE

American Literature Discussion List

Discussion of topics and issues in American literature among a world-wide community.

Listserv mailing list:
List Address: **amlit-l@umcvmb.bitnet**
Subscription Address: **listserv@umcvmb.bitnet**

Art of Writing

Discussions and examples relating to authors and the art of writing.

Usenet:
Newsgroup: **misc.writing**
Newsgroup: **rec.arts.prose**

Bibliographies

Reading lists and bibliographies on many literary subjects, including Arthurian legends, computer ethics, hypertext, medieval Europe, narrative theory and modern drama.

Gopher:
Name: English Server
Address: **english-server.hss.cmu.edu**
Choose: **Bibliographies**

Lonely? Try the Personals.

Bryn Mawr Classical Review

Several hundred articles on classical literature topics.

Gopher:
Name: University of Florida
Address: **gaia.sci-ed.fit.edu**
Choose: **Subject Area Resources | Language Arts**

Classics

Discussions about classics, classical literature, and Latin.

Listserv mailing list:
List Address: **classics@uwavm.bitnet**
Subscription Address: **listserv@uwavm.bitnet**

List Address: **latin-l@psuvm.psu.edu**
Subscription Address: **listserv@psuvm.psu.edu**

Dutch Literature

This moderated group offers a change of scenery with its concentration on Dutch language and literature. You'll find yourself swept up in the culture and atmosphere of the Netherlands.

Usenet:
Newsgroup: **bit.lang.neder-l**

Electronic Antiquity

Provocative articles, reviews, conference news and other information regarding classics.

Gopher:
Name: University of Tasmania
Address: **info.utas.edu.au**
Choose: **Publications | Electronic Antiquity : Communicating The Classics**

English Server

A Gopher dedicated to the sharing of texts in English and other languages. Texts include novels, poems, plays, short stories, autobiographies, essays, speeches, hypertexts, jokes and other items of interest.

Anonymous FTP:
Address: **english-server.hss.cmu.edu**
Path: **/English Server/***

Gopher:
Name: The English Server
Address: **english-server.hss.cmu.edu**

Frederick Douglass

The full text of this narrative of the life of an American writer, orator, abolitionist and former slave.

Gopher:
> Name: University of Minnesota
> Address: **gopher.micro.umn.edu**
> Choose: **Libraries**
> | **Electronic Books**
> | **By Title**

Etext Pointers

Pointers on where to obtain electronic text (etext) on the Internet and elsewhere. This information is from the Usenet **alt.etext** archives and is updated daily.

Anonymous FTP:
> Address: **ftp.spies.com**
> Path: **/alt.etext/***

Gopher:
> Name: Internet Wiretap
> Address: **wiretap.spies.com**
> Choose: **Usenet alt.etext Archives**

Fun Reading

A collection of informative and entertaining stories, interviews, articles and FAQ lists.

Gopher:
> Name: University of Illinois
> Address: **wx.atmos.uiuc.edu**
> Choose: **Documents**
> | **FUN**

Gopher problems?
Read
"The Internet Complete Reference"

Fun Reading

What a pickle. It's Saturday night and you have nothing to do, so you look for something to read. Unfortunately, you've already read every page of *The Internet Complete Reference*, and nothing else looks good. What to do? Connect to the Internet and immerse yourself in something light and diverting.

(Maybe, just maybe, it will let you forget how your ex-significant other took the television set when she left you for that jerk on the rugby team who doesn't even know how to use a computer.)

General Literature

Explore the subtle wonders of mainstream literature. Get frightened, get romantic, get nostalgic: all with a little help from some literary stimuli.

Usenet:
> Newsgroup: **bit.listserv.literary**

Listserv mailing list:
> List Address: **literary@ucf1vm.cc.ucf.edu**
> Subscription Address: **listserv@ucf1vm.cc.ucf.edu**

Information on Authors

Author information, including lists of works available at this FTP site.

Anonymous FTP:
> Address: **ftp.uu.net**
> Path: **/doc/literary/obi/Misc/Books**

A B C D E F G H I J K L M N O P Q R S T U V W X Y Z

Women's Book List

A list of books directly related to the role of women in society, including such topics as sexism, politics, jobs and feminism.

Gopher:
Name: English Server
Address: **english-server.hss.cmu.ecu**
Choose: **Bibliographies**
  | Women's Center Book List

Workshop on Electronic Texts

The Workshop on Electronic Texts drew together experts to compare ideas, beliefs, experiences and, in particular, methods of placing and presenting historical textual materials in computerized form. The proceedings from this and other events are available here, as is information on upcoming events.

Gopher:
Name: University of Maryland
Address: **info.umd.edu**
Choose: **Educational Resources**
  | The Reading Room | Miscellaneous
  | ElecWorkShop

Writer Resource Guide

A list of magazines and newsletters accepting submissions by electronic mail, and other electronic resources for writers.

Anonymous FTP:
Address: **rtfm.mit.edu**
Path: **/pub/usenet/news.answers/writing/resources**

LITERATURE: AUTHORS

Austen

A mailing list for fans of Jane Austen. Includes the discussion of her novels, as well as those of some of her contemporaries, including Fanny Burney, Maria Edgeworth and Maria Wollstonecraft.

Listserv mailing list:
List Address: **austen-l@mcgill1.bitnet**
Subscription Address: **listserv@mcgill1.bitnet**

Baum

Two complete texts by L. Frank Baum, creator of the Wizard of Oz.

Anonymous FTP:
Address: **nic.funet.fi**
Path: **/pub/doc/literary/etext/ozland.txt**

Address: **nic.funet.fi**
Path: **/pub/doc/literary/etext/wizoz.txt**

Bierce

Complete works by Ambrose Bierce, including *Can Such Things Be* and *The Devil's Dictionary*.

Anonymous FTP:
Address: **world.std.com**
Path: **/obi/Ambrose.Bierce/***

Gopher:
Name: The World
Address: **world.std.com**
Choose: **OBI The Online Book Initiative**
  | The Online Books | Ambrose.Bierce

Carroll

Several full texts by Lewis Carroll.

Anonymous FTP:
Address: **nic.funet.fi**
Path: **/pub/doc/literary/etext/alice.txt**

Address: **nic.funet.fi**
Path: **/pub/doc/literary/etext/caroll/***

Address: **nic.funet.fi**
Path: **/pub/doc/literary/etext/jabber.txt**

Address: **nic.funet.fi**
Path: **/pub/doc/literary/etext/looking.txt**

Address: **nic.funet.fi**
Path: **/pub/doc/literary/etext/snark.txt**

Chaucer Mailing List

A mailing list discussion group devoted to the works of Geoffrey Chaucer and English literature and culture during the period 1100-1500.

Internet mailing list:
List Address: **chaucer@unlinfo.unl.edu**
Subscription Address:
  chaucer-request@unlinfo.unl.edu

Dickens

Several complete novels by Charles Dickens.

Anonymous FTP:
Address: **nic.funet.fi**
Path: **/pub/doc/literary/etext/carol.txt**

Address: **nic.funet.fi**
Path: **/pub/doc/literary/etext/chimes.txt**

Address: **nic.funet.fi**
Path: **/pub/doc/literary/etext/cricket.txt**

Doyle

Several complete texts and stories by Sir Arthur Conan Doyle, author of the Sherlock Holmes series.

Anonymous FTP:
Address: **nic.funet.fi**
Path: **/pub/doc/literary/etext/adventures.dyl**

Address: **nic.funet.fi**
Path: **/pub/doc/literary/etext/casebook.dyl**

Address: **nic.funet.fi**
Path: **/pub/doc/literary/etext/doyle/***

Address: **nic.funet.fi**
Path: **/pub/doc/literary/etext/hound.dyl**

Address: **nic.funet.fi**
Path: **/pub/doc/literary/etext/lastbow.dyl**

Address: **nic.funet.fi**
Path: **/pub/doc/literary/etext/magicdoor.dyl**

Address: **nic.funet.fi**
Path: **/pub/doc/literary/etext/memoirs.dyl**

Address: **nic.funet.fi**
Path: **/pub/doc/literary/etext/return.dyl**

Address: **nic.funet.fi**
Path: **/pub/doc/literary/etext/signfour.dyl**

Address: **nic.funet.fi**
Path: **/pub/doc/literary/etext/study.dyl**

Address: **nic.funet.fi**
Path: **/pub/doc/literary/etext/valley.dyl**

The Case of the Missing Password

"It was on a bitterly cold night and frosty morning, towards the end of the winter of '97, that I was awakened by a tugging at my shoulder. It was Holmes. The candle in his hand shone upon his eager, stooping face, and told me at a glance that something was amiss.

"'Come, Watson, come! ' he cried. 'The game is afoot. Not a word! Into your clothes and come! We must track down the missing superuser password. . .'"

But who would steal a password? And what does this have to do with the giant rat of Sumatra? No need to die of suspense: download the stories of Arthur Conan Doyle and see for yourself.

Mansfield

Collection of works by Katherine Mansfield.

Anonymous FTP:
Address: **nic.funet.fi**
Path: **/pub/doc/literary/etext/mansfield/***

Milton

Several works by John Milton.

Anonymous FTP:
Address: **nic.funet.fi**
Path: **/pub/doc/literary/etext/pargain.txt**

Address: **nic.funet.fi**
Path: **/pub/doc/literary/etext/parlost.txt**

A B C D E F G H I J K L M N O P Q R S T U V W X Y Z

Poe

Collection of works by Edgar Allan Poe.

Anonymous FTP:
Address: **ftp.uu.net**
Path: **/doc/literary/obi/Edgar.Allan.Poe/***

Address: **nic.funet.fi**
Path: **/pub/doc/literary/etext/Poe/***

Address: **nic.funet.fi**
Path: **/pub/doc/literary/etext/cask.poe**

Address: **nic.funet.fi**
Path: **/pub/doc/literary/etext/pit.poe**

Address: **nic.funet.fi**
Path: **/pub/doc/literary/etext/telltale.poe**

Pratchett

Archive of information about Terry Pratchett, the well-known author of humorous fantasy-based science fiction novels, and his discworld creations.

Anonymous FTP:
Address: **ftp.cs.pdx.edu**
Path: **/pub/pratchett/***

Saki

Two complete texts, including *Reginald*.

Anonymous FTP:
Address: **nic.funet.fi**
Path: **/pub/doc/literary/etext/reginald.hh**

Address: **nic.funet.fi**
Path: **/pub/doc/literary/etext/russia.hh**

Shakespeare

The full texts of Shakespeare's plays, poems and sonnets.

Anonymous FTP:
Address: **ftp.uu.net**
Path: **/doc/literary/shakespeare/***

Address: **nic.funet.fi**
Path: **/pub/doc/literary/etext/shakespeare/***

Address: **ocf.berkeley.edu**
Path: **pub/Library/Shakeseare**

Gopher:
Name: **University of Minnesota**
Address: **gopher.micro.umn.edu**

Tolkien Discussions.

A mailing list for anyone interested in discussing the life and works of J.R.R. Tolkien.

Listserv mailing list:
List Address: **tolkien@jhuvm.hcf.jhu.edu**
Subscription Address: **listserv@jhuvm.hcf.jhu.edu**

Twain

Several complete texts by Mark Twain, including *Tom Sawyer*, *A Connecticut Yankee in King Arthur's Court*, and others.

Anonymous FTP:
Address: **nic.funet.fi**
Path: **/pub/doc/literary/etext/abroad.mt**

Address: **nic.funet.fi**
Path: **/pub/doc/literary/etext/adam.mt**

Address: **nic.funet.fi**
Path: **/pub/doc/literary/etext/detective.mt**

Address: **nic.funet.fi**
Path: **/pub/doc/literary/etext/ghost.mt**

Address: **nic.funet.fi**
Path: **/pub/doc/literary/etext/niagara.mt**

Address: **nic.funet.fi**
Path: **/pub/doc/literary/etext/pitcairn.mt**

Address: **nic.funet.fi**
Path: **/pub/doc/literary/etext/sawyer.mt**

Address: **nic.funet.fi**
Path: **/pub/doc/literary/etext/yankee.mt**

Virgil

Collection of works in Latin by Virgil.

Anonymous FTP:
Address: **nic.funet.fi**
Path: **/pub/doc/literary/etext/Virgil**

Wells

Complete texts by H.G. Wells.

Anonymous FTP:
Address: **nic.funet.fi**
Path: **/pub/doc/literary/etext/invisman.txt**

Address: **nic.funet.fi**
Path: **/pub/doc/literary/etext/timemach.txt**

Wodehouse

A discussion group for fans of P.G. Wodehouse (pronounced "Woodhouse"). Wodehouse is the creator of many enduring characters, including Bertie Wooster and his valet Jeeves, Mr. Mulliner, Lord Emsworth and the Empress of Blandings, and Stanley Featherstonehaugh ("Fanshaw") Ukridge. The FTP site contains important Wodehouse information, including a full list of all his novels. He who has not met Wodehouse, has not lived a full life.

Anonymous FTP:
Address: **cathouse.org**
Path: **/pub/cathouse/humor/authors/ p.g.wodehouse.***

Usenet:
Newsgroup: **alt.fan.wodehouse**

P.G. Wodehouse was called "the best living writer of English prose". (That was when he was alive, of course.) Take a look at the Wodehouse archives and see what you're missing.

Yeats

The complete works of the Irish poet William Butler Yeats.

Anonymous FTP:
Address: **nic.funet.fi**
Path: **/pub/doc/literary/etext/yeats/***

LITERATURE: COLLECTIONS

Anglo Saxon Tales

Anglo Saxon tales, translated and annotated. Includes such classics as *Beowulf*.

Anonymous FTP:
Address: **world.std.com**
Path: **/obi/Anglo-Saxon/***

Gopher:
Name: The World
Address: **world.std.com**
Choose: **OBI The Online Book Initiative | The Online Books | Anglo-Saxon**

Complete Books in .ZIP Format

Many of the works mentioned elsewhere in this catalog in .ZIP format. Other titles include *The Book of Mormon*, and *Zen and the Art of the Internet*.

Anonymous FTP:
Address: **oak.oakland.edu**
Path: **/pub/misc/books**

Electronic Books

Access Library of Congress records and a number of books in electronic form available to be read or downloaded. Titles include *Aesop's Fables*, *Agrippa*, *Aladdin and the Wonderful Lamp*, *Alice's Adventures in Wonderland*, and the *CIA World Factbook*. Search by author, call letter, title or by specific strings of text. Entries are arranged alphabetically.

Gopher:
Name: University of Minnesota
Address: **gopher.micro.umn.edu**
Choose: **Libraries | Electronic Books**

Electronic Books in ASCII Text

ASCII text versions of more of your favorite novels than you could ever have imagined, all in one place.

Anonymous FTP:
Address: **nic.funet.fi**
Path: **/pub/doc/literary/etext/***

Poetry About Life

A collection of Chinese poetry, including "A Chinese Oath of Friendship" and other ponderings on life.

Gopher:
Name: National Chung Cheng University
Address: **gopher.ccu.edu.tw**
Choose: **miscellanies | Time To Relax**

Want to know what makes the Internet run? Read Internet: RFCs

A
B
C
D
E
F
G
H
I
J
K
L
M
N
O
P
Q
R
S
T
U
V
W
X
Y
Z

Excerpt from the Net...

```
(from the poetry collection at the Chung
Cheng University gopher, Taiwan)

    Oath of Friendship

    Shang Ya!
    I want to be your friend
    For ever and ever without break or decay.
    When the hills are all flat
    And the rivers are all dry.
    When it lightens and thunders in winter,
    When it rains and snows in summer,
    When Heaven and Earth mingle -
    Not till then will I part from you.

    -- Anonymous
       China, 1st centry B.C.
```

Poetry Assortments

A large collection of poetry arranged by author. Includes works of Housman, Jeffers, Millay, O'Shaugnessy, Russell, Whitman, and Yeats.

Anonymous FTP:
>   Address: **ocf.berkeley.edu**
>   Path: **/pub/Library/Poetry**

Gopher:
>   Name: North Dakota State University
>   Address: **chiphead.cc.ndsu.nodak.edu**
>   Choose: **Other Stuff | Fun Stuff | Poems**

Project Gutenberg

Project Gutenberg is planned as a storage- and clearing-house for making books available very cheaply. Much of the work, so far, has focused on classic literature (for which the copyright has expired). They have books by many authors, including Mark Twain, H.G. Wells, and F. Scott Fitzgerald. They also have *The Bible*, *The Book of Mormon*, and *The Koran* in ASCII format. Also available from **info.umnd.edu** is a collection of economic time series data from the federal government, as well as daily and long-term weather forecasts.

Anonymous FTP:
>   Address: **info.umd.edu**
>   Path: **/info/ReadingRoom/Fiction**

>   Address: **mrcnext.cso.uiuc.edu**
>   Path: **/pub/etext**

>   Address: **oes.orst.edu**
>   Path: **/pub/data/etext**

Telnet:
>   Address: **info.umd.edu**

Short Stories

An interesting collection of essays and short stories.

Gopher:
>   Name: Whole Earth Lectronic Link
>   Address: **gopher.well.sf.ca.us**
>   Choose: **Publications**

LITERATURE: TITLES

The Aeneid

The complete text, in Latin, by Virgil.

Anonymous FTP:
>   Address: **ftp.uu.net**
>   Path: **/doc/literary/obi/Classics/texts**

>   Address: **nic.funet.fi**
>   Path: **/pub/doc/literary/etext/Vergil/***

Aesop's Fables

The complete text from Project Gutenberg.

Gopher:
>   Name: University of Minnesota
>   Address: **gopher.micro.umn.edu**
>   Choose: **Libraries | Electronic Books**

Agrippa

The complete text from Project Gutenberg.

Gopher:
>   Name: University of Minnesota
>   Address: **gopher.micro.umn.edu**
>   Choose: **Libraries | Electronic Books | By Title**

Aladdin and the Wonderful Lamp

The complete text from Project Gutenberg.

Gopher:
>   Name: University of Minnesota
>   Address: **gopher.micro.umn.edu**
>   Choose: **Libraries | Electronic Books | By Title**

Why be normal? Read Bizarre

Alice in Wonderland

The complete text of the novel by Lewis Carroll.

Anonymous FTP:
    Address: **ucselx.sdsu.edu**
    Path: **/pub/doc/etext/alice26a.txt**

Gopher:
    Name: University of Minnesota
    Address: **gopher.micro.umn.edu**
    Choose: **Libraries**
      | Electronic Books
      | By Title

*Go ask Alice,
I think she'll know*

Anne of Green Gables

The complete text of the novel by Lucy Montgomery.

Anonymous FTP:
    Address: **nic.funet.fi**
    Path: **/pub/doc/literary/etext/anne.txt**

As a Man Thinketh

The complete text by James Allen.

Anonymous FTP:
    Address: **nic.funet.fi**
    Path: **/pub/doc/literary/etext/thinketh.txt**

The Call of the Wild

The complete text of the novel by Jack London.

Anonymous FTP:
    Address: **nic.funet.fi**
    Path: **/pub/doc/literary/etext/callwild.txt**

A Christmas Carol

The complete text of the tale by Charles Dickens.

Anonymous FTP:
    Address: **nic.funet.fi**
    Path: **/pub/doc/etext/carol.txt**

Have a Dickens of a Time

What could be more heartwarming than snuggling around the fire and reading aloud from *A Christmas Carol?* Download this wonderful tale and make your next holiday season one that your friends and loved ones will treasure forever. (Our favorite part is where the guests are eating dinner and, all of a sudden, they realize that Dr. Franknfurter has actually cooked Eddie the delivery boy.)

The Communist Manifesto

The document by Karl Marx and Friedrich Engels.

Anonymous FTP:
    Address: **nic.funet.fi**
    Path: **/pub/doc/literary/etext/manifesto.txt**

A
B
C
D
E
F
G
H
I
J
K
L
M
N
O
P
Q
R
S
T
U
V
W
X
Y
Z

A Connecticut Yankee in King Arthur's Court

The complete text of the novel by Mark Twain.

Anonymous FTP:
  Address: **nic.funet.fi**
  Path: **/pub/doc/literary/etext/yankee.mt**

Discourse on Reason

The complete text of the essay by Descartes.

Anonymous FTP:
  Address: **nic.funet.fi**
  Path: **/pub/doc/literary/etext/reason.txt**

Dracula

Collection of texts by Bram Stoker.

Anonymous FTP:
  Address: **nic.funet.fi**
  Path: **/pub/doc/literary/etext/dracgst**

  Address: **nic.funet.fi**
  Path: **/pub/doc/literary/etext/dracula.txt**

Essays in Radical Empiricism

The complete text by William James.

Anonymous FTP:
  Address: **nic.funet.fi**
  Path: **/pub/doc/literary/etext/empiricism.txt**

Fairy Tales

Wonderful collection of childhood magic. Tales of huffing and puffing wolves, little pigs, ugly ducklings, dwarves, princesses and thieves. Text of numerous fairy tales including The Little Mermaid, Snow White, The Adventures of Aladdin, Beauty and the Beast, Hansel and Gretel, Jack and the Beanstalk, The Three Little Pigs, The Tin Soldier and many more.

Anonymous FTP:
  Address: **ftp.uu.net**
  Path: **/doc/literary/obi/Fairy.Tales/Grimm**

  Address: **nic.funet.fi**
  Path: **/pub/doc/literary/etext/fariy-tale/***

  Address: **world.std.com**
  Path: **obi/Fairy.Tales/Grimm/***

Far From the Madding Crowd

The complete text of the novel by Thomas Hardy, provided by Project Gutenberg.

Gopher:
  Name: University of Minnesota
  Address: **gopher.micro.umn.edu**
  Choose: **Libraries | Electronic Books | By Title**

The Gift of the Magi

The complete text of the O. Henry story, provided by Project Gutenberg.

Gopher:
  Name: University of Minnesota
  Address: **gopher.micro.umn.edu**
  Choose: **Libraries | Electronic Books | By Title**

Herland

The full text from Project Gutenberg.

Gopher:
  Name: University of Minnesota
  Address: **gopher.micro.umn.edu**
  Choose: **Libraries | Electronic Books | By Title**

Hippocratic Oath and Law

The complete text by Hippocrates.

Anonymous FTP:
  Address: **nic.funet.fi**
  Path: **/pub/doc/literary/etext/hippoc.txt**

Hunting of the Snark

The complete text of the poem by Lewis Carroll.

Anonymous FTP:
  Address: **ucselx.sdsu.edu**
  Path: **/pub/doc/etext/snark11.txt**

Gopher:
  Name: University of Minnesota
  Address: **gopher.micro.umn.edu**
  Choose: **Libraries | Electronic Books | By Title**

The Invisible Man

The complete text of the novel by H.G. Wells.

Anonymous FTP:
  Address: **nic.funet.fi**
  Path: **/pub/doc/literary/etext/invisman.txt**

Jabberwocky

The complete text of the poem by Lewis Carroll.

Anonymous FTP:
    Address: **nic.funet.fi**
    Path: **/pub/doc/literary/etext/jabber.txt**

The Japan That Can Say No

A complete text.

Anonymous FTP:
    Address: **ucselx.sdsu.edu**
    Path: **/pub/doc/etext/japan-that-can-say-no.txt**

Keepsake Stories

The complete text by Walter Scott.

Anonymous FTP:
    Address: **nic.funet.fi**
    Path: **/pub/doc/literary/etext/keepsake.txt**

The Legend of Sleepy Hollow

The complete story by Washington Irving.

Anonymous FTP:
    Address: **University of Minnesota**
    Path: **gopher.micro.umn.edu**

    Address: **nic.funet.fi**
    Path: **/pub/doc/literary/etext/sleepy.txt**

Moby Dick

The complete text of the novel by Herman Melville, provided by Project Gutenberg.

Gopher:
    Name: University of Minnesota
    Address: **gopher.micro.umn.edu**
    Choose: **Libraries** | **Electronic Books** | **By Title**

Make Your Own Literature

Herman Melville labored for years writing *Moby Dick* and now you can read the whole thing for free anytime you want, just by using a Gopher. Better yet, download your favorite chapters and make changes. For example, use **vi** and enter the command **:%s/Dick/Rick/g.** You are now reading *Moby Rick*!

O Pioneers!

The complete text of the novel by Willa Cather, provided by Project Gutenberg.

Gopher:
    Name: University of Minnesota
    Address: **gopher.micro.umn.edu**
    Choose: **Libraries** | **Electronic Books** | **By Title**

Oedipus Trilogy

The complete texts by Sophocles, provided by Project Gutenberg.

Gopher:
    Name: University of Minnesota
    Address: **gopher.micro.umn.edu**
    Choose: **Libraries** | **Electronic Books** | **By Title**

Whatever else you say about Oedipus, you have to admit he *was* nice to his mother.

Paradise Lost

The complete text of the poem by John Milton, provided by Project Gutenberg.

Gopher:
    Name: University of Minnesota
    Address: **gopher.micro.umn.edu**
    Choose: **Libraries** | **Electronic Books** | **By Title**

A B C D E F G H I J K L M N O P Q R S T U V W X Y Z

Peter Pan

The complete text of the story by J. M. Barrie, provided by Project Gutenberg.

Gopher:
Name: University of Minnesota
Address: **gopher.micro.umn.edu**
Choose: **Libraries | Electronic Books | By Title**

The Pit and the Pendulum

The complete text of the story by Edgar Allan Poe.

Anonymous FTP:
Address: **nic.funet.fi**
Path: **/pub/doc/literary/etext/pit.poe**

The Scarlet Letter

The complete text of the novel by Nathaniel Hawthorne, provided by Project Gutenberg.

Gopher:
Name: University of Minnesota
Address: **gopher.micro.umn.edu**
Choose: **Libraries | Electronic Books | By Title**

The Scarlet Pimpernel

The complete text by Baroness Orezy.

Anonymous FTP:
Address: **nic.funet.fi**
Path: **/pub/doc/literary/etext/pimpernel.txt**

Scientific Secrets, 1861

The complete text by Daniel Young.

Anonymous FTP:
Address: **nic.funet.fi**
Path: **/pub/doc/literary/etext/science.txt**

Sherlock Holmes Novels

Collection of texts by Sir Arthur Conan Doyle.

Anonymous FTP:
Address: **ftp.uu.net**
Path: **/pub/literary/obi/Arthur.Conan.Doyle**

Address: **nic.funet.fi**
Path: **/pub/doc/literary/etext/adventures.dyl**

Address: **nic.funet.fi**
Path: **/pub/doc/literary/etext/casebook.dyl**

Address: **nic.funet.fi**
Path: **/pub/doc/literary/etext/hound.dyl**

Address: **nic.funet.fi**
Path: **/pub/doc/literary/etext/lastbow.dyl**

Address: **nic.funet.fi**
Path: **/pub/doc/literary/etext/magicdoor.dyl**

Address: **nic.funet.fi**
Path: **/pub/doc/literary/etext/memoirs.dyl**

Address: **nic.funet.fi**
Path: **/pub/doc/literary/etext/return.dyl**

Address: **nic.funet.fi**
Path: **/pub/doc/literary/etext/signfour.dyl**

Address: **nic.funet.fi**
Path: **/pub/doc/literary/etext/study.dyl**

Address: **nic.funet.fi**
Path: **/pub/doc/literary/etext/valley.dyl**

The Song of Hiawatha

The complete text of the poem by Henry Wadsworth Longfellow, provided by Project Gutenberg.

Gopher:
Name: University of Minnesota
Address: **gopher.micro.umn.edu**
Choose: **Libraries | Electronic Books | By Title**

The Strange Case of Dr. Jekyll and Mr. Hyde

The complete text of the novel by Robert Louis Stevenson, provided by Project Gutenberg.

Gopher:
Name: University of Minnesota
Address: **gopher.micro.umn.edu**
Choose: **Libraries | Electronic Books | By Title**

Through the Looking Glass

The complete text of the novel by Lewis Carroll.

Anonymous FTP:
Address: **ucselx.sdsu.edu**
Path: **/pub/doc/etext/lglass15.txt**

Gopher:
Name: University of Minnesota
Address: **gopher.micro.umn.edu**
Choose: **Libraries | Electronic Books | By Title**

The Time Machine

The complete text of the novel by H.G. Wells, provided by Project Gutenberg.

Gopher:
    Name: University of Minnesota
    Address: **gopher.micro.umn.edu**
    Choose: **Libraries | Electronic Books
    | By Title**

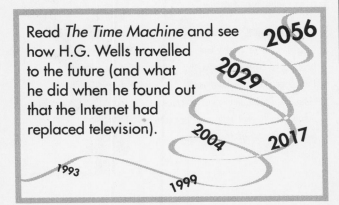

Read *The Time Machine* and see how H.G. Wells travelled to the future (and what he did when he found out that the Internet had replaced television).

1993 1999 2004 2017 2029 2056

Tom Sawyer

Collection of complete *Tom Sawyer* novels by Mark Twain.

Anonymous FTP:
    Address: **nic.funet.fi**
    Path: **/pub/doc/literary/etext/abroad.mt**

    Address: **nic.funet.fi**
    Path: **/pub/doc/literary/etext/detective.mt**

    Address: **nic.funet.fi**
    Path: **/pub/doc/literary/etext/sawyer.mt**

United Nations Declaration of Human Rights

The complete text.

Anonymous FTP:
    Address: **ucselx.sdsu.edu**
    Path: **/pub/doc/etext/un_declaration.txt**

United We Stand

The complete text, provided by Project Gutenberg.

Gopher:
    Name: University of Minnesota
    Address: **gopher.micro.umn.edu**
    Choose: **Libraries | Electronic Books
    | By Title**

War of the Worlds

The complete text of the novel by H.G. Wells.

Anonymous FTP:
    Address: **nic.funet.fi**
    Path: **/pub/doc/literary/etext/warworld.txt**

Wizard of Oz

The complete text of the children's novel *The Wonderful Wizard of Oz* by L. Frank Baum.

Anonymous FTP:
    Address: **nic.funet.fi**
    Path: **/pub/doc/literary/etext/wizoz.txt**

Spare time? Take a look at *The Wonderful Wizard of Oz*, L. Frank Baum's marvellous satire of the Clinton White House.

Wuthering Heights

The complete text of the novel by Emily Brontë.

Anonymous FTP:
    Address: **nic.funet.fi**
    Path: **/pub/doc/literary/etext/wuther.txt**

If you're feeling risque, take a look at the X-Rated Resources

A B C D E F G H I J K L M N O P Q R S T U V W X Y Z

MAGAZINES

AIXpert Magazine

This FTP site houses information about AIX and the IBM RS/6000, including articles from IBM's *AIXpert* magazine.

Anonymous FTP:
Address: **asterix.fi.upm.es**
Path: **/pub/docs/ibm**

Byte Magazine

Back issues of *Byte* magazine.

Anonymous FTP:
Address: **oak.oakland.edu**
Path: **/pub/misc/byte**

Chips Online

Back issues of *Chips* and *Chips Online* magazines.

Anonymous FTP:
Address: **oak.oakland.edu**
Path: **/pub/misc/nardac**

Culture Magazines

Sample articles and subscription information for music, consumer, sports and travel magazines.

Gopher:
Name: The Electronic Newsstand
Address: **gopher.internet.com 2100**
Choose: **Titles Arranged by Category**
 | Culture - Music, Popular, Sport, Travel, etc

E-Zine List

A list of electronic magazines available on the Internet.

Anonymous FTP:
Address: **netcom.com**
Path: **/pub/johnl/zines/e-zine-list**

Electronic Magazines

The Internet has a lot of electronic magazines that you can download whenever you want. No more will you have to put up with all the inconveniences of real magazines, like those subscription forms that fall out when you turn the page, or the perfume ads that smell like one of Zsa Zsa Gabor's bad dreams.

No longer will you have to worry about your name being sold to a mailing list that specializes in junk mail. But the best thing about electronic magazines is that they are free--which makes them ideal for birthday presents.

Electronic Journals Project

A comprehensive collection of all public domain electronic journals currently available on the Internet. A complete list of the collection with description and topic information for each journal is available for easy selection.

Anonymous FTP:
Address: **ftp.cic.net**
Path: **/pub/e-serials/***

Gopher:
Name: Cicnet
Address: **ftp.cic.net**
Choose: **Electronic Serials**

Internet Business Journal

Details about and samples from this publication exploring commercial opportunities in the networking age.

Gopher:
Name: Poniecki Foundation Gopher
Address: **poniecki.berkeley.edu**
Choose: **Info Services**
 | Internet Business Journal

META

META is an electronic networking magazine focusing on the growth and development of the Internet, as well as issues concerning access, privacy, intellectual property and related topics.

Anonymous FTP:
>Address: **ftp.netcom.com**
>Path: **/pub/mlinksva/meta**

Mail:
>Address: **mlinksva@netcom.com**

Mother Jones

Mother Jones is a magazine of investigation and ideas for independent thinkers. It challenges conventional wisdom, exposes abuses of power, helps redefine stubborn problems, and offers fresh solutions. It's online and free.

Anonymous FTP:
>Address: **mojones.com**
>Path: **/pub/***

Gopher:
>Name: Mother Jones Magazine
>Address: **mojones.com**

PC Magazine

The popular Ziff-Davis publication online.

Anonymous FTP:
>Address: **ftp.cco.caltech.edu**
>Path: **/pub/ibmpc/pcmag/**

Phrack

An electronic magazine devoted to hackers. Complete collection of the popular computer underground publication; contains technical and legal information relevant to hacking, phreaking and other underground activities.

Anonymous FTP:
>Address: **aql.gatech.edu**
>Path: **/pub/eff/cud/phrack**

>Address: **etext.archive.umich.edu**
>Path: **/pub/CuD/cud/***

>Address: **ftp.halcyon.com**
>Path: **/pub/mirror/cud/phrack**

>Address: **ftp.netsys.com**
>Path: **/pub/phrack**

>Address: **ftp.uu.net**
>Path: **/doc/literary/obi/Phracks**

**Love to hack?
Love to crack?
Read Phrack.**

Random Zines

A random collection of popular zines, including *Voices from the Net*, *Soapbox*, and *Zig-Zag*.

Anonymous FTP:
>Address: **ftp.spies.com**
>Path: **/Library/Techdoc/Zines/***

Gopher:
>Name: Internet Wiretap
>Address: **wiretap.spies.com**
>Choose: **Wiretap Online Library**
> **| Technical Information**
> **| Zines**

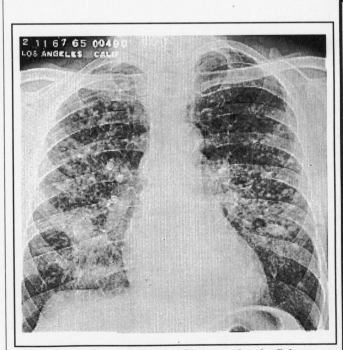

Can you identify this celebrity skeleton? *The Internet Complete Reference* won't help you identify Bones here, but it will show you how easy it is to find and retrieve picture files on the Internet. This image was retrieved via Anonymous FTP from Washington University Saint Louis (**ftp.wustl.edu**) in the directory **/multimedia/images/gif**. The filename is **x-ray.gif**..

A B C D E F G H I J K L M N O P Q R S T U V W X Y Z

Soapbox

Soapbox magazine is a forum for varying and controversial opinions on all subjects.

Anonymous FTP:
Address: **ftp.spies.com**
Path: **/Library/Techdoc/Zines/soapbox/***

Gopher:
Name: Internet Wiretap
Address: **wiretap.spies.com**
Choose: **Wiretap Online Library**
| **Technical Information**
| **Zines**
| **Soapbox**

Sound Site Newsletter

A monthly newsletter for PC sound enthusiasts. Tips on configuration, sound files, programming with sound, and much more.

Anonymous FTP:
Address: **oak.oakland.edu**
Path: **/pub/misc/sound**

Talk Radio

Internet Talk Radio is a new type of publication: a news and information service about the Internet, distributed on the Internet. Internet Talk Radio is modeled on National Public Radio and has a goal of providing in-depth technical information to the Internet.

Internet mailing list:
List Address: **announce@radio.com**
Subscription Address:
announce-request@radio.com

Mail:
Address: **questions@radio.com**
Address: **radio.ora.com**

Usenet:
Newsgroup: **alt.internet.services**

Need a laugh?
Check out Humor

Voices from the Net

An electronic magazine filled with interviews and essays featuring the voices of people from a wide variety of online environments. Entertaining and useful, Net-literature and Net-ethnography combined. An exploration of the odd corners of cyberspace. To subscribe, send mail to the address listed here. To download a back issue, use one of the FTP sites.

Anonymous FTP:
Address: **aql.gatech.edu**
Path: **/pub/Zines/Voices_from_the_Net**

Address: **etext.archive.umich.edu**
Path: **/pub/Zines/Voices**

Address: **ftp.spies.com**
Path: **/Library/Zines**

Mail:
Address: **voices-request@andy.bgsu.edu**
Subject: **Voices from the Net**
Body: **subscribe**

Zines

A collection of many popular zines, including *The Unplastic News*, *Cyberspace Vanguard* and others.

Gopher:
Name: CICnet
Address: **gopher.cic.net**
Choose: **Electronic Serials**

MAIL TO FAMOUS PEOPLE

Douglas Adams

The author of *The Hitchikers's Guide to the Universe* and many other imaginative works has his own Usenet fan club. Drop in, chat with the fans, and maybe even send a line to the grand young man himself.

Mail:
Address: **adamsd@cerf.net**

Usenet:
Newsgroup: **alt.fan.douglas-adams**

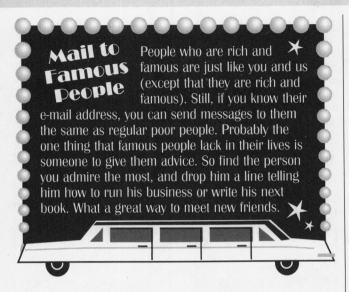

Mail to Famous People

People who are rich and famous are just like you and us (except that they are rich and famous). Still, if you know their e-mail address, you can send messages to them the same as regular poor people. Probably the one thing that famous people lack in their lives is someone to give them advice. So find the person you admire the most, and drop him a line telling him how to run his business or write his next book. What a great way to meet new friends.

Scott Adams

Do you enjoy the *Dilbert* comic strip? Do you like the cute little dog that looks like a balloon with glasses? Then tell the artist himself: Scott Adams.

Mail:
Address: **scott.adams@aol.com**

Beavis and Butt-head

When we think of philosophy, most of us think of Plato, Aristotle, Socrates and the rest of those old folks. "Why," we hear you ask, "aren't there any great philosophers alive today?". Well, there are. Send a note to two of the greatest, and tell them that you, too, hate stuff that sucks.

Mail:
Address: **beavis@mtv.com**
Address: **butthead@mtv.com**

Stewart Brand

Meet Stewart Brand, the original hippie-who-knows-how-to-make-money-without-selling-out-like-Jerry-Ruben. Brand, the creative force behind the *Whole Earth Catalog* and the newer *Whole Earth Review*, is also the man behind the Well, the electronic meeting place that reflects the best of the I-live-north-of-San-Francisco popular culture. Send him a message or check out the Well itself by using their Gopher.

Mail:
Address: **sbb@well.sf.ca.us**

Usenet:
Newsgroup: **gopher.well.sf.ca.us**

Bill Clinton

The President of the United States is a lot more than a good ol' boy from Arkansas: he's the Leader of the Free World, the Commander-in-Chief of the U.S. armed forces, and the Grand Poobah of the Illuminati. Drop him a note and tell him what is wrong with America and how to fix it. (You might also ask him if he knows where Hillary gets her hair done.)

Mail:
Address: **president@whitehouse.gov**

Alan Colmes

Here is the most computer-knowledgeable radio talk show host in America. Drop a note to Alan and let him know how you like his show, his liberal point of view, and his wry sense of humor. Colmes is the inventor of "Radio Graffiti", where anyone can call in and say one sentence about anything they want.

Mail:
Address: **alan@panix.com**
Address: **radio@echony.com**

Adam Curry

Adam Curry, the MTV VJ (video jock) and gossip personality is forging the link between big-time TV-oriented music entertainment and the Internet. Aside from having an Internet mailbox, Curry—somewhat of a computer nerd himself—has established a Gopher and an electronic magazine. For more information, finger him at the address below.

Gopher:
Name: MTV Gopher
Address: **mtv.com**

Mail:
Address: **adam@mtv.com**

Bill Gates

Isn't it great that we all get to live on this Earth at the same time as Bill Gates? Send Mr. Microsoft a note and tell him how much you appreciate his efforts to save mankind.

Mail:
Address: **billg@microsoft.com**

A B C D E F G H I J K L **M** N O P Q R S T U V W X Y Z

Lou Gerstner

It's not easy being the Chairman of IBM. Everybody always wants something from you and nobody loves you just for yourself. Send a message to Lou and tell him what a good guy he is.

Mail:
Address: **lvg@vnet.ibm.com**

Al Gore

No, there is no truth that the Vice President of the United States is really a Turing Machine. (Actually, he couldn't pass the test.) Write him and tell him how nice he looks on TV.

Mail:
Address: **vice-president@whitehouse.gov**

Billy Idol

Write to rock musician Billy Idol, tell him how much you like his music and ask him when will he be doing his Elvis impersonation again. Or maybe you just want to ask him where he gets his hair done.

Mail:
Address: **idol@well.sf.ca.us**

Mike Jittlov

Film maker and animator, creator of such cult films as *Wizard of Speed and Time*, Mike Jittlov is one of those lucky few who have an adoring set of fans, a Usenet fan club group, and an Internet address.

Mail:
Address: **jittlov@gumby.cs.caltech.edu**

Usenet:
Newsgroup: **alt.fan.mike-jittlov**

Mitch Kapor

Introduce yourself to one of the orignal pioneers of the personal computer era: Mitch Kapor, founder of Lotus (they make software, don't they?) and co-founder of the Electronic Frontier Foundation, the staunch defender of your electronic rights.

Mail:
Address: **mkapor@kei.com**

Rush Limbaugh

Rush Limbaugh—the conservative radio and TV commentator with a huge audience of ditto-heads—is more an Act of God than anything else. Send mail to the man who routinely performs with "half his brain tied behind his back". (After all, if he were using his whole brain, he would be on the Internet, wouldn't he, and not CompuServe.)

Mail:
Address: **70277.2502@compuserve.com**

Photographs of famous people are easy to find on the Net. If they've been on TV or had their picture taken, someone has scanned them into a picture file.

Stop whatever you are doing–right now–and send Rush Limbaugh a message. Tell him to make sure that all his listeners buy a copy of **The Internet Yellow Pages.**

Roger McGuinn

Roger McGuinn, singer-songwriter, musician and founder of the Byrds.

Mail:
Address: **71571.672@compuserve.com**

Marvin Minsky

Talk to one of the fathers of Artifical Intelligence. Ask him if he knows if the Vice-President of the U.S. is really a Turing Machine.

Mail:
Address: **minsky@media.mit.edu**

MATHEMATICS

American Mathematical Society

A variety of mathematical topics, including information about Fermat's Last Theorem, mathematical publications, conference information, and access to other mathematical sites.

Gopher:
Name: American Mathematical Society
Address: **e-math.ams.com**

Differential Equations

The Electronic Journal of Differential Equations is a collection of academic papers that discuss all aspects of differential equations and is available in TeX and postscript formats.

Anonymous FTP:
Address: **ftp.unt.edu**
Path: **/EJDE/***

E-Math

The BBS of the American Mathematics Society. Offers conversation, software, and software reviews.

Telnet:
Address: **e-math.ams.com**
Login: **e-math**
Password: **e-math**

General Discussion

A general discussion of things mathematical. Remember, a person who knows his numbers is a person you can count on.

Usenet:
Newsgroup: **sci.math**

GNU Plot

Interactive Unix program for plotting mathematical expressions and data, complete with source.

Anonymous FTP:
Address: **aeneas.mit.edu**
Path: **/pub/gnu/gnuplot***

Address: **sunsite.unc.edu**
Path: **/pub/gnu/gnuplot***

Archie:
Pattern: **gnuplot**

Logic

(1) The Internet is important to the human race. (2) Before you can use the Internet, you must learn how it works. (3) *The Internet Complete Reference* is the best Internet book ever written. Therefore, it follows that (4) anyone who has not bought *The Internet Complete Reference* has not fulfilled his or her obligation as a human being. For more complex questions of logic, read this newsgroup, in which you will find discussions of mathematics, philosophy and computation.

Usenet:
Newsgroup: **sci.logic**

Math Archives Gopher

Most all public domain and shareware software, as well as many other materials that can be used to teach mathematics at the community college, college, and university levels.

Gopher:
Name: University of Tennessee, Knoxville
Address: **archives.math.utk.edu**

MATH ARCHIVES

YES, MATHEMATICS IS TRULY THE QUEEN OF SCIENCES, AND THE MATHEMATICS GOPHER IS TRULY THE QUEEN OF GOPHERS. IF YOU HAVE ANYTHING TO DO WITH LEARNING, TEACHING OR ENJOYING MATH, YOU WILL LOVE THIS GOPHER. FIRST, IT HAS A WEALTH OF INFORMATION AND FREE SOFTWARE. SECOND, PLAYING WITH A GOPHER IS A LOT EASIER THAN ACTUALLY DOING YOUR HOMEWORK. (REMEMBER, A MAN WHO KNOWS HIS NUMBERS IS A MAN YOU CAN COUNT ON.)

A B C D E F G H I J K L M N O P Q R S T U V W X Y Z

Math Articles

Documents on mathematics, including a fuzzy-logic tutorial, FAQs, fractals, Putnam problems, the mathematics of perspective, and other interesting topics.

Anonymous FTP:
Address: **ftp.spies.com**
Path: **/Library/Article/Math/***

Gopher:
Name: Internet Wiretap
Address: **wiretap.spies.com**
Choose: **Wiretap Online Library**
  | **Articles**
  | **Mathematics**

Math and Calculus Programs

Interesting and useful mathematics and calculus programs.

Anonymous FTP:
Address: **wuarchive.wustl.edu**
Path: **/edu/math/msdos/calculus/***

Math and Philosophy

Do you agree that even Frege can be faulted for insufficient tenacity in giving up his program after Russell's discovery of the eponymous paradox? Or do you think that ramified type theory, contextual definition of class abstracts, the doctrine of acquaintance, and the theory of proposition identity are just so much hot air? Sit in with those people who really understand who shaves the barber (if the barber shaves everyone who does not shave himself). Just be careful to behave yourself: someone may prove that you do not really exist.

Usenet:
Newsgroup: **sci.philosophy.tech**

Math Programs for the Mac

An FTP site that contains science and math software for Apple Macintosh computers.

Anonymous FTP:
Address: **info.umd.edu**
Path: **/pub/software/Macintosh/Math-Science/***

Mathematical Research

Keep abreast of what is happening in the world of mathematics. Just the place to send your new proof of Fermat's Last Theorem that *does* fit in the margin of a book.

Usenet:
Newsgroup: **sci.math.research**

MathWorks

Discussions regarding Matlab, the calculation and visualization package from MathWorks.

Usenet:
Newsgroup: **comp.soft-sys.matlab**

Excerpt from the Net...

```
Newsgroups: sci.math, sci.philosophy.tech, sci.lang, sci.logic
Subject: Is this finite or infinite?

> Well, then, if you're an ambitious logician, try your hand at
> describing the anaphoric construction (and finding the indirect
> quotation) in this example:
>      John didn't catch a fish, and he didn't eat it.

This is easy:  Quantify over concepts, and define the relation of things falling under
(singular or natural kind) concepts.  Then proceed to say that there is no object X
falling under the concept of fish, such that John caught X, or John ate X.  (Note that
this analysis works for unicorns just as well.)  As for the scope of indirect quotation,
it is implicit in the intentional aspect of John's sporting and alimentary failure --
since to catch X is to succeed in seeking that X comes in one's possession.  Again, all
of this is exceedingly well known from intensional logic.
```

NetLib

Math software programs via e-mail. Include the line **send index** in the body of an e-mail message.

Mail:
Address: **netlib@ornl.gov**
Address: **netlib@uunet.uu.net**

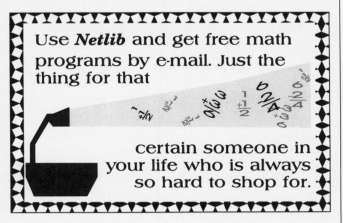

Use *Netlib* and get free math programs by e-mail. Just the thing for that

certain someone in your life who is always so hard to shop for.

Nonlinear Dynamics

Preprints and programs on nonlinear dynamics, signal processing and related subjects, including fractal papers.

Anonymous FTP:
Address: **lyapunov.ucsd.edu**
Path: **/pub/***

Numerical Analysis

It's amazing how many people still don't know a Tchebyshev polynomial from a fourth-order Runge-Kutte algorithm. Join the discussion with people who want more out of life than the simple L2 norm that seems to satisfy a whole world of mathematically-disadvantaged social scientists.

Usenet:
Newsgroup: **sci.math.num-analysis**

Pi to 1 Million Digits

The first one million digits of pi, that mathematical marvel. Provided by Project Gutenberg.

Gopher:
Name: University of Minnesota
Address: **gopher.micro.umn.edu**
Choose: **Libraries**
| Electronic Books
| By Title

Pi to 1.25 Million Digits

The first 1.25 million digits of pi, that mathematical wonder.

Anonymous FTP:
Address: **wuarchive.wustl.edu**
Path: **/doc/misc/pi/***

Society for Industrial and Applied Mathematics

The Society for Industrial and Applied Mathematics (SIAM) Gopher Server provides information about activities and issues of interest to applied and computational mathematicians and to engineers and scientists who use mathematics and computers.

Gopher:
Name:
Society for Industrial and Applied Mathematics
Address: **gopher.siam.org**

Square Root of 2

The square root of 2 to many decimal places.

Gopher:
Name: University of Minnesota
Address: **gopher.micro.umn.edu**
Choose: **Libraries**
| Electronic Books
| By Title

Statistics

When you need a fuzzy clustering algorithm, do you go to a statistical mathematician or a mathematical statistician? Try both. Two complementary newsgroups for people who are approximately right, some or all of the time.

Usenet:
Newsgroup: **sci.math.stat**
Newsgroup: **sci.stat.math**

StatLib Archives

Programs, datasets, instructions and help for statisticians. Include the line **send index** in the body of your mail message.

Gopher:
Name: StatLib Server
Address: **lib.stat.cmu.edu**

Mail:
Address: **statlib@lib.stat.cmu.edu**

StatLib Gopher Server

Presents a Gopher view of the StatLib archives.

Gopher:
> Name: Carnegie Mellon University
> Address: **lib.stat.cmu.edu**
> Choose: **StatLib Gopher Server**

Symbolic Algebra

The invention of symbolic computational programs has added a whole new set of tools to the arsenal of the practicing mathematician. This group discusses such tools, as well as the related mathematical issues. Talk about Mathematica, Maple, Macsyma and Reduce. (My goodness, is Reduce still around? We remember using it back in the mid-1970s. Oh, how symbolic algebra makes one feel old.)

Usenet:
> Newsgroup: **sci.math.symbolic**

Teaching: Elementary and High Schools

If you hated math in school, how do you think your teachers felt? Find out by taking a look at these discussion groups: **.tecmat** for high school, **k12** for teachers in all grades; the **.stat** group for teachers of statistics.

Usenet:
> Newsgroup: **bit.listserv.tecmat-l**
> Newsgroup: **k12.ed.math**
> Newsgroup: **sci.stat.edu**

Weights and Measures

A detailed conversion table including mathematical notation, metric inter-relationships, and metric equivalents.

Gopher:
> Name: Asian Institute of Technology
> Address: **emailhost.ait.ac.th**
> Choose: **Library Resources**
> | **On-line Reference Works**
> | **Other Reference Works**
> | **Weights and Measures**

MEDICINE

AIDS

Acquired Immune Deficiency Syndrome and the HIV virus. Read this moderated newsgroup to keep up to date on the medical treatments of AIDS, including the AIDS daily summary from the Centers for Disease Control and Prevention (CDC) National AIDS Clearinghouse.

Usenet:
> Newsgroup: **sci.med.aids**

AIDS Information via CHAT Database

CHAT (Conversational Hypertext Access Technology) database system. You can ask questions of this database in plain English. It correctly interprets an amazing number of questions and instantly provides answers about AIDS—especially about AIDS in Canada.

Telnet:
> Address: **debra.dgbt.doc.ca**
> Login: **chat**

AIDS Statistics

Center for Disease Control's monthly AIDS Surveillance Reports and other information on AIDS.

Internet mailing list:
> List Address: **aids-stat@wubios.wustl.edu**
> Subscription Address:
> **aids-stat-request@wubios.wustl.edu**

AIDS Treatment News and Facts

AIDS treatment news, access to an AIDS BBS, newsletters, statistics, and much more AIDS-related information.

Gopher:
> Name:
> National Institute of Allergy & Infectious Disease
> Address: **odie.niaid.nih.gov**
> Choose: **AIDS Related Information**

Alternative Medicine

Tired of legal drugs and poor bedside manner? Drop in to the alternative medicine forum where alternative-oriented people share alternative medical tips, alternative home remedies, and alternative approaches to healing. (If you can't make it, send an alternate.)

Usenet:
> Newsgroup: **misc.health.alternative**

Alternative Medicine

Our philosophy is that it is better to not get sick in the first place. Still, if you do, it is nice to know that you have a forum in which you can discuss the types of things that you can only whisper about at the doctor's office. So, next time you need to know how many leeches to use to cure brain cancer, check with your friends on **misc.health.alternative**

Remember the old saying about an apple a day. . .

Anesthesiology

Discussion of topics and dissemination of information related to anesthesiology.

Listserv mailing list:
List Address: **anest-l@ubvm.bitnet**
Subscription Address: **listserv@ubvm.bitnet**

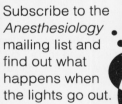

Subscribe to the *Anesthesiology* mailing list and find out what happens when the lights go out.

Ayurvedic Medicine

In Sanskrit, *Ayurveda* means "laws of health", and is the name of one of the four sacred Hindu texts. Ayurvedic medicine is based on Indian traditions over 3000 years old. Read this newsgroup and learn about this ancient healing art and how it is practiced today.

Usenet:
Newsgroup: **alt.health.ayurveda**

Biomedical Engineering

If you ever find medical imaging too boring, this is the place to be: signal processing, biomedical engineering, your cup will runneth over.

Usenet:
Newsgroup: **sci.engr.biomed**

CancerNet

Health and clinical information about cancer and cancer research.

Gopher:
Name: National Institute of Health
Address: **gopher.nih.gov**
Choose: **Health and Clinical Information | CancerNet Information**

Mail:
Address: **cancernet@icicb.nci.nih.gov**

Chronic Fatigue Syndrome

As the song says, "I'm so tired, I haven't slept a wink". Chronic fatigue syndrome is no fun. Join the discussion and share tips, experiences and recommendations.

Listserv mailing list:
List Address: **cfs-l@nihlist.bitnet**
Subscription Address: **listserv@nihlist.bitnet**

Usenet:
Newsgroup: **alt.med.cfs**

Dentistry

Long in the tooth or down in the mouth, everyone is welcome to this discussion on dentists, materials and dental techniques. Whether you need help on deciding if implants are better than a bridge, or you just want to read humorous stories about people who have had their jaws wired shut, nothing is more exciting and breathtaking than modern dentistry.

Usenet:
Newsgroup: **sci.med.dentistry**

A B C D E F G H I J K L M N O P Q R S T U V W X Y Z

Excerpt from the Net...

```
Newsgroup: sci.med.dentistry
Subject: Need stories about jaw wiring

I am looking for humorous anecdotes
about patients who have had their jaws
wired shut,especially for the purpose
of weight control.

Please E-mail me direct at:
xxxxx.ucla.edu

Thank you,
Xxxxxxx Xxxxxxxxx, D.M.D.
```

Developmentally Disabled and Autism

A mailing list for those who are developmentally disabled, their teachers, or anyone interested in the subject.

Listserv mailing list:
　List Address: **autism@sjuvm.bitnet**
　Subscription Address: **listserv@sjuvm.bitnet**

Digital Imaging and Communications

Join discussions of the technical details of digital imaging and communications as practiced in bio-engineering and medicine.

Usenet:
　Newsgroup: **comp.protocols.dicom**

Drugs Information

Read the latest reports and journals from the Food and Drug Administration's database. Called Medline, the database has the latest information.

Telnet:
　Address: **library.umdnj.edu**
　Login: **library**

　Address: **utmem1.utmem.edu**
　Login: **harvey**

E.T. Net

An information system run by the National Library of Medicine. It features conferences on computer aided education in health sciences, hypermedia, expert systems, patient simulations, nursing care, computer hardware and software—including medical shareware.

Telnet:
　Address: **etnet.nlm.nih.gov**
　Login: **etnet**

Epilepsy Information via CHAT Database

A CHAT (Conversational Hypertext Access Technology) database system. You can ask questions of this database in plain English. It correctly interprets an amazing number of questions and instantly provides answers about epilepsy.

Telnet:
　Address: **debra.dgbt.doc.ca**
　Login: **chat**

Forensic Medicine

Articles on forensic medicine, the application of the principles and practice of medicine to the needs of the law, including diagnostic criteria in surgical pathology.

Gopher:
　Name: MedCal
　Address: **gopher.vifp.monash.edu.au**
　Choose: **Medical**
　　| **Forensic Medicine**

General Medical Discussion

Here is the agora of the Usenet medical community. Need to find out the etiology of kidney stones? Need to find out what "etiology" means? This is the place for you. General, free-flowing talk on everything medical. (Does anyone have a cure for a chrono-synclastic infidibulum?)

Usenet:
　Newsgroup: **sci.med**

Genetic Sequence Data Bank

Genetic sequence data, a database search utility, and other databases of interest to molecular biologists.

Gopher:
　Name: National Institute of Health
　Address: **helix.nih.gov**
　Choose: **Molecular Biology Databases**

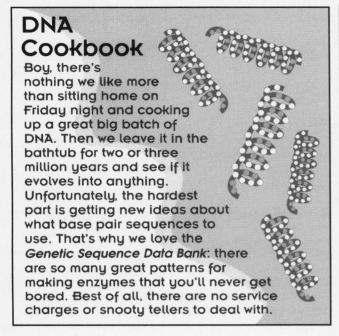

DNA Cookbook

Boy, there's nothing we like more than sitting home on Friday night and cooking up a great big batch of DNA. Then we leave it in the bathtub for two or three million years and see if it evolves into anything. Unfortunately, the hardest part is getting new ideas about what base pair sequences to use. That's why we love the *Genetic Sequence Data Bank*: there are so many great patterns for making enzymes that you'll never get bored. Best of all, there are no service charges or snooty tellers to deal with.

Genetics Bank

A genetics database, including nucleic acid and protein sequence provided by the National Center of Biotechnology Information (part of the National Library of Medicine). Query the database by e-mail.

Mail:
Address: **blast@ncbi.nlm.nih.gov**
Body: **help**

Address: **gene-server@bchs.uh.edu**
Body: **help**

Address: **retrieve@ncbi.nlm.nih.gov**
Body: **help**

Imaging

The technical details of medical imaging are fascinating. Indulge yourself.

Usenet:
Newsgroup: **alt.image.medical**

MEDCAL

The Medical Computer Assisted Learning Resource Archive contains information on research in progress, software packages, developmental tools, and other general information related to this field.

Gopher:
Name: MedCal
Address: **gopher.vifp.monash.edu.au**
Choose: **Medical**
I **MEDCAL - Medical Computer Assisted Learning Resource Archive**

Medical Libraries

Discussions on the care and feeding of medical libraries (and medical librarians).

Usenet:
Newsgroup: **bit.listserv.medlib-l**

Medical Physics

Here is the forum for medical physicists (those nice people who give you radiation therapy). Do they really glow in the dark or is that just an old wives' tale?

Usenet:
Newsgroup: **sci.med.physics**

Medical Resources

A guide to, and large list of, medical resources on the Internet.

Anonymous FTP:
Address: **nic.funet.fi**
Path: **/pub/doc/library/medical_resources.txt.Z**

Medical Software

Macintosh software useful to the health science professional.

Anonymous FTP:
Address: **archie.au**
Path: **/micros/mac/umich/misc/medical/***

Address: **mac.archive.umich.edu**
Path: **/mac/misc/medical/***

Gopher:
Name: MedCal
Address: **gopher.vifp.monash.edu.au**
Choose: **Medical**
I **MEDCAL - Medical Computer Assisted Learning Resource Archive**
I **Software and Demos for downloading**

A
B
C
D
E
F
G
H
I
J
K
L
M
N
O
P
Q
R
S
T
U
V
W
X
Y
Z

Medical Software and Data

An archive of software and documentation aimed at fostering educational and practical uses of computers in medicine and health sciences.

Anonymous FTP:
Address: **ccsun.unicamp.br**
Path: **/pub/medicine/***

Medical Students Forum

Medical students voice their doubts and opinions in this moderated forum. Not a medical student yourself? Not to worry. Tune in and eavesdrop on what the future healers of America are up to.

Usenet:
Newsgroup: **bit.listserv.medforum**

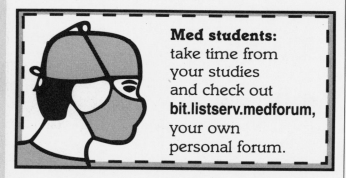

Med students: take time from your studies and check out **bit.listserv.medforum,** your own personal forum.

Medical/Health Information

Offers access to a large number of medical resources from a single menu, including Camis, CancerNet, Medinfo and many more.

Gopher:
Name: Albert Einstein College of Medicine
Address: **gopher.aecom.yu.edu**
Choose: **Internet Resources**
| Medical/Health Information

Mednews

An electronic journal dedicated to what is new and exciting in the field of medicine.

Usenet:
Newsgroup: **bit.listserv.mednews**

National Cancer Center Database (Japan)

Database interfaces for physicians, patients, researchers and other interested people. Other information includes design of clinical trials information, supportive care, cancer screening guidelines, news and general information. A mailing list is also available.

Gopher:
Name: National Cancer Center
Address: **gan.ncc.go.jp**
Choose: **CancerNet service**

National Library of Medicine (NLM) Locator

The locator searches the book holdings database (CATLINE), the audiovisual holdings database (AVLINE), and the journal holdings database (SERLINE) of the U.S. National Library of Medicine. Information is also available on library hours, policies, interlibrary loan and the National Network of Libraries of Medicine (NN/LM).

Gopher:
Name:
Spencer S. Eccles Health Sciences Library Gopher
Address: **el-gopher.med.utah.edu**

Telnet:
Address: **locator.nlm.nih.gov**
Login: **locator**
Password:
Health Sciences Resources on the Internet

Nursing

The Nightingale Gopher is all about nursing, including research, practice, education, nursing publications, professional nursing communications and other nursing resources.

Gopher:
Name: Nightingale
Address: **nightingale.con.utk.edu**

Occupational Medicine

Need to pick out a back-friendly chair or an ergonomic keyboard? This discussion on occupational medicine will be just what the doctor would have ordered if he had thought of it.

Usenet:
Newsgroup: **sci.med.occupational**

Paramedics

If you have been eating an apple a day and you still need help, you may not be able to get the doctor to come over; however, the paramedics are always available. Join the discussion with paramedics and other emergency workers.

Usenet:
Newsgroup: **misc.emerg-services**

PET Scan Image Database

A database of Positron Emission Tomography (PET) scan images for a variety of human medical conditions. Images are accompanied by informative text files. Image files are in JPEG format.

Gopher:
Name: Austin Hospital
Address: **austin.unimelb.edu.au**
Choose: **Digital Image Library**
| **Austin Hospital PET Centre Image Database**

Pharmacy

What a pickle. You are in charge of fund raising for the local PTA and you forgot the recipe for methylenedioxyamphetamine. Ask a pharmacist.

Or maybe you just need a pharmacist joke. (Did you hear about the pill counter who married the bean counter? They had a son who became a CPA, but would only work one hour before or three hours after meals.) Find out why pharmacy is the new glamour profession of the nineties.

Usenet:
Newsgroup: **sci.med.pharmacy**

Politics and Medicine

Talk is cheap, but medical care is not. What happens when an irresistable force (health care reform) meets an immovable object (the health care industry)? Join the ongoing debate and share your story of Uncle Willie and his gallbladder operation.

Usenet:
Newsgroup: **talk.politics.medicine**

TIRED OF EXPENSIVE MEDICAL BILLS? TALK IS CHEAP. DROP IN TO THE **talk.politics.medicine** DISCUSSION GROUP.

Repetitive Stress Injuries

A list for those in the Boston area interested in the Boston RSI (Repetitive Stress Injury) Support Group. Repetitive stress injuries are those such as carpal tunnel syndrome, cumulative trauma disorders, tendonitis and nerve compression, and are caused by repetitive motion.

Internet mailing list:
List Address: **boston-rsi@world.std.com**
Subscription Address:
boston-rsi-request@world.std.com

Sci.Med.AIDS Newsgroup

A mailing list for medical issues related to AIDS as well as some discussion of political and social issues.

Listserv mailing list:
List Address: **aids@rutvm1.bitnet**
Subscription Address: **listserv@rutvm1.bitnet**

Telemedicine

Clinical consulting through computer networks. New technology for the world's second oldest profession.

Usenet:
Newsgroup: **sci.med.telemedicine**

Spare time? Take a look at Games

A B C D E F G H I J K L M N O P Q R S T U V W X Y Z

MILITARY

Defense Conversion Subcommittee

Forums for associations, institutes, think tanks, and consultants for defense conversion. Includes weekly updates, government contacts, Russian conversion issues, and success stories.

Gopher:
Name: University of California San Diego
Address: **infopath.ucsd.edu**
Choose: **News & Services**
  | Economic..
  | Defense Conversion..

Military Collections

Collection of papers and viewpoints about the military, its people, policies and practices, including book reviews and intelligence information.

Gopher:
Name: Whole Earth Lectronic Link
Address: **gopher.well.sf.ca.us**
Choose:
  The Military, its People, Policies, and Practices

Naval Fighting Ships

Information on U.S. battleships and battle cruisers, including specifications and statistics.

Anonymous FTP:
Address: **ftp.spies.com**
Path: **/Gov/US-History/Naval/***

Gopher:
Name: Internet Wiretap
Address: **wiretap.spies.com**
Choose: **Government Docs (US & World)**
  | US Historical Documents
  | Naval Fighting Ships

Navy News Service (NAVNEWS)

An electronic magazine with articles of interest to those in, or interested in, the Navy. Includes good articles on the Internet by famous authors and such items as the air

show schedule for the Blue Angels. Mail for information on how to get on the mailing list and where to FTP files.

Gopher:
Name: Library of Congress
Address: **marvel.loc.gov**
Choose: **Federal Government Information**
  | Federal Information Resources
  | Information by Agency
  | Military Ag

Mail:
Address: **navnews@nctamslant.navy.mil**

Generous movie fans take the time to create images of famous scenes and settings in their favorite movies. This means a wealth of art at your fingertips. You can easily import images you find on the Net into your favorite word-processing program.

Navy Policy Book

The full text of the United States *Navy Policy Book*.

Gopher:
Name: Library of Congress
Address: **gopher.loc.gov**
Choose: **Federal Govt. Information**
  | Fed. Information Resources
  | Info by Agency | Military Agencies
  | The Navy Policy Book

A number of great U.S. Navy ship photographs can be found at the University of North Carolina. The computer is **sunsite.unc.edu** and the path is /pub/academic/history/marshall/maritime/pictures. Some of these images also exist on machines in Taiwan. Use Archie to find them. This image of a WWII destroyer is called **ship4.gif**.

Lonely? Try the Personals

Tattoo

The electronic newspaper of the Australian Defense Force Academy. Read about the daily regimen of cadets and other items of interest.

Gopher:
Name: Australian Defense Force Academy
Address: **ccadfa.cc.adfa.oz.au**
Choose: **ACC Tattoos**

U.S. Code of Military Justice

The first 12 chapters of this legal guide for the military.

Anonymous FTP:
Address: **ftp.spies.com**
Path: **/Gov/UCMJ/***

Gopher:
Name: Internet Wiretap
Address: **wiretap.spies.com**
Choose: **Government Docs**
   | **Uniform Code of Military Justice**

War History

Documents about wars and battles, including the Gulf War, World War II and Hiroshima, Vietnam, secret wars of the CIA, and other conflicts.

Anonymous FTP:
Address: **english-server.hss.cmu.edu**
Path: **/English Server/Progressive/Gulf War/***

Gopher:
Name: The English-Server
Address: **english-server.hss.cmu.edu**
Choose: **Progressive**
   | **Gulf War**

MISCHIEF

Big Book of Mischief

Information on how to make explosives, tennis ball cannons, carbide bombs, how to open locks, and other vital information for the budding soldier of fortune.

Anonymous FTP:
Address: **ftp.spies.com**
Path: **/Library/Untech/tbbom13.txt**

Gopher:
Name: Internet Wiretap
Address: **wiretap.spies.com**
Choose: **Wiretap Online Library**
   | **Questionables**
   | **The Big Book of Mischief v1.3**

Practical Jokes

For serious enjoyment what could be more fun than embarrassing your friends and neighbors by making them look foolish? The dribble glass and plastic vomit are child's play. Check out this newsgroup for new ideas, techniques and experiences with practical jokes. Make your loved ones say "uncle", and make your uncle say, "bork, bork, bork".

Usenet:
Newsgroup: **alt.shenanigans**

Why be normal?
Read Bizarre

Excerpt from the Net...

(from the electronic newspaper of the Australian Defence Force Academy)

```
ACC'S TATTOO FOR 11 DEC 93

Drill timings
Saturday 11 DEC 1993: Band, Pipes and Drums F/up 0845 Assembly Hall

0800: All Graduating Class to parade at the head of the parade ground for "reform"
      rehearsal.

0900: Corps in position to march onto practice parade ground (oval No.4).  Drum Corps
      required -- Band to rehearsals in the Assembly Hall.

1200: Corps dismissed.

NOTE: Everyone is to carry a water bottle on their belt.
```

A
B
C
D
E
F
G
H
I
J
K
L
M
N
O
P
Q
R
S
T
U
V
W
X
Y
Z

Revenge

Landlord got you pissed? Teacher rapped you with a ruler? Your ex-SO (significant other) won't return your only copy of *The Little Prince*? Don't get mad, get even. Join the pros and find out just how smelly a fish in the ventilation duct can be. (Federal regulations require us to remind you of the ancient Chinese saying: "Before you set out for revenge, be sure to dig two graves.")

Usenet:
Newsgroup: **alt.revenge**

Terrorist's Handbook

A few of the techniques and methods employed by people who use terror as a means to achieve their social and political goals.

Anonymous FTP:
Address: **ftp.spies.com**
Path: **/Library/Untech/terror.hb**

Gopher:
Name: Internet Wiretap
Address: **wiretap.spies.com**
Choose: **Wiretap Online Library**
| **Questionables**
| **The Terrorist's Handbook**

Stuff You Are Not Supposed to Know About

Whether you are planning to blow up the World Trade Center, or merely explode a few small devices on the White House lawn, the *Terrorist's Handbook* is an invaluable guide to having a good time. Where else can you get such wonderful ideas about how to use up all that extra ammonium triiodide left over from last year's revolution?

MOVIES

Cinema Discussion List

A mailing list dedicated to the discussion of cinema, in all its aspects. This list hopes to attract a variety of viewpoints and opinions.

Listserv mailing list:
List Address: **cinema-l@auvm.bitnet**
Subscription Address: **listserv@auvm.bitnet**

Film Database

Search a database of synopses, cast lists and other information on thousands of films released before 1987.

Gopher:
Name: Manchester Computing Centre
Address: **info.mcc.ac.uk**
Choose: **Miscellaneous items**
| **Film database**

Mail:
Address: **movie@ibmpcg.co.uk**
Body: **help**

Horror Talk

Love a movie that scares you out of your wits? You're not alone. Join with other fans of horror and scary films in this mailing list forum and talk about all your favorites.

Listserv mailing list:
List Address: **horror@pacevm.dac.pace.edu**
Subscription Address:
listserv@pacevm.dac.pace.edu

Look around. Is anyone watching? Good. Take a look at the X-Rated section. (But remember, you didn't read it here.)

Movie Database Request Server

Perform detailed searches for movies by title, actor, actress or director. This database is large and contains a great deal of information.

Anonymous FTP:
  Address: **refuge.colorado.edu**
  Path: **/pub/tv+movies/lists/***

Mail:
  Address: **movie@ibmpcug.co.uk**
  Body: **help**

Movie Folklore

Interesting folklore about movies, including *The Wizard of Oz, The Little Mermaid, Beauty and the Beast,* and *Faces of Death.*

Anonymous FTP:
  Address: **cathouse.org**
  Path: **/pub/cathouse/urban.legends/movies/***

Images from TV shows and movies are in abundant supply on the Internet. This picture was downloaded via Anonymous FTP from Washington University Saint Louis (**ftp.wustl.edu**). The pathname for this image is **/multimedia/images/gif/1_numbers/3stooges.gif**. If you'd like to find images from movies or cartoons, you can usually find what you want with a little imagination and Archie. For example, try an Archie substring search for **batman**, **beauty**, or **mermaid**.

Movie List

The canonical movie list, and more specific lists, including the James Bond movie list, railway movies, film noir list, Hitchcock information, vampire movie list and others.

Anonymous FTP:
  Address: **ftp.spies.com**
  Path: **/Library/Media/Film/***

Gopher:
  Name: Internet Wiretap
  Address: **wiretap.spies.com**
  Choose: **Wiretap Online Library**
    | **Mass Media** | **Film and Movies**

Reviews

Thousands of reviews of all the popular movies, from a variety of critics.

Anonymous FTP:
  Address: **nic.funet.fi**
  Path: **/pub/culture/tv+film/reviews/***

Gopher:
  Name: The World
  Address: **world.std.com**

  Name: University of Minnesota
  Address: **ashpool.micro.umn.edu**
  Choose: **Fun**
    | **Movies**

Weird Movie List

A long, alphabetical list of weird movies, including descriptions.

Anonymous FTP:
  Address: **ftp.spies.com**
  Path: **/Library/Media/Film/weird.mov**

Gopher:
  Name: Internet Wiretap
  Address: **wiretap.spies.com**
  Choose: **Wiretap Online Library**
    | **Mass Media**
    | **Film and Movies**
    | **Weird Movie List**

MUDs: GENERAL INFORMATION

Administrating MUDs

As a player, if you think it's an inconvenience when your MUD crashes, think how it would be if you were in charge of the machine that crashed it. Learn the ins and outs of being an administrator of a multiple user dimension. How do you start a MUD, and once you get it started, how in the world do you keep it going?

Usenet:
  Newsgroup: **rec.games.mud.admin**

A
B
C
D
E
F
G
H
I
J
K
L
M
N
O
P
Q
R
S
T
U
V
W
X
Y
Z

Announcements

What's new? What's passed away? Every Friday get the latest word on what MUD sites are up and running and which ones have been put to pasture. Did you lose your favorite MUD? Ask around here—someone will know the answer.

Usenet:

Newsgroup: **rec.games.mud.announce**

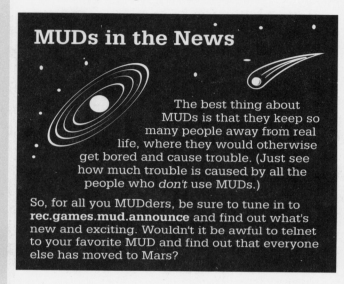

MUDs in the News

The best thing about MUDs is that they keep so many people away from real life, where they would otherwise get bored and cause trouble. (Just see how much trouble is caused by all the people who *don't* use MUDs.)

So, for all you MUDders, be sure to tune in to **rec.games.mud.announce** and find out what's new and exciting. Wouldn't it be awful to telnet to your favorite MUD and find out that everyone else has moved to Mars?

DikuMUDs

A DikuMUD is a text-based, role-playing virtual reality. Slay a dragon, save a princess, drink a magic potion which will kill you (these are all optional, of course). If you love excitement, adventure and fantasy find out what DikuMUDs are all about.

Usenet:

Newsgroup: **rec.games.mud.diku**

German Speakers

Sprechen Sie Deutsch? German-speaking MUDders not only experience the thrill of MUDding, but they can do it in German, making it extra special.

Usenet:

Newsgroup: **alt.mud.german**

LPMUDs

Hack it, slash it, just make sure you clean up afterward. LPMUDs are text-based virtual realities where you can puzzle out a quest for advancement in the game or you can just find monsters to kill. Discover the adventurer

within you. If you are already a hard-core MUDder and want to set up your own, check out **alt.mud.lp** on get tips on how to start.

Usenet:

Newsgroup: **alt.mud.lp**

Newsgroup: **rec.games.mud.lp**

MUD Documents

An interesting selection of information about MUDs, including a history of MUD, inter-MUD communication, a MUD survey, and a paper on social virtual reality in the real world.

Gopher:

Name: University of Stuttgart

Address: **nova.tat.physik.uni-tuebingen.de 4242**

Choose: **Nightfall Gopher Information Services | Documents and papers about MUDs**

MUD Information

A large selection of information all about MUDs and the culture surrounding them, including research articles, clients, FTP sites, MUD lists and descriptions of the various MUDs. It also catorgorizes MUDs into their different types and allows you to connect directly to them from the Gopher.

Gopher:

Name: University of Texas at Austin

Address: **actlab.rtf.utexas.edu**

Choose: **Virtual Spaces: MUD**

MUD List

List of all the Internet MUDs you will ever want to play. Categorizes each MUD and provides both numeric and name addresses, status and any further information (such as how to register).

Anonymous FTP:

Address: **caisr2.caisr.cwru.edu**

Path: **/pub/mud**

The Internet will set you free

MUD as a Psychological Model

A theory discussing MUD as a psychological model, and issues concerning the separation of reality from virtual reality.

Anonymous FTP:
    Address: **ftp.spies.com**
    Path: **/Library/Cyber/realife.mud**

Gopher:
    Name: Internet Wiretap
    Address: **wiretap.spies.com**
    Choose: **Wiretap Online Library**
    | **Cyberspace**
    | **MUD as a Psychological Model**

MUD Usenet Discussion Groups

Immerse yourself in the wonder of multiple user dimension games (MUDs). Text-based virtual realities provide you with an exciting realm in which to socialize or play adventure games. Find out what MUDding is all about, but be warned: The Surgeon General has declared MUDding to be addictive.

Usenet:
    Newsgroup: **alt.mud**
    Newsgroup: **rec.games.mud.misc**

MUDWHO Server

Shows the current players on various MUDs. Each MUDWHO Server will know who is using various MUDs, so check the different servers to see which one keeps track of players on your favorite MUD.

Telnet:
    Address: **actlab.rtf.utexas.edu 6889**
    Address: **af.itd.com 6889**
    Address: **amber.ecst.csuchico.edu 6889**
    Address: **dancer.ethz.ch 6889**
    Address: **nova.tat.physik.uni-tuebingen.de 6889**
    Address: **riemann.math.okstate.edu 6889**

Tiny MUDs

Some MUDders consider adventuring and killing monsters barbaric. Imagine that. These social animals hang out on Tiny MUDs where social skill is a high art. If you are interested in chatting, making friends or other interactive socializing, you'll love Tiny MUDs (including MUSH, MUSE, and MOO).

Usenet:
    Newsgroup: **alt.mud.tiny**
    Newsgroup: **rec.games.mud.tiny**

MUDs: SPECIFIC TYPES

Actuator MUD

Actuator is about building cyberspace. It is for researching and designing drivers, clients, graphics, mudlibs, worlds, networked objects and social interaction.

Telnet:
    Address: **actlab.rtf.utexas.edu 4000**

Actuator MUD Gopher

Browse Actuator MUD, list its users, connect to other MUD Gopher servers, or simply connect to Actuator MUD itself.

Gopher:
    Name: University of Texas at Austin
    Address: **actlab.rtf.utexas.edu 3452**

AlexMUD

The oldest DikuMUD on the Internet, started on March 9th, 1991. Based in Sweden, it has its own distinctive style and depth—which accounts for its popularity.

Telnet:
    Address: **marcel.stacken.kth.se 4000**
    Address: **mud.stacken.kth.se 4000**

Apocalypse

A very popular Diku MUD, with lots of extras. Seven different races, nine different character classes, chit-chat channels, and even color! Check it out.

Telnet:
    Address: **peabrain.humgen.upenn.edu 4000**

BurningDiku

An expanding DikuMUD, with lots of new areas, spells, skills, levels and smarter, tougher monsters.

Telnet:
    Address: **next5.cas.muohio.edu 4000**

Too much spare time?
Explore a MUD

A B C D E F G H I J K L M N O P Q R S T U V W X Y Z

Chupchups

MUDs come in all shapes and sizes. Chupchups is one of those MUDs with a very distinctive shape. It's so distinctive it gets its own newsgroup.

Usenet:
　　Newsgroup: **alt.mud.chupchup**

CoolMud

CoolMud is a distributed, multiuser, object-oriented programmable, world-building environment where players can create their own ideas.

Telnet:
　　Address: **groan.berkeley.edu 8888**

Copper Diku

A friendly, modified DikuMUD with selection of hometown, special city for killers, battle arena, new areas, and even jail for law-breaking players.

Telnet:
　　Address: **copper.denver.colorado.edu 4000**

Dark Shadow's DikuMUD

Based on the *Dragonlance* books (Weis & Hickman), with eight races (including gnomish and kender), ten classes (including druids and monks), guilds, and a Realm of Souls for those who met their fate.

Telnet:
　　Address: **jericho.connected.com 6666**

Deeper Trouble

A classic fantasy-based LPmud with a Tolkienesque theme.

Telnet:
　　Address: **alk.iesd.auc.dk 4242**

DikuMud II

Roam fantastic lands playing human, elf, dwarf, halfling or gnome characters in the official Version Two of the original DikuMud-style MUD.

Telnet:
　　Address: **mud.stacken.kth.se 4242**

Dirt

A classic adventure-style AberMud.

Telnet:
　　Address: **alkymene.uio.no 6715**

Discworld MUD

An LPMud based on the colorful *Discworld* books by the legendary Terry Pratchet. Discworld is where—as the Wombles and Blues will tell you—all your dreams can't come true.

Telnet:
　　Address: **cix.compulink.co.uk 4242**

Discworld MUD Gopher

Allows one to view and find information about players of DiscWorld MUD, and offers easy access to other MUD and entertainment-related Gophers.

Gopher:
　　Name: Compulink
　　Address: **cix.compulink.co.uk 3450**

Game Server

Choose from a multitude of exciting online games, including Bucks, Moria, Tetris, Sokoban, Reversi, Nethack, and many adventure games, including MUDs.

Gopher:
　　Name: University of Stuttgart
　　Address: **rusinfo.rus.uni-stuttgart.de**
　　Choose: **Fun & Game**
　　　| **GamerServer in Tuebingen Login: GAMES**

Telnet:
　　Address: **castor.tat.physik.uni-tuebingen.de**
　　Login: **games**

Choose a MUD

There are so many MUDs out there in Internet-land, how do you ever find them and how do you decide which ones to join? Do it the easy way. Use the *Game Server* at the University of Stuttgart, where you will find enough MUDs to choke a horse.

Hotel California

An interesting place to chill out and chat. "The time has come to talk of many things: of shoes, of ships, of sealing wax, of cabbages and kings!"

Telnet:
>Address: **sachs.cs.colostate.edu 2525**

Island

A MUD with more than a passing resemblance to Oxford University.

Telnet:
>Address: **teaching4.physics.ox.ac.uk 2093**

LambdaMOO

A large and very popular virtual reality, with more varied sections and interesting objects than you'll ever be able to explore. Players are allowed to program and create their own sections.

Telnet:
>Address: **lambda.parc.xerox.com 8888**

MUD Access via Gopher

Access all your favorite MUDs through Gopher. Simply select the MUD you wish to play from the massive selection available and you will be instantly connected. No more messing with lengthy MUD lists.

Gopher:
>Name: Technische Universitaet Clausthal
>Address: **solaris.rz.tu-clausthal.de**
>Choose: **Student-Gopher**
> **| Mud-Servers (for the REAL players!)**

>Name: University of Minnesota
>Address: **gopher.micro.umn.edu**
>Choose: **Fun & Games**
> **| Games**
> **| MUDs**

Nails

A popular and friendly MUD set in a modern day environment and using ANSI color.

Telnet:
>Address: **flounder.rutgers.edu 5150**

Nemesis MUD

Enter the ancient fantasy world of Nemesis and explore its lands, finding the secrets that lie hidden in its depths.

Telnet:
>Address:
>**dszenger9.informatik.tu-muenchen.de 2000**

Nemesis MUD Gopher

Offers lots of information and news about Nemesis MUD, including information about current players, maps, popular Nemesis bulletin boards, and Nemesis programming documentation. Also allows easy access to other LPMud Gophers.

Gopher:
>Name: dszenger9.informatik.tu-muenchen.de
>Address: **7000**

Nightfall MUD

An interactive, text-based, social Virtual Reality. It is an LPMud that allows you to adventure through strange lands solving puzzles, killing monsters and selling treasures on your way.

Telnet:
>Address:
>**nova.tat.physik.uni-tuebingen.de 4242 4242**

Nightfall MUD Information

This Gopher offers information about Nightfall MUD and the MUD culture in general. It has access to the Nightfall MUD statistics and status, and it also allows you to connect to the MUD itself or check who is currently playing.

Gopher:
>Name: University of Stuttgart
>Address: **nova.tat.physik.uni-tuebingen.de 4242**

PernMush

A popular MUD based on the *Pern* novels by Anne McCaffrey.

Telnet:
>Address: **cesium.clock.org 4201**

Want some fun?
Read the Fun section

A B C D E F G H I J K L **M** N O P Q R S T U V W X Y Z

Regenesis

A virtual reality project with special clients available for X Window, Amiga and PCs that allow you to play with graphics.

Telnet:
> Address: **regenesis.lysator.se 7475**

Star Wars

A MUSH-style MUD based on Star Wars, where the Force is always with you.

Telnet:
> Address: **durrance.colorado.edu 4402**

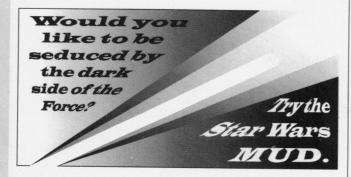

Would you like to be seduced by the dark side of the Force? Try the Star Wars MUD.

TrekMuse

A TinyMuse MUD based on the original *Star Trek* TV series.

Telnet:
> Address: **siher.stanford.edu 1701**

Tsunami

A popular LPMud where "you can't keep a good wave down!"

Telnet:
> Address: **castor.acs.oakland.edu 2777**

Zen

Meditate amidst the smell of incense and the sound of gongs and chanting in the great Zen MOO.

Telnet:
> Address: **cheshire.oxy.edu 7777**

MUSIC

A Cappella

Music without instrumental accompaniment.

Usenet:
> Newsgroup: **alt.music.a-cappella**
> Newsgroup: **rec.music.a-cappella**

Acoustic Guitar Archive

Complete transcriptions (with full lyrics) of guitar music of all kinds, digests, and other related guitar information.

Anonymous FTP:
> Address: **ftp.acns.nwu.edu**
> Path: **/pub/acoustic-guitar/***

Gopher:
> Name: NYSERNet
> Address: **nysernet.org**
> Choose: **Reference Desk**
> | **700 - Arts and Recreation**
> | **780 - Music**
> | **Acoutstic Guitar data**

Acoustic Guitar Digest

Check out this electronic magazine for acoustic guitar buffs.

Anonymous FTP:
> Address: **casbah.acns.nwu.edu**
> Path: **/pub/acoustic-guitar**

Afro-Latin

Music with an African and Latin American influence.

Usenet:
> Newsgroup: **rec.music.afro-latin**

Articles of Music Composition

A number of articles about composing music. Hints, tips, tricks and ideas of all sorts.

Gopher:
> Name: University of Wisconsin Parkside
> Address: **cs.uwp.edu**
> Choose: **Music Archives**
> | **composition**

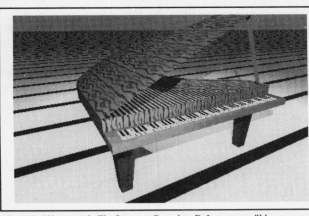

After a half hour with *The Internet Complete Reference*, you'll be an expert with FTP and Archie, and you will be amazed at how much artwork is available on the Net. Millions of hours of artwork in the public domain.

Bagpipes

Archive files and discussion of any topic related to bagpipes, with all manner of Scottish, Irish, English and other instruments being discussed. The FTP site contains FAQs, archives and a bagpipe survey.

Anonymous FTP:
>Address: **cs.dartmouth.edu**
>Path: **/pub/bagpipes/***

Gopher:
>Name: Dartmouth College
>Address: **cs.dartmouth.edu**
>Choose: **Bagpipe Archives**

Internet mailing list:
>List Address: **bagpipes@cs.dartmouth.edu**
>Subscription Address:
>   **bagpipes-request@cs.dartmouth.edu**

Who hasn't heard a real Scotsman playing the bagpipes and not fallen in love with that sensuous, romantic, sophisticated sound that other, more euphonic musicians can only dream of?

Bass

Techniques and equipment for both the double bass and electric bass.

Usenet:
>Newsgroup: **rec.music.makers.bass**

Billboard Magazine's Top 10 Charts

Top 10 charts for pop singles, pop albums, adult contemporary, and rhythm and blues.

Finger:
>Address: **buckmr@rpi.edu**

Bluegrass Music Discussion List

A mailing list for issues related to the International Bluegrass Music Association, and bluegrass music in general, including, but not limited to, recordings, bands, individual performers and live performances.

Listserv mailing list:
>List Address: **bgrass-l@ukcc.bitnet**
>Subscription Address: **listserv@ukcc.bitnet**

Blues

Discussions of blues music and blues performers from Blind Blake and Charley Patton to Robert Cray and Stevie Ray Vaughn.

Listserv mailing list:
>List Address: **blues-l@brownvm.bitnet**
>Subscription Address: **listserv@brownvm.bitnet**

Brass Musicians

A discussion group for people interested in brass musical performance and related topics, especially small musical ensembles of all kinds. Woodwind, percussion and other orchestral types are also welcome.

Internet mailing list:
>List Address: **brass@geomag.gly.fsu.edu**
>Subscription Address:
>   **brass-request@geomag.gly.fsu.edu**

Buying and Selling

Buying and selling musical instruments and equipment, records, tapes and CDs.

Usenet:
>Newsgroup: **rec.music.makers.marketplace**
>Newsgroup: **rec.music.marketplace**

The Bizarre section has some cool stuff

A B C D E F G H I J K L M N O P Q R S T U V W X Y Z

Money for Music

What do you do with the saxophone you bought five years ago and somehow never got around to learning how to play? And what about all those Julie Andrews Christmas albums that are taking up space on your coffee table?

Trade them, sell them, give them away-whatever your favorite means of commerce, gather up your musical extras and drop into the Usenet buy and sell newsgroups. Who knows, maybe you'll run into someone who will really appreciate your collection of Mrs. Miller records.

CDs

General discussion of music and CDs, including what's available, new releases, CDs wanted and for sale, and requests for information.

Usenet:
>Newsgroup: **rec.music.cd**

Celtic

Celtic music, both traditional and modern.

Usenet:
>Newsgroup: **rec.music.celtic**

Christian Music

Contemporary and traditional Christian music.

Usenet:
>Newsgroup: **rec.music.christian**

Clarinet Players Mailing List

News, information, research and teaching, and other items of interest to clarinet players, teachers, students and enthusiasts.

Listserv mailing list:
>List Address: **klarinet@vccscent.bitnet**
>Subscription Address: **listserv@vccscent.bitnet**

Classical Music

Talk to *aficionados* about classical music in general, early preclassical European music, or the music of Shostakovitch.

Usenet:
>Newsgroup: **alt.fan.shostakovich**
>Newsgroup: **rec.music.classical**
>Newsgroup: **rec.music.early**

Classical Music Mailing List

The Classical Music Mailing List was created to discuss classical music of all kinds. All topics and periods are welcome, from Gregorian Chants to George Crumb.

Internet mailing list:
>List Address: **classm-l@brownvm.brown.edu**
>Subscription Address:
>**classm-l-request@brownvm.brown.edu**

Compact Disc Connection

Buy compact discs online, choosing from a selection of more than 65,000 titles. Also view details of current sales, and the top-selling CDs. Accepts Visa and MasterCard.

Telnet:
>Address: **holonet.net cdc**

Composition

Writing music and other lyrical works.

Usenet:
>Newsgroup: **rec.music.compose**

Computerized Music

Exchanging music stored on a computer in MOD/669 format.

Usenet:
>Newsgroup: **alt.binaries.sounds.music**

Computers and Research

Discuss using computers for musical research and composition.

Usenet:
>Newsgroup: **comp.music**

Country and Western

Country and western music—love, marriage, divorce, trucks, dogs, beer, betrayal—good old-fashioned American fun.

Usenet:
Newsgroup: **rec.music.country.western**

Country and Western Music

There is something about the steady thump, thump, twang, twang of country music that is so reassuring. *Country and Western* music serves up a heapin' platter of good ol' American culture at its finest: money, booze and bad love. Just the thing for tired Internet music lovers who have overdosed on bagpipes.

Cyber-Sleaze Mailing List

News and gossip about musicians and bands.

Anonymous FTP:
Address: **mtv.com**
Path: **/pub/sleaze/***

Gopher:
Name: MTV
Address: **mtv.com**
Choose: **sleaze**

Internet mailing list:
List Address: **listproc@mtv.com**
Subscription Address: **listproc-request@mtv.com**

Cyber-Sleaze Report

An abbreviated daily version of the Cyber-Sleaze Mailing List providing the low-down on the music world.

Finger:
Address: **adam@mtv.com**
Address: **hotlist@mtv.com**

Discographies

A large collection of discographies covering many bands and groups, including the Beatles, Genesis, Grateful Dead, New Order, Nirvana, Pink Floyd, Rolling Stones and many others.

Anonymous FTP:
Address: **ftp.spies.com**
Path: **/Library/Music/Disc/***

Gopher:
Name: Internet Wiretap
Address: **wiretap.spies.com**
Choose: **Wiretap Online Library**
| **Music**
| **Discographies**

Who sang what, with whom, and when? Use the Wiretap Gopher and cop some info from the Discographies archive.

Electronic Music

Discussions and digests about electronic music, including composition, criticism, technology, and technique.

Listserv mailing list:
List Address: **emusic-d@american.edu**
Subscription Address: **listserv@american.edu**

List Address: **emusic-l@american.edu**
Subscription Address: **listserv@american.edu**

Electronic Music and Synthesizers

Composing and playing electronic music, particularly music that uses synthesizers and MIDI.

Usenet:
Newsgroup: **alt.emusic**
Newsgroup: **bit.listserv.emusic-l**
Newsgroup: **comp.sys.amiga.audio**
Newsgroup: **rec.music.makers.synth**
Newsgroup: **rec.music.synth**

A
B
C
D
E
F
G
H
I
J
K
L
M
N
O
P
Q
R
S
T
U
V
W
X
Y
Z

Electronic/Industrial Music Zine List

A list of electronic/industrial/techno music-related zines with reviews and contact information for each.

Anonymous FTP:
Address: **ftp.spies.com**
Path: **/Library/Misc/electron.zin**

Gopher:
Name: Internet Wiretap
Address: **wiretap.spies.com**
Choose: **Wiretap Online Library**
| **Miscellaneous**
| **Electronic/Industrial Zine List**

Ethnomusicology Research Digest

A periodical for professionals, librarians and graduate students interested the field of ethnomusicology. (This is, of course, a subject of great global significance.)

Gopher:
Name: University of Maryland
Address: **info.umd.edu**
Choose: **Educational Resources**
| **The Reading Room**
| **Newletters**
| **Ethnomusicology**
| **Digest**

Filk

Science fiction and fantasy-related folk music.

Usenet:
Newsgroup: **alt.music.filk**

Filk Music

Filking is the clever, irreverant art of taking an existing song, gutting it, and creating something new using the same music but different words. Join the rowdy crowd around the campfire as they belt out the ballads.

Usenet:
Newsgroup: **alt.music.filk**

Film Music

Discussions of the music used in movies and television, including music reviews, film composers, film music history and theory, and requests for information about film music.

Listserv mailing list:
List Address: **filmus-iubvm@ucs.indiana.edu**
Subscription Address: **listserv@ucs.indiana.edu**

Folk Music: Archives

Selection of folk music, country blues, fingerstyle guitarists, discographies and lyrics. Also offers lists of folk music societies, radio programs, publications and other FTP sites.

Anonymous FTP:
Address: **ftp.uwp.edu**
Path: **/pub/music/folk/***

Gopher:
Name: University of Wisconsin Parkside
Address: **gopher.uwp.edu**
Choose: **Music Archives**
| **Folk**

Folk Music: The Digital Tradition

The Digital Tradition is a huge database containing the words to over 4000 folk songs. It also contains over 1700 actual tunes that you can play using the speaker in your PC or Macintosh.

Anonymous FTP:
Address: **parcftp.xerox.com**
Path: **/pub/music/digital_tradition/***

Folk Music: Discussion

Folk music of all types.

Usenet:
Newsgroup: **rec.music.folk**

Folk Music: Lyrics

Lyrics to many ancient and new folk songs. Especially interesting are the old English and Scottish songs. The lyrics are arranged, alphabetically by name, in a hierarchy of directories. This site also has many contemporary lyrics, but the old folk songs make it especially interesting.

Anonymous FTP:
Address: **ftp.luth.se**
Path: **/pub/misc/lyrics/folk/***

Funk

Funk, rap, hip-hop, house, soul, R&B, and all their spiritual and commercial relatives.

Usenet:
Newsgroup: **rec.music.funky**

Grind

A digest covering many aspects of grindcore, death metal and heavy thrash music.

Internet mailing list:
> List Address: **grind@unh.edu**
> Subscription Address: **grind-request@unh.edu**

Guitar

Guitar players: check out the discussion groups just for you. Tablature groups for sharing music and lyrics, as well as groups for general guitar, acoustic guitar and classical guitar.

Usenet:
> Newsgroup: **alt.guitar.tab**
> Newsgroup: **rec.music.classical.guitar**
> Newsgroup: **rec.music.makers.guitar**
> Newsgroup: **rec.music.makers.guitar.acoustic**
> Newsgroup: **rec.music.makers.guitar.tablature**

Guitar Archive

Large collection of guitar Tab files, covering thousands of artists and groups, all organized in alphabetical order.

Anonymous FTP:
> Address: **ftp.nevada.edu**
> Path: **/pub/guitar/***

Gopher:
> Name: University of Wisconsin Parkside
> Address: **gopher.uwp.edu**
> Choose: **Music Archives**
> **| Guitar**

Guitar Chords for Popular Songs

Song lyrics and guitar chords for many popular songs. Songs are categorized by group or artist.

Anonymous FTP:
> Address: **ftp.nevada.edu**
> Path: **/pub/guitar**

Women Love Men Who Know When to Stop Playing the Guitar

For men only:
Hey guys, here's a surefire way to win the heart of any woman with half an ear. FTP to the *Guitar Chords* archive and download the info on all your favorite songs. The next time your best girl comes over, show her your treasures and tell her that you are going to sing each one because you know how romantic she is. If she's any kind of music lover, she'll do anything to get you to shut up.

Heavy Metal

Discuss metal and heavy metal music. Achieve total heavy-osity.

Usenet:
> Newsgroup: **alt.rock-n-roll.hard**
> Newsgroup: **alt.rock-n-roll.metal**
> Newsgroup: **alt.rock-n-roll.metal.heavy**
> Newsgroup: **alt.rock-n-roll.metal.progressive**

Indian Music

Classical Hindustani and Carnatic music, as well as general discussions of Indian music.

Usenet:
> Newsgroup: **rec.music.indian.classical**
> Newsgroup: **rec.music.indian.misc**

Jazz

Jazz, the blues and related types of music.

Usenet:
> Newsgroup: **rec.music.bluenote**

Jazz is cool, the Internet is cool, you are cool.

What are you waiting for? Take a look at **rec.music.bluenote.**

Jewish Music

General discussion about Jewish music. Just the thing to listen to while eating chicken soup.

Usenet:
>Newsgroup: **alt.music.jewish**

Label Discographies

A collection of label discographies, including those for 4AD, BMG, DDK and Disney.

Anonymous FTP:
>Address: **ftp.spies.com**
>Path: **/Library/Music/Label/***

Gopher:
>Name: Internet Wiretap
>Address: **wiretap.spies.com**
>Choose: **Wiretap Online Library | Music | Label Discographies**

Lute

Discussion of lute playing and performance. The FTP site contains archives and the source for a Unix and Vax-VMS program to typeset tablature for the lute.

Anonymous FTP:
>Address: **cs.dartmouth.edu**
>Path: **/pub/lute/***

Gopher:
>Name: Dartmouth College
>Address: **cs.dartmouth.edu**
>Choose: **Lute Files**

Internet mailing list:
>List Address: **lute@cs.dartmouth.edu**
>Subscription Address:
> **lute-request@cs.dartmouth.edu**

Lyrics Archive

Massive collection of song lyrics from thousands of artists and groups, with a variety of indexing methods to use when searching.

Anonymous FTP:
>Address: **ftp.uwp.edu**
>Path: **/pub/music/lyrics/***

>Address: **ocf.berkeley.edu**
>Path: **/pub/Library/Lyrics**

Gopher:
>Name: University of Wisconsin Parkside
>Address: **gopher.uwp.edu**
>Choose: **Music Archives | Lyrics**

Music Archives

A massive collection of information about music, including artists, buying guides, picture files, lyrics, FTP site lists and more.

Anonymous FTP:
>Address: **ftp.uwp.edu**
>Path: **/pub/music/***

Gopher:
>Name: University of Wisconsin Parkside
>Address: **gopher.uwp.edu**
>Choose: **Music Archives**

Music Charts

All the latest music charts, including more obscure ones like the Braun European Top 20 Countdown.

Anonymous FTP:
>Address: **mtv.com**
>Path: **/pub/charts/***

Gopher:
>Name: MTV
>Address: **mtv.com**
>Choose: **Charts**

Music Discussion

A mailing list devoted to discussions of all forms and aspects of music, from appreciation to performance.

Listserv mailing list:
>List Address: **allmusic@auvm.bitnet**
>Subscription Address: **listserv@auvm.bitnet**

Music Facts

Facts and lists about all kinds of music, including a list of all-female bands, science fiction music list and various band FAQs.

Anonymous FTP:
>Address: **quartz.rutgers.edu**
>Path: **/pub/music/***

Gopher:
>Name: Rutgers Quartz Text Archive
>Address: **quartz.rutgers.edu**
>Choose: **Music**

Music in General

General discussions about music. Musical ideas, questions and items that have no other place to go.

Usenet:
Newsgroup: **alt.music.alternative**
Newsgroup: **bit.listserv.allmusic**
Newsgroup: **rec.music.misc**

Music Gossip

An exciting, humorous and occasionally informative column of chat from the music world. This document is updated weekly.

Anonymous FTP:
Address: **mtv.com**
Path: **/pub/kenscolumn/***

Gopher:
Name: MTV
Address: **mtv.com**
Choose: **kenscolumn**

Music Library Association

The issues and esoterica of music libraries around the world.

Usenet:
Newsgroup: **bit.listserv.mla-l**

Music List of Lists

The master list for music subjects.

Internet mailing list:
List Address: **mlol@wariat.org**
Subscription Address: **mlol-request@wariat.org**

Music Server

This site has just about anything a music fan might be interested in. Archives by artist name, music databases, classical, folk music, guitar TAB files, lyrics, MIDI files, picture files, release listings, mailing lists and on and on.

Anonymous FTP:
Address: **ftp.uwp.edu**
Path: **/pub/music**

Musicals Lyrics

Lyrics to several musicals, including *Cats*, *Chess*, *Grease*, *Les Miserables*, *Phantom of the Opera*, and *The Rocky Horror Picture Show*.

Anonymous FTP:
Address: **quartz.rutgers.edu**
Path: **/pub/theater/musicals/***

Gopher:
Name: Rutgers Quartz Text Archive
Address: **quartz.rutgers.edu**
Choose: **Theater-Plays and Musicals
| Musicals**

New Age

New Age music—Kitaro, Windham Hill, Steven Halpern, Enya, and so on—performers, recordings and general discussion.

Usenet:
Newsgroup: **alt.fan.enya**
Newsgroup: **alt.music.enya**
Newsgroup: **rec.music.gaffa**
Newsgroup: **rec.music.newage**

New Music

Discover music with a difference as you browse online catalogs and playlists offering music and sound works that stretch the mind.

Gopher:
Name: Whole Earth Lectronic Link
Address: **gopher.well.sf.ca.us**
Choose: **Art and Culture
| New Music**

News

News from the world of music.

Usenet:
Newsgroup: **clari.news.music**
Newsgroup: **rec.music.info**

Percussion

Techniques and equipment for drums and other percussion instruments.

Usenet:
Newsgroup: **rec.music.makers.percussion**

A
B
C
D
E
F
G
H
I
J
K
L
M
N
O
P
Q
R
S
T
U
V
W
X
Y
Z

Performance

All aspects of music making and performance. Be another Bob Dylan, Pete Townshend or Billy Joel.

Usenet:
> Newsgroup: **rec.music.makers**

Music Making Made Modern

Who can forget those fabulous musical film performances of the Lost Generation: Tom Cruise as the ultimate cool dude in "Risky Business"; or Garth, Wayne and the boys treating us to their special rendition of "Bohemian Rhapsody"? We know your secret: you too are a cool dude with unbelievable talent, and all you need is a break. Drop in to the rec.music.makers newsgroup and see what all the other talented Internet musicians are up to.

Performing Classical Music

Discussion for those who perform classical music. Pick up useful hints on style, logistics and deciding how many encores to take. Check out the directions on how to get to Carnegie Hall (practice, practice, practice).

Usenet:
> Newsgroup: **rec.music.classical.performing**

Pipe Organ

A programmable color organ program for the IBM-PC. Allows you to interchange music and graphics.

Anonymous FTP:
> Address: **ftp.cs.pdx.edu**
> Path: **/pub/music/ravel/pip.tar.Z**

Progressive

Progressive music: Yes, Marillion, Asia, King Crimson and so on.

Usenet:
> Newsgroup: **alt.music.progressive**

Punk Rock

Punk rockers, head banging, thrashing, nose studs, dyed hair, and shaved heads—and what ever became of Jello Biafra? Share the punk experience.

Usenet:
> Newsgroup: **alt.punk**

Rap

Rap music: rap, hip hop, gangsta.

Usenet:
> Newsgroup: **alt.rap**

Rave

Immerse yourself in the ultimate techno-culture of music, dancing, drugs, and more illegal and excessive fun than most people can imagine. Learn to be the type of person that your parents warned you about.

Usenet:
> Newsgroup: **alt.rave**

Do you still have some extra brain cells that you don't know what to do with? Mr. Braincell Mr. Braincell Try Rave

Reggae

Reggae, including roots, rockers and dancehall reggae.

Usenet:
> Newsgroup: **rec.music.reggae**

Reviews

Reviews of all types of music. Read the opinions of people who have more knowledge of music in their whole body than you have in your little finger. A moderated group.

Usenet:
> Newsgroup: **rec.music.reviews**

Rock and Classical Music

The melding of rock and classical music. Combining the great art of the past with the nostalgia of the future.

Usenet:
>Newsgroup: **alt.rock-n-roll.symphonic**

Rock and Roll

Rock and roll is here to stay, I dig it till the end. It'll go down in history, just you wait my friend.

Usenet:
>Newsgroup: **alt.rock-n-roll**
>Newsgroup: **alt.rock-n-roll.classic**
>Newsgroup: **alt.rock-n-roll.oldies**

Sid's Music Server

Lists of rare live recordings and CDs for sale. There is also a mailing list available. Send mail for more information.

Mail:
>Address: **mwilkenf@silver.ucs.indiana.edu**
>Subject: **boothelp**

Song Lyrics

Lyrics to popular (and not so popular) songs. This Gopher server has an amazing volume of artists and songs. Directories are arranged alphabetically. Pick a directory for the band or artist. (For example, choose **J** for Elton John, then choose an album, then the song.)

Gopher:
>Name: University of Minnesota
>Address: **gopher.micro.umn.edu**
>Choose: **Fun & Games**
>| **Music**
>| **Music Archives**
>| **Lyrics Archives**

Sonic

The *Sonic Verse Music* magazine highlights underground music and contains record reviews, interviews and much more.

Listserv mailing list:
>List Address: **sonic-l@vm.marist.edu**
>Subscription Address: **listserv@vm.marist.edu**

Strange Sounds

Bizarre, esoteric sounds. Exotic music, skank, thrash, hardcore, industrial, electronic body music: not for those without an industrial-strength auditory cortex.

Usenet:
>Newsgroup: **alt.exotic-music**
>Newsgroup: **alt.music.ebm**
>Newsgroup: **alt.music.hardcore**
>Newsgroup: **alt.music.ska**
>Newsgroup: **alt.thrash**
>Newsgroup: **rec.music.industrial**

Techno/Rave Gopher

Archives, GIF images, media reports, music reviews, ambient music survey and more about raves and techno music.

Gopher:
>Name: Techno/Rave Gopher
>Address: **techno.stanford.edu**

Top (and Bottom) 100 Lists

Various "100" lists, including MTV top 100 videos, top 100 albums, and worst 100 singles of the last 25 years.

Anonymous FTP:
>Address: **ftp.spies.com**
>Path: **/Library/Music/Lists/***

Gopher:
>Name: Internet Wiretap
>Address: **wiretap.spies.com**
>Choose: **Wiretap Online Library**
>| **Music**
>| **Various Top 100 Lists**

Update Electronic Music Newsletter

An electronic newsletter for those interested in electronic music.

Listserv mailing list:
>List Address: **upnews@vm.marist.edu**
>Subscription Address: **listserv@vm.marist.edu**

Used Music Server

Buy, sell or trade CDs, tapes and LPs. You can also subscribe to the mailing list.

Mail:
>Address: **used-music-server@wang.com**
>Subject: **help**

A
B
C
D
E
F
G
H
I
J
K
L
M
N
O
P
Q
R
S
T
U
V
W
X
Y
Z

Videos

Music videos and music video software.

Usenet:
> Newsgroup: **rec.music.video**

Virtual Record Store

Purchase CDs from a large selection of titles covering all kinds of music. The electronic record store is arranged by artist for easy browsing, and the database can be searched by artist, CD title or catalog number.

Gopher:
> Name: Nova Scotia Technology Network
> Address: **nstn.ns.ca**
> Choose: **NSTN Electronic Shopping Mall
> | Virtual Record Store**

The Internet Record Store

HOT PATOOTIE, BLESS MY SOUL.
I REALLY LOVE THAT ROCK AND ROLL.

But wouldn't it be great to buy CDs from the privacy of your own home? Well, you can. Just visit the *Virtual Record Store* and use real money to buy real CDs from real people that you never have to meet.

World Music

Music from around the world: all types, all cultures: everything and anything.

Usenet:
> Newsgroup: **alt.music.world**

MUSIC: PERFORMERS

Allman Brothers

A mailing list on the Allman Brothers Band and its derivatives. Tape trading, tour information and other topics of interest to fans.

Internet mailing list:
> List Address: **allman@world.std.com**
> Subscription Address:
> **allman-request@world.std.com**

Musicians are popular subjects of images. From Paula Abdul to ZZ-Top, they're all on the Net. For a copy of Paula's picture (with a more appropriate head), use Archie to search for **abdul2.gif**.

Art of Noise

A mailing list about the music group the Art of Noise.

Internet mailing list:
> List Address: **aon@polyslo.calpoly.edu**
> Subscription Address:
> **aon-request@polyslo.calpoly.edu**

Concrete Blonde

Discuss the rock group Concrete Blonde and related artists.

Internet mailing list:
List Address: **concrete-blonde@piggy.ucsb.edu**
Subscription Address:
concrete-blonde-request@piggy.ucsb.edu

Alice Cooper

A mailing list for fans of Alice Cooper. Virtually any related topic is appropriate, including news, comments on his music, tour dates, and so on.

Listserv mailing list:
List Address: **alicefan@wkuvx1.bitnet**
Subscription Address: **listserv@wkuvx1.bitnet**

Can you believe that when Alice Cooper was screaming about being eighteen, Harley really was eighteen? Alice fans unite: join the alicefan mailing list and find out who is still caught in a dream.

Bob Dylan

Large archive of information about Bob Dylan, including interviews, details of his life and events for over 30 years, and CD and book lists.

Anonymous FTP:
Address: **ftp.cs.pdx.edu**
Path: **/pub/dylan/***

Favorite Musicians and Music Groups

There are many discussion groups devoted to popular musicians and music groups. Tune in for the latest in concert appearances, reviews, opinions and esoterica. Look for your favorites: AC/DC, Beatles, Bela and the Flecktones, Devo, Bob Dylan, Grateful Dead, Guns 'n Roses, Iron Maiden, Jethro Tull, Marillion, Metallica, Nine-Inch Nails, Oingo Boingo, Phish, Prince, Queen, Rolling Stones, Run-DMC, Rush, Spinal Tap, TMBG, U2 and Frank Zappa.

Usenet:
Newsgroup: **alt.fan.devo**
Newsgroup: **alt.fan.frank-zappa**
Newsgroup: **alt.fan.oingo-boingo**
Newsgroup: **alt.fan.run-dmc**
Newsgroup: **alt.fan.spinal-tap**
Newsgroup: **alt.fan.u2**
Newsgroup: **alt.music.bela-fleck**
Newsgroup: **alt.music.marillion**
Newsgroup: **alt.music.nin**
Newsgroup: **alt.music.prince**
Newsgroup: **alt.music.queen**
Newsgroup: **alt.music.rush**
Newsgroup: **alt.music.tmbg**
Newsgroup: **alt.music.u2**
Newsgroup: **alt.rock-n-roll.acdc**
Newsgroup: **alt.rock-n-roll.metal.gnr**
Newsgroup: **alt.rock-n-roll.metal.ironmaiden**
Newsgroup: **alt.rock-n-roll.metal.metallica**
Newsgroup: **alt.rock-n-roll.stones**
Newsgroup: **info.jethro-tull**
Newsgroup: **rec.music.beatles**
Newsgroup: **rec.music.dylan**
Newsgroup: **rec.music.gdead**
Newsgroup: **rec.music.phish**

Debbie Gibson

A mailing list devoted to fans of Debbie Gibson.

Internet mailing list:
List Address: **btl@bullwinkle.ucdavis.edu**
Subscription Address:
btl-request@bullwinkle.ucdavis.edu

Make sure you are prepared: Read Emergency and Disaster

If you like trouble, take a look at Mischief

A B C D E F G H I J K L **M** N O P Q R S T U V W X Y Z

Grateful Dead Archives

Files of interest to Dead Heads.

Anonymous FTP:
Address: **gdead.berkeley.edu**
Path: **/pub/gdead**

Gopher:
Name: University of California Berkeley
Address: **gdead.berkeley.edu**

Allan Holdsworth

Stimulating discussions on the works of guitarist Allan Holdsworth.

Internet mailing list:
List Address:
atavachron@msuacad.morehead-st.edu
Subscription Address:
atavachron-request@msuacad.morehead-st.edu

Severed Heads

Discussion of the popular Australian band Severed Heads.

Internet mailing list:
List Address: **adolph-a-carrot@andrew.cmu.edu**
Subscription Address:
adolph-a-carrot-request@andrew.cmu.edu

Bruce Springsteen

A mailing list for fans of the Boss.

Listserv mailing list:
List Address: **bstreets@virginia.bitnet**
Subscription Address: **listserv@virginia.bitnet**

XTC

Chalkhills is a mailing list for the discussion of the music and records of the band XTC.

Internet mailing list:
List Address: **chalkhills@presto.ig.com**
Subscription Address:
chalkhills-request@presto.ig.com

**Gopher problems?
Read "The Internet Complete Reference"**

Excerpt from the Net...
(from the Grateful Dead Archives)

```
----------------------------------------------------------------

The Church of Unlimited Devotion is nothing if not eclectic...

The church's name can be found in a song by the Grateful Dead:

        "The Golden Road (to Unlimited Devotion)"

Members of the church -- which is based in Philo, California -- follow this rock band on
most of its tours.  Because of the spinning dance they perform both at concerts and as
part of their religious devotions, they are know as "the Spinners."  They are vegetarian,
and take vows of poverty, chastity and obedience...

----------------------------------------------------------------

How did Jerry Garcia lose his finger ?

While they were chopping wood as children, his brother Tiff accidentally chopped it off
with an axe.

----------------------------------------------------------------
```

NEWS

Australian News

News stories past and present, from Australian newspapers.

Gopher:
> Name: Universite de Montreal
> Address: **megasun.bch.umontreal.ca**
> Choose: **Australiana - News, sport, FAQ's, etc about Australia**
> | **News from Australian Newspapers**

Usenet:
> Newsgroup: **soc.culture.australian**

Clarinet

Many Usenet-like newsgroups devoted to real news. To be able to access Clarinet, your news site must subscribe to it.

Usenet:
> Newsgroups: **clari.***

Current Affairs Magazines

Sample articles and subscription information for business, political and news magazines.

Gopher:
> Name: The Electronic Newsstand
> Address: **gopher.internet.com 2100**
> Choose: **Titles Arranged by Category**
> | **Current Affairs - Business, Politics, News**

Ecuadorian Daily News Summaries

La Prensa newspaper (in Spanish).

Gopher:
> Name:
>   Ministerio de Relaciones Exteriores del Ecuador
> Address: **gopher.mmrree.gov.ec**
> Choose: **PRENSA**

> ## Need a laugh?
> ## Check out Humor

EFFector Online and EFF News

The complete set of *EFFector Online* magazine and EFF News publications, which tackle issues relating to computers, the law and privacy.

Anonymous FTP:
> Address: **ftp.eff.org**
> Path: **/pub/EFF/newsletters/***

Gopher:
> Name: Electronic Frontier Foundation
> Address: **gopher.eff.org**
> Choose: **Electronic Frontier..**
> | **Back issues of EFFector..**

Electronic Newsstand

Easy access to a wide range of interesting information and articles provided by U.S. and worldwide magazine publishers. Electronic Newsstand provides a window into the worlds of politics, science, business, foreign affairs, arts, travel, food and sports.

Gopher:
> Name: The Electronic Newsstand
> Address: **gopher.internet.com 2100**

Marla leaves Donald for a handsome Internet author!! *Special Inside*

The Electronic Newsstand

How many times

have you held up the line in the supermarket reading the *National Enquirer* while everyone else encourages you to either buy it or move on? On the Net, you can take your time. Just connect to the *Electronic Newsstand* Gopher and browse until you're full. No, you won't find the *Enquirer*, but you will find a lot of other interesting items; certainly enough to keep you occupied when you should be working.

President consumes 32 million MacBurgers in effort to boost economy, and gains 576 lbs. as a result.

> ## Spare time?
> ## Take a look at Games

A B C D E F G H I J K L M N O P Q R S T U V W X Y Z

French Language Press Review

French summaries of news reported in the French language press, updated on an almost daily basis.

Gopher:
> Name: Michigan State University
> Address: **gopher.msu.edu**
> Choose: **News & Weather**
> | **Electronic Newspapers**
> | **French Language Press Review**

French News

Daily newsbriefs (in French) about events in France, including a general discussion of the main articles published in the French press on that day, often with extensive quotes from the articles.

Gopher:
> Name: Yale University
> Address: **yaleinfo.yale.edu**
> Choose: **The Internet**
> | **News and weather**
> | **France**

Make News

Instructions on using the Internet to submit press releases, news tips, letters to the editor, op-ed pieces and questions to the *Middlesex News* newspaper, based near Boston.

Gopher:
> Name: The World
> Address: **world.std.com**
> Choose: **Periodicals, Magazines, and Journals**
> | **Middlesex News**
> | **About the Middlesex News**

Middlesex News

General interest newspaper from Metrowest, the high-tech region west of Boston. This electronic newspaper includes movie and restaurant reviews, event guides, tourist information, regular columns and other items of interest.

Gopher:
> Name: The World
> Address: **world.std.com**
> Choose: **Periodicals, Magazines, and Journals**
> | **Middlesex News**

Moscow News

Sample of English articles from the *Moscow News*.

Gopher:
> Name: Michigan State University
> Address: **gopher.msu.edu**
> Choose: **News & Weather**
> | **Electronic Newspapers**
> | **Moscow News**

News Mail Servers

Post to Usenet news via mail.

Mail:
> Address: *newsgroup*@**cs.utexas.edu**

Can't post to Usenet?
Can't post to Usenet?
Can't post to Usenet?

Send articles by mail.
Send articles by mail.
Send articles by mail.

Excerpt from the Net...

(From the "Electronic Newsstand")

The Electronic Newsstand was founded to provide the Internet community with easy access to a wide range of interesting information provided by magazine publishers.

Like traditional newsstands, the Electronic Newsstand is a place where you can browse through many publications and have your interest stimulated by a wide range of subjects. The Electronic Newsstand provides a window on the world of politics, science, business, foreign affairs, the arts, travel food, sports...

Newsletters and Journals Available Through Gopher

A large collection of online newsletters and journals covering art, computing, education, humanities, languages, law, medicine, politics, religion and more. They are all neatly categorized and available through Gopher.

Gopher:
Name: Swedish University Network
Address: **sunic.sunet.se**
Choose: **Library Services**
  | Newsletters & Journals

Name: University of North Texas
Address: **gopher.unt.edu**
Choose: **Remote Information...**
  | Electronic Documents

Parent Trap

A column that features stories of parents about life, love and raising children.

Gopher:
Name: The World
Address: **world.std.com**
Choose: **Periodicals, Magazines, and Journals**
  | Middlesex News
  | Columns
  | The Parent Trap

USA Today

Sample articles from *USA Today*.

Gopher:
Name: Michigan State University
Address: **gopher.msu.edu**
Choose: **News & Weather**
  | Electronic Newspapers
  | USA Today

Telnet:
Address: **freenet-in-a.cwru.edu**
Address: **freenet-in-b.cwru.edu**
Address: **freenet-in-c.cwru.edu**
Address: **yfn.ysu.edu**
Login: **visitor**

Washington Post

Sample articles from the *Washington Post*.

Gopher:
Name: Michigan State University
Address: **gopher.msu.edu**
Choose: **News & Weather**
  | Electronic Newspapers
  | Washington Post

NEWS: WORLD

Croatian Ministry of Foreign Affairs

Daily news, bulletins and flashes, letters, and press releases.

Gopher:
Name: Croatia
Address: **rujan.srce.hr**
Choose: **English Language**
  | Actual News

Israeli News

Articles about the state of Israel, including Israel's Declaration of Independence, conference news and newspaper reports.

Anonymous FTP:
Address: **israel.nysernet.org**
Path: **/israel/Israel_Info/***

Gopher:
Name: NYSERNet
Address: **israel.nysernet.org 71**
Choose: **Israel Projects**
  | Israel Info

Want some fun?
Read the Fun section

Too much spare time?
Explore a MUD

A B C D E F G H I J K L M N O P Q R S T U V W X Y Z

OCEANOGRAPHY

Oceanic (Ocean Network Information Center)

Oceanic data sets, research ship schedules and information, science and program information.

Telnet:
Address: **delocn.udel.edu**
Login: **info**

Oceanography Information

Exchange information with oceanographers and oceanography buffs. From fishery science to the effects of natural and man-made disasters on the ocean's ecology, this is the place to find the information.

Anonymous FTP:
Address: **biome.bio.dfo.ca**
Path: **/pub**

OPERATING SYSTEMS: DOS

4DOS Command Processor

Discussion of the 4DOS command processor, a replacement for the standard COMMAND.COM.

Usenet:
Newsgroup: **comp.os.msdos.4dos**

Desqview

Discussion group devoted to Desqview—the multitasking task manager from Quarterdeck—and related products.

Usenet:
Newsgroup: **comp.os.msdos.desqview**

Lonely?
Try the Personals

Mail and Usenet News

DOS-based mail and Usenet news systems.

Usenet:
Newsgroup: **comp.os.msdos.mail-news**

Miscellaneous DOS Topics

Discussion of topics relating to DOS and DOS machines.

Usenet:
Newsgroup: **comp.os.msdos.misc**

UUCP

Discussion of UUCP for DOS systems.

Usenet:
Newsgroup: **alt.bbs.pcbuucp**

OPERATING SYSTEMS: GENERAL TOPICS

Operating Systems General Discussion

General discussion about operating systems, not carried elsewhere.

Usenet:
Newsgroup: **comp.os.misc**

Research

Research on operating systems and related areas.

Usenet:
Newsgroup: **comp.os.research**

OPERATING SYSTEMS: MICROSOFT WINDOWS

Announcements

This moderated newsgroup contains announcements related to Microsoft Windows.

Usenet:
Newsgroup: **comp.os.ms-windows.announce**

Microsoft Windows

Isn't Windows great? Don't you just love those GPF (General Protection Faults)? And don't you look back with nostalgia on so many of those fabulous UAE's (Unidentified Application Errors)?

Come on guys, no complaining: GPFs and UAEs are just Microsoft's way of telling you to slow down. In fact, we bet that you love Windows so much that you would do anything to keep from missing out on all that's new and keen. Not to worry.

All you have to do is read
comp.os.ms-windows.announce
and you'll never be left behind.

Applications

Discussion about all types of Microsoft Windows applications.

Usenet:
    Newsgroup: **comp.os.ms-windows.apps**

Binaries

Binary (executable) programs for Microsoft Windows, ready to download and run.

Usenet:
    Newsgroup: **comp.binaries.ms-windows**

Sockets

Socket implementations for Microsoft Windows: discussion and programming considerations.

Usenet:
    Newsgroup: **alt.winsock**

Excerpt from the Net...

```
Newsgroup: comp.os.msdos.misc
Subject: What is this hidden file?

>> I have just discovered, on a quest to solve another mystery, the
>> following hidden system file in the root directory:
>>
>>      386spart.par
>>
>> with the incredible size of 12558336.  It carries today's date.
>>
>> What on earth is this file?

> This is a FAQ (frequently asked question).  The file is your 12 Mb
> permanent Windows swapfile.
>
> I wonder, is there an advantage for having a permanent swap file over a
> temporary one?

Yes.

A temporary swap file uses space that was available on your hard drive at the time you
started Windows: you have no control on how large this file will be.  Moreover, the file
may very well be fragmented.

The permanent swap file is constructed only of contiguous blocks on your hard drive.
This provides faster access.  In addition, you can specify how large the file should be.
With contiguous blocks, you will have faster access.  Working with a temporary swap file
may result in a slower speed, just as with a fragmented hard disk.
```

A B C D E F G H I J K L M N O P Q R S T U V W X Y Z

Windows General Discussion

General discusssion about Microsoft Windows. The **.advocacy** newsgroup contains more controversial talk and debate.

Usenet:
Newsgroup: **bit.listserv.win3-l**
Newsgroup: **comp.os.ms-windows.advocacy**
Newsgroup: **comp.os.ms-windows.misc**

Windows Setup

Installation and configuration of Microsoft Windows.

Usenet:
Newsgroup: **comp.os.ms-windows.setup**

WordPerfect

Discussion about WordPerfect for Windows.

Usenet:
Newsgroup: **bit.listserv.wpwin-l**

OPERATING SYSTEMS: MISCELLANEOUS SYSTEMS

AOS

Data General's AOS/VS operating system.

Usenet:
Newsgroup: **comp.os.aos**

CP/M

One of the early microcomputer operating systems, CP/M is the spiritual ancestor of DOS and, in certain parts of the computing world, is still alive today.

Usenet:
Newsgroup: **comp.os.cpm**
Newsgroup: **comp.os.cpm.amethyst**

Geos

The Geos operating system from Geoworks.

Usenet:
Newsgroup: **comp.os.geos**
Newsgroup: **comp.os.msdos.pcgeos**

Lynx

The Lynx realtime operating systems.

Usenet:
Newsgroup: **comp.os.lynx**

Mach

The famous Mach operating system and its ubiquitous kernel, as developed at Carnegie-Mellon University. The newsgroups are for ongoing discussion; the FTP sites contain source code, utilities and documentation.

Anonymous FTP:
Address: **ftp.uu.net**
Path: **/systems/mach/***

Address: **gatekeeper.dec.com**
Path: **/pub/Mach/***

Usenet:
Newsgroup: **comp.os.mach**
Newsgroup: **info.mach**

WANT TO BUILD YOUR OWN OPERATING SYSTEM? NO PROBLEM. START WITH THE MACH KERNEL. IT'S AVAILABLE FOR DOWNLOADING ON THE INTERNET.

Minix

The Minix operating system, designed by Andy Tannenbaum and described in his operating system book. The newsgroup is for ongoing discussion; the FTP site is for archives.

Anonymous FTP:
Address: **oak.oakland.edu**
Path: **/pub/misc/minix**

Usenet:
Newsgroup: **comp.os.minix**

Multics

The infamous Multics operating system, a dinosaur from days gone by at MIT.

Usenet:
Newsgroup: **alt.os.multics**

OS9

OS9 is a realtime, multiuser, multitasking operating system that runs on a wide variety of processors and has very small memory requirements. The family of OS9 operating systems is based on the original OS9, developed by Microware Systems in the 1970s for the 6809 processor. Today, OS9 is supported by various other vendors and a disparate group of programmers around the world.

Usenet:
> Newsgroup: **comp.os.os9**

RSTS

The old, venerable RSTS operating system for DEC's PDP-11 computers.

Usenet:
> Newsgroup: **comp.os.rsts**

V

The V distributed operating system from Stanford. (Historical note: A windowing system named "W" was originally developed for V. W was the ancestor of X Window.)

Usenet:
> Newsgroup: **comp.os.v**

VMS

There are a large number of newsgroups devoted to discussions of various aspects of DEC's VMS operating system, as well as related hardware, software and networking.

Usenet:
> Newsgroup: **bit.listserv.jnet-l**
> Newsgroup: **bit.listserv.vmslsv-l**
> Newsgroup: **comp.os.vms**
> Newsgroup: **gnu.emacs.vms**
> Newsgroup: **news.software.anu-news**
> Newsgroup: **sysmgt**
> Newsgroup: **vmsnet.admin**
> Newsgroup: **vmsnet.alpha**
> Newsgroup: **vmsnet.announce.***
> Newsgroup: **vmsnet.databases.rdb**
> Newsgroup: **vmsnet.decus.***
> Newsgroup: **vmsnet.employment**
> Newsgroup: **vmsnet.infosystems.***
> Newsgroup: **vmsnet.internals**
> Newsgroup: **vmsnet.mail.***
> Newsgroup: **vmsnet.misc**
> Newsgroup: **vmsnet.networks.***
> Newsgroup: **vmsnet.pdp-11**

> Newsgroup: **vmsnet.sources.***
> Newsgroup: **vmsnet.sysmgt**
> Newsgroup: **vmsnet.tpu**
> Newsgroup: **vmsnet.uucp**
> Newsgroup: **vmsnet.vms-posix**

VxWorks

The VxWorks realtime operating system

Usenet:
> Newsgroup: **comp.os.vxworks**

Xinu

The Xinu ("Xinu is Not Unix") operating system from Purdue; from a project organized by Doug Comer.

Usenet:
> Newsgroup: **comp.os.xinu**

OPERATING SYSTEMS: OS/2

Announcements

Announcements related to OS/2.

Usenet:
> Newsgroup: **comp.os.os2.announce**

OS/2 Announcements

Okay, we admit it, we like OS/2. But (we hear you say), don't you miss all those GFPs and UAEs? Isn't it boring to use an operating system that doesn't keep crashing?
Don't despair, OS/2 runs Windows, so you never need feel deprived. But don't run the risk of being left behind: find out what's new and exciting by reading **comp.os.os2.announce.**

(By the way, don't tell anyone, but we use OS/2 mostly to run our DOS programs...shh...it's a secret.)

A
B
C
D
E
F
G
H
I
J
K
L
M
N
O
P
Q
R
S
T
U
V
W
X
Y
Z

Applications

Discussion on all types of OS/2 applications

Usenet:
Newsgroup: **comp.os.os2.apps**

Binaries

Binary (executable) programs for OS/2 ready to download and run.

Usenet:
Newsgroup: **comp.binaries.os2**

Bugs and Fixes

Bug reports and fixes for current versions of OS/2.

Usenet:
Newsgroup: **comp.os.os2.bugs**

Multimedia

Multimedia support and implementation for OS/2.

Usenet:
Newsgroup: **comp.os.os2.multimedia**

Networking

Networking in OS/2 environments.

Usenet:
Newsgroup: **comp.os.os2.networking**

OS/2 Beta Releases

Problems, comments and bugs in OS/2 beta releases.

Usenet:
Newsgroup: **comp.os.os2.beta**

OS/2 General Discussion

General discussion about all aspects of OS/2. The **.advocacy** newsgroup contains more debate and controversial topics.

Usenet:
Newsgroup: **comp.os.os2.advocacy**
Newsgroup: **comp.os.os2.misc**

OS/2 Setup

Installing and configuring OS/2.

Usenet:
Newsgroup: **comp.os.os2.setup**

OS/2 Versions 1.x

Discussion about OS/2 versions 1.0 through 1.3.

Usenet:
Newsgroup: **comp.os.os2.ver1x**

Programming

Programming in the OS/2 environment. The **.porting** newsgroup is devoted to porting software from another system to OS/2.

Usenet:
Newsgroup: **comp.os.os2.programmer**
Newsgroup: **comp.os.os2.programmer.misc**
Newsgroup: **comp.os.os2.programmer.porting**

OPERATING SYSTEMS: SCO

Announcements

This moderated newsgroup contains announcements regarding SCO's products.

Usenet:
Newsgroup: **biz.sco.announce**

Do you use SCO Unix or Open Desktop?

Keep up on the news by reading biz.sco.announce

Binaries

Binary (executable) programs for SCO Xenix, Unix or Open Desktop, ready to download and run.

Usenet:
Newsgroup: **biz.sco.binaries**

Enhanced Feature Supplements

This directory on SCO's FTP server houses feature supplements and bug fixes for SCO's Unix operating systems. The supplements are contained within compressed Unix files and are keyed by floppy disk type (96 or 135 tpi installation drives).

Anonymous FTP:
    Address: **ftp.sco.com**
    Path: **/EFS**

Games

This directory on SCO's FTP server contains games for SCO Unix systems.

Anonymous FTP:
    Address: **ftp.sco.com**
    Path: **/Games**

Hardware Compatibility Handbook

An electronic version of the *Hardware Compatibility Handbook* distributed with SCO products.

Anonymous FTP:
    Address: **ftp.sco.com**
    Path: **/HCH**

Open Desktop

Discussion about SCO's Open Desktop operating system and programming environment.

Usenet:
    Newsgroup: **biz.sco.opendesktop**

SCO General Discussion

General discussion about all of SCO's products.

Usenet:
    Newsgroup: **biz.sco.general**

SCO Talk

Yes, there is a place on the Net for SCO bigots. Tune in to **biz.sco.general** and talk, talk, talk about ODT, Unix and (gasp) Xenix. Where else can you go when it's early Sunday morning and you need to find out just which EISA SCSI host adaptors are best supported under SCO Unix?

SCO Magazine

An electronic magazine for users of SCO's Unix operating systems.

Usenet:
    Newsgroup: **biz.sco.magazine**

Sources

Source programs to run under the various SCO operating systems.

Usenet:
    Newsgroup: **biz.sco.sources**

Support Level Supplements

Bug fixes and enhancements to SCO products. Includes an improved CD-ROM driver, console keyboard driver, TCP/IP daemon and driver, security supplements, an NFS supplement, and so on.

Anonymous FTP:
    Address: **ftp.sco.com**
    Path: **/SLS**

Technical Library Supplements

Experimental and educational files that are, in some cases, components and updates to existing SCO software. Not yet another archive for SCO products, but rather software that only SCO can provide or that is not available elsewhere.

Anonymous FTP:
    Address: **ftp.sco.com**
    Path: **/TLS**

Why be normal?
Read Bizarre

Termcap and Terminfo Changes

Updated termcap and terminfo entries for many terminals.

Anonymous FTP:
>Address: **ftp.sco.com**
>Path: **/Term**

Widget Server

Discussion about the SCO widget server.

Usenet:
>Newsgroup: **biz.sco.wserver**

Xenix

SCO's version of the Xenix operating system.

Usenet:
>Newsgroup: **comp.unix.xenix.sco**

OPERATING SYSTEMS: UNIX IN GENERAL

Dial-up Site List

A long listing of open access dial-up Unix sites, including both fee and no-fee hosts. Contains detailed information on what each site has to offer.

Anonymous FTP:
>Address: **gvl.unisys.com**
>Path: **/pub/nixpub/***

Mail:
>Address: **archive-server@cs.widener.edu**
>Body: **send nixpub long**
>
>Address: **mail-server@bts.com**
>Body: **get pub nixpub**
>
>Address: **nixpub@access.digex.net**

Usenet:
>Newsgroup: **alt.bbs**
>Newsgroup: **comp.bbs.misc**
>Newsgroup: **comp.misc**

DOS Under Unix

Talk and technical questions about all the different ways to run DOS and DOS programs under Unix.

Usenet:
>Newsgroup: **comp.unix.dos-under-unix**

General Unix Discussion

Discussion of miscellaneous Unix topics that don't fit into any other newsgroup.

Usenet:
>Newsgroup: **comp.unix.misc**

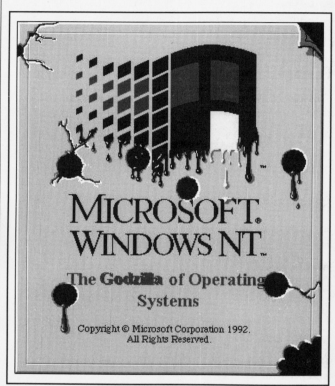

Humorous art and spoofs on common symbols are everywhere. This is **windoze.jpg** from **ftp.wustl.edu** (under **w**).

Mainframes and Large Networks

Technical discussion about Unix systems that run on mainframes or on large networks.

Usenet:
>Newsgroup: **comp.unix.large**

News About Unix

News stories that involve the Unix industry.

Usenet:
>Newsgroup: **clari.nb.unix**

NQS Unix Batch System

A collection of available information about NQS, the most commonly used batch software on Unix. The information is grouped into two areas, that revelant to users of NQS, and that required by adminstrators of systems running NQS.

Gopher:
> Name: Manchester Computing Centre
> Address: **uts.mcc.ac.uk**
> Choose: **NQS...The Unix Batch System**

Open Software Foundation

Gossip, rumors and technical debate regarding the Open Software Foundation and its machinations.

Usenet:
> Newsgroup: **comp.unix.osf.misc**

*What is the **Open Software Foundation** up to and how long until they are disbanded?*

Read all about it in comp.unix.osf.misc

PC and Macintosh Guides

Articles and FAQs on Berkeley Unix, USL Unix, Sun administration, C-Shell, zshell, Unix security and other variants of Unix.

Anonymous FTP:
> Address: **ftp.spies.com**
> Path: **/Library/Techdoc/Unix/***

Gopher:
> Name: Internet Wiretap
> Address: **wiretap.spies.com**
> Choose: **Wiretap Online Library**
> **| Technical Information**
> **| Unix Operating System**

Programming

Questions and answers regarding Unix programming.

Usenet:
> Newsgroup: **comp.unix.programmer**

Questions and Answers

General Unix question and answer forums. Almost all questions should go to the **.questions** newsgroup. The **.wizards** group is only for real experts (stay away). You do not need to post a question to **.wizards** to make sure it is read by an expert; they read both groups.

Usenet:
> Newsgroup: **comp.unix.questions**
> Newsgroup: **comp.unix.wizards**

Security

Discussion of all aspects of Unix security.

Usenet:
> Newsgroup: **comp.security.unix**

Shells

Technical discussion about all the various Unix shells.

Usenet:
> Newsgroup: **comp.unix.shell**

Software and Source Code

A large general-purpose archive of systems software, utilities, and programs that have been published by several popular Unix magazines. Programs include source code and documentation for Unix.

Anonymous FTP:
> Address: **ftp.uu.net**
> Path: **/published/open-systems-today/***

> Address: **ftp.uu.net**
> Path: **/published/unix-review/***

> Address: **ftp.uu.net**
> Path: **/published/unix-world/***

Sources

Source programs to run under Unix. The **.sources** newsgroup contains programs ready to download and compile. The **.unix-sw** group has pointers to Unix software that is available by Anonymous FTP.

Usenet:
> Newsgroup: **comp.sources.unix**
> Newsgroup: **info.unix-sw**

A B C D E F G H I J K L M N O P Q R S T U V W X Y Z

Standards

Discussion about Unix standards, especially the Posix 1003 standards.

Usenet:
> Newsgroup: **comp.std.unix**

Text Formatter

A scaled down nroff/troff style text formatter for Unix systems.

Anonymous FTP:
> Address: **world.std.docm**
> Path: **/src/print/awf/***

Usenet:
> Newsgroup: **comp.sources.unix**

Unix Administration

Discussion of all aspects of Unix administration.

Usenet:
> Newsgroup: **comp.unix.admin**

Unix Internals

Discussion about hacking deep inside of Unix. Not for the faint of heart.

Usenet:
> Newsgroup: **comp.unix.internals**

Unix Manual

Access the Unix manual by searching for keywords.

Wais:
> Database: **unix-manual**

Unix on PC Architectures

Talk and technical questions about running Unix on PCs. The **.16bit** newsgroup is for the older 16-bit machines. The **.32bit** group is for the more modern 32-bit machines.

Usenet:
> Newsgroup: **comp.unix.pc-clone.16bit**
> Newsgroup: **comp.unix.pc-clone.32bit**

User-Friendliness

A discussion of Unix and how it is (or is not) user-friendly. Lots of debate about whether Unix should (or should not be) user-friendly. The newsgroup is for ongoing discussion; the FTP contains a frequently asked question list.

Anonymous FTP:
> Address: **ftp.wfu.edu**
> Path: **/pub/usenet/cuuf.FAQ**

Usenet:
> Newsgroup: **comp.unix.user-friendly**

vi Reference Card

A complete list of all the commands for the popular Unix vi text editor. The commands are suitably grouped into topics, so it's easy to locate the one you need.

Gopher:
> Name: Manchester Computing Centre
> Address: **uts.mcc.ac.uk**
> Choose: **Experimental and New Services**
>   **| VI Reference Card**

RTFM

Yes, RTFM is the longest word in the English language with no vowels. It's also the single most important word in the Internet/Unix community. Originally, R.T.F.M. was an acronym that meant "Read the F. . . . . Manual". (Sorry, we are not allowed to print swear words where your parents might see them.)

Today, RTFM has a more refined meaning: it represents the idea that before you ask a question, you should try to answer it yourself. On the Internet, you are expected to (1) read the frequently asked question (FAQ) list for a Usenet newsgroup before sending in a question for the first time, and (2) check with the Unix manual before asking a question about a Unix command.

The FAQ lists are posted regularly to their respective newsgroups and to **news.answers**. They are also available by Anonymous FTP from **rtfm.mit.edu**. (Look in the directory **/pub/usenet/news.answers**.)

The Unix manual is a different story. All Unix systems should have a built-in command named **man** that will display the documentation for any Unix command. If for some reason this is not available on your system, you can search the Unix manual by using Wais. The name of the Wais database is **unix-manual**.

vi Tutorial

An interactive tutor teaching you all the necessities of the popular Unix vi text editor. The file needs to be captured or downloaded and then used with vi.

Anonymous FTP:
Address: **ftp.mines.colorado.edu**
Path: **/pub/tutorials/vitutor***

Gopher:
Name: Manchester Computing Centre
Address: **uts.mcc.ac.uk**
Choose: **Experimental and New Gopher Services | VI Tutorial**

OPERATING SYSTEMS: UNIX SYSTEMS

A/UX

Apple's version of Unix.

Usenet:
Newsgroup: **comp.unix.aux**

AIX

IBM's version of Unix, running on the RS/6000 and other platforms. The newsgroups are for ongoing discussion; the FTP site contains archives, including articles from *AIXpert* magazine.

Anonymous FTP:
Address: **asterix.fi.upm.es**
Path: **/pub/docs/ibm/***

Usenet:
Newsgroup: **bit.listserv.aix-l**
Newsgroup: **comp.unix.aix**

Amiga

Unix as it runs on Amiga computers.

Usenet:
Newsgroup: **comp.binaries.amiga**
Newsgroup: **comp.sys.amiga.unix**
Newsgroup: **comp.unix.amiga**

Berkeley Software Distribution for PCs

The version of BSD (Berkeley Unix) as ported to the Intel PC architecture. The newsgroups are for ongoing discussion; the FTP site contains source code and documentation.

Anonymous FTP:
Address: **gatekeeper.dec.com**
Path: **/pub/BSD/***

Usenet:
Newsgroup: **comp.os.386bsd.announce**
Newsgroup: **comp.os.386bsd.apps**
Newsgroup: **comp.os.386bsd.bugs**
Newsgroup: **comp.os.386bsd.development**
Newsgroup: **comp.os.386bsd.misc**
Newsgroup: **comp.os.386bsd.questions**

BSD is one of the two ancestors of modern Unix (the other being System V). If you are interested in the version of BSD that runs on PCs, check out the comp.os.386bsd.* newsgroups. If you want, you can even download a free copy of the operating system and run it on your own PC.

Berkeley Unix (BSD)

Berkeley Unix (BSD): one of the two ancestors of modern Unix. The newsgroups are for ongoing discussion; the FTP sites contain source code and documentation.

Anonymous FTP:
Address: **ftp.uu.net**
Path: **/systems/unix/bsd-sources/***

Address: **gatekeeper.dec.com**
Path: **/pub/BSD/***

Usenet:
Newsgroup: **comp.bugs.2bsd**
Newsgroup: **comp.bugs.4bsd**
Newsgroup: **comp.bugs.4bsd.ucb-fixes**
Newsgroup: **comp.unix.bsd**

BSDI

A commercial version of Berkeley Unix (BSD) as implemented by the BSDI company. The **.suit** newsgroup discusses the infamous and mean-spirited lawsuit between AT&T and BSDI.

Usenet:
Newsgroup: **alt.os.bsdi**
Newsgroup: **alt.suit.att-bsdi**
Newsgroup: **info.bsdi.users**

A B C D E F G H I J K L M N O P Q R S T U V W X Y Z

Coherent

Coherent: an economical Unix-like operating system that runs on PCs.

Usenet:
> Newsgroup: **comp.os.coherent**

Cray

Unix systems that run on Cray supercomputers.

Usenet:
> Newsgroup: **comp.unix.cray**

Linux

Linux: the free Unix clone, developed and maintained by Linus Torvalds and a gaggle of hackers around the Internet. Linux was written completely from scratch (using no "official" Unix code) for 386- and 486-based PCs. The world of Linux is huge and is one of the most important (and unsung) achievements in the history of operating system development. The newsgroups are for ongoing discussion; the FTP sites contain source code, documentation and archives.

Anonymous FTP:
> Address: **ftp.informatik.tu-muenchen.de**
> Path: **/pub/Linux/***
>
> Address: **nic.funet.fi**
> Path: **/pub/OS/Linux/***
>
> Address: **sunsite.unc.edu**
> Path: **/pub/Linux/***
>
> Address: **tsx-11.mit.edu**
> Path: **/pub/linux/***

Usenet:
> Newsgroup: **alt.uu.comp.os.linux.questions**
> Newsgroup: **comp.os.linux**
> Newsgroup: **comp.os.linux.admin**
> Newsgroup: **comp.os.linux.announce**
> Newsgroup: **comp.os.linux.development**
> Newsgroup: **comp.os.linux.help**
> Newsgroup: **comp.os.linux.misc**

OSF/1

The flagship operating system from the Open Software Foundation.

Usenet:
> Newsgroup: **comp.unix.osf.osf1**

Solaris

Sun's newer version of Unix.

Usenet:
> Newsgroup: **comp.unix.solaris**

System V

System V: one of the two ancestors of modern Unix.

Usenet:
> Newsgroup: **comp.bugs.misc**
> Newsgroup: **comp.unix.sys3**
> Newsgroup: **comp.unix.sys5.misc**
> Newsgroup: **comp.unix.sys5.r3**
> Newsgroup: **comp.unix.sys5.r4**
> Newsgroup: **comp.unix.sysv386**

Ultrix

One of DEC's versions of Unix.

Usenet:
> Newsgroup: **comp.unix.ultrix**

Xenix

The very old version of Unix designed to run on PCs.

Usenet:
> Newsgroup: **comp.unix.xenix.misc**
> Newsgroup: **comp.unix.xenix.sco**

OPERATING SYSTEMS: WINDOWS NT

Setup

Installing and configuring Windows NT.

Usenet:
> Newsgroup: **comp.os.ms-windows.nt.setup**

Windows NT General Discussion

Discussion about any and all topics involving Microsoft's Windows NT operating system.

Usenet:
> Newsgroup: **comp.os.ms-windows.nt.misc**

HERE IT IS, MICROSOFT'S READY-FOR-PRIME-TIME OPERATING SYSTEM FOR THE EARLY 1990s. THE TROUBLE IS, IT'S THE MID-1990s. NEVER MIND, NT IS HERE AND ALL IS WELL. FOR ALL THE IMPORTANT NEW INFO AND GENERAL NT DISCUSSION, TUNE IN TO comp.os.ms-windows.nt.misc.

ORGANIZATIONS

Association for Computing Machinery

The Association for Computing Machinery (ACM) is the largest and oldest educational and scientific computing organization in the world. Access to current information about the Association's activities is readily available here, including many technical computing areas.

Gopher:
Name: Association for Computing Machinery
Address: **gopher.acm.org**

Electronic Frontier Foundation

The Electronic Frontier Foundation's purpose is to ensure that the new communications technology era is available to everyone, and that everyone's constitutional rights are preserved therein. Plenty of legal information, EFF publications, and many related articles and zines are available here.

Anonymous FTP:
Address: **ftp.eff.org**
Path: **pub/EFF/***

Gopher:
Name: Electronic Frontier Foundation
Address: **gopher.eff.org**

THE ELECTRONIC FRONTIER FOUNDATION

The Electronic Frontier Foundation (EFF) is a non-profit organization dedicated to maintaining your rights within the American electronic infrastructure. They publish an electronic newsletter (*EFFector Online*) that is freely available for reading or downloading, and they furnish expert testimony and financial support in various court cases. Isn't it nice to know that concerned **net.anti-police** are ready to jump in and fight for your right to privacy and access to public information? Why not take a look at some of their publications and see if you want to support them.

History of the Philosophy of Science (HOPOS)

An informal, international working group of scholars who share an interest in promoting serious, scholarly research on the history of the philosophy of science and related topics.

Gopher:
Name: Occidental College
Address: **apa.oxy.edu**
Choose: **Other Societies and Associations | History of Philosophy of Science Working Group (HOPOS)**

If you like science, and you like philosophy, and you like history, you'll just *love* the history of the philosophy of science. Join the rest of the hoposophiles on the Occidental College Gopher.

Hume Society

The Hume Society invites anyone interested in the philosophy and writings of David Hume to become a member. Founded in 1974, the Hume Society is an international organization with approximately 300 members around the world.

Gopher:
Name: Occidental College
Address: **apa.oxy.edu**
Choose: **Other Societies and Associations | The Hume Society**

A B C D E F G H I J K L M N O P Q R S T U V W X Y Z

SEA Gopher

The Society for Electronic Access (SEA) works to educate people about computer networks and how to use them to communicate and to find information. Their Gopher includes a list of U.S. government BBSs, articles, archives and telecom law information.

Gopher:
Name: Panix
Address: **gopher.panix.com**
Choose: **Society for Electronic Access (SEA)**

The Internet will set you free

Excerpt from the Net...

(from the "EFFector Online", the Electronic Frontier Foundation newsletter)

```
*****************************************************************
        ///////////////    ///////////////    ///////////////
        ///              ///              ///
      ////////          ////////          ///////
      ///              ///              ///
      ///////////////    ///              ///
*****************************************************************

EFFector Online Volume 6 No. 1      9/17/1993      editors@eff.org
A Publication of the Electronic Frontier Foundation    ISSN 1062-9424

                -==-==-==-<>-==-==-==-
                  In This Issue:
                Clipper Escrow Agents Chosen
                Barlow's "A Plain Text on Crypto Policy"
                Crypto Conference in Austin
                Virginians Against Censorship
                -==-==-==-<>-==-==-==-


                A Plain Text on Crypto Policy
                    by John Perry Barlow
...the Clipper Chip — now called Skipjack owing to a trademark conflict —- is a
hardware encryption device that the National Security Agency designed under Reagan-Bush.
In April of 1993, it was unveiled by the Clinton Administration and proposed for both
governmental and public use.  Installed in phones or other telecommunications tools,
Skipjack would turn any conversation into gibberish for all but the speaker and his
intended listener, using a secret military algorithm.

Skipjack is unique, and controversial, in that it also allows the agents of government to
listen under certain circumstances.  Each chip contains a key that is split into two
parts immediately following manufacture.  Each half is then placed in the custody of some
trusted institution or "escrow agent".

If, at some subsequent time, some government agency desires to legally listen in on the
owner of the communications device in which the chip has been placed, it would present
evidence of "lawful authority" to the escrow holders. They will reveal the key pairs, the
agency will join them, and begin listening to the subject's unencrypted conversations.

Apparently there are other agencies besides law enforcement who can legally listen to
electronic communications.  The government has evaded questions about exactly who will
have access to these keys, or for that matter, what, besides an judicial warrant,
constitutes the "lawful authority" to which they continually refer.

Skipjack was not well received...

        ==============================================================
            This newsletter is printed on 100% recycled electrons.
```

PEOPLE

Albert Einstein

Discussions of the life and works of Albert Einstein, including topics indirectly related to his life.

Listserv mailing list:
List Address: **epp-l@buacca.bitnet**
Subscription Address: **listserv@buacca.bitnet**

Who's Who in Russia

A large list of important people in Russia.

Anonymous FTP:
Address: **ftp.spies.com**
Path: **/Library/Document/russia.who**

Gopher:
Name: Internet Wiretap
Address: **wiretap.spies.com**
Choose: **Wiretap Online Library**
| Assorted Documents
| Who's Who in Russia

PERSONALS

Backrubs

An interesting and informative collection of postings about recreational massage and backrubbing. Serious massage only; no sex.

Usenet:
Newsgroup: **alt.backrubs**

Bondage

Do you have an itch you just can't scratch? If you're looking for something new to do (or someone new to do something old with), speak up and say what you want. Join the discussion and find yourself someone who will keep you tied up all weekend.

Usenet:
Newsgroup: **alt.personals.bondage**

Electronic Matchmaker

A free, global matching service for anyone over 18 years of age. Fill out the detailed questionnaire and the perfect date could be yours.

Mail:
Address: **perfect@match.com**
Body: **send form**

Meeting People

Welcome to the buffet of personal ads. There is something for everyone, and you can take as much as you like. Non-fattening, hypo-allergenic, 100 percent of your recommended daily allowance of fun and good times. Participate in one of these Usenet groups and maybe you'll meet the man, woman, or none-of-the-above of your dreams.

Usenet:
Newsgroup: **alt.personals**
Newsgroup: **alt.personals.misc**

Romance and the Internet

Are you looking for that special someone?

Or are you looking for someone who is looking for that special someone?

Or would you like to just snoop on people who are looking for that special someone?

As you can see, there are lots of reasons to read the Usenet personal groups.

Give your resume a quick brush up and drop in today.

Need a laugh?
Check out Humor

A B C D E F G H I J K L M N O **P** Q R S T U V W X Y Z

Polyamory

The Law of Romantic Physics states that when there is too much love to go around the excess has to go somewhere. We've found where it goes, and if you want to get some of it to take home with you, feel welcome. Polyamorous people share themselves with you (and you and you and you).

Usenet:
Newsgroup: **alt.personals.poly**

Sex Wanted

Forget love, forget romance. If you're looking to cut to the chase, then cut in here. Don't bother being coy or shy, state what you want and let the good times roll.

Usenet:
Newsgroup: **alt.sex.wanted**

PETS

Animals in the News

Don't take Mr. Ed's word for it. Read the latest news and information on animals.

Usenet:
Newsgroup: **clari.news.interest.animals**

Aquaria

Buyer guides, filter information, magazine list, plant and water quality basics, and much more related to aquarium and fish keeping.

Anonymous FTP:
Address: **caldera.usc.edu**
Path: **/pub/aquaria/***

Bird Keeping

Bird magazines, books, terminology, buying guides, cage and toy reviews, diet and feeding information, training help, and other topics.

Anonymous FTP:
Address: **rtfm.mit.edu**
Path: **/pub/usenet/news.answers/pets-birds-faq/***

Cats

Basic cat care, guide to getting a cat, medical information, behavior problems, entertainment, and much more about cats.

Anonymous FTP:
Address: **rtfm.mit.edu**
Path: **/pub/usenet/news.answers/cats-faq/***

Dogs

Owner guides, puppy needs, health care issues, training tips, behavior understanding, kennel clubs, publications, resources and much more material concerning man's best friend.

Anonymous FTP:
Address: **rtfm.mit.edu**
Path: **/pub/usenet/news.answers/dogs-faq/***

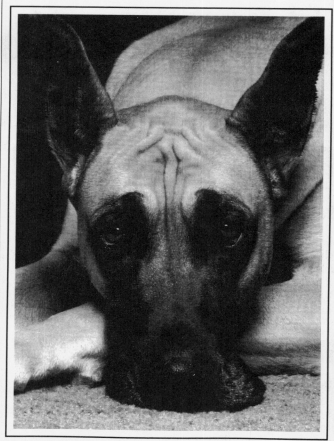

Pet lovers take heart. You're sure to find images of your favorite animals on the Net. From chinchillas to zebras, they're all here. If you think your pet is cuter than this, take a picture and post it for others to enjoy. This one is **saddog.jpg**.

Exotic Pets

Do you have a fondness for exotic pets? Learn about special care for your special animals, including how to breed and feed animals, recognize illnesses, and develop an awareness of safety. Discussion is not limited to reptiles (herpetology).

Usenet:
Newsgroup: **rec.pets.herp**

Fleas and Ticks

Learn how to rid your pet or home of fleas, and how to deal with ticks.

Anonymous FTP:
Address: **rtfm.mit.edu**
Path: **/pub/usenet/news.answers/fleas-ticks**

General Pet Discussion

Learn about a wide variety of pets. Share information and experiences on a range of topics including exotic animals, nutrition, grooming, behavior and veterinary care.

Usenet:
Newsgroup: **rec.pets**

Where the hell are the cool cats? On the Internet, of course. This image is from North Carolina State University (**garfield.catt.ncsu.edu**). The file is **/pub/graphics/images/Animals/kitty.gif**.

Spare time? Take a look at Games

Pet Discussions

Kittens and puppies and birds, oh my! Learn the best methods of caring for your pet. Discover how to pick the best pet, analyze behavior, and find new ideas for making your pet the happiest pet ever. Read advice and anecdotes from experienced animal friends.

Usenet:
Newsgroup: **rec.pets.birds**
Newsgroup: **rec.pets.cats**
Newsgroup: **rec.pets.dogs**

Treatment of Animals

What goes on in the lives of animals? Develop awareness on the use and abuse of animals.

Usenet:
Newsgroup: **talk.politics.animal**

PHILOSOPHY

Philosophical Discussions

Mailing lists for philosophers worldwide, where topics can be discussed and jobs and conference information is shared.

Listserv mailing list:
List Address: **phil-l@vm.ucs.ualberta.ca**
Subscription Address: **listserv@vm.ucs.ualberta.ca**

List Address: **philosed@suvm.syr.edu**
Subscription Address: **listserv@suvm.syr.edu**

List Address: **philosop@yorkvm1.bitnet**
Subscription Address: **listserv@yorkvm1.bitnet**

Do you like to talk about Life and other Important Stuff?

Join one of the *Philosophical Discussions* mailing lists and talk with the pros.

A
B
C
D
E
F
G
H
I
J
K
L
M
N
O
P
Q
R
S
T
U
V
W
X
Y
Z

PHOTOGRAPHY

California Museum of Photography

A sample of some of the photographs on display at the California Museum of Photography.

Gopher:
Name: University of California at Riverside
Address: **galaxy.ucr.edu**
Choose: **Campus Events
  | California Museum of Photography
  | Network Exhibitions**

Photo Database

Material relating to photography, including technique guides, paper and film data sheets, and chemistry formulae and information.

Gopher:
Name: Panix Public Access Unix, New York City
Address: **gopher.panix.com**
Choose: **The Panix Photography Database**

Photography

Lexicon of terms, FAQs, equipment reviews, lens information, useful addresses and phone numbers, and archives to do with photos and cameras.

Anonymous FTP:
Address: **moink.nmsu.edu**
Path: **/rec.photo/***

Address: **rtfm.mit.edu**
Path: **/pub/usenet/news.answers/rec-photo-faq**

Photography Mailing List

Discussion of all aspects of photography, including aesthetics, equipment and shooting technique.

Listserv mailing list:
List Address: **photo-l@buacca.bitnet**
Subscription Address: **listserv@buacca.bitnet**

PHYSICS

European Group for Atomic Spectroscopy

The EGAS organization is open to all European physicists working in the field of atomic physics. It aims to promote international cooperation between its members by the dissemination of information.

Gopher:
Name: EGAS
Address: **ipne.pne.ulg.ac.be**
Choose: **IPNE | EGAS**

Can you name this molecule? Well, at least you can find its picture at Northern Arizona University (**ftp.nau.edu**) in **/graphics/gif/ray**. The filename is **molecule.gif**.

LANL Physics Information Service

An information service for nuclear and particle physics that provides access to nuclear and high-energy physics related preprint listings. Both the abstracts and the papers themselves are available through this Gopher, as well as text searches of the abstracts, authors and titles.

Gopher:
Name: LANL Physics Information Service
Address: **mentor.lanl.gov**

National Nuclear Data Center Online Data Service

All the data you could possibly want regarding nuclear physics and statistical measurements, including radiation levels and other information for the U.S.

Telnet:
Address: **bnlnd2.dne.bnl.gov**
Login: **nndc**

Particles

A list of elementary and fundamental particles, giving the mass, lifetime and properties of each.

Anonymous FTP:
Address: **ftp.spies.com**
Path: **/Library/Document/particle.tbl**

Gopher:
Name: Internet Wiretap
Address: **wiretap.spies.com**
Choose: **Wiretap Online Library**
| **Assorted Documents**
| **Elementary & fundamental particles**

Physics Gopher

Access to physics resources and information, including the areas of astrophysics, general relativity and quantum cosmology, high energy physics, and nuclear theory.

Gopher:
Name: University of Chicago
Address: **granta.uchicago.edu**

The Physics Gopher

Physics is great.

If we didn't have physics, there wouldn't be any gravity or light or sound (and we would all be floating around silently in the dark).

So, when you need to indulge yourself, try the physics Gopher at the University of Chicago: a great source for all types of things physical.

Physics Mailing List

Covers current developments in theoretical and experimental physics, including plasmaphysics, particle physics and astrophysics.

Internet mailing list:
List Address: **physics@qedqcd.rye.ny.us**
Subscription Address:
physics-request@qedqcd.rye.ny.us

Physics Student Discussion List

A mailing list for physics students covering physics experiments, computer simulations and other topics of interest.

Listserv mailing list:
List Address: **phys-stu@uwf.bitnet**
Subscription Address: **listserv@uwf.bitnet**

Theoretical Physics Preprint List

Papers on general relativity and quantum cosmology, and high energy physics.

Anonymous FTP:
Address: **xxx.lanl.gov**
Path: **/gr-qc/***

Address: **xxx.lanl.gov**
Path: **/hep-th/***

Mail:
Address: **gr-qc@xxx.lanl.gov**
Subject: **help**

Address: **hep-th@xxx.lanl.gov**
Subject: **help**

POETRY

Chinese Poetry

A mailing list dedicated to sharing and discussion of Chinese poems.

Listserv mailing list:
List Address: **chpoem-l@ubvm.cc.buffalo.edu**
Subscription Address:
listserv@ubvm.cc.buffalo.edu

Poems

Spirits soar free on the wings of poetry. Show your verse to creative, like-minded people. If you ask, you can get advice, but there are more poems posted than critiqued.

Usenet:
Newsgroup: **rec.arts.poems**

Too much spare time?
Explore a MUD

A B C D E F G H I J K L M N O P Q R S T U V W X Y Z

Poems and Prose

A collection of original poems and prose composed by people on the Internet.

Anonymous FTP:
Address: **quartz.rutgers.edu**
Path: **/pub/origworks/***

Gopher:
Name: Rutgers Quartz Text Archive
Address: **quartz.rutgers.edu**
Choose: **Quartz BBS Original Works Archive**

POLITICS

Bay Area Libertarians

Discussion and announcements of meetings, activities and outings of Libertarians in the San Francisco bay area.

Internet mailing list:
List Address: **ba-liberty@shell.portal.com**
Subscription Address:
ba-liberty-request@shell.portal.com

California Libertarians

Meetings, events, activities, and schedules for the Libertarian party in California.

Internet mailing list:
List Address: **ca-liberty@shell.portal.com**
Subscription Address:
ca-liberty-request@shell.portal.com

Clinton Jokes

A Clinton joke for every occasion. Hillary, Bill, Chelsea, even Socks. No one is spared.

Anonymous FTP:
Address: **cco.caltech.edu**
Path: **/pub/humor/political**

Coalition for Networked Information (CNI)

Search databases for interesting publications, transcripts of congressional sessions, and other political events.

Telnet:
Address: **a.cni.org**
Login: **brsuser**

Conservative Archives

A collection of speeches, talks and papers of prominent conservative thinkers.

Anonymous FTP:
Address: **cathouse.org**
Path: **/pub/cathouse/conservative/***

ARE YOU A POLITICAL CONSERVATIVE?
If not, do you want to know what the conservative intellectuals are up to? Either way, the *Conservative Archives* will well repay your inspection.

Iowa Political Stock Market

Buy and sell shares in political candidates. This is a non-profit research project.

Telnet:
Address: **ipsm.biz.uiowa.edu**

National Research and Education Network Bill

The full text of the Bill for an Information Superhighway, including editorial comments.

Gopher:
Name: University of Minnesota
Address: **gopher.micro.umn.edu**
Choose: **Libraries**
| Electronic Books
| By Title
| NREN

New Republic Magazine

A weekly political opinion magazine. The current issue and back issues are online.

Gopher:
Name: The Internet Company
Address: **gopher.internet.com 2101**

Political Discussions

Mailing lists for serious discussions of U.S. politics.

Listserv mailing list:
List Address: **politics@ucf1vm.cc.ucf.edu**
Subscription Address: **listserv@ucf1vm.cc.ucf.edu**

List Address: **statepol@umab.umd.edu**
Subscription Address: **listserv@umab.umd.edu**

Political Humor

Humor related to politics and politicians.

Anonymous FTP:
Address: **quartz.rutgers.edu**
Path: **/pub/humor/Political/***

Gopher:
Name: Rutgers Quartz Text Archive
Address: **quartz.rutgers.edu**
Choose: **Humor | Political**

Political Implications of the Internet

An article discussing the political and social implications of the Internet.

Anonymous FTP:
Address: **ftp.spies.com**
Path: **/Library/Cyber/cyber.net**

Gopher:
Name: Internet Wiretap
Address: **wiretap.spies.com**
Choose: **Wiretap Online Library | Cyberspace | Political & Social Implications of the Net**

Political Party Platform Statements

The political platform statements of the Democratic, Green and Libertarian political parties.

Gopher:
Name: Internet Wiretap
Address: **wiretap.spies.com**
Choose: **Government Docs | Political Platforms of the US**

Politics and the Network Community

Information concerning several areas of politics, but especially those issues concerning politics, computers and the network community.

Gopher:
Name: Whole Earth Lectronic Link
Address: **gopher.well.sf.ca.us**
Choose: **Politics**

Radio Free Europe/Liberty Research Institute Reports

A daily report of the latest developments in Russia, Central Asia, and Central and Eastern Europe.

Anonymous FTP:
Address: **poniecki.berkeley.edu**
Path: **/pub/polish/publications/RFE-RL/***

Gopher:
Name: Poniecki Foundation Gopher
Address: **poniecki.berkeley.edu**

Name: University of Michigan
Address: **gopher.lib.umich.edu**
Choose: **News Services | Radio Free Europe**

Listserv mailing list:
List Address: **rferl-l@ubvm.cc.buffalo.edu**
Subscription Address:
listserv@ubvm.cc.buffalo.edu

Rush Limbaugh Archives

Frequently asked question list and summaries of this popular radio and TV personality's shows. Show summaries are arranged chronologically by year and month. These archives are part of the Catstyle archives.

Anonymous FTP:
Address: **cathouse.org**
Path: **/pub/cathouse/rush.limbaugh/***

Excerpt from the Net...

(from "Political Implications of the Internet")

I have called the Net the last (accidentally) uncensored mass medium. It does not take a rocket scientist to realize that they decide what appears in newspapers, magazines, books, and on radio and TV, whereas we decide what will appear on the Net...

A B C D E F G H I J K L M N O **P** Q R S T U V W X Y Z

The Mouth that Roared

There's a lot you can say about Rush Limbaugh—the conservative political commentator and talk show host—and just about anyone you meet is ready to say it. Still, you have to admire anyone who can sell 1.4 million books in a month. (Well, maybe you don't have to admire that, but we find it hard not to.) *The Rush Limbaugh Archives* provide a wealth of information for dittoheads around the world. Rush, of course, can't read it because he isn't on the Internet, but you are, so go wild.

Weird Politics and Conspiracy

Lots of documents and archives from some of the more unusual political movements. Includes Arm the Spirit, The Disability Rag, NativeNet archives, Workers World, and more.

Anonymous FTP:
 Address: **red.css.itd.umich.edu**
 Path: **/pub/Politics/***

 Address: **red.css.itd.umich.edu**
 Path: **/pub/Zines/***

POLITICS: INTERNATIONAL

Arms and Disarmament

Politics, peace, war, the cold war, disarmament and related subjects.

Internet mailing list:
 List Address: **arms-d@xx.lcs.mit.edu**
 Subscription Address:
  arms-d-request@xx.lcs.mit.edu

Listserv mailing list:
 List Address: **arms-l@buacca.bitnet**
 Subscription Address: **listserv@buacca.bitnet**

NATO Handbook

Documents explaining NATO (North Atlantic Treaty Organization)—how it works, the future role of the alliance, its organization and structure, and other related information.

Anonymous FTP:
 Address: **ftp.spies.com**
 Path: **/Gov/NATO-HB/***

Gopher:
 Name: Internet Wiretap
 Address: **wiretap.spies.com**
 Choose: **Government Docs (US & World)**
  | NATO Handbook

NATO Press Releases

Press releases and news from NATO, the North Atlantic Treaty Organization.

Anonymous FTP:
 Address: **ftp.spies.com**
 Path: **/Gov/NATO/***

Gopher:
 Name: Internet Wiretap
 Address: **wiretap.spies.com**
 Choose: **Government Docs (US & World)**
  | NATO Press Releases

Treaties and International Covenants

A collection of treaties and convention information, including the Geneva Conventions, League of Nations, Hague Conventions, and The Law of the Sea.

Anonymous FTP:
 Address: **ftp.spies.com**
 Path: **/Gov/Treaties/***

Gopher:
 Name: Internet Wiretap
 Address: **wiretap.spies.com**
 Choose: **Government Docs (US & World)**
  | Treaties and International Covenants

PROGRAMMING

Ada

Public library containing compilers, tools, documentation, FAQs and other software for the Ada programming language, as used by the U.S. Department of Defense.

Anonymous FTP:
Address: **wuarchive.wustl.edu**
Path: **/languages/ada/***

C Programs

Some interesting little C programs for the Unix gurus amongst you, although some require you to have root privileges to run them.

Anonymous FTP:
Address: **ftp.cs.widener.edu**
Path: **/pub/brendan/***

C++ Frequently Asked Questions

Answers to hundreds of the most frequently asked questions about the C++ programming language. Nearly one hundred pages of densely packed information for programmers interested in C++.

Anonymous FTP:
Address: **sun.soe.clarkson.edu**
Path: **/pub/C++/FAQ**

If you're thinking of making the most serious commitment that a computer programmer can make, jumping into C++, stop, take a deep breath, and read the frequently asked question list.

CCMD Source Code in C

The complete source code and makefiles to a user-interface program based on the COMND jsys from TOPS20. This program gives escape completion on many different types of data (filenames, users, groups, keywords, etc.). Columbia's MM (Mail Manager) program is written with it.

Anonymous FTP:
Address: **oak.oakland.edu**
Path: **/pub/misc/ccmd/***

CompuServe B File Transfer Protocol

The complete C source and documentation for implementing the CompuServe B file transfer protocol.

Anonymous FTP:
Address: **oak.oakland.edu**
Path: **/pub/misc/cis/***

Data File Formats

Documents and descriptions of image and data file formats.

Anonymous FTP:
Address: **wuarchive.wustl.edu**
Path: **/doc/graphic-formats/***

Eyes X Window Environment

Eyes is a visual programming environment for X Window, and is useful in the areas of image processing, document recognition, database management, dataflow programming and network analysis.

Anonymous FTP:
Address: **ftp.ulowell.edu**
Path: **/Eyes/***

Free Language Tools

Extensive list of free language tools—with source code—including compilers and interpreters.

Anonymous FTP:
Address: **csd4.csd.uwm.edu**
Path: **/pub/compilers.list**

Gopher:
Name: Pacific Systems Group
Address: **gopher.psg.com**
Choose: **Programming Languages | List of Free Compilers...**

FSP

Information, utilities, and the latest Unix FSP software, the new alternative file transfer protocol to FTP.

Anonymous FTP:
Address: **erratic.bradley.edu**
Path: **/pub/fsp/***

A B C D E F G H I J K L M N O P Q R S T U V W X Y Z

General Discussion

General discussion about DOS programming: tips, questions and answers.

Usenet:
Newsgroup: **alt.msdos.programmer**
Newsgroup: **comp.os.msdos.programmer**

Gnuplot Tutorial

A Postscript file containing a tutorial to teach you the nuances of gnuplot, a graph plotting program.

Anonymous FTP:
Address: **ccosun.caltech.edu**
Path:
/pub/documents/gnuplot-tutorial.ps

Gopher and Utilities for VMS

Collection of VMS files and programs that you can browse or download. Includes the latest Gopher client, compression and archive utilities, and more.

Gopher:
Name: Sam Houston State University
Address: **niord.shsu.edu**
Choose: **VMS Gopher-related file library**

Hello World!

The classic neophyte program in many different languages.

Anonymous FTP:
Address: **ocf.berkeley.edu**
Path: **/pub/Library/Hello_World**

Interactive Fiction

Interactive fiction games, development tools, game solutions and programming examples from the Usenet newsgroups **rec.arts.int-fiction** and **rec.games.int-fiction**.

Anonymous FTP:
Address: **wuarchive.wustl.edu**
Path: **/doc/misc/if-archive/***

Language FAQs

FAQs on many programming languages and tools, including C, C++, Forth, Lisp, Perl, Prolog and Scheme.

Anonymous FTP:
Address: **quartz.rutgers.edu**
Path: **/pub/computer/languages/***

Gopher:
Name: Rutgers Quartz Text Archive
Address: **quartz.rutgers.edu**
Choose: **Computer-Sources, Documentation, Comp.Sci**
| Languages

WE'VE GOT THE ANSWERS TO ALL OF YOUR QUESTIONS
If they are about computer languages, that is. The **quartz** archive at Rutgers University has a wealth of frequently asked question (FAQ) lists about all kinds of languages. Here's an idea: why not connect to the Gopher and check out a programming language you have never heard of? it's a great way to impress a date.

Language List

An extensive list of collected information on more than 2000 computer languages, past and present.

Anonymous FTP:
Address: **ftp.s.u-tokyo.ac.jp**
Path: **/lang/language-list/***

Gopher:
Name: Pacific Systems Group
Address: **gopher.psg.com**
Choose: **Programming Languages**
| List of 'All' Programming...

League for Programming Freedom

An Anonymous FTP site that stores position papers, descriptions of events, and membership information for the League for Programming Freedom (LPF).

Anonymous FTP:
Address: **ftp.cs.widener.edu**
Path: **/pub/lpf/***

Make Tutorial

An easy-to-use introduction to **make**, the C program maintenance utility.

Gopher:
Name: Manchester Computing Centre
Address: **uts.mcc.ac.uk**
Choose: **Experimental and New Services**
| Make: A Tutorial

Obfuscated C Code

Entries for the International Obfuscated C Code Contest, which asked people to write, in 512 bytes or less, the worst complete C program.

Comment: This is an annual contest, so different sites may maintain these files each year. Use Archie and Veronica to find other sites.

Anonymous FTP:
Address: **ftp.white.toronto.edu**
Path: **/pub/obfuscated/***

Archie:
Pattern: **obfuscated**

Obfuscated C Code Winners

The winning entries to the obfuscated C code contest.

Anonymous FTP:
Address: **ftp.uu.net**
Path: **/doc/literary/obi/Nerd.Humor/ObfuscatedC**

Pascal to C Translator

This Unix program translates Pascal programs into C programs, just like that!

Anonymous FTP:
Address: **ccosun.caltech.edu**
Path: /pub/misc/p2c-1.18.tar.Z

Programming Examples

Programming examples, code fragments and helpful hints for many different computer languages.

Anonymous FTP:
Address: **ftp.uu.net**
Path: **/languages/***

Programming for Microsoft Windows

Discussions, questions, answers about the ridiculously easy task of programming under Microsoft Windows. The **.tools** newsgroup is for discussion of programming tools. The **.win32** group is devoted to the Windows 32-bit API.

Usenet:
Newsgroup:
comp.os.ms-windows.programmer.misc
Newsgroup:
comp.os.ms-windows.programmer.tools
Newsgroup:
comp.os.ms-windows.programmer.win32

Programming in Ada

Tips, tricks, utilities, source code and complete programs for users of this programming language.

Anonymous FTP:
Address: **oak.oakland.edu**
Path: **/pub/ada/***

Programming Language Material

Articles and guides on computer languages, including C, Ada and Protolo object code format.

Anonymous FTP:
Address: **ftp.spies.com**
Path: **/Library/Techdoc/Language/***

Gopher:
Name: Internet Wiretap
Address: **wiretap.spies.com**
Choose: **Wiretap Online Library**
| Technical Information
| Languages

Programming Languages

Information on many computer programming languages, including C++, Modula 2, Oberon and Pascal.

Gopher:
Name: Pacific Systems Group
Address: **gopher.psg.com**
Choose: **Programming Languages**

Need information on programming languages?

Try the Pacific System Group's Gopher.

Ravel

A C-like, interpreted programming language for the IBM-PC that directly supports MIDI music constructs. The package includes music files and source code.

Anonymous FTP:
Address: **ftp.cs.pdx.edu**
Path: **/pub/music/ravel/***

A B C D E F G H I J K L M N O P Q R S T U V W X Y Z

TCP/IP Development Tools

This directory contains instructions and C source code for a mail program and for implementing the TCP/IP protocol on PCs and Macintosh computers.

Anonymous FTP:
    Address: **oak.oakland.edu**
    Path: **/pub/misc/ka9q-tcpip/***

Turbo Vision

Programming using Borland's Turbo Vision: text-based object-oriented application libraries and development tools.

Usenet:
    Newsgroup:
        comp.os.msdos.programmer.turbovision

Twisted Code

Humorous articles relating to computer code and languages, including an electronic C Christmas card, funny **man** pages, and a very rude C program.

Anonymous FTP:
    Address: **ftp.spies.com**
    Path: **/Library/Humor/Code/***

Gopher:
    Name: Internet Wiretap
    Address: **wiretap.spies.com**
    Choose: **Wiretap Online Library**
        | **Humor**
        | **Code**

X Window Software Index

An index of public domain software to exploit or enhance the X Window system. It lets you peruse archives and tells you what software exists and where to find it, along with a brief description of each item.

Gopher:
    Name: University of Edinburgh
    Address: **gopher.ed.ac.uk**
    Choose: **Index to public domain X sources**

PSYCHOLOGY

Birthparents of Adoptees

A mailing list provided for communication among birthparents of adopted children.

Listserv mailing list:
    List Address: **brthprnt@indycms.bitnet**
    Subscription Address: **listserv@indycms.bitnet**

Brainwashing

A discussion of the history, problems and techniques of brainwashing, and the ways it is used in modern society.

Anonymous FTP:
    Address: **ftp.spies.com**
    Path: **/Library/Article/Misc/brainwa.txt**

Gopher:
    Name: Internet Wiretap
    Address: **wiretap.spies.com**
    Choose: **Wiretap Online Library**
        | **Articles**
        | **Misc**
        | **The Battle for your Mind: Brainwashing**

Freud's Occult Studies

A paper on Freud's research into the paranormal.

Anonymous FTP:
    Address: **ftp.spies.com**
    Path: **/Library/Fringe/Occult/freud.occ**

Gopher:
    Name: Internet Wiretap
    Address: **wiretap.spies.com**
    Choose: **Wiretap Online Library**
        | **Fringes of Reason**
        | **Occult and Paranormal**
        | **Freud's Studies of the Occult**

Psycgrad Project

A Gopher dedicated to providing graduate students with information about psychology and graduate studies in psychology.

Gopher:
    Name: The Psycgrad Project
    Address: **pand1.uottowa.ca 4010**

Psychology Graduate Student Journal

Professional-level articles in the field of psychology, compiled by and tailored to graduate students.

Listserv mailing list:
List Address: **psygrd-j@acadvm1.uottawa.ca**
Subscription Address:
listserv@acadvm1.uottawa.ca

Psycoloquy

A regularly published collection of articles from all areas of psychology. This resource is sponsored by the American Psychological Association.

Anonymous FTP:
Address: **una.hh.lib.umich.edu**
Path: **/journals/psyc/***

Gopher:
Name: University of Virginia
Address: **gopher.virginia.edu**
Choose: **Library Services**
| **University Library GWIS Collections**
| **Alphabetic Organization**
| **Psycoloquy**

Name: University of Michigan Libraries
Address: **gopher.lib.umich.edu**
Choose: **Social Sciences Resources**
| **Psychology, Sociology, and Anthropology**
| **Psycoloquy**

Excerpt from the Net...

```
(from "The Battle for Your Mind: Brainwashing")

To begin, I want to state the most basic of all facts about
brainwashing:

        In the entire history of man, no one has ever
        been brainwashed and realized, or believed, that
        he had been brainwashed.

Those who have been brainwashed will usually passionately defend their manipulators,
claiming they have simply been "shown the light", or have been transformed in miraculous
ways...

Cults and human-potential organizations are always looking for new converts. To attain
them, they must also create a brain-phase. And they often need to do it within a short
space of time -- a weekend, or maybe even a day.  The following are the six primary
techniques used to generate the conversion.

The meeting or training takes place in an area where participants are cut off from the
outside world...  In human-potential trainings, the controllers will give a lengthy talk
about the importance of "keeping agreements" in life.  The participants are told that if
they don't keep agreements, their life will never work.  It's a good idea to keep
agreements, but the controllers are subverting a positive human value for selfish
purposes.  The participants vow to themselves and their trainer that they will keep their
agreements.  Anyone who does not will be intimidated into agreement or forced to leave.
The next step is to agree to complete training, thus assuring a high percentage of
conversions for the organizations.  They will USUALLY have to agree not to take drugs,
smoke, and sometimes not to eat, or they are given such short meal breaks that it creates
tension.  The real reason for the agreements is to alter internal chemistry, which
generates anxiety and hopefully causes at least a slight malfunction of the nervous
system, which in turn increases the conversion potential.

Before the gathering is complete, the agreements will be used to ensure that the new
converts go out and find new participants.  They are intimidated into agreeing to do so
before they leave.  Since the importance of keeping agreements is so high on their
priority list, the converts will twist the arms of everyone they know, attempting to
talk them into attending a free introductory session offered at a future date by the
organization.  The new converts are zealots. In fact, the inside term for merchandising
the largest and most successful human-potential training is, "sell it by zealot!"...
```

PSYCOLOQUY

What do you do when you have a house guest you are just too busy to entertain? Sit him down at the computer, connect him to a Gopher, and have him read back issues of *Psycoloquy*, a refereed psychology journal.

Just listen to this:
"According to Wallis (1992), philosophers of mind agree that a successful theory of representation must 'describe conditions for representation in nonintentional and nonsemantic terms.' If we restrict representation talk to what goes on in frogs, the visual systems of humans, etc., then perhaps Wallis is right. But once we count beliefs as representations, there is no such agreement. Indeed..."

Your friends will be coming back to visit you, again and again.

SAIDIE - The Intellectual Disability Network

Articles and information about intellectual disabilities; topics include policy, psychology, medicine and education.

Gopher:
Name: MedCal
Address: **gopher.vifp.monash.edu.au**
Choose: **Medical**
  | **SAIDIE - The Intellectual Disability Network**

PUBLICATIONS

Dartmouth College Library Online System

Search and browse a wealth of database files. Get information about titles, authors and publications. You can even search books and periodicals for keywords and view the text.

Telnet:
Address: **library.dartmouth.edu**

Journalism

This Wais site indexes over 10,000 published journals and periodicals.

Wais:
Database: **journalism.periodicals**

Journals with a Difference

Selection of journals covering some of the more unusual topics in life. Includes such publications as *The Unplastic News*, *Athene*, *Scream Baby* and *Quanta*.

Anonymous FTP:
Address: **etext.archive.umich.edu**
Path: **/pub/***

Newsletters, Electronic Journals, Zines

A wide selection of online publications covering biology, computing, health, kids, libraries, networks, politics and space.

Anonymous FTP:
Address: **nigel.msen.com**
Path: **/pub/newsletters/***

Online Publications

Multitudes of online zines, essays and articles covering varied and unusual subjects. Includes articles from such publications as *Mondo 2000*, *Whole Earth Review*, *Locus* and *The Unplastic News*.

Gopher:
Name: Whole Earth Lectronic Link
Address: **gopher.well.sf.ca.us**
Choose: **Publications**

Publisher's Catalogs

Browse catalogs from publishing companies, including Addison-Wesley, MIT Press, O'Reilly, Prentice Hall and others.

Gopher:
Name: University of Virginia
Address: **gopher.virginia.edu**
Choose: **Library Services**
  | **University Library Resources (Alphabetic Organization)**
  | **Publisher's Catalogs**

Whole Earth Review Articles

A selection of articles from the *Whole Earth Review* magazine, which is dedicated to demystification, self-teaching, and to encouraging people to think for themselves.

Gopher:
> Name: Whole Earth Lectronic Link
> Address: **gopher.well.sf.ca.us**
> Choose: **Whole Earth Review, the Magazine**

Zine Reviews

A large collection of reviews from the *Factsheet Five - Electric* zine, covering various and esoteric zines, those opinionated publications with press runs of between 50 and 5000 copies.

Anonymous FTP:
> Address: **nigel.msen.com**
> Path: **/pub/newsletters/Zine-Reviews/F5-E**

Gopher:
> Name: Whole Earth Lectronic Link
> Address: **gopher.well.sf.ca.us**
> Choose: **Publications**
> **| Factsheet Five, Electric**

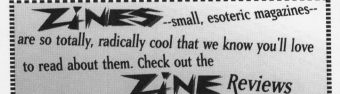

Zines

Collection of zines covering such topics as science fiction, computers, short fiction, poetry and cyberpunk.

Gopher:
> Name: CICnet
> Address: **gopher.cic.net**
> Choose: **Electronic Serials**

PUBLISHING

Association of American University Presses

Electronic publishing and other issues of interest to university presses.

Listserv mailing list:
> List Address: **aaup-l@psuvm.bitnet**
> Subscription Address: **listserv@psuvm.bitnet**

Copy Editors Mailing List

A mailing list for copy editors and other defenders of the King's English who wish to discuss editorial problems, client relations, Internet resources, dictionaries or whatever.

Internet mailing list:
> List Address: **copyediting-l@cornell.edu**
> Subscription Address:
> **copyediting-l-request@cornell.edu**

Electronic Publishing

Important articles about publishing an electronic journal or paper, including ISSN and copyright information, resource guide, and the functions of the Library of Congress.

Anonymous FTP:
> Address: **ftp.spies.com**
> Path: **/Library/Article/Publish/***

> Address: **seq1.loc.gov**
> Path: **/pub/Library.of.Congress/about.LC/***

Gopher:
> Name: Internet Wiretap
> Address: **wiretap.spies.com**
> Choose: **Wiretap Online Library**
> **| Articles**
> **| Electronic Publishing**

McGraw-Hill Internet Resource Area

Samples and introductions for Internet-related books published by McGraw-Hill.

Gopher:
> Name: The Electronic Newsstand
> Address: **gopher.internet.com 2100**
> Choose:
> **Special Projects—(McGraw-Hill, Ventana Press)**
> **| McGraw-Hill Internet Resource Area**

Ventana Press Internet Resource Area

Samples and introductions for Internet-related books and software published by Ventana Press.

Gopher:
> Name: The Electronic Newsstand
> Address: **gopher.internet.com 2100**
> Choose:
> **Special Projects—(McGraw-Hill, Ventana Press)**
> **| Ventana Press Internet Resource Area**

A B C D E F G H I J K L M N O P Q R S T U V W X Y Z

QUOTATIONS

Woody Allen

You probably think that we have a good sense of humor but, actually, all we've done is memorized all of Woody Allen's famous quotes. No reason why you can't do the same.

Anonymous FTP:
Address: **cathouse.org**
Path: **/pub/cathouse/humor/quotes/woody.allen**

Beavis and Butt-head

Is your significant other bringing the inlaws over for dinner tonight? Don't worry about getting caught short with nothing to say. Take a look at some quotes from Beavis and Butt-head, two of America's foremost cultural philosophers.

Anonymous FTP:
Address: **quartz.rutgers.edu**
Path: **/pub/tv+movies/beavis/bnb-quotes**

Gopher:
Name: Rutgers University
Address: **quartz.rutgers.edu**
Choose: **Television and Movies**
| **Beavis**
| **Bnb-quotes**

Bible Quotes

Quotations from the Bible, courtesy of *Christian Computing* magazine.

Gopher:
Name: University of Alabama
Address: **twinbrook.cis.uab.edu**

Lenny Bruce

Here's a man who knew how to talk dirty and influence people. Lenny Bruce was truly one of the illegitimate fathers of modern popular culture. You can draw a straight line from Lenny through George Carlin right to Beavis and Butt-head. But what would be the point?

Anonymous FTP:
Address: **cathouse.org**
Path: **/pub/cathouse/humor/standup/lenny.bruce**

Andrew Dice Clay

If you're tired of plain old traditional nursery rhymes, read what Andrew Dice Clay has to say about Mother Hubbard and what else was bare besides her cupboard.

Anonymous FTP:
Address: **cathouse.org**
Path: **/pub/cathouse/humor/standup/**
andrew.dice.clay

Rodney Dangerfield

We get no respect. We went to use our Internet account the other day and found that somebody had changed our username to **shicklegruber**. But we've got nothing to complain about; take a look at what Rodney has to say.

Anonymous FTP:
Address: **cathouse.org**
Path: **/pub/cathouse/humor/standup/**
rodney.dangerfield

FOR MEN ONLY

Hey guys, need a quick way to impress a woman?

If she is under 20 years old, quote Beavis and Butt-head.

If she is between 20 and 30, quote Jerry Seinfeld.

If she is between 30 and 40, quote Steven Wright.

If she is between 40 and 50, quote Woody Allen.

If she is over 50, quote Rodney Dangerfield.

W.C. Fields

Even today, W.C. Fields' wit is legendary. After all, anyone who hates kids, dogs and books for dummies can't be all that bad.

Anonymous FTP:
Address: **cathouse.org**
Path: **/pub/cathouse/humor/quotes/w.c.fields**

Fortune Quotes

A large collection of quotes for fortune programs. Includes weasel quotes, strong quotes, Moriarty quotes and fortune cookies.

Anonymous FTP:
Address: **quartz.rutgers.edu**
Path: **/pub/computer/fortune/***

Gopher:
Name: Rutgers Quartz Text Archive
Address: **quartz.rutgers.edu**
Choose:
    Computer-Sources, Documentation, Comp.Sci
    | Fortune

Samuel Goldwyn

Are all the Samuel Goldwyn quotes real? We can tell you in two words: a pocryphal.

Anonymous FTP:
Address: **cathouse.org**
Path: **/pub/cathouse/humor/quotes/sam.goldwyn**

David Letterman

Everybody who loves David Letterman loves his top ten lists. But what do you do in the middle of the night when you wake up in a sweat because you can't remember what was number 5 on the list of top ten Dear Abby letter signatures from July 23, 1987? No problem. Connect to the Internet and the information is only a few keystrokes away.

Anonymous FTP:
Address: **quartz.rutgers.edu**
Path: **/pub/tv+movies/letterman/top-ten**

Gopher:
Name: Rutgers University
Address: **quartz.rutgers.edu**
Choose: **Television and Movies**
    | Letterman
    | Top-ten

Excerpt from the Net...

(from the "Fortune Quotes" archive)

```
Tie?  You want me to wear a TIE?  Listen: there's only one time in a man's life when he
should have a rope knotted around his neck, and that time ain't yet come for me.
    -- Canada Bill Jones

The secret of my success is that at a very early age I discovered that I'm not God.
    -- Oliver Wendell Holmes

...Fortunately, AT&T couldn't sell drugs at a Grateful Dead show.
    -- Bob Stratton

Time, because it is so fleeting, time, because it is beyond recall, is the most precious
of human goods, and to squander it is the most delicate form of dissipation in which man
can indulge.
    -- W. Somerset Maugham, "The Bum"

A fool with a spreadsheet is still a fool.
    -- Paul Abrahams

I love deadlines.  I like the whooshing sound they make as they fly by.
    -- Douglas Adams

Emacs is not an editor.  Emacs is a way of thinking about the world and, as such, is a
way of thinking about editors.  The process of editing is Emacs, but Emacs is more than
the process of editing.

When you ask what Emacs does, you are asking a question with no answer, because Emacs
doesn't do, it is done to.  Emacs just is.
...I hope this makes things clearer.
    -- Scott Dorsey

Not only did they all laugh at Christopher Columbus, they also laughed at Bozo the Clown.
    -- Peter Reiher

Shouldn't "anal rententive" have a hyphen?
    -- unidentified passing t-shirt
```

Groucho Marx

Groucho Marx was one of America's funniest funny men. Check out some of his quotes, and maybe you can pass them off as your own.

Anonymous FTP:
    Address: **cathouse.org**
    Path: **/pub/cathouse/humor/standup/groucho.marx**

**Make sure you are prepared:
Read
Emergency and Disaster**

Excerpt from the Net...

              (from the Samuel Goldwyn quotation archive)

```
------------------------------------------------------------------------
Note: Samuel Goldwyn was an American immigrant who became one of the most powerful film
producers in Hollywood.  He controlled MGM (Metro-Goldwyn-Mayer) and was well-known for
his emminently quotable remarks, many of which are, no doubt, apocryphal.
------------------------------------------------------------------------

"It rolled off my back like a duck."

[When told his son was getting married]
"Thank heaven.  A bachelor's life is no life for a single man."

"I can give you a definite maybe."

"Gentleman, include me out."

"A verbal contract isn't worth the paper its printed on."

Bookkeeper:  Mr. Goldwyn, our files are bulging with paperwork we no longer need.  May I
             have your permission to destroy all records before 1945?
Goldwyn:  Certainly.  Just be sure to keep a copy of everything.

"I can tell you in two words: im possible."

[On being told that a friend had named his son Sam, after him]
"Why did you do that?  Every Tom, Dick and Harry is named Sam!"

"I paid too much for it, but its worth it."

"Don't worry about the war.  It's all over but the shooting."

"Gentlemen, for your information, I have a question to ask you."

"I read part of it all the way through."

"If I could drop dead right now, I'd be the happiest man alive."

"I never put on a pair of shoes until I've worn them at least five years."

"I don't think anyone should write their autobiography until after they're dead."

"Anyone who goes to a psychiatrist ought to have his head examined.

"Gentlemen, listen to me slowly."

[in discussing Lillian Helman's play, "The Children's Hour"]
  Goldwyn:  Maybe we ought to buy it?
Associate:  Forget it, Mr. Goldwyn, its about Lesbians.
  Goldwyn:  That's okay, we'll make them Americans.
```

Norm Peterson from Cheers

One of the troubles with witty sayings is that they are often too difficult to understand if you've been drinking too much beer. Just the time to download a few Normisms ("How's life in the fast lane, Norm? Beats me, I can't find the on-ramp.").

Anonymous FTP:
Address: **quartz.rutgers.edu**
Path: **/pub/tv+movies/cheers/norm-sayings**

Gopher:
Name: Rutgers University
Address: **quartz.rutgers.edu**
Choose: **Television and Movies**
  | **Cheers**
  | **Norm-sayings**

Quotation Reference Books

A comprehensive bibliography of books of quotations. Why waste your time being creative when borrowing is so much easier?

Anonymous FTP:
Address: **quartz.rutgers.edu**
Path: **/pub/books/quote-books**

Gopher:
Name: Rutgers University
Address: **quartz.rutgers.edu**
Choose: **Book FAQs and Info**
  | **Quote-books**

Quotations Archive

A large selection of quotes from all walks of life.

"Truth is more of a stranger than fiction."
  -Mark Twain.

Anonymous FTP:
Address: **wilma.cs.brown.edu**
Path: **pub/alt.quotations/Archive/***

Usenet:
Newsgroup: **alt.quotations**

Lonely?
Try the Personals

Quotation Archives

The Internet has a number of Anonymous FTP sites at which you can find all kinds of quotations. Just the thing for spicing up your conversation and enhancing your reputation. Here is a typical example showing how it works.

[You are talking to your teacher or boss.]

Teacher/Boss:
So what do you have to say for yourself?

[At this point you repeat a quote that you downloaded the night before from one of the Internet quotation archives.]

You:
Well, I think blah, blah blah, blah, blah...

Teacher/Boss:
Wow, you really are terrific. I'm going to give you an A (or a raise).

Very good looking woman/man who happens to be listening:
You are an unbelievably attractive person. Would you like to have dinner with me tonight?

Ren and Stimpy

Do you know the Ren and Stimpy fan club oath? Well, you should. Check out the Ren and Stimpy quotes and find all kinds of good stuff.

Anonymous FTP:
Address: **quartz.rutgers.edu**
Path: **/pub/tv+movies/renstimpy/quotes**

Gopher:
Name: Rutgers University
Address: **quartz.rutgers.edu**
Choose: **Television and Movies**
  | **Renstimpy**
  | **Quotes**

A B C D E F G H I J K L M N O P Q R S T U V W X Y Z

Seinfeld

Too many people spend too much time watching Jerry Seinfeld and his friends on TV when they should be reading *The Internet Complete Reference*. But what can we do about it? Probably nothing, so you might as well use the Internet to download all those swell quotes that sounded so good the night before the morning after.

Anonymous FTP:
> Address: **quartz.rutgers.edu**
> Path: **/pub/tv+movies/seinfeld/Quotes**

Gopher:
> Name: Rutgers University
> Address: **quartz.rutgers.edu**
> Choose: **Televison and Movies**
> | **Seinfeld**
> | **Quotes**

Star Trek

Damn it Jim, we're Internet writers, not trivia buffs! If you want to get quotes from the original *Star Trek*, *The Next Generation*, the *Star Trek* movies or *Deep Space 9*, you'll have to get them yourself.

Anonymous FTP:
> Address: **quartz.rutgers.edu**
> Path: **/pub/tv+movies/startrek/trek-quotes**

Finger:
> Address: **franklin@ug.cs.dal.ca**

Gopher:
> Name: Rutgers University
> Address: **quartz.rutgers.edu**
> Choose: **Television and Movies**
> | **Startrek**
> | **Trek-quotes**

Mark Twain

Everybody talks about putting up an archive site for Mark Twain quotations, but nobody does anything about it. Except that Jason Heimbaugh has done something about it. Take a look at Jason's Cathouse archives, and see what the father of modern American literature (Mark Twain, not Jason) has to say for himself.

Anonymous FTP:
> Address: **cathouse.org**
> Path: **/pub/cathouse/humor/quotes/mark.twain**

Oscar Wilde

According to Oscar Wilde, the only way to get rid of a temptation is to yield to it. So don't wait, rush out and buy 10 copies of *The Internet Complete Reference*.

Anonymous FTP:
> Address: **cathouse.org**
> Path: **/pub/cathouse/humor/quotes/oscar.wilde**

Steven Wright

Probably one of the things that makes you so popular is your ability to tell Steven Wright jokes at parties. But what do you do when you run out of material? Here's a large archive of Steven Wright quotations that will last you for years.

Anonymous FTP:
> Address: **cathouse.org**
> Path: **/pub/cathouse/humor/standup/steven.wright**

Why be normal? Read Bizarre

The Internet supports the three most important pillars of popular culture: sex, lies and video tape.

(For more information, take a look at Sexuality, Politics and Television.)

RELIGION: ALTERNATIVE

Ahmadiyya

Learn about Ahmadiyya, a messianic movement based on the principles of the Qur'an and founded in the late nineteenth century by Ghulam Ahmad Qadiyani. Unlike traditional Muslims, adherents of Ahmadiyya believe Qadiyani to be a prophet after Muhammad.

Usenet:
Newsgroup: **alt.sect.ahmadiyya**

Baha'i Faith

Who was Baha'u'llah (a.k.a. Mirza Husayn Ali)? What did he do in Iran in the mid-nineteenth century that was so important? Was he really the Bab (with a direct line to the twelfth Imam)? Learn about the message of the Baha'u'llah and the Baha'i view of life. Read quotes from Baha'i scriptures and discuss such topics as gender equality and spiritual revelations. The newsgroup is moderated.

Usenet:
Newsgroup: **soc.religion.bahai**

Internet mailing list:
List Address: **bahai-faith@oneworld.wa.com**
Subscription Address:
bahai-faith-request@oneworld.wa.com

Baha'i Faith Archives

Introduction to the Baha'i faith, including Baha'i teachings, early history, recent history, and current status and references.

Anonymous FTP:
Address: **ftp.spies.com**
Path: **/Library/Article/Religion/bahai.int**

Gopher:
Name: Internet Wiretap
Address: **wiretap.spies.com**
Choose: **Wiretap Online Library**
| **Articles**
| **Religion and Philosophy**
| **Introduction to Baha'i Faith**

Lonely? Try the Personals

Brother Jed

Follow the comings and goings of Brother Jed (George E. Smock) as his itinerent travels take him from campus to campus throughout America, spreading the word that Christianity is incompatible with homosexuality, long hair, drugs and rock music. (Yes, this is true. Would we make up something like this?)

Usenet:
Newsgroup: **alt.brother-jed**

Eckankar

Join Eckists as they explore visualization, reality and waking dreams. Book lists, exercises and historical origins are a few of the topics covered.

Usenet:
Newsgroup: **alt.religion.eckankar**

Kriya Yoga

An introduction to the original Kriya practice and the keys of the Kriya path.

Anonymous FTP:
Address: **ftp.spies.com**
Path: **/Library/Article/Religion/kriya.yog**

Gopher:
Name: Internet Wiretap
Address: **wiretap.spies.com**
Choose: **Wiretap Online Library**
| **Articles**
| **Religion and Philosophy**
| **Original Kriya Yoga at a Glance**

Magick, Occultism and Satanism

Open discussions about everything related to magick, Satanism and the occult.

Usenet:
Newsgroup: **alt.horror.cthulhu**
Newsgroup: **alt.magick**
Newsgroup: **alt.necromicon**
Newsgroup: **alt.religion.sabaean**
Newsgroup: **alt.satanism**

A B C D E F G H I J K L M N O P Q R S T U V W X Y Z

Tired of mainstream religion?

Try **Magick, Occultism and Satanism.**

New Age

New Age believers encourage awareness, positive thinking and healing with the mind. Information on many other New Age topics available as well.

Usenet:
> Newsgroup: **talk.religion.newage**

Occult

No more will you wonder if the supernatural and existence-beyond-existence is real or just a figment of your reality. Join the discussion about things hidden and esoteric and learn about the history and theory of the occult.

Listserv mailing list:
> List Address: **arcana@unccvm.bitnet**
> Subscription Address: **listserv@unccvm.bitnet**

Paganism

What are pagans about? Read the history, rituals, ethics and methods of worship relating to paganism.

Internet mailing list:
> List Address: **pagan@drycas.club.cc.cmu.edu**
> Subscription Address:
> **pagan-request@drycas.club.cc.cmu.edu**

Usenet:
> Newsgroup: **alt.pagan**

Sabaean Religious Order

The origins, history and philosophy of the Sabaeans and Sheba.

Usenet:
> Newsgroup: **alt.religion.sabaean**

Excerpt from the Net...

```
Newsgroups: alt.magick
Subject: Magick is better than Science

It is necessary to doubt something.  The first clue to this is your own body: it
expressly denies the belief that holding your hand in a flame isn't painful...  You just
can't live life believing everything, and it is necessary to doubt some things...

Now that you politely agree with me that it is necessary to doubt some things, I'm going
to rudely suggest that there is no basis for believing anything.  Even more rudely, I'm
going to state that Science, that default religion of our modern Western tradition, has
no basis for demanding belief in any of the statements it cherishes as laws.

Here's where Science breaks down, and how Magick can pick up the pieces:

    (1) Science denies its own Magickal roots...

    (2) Science denies personal reality, but cannot establish an objective reality...

    (3) Science cannot deal with the fact that existence is absurd...

    (4) Science removes itself from the sphere of human morality and responsibility...

So here I give the challenge:

Show how Science can deal with these deficiencies without recognition of some sense of
Magick to restore meaning to our lives.
```

Satanism

Discover what Satanists feel are the misconceptions about their beliefs. See what Satanism means and discuss how Satanists feel it relates to Christianity. Other topics include music, books and news items.

Usenet:
> Newsgroup: **alt.satanism**

Scientology

Invite yourself into the house that Ron built: Scientology and Dianetics. Learn about becoming a *clear*: eliminate all your engrams, your first step towards becoming an operating thetan. Find out what is new and exciting in this oft-misunderstood marriage of science, religion, applied psychology, and science fiction. (Be sure to take along plenty of money.)

Usenet:
> Newsgroup: **alt.clearing.technology**
> Newsgroup: **alt.religion.scientology**

Shamanism

Delve into the natural spiritual practices of the shaman. Discover the full range of the shamanic experience, which includes such things as drumming, vision quests and visiting sacred sites.

Usenet:
> Newsgroup: **alt.religion.shamanism**
> Newsgroup: **soc.religion.shamanism**

Society of Friends

Commonly referred to as Quakers, Friends illustrate their natural way of living in ways such as environmentalism and the prevention of violence.

Usenet:
> Newsgroup: **soc.religion.quaker**

Unitarianism

Share thoughts and opinions with the people who address their prayers "to whom it may concern". Discuss issues of interest to members of the Unitarian-Universalist church: the most free-thinking, tolerant, diverse and intellectual group of people since the Nixon White House.

Usenet:
> Newsgroup: **bit.listserv.uus-l**

Wicca

Documents detailing the Wiccan tradition branch of the occult, including spells, beliefs, exercises and much more.

Anonymous FTP:
> Address: **nic.funet.fi**
> Path: **/pub/doc/occult/wicca/***

RELIGION: TRADITIONAL

Articles on Religion

Numerous documents and discussions, including an atheist manifesto, religion in American schools, Gideons, Mormonism, Baha'i faith, shamanism, Vedic civilization and Taoism.

Anonymous FTP:
> Address: **ftp.spies.com**
> Path: **/Library/Article/Religion/***

Gopher:
> Name: Internet Wiretap
> Address: **wiretap.spies.com**
> Choose: **Wiretap Online Library**
> | **Articles**
> | **Religion and Philosophy**

Atheism

If you are one of those people that think "god" is just "dog" spelled backwards, this may be the group for you. Discuss how, why and where there is no God, and what this means for ordinary people who must pay their bills and remember their computer passwords. Atheists take their beliefs seriously and so should you.

Usenet:
> Newsgroup: **alt.atheism**
> Newsgroup: **alt.atheism.moderated**

Atheism Archives

Introduction to atheism, including FAQs, logical arguments and a list of atheist resources.

Anonymous FTP:
> Address: **rtfm.mit.edu**
> Path: **/pub/usenet/alt.atheism/***

Usenet:
> Newsgroup: **alt.atheism**

A
B
C
D
E
F
G
H
I
J
K
L
M
N
O
P
Q
R
S
T
U
V
W
X
Y
Z

Atheist Manifesto

Arguments in support of atheism.

Anonymous FTP:
Address: **ftp.spies.com**
Path: **/Library/Article/Religion/atheist.mf**

Gopher:
Name: Internet Wiretap
Address: **wiretap.spies.com**
Choose: **Wiretap Online Library**
  | **Articles**
  | **Religion and Philosophy**
  | **Atheist Manifesto**

Baptist Discussion List

A list for the discussion of any and all topics relating to the Baptist experience. It includes all nationalities and denominations of Baptists, and is a forum for sharing information, ideas and opinions.

Listserv mailing list:
List Address: **baptist@ukcc.bitnet**
Subscription Address: **listserv@ukcc.bitnet**

Bible Browser for Unix

A program for browsing the Bible.

Anonymous FTP:
Address: **cs.arizona.edu**
Path: **/icon/contrib/bibl_tar.Z**

Bible Online

The complete Bible, online with a Gopher interface. There actually are many places where you can read the Bible online. Use Veronica to find other sites.

Gopher:
Name: University of Minnesota
Address: **joeboy.micro.umn.edu**
Choose: **Ebooks**
  | **By Title**
  | **King James Bible**

The Internet will set you free

Excerpt from the Net...

```
Newsgroup: alt.atheism
Subject: Question for fellow atheists

> Although I am an atheist, I have always been fascinated by the
> beliefs of religions around the world.  Is this unusual for an
> atheist?
>
> I do not believe in God, but I see in the world's religions some
> vital information and insight into the nature of man.  When I explore
> various religions -- taking them as metaphors -- I learn a great deal
> about myself and my fellow human beings.  I have assumed that most
> atheists are more interested and educated in the world's religions,
> even after their acceptance of atheism, than most followers of
> individual faiths.  Is this true?

I don't know.  It's hard to speak authoritatively for "most atheists".
Certainly among those who participate in discussions of religion and atheism on the Net,
this seems to be the case.

In my own case, early exposure to other religions was instrumental in the development of
my atheism.  I was always interested by religious mythology, both as story and as it
related to the development of our culture.

Interestingly, I tended to give a fairly wide berth to Christianity and the major modern
religions until around the time I started participating in alt.atheism.  Since then, it's
been a fairly major topic with me.

--
"A little rudeness and disrespect can elevate a meaningless interaction to a battle of
 wills and add drama to an otherwise dull day." -- Calvin
```

THE BIBLE

By far, the most popular book in the history of mankind is the Bible (even more popular than *The Internet Complete Reference*). If you are a Bible scholar, or even a casual reader, you will be glad to know that the entire bible is available on the Net for downloading and perusing.

Bible Program

The complete online Bible program, with instructions for installation on an IBM-PC or Mac.

Anonymous FTP:
Address: **wuarchive.wustl.edu**
Path: **/doc/bible/***

Bible Promises Macintosh Hypercard Stack

A Hypercard program for the Macintosh.

Anonymous FTP:
Address: **f.ms.uky.edu**
Path: **/pub/mac/hypercard/
bible-promise-stack.cpt.bin**

Bible Quiz Game

Over a thousand questions about the Bible.

Anonymous FTP:
Address: **oak.oakland.edu**
Path: **/pub/msdos/bible/bibleq.zip**

Bible Quotes

Quotations from the Bible, courtesy of *Christian Computing* magazine.

Gopher:
Name: University of Alabama
Address: **twinbrook.cis.uab.edu**
Choose: **The Continuum
| The Gabriel's Horn**

Bible Retrieval System for Unix

A Bible query system for Unix systems.

Anonymous FTP:
Address: **ftp.uu.net**
Path: **/doc/literary/obi/Religion/
Bible.Retrieval.System/***

Bible Search Program

Bible search utilities.

Anonymous FTP:
Address: **oak.oakland.edu**
Path: **/pub/msdos/bible/bible14.zip**

Bible Search Tools

Assorted Bible search utilities.

Anonymous FTP:
Address: **oak.oakland.edu**
Path: **/pub/msdos/bible/kjv-tool.zip**

Bible Study Discussion

A discussion group for those interested in active study and interpretation of the Bible.

Usenet:
Newsgroup: **soc.religion.christian.bible-study**

Bible Text

The complete text of the Bible.

Anonymous FTP:
Address: **oak.oakland.edu**
Path: **/pub/msdos/bible/journey.zip**

Address: **ocf.berkeley.edu**
Path: **/pub/Library/Religion**

Wais:
Database: **Bible**

Why be normal?
Read Bizarre

A B C D E F G H I J K L M N O P Q R S T U V W X Y Z

Bible Translations

The Bible online in German, English, Swahili and Swedish.

Anonymous FTP:
    Address: **ftp.spies.com**
    Path: **/Library/Religion/Bible/***

Gopher:
    Name: Internet Wiretap
    Address: **wiretap.spies.com**
    Choose: **Wiretap Online Library**
     | **Religion**
     | **Bible**

Bible Verses

A memory resident pop-up program for DOS computers.

Anonymous FTP:
    Address: **oak.oakland.edu**
    Path: **/pub/msdos/bible/biblepop.zip**

Bible Word and Phrase Counts of the King James Version

Word counts, phrase counts and other statistics for the King James Bible.

Anonymous FTP:
    Address: **oak.oakland.edu**
    Path: **/pub/msdos/bible/kjvcount.txt**

Bible Stats

Ahoy Bible scholars: if you are interested in analyzing the Bible from a statistical point of view, raw material is easy to come by on the Net. In just a few minutes, you can download all the word and phrase counts for the King James Bible. Great for programmers who want to devise their own computer analysis.

Give it a try and, who knows, maybe you'll be able to prove that the Bible was really written by Sir Francis Bacon.

Biblical Search and Extraction Tool

Bible search utilities.

Anonymous FTP:
    Address: **oak.oakland.edu**
    Path: **/pub/msdos/bible/refrkjv1.txt**

Biblical Timeline

A Jewish biblical timeline, based on the ages shown in the Torah.

Anonymous FTP:
    Address: **ftp.spies.com**
    Path: **/Library/Article/Religion/biblical.tl**

Gopher:
    Name: Internet Wiretap
    Address: **wiretap.spies.com**
    Choose: **Wiretap Online Library**
     | **Articles**
     | **Religion and Philosophy**
     | **Biblical Timeline**

Who did what, when, and to whom?
Take a look at the *Biblical Timeline* and bring some order to the chaos.

Book of Mormon

The complete text of the Book of Mormon.

Anonymous FTP:
    Address: **ftp.uu.net**
    Path: **/systems/symtel20/msdos/mormon/bom.zip**

    Address: **ocf.berkeley.edu**
    Path: **/pub/Library/Religion/Book_of_Mormon**

Wais:
    Database: **Book_of_Mormon**

Buddhism

Lots of documents about different types of Buddhism and Taoism, including e-mail addresses of individuals and organizations interested in Buddhism and Zen around the world.

Anonymous FTP:
    Address: **coombs.anu.edu.au**
    Path: **/coombspapers/otherarchives/**
      electronic-buddhist-archives/*

Buddhism Discussion Group

A mailing list to exchange information and views about Buddhism.

Listserv mailing list:
List Address: **buddha-l@ulkyvm.bitnet**
Subscription Address: **listserv@ulkyvm.bitnet**

Catholic Evangelism

A mailing list about Catholic evangelism, church revitalization, and the preservation of Catholic teachings, traditions and values.

Internet mailing list:
List Address: **catholic-action@vpnet.chi.il.us**
Subscription Address:
catholic-action-request@vpnet.chi.il.us

Catholicism

Information and articles on the Catholic Church, including its rituals, Vatican II material and statements of the popes.

Anonymous FTP:
Address: **ftp.spies.com**
Path: **/Library/Religion/Catholic/***

Gopher:
Name: Internet Wiretap
Address: **wiretap.spies.com**
Choose: **Wiretap Online Library**
| Religion
| Catholic

Christia

Free-spirited discussions about practical Christian life among strongly motivated Christians who agree to disagree. Immerse yourself in the everyday culture of people who practice their religion with the volume turned up.

Usenet:
Newsgroup: **bit.listserv.christia**

Christianity

Discover important topics on Christianity. Fundamentalism, Evangelism, inter-faith marriages, the Trinity, biblical history, tithing, holidays and the effects of the New Age movement are just a taste of what you will find.

Usenet:
Newsgroup: **soc.religion.christian**

Coptic

Material on the Coptic Lectionary.

Anonymous FTP:
Address: **ftp.spies.com**
Path: **/Library/Religion/Coptic/***

Address: **pharos.bu.edu**
Path: **/CN/***

Gopher:
Name: Internet Wiretap
Address: **wiretap.spies.com**
Choose: **Wiretap Online Library**
| Religion
| Coptic

Croatian Christian Information Service

An organization established to collect and distribute information about Christian church life. News distributions from various religious communities with regard to social, cultural and scientific issues that are of interest to Christians in Croatia and elsewhere.

Gopher:
Name: Croatia
Address: **rujan.srce.hr**
Choose: **English Language**
| Information - Various Institutions..
| Christian Information Service

Eastern Religions

If you are interested in Eastern enlightenment, read about Buddhism, Hinduism and other Eastern religions. Often, points are related through the tradition of parable, illustrating the beauty of the spiritual path. This group is moderated. (What is the sound of one hand holding open an Internet book?)

Usenet:
Newsgroup: **soc.religion.eastern**

The Electric Mystic's Guide to the Internet

A complete bibliography of electronic documents, online conferences, serials, software and archives relevant to religious studies.

Anonymous FTP:
Address: **panda1.uottawa.ca**
Path: **/pub/religion/electric-mystics-guide**

A B C D E F G H I J K L M N O P Q R S T U V W X Y Z

Gabriel's Horn

Returns a Bible verse from the Old or New Testament.

Telnet:
>   Address: **138.26.65.78 7777**

Need some quick inspiration? Try Gabriel's Horn

Genesis

A study aid and reference for the King James Bible.

Anonymous FTP:
>   Address: **oak.oakland.edu**
>   Path: **/pub/msdos/bible/genaidc.zip**

GRASS Mailing List

The Generic Religions and Secret Societies (GRASS) mailing list is a forum for the development of religions and secret societies for use in role-playing games.

Mail:
>   Address: **grass-server@wharton.upenn.edu**
>   Body: **subscribe** *your name*

Hebrew Quiz

A biblical Hebrew language tutor.

Anonymous FTP:
>   Address: **oak.oakland.edu**
>   Path: **/pub/msdos/hebrew/hebquiz.zip**

Hinduism

A moderated discussion group devoted to practice and scriptures of Hinduism.

Usenet:
>   Newsgroup: **bit.listserv.hindu-d**

History of American Catholicism

A mailing list for those interested in the history of American Catholicism.

Listserv mailing list:
>   List Address: **amercath@ukcc.bitnet**
>   Subscription Address: **listserv@ukcc.bitnet**

Islam

Discuss a variety of issues that are important in the Islamic faith. While topics cover the Qur'an (Koran), judgement day, Jesus, prophets and religious traditions, there is also spirited discussion regarding current events in the Middle East. This group is moderated.

Usenet:
>   Newsgroup: **soc.religion.islam**

Issues in Religion

Sit in on discussions that are religious, ethical and moral in nature. Talk includes reference to scriptures and parables, but much of it concerns heavily debatable topics—for example, does the Pope use the Internet?—all of which makes for lively banter.

Usenet:
>   Newsgroup: **talk.religion.misc**

Jainism

A course on the fundamentals of Jainism, human virtues and articles on Jainism, with other related material.

Anonymous FTP:
>   Address: **ftp.spies.com**
>   Path: **/Library/Religion/Jainism/***

Gopher:
>   Name: Internet Wiretap
>   Address: **wiretap.spies.com**
>   Choose: **Wiretap Online Library**
>   **| Religion**
>   **| Jainism**

Jewish Culture and Religion

Enjoy a mix of culture and religion. This lively group covers a wide range of topics including the Torah, keeping kosher, traditions, history, and Middle Eastern current events. Learn how to offer too much food to people who visit you.

Usenet:
>   Newsgroup: **soc.culture.jewish**

Jewish Mailing List

A list focusing on issues and questions of concern to observant Jews.

Listserv mailing list:
    List Address: **baltuva@mcgill1.bitnet**
    Subscription Address: **listserv@mcgill1.bitnet**

King James Bible

The full text of the King James Bible, provided by Project Gutenberg.

Anonymous FTP:
    Address: **ftp.uu.net**
    Path: **/doc/literary/obi/Religion/KingJamesBible**

Gopher:
    Name: University of Minnesota
    Address: **gopher.micro.umn.edu**
    Choose: **Libraries**
      | Electronic Books
      | By Title
      | King James Bible

Koran (or Quran)

The complete text of the Koran.

Anonymous FTP:
    Address: **etext.archive.umich.edu**
    Path: **/pub/Religious.Texts/Quran/***

    Address: **ocf.berkeley.edu**
    Path: **/pub/Library/Religion/Koran**

    Address: **oes.orst.edu**
    Path: **/pub/data/etext/koran/koran**

Wais:
    Database: **Quran**

Make sure you are prepared: Read Emergency and Disaster

The Quran

Strictly speaking, the Quran (Islamic Holy text) should be read in the original Arabic and is not considered to be correct when translated into another language. Still, if your Arabic skills are a bit rusty, you might get more out of reading the Quran in English. Download it and give it a try. Hint: If you want to search for a particular verse, use Wais. (Allaah yusallimukum.)

Moorish Orthodox Church

A history and catechism of the Moorish Orthodox Church of America.

Anonymous FTP:
    Address: **ftp.spies.com**
    Path: **/Library/Article/Religion/moorish.usa**

Gopher:
    Name: Internet Wiretap
    Address: **wiretap.spies.com**
    Choose: **Wiretap Online Library**
      | Articles
      | Religion and Philosophy
      | Moorish Orthodox Church in the USA

Mormon

Material on the Mormon doctrine and covenant, the Book of Mormon, and the Mormon scriptures.

Anonymous FTP:
    Address: **ftp.spies.com**
    Path: **/Library/Religion/Mormon/***

Gopher:
    Name: Internet Wiretap
    Address: **wiretap.spies.com**
    Choose: **Wiretap Online Library**
      | Religion
      | Mormon

A
B
C
D
E
F
G
H
I
J
K
L
M
N
O
P
Q
R
S
T
U
V
W
X
Y
Z

Period Calendar

A guide to taking modern month-and-day dates and converting them to old church-style dating by feasts and seasons.

Anonymous FTP:
Address: **ftp.spies.com**
Path: **/Library/Document/calendar.sca**

Gopher:
Name: Internet Wiretap
Address: **wiretap.spies.com**
Choose: **Wiretap Online Library**
  | **Assorted Documents**
  | **Creative Anachronism Period Calendar**

Practical Christian Life

A mailing list for discussions on practical Christian life.

Listserv mailing list:
List Address: **christia@finhutc.bitnet**
Subscription Address: **listserv@finhutc.bitnet**

Religious Denominations

Material on many Christian denominations, including Anglican, Catholic, Coptic, Mormon, Presbyterian and others.

Anonymous FTP:
Address: **ftp.spies.com**
Path: **/Library/Religion/***

Gopher:
Name: Internet Wiretap
Address: **wiretap.spies.com**
Choose: **Wiretap Online Library | Religion**

Religious News

Read what's going on with religion and religious leaders of the world. This is where you will find the facts on current religious events.

Usenet:
Newsgroup: **clari.news.religion**

Religious Studies Publications

An electronic journal that disseminates table of contents, abstracts, reviews and ordering information on new and recently printed and electronic publications relevant to religious studies.

Listserv mailing list:
List Address: **contents@uottawa.bitnet**
Subscription Address: **listserv@uottawa.bitnet**

Vedic Civilization

Examples of Vedic ideas concerning time and human longevity, as detailed by the Vedic literature of India.

Anonymous FTP:
Address: **ftp.spies.com**
Path: **/Library/Article/Religion/marriage.ved**

Address: **ftp.spies.com**
Path: **/Library/Article/Religion/vedic.txt**

Address: **ftp.spies.com**
Path: **/Library/Article/Religion/vedic.wst**

Gopher:
Name: Internet Wiretap
Address: **wiretap.spies.com**
Choose: **Wiretap Online Library**
  | **Articles**
  | **Religion and Philosophy**
  | **Vedic Civilization**

ROMANCE

Couples

It's the best of times, it's the worst of times. Relationships have their ups and downs, but, like a roller coaster, it's fun and thrilling, makes you afraid and makes you laugh. See what is going on in the lives of other couples. Get ideas for romantic outings, anniversaries, how to patch up a fuss, or what to do with in-laws.

Usenet:
Newsgroup: **soc.couples**

Men and Women

We all got along fine when we were algae. But somewhere between floating gently on a lake and the invention of the bikini, men and women started to have their differences. Get up close and personal. See what the factions are saying about each other. It's not too much of a secret since there is a lot of cross-posting.

Usenet:
Newsgroup: **soc.men**
Newsgroup: **soc.women**

This is the first book of the rest of your life.

Penpals

It's so much fun to make new friends. Get a penpal (or two or three) and find out what is going on outside your world. Stick close to home or experience the other side of the world through someone else's eyes. Take a little time and reach out to someone.

Usenet:
> Newsgroup: **soc.penpals**

Polyamory

Whether it's a big heart or a big ego, if you have the desire to love more than one person at a time you can be in for quite a wild, emotional ride. Don't get caught with your pants down. Learn the pros and cons of polyamory from some of the pros.

Usenet:
> Newsgroup: **alt.polyamory**

Romance

Have you noticed life isn't quite like the covers of paperback romance novels (or the inside of the romance novels, for that matter)? Do something about that by generating a romantic fire with others who mourn the death of romance. Remember Cyrano de Bergerac and his words that could melt the hair off a moose? Where do you think he got his start?

Usenet:
> Newsgroup: **alt.romance**
> Newsgroup: **alt.romance.chat**

Romance Readers Anonymous

You've been sucked in. It's impossible to walk past a rack of romance novels without picking up at least one. The bronzed man holding the lithe woman with the heaving bosom makes your heart beat quickly, loud enough for everyone else in the store to hear. The television has cobwebs and you haven't been out of the house in months since you got a subscription to Romance of the Week. Get help now. You are not alone.

Usenet:
> Newsgroup: **bit.listserv.rra-l**

Singles

Your mother probably said that anyone you can pick up in a bar is not someone with whom you want to develop a serious relationship. (What you didn't want to tell her was that you weren't looking for a serious relationship.) In the event that you change your mind, stop in at the nicest singles hangout in Usenet and find that special someone.

Usenet:
> Newsgroup: **soc.singles**

Weddings

Don't let your wedding be a remake of *Father of the Bride* (or the Bay of Pigs). Learn what is proper and what is not. Find out shortcuts from folks who have done this before (or again and again). Topics cover a wide range, such as invitations, RSVPs, dresses, parties, garters, underclothes and much more.

Usenet:
> Newsgroup: **alt.wedding**

Getting Married?

Getting married can be a lot of work, so why not let your friends on the Net make it easier? Drop in to **alt.wedding** and read about all those little hints and tips that can make your special day even more special. If you have already taken the plunge, maybe you'd like to share your experiences with the neophytes.

(In any event, we suggest that if you are going to get married, do it in the evening. That way, if it doesn't work out, at least you haven't blown a whole day.)

Why be normal?
Read Bizarre

Make sure you are prepared:
Read Emergency and Disaster

A B C D E F G H I J K L M N O P Q **R** S T U V W X Y Z

SCIENCE

Annealing

Discussion of simulated annealing techniques and analysis, as well as other related issues, including stochastic optimization, Boltzmann machines, metricity and more.

Internet mailing list:
List Address: **anneal@sti.com**
Subscription Address: **anneal-request@sti.com**

Anthropology Mailing List

Discussions of various techniques and fields of research in anthropology, including computation in anthropology, graphics in archaeology, programs anthropologists use, and so on.

Listserv mailing list:
List Address: **anthro-l@ubvm.bitnet**
Subscription Address: **listserv@ubvm.bitnet**

Aquaculture Discussion List

A mailing list on farming aquatic species, including what is involved, technology, problems and solutions, and who is doing it now, and where.

Listserv mailing list:
List Address: **aqua-l@uoguelph.bitnet**
Subscription Address: **listserv@uoguelph.bitnet**

Global Positioning System

Information on the Australian global positioning navigation system, including the locations of base stations and other topics of interest.

Gopher:
Name: Australian Environmental Resources
Information Network
Address: **kaos.erin.gov.au**
Choose: **ERIN Information**
  l Global Positioning System

History of Science and Technology (HOST)

A biannual journal that features articles, research notes, communications, book reviews, and electronic resource information.

Anonymous FTP:
Address: **epas.utoronto.ca**
Path: **/pub/ihpst/***

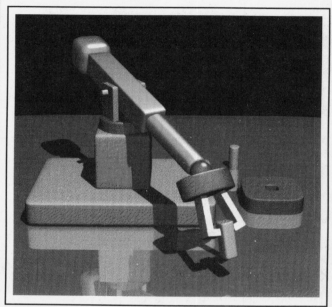

Simulating the operation of machines that aren't even built is a major application of computers in the world of engineering and science. Combine this technology with graphics and you get pictures of things that have never existed! This image was retrieved from Northern Arizona University. The file is **/graphics/gif/ray/robotarm.gif**.

International System of Units

A list of SI units, conversion of non-SI units to SI units, fundamental constants and elemental unit definitions.

Anonymous FTP:
Address: **ftp.spies.com**
Path: **/Library/Document/si.tbl**

Gopher:
Name: Internet Wiretap
Address: **wiretap.spies.com**
Choose: **Wiretap Online Library**
  l Assorted Documents
  l International System of Units

Mini-Journal of Irreproducible Results

Humorous news about overly stimulating research and ideas.

Listserv mailing list:
List Address: **mini-jir@mitvma.mit.edu**
Subscription Address: **listserv@mitvma.mit.edu**

National Science Foundation Publications

Access the publications of the National Science Foundation, including award information, letters, program guidelines and reports for each directorate.

Gopher:
    Name: National Science Foundation
    Address: **stis.nsf.gov**

Periodic Table of the Elements

Download this graphical DOS program to display your very own version of the periodic table. For detailed information about any element, simply move to it and press ENTER.

Anonymous FTP:
    Address: **freebsd.cdrom.com**
    Path: **/.1/games/msdos/educate/periodic.zip**

    Address: **ftp.edvz.univie.ac.at**
    Path: **/pc/dos/chemistry/periodic.zip**

Archie:
    Pattern: **periodic.zip**

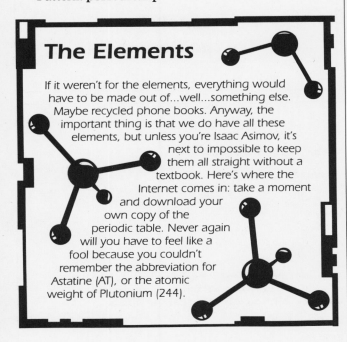

The Elements

If it weren't for the elements, everything would have to be made out of...well...something else. Maybe recycled phone books. Anyway, the important thing is that we do have all these elements, but unless you're Isaac Asimov, it's next to impossible to keep them all straight without a textbook. Here's where the Internet comes in: take a moment and download your own copy of the periodic table. Never again will you have to feel like a fool because you couldn't remember the abbreviation for Astatine (AT), or the atomic weight of Plutonium (244).

Periodic Table of the Elements (Online)

An online periodic table of the elements. A handy tool to have, since the periodic table changes so frequently.

Telnet:
    Address: **camms2.caos.kun.nl 2034**

Science Fraud

A mailing list dedicated to the discussion of fraud in science, including current and recent events, and historic accounts of fraudulent science. Also available is a database on fraud in science with over 4000 references.

Listserv mailing list:
    List Address: **scifraud@albnyvm1.bitnet**
    Subscription Address: **listserv@albnyvm1.bitnet**

Science Magazines

Sample articles and subscription information for science-related magazines.

Gopher:
    Name: The Electronic Newsstand
    Address: **gopher.internet.com 2100**
    Choose: **Titles Arranged by Category**
    | Science - Ecology, General

Science Resource Guides

Internet resource guides for agriculture, biological sciences, computing, earth sciences, health sciences, mathematics and physical sciences.

Anonymous FTP:
    Address: **una.hh.lib.umich.edu**
    Path: **/inetdirs/sciences/***

Gopher:
    Name: University of Michigan
    Address: **una.hh.lib.umich.edu**
    Choose: **inetdirs**
    | Guides on the Sciences (UMich)

Science and Technology Information System

STIS offers discussion, help and a number of interesting topics for people interested in science and technology.

Telnet:
    Address: **stis.nsf.gov**
    Login: **public**

Scientific Articles

Contains some interesting online science articles and book reviews, such as a scientific article about forecasting eclipses.

Gopher:
    Name: Whole Earth Lectronic Link
    Address: **gopher.well.sf.ca.us**
    Choose: **Science**

A B C D E F G H I J K L M N O P Q R S T U V W X Y Z

Scientific Ponderings

A collection of science articles covering topics such as perpetual motion, cold nuclear fusion in condensed matter, and quantum information processing in animals.

Anonymous FTP:
> Address: **ftp.spies.com**
> Path: **/Library/Article/Sci/***

Gopher:
> Name: Internet Wiretap
> Address: **wiretap.spies.com**
> Choose: **Wiretap Online Library**
> | **Articles**
> | **Science**

Look around. Is anyone watching? Good. Take a look at the X-Rated section. (But remember, you didn't read it here.)

The Scientist

Online version of current issues of *The Scientist*, a biweekly tabloid newspaper for science professionals.

Anonymous FTP:
> Address: **ds.internic.net**
> Path: **/pub/the-scientist/***

Gopher:
> Name: The Jackson Laboratory
> Address: **hobbes.jax.org**
> Choose: **The Scientist - Newsletter**

> Name: University of Florida
> Address: **gaia.sci-ed.fit.edu**
> Choose: **Subject Area Resources**
> | **Educational TV**
> | **The Scientist — Newsletter**

Wais:
> Database: **the-scientist**

**Lonely?
Try the Personals**

Excerpt from the Net...

(from the collection of scientific ponderings on the "Wiretap" gopher)

```
        OBSERVATION OF COLD NUCLEAR FUSION IN CONDENSED MATTER
                        by S. E. Jones et al

                    Department of Physics and Chemistry
                    Brigham Young University -- Utah, USA


                          March 23, 1989
```

Fusion of isotopic hydrogen nuclei is the principal means of producing energy in the high-temperature interior of stars. In relatively cold terrestrial conditions, the nuclei are clothed with electrons and approach one another no closer than allowed by the molecular Coulomb barrier...

We have discovered a means of inducing nuclear fusion without the use of either high temperatures or radioactive muons. We will present direct experimental results as well as indirect geological evidence for the occurrence of cold nuclear fusion.

DETECTION OF COLD FUSION NEUTRONS

We have observed deuteron-deuteron fusion at room temperature during low-voltage electrolytic infusion of deuterons into metallic titanium or palladium electrodes...

Scientist's Workbench

An X Window based application designed to bring together a set of tools for enhancing the development, testing and execution of scientific codes.

Anonymous FTP:
    Address: **info.tc.cornell.edu**
    Path: **/pub/swb/***

Gopher:
    Name: Cornell University
    Address: **gopher.tc.cornell.edu**
    Choose: **Anonymous FTP**
      | Scientist's Workbench

A Theory on the Origin of the Universe

A document by Stephen Hawking discussing his theory on the origin of the universe.

Gopher:
    Name: University of Illinois
    Address: **wx.atmos.uiuc.edu**
    Choose: **Documents**
      | FUN
      | hawking.origin

Do you like the universe? (It's always been one of *our* favorite places.)

If so, read what Steven Hawking has to say about it.

A Theory Regarding Black Holes

A document by Stephen Hawking discussing his theory about black holes.

Gopher:
    Name: University of Illinois
    Address: **wx.atmos.uiuc.edu**
    Choose: **Documents**
      | FUN
      | hawking.black.holes

SCIENCE FICTION

Announcements

Attention science fiction buffs! Find out what's up and coming in sci-fi land. This moderated group will provide you with all the information you need on new movies, books, television shows—anything that is new in science fiction.

Usenet:
    Newsgroup: **rec.arts.sf.announce**

Science fiction fanatics: keep up on what's happening by reading **rec.arts.sf.announce.**

Fandom

Fans from all over the world live, eat and breathe science fiction. They travel in packs, eager to suck the nectar out of the sci-fi flower. If you have a taste for something out of the ordinary, join the crowd, go to cons, and be a groupie.

Usenet:
    Newsgroup: **alt.fandom.cons**
    Newsgroup: **rec.arts.sf.fandom**

Fans of Writers

Lose yourself in the fantasy worlds that come pouring out of the minds of great science fiction writers. Anne McCaffrey, Piers Anthony and Terry Pratchett are creators who have a strong following of worshippers. No tithing is necessary, only a true devotion and a love of the unusual.

Usenet:
    Newsgroup: **alt.fan.pern**
    Newsgroup: **alt.fan.piers-anthony**
    Newsgroup: **alt.fan.pratchett**

Fantasy, Science Fiction, and Horror Calendar

A calendar of upcoming events in the U.S. in the worlds of science fiction, fantasy and horror. Updated regularly.

Gopher:
    Name: Panix Public Access Unix
    Address: **gopher.panix.com**
    Choose: **Fantasy, SF, and Horror Calendar**

A B C D E F G H I J K L M N O P Q R S T U V W X Y Z

Fanzines

Get out of the mainstream and discover the zest and originality of science fiction fanzines: small, personal, opinionated publications that cover a specific topic. Quench your thirst for the intriguing.

Usenet:
Newsgroup: **rec.mag.fsf**

Infinity City

A series of science fiction books about Infinity City, an incredible world within a black hole. These books were written by Douglas K. Bell, who will mail you an electronic copy free of charge. The first three books in the series are *Van Gogh in Space*, *Jason the Rescuer*, *Search for Katz*, but there is a lot more. For information, send mail to Doug at the address below.

Mail:
Address: **dougbell@netcom.com**

Movies

You just saw the best movie ever, and you have to tell someone or you'll explode. You can either run screaming through the parking lot of the movie theater and risk being arrested for disturbing the peace, or you can tell the rest of the sci-fi movie fans on the Internet.

Usenet:
Newsgroup: **rec.arts.sf.movies**

Mystery Science Theatre 3000

There are worse things in life than being consigned to review bad sci-fi for your entire life. Experience the hilarity of *Mystery Science Theatre 3000* with other fans.

Usenet:
Newsgroup: **alt.tv.mst3k**

Red Dwarf

Delight in this British science fiction comedy. A man, a hologram and something evolved from a cat make their bewildered way through the universe.

Usenet:
Newsgroup: **alt.tv.red-dwarf**

Reviews

Don your beret, light up your pipe, and launch into a review of the best and worst of science fiction. Don't hesitate to tell how you feel, because no one else will. Sometimes sublime, but more often not, reviews are always revealing and informative.

Usenet:
Newsgroup: **rec.arts.sf.reviews**

Sci-Fi Books

Popularity rating for science fiction books, followed by a large bibliography arranged by author.

Anonymous FTP:
Address: **ftp.spies.com**
Path: **/Library/Media/Sci-Fi/books.sf**

Gopher:
Name: Internet Wiretap
Address: **wiretap.spies.com**
Choose: **Wiretap Online Library**
I **Mass Media**
I **Science Fiction and Fantasy**
I **Science Fiction Books (poll & biblio)**

Sci-Fi Lovers

Discussions of any science fiction or fantasy-related subjects, ranging from stories, reviews and conventions, to movies and television.

Anonymous FTP:
Address: **gandalf.rutgers.edu**
Path: **/pub/sfl/***

Internet mailing list:
List Address: **sf-lovers@rutgers.edu**
Subscription Address:
sf-lovers-request@rutgers.edu

Science and Science Fiction

Stretch your mind by pushing your imagination to the limit. How real is the science in science fiction? A wide variety of topics are covered, such as the possibility of forcefields, transcendental engineering, and Hawking radiation. Invent your own theories or pick apart someone else's.

Usenet:
Newsgroup: **rec.arts.sf.science**

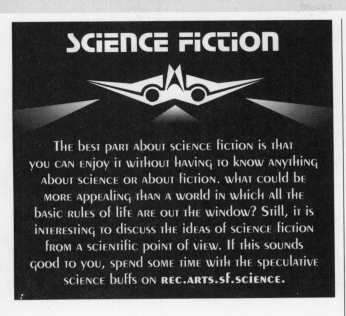

The best part about science fiction is that you can enjoy it without having to know anything about science or about fiction. What could be more appealing than a world in which all the basic rules of life are out the window? Still, it is interesting to discuss the ideas of science fiction from a scientific point of view. If this sounds good to you, spend some time with the speculative science buffs on **rec.arts.sf.science**.

Science Fiction and Fantasy

Articles, guides, FAQs, reading lists and other documents regarding science fiction, fantasy and cyberpunk.

Anonymous FTP:
>   Address: **ftp.spies.com**
>   Path: **/Library/Media/Sci-Fi/***

Gopher:
>   Name: EUnet in Slovakia
>   Address: **gopher.eunet.sk**
>   Choose: **Archive of EUnet Slovakia
> | Science Fiction Archive**
>
>   Name: Internet Wiretap
>   Address: **wiretap.spies.com**
>   Choose: **Wiretap Online Library
> | Mass Media
> | Science Fiction and Fantasy**

Science Fiction Forum

Science fiction isn't a hobby: it's a lifestyle. Are you one of those people whose walls and cabinets (and floors) are covered with sci-fi books, magazines, tapes and memorabilia? Scoot all of it out of the way so you can get to the computer and find your sci-fi soul companions. Anything science fiction goes.

Usenet:
>   Newsgroup: **rec.arts.sf.misc**

Science Fiction Marketplace

Are you looking to trade your extra copy of the "Pegasus" episode of *Battlestar Galactica* for a signed copy of a *Friday* print by Whelan? Shop at the science fiction flea market—rare commodities for rare people. Buy, sell or trade. Display your merchandise in this shoplifter-free environment.

Usenet:
>   Newsgroup: **rec.arts.sf.market**

Star Wars

What would happen if... ? Speculation abounds regarding the *Star Wars* universe. *Star Wars* fans reinvent the movie daily, wondering what would happen if certain characters had done things differently. Discover inconsistencies you may have missed in the movies and learn what has happened to everyone involved from the big screen to the cutting room floor.

Usenet:
>   Newsgroup: **rec.arts.sf.starwars**

Television

It's natural to feel like you can never get enough science fiction. Your mouth goes dry, your hands press continually on the remote control even thought you know it will not make science fiction magically appear before you. You need a source or you are going to lose your mind. When you can't find it on the tube, seek your sci-fi television support group and get a quick fix.

Usenet:
>   Newsgroup: **rec.arts.sf.tv**

Writing

Allow yourself to linger on the words, your eyes playing gently back and forth across the pages of your latest sci-fi novel. There is something tangible about a book that you just can't get from television or movies. Discuss your favorite book, hear about someone else's. Find out what's new and what is hopelessly out of print.

Usenet:
>   Newsgroup: **rec.arts.sf.written**

A B C D E F G H I J K L M N O P Q R S T U V W X Y Z

SECRET STUFF

Easter Eggs

Instructions on how to view secret screens (easter eggs) in many PC and Macintosh software products.

Anonymous FTP:
　　Address: **ftp.spies.com**
　　Path: **/Library/Techdoc/Micro/secret.scr**

Gopher:
　　Name: Internet Wiretap
　　Address: **wiretap.spies.com**
　　Choose: **Wiretap Online Library**
　　　│ **Technical Information**
　　　│ **PCs and Macintoshes**
　　　│ **Secret Screen Cheat Sheet**

Macintosh Secret Tricks List

Details of amusing and interesting hidden screens in Macintosh programs.

Anonymous FTP:
　　Address: **ftp.spies.com**
　　Path: **/Library/Techdoc/Micro/macintos.sec**

Gopher:
　　Name: Internet Wiretap
　　Address: **wiretap.spies.com**
　　Choose: **Wiretap Online Library**
　　　│ **Technical Information**
　　　│ **PCs and Macintoshes**
　　　│ **Macintosh Secret Tricks List**

Are you a Mac person? Take a look at the **Macintosh Secret Tricks List** *and amaze your friends.*

Questionables

Information and material of a questionable nature, including articles on ATM secret codes, garage door opener plans, pyrotechnics, police scanner codes, and pay-TV decoder plans.

Anonymous FTP:
　　Address: **ftp.spies.com**
　　Path: **/Library/Untech/***

Gopher:
　　Name: Internet Wiretap
　　Address: **wiretap.spies.com**
　　Choose: **Wiretap Online Library**
　　　│ **Questionables**

SEX

Amputee Fetish

It's not what you've got that's so sexy, it's what you don't have that counts. Join the discussion and find out what's so attractive about the person who doesn't have everything.

Usenet:
　　Newsgroup: **alt.sex.fetish.amputee**

Bestiality

Dog is not just man's best friend. Find out the how, what, when, where, and for-heaven's-sake-why of bestiality. Learn why platform shoes have never quite gone out of style. For those with a more exotic animal fetish, check out the **barney** group and discover what really makes that dinosaur so lovable.

Usenet:
　　Newsgroup: **alt.sex.bestiality**
　　Newsgroup: **alt.sex.bestiality.barney**

Bondage

All tied up with no place to go? You're in the right place. If having the most toys means having the most fun, then this is the zenith of extracurricular sexual activity. Read stories, share experiences and discuss techniques and safety tips. If you love something, set it free; if it comes back to you, tie it up again.

Usenet:
　　Newsgroup: **alt.sex.bondage**

Diaper Fetish

Some people don't have a preference between cloth or plastic. Some like the velcro tabs, some like safety pins, some like really sticky duct tape. But no matter what your preference, always remember the diaper fetish motto: Doodoo it to them before they can doodoo it to you.

Usenet:
　　Newsgroup: **alt.sex.fetish.diapers**

A B C D E F G H I J K L M N O P Q R S T U V W X Y Z

Discussion of Sex Stories

Stories of sexual encounters are discussed in the Usenet newsgroup **alt.sex.stories**.

Usenet:
Newsgroup: **alt.sex.stories.d**

Exhibitionism

If you've got it, flaunt it. Or even if you don't have it, flaunt it. Exhibitionism is not for the faint of heart. Be gutsy, be bold. Hear stories of the exploits of the daring. Bring your own raincoat.

Usenet:
Newsgroup: **alt.sex.exhibitionism**

Fat Fetish

Do you find the 90s' body image preposterous? Don't continue to mourn the lost days when Rubenesque women were the norm. Revel in the rich, full quality of people who are fat and proud of it.

Usenet:
Newsgroup: **alt.sex.fetish.fa**

Foot Fetish

You don't have to be a shoe salesman to enjoy yourself here. Experience the sensuous excitement of a well-shined pump wrapped around a delicately stockinged foot with deliciously painted toenails.

Usenet:
Newsgroup: **alt.sex.fetish.feet**

Hair Fetish

Montel Williams and Jean-Luc Picard hold no appeal for you. If it's not hairy, it's not interesting. Don't think you're alone in your fantasies about Cousin It.

Usenet:
Newsgroup: **alt.sex.fetish.hair**

Kama Sutra

The love teachings of the Kama Sutra describe a wide variety of sex positions and techniques, including the Flag of Cupid, Aphrodite's Delight, and the Monkey.

Anonymous FTP:
Address: **quartz.rutgers.edu**
Path: **/pub/sex/kama.sutra**

Gopher:
Name: Rutgers Quartz Text Archive
Address: **quartz.rutgers.edu**
Choose: **Sex**
| **kama.sutra**

Got too much stuff?
Need some more stuff?
Try
Buying and Selling

Make sure you are prepared:
Read
Emergency and Disaster

Excerpt from the Net...

(from the Kama Sutra, available via Anonymous FTP and Gopher)

To Enslave a Lover:

Leaves caught as they fall from trees
and powdered with peacock-bone
and fragments of a corpse's winding-sheet
will, when dusted lightly
on the love organ, bewitch any woman living.

The Kama Sutra

Is that special something missing from your relationship? Maybe what you need is a little pick-me-up that goes beyond advice from Dr. Ruth. The Kama Sutra is an ancient text that describes things that have to be seen to be believed. (Unfortunately, you'll probably never see them.) Still, when you're sitting at home bored to distraction, there is probably some solace to be drawn in reading about adventurous techniques that have the potential to make the art of lovemaking even more fun than hanging out at the mall or watching Monday night football.

Law, Crime and Sex

Discussion of sex crimes, trials and the law.

Usenet:
Newsgroup: **clari.news.law.crime.sex**

Limericks

A collection of sex-related limericks.

Anonymous FTP:
Address: **quartz.rutgers.edu**
Path: **/pub/humor/limericks**

Gopher:
Name: Rutgers Quartz Text Archive
Address: **quartz.rutgers.edu**
Choose: **Humor**
| Limericks

Masturbation

You waited too late to get a date for Friday night. No big deal. Light a candle, fix a romantic dinner, watch a movie with yourself. There's nothing like a little peaceful reflection. When the mood is right, you can make your move without all the worry about offending anyone, being sensitive, catching germs or calling in the morning. It's safe, it's reliable and Ann Landers says it's okay.

Usenet:
Newsgroup: **alt.sex.masturbation**

Movies

Step aside, Siskel and Ebert. Meet the pros: people who really know their films intimately. Learn what movies are hot and what movies are not worth warming up the television. Who are the superstars of sexy films and what movies actually have a plot? Bone up on your erotic movie trivia.

Usenet:
Newsgroup: **alt.sex.movie**

Oriental Fetish

Worship the exotic. Experience the mystery of the Far East by plunging yourself head first into its people and culture. Learn the secrets of Oriental sexuality.

Usenet:
Newsgroup: **alt.sex.fetish.orientals**

Pantyhose and Stockings

Soft, sleek, sensual... and more. Talk to the people who really appreciate what the well-dressed leg is wearing this season. Share your opinions and read provocative stories.

Usenet:
Newsgroup: **alt.pantyhose**

Playboy Centerfolds

Names and vital statistics for U.S.-edition Playboy centerfolds and playmates.

Anonymous FTP:
Address: **ftp.spies.com**
Path: **/Library/Article/Sex/playboy.l***

Gopher:
Name: Internet Wiretap
Address: **wiretap.spies.com**
Choose: **Wiretap Online Library**
| Articles
| Sex
| Playboy Centerfolds

This image was downloaded via Anonymous FTP from Washington University Saint Louis (**ftp.wustl.edu**). The filename is **gender.gif**. We had a much more exciting illustration here, but the political correctness police won that round. (Someday, we are going to have to publish *The Uncensored Internet Yellow Pages*.)

Anonymous FTP:
> Address: **ftp.spies.com**
> Path: **/Library/Article/Sex/polyamor.txt**

Gopher:
> Name: Internet Wiretap
> Address: **wiretap.spies.com**
> Choose: **Wiretap Online Library**
>> | **Articles**
>> | **Sex**
>> | **Polyamory**

Polyamory

An article describing this lifestyle, in which multiple intimate relationships are pursued simultaneously.

NEED TO CONVINCE YOUR COMPANY THAT THE INTERNET IS CRUCIAL TO YOUR ECONOMIC FUTURE?

JUST SHOW THEM HOW EASY IT IS TO ACCESS THE VITAL STATISTICS FOR PLAYBOY CENTERFOLDS.

Excerpt from the Net...

(from a story posted to alt.pantyhose)

I was still reeling from the shock...I thought I'd seen everything that might ruin our marriage, but we've stuck together through thick and thin. Through sickness and health. Except for now.

"Stephanie...", I stammered. "You know that lesbianism doesn't bother me, but why did you wait after all this time to admit this to me? I'm your HUSBAND!"...

My head was a soup of confused feelings...the one person who meant more to me than anything may very well have made our marriage a lie. A good part of my life will have to be ripped away from me, unless I made some sacrifices to keep her in my life...

"Stephanie," I asked, mentally preparing myself for what I was about to do, "Would it be easier for you if I were a woman?"

Her eyes lit up like Christmas tree lights, and I could see that she was fascinated with this idea, a chance to save our marriage. "You would do that for me? That's, that's wonderful..."

Anyway, that's how all this started. I am going over that episode in my mind again as I now stand in the bedroom, showered, fully shaved, and powdered, trying to tell myself that this is for our marriage, and to at least give this scheme a chance....

"Okay, first you take one of the stocking legs and gather it up to the toe, like this," Stephanie explained, demonstrating with her pair, gathering the leg up with her thumbs which I emulated. "Then, you put your toes in, straightening out the toe seam across the toes. Personally, I like to put the seam just under the toes, so if you take off your shoes the seam will be invisible." I tried to follow her example as she put them on her smooth legs...

A
B
C
D
E
F
G
H
I
J
K
L
M
N
O
P
Q
R
S
T
U
V
W
X
Y
Z

Prostitute Prices

Detailed prostitute prices for many cities around the world.

Anonymous FTP:
  Address: **ftp.spies.com**
  Path: **/Library/Article/Sex/whore.pr**

Gopher:
  Name: Internet Wiretap
  Address: **wiretap.spies.com**
  Choose: **Wiretap Online Library**
    | **Articles**
    | **Sex**
    | **Whore Prices**

Purity Tests

A selection of fun purity tests to determine your sexual purity rating.

Anonymous FTP:
  Address: **ftp.spies.com**
  Path: **/Library/Article/Sex/purity***

  Address: **ftp.std.com**
  Path: **/pub/purity/***

  Address: **nic.funet.fi**
  Path: **/pub/doc/fun/tests/purity***

  Address: **quartz.rutgers.edu**
  Path: **/pub/purity/***

Archie:
  Pattern: **purity***

Gopher:
  Name: Internet Wiretap
  Address: **wiretap.spies.com**
  Choose: **Wiretap Online Library**
    | **Articles**
    | **Sex**
    | **The 1500 Question Purity Test**

Questions and Answers

All your wildest questions answered, including a special list of FAQs for sex wizards. Includes sex terms and acronyms, purity test guides, and much more.

Anonymous FTP:
  Address: **rtfm.mit.edu**
  Path: **/pub/usenet/news.answers/alt-sex/***

Sex Experts

You're in the heat of the moment and a problem arises. What do you do? There's no time to write a letter to Dear Abby. Admittedly, this is not going to happen often, but if you want answers or information from sex experts, they are available with a few keystrokes. Don't you wish everything was that easy?

Usenet:
  Newsgroup: **alt.sex.wizards**

Sex-Related Articles

Lots of interesting articles, including purity tests, FAQs, Playboy centerfold lists, strip joint reviews, smurfs code, prostitute pricing, and other information.

Anonymous FTP:
  Address: **ftp.spies.com**
  Path: **/Library/Article/Sex/***

Gopher:
  Name: Internet Wiretap
  Address: **wiretap.spies.com**
  Choose: **Wiretap Online Library**
    | **Articles**
    | **Sex**

Sex-Related Humor

Humor about sex, including bedroom golf, pick-up lines and sex colors.

Anonymous FTP:
  Address: **quartz.rutgers.edu**
  Path: **/pub/humor/Sex/***

Gopher:
  Name: Rutgers Quartz Text Archive
  Address: **quartz.rutgers.edu**
  Choose: **Humor**
    | **Sex**

Sex and Humor

Yes, it's true, sex is funny (if you do it right). For a nice collection of instantly-available sex-related humor, try the *Quartz* Gopher and archive. just the place to look for interesting stories before you go to a family reunion.

Sex Talk

What's the weirdest place you have ever had sex? Care to share? Even if you don't, there are hoardes of people who do. Not only will they tell you the weirdest place, but the weirdest accident they've ever had during sex, how many times they had sex, and what was going on around them before, during and after. Be informed as you are entertained. Read about birth control, STDs, virginity (or lack thereof), and other topics of a sexual nature.

Usenet:
    Newsgroup: **alt.sex**

> ## No matter who you are or what you believe, somewhere on the Internet, there are people like you.

Sex Wanted

Caress your keyboard as the words flow smoothly out on the screen and onto someone else's. Electronically communicate your desires, whatever they may be, to others who are seeking erotica, textual intimacy or a meeting in the flesh.

Usenet:
    Newsgroup: **alt.sex.wanted**

Sexual Massage

Discover the exotic arts of yoni and lingam massage.

Anonymous FTP:
    Address: **ftp.spies.com**
    Path: **/Library/Article/Sex/massage.txt**

Gopher:
    Name: Internet Wiretap
    Address: **wiretap.spies.com**
    Choose: **Wiretap Online Library**
        | Articles
        | Sex
        | Yoni Massage How-To

Excerpt from the Net...

```
Newsgroup: alt.sex
Subject: Is this sexy or what?

> ...it is a decoy.  I also found something in my smoke detector even
> more sinister, a cylindrical metalic case which cannot be opened and
> is covered with warnings and threats with vague references to radio
> activity...

Yes, if you open the secret metallic cylinder, you will find a fascinating substance.  It
may take some work to open the box up, but you should be able to pry it with a
screwdriver.  The substance in the smoke detector -- Hydropolyruthenium -- has some
amazing properties.

This substance was shown to the U.S. government by those almond-eyed aliens without any
hair, but superdeveloped brains and telepathic ability.  By eating enough of this
substance, a transformation takes place in humans.  They begin to lose their hair and
exhibit telepathic abilities.

It is this radio frequency wave which may be used to listen in on folks.  By eating the
substance and gaining those abilities, one can not only listen in to other's thoughts at
will, but shield oneself from others listening in (like the government).

Our government has a secret division of people who have developed this ability and patrol
the streets listening in on people where there aren't "smoke detectors".  These folks are
almost always completely bald and usually wear baseball caps.  Their eyes are larger than
normal.

I'm posting this anonymously for obvious reasons.
```

A
B
C
D
E
F
G
H
I
J
K
L
M
N
O
P
Q
R
S
T
U
V
W
X
Y
Z

Sounds

Audio excitement.

Usenet:
Newsgroup: **alt.sex.sounds**

Spanking

Have you ever been sitting around the house and suddenly you think, "Hmm, I need a good spanking"? Don't feel alone, we've all had that experience (not really, but you can think that). Gather around others who like to take physical intimacy to another dimension. You'll recognize them: they're the ones who can't sit down.

Usenet:
Newsgroup: **alt.sex.spanking**

Stories

There's nothing like curling up with a provocative story and a hot cup of tea or a little classical music. You won't find tea or good music here, but you will never want for a good, sexy story (or a bad one, for that matter). Stories range from mildly erotic mainstream to bold, raunchy kink. There's something for everyone. And if you like to hang around afterwards over coffee or a smoke and discuss the literary merits of the writing, check out **alt.sex.stories.d** for discussion.

Usenet:
Newsgroup: **alt.sex.stories**
Newsgroup: **alt.sex.stories.d**

Strip Joint Reviews

Detailed reviews of many U.S. and Canadian strip joints.

Anonymous FTP:
Address: **ftp.spies.com**
Path: **/Library/Article/Sex/strip.rv**

Gopher:
Name: Internet Wiretap
Address: **wiretap.spies.com**
Choose: **Wiretap Online Library**
| Articles | Sex
| Review of Strip Joints

Urban Sex Legends

Amusing stories and urban legends with a sexual twist.

Anonymous FTP:
Address: **cathouse.org**
Path: **/pub/cathouse/urban.legends/sex/***

Voyeurism

There's something exciting about forbidden observation: peeking through the slats of the venetian blinds, pressing your ear against the cool, smooth wall, opening the door just a crack and watching. If you are more of a watcher than a doer, or you like doing while watching, post your thoughts, ideas and stories here.

Usenet:
Newsgroup: **alt.sex.voyeurism**

Do you like to watch? Take a peek at alt.sex.voyeurism.

Wanted

Requests for erotica, either literary or in the flesh.

Usenet:
Newsgroup: **alt.sex.wanted**

Watersports

If you are looking for a good place to discuss your skill as a water-skier, go someplace else. For watersports of a more personal nature, like enemas and related fetishes, this is your place.

Usenet:
Newsgroup: **alt.sex.fetish.watersports**

Wizards

Discussion group for difficult or complex sex questions. Ask whatever you want and people who really know what they are talking about will answer. No more will you have to suffer from ignorance or lack of ideas. But don't be silly or childish, these people take their sex seriously.

Usenet:
Newsgroup: **alt.sex.wizards**

A
B
C
D
E
F
G
H
I
J
K
L
M
N
O
P
Q
R
S
T
U
V
W
X
Y
Z

Real Answers About Real Sex

If you are interested in sex, drop in to alt.sex.wizards. There you will find a whole bunch of friendly, knowledgeable people ready to discuss sex without blushing. For a real treat, keep your eye out for the frequently asked question (FAQ) list.

No matter how experienced you are, we bet that you'll find something new to pique your interest. (And maybe, if you're lucky, someone will explain to you what a "Mexican Cartwheel" is.)

SEXUALITY

Abuse and Recovery

Here is a safe place where you will be welcome. Spend some time reading stories of hurt as well as stories of healing. Sexual abuse brings people together with sadness and anger, but sharing and caring can inspire you to comfort and recovery.

Usenet:
Newsgroup: **alt.sexual.abuse.recovery**

Coming Out

Discussion of the process through which individuals come to terms with their lesbian or gay sexual orientations.

Gopher:
Name: Healthline Gopher Server
Address: **selway.umt.edu 700**
Choose: **Sexuality
| Coming Out**

Telnet:
Address: **selway.umt.edu**
Login: **health**

Gay FTP Site

Gay and lesbian stories, campaign information, queer resources directory, mailing lists, laws, AIDS information, event guide, newspaper articles and much more.

Anonymous FTP:
Address: **nifty.andrew.cmu.edu**
Path: **/pub/***

Homosexuality

Of alternative lifestyles, politics and homosexuality, and encounters with members of the same sex (MOTSS).

Usenet:
Newsgroup: **alt.homosexual**
Newsgroup: **alt.politics.homosexuality**
Newsgroup: **alt.sex.motss**

Kinsey Questions and Answers

Read features from the Kinsey Institute and get real answers from the real pros. Why pick up your information from the gutter when Usenet is only a few keystrokes away?

Usenet:
Newsgroup: **clari.feature.kinsey**

Lesbian, Gay and Bisexual Mailing Lists

List of more than 50 lesbian, gay, bisexual and transgender mailing lists, and information about each.

Anonymous FTP:
Address: **nifty.andrew.cmu.edu**
Path: **/pub/QRD/qrd/info/RESOURCES/
network/EMAIL/***

Address: **vector.intercon.com**
Path:
/pub/QRD/info/RESOURCES/network/EMAIL/*

Politics

For some reason, politics and sex are inseparable (and it's not just the Kennedys). What do Gennifer Flowers, Donna Rice and Jessica Hahn know that Dr. Ruth has never figured out? Join the discussion and see what strange bedfellows politics and sex really make.

Usenet:
Newsgroup: **alt.politics.sex**

Queer Resource Directory

FTP site for gay interests and issues, including rights and AIDS information.

Anonymous FTP:
Address: **nifty.andrew.cmu.edu**
Path: **/pub/QRD**

Wais:
Database: **Queer-Resources**

Sex in the News

Sex isn't just fun and games (mostly, but not completely). When it's time to find out the hard news on the facts of life, turn to these two Clarinet newsgroups for your fix.

Usenet:
Newsgroup: **clari.news.law.crime.sex**
Newsgroup: **clari.news.sex**

Sexual Assault and Sexual Abuse Recovery

Documents and discussions to help deal with traumatic experiences, recover from sexual assault, and prevent acquaintance and date rape.

Gopher:
Name: Healthline Gopher Service
Address: **selway.umt.edu 700**
Choose: **Sexual Assault Recovery Service (SARS)**

Telnet:
Address: **selway.umt.edu**
Login: **health**

Usenet:
Newsgroup: **alt.sexual.abuse.recovery**

Sexual Identity and Gender Identity Glossary

Basic information and a glossary of words and terms used in the gay and bisexual communities.

Anonymous FTP:
Address: **ftp.spies.com**
Path: **/Library/Article/Sex/lesbian.dic**

Gopher:
Name: Internet Wiretap
Address: **wiretap.spies.com**
Choose: **Wiretap Online Library**
  I Articles
  I Sex
  I Les/Bi/Gay & Transgender Glossary

Transgender

Changing your gender is not an easy thing to do. (Now that's an understatement.) Talk with people who think it's okay for you to be who you really are. Here is an informative forum with technical and emotional support for anyone in the transgender process.

Usenet:
Newsgroup: **alt.transgendered**

SOCIOLOGY AND MYTHOLOGY

Alternate Institutions

A mailing list on alternative ways to run conversations, countries, households, markets and so on.

Internet mailing list:
List Address: **altinst@cs.cmu.edu**
Subscription Address: **altinst-request@cs.cmu.edu**

Amazons International

Amazons of the world unite! *Amazons International* is an electronic digest newsletter for, about, and by Amazon women.

Internet mailing list:
List Address: **amazons@math.uio.no**
Subscription Address:
  amazons-request@math.uio.no

Arachnet Electronic Journal of Virtual Culture

A forum for communication that includes electronic mail, conferences and journals.

Listserv mailing list:
List Address: **arachnet@kentvm.bitnet**
Subscription Address: **listserv@kentvm.bitnet**

Social Sciences Resource Guides

Internet resource guides for education, anthropology, bisexuality, business, economics, geography, government, journalism, law, library, social science and women's studies.

Anonymous FTP:
Address: **una.hh.lib.umich.edu**
Path: **/inetdirs/socsciences/***

Gopher:
Name: University of Michigan
Address: **una.hh.lib.umich.edu**
Choose: **inetdirs**
| **Guides on the Social Sciences (UMich)**

Sociological Issues

Articles about subjects such as neolithic warfare, anarchy, Celtic mythology, history of the Red Army Faction and more.

Anonymous FTP:
Address: **ftp.spies.com**
Path: **/Library/Article/Socio/***

Gopher:
Name: Internet Wiretap
Address: **wiretap.spies.com**
Choose: **Wiretap Online Library**
| **Articles**
| **Sociological Issues**

Urban Folklore

FAQs, articles and lists relating to computer, urban and college folklore.

Anonymous FTP:
Address: **quartz.rutgers.edu**
Path: **/pub/folklore/***

Gopher:
Name: Rutgers Quartz Text Archive
Address: **quartz.rutgers.edu**
Choose: **Folklore - Urban and Other**

Urban Legends

Stories, trivia, old wives' tales, and a place for confirming or disproving beliefs and rumors of all kinds.

Anonymous FTP:
Address: **balder.nta.no**
Path: **/pub/alt.folklore.urban/***

Address: **cathouse.org**
Path: **/pub/cathouse/urban.legends/***

Usenet:
Newsgroup: **alt.folklore.urban**

Excerpt from the Net...

```
Newsgroup: alt.transgendered
Subject: Mirrors

Who was he?  The strange man in the mirror.  I never knew.  I laughed with him sometimes,
cried with him more, yet I never knew who he was. We often stared at each other but he
never spoke to me or betrayed his secrets to me.

I've heard that some people believe the mirror holds their soul and provides them a short
visitation of it.  Yet each time I came to the mirror, I was met by this cold stranger.
I was forced by him to search within me to find my soul.

After long searching I finally came to her, sealed behind many walls and buried beneath
tears and lies.  I looked to her and cried, embracing her after so long.  I began tending
her wounds and helped her from that place, giving her freedom.  She smiled and rose,
filling me and embracing me.  Now when I meet the mirror, I see her and she smiles
tenderly to me.  We share our thoughts and secrets.  I speak fondly to her and feel her
reply.

But I wonder what happened to the man in the mirror and who he was.  I wish I could have
known him and spoken to him.  He is gone forever now.  Perhaps he never existed, except as
the guardian protecting my soul until she was strong enough to stand alone.
```

SOFTWARE

ASK-Software-Informationssystem

Bilingual BBS offering database searches for software, news, and information. Choose option 3 on the main menu to change from German to English.

Telnet:
Address: **askhp.ask.uni-karlsruhe.de**
Login: **ask**
Password: **ask**

Encryption

Encryption routines and software. Information, algorithms, hardware and other related material.

Anonymous FTP:
Address: **nic.funet.fi**
Path: **/pub/crypt/***

Do you like to be mysterious? Check the *Encryption* archive for everything you need to send and receive secret messages, even if you don't have a Masked Avenger Secret Decoder Ring.

GNU

A large, multifaceted software project to create and distribute free software.

Usenet:
Newsgroup: **gnu.***

GNU for PCs

GNU-style programs and utilities for the PC, including **emacs**, **make**, **grep**, **sed** and **sort**.

Anonymous FTP:
Address: **wuarchive.wustl.edu**
Path: **/systems/ibmpc/gnuish/***

Graphics Software Search

Search and retrieve graphics software and data with this Gopher tool, including FTP sites, bibliography, FAQs and other resources.

Gopher:
Name: Johns Hopkins University
Address: **merlot.welch.jhu.edu**
Choose: **Search and Retrieve Software**
| Search and Retrieve Graphics Software and Data

Info und Softserver

Journals, Unix programs and utilities, recipes, online cookbook. A bilingual (but mostly German) BBS.

Telnet:
Address: **rusinfo.rus.uni-stuttgart.de**
Login: **info**

Jewish Software

Jewish and Hebrew software and materials for the Macintosh, MS-DOS computers and Unix systems.

Anonymous FTP:
Address: **israel.nysernet.org**
Path: **/israel/***

NCSA Telnet

A TCP/IP package for PCs.

Anonymous FTP:
Address: **ftp.ncsa.uiuc.edu**
Path: **/PC/Collage**

Nutshell Code

Many of the tools and programs discussed in various O'Reilly handbooks.

Anonymous FTP:
Address: **ftp.ora.com**
Path: **/pub/examples**

Address: **ftp.uu.net**
Path: **/published/oreilly**

OS/2 Archive

Archiving programs, communications programs, demos, drivers, editors, games, graphics, patches, utilities and other software for all versions of OS/2.

Anonymous FTP:
> Address: **ftp-os2.nmsu.edu**
> Path: **/os2/***

PC Software Search

Search and retrieve MS-DOS software from popular FTP sites by either browsing or using program description keyword search.

Gopher:
> Name: Johns Hopkins University
> Address: **merlot.welch.jhu.edu**
> Choose: **Search and Retrieve Software**
> **| Search and Retrieve DOS Software**

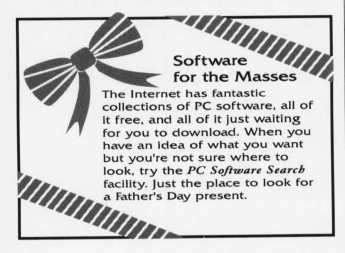

Software for the Masses

The Internet has fantastic collections of PC software, all of it free, and all of it just waiting for you to download. When you have an idea of what you want but you're not sure where to look, try the *PC Software Search* facility. Just the place to look for a Father's Day present.

PERL Archives

Scripts, FAQs, hints, help guides, source and more for PERL, the Practical Extraction and Report Language.

Anonymous FTP:
> Address: **convex.com**
> Path: **/pub/perl/***
>
> Address: **coombs.anu.edu.au**
> Path: **/pub/perl/***
>
> Address: **ftp.demon.co.uk**
> Path: **/pub/perl/***
>
> Address: **ftp.ee.umanitoba.ca**
> Path: **/pub/msdos/perl/***
>
> Address: **ftp.metronet.com**
> Path: **/pub/perl/***

Gopher:
> Name: Texas Metronet
> Address: **gopher.metronet.com**
> Choose: **The PERL programming language**

PERL Scripts

PERL (Practical Extraction and Report Language) scripts for many purposes, including system administration, database tools, menu applications, processes and networks.

Anonymous FTP:
> Address: **ftp.metronet.com**
> Path: **/pub/perl/scripts/***

Gopher:
> Name: Texas Metronet
> Address: **gopher.metronet.com**
> Choose: **The PERL programming language**
> **| PERL Scripts for Many Purposes**

Searching for Software

The links and directories here will allow you to easily search for and retrieve software from FTP archives all over the world.

Gopher:
> Name: Johns Hopkins University
> Address: **merlot.welch.jhu.edu**
> Choose: **Search and Retrieve Software**

SIMTEL20 Software Archives

A huge repository of all types of software for all types of computers. These archives are mirrored at many sites around the world.

Anonymous FTP:
> Address: **ftp.uu.net**
> Path: **/systems/simtel20/***

Software Archives

Information about archive sites around the Internet from which you can download programs via Anonymous FTP. The **announce** newsgroup is moderated and contains announcements regarding DOS archives. The **.d** group is for the discussion of related topics. This is a good place to ask where a particular program is available.

Usenet:
> Newsgroup: **comp.archives.msdos.announce**
> Newsgroup: **comp.sources.***
> Newsgroup: **comp.sources.d**

A B C D E F G H I J K L M N O P Q R S T U V W X Y Z

Software Sites

Some of the most well-known software archive sites. They contain far more than we could ever print in this book. Good for weeks of exploration.

Anonymous FTP:
Address: **bongo.cc.utexas.edu**
Path: **/pub/***

Address: **export.lcs.mit.edu**
Path: **/pub/***

Address: **ftp.rahul.net**
Path: **/pub/***

Address: **ftp.uu.net**
Path: **/systems/***

Address: **ftp.uu.net**
Path: **/systems/simtel20/***

Address: **garbo.uwasa.fi**
Path: **/pub/***

Address: **nic.funet.fi**
Path: **/pub/***

Address: **oak.oakland.edu**
Path: **/pub/***

Address: **wuarchive.wustl.edu**
Path: **/pub/***

System Software

Large software and documentation archives for numerous systems, including Xenix, Unix, Sinclair, Novell, MS-DOS, HPUX, Apple2 and VAX-VMS.

Anonymous FTP:
Address: **wuarchive.wustl.edu**
Path: **/systems/***

TeX Text Typesetter

Bundles of information about TeX, the software system written by Donald Knuth to typeset text, including access to archives, font information, FAQ lists and LaTeX information.

Gopher:
Name: Sam Houston State University
Address: **niord.shsu.edu**
Choose: **TeX-related Materials**

Thesaurus Construction Program

Tim Craven's thesaurus construction program for the IBM-PC. Assists in creating, modifying, viewing and printing out a small thesaurus. Includes source code and is in self-extracting archive form.

Anonymous FTP:
Address: **nic.funet.fi**
Path: **/pub/doc/library/thesauri.exe**

> There's something undeniably attractive about someone who has created their own thesaurus. And now, you can be that person. Just download the *Thesaurus Construction Program* and even Roget will eat your dust.

VAX/VMS Software List

An extensive list with hundreds of software applications for VAX/VMS systems and where to find them.

Comment: Restrict FTP usage to times other than weekdays 10 A.M. to 10 P.M. PST (GMT-0800).

Anonymous FTP:
Address: **pomona.claremont.edu**
Path: **/vax_list.dir/vax_list.txt**

Gopher:
Name: ISW, National Chung Cheng Univ.
Address: **isw2.sw.ccu.edu.tw**
Choose: **VAX/VMS Public Domain Files**
  | The VAX Software List

Mail:
Address: **vmsserv@pomona.claremont.edu**
Body: **send vax_list.package**

X-10 Protocol

Technical information about the X-10 remote control standard.

Anonymous FTP:
Address: **oak.oakland.edu**
Path: **/pub/misc/x-10/***

ZIB Electronic Library

Software, hot links to NetLib, archives and catalogs.

Telnet:
Address: **elib.zib-berlin.de**
Login: **elib**

Zmodem

Complete C source, including makefiles, for the **sz** and **rz** Unix programs for sending and receiving with the Xmodem, Ymodem, and Zmodem protocols. You can download these programs and type **make** to produce the executables.

Anonymous FTP:
   Address: **oak.oakland.edu**
   Path: **/pub/misc/zmodem**

SOFTWARE: ARCHIVES

Amiga

Demos, games, utilities, programming tools, mailing list information and documentation for people with Commodore Amiga computers.

Anonymous FTP:
   Address: **wuarchive.wustl.edu**
   Path: **/systems/amiga/***

Gopher:
   Name: EUnet in Slovakia
   Address: **gopher.eunet.sk**
   Choose: **Archive of EUnet Slovakia**
      | Amiga Archive

Apple II Archives

A large archive of games, demos, utilities, source code and other material for the Apple II range of computers.

Anonymous FTP:
   Address: **ccosun.caltech.edu**
   Path: **/pub/apple2/***

Atari

Bundles of programs, source code, graphics, sounds, magazines and documentation for the Atari ST range of computers.

Anonymous FTP:
   Address: **wuarchive.wustl.edu**
   Path: **/systems/atari/***

Commodore 64/128 Archives

Large archive of information, graphics, games, utilities and other material for the Commodore 64 and Commodore 128 computers.

Anonymous FTP:
   Address: **ccosun.caltech.edu**
   Path: **/pub/rknop/***

CPM Archives

Tips, tricks, utilities, source code and complete programs for users of CPM computers.

Anonymous FTP:
   Address: **oak.oakland.edu**
   Path: **/pub/cpm/***

DECUS Library

A library catalog of software for various operating systems. Includes utilities, programs and games for CPM, DEC, Ultrix and VAX.

Gopher:
   Name: La Trobe University
   Address: **gopher.latrobe.edu.au**
   Choose: **Computing Services**
      | DECUS Library

Garbo (University of Vaasa, Finland)

Software, software, software! This Anonymous FTP site has tons of software for DOS, Windows, Macs and Unix machines. Demos, utilities, screen savers, fonts, bitmaps, icons, games, patches, and programs from astronomy and business to virus interceptors, and more games.

Anonymous FTP:
   Address: **garbo.uwasa.fi**
   Path: **/mac/***

   Address: **garbo.uwasa.fi**
   Path: **/next/***

   Address: **garbo.uwasa.fi**
   Path: **/pc/***

   Address: **garbo.uwasa.fi**
   Path: **/unix/***

   Address: **garbo.uwasa.fi**
   Path: **/windows/***

A
B
C
D
E
F
G
H
I
J
K
L
M
N
O
P
Q
R
S
T
U
V
W
X
Y
Z

Macintosh Archives

Tips, tricks, utilities, source code and complete programs for users of Macintosh computers.

Anonymous FTP:
Address: **oak.oakland.edu**
Path: **/pub2/macintosh/***

PC Archives

Probably one of the largest collections of IBM-PC related material to ever exist in one place. Mirrors from several other large sites also. You name it, it's here.

Anonymous FTP:
Address: **wuarchive.wustl.edu**
Path: **/systems/ibmpc/***

PC Game Archives

Central repository for the PC gaming community, containing all manner of freely distributable games and accessories that run under MS-DOS or MS-Windows.

Anonymous FTP:
Address: **ftp.ulowell.edu**
Path: **/msdos/Games/***

Address: **wuarchive.wustl.edu**
Path: **/systems/ibmpc/msdos-games/***

The Internet has some fascinating Frequently Asked Question (FAQ) Lists.

When you have a spare moment, find a FAQ list that looks interesting and read it.

PC Games for You

It's a sad day when you run out of new games for your PC and you are left with no alternative but to actually do some work.

But, as an Internet user, this unfortunate situation will never happen to you. All you have to do is look in the **PC Game Archives** and you will find enough diversions to keep you busy until it is time to retire.

Sinclair Archives

Dedicated to those wonderful creations of Clive Sinclair. If you're looking for information or specs for a ZX-81, QL or Cambridge Z88, this is the place to find it.

Anonymous FTP:
Address: **wuarchive.wustl.edu**
Path: **/systems/sinclair/***

TeX Archives

Large repository of TeX-related material, accumulated by the Comprehensive TeX Archive Network (CTAN). It offers TeX digests, documentation, fonts, graphics, listings, macros and much more.

Anonymous FTP:
Address: **ftp.shsu.edu**
Path: **/tex-archive/***

Unix C Archive

More serious software for Unix than you could ever imagine, much of it written in C or related tools and complete with source. Included are database utilities, editors, graphics, languages and much more.

Anonymous FTP:
    Address: **wuarchive.wustl.edu**
    Path: **/systems/unix/unix-c/***

SOFTWARE: DOS

HENSA Software Archive

Higher Education National Software Archive (HENSA) for microcomputers.

Gopher:
    Name: Hensa PD Software Archive
    Address: **micros.hensa.ac.uk**

This artistic image is called **avn_ati.gif** and is available from Northern Arizona University, Washington University, St. Louis, and the University of Missouri, Kansas City (**ftp.cstp.umkc.edu**).

**There are a lot of books that you can download for free on the Internet.
See the Literature sections for details.**

Waffle BBS Software

A collection of software for use with Waffle BBS, an MS-DOS BBS package.

Anonymous FTP:
    Address: **ftp.spies.com**
    Path: **/waffle/***

Gopher:
    Name: Internet Wiretap
    Address: **wiretap.spies.com**
    Choose: **Waffle BBS Software**

SOFTWARE: INTERNET

Archie Clients

Client programs for accessing Archie servers.

Anonymous FTP:
    Address: **ftp.cs.widener.edu**
    Path: **/pub/archie/***

Gopher Clients

Client programs for accessing Gopher servers. The addresses for downloading Gopher clients are given in the Gopher FAQ.

Anonymous FTP:
    Address: **rtfm.mit.edu**
    Path: **/pub/usenet/news.answers/gopher-faq**

IRC II Client

IRC II help files and clients for Unix and VMS. If you telnet to the telnet site, the necessary files are downloaded and compiled automatically. You must, however, follow the telnet command with the characters 1 | sh, as shown.

Anonymous FTP:
    Address: **cs.bu.edu**
    Path: **/irc/clients**

    Address: **slopoke.mlb.semi.harris.com**
    Path: **/pub/irc/***

Telnet:
    Address: **sci.dixie.edu 1 | sh**

A
B
C
D
E
F
G
H
I
J
K
L
M
N
O
P
Q
R
S
T
U
V
W
X
Y
Z

IRC (Internet Relay Chat) is absolutely fantabulous, but to use it you need an IRC client program. If there isn't one already installed on your system, you can download one for yourself.

(Note: Be nice, though, and ask the system manager first. Some managers do not want people using IRC.)

NUPop

NUPop provides a suite of Internet services in a menu-driven format, including electronic mail, file transfer, remote login, Gopher, user lookup, webster, ping and remote password change.

Anonymous FTP:
Address: **ftp.acns.nwu.edu**
Path: **/pub/nupop**

Wais Clients

A Wais client is a program used to access a Wais server. Information about downloading Wais clients can be found in the Wais frequently asked question (FAQ) list.

Anonymous FTP:
Address: **rtfm.mit.edu**
Path: **/pub/usenet/news.answers/wais-faq**

World Wide Web Browsers

A browser is a program used to access the World Wide Web. You can download a browser via Anonymous FTP. The xmosaic browser, used with X Window, can be found at the first address listed below. Browsers for all other systems can be found at the second address.

Anonymous FTP:
Address: **ftp.ncsa.uiuc.edu**
Path: **/Web/***

Address: **info.cern.ch**
Path: **/pub/www**

SOFTWARE: MACINTOSH

Apple Macintosh System 7 Operating System

Not System 7.1, but System 7.0 is available by Anonymous FTP.

Anonymous FTP:
Address: **ftp.apple.com**
Path: **/dts/mac/sys.soft/***

Applications

Discussion about all types of Macintosh applications. The **.apps** newsgroup is for talk about any type of application; **.word** is for word processing; **.comm** is for communications; and **.databases** is for database systems.

Usenet:
Newsgroup: **bit.mailserv.word-mac**
Newsgroup: **comp.sys.mac.apps**
Newsgroup: **comp.sys.mac.comm**
Newsgroup: **comp.sys.mac.databases**

Binaries

This moderated newsgroup contains binaries (executable Macintosh programs) ready to download and run.

Usenet:
Newsgroup: **comp.binaries.mac**

Eudora

Eudora is an Internet mail program for the Macintosh. It uses the POP and SMTP protocols. Eudora allows users sitting at their own Mac to connect to a Unix machine and get/send mail without actually having to login and use Unix.

Anonymous FTP:
Address: **ftp.qualcomm.com**
Path: **/pub/eudora**

Games

What's the point of having a computer without games? Join this discussion group to talk about all aspects of Macintosh games: which ones are best, which ones to avoid, copy protection issues, as well as hints and tricks.

Usenet:
Newsgroup: **comp.sys.mac.games**

Hypercard

Talk about all kinds of issues related to the Macintosh Hypercard: the stack-oriented hypertext system.

Usenet:
Newsgroup: **comp.sys.mac.hypercard**

Mac FTP List

A large list of Anonymous FTP sites that contain many files and programs for the Apple Macintosh. This document also contains information and advice for downloading and running Mac software from the Internet.

Anonymous FTP:
Address: **ftp.sunet.se**
Path: **/pub/mac/info/comm/mac-ftp-list***

Address: **ftp.wustl.edu**
Path:
/systems/mac/info-mac/Old/report/mac-ftp-list*

Archie:
Pattern: **mac-ftp-list**

Gopher:
Name: Saitama University
Address: **gopher.cent.saitama-u.ac.jp**
Choose: **FTP | mac-ftp-list**

Free Mac Stuff

There are lots and lots (and lots and lots) of free Macintosh software and files available on the Net. Many of these programs are collected together in the various Macintosh FTP archives. If you are not exactly sure what you want, try using the Macintosh software search Gopher. No need to pay for programs when you are on the Net.

Macintosh Software Search

Browse, search by keyword and retrieve Macintosh software from popular FTP archives.

Gopher:
Name: Johns Hopkins University
Address: **merlot.welch.jhu.edu**
Choose: **Search and Retrieve Software
| Search and Retrieve Macintosh Software**

Object-Oriented Programming

Object-oriented programming is just like regular programming except that you look at everything differently, write your programs differently, maintain them differently, and think with a different part of your temporal lobe. Join the discussion and talk about object-oriented tools, techniques and problems. The **.misc** newsgroup is for general discussion of Macintosh object-oriented programming. The **.macapp3** group is devoted to Version 3 of the MacApp system. The **.tcl** group is for discussion of the Think Class Libraries.

Usenet:
Newsgroup: **comp.sys.mac.oop.macapp3**
Newsgroup: **comp.sys.mac.oop.misc**
Newsgroup: **comp.sys.mac.oop.tcl**

Programming

Macintosh programming: tips, questions and answers. The **.lisp** newsgroup is for Lisp programming. The **.mac** group is for general discussion about all aspects of programming.

Usenet:
Newsgroup: **comp.lang.lisp.mcl**
Newsgroup: **comp.sys.mac.programmer**

Software for Macintosh

Archives of Macintosh software.

Anonymous FTP:
Address: **ftp.uu.net**
Path: **/systems/mac**

Address: **sumex-aim.stanford.edu**
Path: **/***

System Software

This is the place for discussion about all aspects of the Macintosh system software (such as Finder and Multifinder), as well as working with disks, what to do about viruses, and on and on.

Usenet:
Newsgroup: **comp.sys.mac.system**

A
B
C
D
E
F
G
H
I
J
K
L
M
N
O
P
Q
R
S
T
U
V
W
X
Y
Z

SOFTWARE: PC

Applications

Discussion about all types of DOS applications. The **.dbase** newsgroup is for dBase applications; **.wpcorp** is for WordPerfect products; **.word** is for word processing in general; and **.apps** is for any and all PC applications.

Usenet:
Newsgroup: **bit.listserv.dbase-l**
Newsgroup: **bit.listserv.wpcorp-l**
Newsgroup: **bit.mailserv.word-pc**
Newsgroup: **comp.os.msdos.apps**

Archives

These Usenet newsgroups contain information about archive sites around the Internet from which you can download programs via Anonymous FTP. The **.announce** newsgroup is moderated and contains announcements regarding DOS archives. The **.d** group is for the discussion of related topics. This is a good place to ask where a particular program is available.

Usenet:
Newsgroup: **comp.archives.msdos.announce**
Newsgroup: **comp.archives.msdos.d**
Newsgroup: **comp.binaries.ibm.pc.archives**

Binaries

These newsgroups contain binaries (executable DOS programs) ready to download and run, as well as information about binaries. The **.d** newsgroup is for discussion only. The **.wanted** group is the place to ask if anyone has a particular program.

Usenet:
Newsgroup: **comp.binaries.ibm.pc**
Newsgroup: **comp.binaries.ibm.pc.d**
Newsgroup: **comp.binaries.ibm.pc.wanted**

Demo Software

A forum devoted to all aspects of creating and using demos: programs that showcase the skills of the programmer and the capabilties of the hardware. As you will see, demo-ing is a well-developed, popular pastime. Sit in with the pros and learn how to show off with flair. (Video programmers: keep an eye out for the Mode X frequently asked question list and learn the secrets of VGA programming.)

Usenet:
Newsgroup: **comp.sys.ibm.pc.demos**

Games

If God didn't want us to use our PCs for games, he wouldn't have given us so many game discussion groups. The **.games** and **.misc** newsgroups are for general talk about all types of PC games: for DOS, Windows and OS/2. The **.announce** group is moderated and contains announcements of interest to the PC games community. Look for the PC Games frequently asked question list, posted regularly to this group. The FAQ is also available by Anonymous FTP. The other groups are for particular types of games (**.rpg** means role-playing games).

Usenet:
Newsgroup: **comp.sys.ibm.pc.games**
Newsgroup: **comp.sys.ibm.pc.games.action**
Newsgroup: **comp.sys.ibm.pc.games.adventure**
Newsgroup: **comp.sys.ibm.pc.games.announce**
Newsgroup: **comp.sys.ibm.pc.games.flight-sim**
Newsgroup: **comp.sys.ibm.pc.games.misc**
Newsgroup: **comp.sys.ibm.pc.games.rpg**
Newsgroup: **comp.sys.ibm.pc.games.strategic**

KEEP UP ON THE NEWEST AND COOLEST IN THE PC GAME WORLD. READ THE **comp.sys.ibm.pc.games.*** NEWSGROUPS.

TCP/IP

TCP/IP is the glue that holds the Internet together. If you want to have your PC actually be on the Internet, it will have to run some type of TCP/IP software. This newsgroup is for discussion of the zillions and zillions of technical considerations that are unavoidably relevant. A good way to start is by reading the FAQ list, which is posted regularly to the newsgroup and is avaiable from the FTP site. Don't get discouraged: all things come to those who think.

Usenet:
Newsgroup: **comp.protocols.tcp-ip.ibmpc**

SOFTWARE: UNIX

Calendar of Days

A large list of important days and holidays that you can view or use as input for the Unix calendar program.

Anonymous FTP:
Address: **ftp.spies.com**
Path: **/Library/Document/calendar.dat**

Gopher:
Name: Internet Wiretap
Address: **wiretap.spies.com**
Choose: **Wiretap Online Library**
  | **Assorted Documents**
  | **Calendar of Days (Holidays, Anniv, etc.)**

con

con is a perl script that facilitates connecting to another site with FTP, mail, Telnet, rlogin/rsh, ping, traceroute, finger and talk. It was written so users wouldn't have to have a mess of aliases and functions just so they could easily connect to a machine in one of the ways described above. Instead, all this info is contained in one file, and **con** makes intelligent guesses on what you want to do.

Anonymous FTP:
Address: **athene.uni-paderborn.de**
Path: **/news/comp.sources.unix/volume26/con**

Address: **usc.edu**
Path:
  /archive/usenet/sources/comp.sources.unix/ volume26/con

delete/undelete

This is the MIT Athena delete/undelete package which allows users to undelete deleted files in Unix. The package replaces the standard Unix **rm** command and keeps a copy of each file users delete with it.

Anonymous FTP:
Address: **charon.mit.edu**
Path: **/pub/delete**

Address: **lth.se**
Path: **/pub/usenet/source.unix/volume22/undel2**

The Internet will set you free.

Elm

The Elm mail program is a popular electronic mail agent used at most major universities and many other sites.

Anonymous FTP:
Address: **ftp.eu.net**
Path: **/mail/elm**

Address: **lth.se**
Path: **/pub/mail/elm**

Elvis

A clone of vi, the standard Unix editor, available with source for BSD Unix, AT&T SysV Unix, SCO Xenix, Minix, MS-DOS, Atari TOS and others.

Anonymous FTP:
Address: **aeneas.mit.edu**
Path: **/pub/gnu/elvis-1***

Address: **sunsite.unc.edu**
Path: **/pub/gnu/elvis-1***

Archie:
Pattern: **elvis-1***

Emacs Editor

Source code to an excellent text editor. Emacs is a widely used editor with many nifty features; however, it does consume some disk space.

Anonymous FTP:
Address: **aeneas.mit.edu**
Path: **/pub/gnu/emacs-18***

Address: **prep.ai.mit.edu**
Path: **/pub/gnu**

Address: **sol.cs.ruu.nl**
Path: /GNU/emacs

Address: **sunsite.unc.edu**
Path: **/pub/gnu/emacs-18***

Archie:
Pattern: **emacs-18**

A B C D E F G H I J K L M N O P Q R S T U V W X Y Z

Emacs = Life

Jumping into Emacs is one of the biggest intellectual commitments you will make in your life (and you won't even need a prenuptial agreement). Emacs creates a world of its own from which you can edit text files, write and debug programs, read the Usenet news, and generally live high on the Unix hog. The source for Emacs is readily available, so you can look inside and customize it up the wazoo.

Fax-3 Fax Software

Group 3 fax transmission and reception services for a networked Unix system with faxmodem.

Anonymous FTP:
>   Address: **aeneas.mit.edu**
>   Path: **/pub/gnu/fax-3***

>   Address: **sunsite.unc.edu**
>   Path: **/pub/gnu/fax-3***

Archie:
>   Pattern: **fax-3**

FlexFAX

Facsimile software source code for Unix systems allowing sending, receiving and polled retrieval of faxes.

Anonymous FTP:
>   Address: **sgi.com**
>   Path: **/sgi/fax/v2.2.src.tar.Z**

gawk

gawk is the GNU version of **awk**, with a number of new features. **gawk** programs are often faster and more reliable than a comparable **awk** program.

Anonymous FTP:
>   Address: **cs.dal.ca**
>   Path: **/comp.archives/gawk**

>   Address: **prep.ai.mit.edu**
>   Path: **/pub/gnu/gawk-2.15.2.tar.gz**

>   Address: **prep.ai.mit.edu**
>   Path: **/pub/gnu/gawk-doc-2.15.2.tar.gz**

gcc

gcc is the GNU ANSI C compiler. It is compatible with the original **cc** and is widely used all over the world as a standard Unix C compiler.

Anonymous FTP:
>   Address: **prep.ai.mit.edu**
>   Path: **/pub/gnu/gcc-2.4.5.tar.gz**

>   Address: **sunsite.unc.edu**
>   Path: **/pub/gnu/gcc-2.4.5.tar.gz**

Ghostscript

Ghostscript is the GNU Postscript clone. If you need something done in PS, Ghostscript will do it for you.

Anonymous FTP:
>   Address: **prep.ai.mit.edu**
>   Path: **/pub/gnu/ghostscript-2.6.1.tar.gz**

>   Address: **relay.iunet.it**
>   Path: **/gnu/ghostscript**

GNU Archives

A large archive of software and source created by the GNU Project.

Anonymous FTP:
>   Address: **aeneas.mit.edu**
>   Path: **/pub/gnu/***

>   Address: **sunsite.unc.edu**
>   Path: **/pub/gnu/***

Archie:
>   Pattern: **gnu**

GNU C Compiler

A portable optimizing compiler that supports ANSI C, C++ and Objective C languages, and that can produce position-independent code for several types of CPUs.

Anonymous FTP:
>   Address: **aeneas.mit.edu**
>   Path: **/pub/gnu/gcc-2**

>   Address: **sunsite.unc.edu**
>   Path: **/pub/gnu/gcc-2**

Archie:
>   Pattern: **gcc-2**

GNU File Compression Utilities

The GNU compression utility that compresses files to a **.Z** extension, and the decompression utility that restores files to their original condition.

Anonymous FTP:
> Address: **garbo.uwasa.fi**
> Path: **/pub/pc/unix/gzip124.zip**

GNU Shell Utilities

A collection of Unix commands that are frequently run from the command line or in shell scripts.

Anonymous FTP:
> Address: **aeneas.mit.edu**
> Path: **/pub/gnu/shellutils***

> Address: **sunsite.unc.edu**
> Path: **/pub/gnu/shellutils***

Archie:
> Pattern: **shellutils***

GNU Software Search

Search and retrieve software from Project GNU, a large software project creating and freely distributing software.

Gopher:
> Name: Johns Hopkins University
> Address: **merlot.welch.jhu.edu**
> Choose: **Search and Retrieve Software**
> **| Search and Retrieve GNU Software**

gnuchess

gnuchess is a chess game for GNU systems. It comes with both ASCII and graphic X Window versions.

Anonymous FTP:
> Address: **prep.ai.mit.edu**
> Path: **/pub/gnu/gnuchess-3.1.tar.gz**

> Address: **prep.ai.mit.edu**
> Path: **/pub/gnu/gnuchess-4.0pl62.tar.gz**

> Address: **prep.ai.mit.edu**
> Path: **/pub/gnu/gnuchess-for-windows.tar.gz**

> Address: **relay.iunet.it**
> Path:
> **/disk0/comp.sources/misc/Volume22/**
> **gnuchess**

gnuplot

gnuplot is the GNU plotting/graphics package. Many university students use this useful utility.

Anonymous FTP:
> Address: **cs.huji.il**
> Path: **/pub/graphics/gnuplot**

> Address: **prep.ai.mit.edu**
> Path: **/pub/gnu/gnuplot3.5.tar.gz**

HENSA Software Archive

Higher Education National Software Archive (HENSA) for Unix systems.

Gopher:
> Name: Hensa PD Software Archive
> Address: **unix.hensa.ac.uk**

Mail:
> Address: **archive@unix.hensa.ac.uk**
> Body: **help**

Internationalized xgopher

A Sun-4 binary package of the internationalized xgopher client that allows X Window to use Japanese and other multibyte characters.

Anonymous FTP:
> Address: **ftp.cs.keio.jp**
> Path: **/pub/inet/gopher/JAPANESE/***

joe Editor

joe stands for "Joe's own editor". It is designed for beginning Unix users and is simple to use.

Anonymous FTP:
> Address: **ftp.germany.eu.net**
> Path: **/pub/applications/textproc/editors**

> Address: **keos.helsinki.fi**
> Path: **/pub/archives/alt.sources/joe**

A
B
C
D
E
F
G
H
I
J
K
L
M
N
O
P
Q
R
S
T
U
V
W
X
Y
Z

> Is Emacs too much of a commitment?
>
> Is **vi** too much for your corpus callosum?
>
> Try **joe**, a Unix text editor for beginners.

Kterm

Kterm is an X.11 terminal emulator that can handle Japanese, Chinese and Korean text. Kterm comes as C source code for Unix X Window workstations.

Anonymous FTP:
    Address: **bash.cc.keio.ac.jp**
    Path: **/pub/mirror/X11-contrib/kterm***

    Address: **export.lcs.mit.edu**
    Path: **/contrib/kterm***

less

less is a paging program similar to the standard Unix **more** program. Named **less** as a play on the name **more**, **less** actually provides more functionality than **more**. In other words, **less** is more.

Anonymous FTP:
    Address: **lth.se**
    Path: **/pub/usenet/source.unix/volume16/less5**

    Address: **sun.soe.clarkson.edu**
    Path: **/pub/src/less**

Multiverse

X Window-based multiuser graphical environment with sample worlds, complete with source.

Anonymous FTP:
    Address: **ftp.u.washington.edu**
    Path: **/public/virtual-worlds/multiverse/***

nenscript

Format an ASCII file and convert it to Postscript. nenscript will beautify your ASCII printouts. This is great for printing source code.

Anonymous FTP:
    Address: **dutepp0.et.tudelft.nl**
    Path: **/pub/Unix/PostScript/nenscript.tar.Z**

    Address: **walton.maths.tcd.ie**
    Path: **/src/misc/enscript**

nn

nn, which stands for No News (is good news), is a replacement for the standard Unix newsreader **rn. nn** makes the user sift through as little material as possible and is a robust and highly configurable newsreader.

Anonymous FTP:
    Address: **ee.utah.edu**
    Path: **/nn**

    Address: **lth.se**
    Path: **/pub/usenet/source.unix/volume22/nn6.4**

Oleo

An excellent spreadsheet program for X Window and character-based terminals. Oleo can generate embedded PostScript renditions of spreadsheets.

Anonymous FTP:
    Address: **aeneas.mit.edu**
    Path: **/pub/gnu/oleo***

    Address: **sunsite.unc.edu**
    Path: **/pub/gnu/oleo***

Archie:
    Pattern: **oleo**

Perl

Perl (for Practical Extraction and Report Language) is a very popular replacement for the **awk** and **sed** text formatting languages.

Comment: The convex site doesn't store the source code, but does have many scripts and a tutorial on how to use Perl.

Anonymous FTP:
    Address: **convex.com**
    Path: **/pub/perl**

    Address: **prep.ai.mit.edu**
    Path: **/pub/gnu/perl-4.036.tar.gz**

Perl: The Ultimate Programming Language
(sort of)

Perl is the holy grail of programming languages (at least for a few years) -- powerful enough to do just about anything you want; obtuse enough to collect a cult-like band of followers; and complex enough to challenge even the most talented of hackers. If you like programming, if you like Unix, and if you know how to program the shell, then Perl is for you.

As Socrates once said:

System managers love Perl.

Everybody loves system managers.

Therefore, everybody loves Perl.

Perhaps another way to put it is that Perl is to the 1990s, what APL was to the 1970s.

Pine

The Pine mailer is a popular mail program.

Anonymous FTP:
Address: **emx.cc.utexas.edu**
Path: **/pub/mnt/source/mail/pine**

Address: **lth.se**
Path: **/pub/mail/pine**

Pine Mailer Demo

Try out an almost full-featured version of the Pine mailer program. This demo package allows the user to send mail messages for demonstration purposes.

Telnet:
Address: **demo.cac.washington.edu**
Login: **pinedemo**

procmail

procmail is a filtering package for incoming and outgoing mail messages. Some mailers have their own packages built in, but you can use **procmail** externally.

Anonymous FTP:
Address: **ftp.eu.net**
Path: **/pub/mail/procmail.tar.gz**

Address: **lth.se**
Path:
/pub/netnews/sources.misc/volume28/procmail

pty

pty is a neat program that allows you to run processes on a pseudo-tty (a **pty**). Like **screen**, processes running in a **pty** will continue to run after you log out.

Anonymous FTP:
Address: **archive.cis.ohio-state.edu**
Path: **/pub/comp.sources.unix/Volume23**

Address: **lth.se**
Path: **/pub/usenet/sources.unix.volume25/pty4**

rn/trn

rn (for Read News) and **trn** (for Threaded Read News) are widely used newsreaders on the Internet. **trn** is the threaded version of **rn**.

Anonymous FTP:
Address: **archive.cis.ohio-state.edu**
Path: **/pub/rn/trn**

Address: **lth.se**
Path: **/pub/usenet/source.unix/volume25/trn**

screen

screen is a program that allows Unix users to split a vt100-style terminal screen into multiple sessions and hot-key between them. **screen** works great with dial-up connections and terminal emulation.

Anonymous FTP:
Address: **aeneas.mit.edu**
Path: **/pub/gnu/screen-3***

Address: **faui43.informatik.uni-erlangen.de**
Path: **/pub/utilities/screen/screen-3.5.2.tar.gz**

Address: **prep.ai.mit.edu**
Path: **/pub/gnu/screen-3.5.2.tar.gz**

Address: **sunsite.unc.edu**
Path: **/pub/gnu/screen-3***

Archie:
Pattern: **screen-3***

A
B
C
D
E
F
G
H
I
J
K
L
M
N
O
P
Q
R
S
T
U
V
W
X
Y
Z

Shells: bash

The "Bourne again shell" is a great improvement over **sh** and is ideal for interactive work.

Comment: **.gz** requires **gzip** to uncompress. **bash-1.13** is due out soon.

Anonymous FTP:
Address: **cs.ubc.ca**
Path: **/pub/unix/shells/bash**

Address: **prep.ai.mit.edu**
Path: **/pub/gnu/bash-1.12.tar.gz**

Shells: pdksh

A public domain version of the popular **ksh**.

Anonymous FTP:
Address: **keos.helsinki.fi**
Path: **/pub/archives/comp.sources.misc/ksh**

Address: **usc.edu**
Path:
/archive/usenet/sources/comp.sources.misc/ volume34

Shells: rc

rc is a simple, elegant shell written for people who want speed and efficiency in their shell scripts without all the interactive glitter.

Anonymous FTP:
Address: **archone.tamu.edu**
Path: **/pub/rc/rc-1.4.tar.Z**

Address: **keos.helsinki.fi**
Path: **/pub/archives/comp.sources.misc/rc**

Unix users: Do you want a sleek, well-designed shell created for smart people who like to program?

Try rc.

Shells: tcsh

tcsh is a vast improvement over **csh** for interactive work. It is backwards compatible with the C Shell but includes command and filename completion.

Anonymous FTP:
Address: **midway.uchicago.edu**
Path: **/pub/unix/tcsh**

Address: **tesla.ee.cornell.edu**
Path: **/pub/tcsh**

Shells: zsh

zsh is often regarded as the best interactive Unix shell available.

Anonymous FTP:
Address: **princeton.edu**
Path: **/pub/zsh/zsh2.3.1.tar.Z**

Address: **relay.iunet.it**
Path: **/disk0/unix/shells/zsh**

Smalltalk

The GNU implementation of Smalltalk, the original object-oriented programming language, complete with source code.

Anonymous FTP:
Address: **aeneas.mit.edu**
Path: **/pub/gnu/smalltalk***

Address: **sunsite.unc.edu**
Path: **/pub/gnu/smalltalk***

Archie:
Pattern: **smalltalk**

Tgif Image Drawing Software

Tgif is a drawing tool for X Window systems that supports hierarchical construction of drawings.

Anonymous FTP:
Address: **cs.ucla.edu**
Path: **/pub/tgif/***

Top

Top is a Unix system administration program that provides continual reports on the state of a system, including a list of the most CPU-intensive processes.

A
B
C
D
E
F
G
H
I
J
K
L
M
N
O
P
Q
R
S
T
U
V
W
X
Y
Z

Anonymous FTP:
Address: **eecs.nwu.edu**
Path: **/pub/top**

X Window Source Archives

A huge collection of X Window source code and programs.

Anonymous FTP:
Address: **export.lcs.mit.edu**
Path: **/contrib**

Address: **ftp.uu.net**
Path: **/pub/window-sys/X/contrib**

xgrabsc—X Window Utility

xgrabsc allows X Window users to capture rectangular screen images and store them in graphic files.

Anonymous FTP:
Address: **kappa.rice.edu**
Path: **/X11R4/bin/xgrabsc**

Address: **relay.iunet.it**
Path: **/disk0/comp.sources/x/Volume9**

xv

This interactive image viewer for X Window will allow you to display and manipulate many different image formats and convert between them.

Anonymous FTP:
Address: **relay.iunet.it**
Path: **/disk0/comp.sources/x/Volume10**

Address: **src.doc.ic.ac.uk**
Path: **/usenet/comp.sources.x/volume10**

xwd, xwud (X Window Dump/Undump Image Utilities)

These two programs are X Window utilities that allow you to dump and undump an image to a file to be viewed later.

Anonymous FTP:
Address: **bongo.cc.utexas.edu**
Path: **/source/X11R5/mit/clients/xwud**

Address: **cs.tut.fi**
Path: **/pub/src/X/X11R5/mit/clients/xwud**

ytalk

ytalk is similar to the Unix **talk** and **ntalk** programs, but **ytalk** allows Unix users to talk with more than one person at the same time. It is compatible with both **talk** and **ntalk**, so remote users that you **ytalk** to don't have to have **ytalk** themselves.

Anonymous FTP:
Address: **bongo.cc.utexas.edu**
Path: **/pub/ytalk/***

Address: **sun.soe.clarkson.edu**
Path: **/pub/src/ytalk/***

Happy Talk With ytalk

We love talking to friends all over the Internet, and our favorite program is **ytalk** (a replacement for **talk** and **ntalk**).

If your Unix system does not already have **ytalk**, ask your system manager to install it, or download the program and do the job yourself.

For more information, see *The Internet Complete Reference.*

SOFTWARE: UTILITIES

ARJ Utilities

Utilities to un-ARJ those .ARJ files, for Unix, VMS, IBM-PC, Mac and Amiga.

Anonymous FTP:
Address: **ftp.rahul.net**
Path: **/pub/atman/UTLCD-preview/unarjers/***

This is the first book of the rest of your life.

ASCII Table

The complete ASCII code table, including control character abbreviations. ASCII stands for the American Standard Code for Information Interchange.

Gopher:
    Name: University of Surrey
    Address: **gopher.cpe.surrey.ac.uk**
    Choose: **Misc Technical notes**
      | ASCII table

Automatic Login Executor (ALEX)

A slick C-Shell program that you can run on a Unix system to automate your Internet explorations. This amazing collection of shell scripts was written by a high school student in ten weeks.

Anonymous FTP:
    Address: **dftsrv.gsfc.nasa.gov**
    Path: **/alex/csh-alex/***

Benchmark Software

Results and summaries of benchmark programs that have been run on various computers, including Dhrystone 1.1, hanoi.c and heapsort.c.

Anonymous FTP:
    Address: **ftp.spies.com**
    Path: **/Library/Techdoc/Bench/***

Gopher:
    Name: Internet Wiretap
    Address: **wiretap.spies.com**
    Choose: **Wiretap Online Library**
      | Technical Information
      | Benchmarks

Chinese Telnet

A modified version of the telnet program for the PC. This version uses the eighth bit of every byte to be able to display Chinese characters.

Anonymous FTP:
    Address: **ftp.ccu.edu.tw**
    Path: **/pub/ncsa/***

    Address: **moers2.edu.tw**
    Path: **/chinese-pub/ncsa/***

Chinese Text Viewer

A shareware system for the PC that allows you to view Chinese text and documents.

Anonymous FTP:
    Address: **ftp.ccu.edu.tw**
    Path: **/pub/chinese-sys/***

    Address: **moers2.edu.tw**
    Path: **/chinese-pub/chinese-sys/***

Displaying Chinese Documents

Instructions for displaying Chinese documents on a PC, Macintosh or X Window system.

Gopher:
    Name: National Chung Cheng University
    Address: **gopher.ccu.edu.tw**
    Choose: **About the Gopher | About this Gopher**

Displaying Hangul (Korean) Documents

Instructions for displaying Hangul, or Korean, documents on a PC, Macintosh or X Window system.

Anonymous FTP:
    Address: **ftp.kaist.ac.kr**
    Path: **/pub/hangul/FAQ**

    Address: **ftp.kaist.ac.kr**
    Path: **/pub/news/Hangulnews.eng**

Displaying Japanese Documents

Instructions for displaying Japanese documents on a PC, Macintosh or X Window system.

Gopher:
    Name: Keio University, Science and Technology
    Address: **bash.cc.keio.ac.jp**
    Choose: **Japanese | How to read Japanese files**

DOS uudecode

A DOS version of the popular Unix **uudecode** program.

Anonymous FTP:
    Address: **oak.oakland.edu**
    Path: **/pub/msdos/decode**

Free Compilers

A list of free compilers and compiler building tools.

Anonymous FTP:
    Address: **wombat.doc.ic.ac.uk**
    Path: **/pub/FreeCompilers.gz**

Gopher:
    Name: Imperial College
    Address: **wombat.doc.ic.ac.uk**
    Choose: **Free Compilers list**

Gzip

New compression program free of known patents and copyrights, used on all archived GNU software, and becoming increasingly popular on many archive sites. Used to compress and uncompress **.gz** files.

Anonymous FTP:
Address: **aeneas.mit.edu**
Path: **/pub/gnu/gzip***

Address: **athene.uni-paderborn.de**
Path: **/unix/gnu/gzip**

Address: **prep.ai.mit.edu**
Path: **/pub/gnu/gzip-1.2.4.tar.gz**

Address: **sunsite.unc.edu**
Path: **/pub/gnu/gzip***

Archie:
Pattern: **gzip***

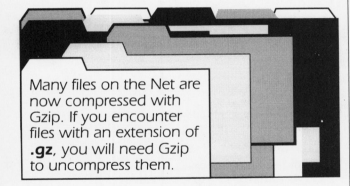

Many files on the Net are now compressed with Gzip. If you encounter files with an extension of **.gz**, you will need Gzip to uncompress them.

Hangul (Korean) Software Tools

Emulators, editors, and fonts to read and compose in Hangul, the Korean language.

Anonymous FTP:
Address: **ftp.kaist.ac.kr**
Path: **/pub/hangul***

Ispell

Interactive Unix spelling corrector based on the "ITS SPELL" program and available with source.

Anonymous FTP:
Address: **aeneas.mit.edu**
Path: **/pub/gnu/ispellz***

Address: **sunsite.unc.edu**
Path: **/pub/gnu/ispell***

Archie:
Pattern: **ispell**

OS/2 Utilities

Utility programs for OS/2, including replacements for CMD.EXE, Phil Katz' PKZIP for OS/2, and other useful programs.

Anonymous FTP:
Address: **oak.oakland.edu**
Path: **/pub/misc/os2**

PC Archiving Utilities

Collection of the ARJ, LHA, ZIP and ZOO common PC archive programs for MS-DOS.

Anonymous FTP:
Address: **ftp.ulowell.edu**
Path: **/msdos/Archivers/***

PC Utilities

Lots of PC utilities and files from *PC Magazine*'s Interactive Reader Service.

Anonymous FTP:
Address: **ftp.cso.uiuc.edu**
Path: **/pc/pcmag/***

PC Video Card Drivers

Get the latest version drivers for Diamond Video, ATI and many other popular video graphics cards.

Anonymous FTP:
Address: **extreme.cica.indiana.edu**
Path: **/pub/pc/win3/drivers/video/***

Source Code for Unix Utilities

Source code for Unix and X Window utilities such as **uuencode**, **uudecode**, **xxencode**, **xxdecode**, **whois**, **uucat** and **more**.

Anonymous FTP:
Address: **oak.oakland.edu**
Path: **/pub/misc/unix**

A B C D E F G H I J K L M N O P Q R **S** T U V W X Y Z

See What's Inside

Have you ever wondered how all those famous Unix utilities actually work? Download the source code and take a look for yourself.

**Secrets are for weenies.
Unix is cool.**

VESA Driver

A universal VESA driver for PCs.

Anonymous FTP:
> Address: **wuarchive.wustl.edu**
> Path: **/systems/msdos/garbo/
> graphics/svgakt41.zip**

Visual Basic Runtime Modules

Many newer shareware programs require you to have certain runtime files. Programs written with Microsoft Visual Basic require runtimes called VBRUN100.EXE, VBRUN200.EXE or VBRUN300.EXE. Here are a few sources for these files.

Comment: Substitute the **?** in the paths below with **1**, **2**, or **3**, depending on the runtime version you need.

Anonymous FTP:
> Address: **gatekeeper.dec.com**
> Path: **/.2/micro/msdos/simtel20/
> windows3/vbrun?00.zip**

> Address: **swdsrv.edvz.inivie.ac.at**
> Path: **/pc/dos/windows3/vbrun?00.zip**

Archie:
> Pattern: **vbrun?00.zip**

VMS Utilities

Collection of various utilities for VMS, including **diff**, **grep**, **more** and others.

Anonymous FTP:
> Address: **ftp.cs.widener.edu**
> Path: **/pub/vms/***

WinPkt

WinPkt is a packet driver interface between Windows 3 Enhanced mode applications and a real packet driver. This is an assembly language program.

Anonymous FTP:
> Address: **bongo.cc.utexas.edu**
> Path: **/microlib/dos/network/.cap/winpkt.zip**

> Address: **oxy.edu**
> Path: **/public/msdos_programs/winpkt.zip**

SOFTWARE: WINDOWS

InfoPop

A hypertext guide to using the Internet in a clever Microsoft Windows help file format. Includes some history, as well as a list of resources.

Anonymous FTP:
> Address: **ftp.gmu.edu**
> Path: **/pub/library/ipwin112.exe**

Archie:
> Pattern: **infopop**

Unix uudecode for Windows

A graphical Windows-based version of the popular, and very necessary, Unix **uudecode** program.

Anonymous FTP:
> Address: **ftp.cica.indiana.edu**
> Path: **/pub/pc/win3/util**

Windows Utilities

Applications, tips, utilities, drivers and bitmaps for Windows.

Anonymous FTP:
> Address: **ftp.cica.indiana.edu**
> Path: **/pub/pc/win3/***

> Address: **wuarchive.wustl.edu**
> Path: **/systems/ibmpc/win3/***

SPACE

Aeronautics and Space Articles

NASA articles, space launch list, Japanese aircraft code names, shuttle disaster article, space acronyms and other items of interest.

Anonymous FTP:
Address: **ftp.spies.com**
Path: **/Library/Article/Aero/***

Gopher:
Name: Internet Wiretap
Address: **wiretap.spies.com**
Choose: **Wiretap Online Library**
 | Articles | Aeronautics and Space

Space images are very popular items. This one is **spacewalk** and it's available in a number of formats, including GIF, JPEG and LZH. Often, archive files are stored on Unix computers where long filenames are allowed. If you're looking for files to download to PCs, you may want to look for shorter names. For example, this image exists in many archives as **spacewal.gif** due to DOS' eight character limitation. Using Archie to search for **spacewalk** won't find **spacewal**.

Astro/Space Acronyms

An acronym list, useful for translating commonly appearing acronyms in the space-related Usenet newsgroups.

Anonymous FTP:
Address: **ftp.spies.com**
Path: **/Library/Article/Aero/space.ac**

Gopher:
Name: Internet Wiretap
Address: **wiretap.spies.com**
Choose: **Wiretap Online Library**
 | Articles
 | Aeronautics and Space
 | Astro/Space Frequently Seen Acronyms

EnviroNet

A menu-driven, user-friendly space environment resource with space data as text, graphics and tables.

Telnet:
Address: **envnet.gsfc.nasa.gov**
Login: **envnet**
Password: **henniker**

European Space Agency

The Data Dissemination Network of the European Space Agency (ESA). Offers information retrieval services, prototype international directory, and other information and services.

Telnet:
Address: **esrin.esa.it**

FIFE Information System

Scientific data from satellites, space flights, and other databases.

Telnet:
Address: **pldsg3.gsfc.nasa.gov**
Login: **fifeuser**

Frequently Asked Questions About Space

Get answers to the most frequently asked questions (FAQs) regarding NASA, spaceflight, and astrophysics.

Anonymous FTP:
Address: **ames.arc.nasa.gov**
Path: **/pub/SPACE/FAQ**

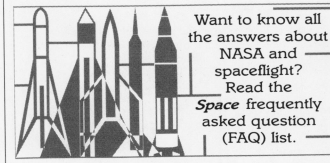

Want to know all the answers about NASA and spaceflight? Read the *Space* frequently asked question (FAQ) list.

General Space Talk

Talk, talk, talk about everything under the sun (and the sun as well). Discuss all manner of space-oriented topics with aficionados around the world.

Usenet:
Newsgroup: **sci.space**

Goddard Space Flight Center

Contains lots of news, images, pictures, information and other resources connected with NASA and the Goddard Space Flight Center.

Gopher:
Name: NASA Goddard Space Flight Center
Address: **gopher.gsfc.nasa.gov**

Hubble Space Telescope

The Space Telescope Electronic Information System (STEIS) contains information for Hubble Space Telescope proposers and observers. It offers documents, status reports, plans and weekly summaries. Get the daily update on the scheduled events and the outcome of experiments with the beleaguered Hubble Space Telescope.

Anonymous FTP:
Address: **stsci.edu**
Path: **/stsci/steis/***

Gopher:
Name:
Space Telescope Electronic Information System
Address: **stsci.edu**

Telnet:
Address: **stinfo.hq.eso.org**
Login: **stinfo**

Lunar and Planetary Institute

The Institute is near the NASA Johnson Space Center and includes a computing center, extensive collections of lunar and planetary data, an image processing facility, an extensive library, a publishing facility, and facilities for workshops and conferences. Current topics include the origin and early evolution of the solar system; studies of the moon, meteorites, and the Earth; and the outer solar system, with emphasis on studies of icy satellites.

Telnet:
Address: **lpi.jsc.nasa.gov**
Login: **lpi**

NASA Extragalactic Database (NED)

At present, NED contains extensive cross-identifications for over 200,000 objects—galaxies, quasars, infrared and radio sources, etc. NED provides positions, names and basic data (e.g., magnitudes, redshifts), as well as bibliographic references, abstracts and notes.

Telnet:
Address: **ned.ipac.caltech.edu**
Login: **ned**

NASA News

Up-to-date information on the status of current spacecraft in space and other NASA happenings. Find out about the new discoveries made with the space-based Hubble telescope and unmanned probes launched towards distant planets and galaxies.

Finger:
Address: **nasanews@space.mit.edu**

Space shuttle images are widely available on the Net. This one is called **shuttlelaunch.gif** and you can find it at Northern Arizona University (**ftp.nau.edu**) in the directory **/graphics/gif/digi**. Don't forget that when you download a file with a long name like this to a PC, the filename will be shortened.

nasalogo is available in GIF, HQX and MAC formats from the University of Western Ontario (**ftp.engrg.uwo.ca**) and NASA (**ames.arc.nasa.gov**). At UWO, it's in the directory **/pub/gifpics**. At NASA, it's in **/pub/SPACE/MAGELLAN**.

NASA NEWS

NASA (the National Aeronautics and Space Administration) is always up to something. Now you can be in the loop. Just finger the magic address (**nasanews@space.mit.edu**) and get the straight poop from the official American space people. Be aware, though, that this is *official* NASA info, so you may not find out much about the government's coverup of secret alien contacts.

Hint for Unix users: If the output goes by too fast, pipe it to a paging program. The one that works best for us is **less**. Try:
finger nasanews@space.mit.edu | less

If this doesn't work, press CTRL-S to pause the display, and CTRL-Q to continue.

NASA Spacelink

History, current events, projects and plans at NASA.

Telnet:
>   Address: **spacelink.msfc.nasa.gov**

NASDA

The National Space Development Agency of Japan (NASDA) is the Japanese equivalent of NASA.

Telnet:
>   Address: **nsaeoc.eoc.nasda.go.jp**
>   Login: **nasdadir**

News About Space

Keep current on the final frontier. Read all the latest news about space, astronomy and spaceflight.

Usenet:
>   Newsgroup: **clari.tw.space**
>   Newsgroup: **sci.space.news**

NOAA Earth Systems Data Directory

The NESDD is an information resource for identification, location and overview descriptions of earth-science data sets (data from satellites).

Telnet:
>   Address: **esdim1.nodc.noaa.gov**
>   Login: **noaadir**

>   Address: **nodc.nodc.noaa.gov**
>   Login: **noaadir**

NSSDC's Online Data & Information Service

NODIS provides menu-based access to data and information services provided by NSSDC and by the Space Physics Data Facility. Primarily through the multidisciplinary Master Directory, NODIS also describes and enables electronic access (E-links) to data/information/systems remote to NSSDC.

Telnet:
>   Address: **nssdc.gsfc.nasa.gov**
>   Login: **nodis**

Politics of Space

Do people belong in space? Is all the money worth it? What should we be doing and who should we be doing it with? Discuss non-technical issues pertaining to space exploration. Wax philosophic without having to get your feet wet.

Usenet:
>   Newsgroup: **talk.politics.space**

SEDS

SEDS (Students for the Exploration and Development of Space) is a student club devoted to the discussion and study of space. Meet people from SEDS chapters around the world. Find out all the latest space news and what SEDS members are up to.

Usenet:
>   Newsgroup: **bit.listserv.seds-l**
>   Newsgroup: **bit.listserv.sedsnews**

Smithsonian Astrophysical Observatory (ASCinfo)

The ASCinfo system is an online bulletin board service that makes a collection of ASC documentation files available to the astronomical community. ASCinfo

A B C D E F G H I J K L M N O P Q R S T U V W X Y Z

resides at the Smithsonian Astrophysical Observatory and is accessible to any user over the Internet.

Telnet:
Address: **asc.harvard.edu**
Login: **ascinfo**

Southwest Data Display and Analysis System

SDDAS offers scientific data and analysis services. It also provides high resolution graphic servers, including X Window servers for data displays.

Telnet:
Address: **espsun.space.swri.edu 540**

Space Digest

The international Space Digest archive site.

Anonymous FTP:
Address: **julius.cs.qub.ac.uk**
Path: **/pub/SpaceDigestArchive**

Space Newsletter

Selection of newsletters about the final frontier, including *Space News*, *Satscan* and *Biosphere*.

Anonymous FTP:
Address: **nigel.msen.com**
Path: **/pub/newsletters/Space/***

Excerpt from the Net...

```
Newsgroup: talk.politics.space
Subject: NASA knows about Nazi Moon Base. Important.
```

```
                    GERMAN MOON BASE, 1942
    ================================================
```

The Germans landed on the Moon in 1942 using larger exo-atmospheric rocket saucers.

The rocket craft was built in diameters of 15 and 50 meters, and the turbine powered craft was designed as an inter-planetary exploration vehicle. The craft had a diameter of 60 meters, had 10 stories of crew compartments, and stood 45 meters high.

Everything NASA has told the world about the Moon is a lie and it was done to keep the exclusivity of the club from joinings by the third world countries.

In my extensive research of dissident American theories about the physical conditions on the Moon, I have proven beyond the shadow of a doubt that there is atmosphere, water and vegetation, and that man does not need a space suit to walk on the Moon. A pair of jeans, a pullover and sneakers are just about enough. All these physical conditions make it a lot easier to build a Moon base.

Ever since their first day of landing on the Moon, the Germans started boring and tunneling under the surface, and by the end of the war there was a small Nazi research base on the Moon. A free energy tachyon drive craft was used after 1944 to haul people, material, and the first robots to the construction site on the Moon.

After the end of the war in May 1945, the Germans continued their space effort from their south polar colony of Neu Schwabenland. When Russians and Americans secretly landed jointly on the Moon in the early fifties with their own saucers, they spent their first night there as guests of the Nazi underground base.

In the sixties a massive Russian/American base had been built on the Moon, and it now has a population of 40,000 people. I have discovered a photograph of their underground space control center there, and I am working to make it available in GIF format.

This is very sensitive information and I am sharing it with you at great risk. If you intend to save this information or share it with others, please delete my name and site location from the headers.

Space Shuttle

Keep up to date on what the space shuttle is doing and what we are doing with the space shuttle.

Usenet:
Newsgroup: **sci.space.shuttle**

What in heaven's name is going on in the space shuttle?

Read **sci.space.shuttle** and keep up with the only government employees who are paid to get high.

SpaceMet

A science and space-related BBS with a heavy interest in space exploration. Includes information from NASA.

Telnet:
Address: **spacemet.phast.umass.edu**

SpaceNews

A weekly finger report with information on current and upcoming shuttle missions, as well as other current information of interest regarding NASA, space and space flight.

Finger:
Address: **magliaco@pilot.njin.net**

SPORTS AND ATHLETICS

.44 Magnum

A variety of recommendations and comments about bullets, powders and loads for the .44 Magnum.

Anonymous FTP:
Address: **ftp.spies.com**
Path: **/Library/Article/Misc/magnum.44**

Gopher:
Name: Internet Wiretap
Address: **wiretap.spies.com**
Choose: **Wiretap Online Library**
| Articles | Misc | Magnum .44 Summary

Aikido Dojos Throughout the World

A list of hundreds of Aikido dojos worldwide. Dojos in the U.S. are listed first, followed by dojos in other countries. The list covers all styles and affiliations of this popular Japanese martial art.

Anonymous FTP:
Address: **iuvax.cs.indiana.edu**
Path: **/pub/aikido/***

Address: **moose.cs.indiana.edu**
Path: **/pub/aikido/***

Australian Rules Football

A summary of the most frequently applied rules in Australian rules football.

Anonymous FTP:
Address: **ftp.spies.com**
Path: **/Library/Article/Sports/rules.afl**

Gopher:
Name: Internet Wiretap
Address: **wiretap.spies.com**
Choose: **Wiretap Online Library**
| Articles | Sports
| Summary of Rules for Australian Football

Australian Sporting News

Stay up-to-date with the latest Australian sporting events and results.

Gopher:
Name: MegaGopher
Address: **megasun.bch.umontreal.ca**
Choose: **Australiana - News, sport, FAQs, etc.**
about Australia | Australian sports news

Baseball Schedule

Get the day's game schedule for your favorite major league baseball teams. Enter **help** for help. Full schedules are also available.

Telnet:
Address: **culine.colorado.edu 862**

Baseball Scores

Get major league baseball scores by mail.

Mail:
Address: **jtchern@ocf.berkeley.edu**
Subject: **mlb**

A B C D E F G H I J K L M N O P Q R S T U V W X Y Z

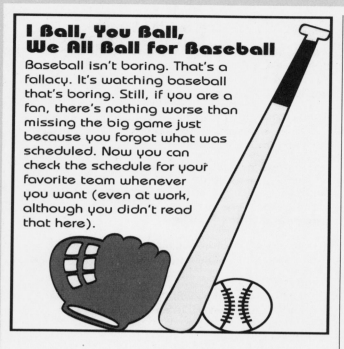

I Ball, You Ball, We All Ball for Baseball

Baseball isn't boring. That's a fallacy. It's watching baseball that's boring. Still, if you are a fan, there's nothing worse than missing the big game just because you forgot what was scheduled. Now you can check the schedule for your favorite team whenever you want (even at work, although you didn't read that here).

Bicycle Mailing List

Local, state and national bicycling issues, especially for Santa Cruz County, California. Public hearings and government meetings are announced and reported.

Internet mailing list:
List Address: **bikepeople@ce.ucsc.edu**
Subscription Address:
bikepeople-request@ce.ucsc.edu

Climbing

Open discussion about climbing techniques, specific climbs and competition announcements.

Usenet:
Newsgroup: **rec.climbing**

Cricket

Mailing list featuring the scoresheets of first class cricket matches and itineraries of the tours. The list is gatewayed to the Usenet newsgroup **rec.sport.cricket.scores**.

Listserv mailing list:
List Address: **cricket@vm1.nodak.edu**
Subscription Address: **listserv@vm1.nodak.edu**

Cycling

FAQs, interesting information, racing details, bike guides, technical hints, general tips and more from the world of cycling.

Anonymous FTP:
Address: **draco.acs.uci.edu**
Path: **/pub/rec.bicycles/***

Address: **rtfm.mit.edu**
Path:
/pub/usenet/news.answers/bicycles-faq/*

Address: **ugle.unit.no**
Path: **/local/biking/***

Cycling in Canada

Information, discussion groups, pictures, programs and more for cycling enthusiasts. This FTP site is in Canada and has great data about routes, rules and routines for biking in Canada (especially Nova Scotia).

Anonymous FTP:
Address: **biome.bio.dfo.ca**
Path: **/pub/cycling/***

Disc Sports

FAQs, archives, contact information, rules, championship history and more for Ultimate, Disc Golf and other disc-related sports.

Anonymous FTP:
Address: **ftp.cs.wisc.edu**
Path: **/pub/ultimate/***

Football Stadiums

A list of the U.S. football stadiums, their capacities and the teams that play there.

Anonymous FTP:
Address: **ftp.spies.com**
Path: **/Library/Article/Sports/stadium.lis**

Gopher:
Name: Internet Wiretap
Address: **wiretap.spies.com**
Choose: **Wiretap Online Library**
| **Articles**
| **Sports**
| **Stadium Listing**

Hiking

Articles and guides about hiking and the great outdoors. Includes hiking songs, a snakebite guide, campfire lore, water filtering information and other topics of interest to campers.

Anonymous FTP:
 Address: **ftp.spies.com**
 Path: **/Library/Article/Outdoors/***

Gopher:
 Name: Internet Wiretap
 Address: **wiretap.spies.com**
 Choose: **Wiretap Online Library**
 | **Articles**
 | **Backcountry and Outdoors**

Hockey Archive

Press releases, scores, GIF and JPEG images, standings, rosters and archives of college hockey mailing lists.

Anonymous FTP:
 Address: **andy.bgsu.edu**
 Path: **/pub/Hockey/***

Martial Arts

Archive of aikido-related material, including dojo addresses around the world.

Anonymous FTP:
 Address: **cs.ucsd.edu**
 Path: **/pub/aikido/***

NBA Schedule

Get the day's game schedule for your favorite NBA basketball teams. Enter **help** for help. Full schedules are also available.

Telnet:
 Address: **culine.colorado.edu 859**

NFL Schedule

Get the day's game schedule for your favorite NFL football teams. Enter **help** for help. Full schedules are also available.

Telnet:
 Address: **culine.colorado.edu 863**

NFL Scores/Standings/Lines

Get the current standings as well as the final scores to the weekend's games.

Finger:
 Address: **nfl@spam.wicat.com**
 Address: **nflline@spam.wicat.com**

NHL Schedule

Get the day's game schedule for your favorite NHL hockey teams. Enter **help** for help. Full schedules are also available.

Telnet:
 Address: **culine.colorado.edu 860**

Paddling

Terminology, river ratings, equipment information, safety guides, books and addresses for canoeing, kayaking and rafting.

Anonymous FTP:
 Address: **rtfm.mit.edu**
 Path: **/pub/usenet/news.answers/paddling-faq**

Scouting

Scouting material for both scouts and leaders, including campfire songs, games, history, world news, unit administration information and official policies.

Anonymous FTP:
 Address: **ftp.ethz.ch**
 Path: **/rec.scouting/***

 Address: **rtfm.mit.edu**
 Path: **/pub/usenet/news.answers/scouting/***

Scuba Diving

Equipment reviews, magazine list, buying guide, huge archives and lots of related material about scuba diving, snorkeling, dive travel and other underwater activities.

Anonymous FTP:
 Address: **ames.arc.nasa.gov**
 Path: **/pub/SCUBA/***

 Address: **rtfm.mit.edu**
 Path: **/pub/usenet/rec.answers/scuba-faq**

A B C D E F G H I J K L M N O P Q R **S** T U V W X Y Z

Immerse yourself in the world of scuba diving: there are some great FTP archives and an informative frequently asked question (FAQ) list just waiting for you.

Skating

Origins, equipment reviews, technique instructions, maintenance advice, FAQs, location lists and much more for in-line (rollerblading), roller figure, and speed skating.

Anonymous FTP:
    Address: **rtfm.mit.edu**
    Path: **/pub/usenet/news.answers/rec-skate-faq/***

Skiing

Get ski conditions and read frequently asked questions about skiing in Utah, Wyoming and Idaho.

Anonymous FTP:
    Address: **ski.utah.edu**
    Path: **/skiing**

Skydiving

FAQs about skydiving, learning to skydive, and the newsgroup **rec.skydiving**.

Anonymous FTP:
    Address: **rtfm.mit.edu**
    Path: **/pub/usenet/news.answers/skydiving-faq**

Soccer Rules

Rules of the game and a universal guide for referees, as authorized by FIFA, the governing body of international soccer.

Anonymous FTP:
    Address: **ftp.spies.com**
    Path: **/Library/Article/Sports/soccer.rul**

Gopher:
    Name: Internet Wiretap
    Address: **wiretap.spies.com**
    Choose: **Wiretap Online Library**
    | **Articles | Sports**
    | **FIFA Rules of Soccer**

Sports Articles

Stadium listings, rosters, results, schedules, rules, history and more about stadium sports.

Anonymous FTP:
    Address: **ftp.spies.com**
    Path: **/Library/Article/Sports/***

Gopher:
    Name: Internet Wiretap
    Address: **wiretap.spies.com**
    Choose: **Wiretap Online Library**
    | **Articles**
    | **Sports**

Sports Schedules

Easy access to professional football, hockey, basketball and baseball schedules from this single menu.

Gopher:
    Name: Ball State University
    Address: **gopher.bsu.edu**
    Choose: **Professional Sports Schedules**

Sports Statistics

Statistics for baseball (MLB), basketball (NBA), football (NFL), and hockey (NHL).

Anonymous FTP:
    Address: **wuarchive.wustl.edu**
    Path: **/doc/misc/sports/***

Windsurfing

Information on windsurfing at various areas in the United States. Get the scoop on windsurf shops, launch sites and conditions. You can also participate in lively discussions and download cool windsurfing bitmaps.

Anonymous FTP:
    Address: **lemming.uvm.edu**
    Path: **/rec.windsurfing**

The skydiving image on this page was found at the University of Florida (**ftp.eng.ufl.edu**) in the directory **/skydive/gifs**.

Wrestler List

A list of WWF and WCW wrestlers and their managers.

Anonymous FTP:
Address: **ftp.spies.com**
Path: **/Library/Article/Sports/wrestle.wwf**

Gopher:
Name: Internet Wiretap
Address: **wiretap.spies.com**
Choose: **Wiretap Online Library**
  | Articles | Sports
  | WWF and WCW Names and Managers

XV Commonwealth Games

Information about the Commonwealth Games—an international athletic competition.

Gopher:
Name: The Community Learning Network
Address: **cln.etc.bc.ca**
Choose: **The Community Learning Network (BC)**
  | Special Projects for the CLN (CLN.ETC)
  | XV Commonwealth Games - Online
    Youth and Ed

STAR TREK

Conventions and Memorabilia

Dress up funny and romp around with other people dressed up like *Star Trek* characters. Conventions are a great place to really experience Trekker fandom. Discover where to get a replica of that communicator you love or collect the one action figure you were missing from your set.

Usenet:
Newsgroup: **rec.arts.startrek.fandom**

> Ok, we know that you have a life – it's just that your life is built around Star Trek. Why waste your time with non-Trekkers? The only resonable place to hang out is **rec.arts.startrek.fandom**.

Future Technologists

You look back and laugh at old sci-fi from the '50s. How close are we getting to *Star Trek*? Speculate how our technological process compares with the technology dreamed up in the creative minds of *Star Trek* writers.

Usenet:
Newsgroup: **rec.arts.startrek.tech**

Games

Don't just watch *Star Trek*, live it! Command your own ship with Xtrek and match wits with the computer or go head to head (or torpedo to torpedo) with others like you on Netrek, the networking version of the game. Both newsgroups cover such topics as tactics, experiences and troubleshooting software.

Usenet:
Newsgroup: **alt.games.xtrek**
Newsgroup: **rec.games.netrek**

Klingons

Ignore the subtitles in the movies: learn to speak Klingon. Explore the culture that devoted fans have worked so hard to develop. Find a variety of interesting topics like Klingon love poetry, haiku, and thoughts on Kronos as the homeworld.

Usenet:
Newsgroup: **alt.startrek.klingon**

A B C D E F G H I J K L M N O P Q R S T U V W X Y Z

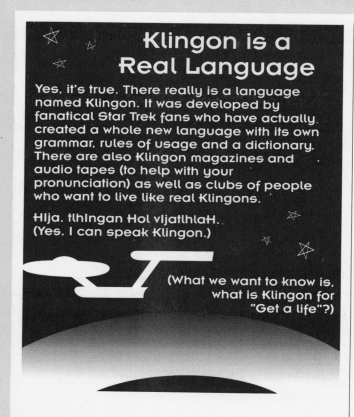

Klingon is a Real Language

Yes, it's true. There really is a language named Klingon. It was developed by fanatical Star Trek fans who have actually created a whole new language with its own grammar, rules of usage and a dictionary. There are also Klingon magazines and audio tapes (to help with your pronunciation) as well as clubs of people who want to live like real Klingons.

HIja. tlhIngan Hol vIjatlhlaH. (Yes. I can speak Klingon.)

(What we want to know is, what is Klingon for "Get a life"?)

Star Trek General Discussion

Light and lively debate volleys, occasionally turning warm, then hot as you defend your favorite episode or character. Talk turns to old shows, bloopers, insider information on actors' lives, and burning questions like, "Why is Lt. Worf still only a Lieutenant?".

Usenet:
Newsgroup: **rec.arts.startrek.misc**

Star Trek Information and Trivia

Everything you need to know about *Star Trek*, including Klingon vocabulary, *Deep Space Nine*, original *Star Trek*, and *Next Generation* guides, listings, a spelling list, a timeline, stardates, drinking games and other important information.

Anonymous FTP:
Address: **ftp.spies.com**
Path: **/Library/Media/Trek/***

Gopher:
Name: Internet Wiretap
Address: **wiretap.spies.com**
Choose: **Wiretap Online Library**
  | **Mass Media**
  | **Star Trek**

Star Trek Quotes

Quotes from the popular TV show.

Finger:
Address: **franklin@ug.cs.dal.ca**

Star Trek Reviews

Nobody can review *Star Trek* like a Trekker. Read what fans think about the latest books, movies and shows (but watch out for spoilers!).

Usenet:
Newsgroup: **rec.arts.startrek.reviews**

Star Trek Universe

This moderated group offers in-depth and accurate information on the universe as it relates to *Star Trek*. Read press releases, episode credits, synopses and factual articles. Since all posts are filtered through a moderator, you can be assured of the reliability of what you read. Queries are best moved to one of the other *Star Trek* groups. All the articles that have been posted to the Usenet newsgroup are available by Anonymous FTP.

Anonymous FTP:
Address: **scam.berkeley.edu**
Path: **/misc/trek-info/***

Usenet:
Newsgroup: **rec.arts.startrek.info**

Stories and Parodies

If you can't get enough of *Star Trek* on television or in movies and books, check out this corner of the Usenet universe. Creative and witty individuals post stories and parodies related to *Star Trek*. Often FAQ lists on submissions are posted containing tips for writing for *Star Trek: The Next Generation* and *Deep Space Nine*, where to send submissions, what to do and what not to do when writing.

Usenet:
Newsgroup: **alt.startrek.creative**

What's Happening

Learn what's going on in the world of *Star Trek*. Fans report rumors and facts of current events—new shows, books and movies. Get the latest word and keep up with the Bones.

Usenet:
Newsgroup: **rec.arts.startrek.current**

TECHNOLOGY

Artificial Intelligence

Technical papers, journals, and surveys about artificial intelligence, robotics and neural networks.

Anonymous FTP:
Address: **flash.bellcore.com**
Path: **/pub/ai/***

Address: **ftp.uu.net**
Path: **/pub/ai/***

Address: **gargoyle.uchicago.edu**
Path: **/pub/artificial_intelligence/***

Address: **solaria.cc.gatech.edu**
Path: **/pub/ai/***

The original Apple was one ugly computer. At least this one was. Thank goodness the woody thing didn't stick with computers. This picture is **apple1.gif** and its widely available. We got our copy from the Computer Science Department at Tampere University of Technology in Finland. You can also find it in Sweden, Taiwan and the U.S.

Audio

Mail order surveys, lists and related information for the art and science of audio.

Anonymous FTP:
Address: **ssesco.com**
Path: **/pub/rec.audio/***

Canada Department of Communications

CHAT (Conversational Hypertext Access Technology) database system. You can ask questions of this database in plain English. It correctly interprets an amazing number of questions and instantly provides answers about the Canadian Department of Communications. The Canadian DOC manages radio in Canada, participates in high-tech ventures, and promotes Canada's cultural infrastructure through communications.

Telnet:
Address: **debra.dgbt.doc.ca**
Login: **chat**

Hot off the Tree (HOTT)

A weekly publication containing excerpts and summaries of information technology articles.

Comment: For the telnet site, type **show hott** after logging in.

Listserv mailing list:
List Address: **hott-list@ucsd.edu**
Subscription Address: **listserv@ucsd.edu**

Telnet:
Address: **melvyl.ucop.edu**
Login: *your terminal type*

National Institute of Standards and Technology

A Gopher server funded and operated by the National Institute of Standards and Technology (NIST). This Gopher is primarily for organizations and employees of NIST, but is made available to the entire Gopher network and its users. The NIST Gopher contains information on applied and computational mathematics at NIST, as well as other information primarily of interest to those involved with NIST.

Gopher:
Name:
National Institute of Standards and Technology
Address: **gopher-server.nist.gov**

Photonics

Documents, reports and other information regarding optical computing research and technology.

Gopher:
Name:
Colorado State University Optical Computing Lab
Address: **sylvia.lance.colostate.edu**

Video Laserdiscs

Introduction to video laserdisc technology, media quality reports, how-to reports, care, repair and retail sources—everything you could want to know about this technology.

Telnet:
Address: **panda.uiowa.edu**

A B C D E F G H I J K L M N O P Q R S T U V W X Y Z

Virtual Reality

Papers, FAQs and bibliographies concerning virtual reality.

Anonymous FTP:
Address: **ftp.u.washington.edu**
Path: **/public/VirtualReality/***

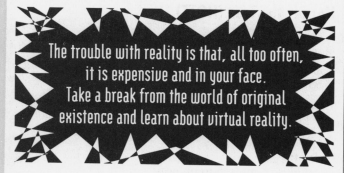

The trouble with reality is that, all too often, it is expensive and in your face. Take a break from the world of original existence and learn about virtual reality.

Virtual Reality Archive

FAQs, bibliographies, software, papers and other material related to virtual worlds and virtual reality.

Anonymous FTP:
Address: **ftp.u.washington.edu**
Path: **/public/virtual-worlds/***

Virtual Reality Mailing List

Open discussion and news about everything to do with virtual reality.

Listserv mailing list:
List Address: **virtu-l@uiucvmd.bitnet**
Subscription Address: **listserv@uiucvmd.bitnet**

TELECOMMUNICATIONS

Amiga Telecom

Discussions about telecommunications for Amiga computer systems.

Usenet:
Newsgroup: **comp.sys.amiga.telecomm**

Lonely? Try the Personals.

Cell-Relay Communications

Cell-relay products and technology.

Usenet:
Newsgroup: **comp.dcom.cell-relay**

Clarinet News

Current news about the world of telecommunications, phones, satellites and so on.

Usenet:
Newsgroup: **clari.nb.telecom**
Newsgroup: **clari.tw.telecom**

Data Communications Servers

Selecting and operating data communications servers.

Usenet:
Newsgroup: **comp.dcom.servers**

Fax Technology

Fax equipment, including computer hardware and software, and technical specifications and protocols.

Usenet:
Newsgroup: **comp.dcom.fax**

International Telecommunications Union

Information about the global development of telecommunications, including documents, infobases, press releases, news and other services.

Gopher:
Name: International Telecommunications Union
Address: **info.itu.ch**

IP (Internet Protocol)

Discussions of the technical aspects of the IP protocol (the underlying mechanism for moving data around the Internet).

Usenet:
Newsgroup: **alt.dcom.telecom.ip**

ISDN

Issues and technology relating to ISDN (Integrated Services Digital Network).

Usenet:
Newsgroup: **comp.dcom.isdn**

PC Communications and Modems

Serial port specifications, modem technical notes, and answers to telecom FAQs.

Anonymous FTP:
Address: **ftp.spies.com**
Path: **/Library/Techdoc/Comm/***

Gopher:
Name: Internet Wiretap
Address: **wiretap.spies.com**
Choose: **Wiretap Online Library**
  | Technical Information
  | Communications and Modems

Telecom Discussions

Discussions about all manner of telecommunications, including the telephone system.

Usenet:
Newsgroup: **alt.dcom.telecom**

Telecommunications Digest

A moderated digest containing articles about the phone system and telecommunications.

Usenet:
Newsgroup: **comp.dcom.telecom**

Telecommunications News

News of recent developments and technology in the Japanese telecommunications industry.

Gopher:
Name: Nippon Telegraphic and Telephone Corp.
Address: **gopher.ntt.jp**
Choose: **NTT News**
  | NTT News Release

TELEPHONES

Area Codes Guide

A guide to U.S. area codes, listing not only the corresponding regions, but also discussing special area codes and the companies involved.

The Internet will set you free.

Anonymous FTP:
Address: **ftp.spies.com**
Path: **/Library/Document/areacode.txt**

Gopher:
Name: Internet Wiretap
Address: **wiretap.spies.com**
Choose: **Wiretap Online Library**
  | Assorted Documents
  | Telecom Digest Guide to Area Codes

Phone-Number-to-Word Translator

Unix C source code to an interesting program that converts phone numbers into words.

Anonymous FTP:
Address: **gatekeeper.dec.com**
Path: **/pub/usenet/comp.sources.misc/ volume12/telewords/***

Your Telephone Number Secrets Unmasked

You know that it is possible to convert your phone number from numbers to letters: 2=A, B or C; 3=D, E or F; and so on. But have you ever taken your personal number and tried all possible combinations to see if they spell anything cool? If so, you will find that there are a lot of combinations. But why should you sweat when you have a computer? Download the phone-number-to-word translating program and let the machine do the work. Maybe you'll get lucky. One person that we know found out that her number spelled out "SEX-YOGA". (You can imagine what this did for her social life.)

Hint: The program is useful for helping to remember any numbers that are entered on a telephone-like keypad, such as your ATM secret code.

RING RING

A B C D E F G H I J K L M N O P Q R S T U V W X Y Z

Phonecards

All about those cards you use instead of coins in public phones. Lists of phone card collections, manufacturer lists and chip diagram pictures of phone cards.

Anonymous FTP:
> Address: **nic.funet.fi**
> Path: **/pub/doc/telecom/phonecard/***

Russian Phone Directory

A phone directory of the former Soviet Union. This file contains both a database of phone information and a program to access the data. The file is a self-extracting DOS .EXE file.

Anonymous FTP:
> Address: **kekule.osc.edu**
> Path:
>   **/pub/russian/phone-directory/phonedir.exe**

> Address: **moose.cs.indiana.edu**
> Path: **/pub/phonedir/phonedir.exe**

Telefax Country Codes

List of the international telephone and fax dialing codes for different countries.

Anonymous FTP:
> Address: **nic.funet.fi**
> Path: **/pub/doc/telecom/telefax_country_codes**

Telephone Privacy

An article that provides detailed information on how to ensure better telephone privacy.

Gopher:
> Name: Oregon State University
> Address: **gopher.fsl.orst.edu**
> Choose: **Other Sources of Information**
>   **| Hugo's Soapbox**
>   **| A Way to Gain Phone Privacy**

Toll-free Phone Numbers for Computer Companies

This file contains toll-free phone numbers for many companies in the computer industry.

Anonymous FTP:
> Address: **oak.oakland.edu**
> Path: **/pub/misc/telephone/tollfree.num**

Toll-free Phone Numbers for Non-Profit Organizations

This file contains a list of toll-free numbers for non-profit organizations and crisis hotlines.

Anonymous FTP:
> Address: **oak.oakland.edu**
> Path: **/pub/misc/telephone/1800help.inf**

U.S. Telephone Area Code Program

A Unix program and area code database for providing area code information gracefully and efficiently. Whether you know the area code and need to find out the location or you know the location and need the area code, this program will provide the answer instantly.

Anonymous FTP:
> Address: **lcs.mit.edu**
> Path: **/telecom-archives/areacodes**

U.S. Telephone Area Codes

Find a specific area code or list all the area code districts in the United States.

Gopher:
> Name: NASA Goddard Space Flight Center
> Address: **gopher.gsfc.nasa.gov**
> Choose: **Virtual Reference Shelf**
>   **| US telephone areacodes**

TELEVISION

Beavis and Butt-head

ASCII art, episode listings, interviews, and quotes from and about the MTV show *Beavis and Butt-head*.

Anonymous FTP:
> Address: **quartz.rutgers.edu**
> Path: **/pub/tv+movies/beavis/***

Gopher:
> Name: Rutgers Quartz Text Archive
> Address: **quartz.rutgers.edu**
> Choose: **Television and Movies**
>   **| Beavis**

Cable TV

A mailing list for anyone interested in any topic related to cable television programming, technology or regulation.

Internet mailing list:
List Address: **catv@quack.sac.ca.us**
Subscription Address:
catv-request@quack.sac.ca.us

Cartoons

Cartoon, comics and animation-related materials, including a list of Warner Brothers cartoons, a *Simpsons* guide, Asterix annotations, anime articles and a *Peanuts* bibliography.

Anonymous FTP:
Address: **ftp.spies.com**
Path: **/Library/Media/Anime/***

Gopher:
Name: Internet Wiretap
Address: **wiretap.spies.com**
Choose: **Wiretap Online Library**
| **Mass Media**
| **Comics and Japanese Anime**

We like cartoons, and we bet that you do too. If so, check out the cartoon archive on the Wiretap Gopher.

Cheers

Episode guides, theme music, Norm sayings, and other trivia from the classic *Cheers* television series.

Anonymous FTP:
Address: **nic.funet.fi**
Path: **/pub/culture/tv+film/Cheers/***

Gopher:
Name: Rutgers University
Address: **quartz.rutgers.edu**
Choose: **Television and Movies**
| **Cheers**

Clarissa Explains

Discussion of the Nickelodeon TV show *Clarissa Explains It All*.

Internet mailing list:
List Address: **clarissa@ferkel.ucsb.edu**
Subscription Address:
clarissa-request@ferkel.ucsb.edu

David Letterman

How to send mail to Dave, get tickets to the show, and get the Top Ten lists. Valuable sources of information about skits, stunts, guests, music, and, of course, Dave himself.

Anonymous FTP:
Address: **quartz.rutgers.edu**
Path: **/pub/tv+movies/letterman/***

Address: **rtfm.mit.edu**
Path: **/pub/usenet/news.answers/letterman/faz.Z**

Usenet:
Newsgroup: **alt.fan.letterman**

The David Letterman archives have all kinds of funny material, including Letterman's top ten lists, a summary of the last show and other episodes, the David Letterman songbook, and so on. This image is from NAU (**ftp.nau.edu**) in the file **/graphics/gif/people/lettrman.gif**.

MTV

A slick FTP site and Gopher with tons of news and entertainment from MTV and the music industry.

Comment: This resource is not affiliated with the MTV network.

A
B
C
D
E
F
G
H
I
J
K
L
M
N
O
P
Q
R
S
T
U
V
W
X
Y
Z

Anonymous FTP:
Address: **mtv.com**
Path: **/pub/***

Gopher:
Name: MTV
Address: **mtv.com**

MTV Schedules

A programming schedule for the MTV network, including MTV Europe.

Anonymous FTP:
Address: **mtv.com**
Path: **/pub/schedules/***

Gopher:
Name: MTV
Address: **mtv.com**
Choose: **schedules**

Nielsen TV Ratings

Weekly TV ratings according to the Nielsen rating system.

Finger:
Address: **normg@halcyon.halcyon.com**

Gopher:
Name: CNS, Inc.
Address: **cns.cscns.com**
Choose: **CNS Main Gopher
| Entertainment - Nielsen TV Ratings**

Northern Exposure

Episode guides and summaries, FAQs, music guides, a quotes list, discussions, and other points of interest regarding the *Northern Exposure* television show.

Anonymous FTP:
Address: **jhunix.hcf.jhu.edu**
Path: **/pub/usagi/***

Address: **rtfm.mit.edu**
Path: **/pub/usenet/news.answers/
northern-exposure-faq**

Address: **tmn.com**
Path: **/pub/MetaNet/Nexp/***

Internet mailing list:
List Address: **trebuchet@noao.edu**
Subscription Address:
trebuchet-request@noao.edu

Usenet:
Newsgroup: **alt.tv.northern-exp**

Official David Letterman Song Book

Lyrics to all your favorite songs from David Letterman's TV show, such as the theme song as sung by Bill Murray and Paul Shaffer, the Viewer Mail Theme, and the Strong Guy, the Fat Guy, the Genius. A hilarious compilation by Keith Rice.

Anonymous FTP:
Address: **quartz.rutgers.edu**
Path: **/pub/tv+movies/letterman/songbook.z**

Address: **rtfm.mit.edu**
Path:
**/pub/usenet/news.answers/letterman/
songbook**

Mail:
Address: **mail-server@rtfm.mit.edu**
Body:
**send usenet/news.answers/letterman/
songbook**

Parker Lewis

All about the *Parker Lewis* television series, including scripts, pictures, sounds, digests, cast lists and more.

Anonymous FTP:
Address: **ftp.cs.pdx.edu**
Path: **/pub/flamingos/***

Ren and Stimpy Show Archives

Fans of Ren and Stimpy can read all about these cartoon characters. The popularity of the *Ren and Stimpy Show* is largely due to its wit and its shameless display of physical functions like nose-picking and farting. The site has a FAQ, a guide and an encyclopedia.

Anonymous FTP:
Address: **aug3.augsburg.edu**
Path: **/files/text_files/ren***

Why be normal?
Read Bizarre.

Seinfeld

The official *Seinfeld* archive offering quotes, sounds, episode guides, FAQs and pictures.

Anonymous FTP:
    Address: **quartz.rutgers.edu**
    Path: **/pub/tv+movies/seinfeld/***

Gopher:
    Name: Rutgers Quartz Text Archive
    Address: **quartz.rutgers.edu**
    Choose: **Television and Movies**
     | Seinfeld

Series and Sitcoms

Episode guides, lists, FAQs, scripts, and much more about films and television series, including *Star Trek*, *Cheers*, *Bladerunner*, *Twin Peaks*, *Monty Python* and many more.

Anonymous FTP:
    Address: **nic.funet.fi**
    Path: **/pub/culture/tv+film/***

Make sure you are prepared: Read Emergency and Disaster.

Series Guides and Facts

Material, FAQs, and guides for many television programs and movies, including *The Twilight Zone*, *Tiny Toons*, *Quantum Leap*, *M*A*S*H*, and *Ren and Stimpy*.

Anonymous FTP:
    Address: **quartz.rutgers.edu**
    Path: **/pub/tv+movies/***

Gopher:
    Name: Rutgers Quartz Text Archive
    Address: **quartz.rutgers.edu**
    Choose: **Television and Movies**

Television and the Internet

We know that *you* don't waste your time watching television. Still, you probably have a few friends who do, so why not tip them off to the Internet's TV resources. The Quartz Gopher has a great TV section, as well as pointers to other archive sites. You can spend all day browsing...sorry...we mean your *friends* can spend all day browsing in a cornucopia of TV trivia, episode descriptions, and frequently asked question (FAQ) lists.

Excerpt from the Net...

```
          (from the television archives at nic.funet.fi)

                  The Star Trek Prime Directive
          ===============================
```

"As the right of each sentient species to live in accordance with its normal cultural evolution is considered sacred, no Star Fleet personnel may interfere with the healthy development of alien life and culture.

"Such interference includes the introduction of superior knowledge, strength, or technology to a world whose society is incapable of handling such advantages wisely.

"Star Fleet personnel may not violate this Prime Directive, even to save their lives and/or their ship, unless they are acting to right an earlier violation or an accidental contamination of said culture.

"This directive takes precedence over any and all other considerations, and carries with it the highest moral obligation."

A
B
C
D
E
F
G
H
I
J
K
L
M
N
O
P
Q
R
S
T
U
V
W
X
Y
Z

The Simpsons

Get the lowdown on the popular animated TV show *The Simpsons*. Bone up on *Simpsons* trivia. This FTP site maintains summaries of each episode, biographies of the characters and series schedules.

Anonymous FTP:
Address: **ftp.cs.widener.edu**
Path: **/pub/simpsons**

Star Trek Archives

Quotes, parodies, episodes, reviews and more.

Anonymous FTP:
Address: **ftp.uu.net**
Path: **/doc/literary/obi/Star.Trek.Stories**

Address: **ftp.uu.net**
Path: **/usenet/rec.arts.startrek**

Star Trek Reviews and Synopses

Synopses and reviews for every episode of *Star Trek: The Next Generation* and *Deep Space Nine*, by Timothy Lynch.

Telnet:
Address: **panda.uiowa.edu**

Tiny Toons Adventures

Pictures, sound files, guides, cast listings, production credits and numbers, episode title indexes, and commentaries from and about the *Tiny Toon Adventures* cartoons.

Anonymous FTP:
Address: **utpapa.ph.utexas.edu**
Path: **/pub/tta/***

Usenet:
Newsgroup: **alt.tv.tiny-toon**

Tiny Toons Episodes

Plot summaries for each episode of *Tiny Toon Adventures*, including production numbers, air dates and animation houses.

Anonymous FTP:
Address: **ftp.coe.montana.edu**
Path: **/pub/TV/Guides/tinytoons.txt.Z**

TV Episode Guides

Episode guides for many TV series, including *Alf*, *Doctor Who*, *Miami Vice*, *The Twilight Zone*, *Parker Lewis*, *Quantum Leap* and *Twin Peaks*.

Anonymous FTP:
Address: **ftp.spies.com**
Path: **/Library/Media/Tv/***

Gopher:
Name: Internet Wiretap
Address: **wiretap.spies.com**
Choose: **Wiretap Online Library**
 | Mass Media
 | Television

TV Schedules

Schedules for the Sci-Fi Channel and information on the commercial custom viewer that permits subscribers to receive detailed, personalized TV listing guides via fax or e-mail.

Gopher:
Name: Vortex Technology
Address: **vortex.com**
Choose: *** **TV/Film/Video** ***

U.K. Television

Searches, contact information and detailed notes on U.K. television-related addresses, including program production information.

Gopher:
Name: University of Manchester
Address: **uts.mcc.ac.uk**
Choose: **Gopher Services**
 | Useful UK Television Related Addresses

UK Sitcom List

A complete list of all sitcoms that have ever been made in the UK and broadcast on UK terrestrial TV.

Gopher:
Name: Manchester Computing Centre
Address: **info.mcc.ac.uk**
Choose: **Miscellaneous**
 | The definitive list of UK sitcoms

TRAVEL

Amtrak Trains

A comprehensive list of Amtrak trains, including train numbers, names, originations, destinations and the days of service for each.

Anonymous FTP:
Address: **ftp.spies.com**
Path: **/Library/Document/amtrak.lis**

Gopher:
Name: Internet Wiretap
Address: **wiretap.spies.com**
Choose: **Wiretap Online Library**
  | **Assorted Documents**
  | **Amtrak Trains**

AMTRAK IS THE NATIONAL RAILWAY ORGANIZATION OF THE UNITED STATES. FOR AN ONLINE LISTING OF AMTRAK'S SCHEDULED SERVICE, TRY THE WIRETAP GOPHER.

International Travel Health Advice

For those traveling to lands afar: a guide to vaccinations, immunizations, and illnesses abroad.

Gopher:
Name: Healthline Gopher Service
Address: **selway.umt.edu 700**
Choose: **General Health Information**
  | **Health Information for International Travel**

Telnet:
Address: **selway.umt.edu**
Login: **health**

This is the first book of the rest of your life.

Journeys and Destinations

Articles pertaining to journeys and travels, including the amusing "Tourist Traps in the U.S.", life in a virtual community, Arizona and New Mexico travelogues, Cancun tales, a prison saga and other interesting stories.

Anonymous FTP:
Address: **ftp.spies.com**
Path: **/Library/Article/Journey/***

Gopher:
Name: Internet Wiretap
Address: **wiretap.spies.com**
Choose: **Wiretap Online Library**
  | **Articles**
  | **Journeys and Travels**

On the Internet, you can find images of exotic places and interesting people. This one, entitled **fijichief.gif** is at Northern Arizona (**ftp.nau.edu**) in the directory **/graphics/gif/people**. Note: When you download this to a PC, the name gets shortened to **fijichie.gif**.

New York City

"The Hitchhiker's Guide to the Big Apple" is an extensive guide of sights to see and things to do in New York City, including hotel, restaurant, club, shopping and subway guides.

Anonymous FTP:
Address: **quartz.rutgers.edu**
Path: **/pub/nyc/***

Gopher:
Name: Rutgers Quartz Text Archive
Address: **quartz.rutgers.edu**
Choose:
  NYC - The Net-Person's Guide to New York City

A B C D E F G H I J K L M N O P Q R S T U V W X Y Z

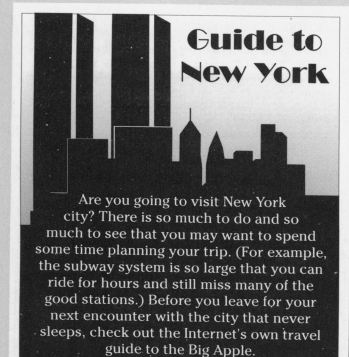

Guide to New York

Are you going to visit New York city? There is so much to do and so much to see that you may want to spend some time planning your trip. (For example, the subway system is so large that you can ride for hours and still miss many of the good stations.) Before you leave for your next encounter with the city that never sleeps, check out the Internet's own travel guide to the Big Apple.

Hint from Harley: go to Carnegie's Deli (the one in *Broadway Danny Rose*) and order the chicken soup.

Subway Navigator

Find the right route in the subways of several of the world's largest cities, including subways in France, Germany, Spain and Canada.

Gopher:
Name: Universites P. & M. Curie
Address: **gopher.jussieu.fr**
Choose: **Indicateur des metros**
 | Subway indicator

Telnet:
Address: **metro.jussieu.fr 10000**

**Got too much stuff?
Need some more stuff?
Try
Buying and Selling**

Tourism Offices

Details on how to get tourist information for a number of destinations, and a directory of tourist information offices worldwide.

Anonymous FTP:
Address: **quartz.rutgers.edu**
Path: **/pub/misc/tourist-info-offices**

Gopher:
Name: Rutgers Quartz Text Archive
Address: **quartz.rutgers.edu**
Choose: **Miscellaneous**
 | tourist-info-offices

Travel Information

Get travel information and personal accounts about a number of destinations. Travelers post detailed accounts of their vacations, including places to go, places to avoid, where and what to eat, reviews of hotels and much more.

Anonymous FTP:
Address: **ftp.cc.umanitoba.ca**
Path: **/pub/rec-travel/**

Travel Resources

Guides to travel information resources available on the Internet. Consists of a large list of mailing lists, FTP sites and Listservs of interest to travelers.

Anonymous FTP:
Address: **rtfm.mit.edu**
Path: **/pub/usenet/rec.answers/travel/ftp-archive**

Address: **rtfm.mit.edu**
Path: **/pub/usenet/rec.answers/travel/online-info**

U.S. State Department Travel Advisories

Extensive information on current and past travel advisories for those interested in traveling abroad. Each factsheet contains the addresses and phone numbers of American consulates, as well as passport, visa and government information, and crime data. Files are arranged alphabetically by country name.

Gopher:
Name: St. Olaf College
Address: **gopher.stolaf.edu**
Choose: **Internet Resources**

TRIVIA

Answer Guys

Do you have a nagging question you can't seem to get an answer to? Try the Answer Guys with the *Middlesex News* electronic newspaper.

Gopher:
Name: The World
Address: **world.std.com**
Choose: **Periodicals, Magazines, and Journals**
l **Middlesex News**
l **Columns**
l **The Answer Guys**

Coin Toss

Need to toss a coin, but don't have one? No problem; Gopher here and simulate it.

Gopher:
Name: University of Alabama
Address: **twinbrook.cis.uab.edu**
Choose: **The Continuum**
l **Coin Toss**

Coke Servers

Interesting places to finger for trivial information.

Finger:
Address: **@coke.elab.cs.cmu.edu**
Address: **bargraph@coke.elab.cs.cmu.edu**
Address: **cocacola@columbia.edu**
Address: **coke@cmu.edu**
Address: **coke@cs.cmu.edu**
Address: **coke@cs.wisc.edu**
Address: **coke@gu.uwa.edu.au**
Address: **coke@xcf.berkeley.edu**
Address: **drink@drink.csh.rit.edu**
Address: **graph@drink.csh.rit.edu**
Address: **info@drink.csh.rit.edu**
Address: **mnm@coke.elab.cs.cmu.edu**
Address: **pepsi@columbia.edu**

Questions and Answers

Okay, we all know that Richie Petrie's middle name is Rosebud and that it stands for "Robert Oscar Sam Edward Benjamin Ulysses David". But what was Rob and Laura's address? How about the Ricardos' phone number? Join the pros and test your trivia skill. TV, radio, music, film, Internet books—all the great cultural achievements of mankind are grist for those who pursue the trivial.

Usenet:
Newsgroup: **rec.games.trivia**

Today's Events in History

Important historical events that happened on today's date in years gone by.

Finger:
Address: **copi@oddjob.uchicago.edu**

Gopher:
Name: Manchester Computing Centre
Address: **uts.mcc.ac.uk**
Choose: **Today's events in history**

Name: University of Alabama
Address: **twinbrook.cis.uab.edu**
Choose: **The Continuum**
l **Today in History**

Mail:
Address: **geiser@pictel.com**

Unofficial Smiley Dictionary

This Smiley Dictionary is one of the most complete lists of smileys available on the Internet. Do you feel ;-) or :-(or just :-I ?

Gopher:
Name: Universitaet des Saarlandes
Address: **pfsparc02.phil15.uni-sb.de**
Choose: **INFO-SYSTEM BENUTZEN**
l **Fun**
l **Cartoons**
l **Smilies :-)**

The only place where Politics comes before Star Trek is in the Internet Yellow Pages.

The Internet has lots of free software. Check out Computers, Software and Operating Systems.

A B C D E F G H I J K L M N O P Q R S **T** U V W X Y Z

USENET

Anonymous Posting Service

Post messages to Usenet groups anonymously. To find out how, send mail to the address below.

Mail:
　　Address: **help@anon.penet.fi**

Being Anonymous

There are many reasons why you might wish to post Usenet articles anonymously. For example, you might want to contribute personal comments to one of the sex-oriented groups. Or, you might not want your employer or system manager (or significant other) to know the nature of your postings.

In order to protect the right of anyone to say whatever they want without fear of retribution, an anonymous posting service has been set up. Once you register, you will be given a user number and all correspondence will be carried out using that number. Moreover, once you post an article anonymously, people will be able to send you mail commenting on the article, without knowing who you are.

This service is an important one and -- as you can imagine -- there are all sorts of self-righteous zealots who would love to shut it down. Please use your intelligence and do not abuse the system.

Creating Alternative Hierarchy Newsgroups

FAQs and guidelines for creating a new **alt** Usenet newsgroup.

Anonymous FTP:
　　Address: **rtfm.mit.edu**
　　Path: **/pub/usenet/news.answers/alt-config-guide**

Creating Standard Newsgroups

Instructions for creating a new mainstream Usenet newsgroup.

Anonymous FTP:
　　Address: **rtfm.mit.edu**
　　Path: **/pub/usenet/news.answers/
　　　creating-newsgroups/***

European Usenet

Read European and British Usenet newsgroups through this Gopher-based newsreader.

Gopher:
　　Name: University of Birmingham
　　Address: **gopher.bham.ac.uk**
　　Choose: **Usenet News Reader
　　 | European/UK Groups**

FAQ Searches and Archives

Search and browse some or all of the Usenet FAQs, as posted to the **news.answers** newsgroup, from this easy-access Gopher menu.

Gopher:
　　Name: Johns Hopkins University
　　Address: **merlot.welch.jhu.edu**
　　Choose: **Usenet News and FAQs
　　 | All FAQs (Frequently Asked Questions)
　　　Searches and Archives**

Frequently Asked Question (FAQ) Lists

Collections of frequently asked questions from many Usenet newsgroups.

Anonymous FTP:
　　Address: **rtfm.mit.edu**
　　Path: **/pub/usenet/news.answers/***

Lonely? Try the Personals.

Frequently Asked Questions (Master List)

The master list of FAQ lists. Includes cross references to Usenet news groups and Internet resources.

Anonymous FTP:
Address: **rtfm.mit.edu**
Path: **/pub/usenet/news.answers/index**

Hangul Newsgroups

Read the Hangul Usenet groups from Korea.

Gopher:
Name: Korea Network Information Center
Address: **gopher.nic.nm.kr**
Choose: **USENET Newsgroups**
  | **Hangul News Groups**

Japanese Usenet

Check out Usenet in Japan. It's in Japanese.

Comment: Requires a software client to read Japanese text. See the Software: Utilities category.

Gopher:
Name: National Institute for Physiological Sciences
Address: **gopher.nips.ac.jp**
Choose: **A. Netnews**

List of Periodic Informational Postings

This multipart list has an entry for informational articles posted periodically to Usenet groups. The list includes FAQs, forms, and other regular postings.

Anonymous FTP:
Address: **rtfm.mit.edu**
Path: **/pub/usenet/news.answers/**
  periodic-postings/part*

Newsgroup Descriptions

Detailed descriptions of most of the Usenet groups and categories.

Telnet:
Address: **kufacts.cc.ukans.edu**
Login: **kufacts**

NNTP News Servers

The master list of publicly accessible NNTP servers that allow you to post to Usenet news via telnet.

Finger:
Address: **lesikar@tigger.stcloud.msus.edu**

Publicly Accessible News Servers

A long list of publicly accessible news servers, accessible via Telnet, FTP, FTPmail, FSP and X.25, and bookmarks for Gopher sites that provide access to Usenet.

Finger:
Address: **lesikar@tigger.stcloud.msus.edu**

Risks of Posting to Usenet

A story describing how a posting to Usenet resulted in a call from a U.S. Air Force base and an interesting visit from the FBI.

Anonymous FTP:
Address: **ftp.spies.com**
Path: **/Library/Article/Rights/posting.rsk**

Gopher:
Name: Internet Wiretap
Address: **wiretap.spies.com**
Choose: **Wiretap Online Library**
  | **Articles**
  | **Civil Rights and Liberties**
  | **Risks of Posting to Usenet**

Usenet Descriptions

Search Usenet newsgroup descriptions to quickly and easily find newsgroups related to a subject or topic of interest.

Gopher:
Name: Nova Scotia Technology Network
Address: **nstn.ns.ca**
Choose: **Internet Resources**
  | **Search Usenet Newsgroup Descriptions**

Why be normal? Read Bizarre.

The Internet will set you free.

A B C D E F G H I J K L M N O P Q R S T U V W X Y Z

Usenet Finger Utility

Lists of FAQ lists, Internet resources and periodic postings to Usenet newsgroups.

Finger:
   Address: **nichol@stavanger.sgp.slb.com**

Usenet Groups with a Difference

A list of Usenet groups that are connected with interaction, interfaces, and agency, for those of you looking for the real Net News.

Gopher:
   Name: University of Texas at Austin
   Address: **actlab.rtf.utexas.edu**
   Choose: **USENET**
    ⏐ USENET Groups related to...

Usenet News via E-mail

Allows you to post to Usenet via e-mail.

Comment: Replace periods in a newsgroup name with hyphens. Example: **alt.bbs** becomes **alt-bbs**.

Mail:
   Address: *newsgroup@cs.utexas.edu*

Would you like to post to a Usenet group that is not carried on your system? Do it by mail.

Usenet News via Gopher

Allows you to read Usenet news through Gopher.

Gopher:
   Name: Michigan State University
   Address: **gopher.msu.edu**
   Choose: **News & Weather**
    ⏐ USENET News

   Name: University of Birmingham
   Address: **gopher.bham.ac.uk**
   Choose: **Usenet News Reader**

Usenet Olympics

Parodies of Usenet and its inhabitants, combined into a single file covering each year.

Anonymous FTP:
   Address: **ocf.berkeley.edu**
   Path: **/pub/Usenet_Olympics/***

Usenet Word Statistics

A list of the 1000 most common words used on Usenet over the period of a year, along with their percentages of occurence.

Anonymous FTP:
   Address: **ftp.spies.com**
   Path: **/Library/Article/Language/top1000.use**

Gopher:
   Name: Internet Wiretap
   Address: **wiretap.spies.com**
   Choose: **Wiretap Online Library**
    ⏐ Articles
    ⏐ Language
    ⏐ Top 1000 Words used on Usenet

Excerpt from the Net...

(from Usenet Word Statistics)

A total of 343,945,617 words were scanned from Usenet articles and a count was kept of how many times each word was used. (A "word" is a separate entity, consisting of one or more characters.)

Here are the top 10:

```
     1) the
     2) to
     3) of
     4) a
     5) I
     6) and
     7) is
     8) in
     9) that
    10) it
```

Other notable words on the list were:

```
   706) r
   710) t
   690) f
    80) m
```

Worldwide Usenet

Read Usenet newsgroups, including many local and regional newsgroups from around the world, such as Australian, European, South American, and specific U.S. state newsgroups.

Gopher:
Name: Johns Hopkins University
Address: **merlot.welch.jhu.edu**
Choose: **Usenet News and FAQs**
| Read USENET News Groups

USENET CURIOSITIES

Cascades

Every once in a while, someone will reply to a silly one-line message with another silly one-line message. Another person will follow up with a third silly one-line message, and (let the trumpets sound) a *cascade* is born. Cascades have a life and an appeal all their own. If you are one of those lucky persons whose sense of taste is so highly developed as to make you an aficionado of cascades, then you will want to tune into this newsgroup where you can cascade until you burst.

Usenet:
Newsgroup: **alt.cascade**

Flames

A *flame* is a complaint, or a complaint about a complaint. Join this group and play with people who complain for a living.

Usenet:
Newsgroup: **alt.flame**

Kibo

Kibo, mythical net-god, is rumored to be omnipresent on the Net. Post any Usenet article with the word "Kibo" to any newsgroup: Kibo will find it and answer. Who exactly is Kibo? That's for us to know and for you to find out. Join in the worship and try to prove (or disprove) Kibo's existence.

Usenet:
Newsgroup: **alt.religion.kibology**

Usenet Junkies

If something is worth doing, it's worth doing to excess. When Usenet becomes a bit too much and you feel your sanity slipping away like an Arab who has folded his tent, check out this support group for Usenet junkies who can't say no.

Usenet:
Newsgroup: **alt.usenet.recovery**

Weird Places to Hang Out on Usenet

Among the thousands of Usenet newsgroups, there are a few strange places to hang out where anything goes. These are newsgroups that were started as a joke, or real newsgroups that have been abandoned by the original settlers. Check out one of these groups and meet the squatters. Sort of the free-trade zone of Usenet commerce. (In fact, there are some newsgroups that are so secret, we can't even tell you about them.)

Usenet:
Newsgroup: **alt.1d**
Newsgroup: **alt.bogus.group**
Newsgroup: **alt.non.sequiter**
Newsgroup: **alt.religion.monica**
Newsgroup: **alt.rmgroup**

A B C D E F G H I J K L M N O P Q R S T U V W X Y Z

The Internet has some fascinating Frequently Asked Question (FAQ) Lists. When you have a spare moment, find a FAQ list that looks interesting and read it.

VIDEO GAMES

ACM

A LAN-based flight combat game.

Anonymous FTP:
Address: **ftp.x.org**
Path: **contrib/acm-4.0.tar.Z**

AD&D Character Creator

A Windows 3.1 character creator for Advanced Dungeons and Dragons.

Anonymous FTP:
Address: **wuarchive.wustl.edu**
Path: **/pub/msdos_uploads/games/creator.zip**

Air Warrior

Files and patches to improve the cockpit detail in some of the planes in the video game Air Warriors. Also, a program that can manipulate the pilot roster. Air Warrior is a PC flight simulator that makes full use of SVGA video and sound cards.

Anonymous FTP:
Address: **cactus.org**
Path: **/pub/genie/airwar/***

Air Warrior Flight Simulator

Fly head-to-head against other Air Warrior aces in this exciting WWII fighter simulation. Download this file for information and the program you need to play Air Warrior over the Internet.

Anonymous FTP:
Address: **cactus.org**
Path: **/pub/IHHD/dialer1.6.3.shar**

Air Warriors Front End

The PC version of the Air Warriors front end for flying over the Internet.

Anonymous FTP:
Address: **cs.uwp.edu**
Path: **/pub/incoming/games/airpc209.zip**

Android Pinball

Who is really controlling that ball? Pinball wizards, you may have met your match here.

Anonymous FTP:
Address: **wuarchive.wustl.edu**
Path: **/pub/msdos_uploads/games/0pinball.zip**

Anime Video Games

A list of anime-related video games available for many game systems. Includes a list of U.S. stores that sell Japanese video game cartridges.

Anonymous FTP:
Address: **romulus.rutgers.edu**
Path: **/pub/anime/misc/Anime-games**

Apogee Games

A multitude of fantastic games from Apogee, including such favorites as Captain Keen and Cosmo.

Anonymous FTP:
Address: **world.std.com**
Path: **/src/msdos/games/apogee**

Arcade Video Game Tricks

A large list of tricks and cheats for many of the classic video arcade games. Lists are arranged by skill level (i.e., beginner, intermediate, and advanced).

Anonymous FTP:
Address: **ftp.spies.com**
Path: **/game_archive/cheatList/***

Gopher:
Name: Internet Wiretap
Address: **wiretap.spies.com**
Choose: **Video Game Archive
| cheatList**

Atari Archive

Huge archive for all Atari computers, including the 8-bit machines, ST range, Falcon and Lynx.

Anonymous FTP:
Address: **atari.archive.umich.edu**
Path: **/atari/***

Batltris

A PC-based game for those Tetris fans who want a little bit more. You play Batltris on two PCs connected with a null modem cable. The game is like Tetris, but you have other options, such as flipping over your opponent's game board.

Anonymous FTP:
Address: **wuarchive.wustl.edu**
Path: **/pub/games/batltris.zip**

Bip Bop 2

A VGA Breakout-like game for DOS.

Anonymous FTP:
 Address: **wuarchive.wustl.edu**
 Path: **/pub/msdos_uploads/games/bigbop2.zip**

Bolo

A FAQ list explaining how to play Bolo, a sixteen player, graphical, networked, realtime tank battle game for the Macintosh.

Anonymous FTP:
 Address: **rtfm.mit.edu**
 Path:
 /pub/usenet/news.answers/games/bolo-faq

Bolo Tracker

A program that keeps track of and reports on all the bolo games currently under way, including the number of players and sides, and the number of neutral bases and pills available. It also gives addresses and IP numeric addresses to join these games.

Telnet:
 Address: **gwis.circ.gwu.edu 1234**

Boulder Bash

The DOS version of the popular Boulder Bash game for VGA.

Anonymous FTP:
 Address: **wuarchive.wustl.edu**
 Path: **/pub/msdos_uploads/games/boulder.zip**

Civilization Editor

An editor for the popular DOS game Civilization.

Anonymous FTP:
 Address: **wuarchive.wustl.edu**
 Path: **/pub/msdos_uploads/games/civedit1.zip**

Civilization Hack

This program allows you to modify many of the elements and characteristics of Civilization, such as unit movements, strengths and so on.

Anonymous FTP:
 Address: **wuarchive.wustl.edu**
 Path: **/pub/msdos_uploads/games/civhack1.zip**

Cuboid 4

A DOS VGA game based on Rubik's Cube.

Archie:
 Pattern: **cuboid4.zip**

The World of Bolo

Bolo is a magnificent computer game -- developed by a programmer named Stuart Cheshire -- in which you play against other people over a network. Bolo is like chess in that it is simple to learn, but difficult to master. There are Bolo players (and fanatics) all over the Internet who have developed sophisticated systems of strategies and ethos, and whose devotion to this pastime transcends the ordinary.

The idea of Bolo is to control a tank that travels around a landscape (called a "map") containing trees, water, swamps, roads and so on. The map also contains "pillboxes" and "bases", structures which have certain characteristics and important strategic value. Your tank has bullets and shields, which you can use for offense and defense, respectively.

It takes a while to learn how to play Bolo well, but if you like strategy and arcade games, any time you put in will be well repaid. Remember, you play in real time against other people, and much of the strategy involves making (and breaking) alliances, and anticipating the actions of the other players. It is not unknown to hear of serious players working in teams during 12-hour long games.

To play Bolo, you need (1) a Macintosh (and only a Macintosh), and (2) a network connection to other Bolo players. This connection can be on your local network or on the Internet. However, the Internet connection should be direct; a phone hookup, even with SLIP or PPP, will be too slow. Before you start, be sure to read the frequently asked question (FAQ) list and the documentation.

A
B
C
D
E
F
G
H
I
J
K
L
M
N
O
P
Q
R
S
T
U
V
W
X
Y
Z

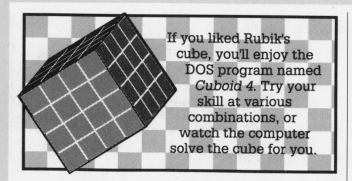

If you liked Rubik's cube, you'll enjoy the DOS program named *Cuboid 4*. Try your skill at various combinations, or watch the computer solve the cube for you.

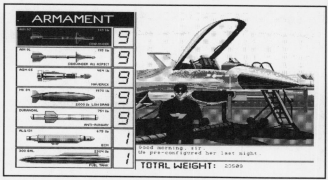

The Internet is a marvelous source for items of interest to the game player. Just teach yourself how to use Anonymous FTP and you can find not only free software and shareware games, but utilities, hints, cheats, additional scenery, missions and more. This image you see here is **cockpit.gif** from Northern Arizona University (**ftp.nau.edu**). If you use Archie to search for **cockpit**, you will find much more specific images, such as **F111C-cockpit.jpg** and **falconcockpit.gif**.

Doom FAQ List

A FAQ file on the game Doom, by ID Software.

Anonymous FTP:
   Address: **wuarchive.wustl.edu**
   Path: **/pub/msdos_uploads/games/doomfaq2.zip**

Dune Utilities

Scenario and game editors and savers for Dune.

Anonymous FTP:
   Address: **wuarchive.wustl.edu**
   Path: **/pub/msdos_uploads/games/dune2ed2.zip**

Euclid I

A 3D strategy game with a multilevel playing board similar to the one in the original *Star Trek* series.

Anonymous FTP:
   Address: **wuarchive.wustl.edu**
   Path: **/pub/msdos_uploads/games/euclid10.zip**

Falcon 3.0 Scenarios

Chad scenarios and utilities for the popular Falcon 3.0 flight simulator.

Anonymous FTP:
   Address: **cactus.org**
   Path: **/pub/falcon3/f3chad.zip**

Falcon 3.0 Upgrades

Upgrade files and utility programs for Falcon 3.0, a popular PC flight simulator from Spectrum HoloByte.

Anonymous FTP:
   Address: **onion.rain.com**
   Path: **/pub/falcon3**

Fleet Defender

A demonstration program for a new game which is rapidly gaining in popularity.

Anonymous FTP:
   Address: **wuarchive.wustl.edu**
   Path: **/pub/msdos_uploads/
      game_demos/mpsf14.zip**

Flight Simulators

Don't worry if you can't fly a plane; simulators are the next best thing. Be bold, be daring, get crazy and never have to worry about the ejection button. The **.flight-sim** newsgroup concentrates on PC flight simulators, touching such topics as bugs and bug fixes, simulator missions and objectives, and game reviews. If your interest in simulation goes beyond games, check out **.simulators**, which deals with flight simulation on all levels.

Usenet:
   Newsgroup: **comp.sys.ibm.pc.games.flight-sim**
   Newsgroup: **rec.aviation.simulators**

Game Demos

Demos of the shareware games Chase, HXINTINT, Risk and Solo.

Anonymous FTP:
Address: **wuarchive.wustl.edu**
Path: **/pub/msdos_uploads/games/lmsgames.zip**

Game Developer's Magazine

An electronic magazine devoted to game developers and programmers.

Anonymous FTP:
Address: **wuarchive.wustl.edu**
Path: **/pub/msdos_uploads/games/gdm1.zip**

Goldrunner

An arcade-style VGA game for DOS.

Anonymous FTP:
Address: **wuarchive.wustl.edu**
Path: **/pub/msdos_uploads/games/unrgrnn.zip**

Head-to-Head Game Mailing Lists

A mailing list for people interested in multiuser, realtime PC games you can play over the Internet.

Listserv mailing list:
List Address: **ihhd@cactus.org**
Subscription Address: **listserv@cactus.org**

Home Video Games History

The history of video games, including all the interesting turns and events that make today's games what they are.

Anonymous FTP:
Address: **ftp.spies.com**
Path: **/Library/Media/Games/videogam.his**

Gopher:
Name: Internet Wiretap
Address: **wiretap.spies.com**
Choose: **Wiretap Online Library**
  | Mass Media
  | Games and Video Games
  | Home Video Games History

Existential Relief for Home Video Players

If you are a home video game fanatic, you may feel a philosophical angst at spending so much of your time in the game world; so much so that you lose a sense of your past. This need not be a problem. Simply take a look at the home video games history and find out how the game that you are using today is part of a proud tradition dating way, way back to the early 1970s. No longer will you feel detached from your culture simply because you spend all your time in front of the tube killing bad guys.

Howitzer94

A Super-VGA game for PCs where tanks do battle on a 2D field in real time.

Anonymous FTP:
Address: **wuarchive.wustl.edu**
Path: **/pub/games/hwitz094.exe**

Imperium Rex

Your basic world domination game, for one to three players.

Anonymous FTP:
Address: **wuarchive.wustl.edu**
Path: **/pub/msdos_uploads/games/rex101.zip**

Killer List of Video Games

A huge list of coin-operated video and arcade games, including descriptions and comments on each.

Anonymous FTP:
Address: **ftp.spies.com**
Path: **/Library/Media/Games/videogam.lis**

Gopher:
Name: Internet Wiretap
Address: **wiretap.spies.com**
Choose: **Wiretap Online Library**
  | Mass Media
  | Games and Video Games
  | The Killer List of Video Games

Lynx Cheats

Cheat sheets and passwords for Atari Lynx video games.

Anonymous FTP:
    Address: **atari.archive.umich.edu**
    Path: **/atari/Lynx/cheats.zoo**

Masters of Orion

The latest patch to Masters of Orion, a Microprose game.

Anonymous FTP:
    Address: **wuarchive.wustl.edu**
    Path: **/pub/msdos_uploads/games/moo0927.zip**

Megatron VGA

A two-player VGA modem combat game that uses ray-trace graphics and sound cards. 386 or 486 computers and 14.4 K bps modems are recommended

Anonymous FTP:
    Address: **wuarchive.wustl.edu**
    Path: **/pub/msdos_uploads/games/mega612.zip**

Microsoft Flight Simulator

Tons of files for Microsoft Flight Simulator, including scenery of dozens of cities and regions throughout the world (check out the Hawaiian Islands). Also, static display files, aircraft (both civil and military) and utility programs.

Comment: For the second site, type **cd xevious:** (note the colon). Then you can get and display files in the usual manner.

Anonymous FTP:
    Address: **ftp.iup.edu**
    Path: **flight-sim/***

    Address: **ftp.iup.edu**
    Path: **xevious:/***

    Address: **wuarchive.wustl.edu**
    Path: **/pub/msdos_uploads/games/sewa100.zip**

Minerva

Simply the best DOS VGA minesweeper game. (At least the game's author thinks so.)

Anonymous FTP:
    Address: **wuarchive.wustl.edu**
    Path: **/pub/msdos_uploads/games/mines10e.zip**

Mortal Kombat

Discuss strategy with the masters of this popular arcade game.

Gopher:
    Name: University of Minnesota
    Address: **gopher.micro.umn.edu**
    Choose: **Fun & Games**
        | **Games**
        | **Arcade Games**
        | **Mortal Kombat**

NetHack for OS/2

The latest version of NetHack, compiled for OS/2 2.x.

Anonymous FTP:
    Address: **wuarchive.wustl.edu**
    Path: **/pub/msdos_uploads/games/os2nh—.zip**

NetHack Graphics

An EGA/VGA front end for the popular Internet game NetHack.

Anonymous FTP:
    Address: **wuarchive.wustl.edu**
    Path: **/pub/msdos_uploads/games/chrhac23.zip**

Prairie Dog Hunt for Windows

A refreshingly politically incorrect shoot-'em-up game for Windows. Choose between a pellet gun, .44 magnum, or shotgun to blow away cute little prairie critters that pop out of their mounds. Be quick, though, or they'll give you rabies before you get them all.

Anonymous FTP:
    Address: **extreme.cica.indiana.edu**
    Path: **/pub/pc/win3/games/windog10.zip**

Archie:
    Pattern: **windog10.zip**

**Make sure you are prepared:
Read
Emergency and Disaster**

Prince of Persia

A cheat utility for Prince of Persia.

Anonymous FTP:
    Address: **wuarchive.wustl.edu**
    Path: **/pub/msdos_uploads/games/pcheat.zip**

Privateer Cheat

Give your Privateer character 16 million credits!

Anonymous FTP:
    Address: **wuarchive.wustl.edu**
    Path: **/pub/msdos_uploads/games/whmbpvct.zip**

Queen for Windows

A card game for Windows 3.x.

Anonymous FTP:
    Address: **wuarchive.wustl.edu**
    Path: **/pub/msdos_uploads/games/queenwin.zip**

𝔐icrosoft Window users: try *Queen*, a card game written for Windows.

Rad

A simple, two-player VGA "shoot-everything-that-moves" game.

Anonymous FTP:
    Address: **wuarchive.wustl.edu**
    Path: **/pub/msdos_uploads/games/rad11.zip**

Sega Game Secrets

A lists of secrets and cheats for Sega Genesis and Sega CD video games.

Anonymous FTP:
    Address: **rtfm.mit.edu**
    Path: **/pub/usenet/news.answers/games/
    video-games/sega/***

Super Secret Stuff for Sega Supporters

Attention Sega game players: Wouldn't you like to know all the secret stuff that the men in suits want desperately to keep hidden? Of course you do, and now you can have it all. Just use Anonymous FTP to connect to the Usenet archive (**rtfm.mit.edu**), and the secret list of special stuff is yours for the downloading.

Sega Hardware

Details and information about Sega video game systems hardware, including Genesis joystick pinouts and Genesis hardware internals.

Anonymous FTP:
    Address: **ftp.spd.louisville.edu**
    Path: **/pub/sega/***

Snackman

A great Pac Man knockoff with Sound Blaster support.

Anonymous FTP:
    Address: **wuarchive.wustl.edu**
    Path: **/pub/msdos_uploads/games/snackman.zip**

Spear of Destiny

A whopping 21 new levels to the Wolf-3D sequel Spear of Destiny.

Anonymous FTP:
    Address: **wuarchive.wustl.edu**
    Path: **/pub/msdos_uploads/games/sod_cc1.zip**

A
B
C
D
E
F
G
H
I
J
K
L
M
N
O
P
Q
R
S
T
U
V
W
X
Y
Z

Streetfighter 2

A FAQ list and strategies for this popular beat-'em-up video game.

Anonymous FTP:
Address: **mrcnext.cso.uiuc.edu**
Path: **/pub/local/sf2/***

SuperBlox

A VGA game similar to Tetris.

Anonymous FTP:
Address: **wuarchive.wustl.edu**
Path: **/pub/msdos_uploads/games/sblox.zip**

Turoid

A new paddle-ball game with VGA and Sound Blaster support.

Anonymous FTP:
Address: **wuarchive.wustl.edu**
Path: **/pub/msdos_uploads/games/turoid11.zip**

Ultima Underworld

Cheats, tips and tricks for Ultima Underworld I and II.

Anonymous FTP:
Address: **wuarchive.wustl.edu**
Path: **/pub/msdos_uploads/games/uwcheats.zip**

Vectrex Arcade System

Service manual, games, music, instructions, internals guide, programming notes, and more relating to the Vectrex Arcade System.

Anonymous FTP:
Address: **csus.edu**
Path: **/pub/vectrex/***

**Why be normal?
Read Bizarre**

Video Game Archive

Archive of material related to video games, including images of ROMs from arcade video games, repair hints, game lists, switch settings, cheats, FAQs and other items of interest.

Anonymous FTP:
Address: **ftp.spies.com**
Path: **/game_archive/***

Gopher:
Name: Internet Wiretap
Address: **wiretap.spies.com**
Choose: **Video Game Archive**

Video Game Discussions

Discussion groups relating to many popular video and arcade games.

Usenet:
Newsgroup: **rec.games.video.arcade**

Video Games FAQs

Questions and answers about video game systems, equipment, magazines, cartridges, cheats, terms, developments, problems and more.

Anonymous FTP:
Address: **rtfm.mit.edu**
Path: **/pub/usenet/news.answers/games/video-games/faq/***

Video Poker Tutor

A tutorial for Video Poker.

Anonymous FTP:
Address: **wuarchive.wustl.edu**
Path: **/pub/msdos_uploads/games/vptutor.zip**

War in Russia

A new version of War in Russia.

Anonymous FTP:
Address: **wuarchive.wustl.edu**
Path: **/pub/msdos_uploads/games/wirx1.zip**

The Internet will set you free

Wolf-3D

An amazing 59 new levels for Wolf-3D.

Anonymous FTP:
  Address: **wuarchive.wustl.edu**
  Path: **/pub/msdos_uploads/games/w3d_cc1.zip**

Wolf-3D has got to be one of the most amazing computer video games ever. And now you can download free descriptions for many more levels of find-em-and-shoot-em-before-they-get-you adventures.

Excerpt from the Net...

(from the Video Game Archive)

[The following is from a frequently asked question (FAQ) list, explaining the best
[strategies for buying a used video game.]

Q: What happened to my favourite game while it was at the arcade, and where did it go
[when it left?
A: Here's a rough sketch, based on the authors' experiences, of what the first few years
[of a game's life is like.

An OPERATOR (the owner of video arcade games) makes money by buying video games for
$2500-$3000 and running them for several months... After the first week of operation, the
operator will probably have $200-$400 inside. If a game costs $3200 and the operator
gets $200/week, it takes the operator 16 weeks to make back his original investment.
Anything that comes in after that is pure profit.

Unless you can offer the operator more than he will make from a machine over the next
three months or so, you can forget it. This is why you never hear of anybody buying new
machines from an operator.

Q: What makes operators tick?
A: Very simply. In fact, one word will suffice: MONEY.

Q: So this is the MONEY principle, right?
A: Right. The MONEY principle is simple: OPERATORS LOVE MONEY.

It's a simple rule, but its importance cannot be overstated. MONEY gets you in the door,
MONEY talks to the operator, MONEY pays your way when you're inside, and MONEY can even
help you get your favourite game away from the operator at the lowest price possible.
The strategy section of this FAQ will describe all of this (and more) in detail.

Operators own games for one reason: to make MONEY. If operators were allowed to run
porno shows on their games in order to collect quarters, they'd do it. Operators are not
interested in the art of game design. They are not interested in the impact that these
games have had upon society. And they are certainly not interested in packaging up the
boards for your favourite game and sending it halfway across the country -- not for you
or anyone else -- not when he can make several times as much money by sitting back and
letting players pump quarters into his games.

        AGAIN, ONLY ONE THING MATTERS TO OPERATORS:
    GETTING THE MOST MONEY OUT OF THE GAMES THEY OWN

        Read that sentence again.

You and I, however, only want to wrestle our favourite games away from these "operators".
So how do we do it? Suffice to say that whatever the answer is, it lies in MONEY. This
should be kept in mind as you read the remainder of this FAQ, and should be foremost in
your mind whenever you deal with an operator...

A
B
C
D
E
F
G
H
I
J
K
L
M
N
O
P
Q
R
S
T
U
V
W
X
Y
Z

WEATHER

Coping with a Flood-Damaged Home or Farm

Information and pointers on cleaning up after a flood. Good advice from people who have learned the hard way.

Telnet:
Address: **exnet.iastate.edu**
Login: **flood**

Gray's Atlantic Seasonal Hurricane Forecast

Provides 1944-to-date seasonal means and current year forecast for the number of named storms, named storm days, hurricanes, hurricane days, major hurricanes, destruction potential and so on.

Finger:
Address: **forecast@typhoon.atmos.colostate.edu**

Hourly Auroral Activity Status Report

Get the latest reports on the activities of the Aurora Borealis (northern lights). Reports watches and warnings. This information is updated hourly.

Finger:
Address: **aurora@xi.uleth.ca**

Japanese Weather

Daily weather reports and satellite images in GIF format.

Gopher:
Name: National Institute for Physiological Sciences
Address: **gopher.nips.ac.jp**
Choose: **Weather JAPAN**

National Weather Service Forecasts

Weather reports for geographical regions, as well as reports categorized by weather type (i.e., storm fronts, severe storms, satellite images, Canada, Caribbean, etc.).

Gopher:
Name: University of Illinois
Address: **wx.atmos.uiuc.edu**

Name: University of Minnesota
Address: **ashpool.micro.umn.edu**
Choose: **Weather**

NOAA Earth Systems Data Directory

The NESDD is an information resource for identification, location and overview descriptions of Earth Science Data Sets (data from satellites).

Telnet:
Address: **esdim1.nodc.noaa.gov**
Login: **noaadir**

Address: **nodc.nodc.noaa.gov**
Login: **noaadir**

NOAA Space Environment Services Center

A database of space environment reports, including solar forecasts and activity reports.

Telnet:
Address: **selvax.sel.bldrdoc.gov**
Login: **sel**

Satellite Images

Display Meteosat satellite images and general interest weather information on your X Window terminal.

Comment: The first time, you will be asked to send mail to **meteo-window@csp.it** with the numerical address of your graphics terminal (must be running X Window).

Telnet:
Address: **cspnsv.csp.it 5000**

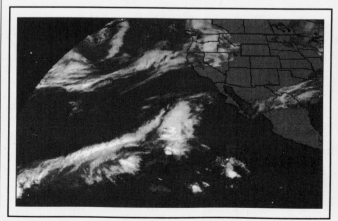

If you use a Unix computer with X Window, you can telnet to port 5000 at **cspnsv.csp.it** to display satellite images on your system. Satellite image files are also widely available from NOAA, NASA, and the National Weather Service.

Solar and Geophysical Reports

Get the latest reports on solar activity. Reports watches and warnings. Information is extensive and includes numerous text graphs and tabular data. This information is updated every three hours.

Finger:
Address: **daily@xi.uleth.ca**
Address: **solar@xi.uleth.ca**

Surface Analysis and Weather Maps

This Anonymous FTP site carries current surface analysis and infrared weather maps. Maps are updated often; old maps are not archived. Maps are mostly in GIF format.

Anonymous FTP:
Address: **vmd.cso.uiuc.edu**
Path: **WX/**

Weather Reports

Get up-to-date weather reports for any location on the planet. An easy-to-use interface guides you through the process of selecting a city or location, and then viewing the weather report onscreen or downloading it to your computer.

Telnet:
Address: **downwind.sprl.umich.edu 3000**

Weather Reports (Australia)

Current weather, forecasts, recent trends and future developments, including boating and coastal conditions, river and solar reports for all parts of Australia.

Telnet:
Address: **vicbeta.vic.bom.gov.au 55555**

Weather Reports (Canada)

Weather forecasts and extended forecasts for all areas of Canada.

Gopher:
Name: Novia Scotia Technology Network
Address: **nstn.ns.ca**
Choose: **Canadian Weather Forecasts**

WORLD CULTURES

African Forum

A mailing list forum for the discussion of issues and topics of interest to Africans, both in Africa and elsewhere.

Listserv mailing list:
List Address: **africa-l@brufmg.bitnet**
Subscription Address: **listserv@brufmg.bitnet**

Arab Press Newsletter

An electronic monthly newsletter of the Arab press. Includes unedited quotes from Arab press members from around the world.

Internet mailing list:
List Address:
arab-press@jerusalem1.datasrv.co.il
Subscription Address:
arab-press-request@jerusalem1.datasrv.co.il

Argentina

All about Argentina: the food, the culture and anything else you'd like to know.

Internet mailing list:
List Address: **argentina@ois.db.toronto.edu**
Subscription Address:
argentina-request@ois.db.toronto.edu

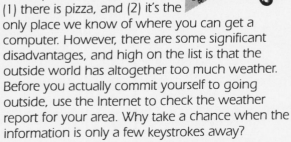

The Outside World

Living on the Internet is fine, but the outside world has two important advantages: (1) there is pizza, and (2) it's the only place we know of where you can get a computer. However, there are some significant disadvantages, and high on the list is that the outside world has altogether too much weather. Before you actually commit yourself to going outside, use the Internet to check the weather report for your area. Why take a chance when the information is only a few keystrokes away?

Australiana

News, sports, FAQs, pictures, radio information, statistics, film guides and more about Australia.

Gopher:
    Name: Universite de Montreal
    Address: **megasun.bch.umontreal.ca**
    Choose: **Australiana - News, sports, FAQs, etc. about Australia**

Baltic Republics Discussion List

A mailing list to facilitate communications to, with, and about the Baltic Republics of Lithuania, Latvia and Estonia.

Listserv mailing list:
    List Address: **balt-l@ubvm.bitnet**
    Subscription Address: **listserv@ubvm.bitnet**

Bosnia

A daily mailing list covering news, events and discussion of Bosnia and Hercegovina. The list is run by volunteers and submissions in either English or Bosnian are accepted.

Internet mailing list:
    List Address: **bosnet@math.lsa.umich.edu**
    Subscription Address:
      bosnet-request@math.lsa.umich.edu

Brazil

A mailing list for general discussion and information about Brazil. Portuguese is the main language of the discussion.

Internet mailing list:
    List Address: **brasil@cs.ucla.edu**
    Subscription Address: **brasil-request@cs.ucla.edu**

Central America Discussion List

A mailing list for students in and from Central American countries, especially Panama and Costa Rica.

Listserv mailing list:
    List Address: **centam-l@ubvm.bitnet**
    Subscription Address: **listserv@ubvm.bitnet**

The Internet will set you free

Central European Development

A mailing list for issues of relevance to regional development and regional development research in Central Europe, including a wide range of disciplines from regional science to economic geography.

Listserv mailing list:
    List Address: **cerro-l@aearn.bitnet**
    Subscription Address: **listserv@aearn.bitnet**

Country Statistics

Detailed statistical information on nearly every country in the world.

Gopher:
    Name: Universite de Montreal
    Address: **megasun.bch.umontreal.ca**
    Choose: **Australiana - News, sports, FAQs, etc. about Australia | Other Countries' Statistics**

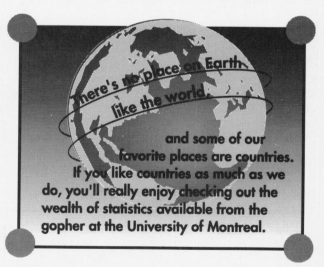

There's no place on Earth like the world.

and some of our favorite places are countries. If you like countries as much as we do, you'll really enjoy checking out the wealth of statistics available from the gopher at the University of Montreal.

Croatian Foreign Press Bureau

The Croatian Information Centre is an independent, non-profit, non-political, and non-governmental cultural and educational institution with the goal of spreading the truth about Croatia and the Croatian nation throughout the world.

Gopher:
    Name: Croatia
    Address: **rujan.srce.hr**
    Choose: **English Language**
      | Information - Subject Tree
      | News - Daily..
      | Foreign Press Bureau

European Community

Discussions of the European Community and about Europe in general.

Listserv mailing list:
    List Address: **ec@trmetu.bitnet**
    Subscription Address: **listserv@trmetu.bitnet**

French Chat

Causerie is French for talk or chat, and this list is dedicated to fun conversations in French.

Listserv mailing list:
    List Address: **causerie@uquebec.ca**
    Subscription Address: **listserv@uquebec.ca**

Greece

Tourist information about Greece, including hotels, driving, visa requirements, health care, phone system, education and scenic pictures.

Gopher:
    Name: Colorado State University Optical
      Computing Lab
    Address: **sylvia.lance.colostate.edu**
    Choose: **Greece**

Hindu Names

A large list of Hindu names and their meanings.

Anonymous FTP:
    Address: **ftp.spies.com**
    Path: **/Library/Article/Language/hindu.nam**

Gopher:
    Name: Internet Wiretap
    Address: **wiretap.spies.com**
    Choose: **Wiretap Online Library**
      | Articles
      | Language
      | List of Hindu Names

Inter-Tribal Network (ITN)

A server for Native American interests, including information on taxpayer funds allocated to American Indians, festivals, holidays and recent policy descriptions.

Gopher:
    Name: CNS, Inc.
    Address: **cns.cscns.com**
    Choose: **Inter-Tribal Network**
      (The ITN Network for Native Americans)

Israel Project

The New York Israel Project is an online Jewish information service which provides Jewish religious, educational and social service information and resources.

Anonymous FTP:
    Address: **israel.nysernet.org**
    Path: **/israel/***

Gopher:
    Name: NYSERNet
    Address: **israel.nysernet.org 71**

Italy

A map of Europe, maps of Italy, and Italian national statistics on residents by age, sex, education, literacy, employment and marital status.

Gopher:
    Name: CINECA—Interuniversity Computer Center
    Address: **vm.cineca.it**
    Choose: **Information and Data about Italy**

Japan

Japanese language and culture-related material, including programs and documentation for processing Japanese language documents with computers.

Anonymous FTP:
    Address: **nic.funet.fi**
    Path: **/pub/culture/japan/***

The Internet is an excellent resource for artistic drawings of scenery and landscapes that you can use to illustrate or adorn your own work. This image is **mthood.gif** and it's widely available. This copy came from Japan (**ftp.kuis.kyoto-u.ac.jp**) in the directory **/MSDOS/simtel20-archive/gif**.

A
B
C
D
E
F
G
H
I
J
K
L
M
N
O
P
Q
R
S
T
U
V
W
X
Y
Z

Japan Information

This Gopher resource provides tourist information, information about events, radio schedules and directories. Also available are the Japanese constitution and other important Japanese documents and information.

Gopher:
Name: Nippon Telegraphic and Telephone Corp.
Address: **gopher.ntt.jp**
Choose: **JAPAN Information**

Japanese Constitution

The complete 1946 constitution of Japan. The constitution has 11 chapters in both English and Japanese.

Comment: The Japanese text is in shift JIS kanji code, and without correct software appears garbled.

Gopher:
Name: Nippon Telegraph and Telephone Corp.
Address: **gopher.ntt.jp**
Choose: **JAPAN Information**
 | **Introduction**
 | **Constitution**

Japanese Event Calendar

A comprehensive list and detailed information about major upcoming events, lectures, symposiums, workshops, and conferences to be held in Japan. The calendar has both English and Japanese versions.

Comment: The Japanese text is in shift JIS kanji code, and without correct software appears garbled.

Gopher:
Name: Nippon Telegraph and Telephone Corp.
Address: **gopher.ntt.jp**
Choose: **JAPAN Information**
 | **Calendar**

Make sure you are prepared: Read Emergency and Disaster

JewishNet

Software resources, libraries and catalogs, reading lists, and other servers and archives of Jewish and Hebrew interest.

Telnet:
Address: **vms.huji.ac.il**
Login: **jewishnet**

Malaysia, Singapore, and Islam News

A list for news only (no discussions) about Malaysia, Singapore, Islam, and other Asian countries when it is of interest to Malaysians or Singaporeans.

Listserv mailing list:
List Address: **berita-l@uiucvmd.bitnet**
Subscription Address: **listserv@uiucvmd.bitnet**

New Zealand

Everything you could want to know about beautiful New Zealand. Statistics on population, economy, politics, geography, climate, shopping and other tourist information.

Gopher:
Name: Wellington City Council
Address: **gopher.wcc.govt.nz**
Choose: **New Zealand information**

NY-Israel Project

A network for Jewish religious, educational and social service organizations worldwide. Includes interesting lists, articles and information on politics and libraries, as well as extensive information on how to make *aliyah* (emigrate to Israel), including housing information, military service policies, and what to expect when you get there.

Gopher:
Name: NYSERNet
Address: **israel.nysernet.org 71**

Lonely? Try the Personals

Radio Japan

Broadcast schedule and introductory information in over 22 languages for Radio Japan, the Japanese overseas broadcasting service.

Gopher:
Name: Nippon Telegraph and Telephone Corp.
Address: **gopher.ntt.jp**
Choose: **JAPAN Information**
| **Radio Japan**

Russia

About the Russian language and culture, including a literature guide, computer-related material, glossaries and word lists, recipes, jokes, lyrics, politics and translation information.

Anonymous FTP:
Address: **nic.funet.fi**
Path: **/pub/culture/russian/***

San Francisco Bay Area

This newsgroup and FAQ are focused primarily on the San Francisco Bay Area, but most of the information is applicable to any area. The FAQ contains information on publications, Usenet, FAQ archives, Gopher, mail, **uucp** and much more.

Anonymous FTP:
Address: **ftp.spies.com**
Path: **/ba.internet/FAQ**

Usenet:
Newsgroup: **ba.internet**

Southern United States

Bubba is devoted to the conversational language, culture, lifestyles, history and humor of the southern United States.

Internet mailing list:
List Address: **bubba-l@knuth.mtsu.edu**
Subscription Address:
bubba-l-request@knuth.mtsu.edu

This is the first book of the rest of your life

Soviet Archives

English translations of newly opened Soviet archives, including documents about the secret police, attacks on intelligentsia, famine, the cold war and other topics.

Anonymous FTP:
Address: **seq1.loc.gov**
Path: **/pub/soviet.archive/***

Gopher:
Name: University of Virginia
Address: **gopher.virginia.edu**
Choose: **Library Services**
| **University Library Resources (Alphabetic Organization)**
| **Soviet Archive Exhibit, Library of Congress**

Thailand

FAQs regarding Thailand, travel information and economic and demographic data.

Gopher:
Name: Asia Institute of Technology
Address: **emailhost.ait.ac.th**
Choose: **Asian Institute of Technology Campus Info | Thailand Info**

Usenet:
Newsgroup: **soc.culture.thai**

Usenet Cultural Groups

About the languages, culture, people, customs and many other aspects of countries around the world.

Usenet:
Newsgroup: **soc.culture.***

Got too much stuff?
Need some more stuff?
Try
Buying and Selling

A
B
C
D
E
F
G
H
I
J
K
L
M
N
O
P
Q
R
S
T
U
V
W
X
Y
Z

World Constitutions

The constitutions and basic laws for many countries around the world, including Germany, Hong Kong, United States, Canada, China, Hungary, Slovak Republic, the English Bill of Rights, Magna Carta, and John at Runnymede.

Anonymous FTP:
Address: **ftp.spies.com**
Path: **/Gov/World/***

Gopher:
Name: Internet Wiretap
Address: **wiretap.spies.com**
Choose: **Government Docs (US & World)**
  | World Constitutions

World Heritage List

A list of both cultural and natural historic sites, properties and cities around the world, as approved by UNESCO's World Heritage Committee.

Anonymous FTP:
Address: **ftp.spies.com**
Path: **/Library/Document/heritage.lis**

Gopher:
Name: Internet Wiretap
Address: **wiretap.spies.com**
Choose: **Wiretap Online Library**
  | Assorted Documents
  | UNESCO's World Heritage List

WRITING

CyberPunk

Step through a portal to another dimension, a cyberpunk world where darkness, depression and danger are the norm. Lovers of cyberpunk sling slang around like literary fly-fishing lures. If you love high-tech, heavy metal punk, you will love the virtual reality of cyberpunk.

Usenet:
Newsgroup: **alt.cyberpunk.chatsubo**

> # Why be normal?
> # Read Bizarre

Dr. Who

Who is that odd fellow bedecked in a voluminous overcoat and mile-long neck scarf? Who, that's who. Hop in your tardis and join the Dr. Who following with creative stories based on the adventures of the happy-go-unlucky doctor. (But we thought Who was on first...)

Usenet:
Newsgroup: **alt.drwho.creative**

Erotica

Stimulate more than your mind. Wrap your brain around sensuously stated sentences and pleasantly playful paragraphs. Slide slowly into the warm depths of the written word. Allow yourself to be swept up in the moment as your fingers press against the keyboard and your screen casts its gentle reflections on your skin.

Usenet:
Newsgroup: **alt.sex.stories**
Newsgroup: **alt.sex.stories.d**
Newsgroup: **rec.arts.erotica**

EROTICA

What a nice word for such an earthy subject. The Internet is full of people who enjoy sex and some of them write stories. You can share those stories in the privacy of your own home just by reading Usenet newsgroups. Be careful though, if you take your computer into the hot tub you might be in for a shocking experience.

Fantasy Role-Playing

Magic, mystery and adventure await you once you step across the line that separates fantasy from reality. Tag along with role-players in Dragon's Inn, Haven's Rest and Cloven Shield as they weave a web of tales in front of this virtual fireplace.

Usenet:
Newsgroup: **alt.dragons-inn**
Newsgroup: **alt.pub.cloven-shield**
Newsgroup: **alt.pub.havens-rest**
Newsgroup: **rec.games.frp.archives**

Manga and Anime

Discover the charm of Japanese animation and storytelling in the form of anime and manga. These two artforms combine words and pictures to create quick and lively stories. You don't have to know Japanese to love these wonderful works of story art.

Usenet:
>   Newsgroup: **rec.arts.anime.stories**
>   Newsgroup: **rec.arts.manga**

Prose

These bite-sized morsels of prose make the perfect afternoon brain snack. No matter what tickles your fancy, the variety of stories will have something for you. Read or share, it's up to you: just remember, if you don't use it, you'll lose it. The **.prose** newsgroups are for stories and articles. The **.d** newsgroup is for discussion.

Usenet:
>   Newsgroup: **alt.prose**
>   Newsgroup: **alt.prose.d**
>   Newsgroup: **rec.arts.prose**

Star Trek

Beam aboard for Mr. Spock's wild ride. You will find yourself engaged in raucous laughter at *Star Trek* parodies, so don't read this group while in the library, lest you be subjected to some severe ear-twisting by a librarian with a tight bun on her head. Stick to the safer, more suspenseful stories that will keep you on the edge of your seat while the *Star Trek* crew race through the universe, boldly taking you where no one has gone before.

Usenet:
>   Newsgroup: **alt.startrek.creative**

Star Trek fans:
When the television episodes, videos, movies, books and conventions just aren't enough, turn to Usenet and read original stories based on the *Star Trek* universe.

Excerpt from the Net...

```
Newsgroup: alt.pub.dragons-inn
Subject: Guess What's Coming to Dinner

Synopsis:
     The party members have been ambushed at a dinner given by their host, the vampire
     Pericles.  A great battle has just begun...

Unable to enjoy her food and not really interested in dessert, Matte had just begun to
try to excuse herself from the table when the servants attacked.  Halfway out of her seat
already, she quickly leapt upon her chair and picked up a piece of cutlery from the
table.  She attempted to hit one of the creatures attacking Moria on the opposite side of
the room, but was picked up from behind as she drew her arm back, the knife falling
harmlessly to the floor.

Matte felt the grip of the armoured servant tighten as she was lifted from her feet.  The
creature's grasp was very firm, and she was unable to free herself to conjure assistance
or use her weapon.  She grunted and kicked at her captor but to no avail.

Suddenly, she felt the iron grip give way as she landed on her feet and heard the clatter
of armour fall to the floor above the din of battle in the room.

She turned to see Tomonobu behind her, his sword flashing at more armoured servants
further away.  "Rescuing you is getting to be a habit, Little One," he said as he moved
away to deal with problems of his own...
```

A
B
C
D
E
F
G
H
I
J
K
L
M
N
O
P
Q
R
S
T
U
V
W
X
Y
Z

X-RATED RESOURCES

Erotic Pictures

There are LOTS and LOTS of X-rated pictures posted to Usenet newsgroups, so you will never have to go without. In order to download the pictures, you will need to be able to use a newsreader program to find and save the appropriate articles. Most pictures are broken into parts and **uuencoded**, each part being posted as a separate article. You must put together the parts and then **uudecode** the resultant file in order to re-create the original picture (which is usually in GIF or JPEG format). In order to look at the picture, you will need a GIF or JPEG viewer program. If you need help with any of this, get our book *The Internet Complete Reference* (published by Osborne/McGraw-Hill) and read Chapter 18.

Usenet:

    Newsgroup: **alt.binaries.pictures.erotica**
    Newsgroup: **alt.binaries.pictures.erotica.blondes**
    Newsgroup: **alt.binaries.pictures.erotica.female**
    Newsgroup: **alt.binaries.pictures.erotica.male**
    Newsgroup: **alt.binaries.pictures.erotica.orientals**
    Newsgroup: **alt.sex.pictures**
    Newsgroup: **alt.sex.pictures.female**
    Newsgroup: **alt.sex.pictures.male**

LOVE TO THINK?

Smart, willing, intellectual women are on standby and eager to talk to you. Let us turn you on to a little Shakespeare or – for those of you into hardcore – some James Joyce. Feel free to be yourself. All that is on *our* minds is to stimulate *you* into some intellectual action. We'll talk about anything... quadratic equations, Unix, objectivism, post-modernist sculpture, the current political administration, Archie searching, or the Big Bang theory.

Call now and fill our heads with ideas.
Phone (900) 4-BRAINS or telnet to 127.0.0.1.
Only $12.95 per minute.
Student discounts available.
Special rates for readers of
The Internet Complete Reference.

Erotic Sounds

If you have a computer that can play sounds, you can download sounds to play with. Not as much fun as making your own, but you can play them over and over, whenever you want.

Usenet:

    Newsgroup: **alt.sex.sounds**

Fetishes

Don't feel alone just because you have certain preferences. There are lots of people like you out there and they are ready to share. Even if you don't have a fetish or a strange desire, you may enjoy reading about people who do. Maybe you'll get some new ideas. (By the way, the **.fa** newsgroup is for those who like fat people.)

Excerpt from the Net...

```
Newsgroup: alt.sex.fetish.feet
Subject: Stereotypes


Although I've enjoyed reading this newsgroup from its beginning, I've never been
comfortable with its name...

I suppose it's a matter of degree. I may like catching glimpses of a woman's bare feet,
someone else may like sucking her toes, and a third likes high heels and painted
toenails, but we're all lumped together as "foot fetishists" with those who cannot get
sexually excited without some contact with feet.

The Net is certainly big enough for all tastes, many of which I may personally find
distasteful, but I agree that the stereotype of the "foot fetishist" as a grovelling
submissive is in large part wrong.

There's got to be a better name for this interest.
```

Usenet:
Newsgroup: **alt.sex.bestiality**
Newsgroup: **alt.sex.bondage**
Newsgroup: **alt.sex.exhibitionism**
Newsgroup: **alt.sex.fetish.amputee**
Newsgroup: **alt.sex.fetish.diapers**
Newsgroup: **alt.sex.fetish.fa**
Newsgroup: **alt.sex.fetish.feet**
Newsgroup: **alt.sex.fetish.hair**
Newsgroup: **alt.sex.fetish.orientals**
Newsgroup: **alt.sex.fetish.watersports**
Newsgroup: **alt.sex.spanking**
Newsgroup: **alt.sex.voyeurism**

General Sex Discussion

On Usenet, the discussion about sex ranges from serious to XXX-rated. The **alt.sex** group is for just about any topic you want. The **.wizards** group is for serious questions, serious sex experts and would-be serious sex experts. (But don't let yourself get too serious.)

Usenet:
Newsgroup: **alt.sex**
Newsgroup: **alt.sex.wizards**

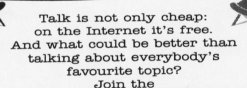

Talk is not only cheap:
on the Internet it's free.
And what could be better than
talking about everybody's
favourite topic?
Join the
General Sex Discussion
on Usenet and experience
the freedom of real talk
about real topics.

Index of Erotic Stories

An ambitious fellow named Ed Stauff maintains an index of the stories posted to **rec.arts.erotica**, **alt.sex** and **alt.sex.stories**. Each listing includes the title of the story, the author's name, the size, and the archive name from **rec.arts.erotica** (if there is one). There is also a brief synopsis or review. This index is posted at irregular intervals to **alt.sex** and **alt.sex.stories**. Note: Ed does not have an archive of all the stories, so don't bother asking him to send one to you. (Also, don't ask him to mail you a copy of the index; wait for it to be posted.)

Usenet:
Newsgroup: **alt.sex**
Newsgroup: **alt.sex.stories**
Newsgroup: **rec.arts.erotica**

Kama Sutra

The Kama Sutra is perhaps the most well-known erotic self-help book. See what the ancient commentators have to teach you about mankind's oldest pastime.

Anonymous FTP:
Address: **quartz.rutgers.edu**
Path: **/pub/sex/kama.sutra**

Gopher:
Name: Rutgers Quartz Text Archive
Address: **quartz.rutgers.edu**
Choose: **Sex | kama.sutra**

Limericks

Probably sometime, somewhere, somebody actually did write a limerick that wasn't dirty. If so, it's not here.

Anonymous FTP:
Address: **quartz.rutgers.edu**
Path: **/pub/humor/limericks**

Gopher:
Name: Rutgers Quartz Text Archive
Address: **quartz.rutgers.edu**
Choose: **Humor | Limericks**

Purity Tests

Purity tests have long been a staple of the Usenet humor groups. These tests consist of many sexually-oriented questions designed to help you find out just how "pure" you are. Hint: The best such test is the 400-question one.

Anonymous FTP:
Address: **ftp.spies.com**
Path: **/Library/Article/Sex/purity***

Address: **ftp.std.com**
Path: **/pub/purity/***

Address: **nic.funet.fi**
Path: **/pub/doc/fun/tests/purity***

Address: **quartz.rutgers.edu**
Path: **/pub/purity/***

Archie:
Pattern: **purity**

Gopher:
Name: Internet Wiretap
Address: **wiretap.spies.com**
Choose: **Wiretap Online Library**
   | Articles
   | Sex
   | The 400 Question Purity Test

A
B
C
D
E
F
G
H
I
J
K
L
M
N
O
P
Q
R
S
T
U
V
W
X
Y
Z

Sex-Related Gopher Resources

Here is a wonderful Gopher that contains all kinds of sexually-oriented material (as well as a wealth of other fascinating information). Whether you need to check the price of a prostitute in Halifax, Canada, or just read a review of your favorite strip joint, this is the place to be.

Anonymous FTP:
    Address: **ftp.spies.com**
    Path: **/Library/Article/Sex/***

Gopher:
    Name: Internet Wiretap
    Address: **wiretap.spies.com**
    Choose: **Wiretap Online Library**
      | Articles | Sex

Sex Stories

There comes a time in everyone's life when you get tired of reading Internet books. The next time you are looking for some fresh stimulation, turn to the Usenet newsgroups devoted to sharing erotic stories. (The **rec** newsgroup is moderated.)

Usenet:
    Newsgroup: **alt.pantyhose**
    Newsgroup: **alt.sex**
    Newsgroup: **alt.sex.stories**
    Newsgroup: **rec.arts.erotica**

Sexy Stories

Life is so short and, one day, you will come to the realization that there are more good things to read than you will have time for. What a waste it would be if you got to the end of your life and discovered that there was a huge backlog of sexy stories floating around the Internet. Don't let your life become a meaningless charade. Start reading today.

Excerpt from the Net...

(from the limerick collection on the "quartz" Gopher)

A pretty young maiden from France
Decided she'd "just take a chance".
    She let herself go
    For an hour or so
And now all her sisters are aunts.

Sex Story Archives

Some sex stories from **alt.sex**, **alt.sex.stories** and **rec.arts.erotica** are available via mail. To find out how it all works, send mail to one of the addresses below. (Note: There is no Anonymous FTP service from these sites and none is planned. It would overwhelm the network, so don't even ask.)

Mail:
    Address: **help@dithots.lonestar.org**

    Address: **server@hermes.acm.rpi.edu**
    Body: **help**

Sexual Humor

We all know that the best jokes are dirty. Here are some good ones.

Anonymous FTP:
    Address: **quartz.rutgers.edu**
    Path: **/pub/humor/Sex/***

Gopher:
    Name: Rutgers Quartz Text Archive
    Address: **quartz.rutgers.edu**
    Choose: **Humor**
      | Sex

Sexual Massage

There is a technique, developed by Eastern know-it-alls, that is pretty good when it comes to one-size-fits-all self-help. Take a look at this article and learn the ins and outs of Yoni and Lingam massage. (*Yoni* and *Lingam* are Sanskrit words. We can't print what they mean in English, so you will have to investigate for yourself.)

Anonymous FTP:
    Address: **ftp.spies.com**
    Path: **/Library/Article/Sex/massage.txt**

Gopher:
    Name: Internet Wiretap
    Address: **wiretap.spies.com**
    Choose: **Wiretap Online Library**
      | Articles
      | Sex
      | Yoni Massage How-To

Lonely? Try the Personals

YOUTH

Child Support

How do you feel about the issues of custody and child support? Find out the thoughts of others affected by these issues and learn about current legislation.

Usenet:
Newsgroup: **alt.child-support**

Childcare Newsletters

Selection of newsletters about kids and childcare in general.

Anonymous FTP:
Address: **nigel.msen.com**
Path: **/pub/newsletters/Kids/***

Interesting Projects for Young Children

The Schoolnet Gopher at Carleton University (Ottawa, Canada) has a wealth of resources for kids, parents and teachers. The *Cool Things to Try* section has ideas for interesting projects that you can do with your youngsters. for example, using common household articles, you can make your own thyxotropic substance. Not only will your kids have fun, but somebody (whose name we won't mention) might even learn something by accident.

Cool Things to Try

Have fun with a potato-powered clock, a liquid that changes to a solid under pressure, and other cool experiments.

Gopher:
Name: Schoolnet Gopher
Address: **gopher.carleton.ca**
Choose: **Schoolnet gopher**
| **Kindergarten to Grade 6 Corner**
| **Cool things to try...**

Disney

FAQs about Disneyland, lyrics to Disney songs, EuroDisney reports, and other material from the Magic Kingdom.

Anonymous FTP:
Address: **quartz.rutgers.edu**
Path: **/pub/disney/***

Gopher:
Name: Rutgers Quartz Text Archive
Address: **quartz.rutgers.edu**
Choose: **Disney - The Wonderful World of Disney**

You can even find nature pictures on the Internet. Animal pictures are great because animals don't read law books and think up reasons to sue you. This image is **zebra.gif** from Washington University Saint Louis (**ftp.wustl.edu**).

Lonely?
Try the Personals

Why be normal?
Read Bizarre

A B C D E F G H I J K L M N O P Q R S T U V W X Y Z

General Children

Kids say the darnedest things. Impart your information and experience regarding children from the cradle onward. Anecdotes, advice on doctors, behavior, activities, discipline and schooling legislation are just a few of the topics covered.

Usenet:
    Newsgroup: **misc.kids**

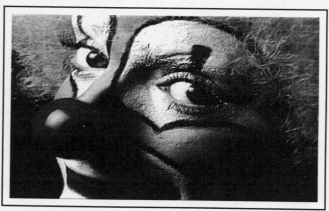

This picture is **clown.gif** from Singapore (**solomon.technet.sg**) in the directory **/pub/NUS/0/pc/msdos/gif**, but it's also in many other locations. For other locations and other clowns, use Archie to search for **clown**.

Great Beginnings

A newsletter that provides tips to help make the job of parenting easier and more rewarding.

Gopher:
    Name: University of Delaware
    Address: **lobster.mis.udel.edu**
    Choose: **UD Department & College Information Services**
       | **AGINFO: College of Agricultural Sciences**
       | **Newsletters**
       | **Great Beginning**

Make sure you are prepared: Read Emergency and Disaster

Excerpt from the Net...

```
Newsgroups: misc.kids
Subject: Re: "My daddy dressed me"

>> Well, Carrie's Daddy dressed her yesterday, and what a combination
>> he came up with!  She was wearing a pair of overalls, bright red
>> with...
>>
>> Normally, if Daddy dresses the kids, I leave on what he puts on
>> them, not wanting to belittle his efforts.  But normally he does
>> better than yesterday.

> I've been away from misc.kids for a while and, on tuning in today, it
> is disappointing to see that this sexist crap is still going on.  The
> traditional "this colour goes with that" attitude has clearly long
> been dropped from fad wear, in which any and every colour is worn
> together.

Sorry, but I have to disagree.  While I personally do not care if my son matches when he
plays, my wife and I do try to make sure he "matches" if we go out.  (Of course, I tend
to have a little more liberal interpretation of what matches than my wife does, but that
seems to be common given the father/mother responses. :-)

Now, I'm not saying it is important for a young child to match.  I don't place that much
weight on it.  However, one of the things I see later on in life, especially with males,
is that wearing the appropriate clothes to work/interviews, etc, one feels much more
confident when one isn't concerned about whether their tie matches their suit or if it
clashes...
```

How to Recycle Paper

A fun guide that teaches kids how to make paper from recycled trash and old paper.

Gopher:
>   Name: Schoolnet Gopher
>   Address: **ernest.ccs.carleton.ca**
>   Choose: **Kindergarten to Grade 6 Corner**
> | **Cool things to try...**
> | **Learn How to Make Your Own Recycled Paper!**

KidArt

A gallery of computer art presenting works by kids. Pictures are stored in GIF format, but the gallery supports MS-DOS, Mac, Amiga, Apple II and Atari systems.

Gopher:
>   Name: KIDLINK Gopher
>   Address: **kids.ccit.duq.edu**
>   Choose: **KIDART Computer Art Gallery**

Kidlink

An educational project to encourage children between the ages of 10 and 15 to get involved in global dialog through e-mail, IRC and other telecommunications technologies.

Gopher:
>   Name: KIDLINK Gopher!
>   Address: **kids.ccit.duq.edu**

HEY KIDS!

THERE'S A SPECIAL PLACE FOR YOU ON THE INTERNET. IF YOU'RE BETWEEN 10 AND 15, CONNECT TO THE KIDLINK GOPHER AND TALK WITH OTHER KIDS FROM ALL OVER THE WORLD. (NO ADULTS ALLOWED.)

KIDS

A spin-off of the KIDSPHERE mailing list, KIDS exists for children to post messages to other children around the world. Send a mail message to the below address to join.

Mail:
>   Address: **joinkids@vms.cis.pitt.edu**

Kids and Computers

Keep kids on the cutting edge by finding the best kid-friendly computers and software.

Usenet:
>   Newsgroup: **misc.kids.computer**

Missing Children

Help locate a missing child. Read descriptions of missing children that have been posted by concerned individuals.

Usenet:
>   Newsgroup: **alt.missing-kids**

News on Children

What is going on with children these days? Read news regarding children and parenting.

Usenet:
>   Newsgroup: **clari.news.children**

News on the Family

Keep current on issues concerning the family, child abuse, and more.

Usenet:
>   Newsgroup: **clari.news.issues.family**

Parents and Teens

What works? What doesn't? Share your experiences with other parents, give advice, ask questions.

Usenet:
>   Newsgroup: **alt.parents-teens**

Scouting

What are good fundraisers, and where are the cool summer camps? Find out more about the traditions and activities of Scouting.

Usenet:
>   Newsgroup: **rec.scouting**

Young People Talk

Kids, create a safe space for self-discovery, exploring the thoughts and ideas of your peers.

Usenet:
>   Newsgroup: **alt.kids-talk**

A B C D E F G H I J K L M N O P Q R S T U V W X Y Z

ZOOLOGY

Camel Research

A mailing list created by the Camel Research Center at King Faisal University, Saudi Arabia, for the purpose of furthering camel knowledge and awareness.

Listserv mailing list:
List Address: **camel-l@sakfu00.bitnet**
Subscription Address: **listserv@sakfu00.bitnet**

Census of Australian Vertebrate Species

A database of articles on Australian animals. The articles in the database are categorized, and can be accessed by family, genus, species, common name, scientific name, or the name of the article's author.

Gopher:
Name: Australian Biological Resources Study
Address: **kaos.erin.gov.au**
Choose: **Biodiversity**
  | **Census of Australian Vertebrate Species**

Camels and You

It's sad that so many people have to go through life knowing so little about these large ruminant quadrupeds. But, as an Internet user, nothing can stand in the way of your overall happiness. All you have to do is subscribe to the **camel-l** mailing list and you will be privy to some of the best camel-oriented discussion this side of the Sahara Desert. ("Camels: We bust our hump for you...")

Excerpt from the Net...

(from the Census of Australian Vertebrate Species -- February 1993)

Family	Genus	Species
============	=========	==========
Acanthizidae	Acanthiza	apicalis
Acanthizidae	Acanthiza	chrysorrhoa
Acanthizidae	Acanthiza	ewingii
Acanthizidae	Acanthiza	inornata
...2177 lines omitted...		
Zosteropidae	Zosterops	citrinella
Zosteropidae	Zosterops	lateralis
Zosteropidae	Zosterops	lutea
Zosteropidae	Zosterops	strenua

Ask Wendy

Dear Wendy,

I am a 22 year-old Landscape Architecture student from Deadgrass, Iowa. My problem is that my parents own a big farm and when my boyfriend comes to visit, he likes to spend more time with the animals than with me. I have tried everything I can think of – new hairstyle, different makeup, expensive perfume – but nothing seems to help. What else can I do?

LOST IN DEADGRASS

Dear Lost,

Back when I was in college at the Fayetteville School of Animal Grooming, I dated a veterinarian who spent all of his free time at the Petting Zoo. I thought that if I adopted a houseful of pets, he would spend more time at my place. But all I ended up with was a cat food bill the size of Oklahoma. Take my advice, the best way to capture your boyfriend's attention is to give him what he really wants. Try fixing his favorite meal and serving it in a bowl on the floor. This will keep him from begging at the table.

A
B
C
D
E
F
G
H
I
J
K
L
M
N
O
P
Q
R
S
T
U
V
W
X
Y
Z

Usenet Newsgroups

This section of the book contains a master list of Usenet newsgroups. We would like to take a few moments to explain this list and to give you some helpful information. However, if you want a full explanation of what Usenet is and how it works, or if you need instructions on how to read the news, we will have to refer you to our other book, *The Internet Complete Reference,* also published by Osborne/McGraw-Hill.

Generally speaking, we can divide Usenet newsgroups into two categories: those that are carried all over the world, and those that are of local or regional interest. This list contains only the worldwide groups that were current at the time we prepared this book.

As you can see, Usenet newsgroup names consist of a number of words or terms, separated by a period. For example:

`comp.admin.policy`

The first word is called the *hierarchy*. The name of the hierarchy tells you what type of group you are looking at. For example, all the groups in the **comp** hierarchy have something to do with computers. Altogether, the worldwide newsgroups are divided into 18 different hierarchies.

Of the 18 hierarchies, 7 are *mainstream* and 11 are *alternative*. (These are shown in Tables 1 and 2.) Most Usenet sites carry all the mainstream groups. However, not all sites carry the alternative groups. The reason is that new alternative newsgroups can be created by anyone who knows how to do it.

Mainstream groups can only be created after a well-defined, deliberative process. Thus, you will find many more exotic groups in the alternative hierarchy. However, not all system managers will carry them.

What can you do if you see a newsgroup in the list that you can't find on your system? You have two choices.

Hierarchy	Number of Groups
comp	526
misc	42
news	22
rec	295
sci	87
soc	97
talk	21
TOTAL	1090

Table 1. *Mainstream Usenet Newsgroup Hierarchies*

Hierarchy	Number of Groups
alt	774
bionet	47
bit	211
biz	35
ddn	2
gnu	28
ieee	12
info	40
k12	36
u3b	5
vmsnet	35
TOTAL	1225

Table 2. *Alternative Usenet Newsgroup Hierarchies*

First, you can (politely) ask your system manager if he or she could start carrying the newsgroup. Second, you can get an account on a system that has a better selection.

So far, all the hierarchies we have mentioned are free to anyone on the Internet. However, there is one hierarchy that costs money. It is called **clari** and it is furnished by a private company called Clarinet.

The **clari** hierarchy contains newsgroups that have real news (like in a newspaper). Clarinet gets their information from a variety of sources, including a live news wire. They edit and repackage the articles into Usenet format, and then send them out over the Internet. If your organization subscribes to Clarinet, the **clari** newsgroups will be available to you and you can read them in the same way as you read the regular Usenet newsgroup. Although your organization pays money for this service, there is no special charge for you.

So, how many newsgroups are there?

As you can see from Table 1, there are 1090 mainstream newsgroups. From Table 2, we see that there are 1225 alternative groups. Thus, there are a total of 2315 worldwide newsgroups. (Or rather, there were at the time we wrote this book.) Clarinet has 239 newsgroups. Thus, potentially, there is a grand total of 2554 non-local Usenet newsgroups.

As you might imagine, new newsgroups are added all the time and any list, no matter how comprehensive, will be out of date. As a public service, several master lists of newsgroups are posted to **news.lists** periodically. At any time, you can look for these lists:

```
List of Active Newsgroups, Part I
List of Active Newsgroups, Part II
Alternative Newsgroup Hierarchies, Part I
Alternative Newsgroup Hierarchies, Part II
```

You can also download the lists via Anonymous FTP from **rtfm.mit.edu** by using the following paths:

```
/pub/usenet/news.answers/active-newsgroups/part1
/pub/usenet/news.answers/active-newsgroups/part2
/pub/usenet/news.answers/alt-hierarchies/part1
/pub/usenet/news.answers/alt-hierarchies/part2
```

Be aware, however, that these lists are not as good as the list in this book. In order to prepare our list, we carefully checked it against various systems to pick up any newsgroups that were not included. Then, we eliminated the names of spurious groups that had somehow found their way onto the list. Finally, we rewrote many of the annotations to make sure that the newsgroup descriptions were consistent and informative.

ALT

`alt.1d`	"One-dimensional imaging": in reality, bizarre nonsense
`alt.3d`	Three-dimensional imaging
`alt.abortion.inequity`	The inequity of abortion
`alt.abuse-recovery`	Helping victims of abuse recover (Moderated)
`alt.abuse.offender.recovery`	Helping offenders recover
`alt.abuse.recovery`	Helping victims of abuse recover (Moderated)
`alt.activism`	Activities for activists
`alt.activism.d`	A place to discuss issues in `alt.activism`
`alt.activism.death-penalty`	Opposition to capital punishment
`alt.adoption`	For those involved with or contemplating adoption
`alt.aeffle.und.pferdle`	German TV cartoon characters
`alt.agriculture.fruit`	Fruit farming and agriculture
`alt.agriculture.misc`	Agriculture and farming
`alt.aldus.freehand`	Aldus Freehand software
`alt.aldus.misc`	Other Aldus software products
`alt.aldus.pagemaker`	All about Aldus PageMaker
`alt.alien.visitors`	Space aliens on Earth, abduction, government coverup
`alt.amateur-comp`	The Amateur computerist
`alt.angst`	Anxiety in the modern world
`alt.anonymous`	The virtues and benefits of anonymity
`alt.answers`	Frequently asked questions about the `alt` groups
`alt.appalachian`	Appalachian regional issues
`alt.aquaria`	Aquariums and tropical fish
`alt.archery`	Archery
`alt.architecture`	Building design/construction and related topics
`alt.architecture.alternative`	Non-traditional building designs
`alt.artcom`	Artistic community, arts and communication
`alt.asian-movies`	Movies from Hong Kong, Taiwan and China
`alt.astrology`	Astrology
`alt.atheism`	Atheism
`alt.atheism.moderated`	Atheism (Moderated)
`alt.authorware`	Authorware software
`alt.autos.antique`	All facets of older automobiles
`alt.autos.rod-n-custom`	Souped-up and customised autos
`alt.bacchus`	The Bachhus organization for lovers of wine
`alt.backrubs`	Massage and back rubs
`alt.barney.dinosaur.die.die.die`	Hate and excoriation of Barney the Dinosaur
`alt.bbs.ads`	Ads for various computer BBSs
`alt.bbs.allsysop`	A forum for BBS system operators (sysops)
`alt.bbs.doors`	BBSs and external programs (doors)
`alt.bbs.first-class`	The First Class Macintosh GUI BBS
`alt.bbs.internet`	BBS systems accessible via the Internet
`alt.bbs.lists`	Postings of regional BBS listings
`alt.bbs.lists.d`	Regional BBS listings
`alt.bbs.majorbbs`	The Major BBS

`alt.bbs.metal`	The METAL telecomm environment
`alt.bbs.pcboard`	The PCBoard BBS
`alt.bbs.pcbuucp`	UUCP for DOS systems
`alt.bbs.searchlight`	Searchlight BBS systems
`alt.bbs.unixbbs`	Bulletin Board Systems under Uniclones
`alt.bbs.waffle`	The Waffle BBS
`alt.bbs.wildcat`	The Wildcat BBS
`alt.beadworld`	Beads
`alt.beer`	Beer and related beverages
`alt.best.of.internet`	Reposts of the best articles from other newsgroups
`alt.bigfoot`	The mythical Bigfoot animal/man/monster
`alt.binaries.multimedia`	Sound, text and graphics data rolled in one
`alt.binaries.pictures`	Pictures (suitable for displaying on a computer)
`alt.binaries.pictures.d`	Discussion about pictures
`alt.binaries.pictures.erotica`	Pictures: erotic
`alt.binaries.pictures.erotica.blondes`	Pictures: erotic blonds
`alt.binaries.pictures.erotica.d`	Discussion about erotic blond pictures
`alt.binaries.pictures.erotica.female`	Pictures: erotic women
`alt.binaries.pictures.erotica.male`	Pictures: erotic men
`alt.binaries.pictures.erotica.orientals`	Pictures: erotic Asians
`alt.binaries.pictures.fine-art.d`	Discussion about fine art pictures (Moderated)
`alt.binaries.pictures.fine-art.digitized`	Pictures: fine art (Moderated)
`alt.binaries.pictures.fine-art.graphics`	Pictures: graphics (Moderated)
`alt.binaries.pictures.fractals`	Pictures: fractals
`alt.binaries.pictures.misc`	Pictures: miscellaneous
`alt.binaries.pictures.supermodels`	Pictures: supermodels
`alt.binaries.pictures.tasteless`	Pictures: tasteless
`alt.binaries.pictures.utilities`	Programs for scanning and viewing picture files
`alt.binaries.sounds.d`	Discussion about digitized sounds
`alt.binaries.sounds.misc`	Sounds: all types
`alt.binaries.sounds.music`	Sounds: music
`alt.birthright`	Birthright Party propaganda
`alt.bitterness`	Bitterness
`alt.bogus.group`	Silliness and bogus thoughts
`alt.bonsai`	The art of bonsai
`alt.books.anne-rice`	Anne Rice's books
`alt.books.deryni`	Katherine Kurtz's books, esp. the Deryni series
`alt.books.isaac-asimov`	Isaac Asimov's books
`alt.books.reviews`	Reviews of all kinds of books
`alt.books.technical`	Technical books
`alt.boomerang`	Technology and use of the boomerang
`alt.brother-jed`	The born-again minister touring U.S. campuses
`alt.business.misc`	Business and commerce of all kinds
`alt.business.multi-level`	Multilevel marketing businesses
`alt.cable-tv.re-regulate`	Regulation of TV networks and cable
`alt.cad`	Computer aided design
`alt.cad.autocad`	CAD as practiced by customers of Autodesk

alt.california	All about California
alt.callahans	Callahan's bar for puns and fellowship
alt.cascade	Long, silly followup articles (cascades)
alt.cd-rom	Optical storage devices (specifically CD-ROM)
alt.censorship	Restricting speech and press
alt.cereal	Breakfast cereals
alt.cesium	Trivia relating to the element cesium
alt.chess.ics	The Internet chess server
alt.child-support	Child support
alt.chinchilla	Chinchilla farming and cultivation
alt.chinese.text	Postings in Chinese; Chinese language software
alt.chinese.text.big5	Posting in Chinese [BIG 5]
alt.clearing.technology	The clearing process used by Scientologists
alt.co-evolution	The Whole Earth Review and associated lifestyles
alt.co-ops	Cooperatives
alt.cobol	Programming in Cobol
alt.collecting.autographs	Autograph collectors and enthusiasts
alt.college.college-bowl	College Bowl competition
alt.college.food	Dining halls, cafeterias, mystery meat, and more
alt.colorguard	Marching bands, etc
alt.comedy.british	British humour
alt.comedy.firesgn-thtre	Firesign Theatre: 1970s comedy/satire group
alt.comics.batman	Batman comics
alt.comics.buffalo-roam	A postscript comic strip
alt.comics.elfquest	W. and R. Pini's Elfquest comics
alt.comics.lnh	Interactive net.madness in the superhero genre
alt.comics.superman	Superman comics
alt.comp.acad-freedom.news	Academic freedom related to computers (Moderated)
alt.comp.acad-freedom.talk	Academic freedom issues related to computers
alt.comp.databases.xbase.clipper	Clipper version of xbase programming
alt.comp.fsp	The FSP file transport protocol
alt.comp.hardware.homebuilt	Building your own computer hardware
alt.computer.consultants	Computer consultants and contrators
alt.config	Discussion about alternate newsgroups
alt.consciousness	All about consciousness
alt.conspiracy	Conspiracy theories
alt.conspiracy.jfk	The Kennedy assassination
alt.control-theory	Control system theory and practice
alt.cosuard	Council of Sysops, Users Against Rate Discrimination
alt.cult-movies	Movies with a cult following
alt.cult-movies.rhps	Rocky Horror Picture Show
alt.cult-movies.rocky-horror	Rocky Horror Picture Show
alt.culture.alaska	Alaska
alt.culture.argentina	Argentina
alt.culture.austrian	Austria
alt.culture.electric-midget	Midgets
alt.culture.hawaii	Hawaii

alt.culture.indonesia	Indonesia
alt.culture.internet	The Internet
alt.culture.karnataka	The Indian state of Karnataka
alt.culture.kerala	People of Keralite origin and the Malayalam language
alt.culture.ny-upstate	Upstate New York
alt.culture.oregon	Oregon
alt.culture.theory	Cultural theory and current practical problems
alt.culture.tuva	The Republic of Tannu Tuva
alt.culture.us.asian-indian	Asian Indians in the U.S. and Canada
alt.culture.us.southwest	Southwest United States
alt.culture.usenet	The Usenet culture
alt.current-events.bosnia	Bosnia-Herzegovina
alt.current-events.haiti	Haiti
alt.current-events.russia	Russia
alt.current-events.somalia	Somalia
alt.cyb-sys	Cybernetics and Systems
alt.cyberpunk	Computer-mediated high-tech lifestyle
alt.cyberpunk.chatsubo	Literary virtual reality in a cyberpunk hangout
alt.cyberpunk.movement	Cybernizing the universe
alt.cyberpunk.tech	Cyberspace and cyberpunk technology
alt.cyberspace	Cyberspace and how it should work
alt.dads-rights	Rights of fathers trying to win custody in court
alt.dcom.catv	Data communications and equipment
alt.dcom.telecom	Telecommunications technology
alt.dcom.telecom.ip	IP (Internet Protocol) telecommunications
alt.dear.whitehouse	Comments on American White House policy
alt.decathena	The DEC Athena
alt.desert-storm	The war against Iraq in Kuwait
alt.desert-storm.facts	Factual information on the Gulf War
alt.desert-thekurds	What's happening to the Kurds in Iraq
alt.destroy.the.earth	Fans of destruction
alt.devilbunnies	Real and imaginary bunnies who cause trouble
alt.discordia	Fans of social discord
alt.discrimination	Quotas, affirmative action, bigotry, persecution
alt.divination	Divination techniques (I Ching, Tarot, runes, etc)
alt.dragons-inn	Role-playing/story telling at the Dragons Inn Pub
alt.dreams	Dreams what do they mean? and so on
alt.drugs	Recreational pharmaceuticals and related flames
alt.drugs.caffeine	Caffeine, the world's most-used stimulant drug
alt.drumcorps	Drum and bugle corps
alt.drwho.creative	Stories about Dr. Who
alt.education.bangkok	Education issues in Thailand
alt.education.bangkok.cmc	Education issues in Thailand
alt.education.bangkok.databases	Education issues in Thailand
alt.education.bangkok.planning	Education issues in Thailand
alt.education.bangkok.research	Education issues in Thailand
alt.education.bangkok.student	Education issues in Thailand

`alt.education.bangkok.theory`	Education issues in Thailand
`alt.education.disabled`	Learning experiences for the disabled
`alt.education.distance`	Learning over networks, etc
`alt.education.ib`	International Baccalaureate diploma program
`alt.education.ib.tok`	International Baccalaureates in theory of knowledge
`alt.education.research`	Research into education
`alt.elvis.king`	Elvis Presley
`alt.emulators.ibmpc.apple2`	Emulating a PC with an Apple
`alt.emusic`	Electronic music
`alt.engr.explosives`	Building your own bombs
`alt.etext`	Electronic text
`alt.evil`	Tales from the dark side
`alt.exotic-music`	Exotic and esoteric music
`alt.exploding.kibo`	People who like to blow things up
`alt.extropians`	Extropians
`alt.fan.alok.vijayvargia`	Alok Vijayvargia
`alt.fan.amy-fisher`	Amy Fisher and the famous trial
`alt.fan.asprin`	Robert Lynn Asprin
`alt.fan.bgcrisis`	Bubble Gum Crisis animation
`alt.fan.bill-gates`	Bill Gates of Microsoft
`alt.fan.bugtown`	Bugtown/Posts/Savage Henry comics
`alt.fan.chris-elliott`	Chris Elliott
`alt.fan.dale-bass`	Dale Bass, baseless refuter of *Scientific American*
`alt.fan.dan-quayle`	Dan Quayle, former U.S. Vice President
`alt.fan.dan-wang`	Dan Wang
`alt.fan.dave_barry`	Dave Barry, humorist
`alt.fan.devo`	Devo, alternative rock group
`alt.fan.dice-man`	Andrew Dice Clay, comedian
`alt.fan.dick-depew`	Dick Depew
`alt.fan.disney.afternoon`	Disney afternoon characters and shows
`alt.fan.douglas-adams`	Douglas Adams, writer
`alt.fan.dune`	Frank Herbert's Dune books
`alt.fan.eddings`	David Eddings, writer
`alt.fan.enya`	Enya music
`alt.fan.firesign-theatre`	Firesign Theatre: 1970s comedy/satire group
`alt.fan.frank-zappa`	The late Frank Zappa, bizarre musician
`alt.fan.furry`	Furry animals, anthropomorphized and stuffed
`alt.fan.g-gordon-liddy`	G. Gordon Liddy
`alt.fan.goons`	The Goon show, radio comedy
`alt.fan.greaseman`	Doug Tracht, disc jockey
`alt.fan.hofstadter`	Douglas Hofstadter, computer scientist and writer
`alt.fan.holmes`	Sherlock Holmes
`alt.fan.howard-stern`	Howard Stern, abrasive radio and TV personality
`alt.fan.itchy-n-scratchy`	Bart Simpson's favorite TV cartoon
`alt.fan.james-bond`	James Bond
`alt.fan.jen-coolest`	People who are named Jennifer
`alt.fan.jimmy-buffett`	Jimmy Buffett, country singer

alt.fan.joel-furr	Joel Furr
alt.fan.john-palmer	John Palmer
alt.fan.karla-homolka	Karla Homolka, Canadian murderer
alt.fan.kent-montana	The Kent Montana Book Series
alt.fan.kevin-darcy	Kevin Darcy
alt.fan.laurie.anderson	Laurie Anderson, performance artist
alt.fan.lemurs	Lemurs, monkey-like mammals from Madagascar
alt.fan.lemurs.cooked	Weird talk, lemur and non-lemur
alt.fan.letterman	David Letterman, TV personality
alt.fan.madonna	Madonna, singer etc
alt.fan.mike-jittlov	Mike Jittlov, animator
alt.fan.monty-python	Monty Python's Flying Circus, humor group
alt.fan.naked-guy	Andrew Martinez, the Naked Guy at U.C. Berkeley
alt.fan.nathan.brazil	The hero of a Jack Chalker novel
alt.fan.noam-chomsky	Noam Chomsky, linguist and political dissident
alt.fan.oingo-boingo	Oingo Boingo, pop music group
alt.fan.pern	Anne McCaffery's science fiction oeuvre
alt.fan.piers-anthony	Piers Anthony, science fiction author
alt.fan.pratchett	Terry Pratchett, science fiction humor writer
alt.fan.q	The Qmnipotent Qne
alt.fan.ren-and-stimpy	Ren and Stimpy
alt.fan.robert-jordan	Robert Jordan, writer of fantasy sagas
alt.fan.ronald-reagan	Ronald Reagan, ex-actor, former president of U.S.
alt.fan.rumpole	Rumpole
alt.fan.run-dmc	Run-DMC, rap music group
alt.fan.rush-limbaugh	Rush Limbaugh, conservative talk show host
alt.fan.serdar-argic	Armenia, Turkey, genocide
alt.fan.shostakovich	Shostakovitch, classical music composer
alt.fan.spinal-tap	Spinal Tap, fictitious movie rock group
alt.fan.tank-girl	Tank girl
alt.fan.tolkien	J.R.R. Tolkein, fantasy writer
alt.fan.tom-robbins	Tom Robbins, novelist
alt.fan.tom_peterson	Tom Peterson from Portland, Oregon
alt.fan.u2	U2, Irish rock music group
alt.fan.wal-greenslade	Wal Greenslade, the BBC Home Service
alt.fan.warlord	The War Lord of the West Preservation Fan Club
alt.fan.wodehouse	P.G. Wodehouse (pronounced "Woodhouse"), humorist
alt.fan.woody-allen	Woody Allen, film maker, writer, comedian
alt.fandom.cons	Conventions, science fiction and others
alt.fandom.misc	Other topics for fans of various kinds
alt.fashion	The fashion industry
alt.feminism	Like soc.feminism, only different
alt.filepro	Filepro 4GL database
alt.filesystems.afs	Andrew file system from Carnegie Mellon University
alt.fishing	Fishing as a hobby and sport
alt.flame	Complaints, and complaints about complaints
alt.flame.roommate	Stories about troublesome roommates

`alt.flame.sean-ryan`	Detractors of Sean Ryan
`alt.folklore.college`	Collegiate humor
`alt.folklore.computers`	Stories & anecdotes about computers (some true!)
`alt.folklore.ghost-stories`	Ghost stories
`alt.folklore.herbs`	Herbs and their uses
`alt.folklore.info`	Current urban legends and other folklore
`alt.folklore.science`	The folklore of science, not the science of folklore
`alt.folklore.urban`	Urban legends, a la Jan Harold Brunvand
`alt.food.cocacola`	Various types of Coca-Cola
`alt.food.fat-free`	Fat-free food
`alt.food.mcdonalds`	Food from McDonalds restaurants
`alt.food.sugar-cereals`	Sugary breakfast cereals
`alt.forgery`	One place for all forgeries, crossposting encouraged
`alt.fractal-design.painter`	Creating fractals with Painter software
`alt.fractals`	Fractals
`alt.fractals.pictures`	Pictures: fractals
`alt.galactic-guide`	Entries for actual Hitchhiker's Guide to the Galaxy
`alt.games.frp.dnd-util`	Utility programs for automated Dungeons and Dragons
`alt.games.frp.live-action`	Live-action gaming
`alt.games.gb`	Galactic Bloodshed conquest game
`alt.games.lynx`	The Atari Lynx
`alt.games.mk`	Mortal Kombat video game
`alt.games.mornington.cresent`	Fans of a game
`alt.games.omega`	Computer game Omega
`alt.games.sf2`	Video game Street Fighter 2
`alt.games.tiddlywinks`	Game of Tiddlywinks
`alt.games.torg`	Gateway for TORG mailing list
`alt.games.vga-planets`	Tim Wisseman's VGA Planets
`alt.games.video.classic`	From early TV remote controls to Space Invaders, etc
`alt.games.whitewolf`	Whitewolf story-telling fantasy games
`alt.games.xpilot`	Xpilot, X Window game
`alt.games.xtrek`	Star Trek game for X Window
`alt.gathering.rainbow`	The annual Rainbow Gathering
`alt.geek`	Geeks (nerds who are dull)
`alt.genealogy`	Geneology
`alt.good.morning`	Nice people saying "Good Morning" to one another
`alt.good.news`	Good news (really!)
`alt.gopher`	The Internet Gopher (menu-driven information)
`alt.gorets`	Imaginary and not so imaginary silliness
`alt.gothic`	The gothic movement, things mournful and dark
`alt.gourmand`	Recipes and cooking information (Moderated)
`alt.grad-student.tenured`	Grad students who never seem to graduate
`alt.graphics`	Computer graphics
`alt.graphics.pixutils`	Pixmap utilities
`alt.great-lakes`	The Great Lakes and adjacent places
`alt.guitar`	Guitar
`alt.guitar.bass`	Bass Guitar

`alt.guitar.tab`	Music and lyrics (tablature) for guitar fans
`alt.hackers`	Projects currently under development (Moderated)
`alt.happy.birthday.to.me`	Newsgroup to read on your birthday
`alt.health.ayurveda`	Ayurvedic (East Indian) medicine
`alt.hemp`	Marijuana
`alt.heraldry.sca`	Heraldry in the Society of Creative Anachronism
`alt.history.living`	The hobby of living history
`alt.history.what-if`	Historical conjecture
`alt.homosexual`	Homosexuality
`alt.horror`	The horror genre
`alt.horror.cthulhu`	Mythos/role-playing based on H.P.Lovecraft's *Cthulhu*
`alt.horror.werewolves`	Werewolves
`alt.hotrod`	High speed automobiles (Moderated)
`alt.housing.nontrad`	Non-traditional housing concepts
`alt.hurricane.andrew`	The 1992 Florida hurricane disaster
`alt.hypertext`	Hypertext
`alt.hypnosis`	Hypnosis
`alt.illuminati`	Conspirisy, political and financial intrigue
`alt.image.medical`	Medical imaging
`alt.india.progressive`	Progressive politics in India (moderated)
`alt.individualism`	Philosophies where individual rights are paramount
`alt.industrial`	The Industrial Computing Society
`alt.info-science`	Library science
`alt.info-theory`	Information theory
`alt.internet.access.wanted`	People looking for Internet access information
`alt.internet.services`	The various Internet services
`alt.internet.talk.radio`	Internet Talk Radio and the Geek of the Week show
`alt.irc`	Internet Relay Chat
`alt.irc.ircii`	The IRC II client program
`alt.irc.recovery`	Recovery from too much IRC
`alt.japanese.text`	Japanese articles and text
`alt.journalism`	Of and by journalists
`alt.journalism.criticism`	Criticism of journalists and the media
`alt.journalism.music`	Music journalism
`alt.ketchup`	Ketchup and related items
`alt.kids-talk`	Discussion among children
`alt.kill.the.whales`	Killing whales and why it is not so bad
`alt.lang.apl`	APL programming language
`alt.lang.asm`	Various types of Assembly languages
`alt.lang.awk`	The Unix language awk scripting language
`alt.lang.basic`	Basic programming language
`alt.lang.cfutures`	The future of the C programming language
`alt.lang.intercal`	The Intercal programming language
`alt.lang.ml`	The ML and SML symbolic programming languages
`alt.lang.teco`	The TECO editor language
`alt.law-enforcement`	Laws of all types, police and jails
`alt.lemmings`	Lemmings, computer game

`alt.letzebuerger`	Luxembougish, the traditional language of Luxemburg
`alt.life.internet`	The Internet as an institution of human culture
`alt.locksmithing`	Locksmithing locks, keys, etc
`alt.lucid-emacs.bug`	Bug reports about Lucid Emacs
`alt.lucid-emacs.help`	Question and answer forum for Lucid Emacs
`alt.lycra`	Clothes made of Lycra, Spandex, etc
`alt.magic`	Stage magic
`alt.magick`	Supernatural arts
`alt.managing.techsupport`	Managing technical support
`alt.manga`	Non-Western comics
`alt.manufacturing.misc`	Manufacturing
`alt.materials.simulation`	Computer modeling of materials (Moderated)
`alt.mcdonalds`	Food from McDonalds restaurants
`alt.med.cfs`	Chronic fatigue syndrome
`alt.meditation`	Meditation
`alt.meditation.transcendental`	Transcendental meditation
`alt.messianic`	Messianic traditions
`alt.military.cadet`	Military school cadets
`alt.mindcontrol`	Mind control (You will buy 10 copies of this book!)
`alt.misanthropy`	Hatred and distrust toward all
`alt.missing-kids`	Locating missing children
`alt.models`	Model building, design, etc
`alt.motorcycles.harley`	Harley-Davidson motorcycles
`alt.msdos.programmer`	Tips, questions and answers for DOS programming
`alt.mud`	Multiuser dimension games
`alt.mud.bsx`	MUD systems on BSX VR
`alt.mud.chupchups`	A MUD game called chupchups
`alt.mud.german`	For German-speaking MUDers
`alt.mud.lp`	Help setting up a MUD
`alt.mud.tiny`	Fans of small MUD sites
`alt.music.a-cappella`	Unaccompanied singing
`alt.music.alternative`	Alternative music
`alt.music.bela-fleck`	Bela and the Flecktones
`alt.music.canada`	Canadian music
`alt.music.ebm`	Industrial/electronic body music/cyberculture "music"
`alt.music.enya`	Gaelic set to spacey music
`alt.music.filk`	SciFi/fantasy-related folk music
`alt.music.hardcore`	Hard core music fans
`alt.music.jewish`	Jewish music
`alt.music.marillion`	Marillion, pop music group
`alt.music.nin`	Nine Inch Nails, one-person gothic music group
`alt.music.prince`	Prince, pop singer
`alt.music.progressive`	Music such as Yes, Marillion, Asia, King Crimson
`alt.music.queen`	Queen, pop music group
`alt.music.rush`	Rush, pop music group
`alt.music.ska`	Ska (skank) music, bands, and so on
`alt.music.tmbg`	They Might Be Giants

alt.music.u2	U2, Irish pop music group
alt.music.world	Music from around the world
alt.mythology	Mythlogy
alt.national.enquirer	*National Enquirer* newspaper
alt.native	Indigenous peoples of the world
alt.necktie	Neckties
alt.netgames.bolo	The game of bolo
alt.news-media	The news media
alt.news.macedonia	News and current affairs in Macedonia
alt.non.sequitur	Interesting bits of imaginitive writing + much junk
alt.online-service	Large commercial online services
alt.org.pugwash	Technological issues from a social stance
alt.os.bsdi	BSD (Berkeley) Unix as implemented by BSDI
alt.os.multics	The Multics operating system
alt.out-of-body	Out of body experiences
alt.overlords	Office of the Omnipotent Overlords of the Omniverse
alt.pagan	Paganism
alt.pantyhose	Talk about pantyhose
alt.paranet.abduct	Stories of abductions by aliens
alt.paranet.paranormal	Paranormal experiences
alt.paranet.science	The theories behind paranormal events
alt.paranet.skeptic	Skeptics explain and refute paranormal stories
alt.paranet.ufo	UFO sightings
alt.paranormal	Phenomena which are not scientifically explicable
alt.parents-teens	Parent-teenager relationships
alt.party	Parties, celebration and general debauchery
alt.pcnews	PCNews software
alt.peeves	Pet peeves and related topics
alt.periphs.pcmcia	Credit card-sized plug-in peripherals for PCs
alt.personals	General personal ads
alt.personals.ads	More personal ads
alt.personals.bondage	Personals bondage
alt.personals.misc	Personals miscellaneous
alt.personals.poly	Personals multiple people
alt.philosophy.objectivism	The Ayn Rand-derived philosophy of Objectivism
alt.planning.urban	Urban planning
alt.politics.british	Politics: Great Britain
alt.politics.bush	George Bush, former U.S. President
alt.politics.clinton	Bill Clinton, Hillary's husband
alt.politics.correct	Political correctness
alt.politics.democrats	Politics, Democrats
alt.politics.democrats.clinton	Politics, Democrats and Bill Clinton
alt.politics.democrats.d	Politics, discussion about Democrats
alt.politics.democrats.governors	Politics, Democrats and governors
alt.politics.democrats.house	Politics, House of Representatives
alt.politics.democrats.senate	Politics, Senate
alt.politics.ec	The European Community

alt.politics.economics	Economics
alt.politics.elections	Elections
alt.politics.equality	Political equality
alt.politics.europe.misc	European politics
alt.politics.greens	Green party politics and activities worldwide
alt.politics.homosexuality	Politics and homosexuality
alt.politics.india.communist	Communism in India
alt.politics.india.progressive	Progressive Indian politics
alt.politics.italy	Politics, Italy
alt.politics.libertarian	The libertarian ideology
alt.politics.media	Politics and the communications media
alt.politics.org.batf	U.S. Bureau of Alcohol, Tobacco and Firearms
alt.politics.org.cia	U.S. Central Intelligence Agency
alt.politics.org.covert	Covert organizations around the world
alt.politics.org.fbi	U.S. Federal Bureau of Investigation
alt.politics.org.misc	Political organizations
alt.politics.org.nsa	U.S. National Security Agency
alt.politics.org.un	Politics at the United Nations
alt.politics.perot	Ross Perot and related issues
alt.politics.radical-left	The radical left
alt.politics.reform	Political reform
alt.politics.sex	Politics and sex
alt.politics.usa.constitution	U.S. Constitutional politics
alt.politics.usa.misc	Miscellaneous U.S. politics
alt.politics.usa.republican	The U.S. Republican party
alt.politics.vietnamese	Politics and Vietnam
alt.polyamory	Multiple love relationships
alt.postmodern	Postmodernism, semiotics, deconstruction, etc
alt.president.clinton	U.S. President Bill Clinton
alt.prisons	Prisons and prison life
alt.privacy	Privacy issues in cyberspace
alt.privacy.anon-server	Anonymous Usenet postings
alt.privacy.clipper	The Clipper encoding chip
alt.prophecies.nostradamus	Nostradamus' predictions and score card
alt.prose	Original writings, fiction and otherwise
alt.prose.d	Discussion of alt.prose articles
alt.psychoactives	Psychoactive drugs, legal and illegal
alt.psychology.personality	Personality taxonomy, such as Myers-Briggs
alt.pub.cloven-shield	Role-playing stories
alt.pub.dragons-inn	A computer fantasy environment
alt.pub.havens-rest	Role-playing stories
alt.pulp	Pulp-genre stories and characters
alt.punk	Punk rock
alt.ql.creative	*Quantum Leap* TV show and creative thought
alt.quotations	Famous (and not so famous) quotes
alt.radio.networks.npr	U.S. National Public Radio
alt.radio.pirate	Pirate radio stations

alt.radio.scanner	Scanning radio receivers
alt.rap	Rap music
alt.rap-gdead	The Grateful Dead and Rap (music)
alt.rave	Techno-culture music, dancing, drugs, dancing
alt.recovery	Recovery programs (AA, ACA, GA, etc)
alt.recovery.codependency	Codependency
alt.religion.all-worlds	The Church of All Worlds, from Heinlein's book
alt.religion.computers	Computing as a Way of Life
alt.religion.eckankar	Eckanker, as founded by Sri Paul Twitchell in 1965
alt.religion.emacs	Emacs as a Way of Life
alt.religion.kibology	Silliness based on the mythical Kibo
alt.religion.monica	Net-venus Monica and her works
alt.religion.sabaean	The Sabaean religious order
alt.religion.santaism	Christmas and Santa Claus
alt.religion.scientology	Scientology and Dianetics
alt.religion.shamanism	Shamanism
alt.revenge	Revenge and how to do it
alt.revisionism	Changing interpretations of history
alt.revolution.counter	Counter-revolutionary issues
alt.rhode_island	The U.S. state of Rhode Island
alt.rmgroup	For the people who like to rmgroup/newgroup things
alt.rock-n-roll	General rock and roll
alt.rock-n-roll.acdc	AC/DC, music group
alt.rock-n-roll.classic	Classical rock music
alt.rock-n-roll.hard	Hard rock
alt.rock-n-roll.metal	General metal rock music
alt.rock-n-roll.metal.gnr	Heavy metal rock music
alt.rock-n-roll.metal.heavy	More heavy metal rock music
alt.rock-n-roll.metal.ironmaiden	Iron Maiden, music group
alt.rock-n-roll.metal.metallica	Metallica, music group
alt.rock-n-roll.metal.progressive	Progressive metal rock
alt.rock-n-roll.oldies	Rock and roll music from 1950-1970
alt.rock-n-roll.stones	The Rolling Stones, music group
alt.rock-n-roll.symphonic	Rock and classical music
alt.rodney-king	The L.A. riots and the aftermath
alt.romance	The romantic side of love
alt.romance.chat	Romantic talk
alt.rush-limbaugh	Rush Limbaugh, conservative radio talk show host
alt.satanism	Talk about Satan
alt.satellite.tv.europe	European satellite TV
alt.satellite.tv.forsale	Satellite TV equipment, wanted and for sale
alt.save.the.earth	Environmentalist causes
alt.sb.programmer	Programming the Sound Blaster card for PCs
alt.sci.astro.aips	The Astronomical Image Processing System
alt.sci.astro.figaro	The Figaro data-reduction package
alt.sci.astro.fits	Programming with FITS
alt.sci.physics.acoustics	Acoustics

`alt.sci.physics.new-theories`	New scientific theories you won't find in journals
`alt.sci.planetary`	Planetary science
`alt.sci.sociology`	Sociology
`alt.sci.tech.indonesian`	Technology discussed in Indonesian
`alt.sect.ahmadiyya`	The Ahmadiyyat sect of Islam
`alt.security`	Building and autombile security systems
`alt.security.index`	Good references to {alt,misc}.security (Moderated)
`alt.security.keydist`	Exchange of keys for public key encryption systems
`alt.security.pgp`	The Pretty Good Privacy encryption package
`alt.security.ripem`	A secure electronic mail system
`alt.sega.genesis`	The Genesis video game
`alt.self-improve`	Self-improvement
`alt.sewing`	Sewing
`alt.sex`	General discussion about sex
`alt.sex.bestiality`	Sex: bestiality
`alt.sex.bestiality.barney`	Crude comments about Barney the Dinosaur
`alt.sex.bondage`	Sex: bondage
`alt.sex.exhibitionism`	Sex: exhibitionism and people who make noise
`alt.sex.fetish.amputee`	Sex: amputee fetishes
`alt.sex.fetish.diapers`	Sex: diaper fetishes
`alt.sex.fetish.fa`	Sex: fat people
`alt.sex.fetish.feet`	Sex: foot fetishes
`alt.sex.fetish.hair`	Sex: hair fetishes
`alt.sex.fetish.orientals`	Sex: oriental people
`alt.sex.fetish.watersports`	Sex: enemas and related fetishes
`alt.sex.masturbation`	Sex: masturbation
`alt.sex.motss`	Sex: homosexuality (members of the same sex)
`alt.sex.movies`	Sex: movies
`alt.sex.pictures`	Pictures: erotic
`alt.sex.pictures.d`	Discussion about erotic pictures
`alt.sex.pictures.female`	Pictures: erotic women
`alt.sex.pictures.male`	Pictures: erotic men
`alt.sex.sounds`	Erotic sounds
`alt.sex.spanking`	Sex: spanking
`alt.sex.stories`	Sex: stories (no discussion)
`alt.sex.stories.d`	Discussion about sexual stories
`alt.sex.voyeurism`	Sex: voyeurism
`alt.sex.wanted`	Requests for erotica, literary or in the flesh
`alt.sex.wizards`	Questions for sex experts
`alt.sexual.abuse.recovery`	Helping others deal with traumatic experiences
`alt.shenanigans`	Practical jokes, pranks, etc
`alt.showbiz.gossip`	Gossip about the entertainment industry
`alt.sigma2.height`	Very short or tall people (> 2 standard deviations)
`alt.skate`	Skating
`alt.skate-board`	Skate-boarding
`alt.skinheads`	The skinhead culture/anti-culture
`alt.skunks`	Skunks

`alt.slack`	The Church of the Subgenius
`alt.slick.willy.tax.tax.tax`	Taxes, U.S. President Bill Clinton, and whining
`alt.smokers`	Smoking as a pastime
`alt.snail-mail`	Regular postal system mail
`alt.snowmobiles`	Snowmobiles
`alt.soc.ethics`	Ethics
`alt.society.anarchy`	Anarchy
`alt.society.ati`	The Activist Times Digest (Moderated)
`alt.society.civil-disob`	Civil disobedience
`alt.society.civil-liberties`	Individual rights
`alt.society.civil-liberty`	Civil libertarians
`alt.society.conservatism`	Social, cultural, and political conservatism
`alt.society.foia`	The U.S. Freedom of Information Act
`alt.society.futures`	The future of society
`alt.society.generation-x`	Generation X: those born 1960 to early-1970s
`alt.society.resistance`	Political talk resistance
`alt.society.revolution`	Political talk revolution
`alt.society.sovereign`	Political talk sovereignty
`alt.soft-sys.tooltalk`	ToolTalk
`alt.sources`	Free computer programs, unmoderated, caveat emptor
`alt.sources.amiga`	Technically-oriented Amiga PC programs
`alt.sources.d`	Discussion about programs that have been posted
`alt.sources.index`	Good references to free programs
`alt.sources.patches`	Corrections to programs, from non-bugs groups
`alt.sources.wanted`	Requests for programs
`alt.spam`	Cooking with Spam, a type of processed meat
`alt.sport.bowling`	Bowling
`alt.sport.bungee`	Bungee cord jumping
`alt.sport.darts`	Darts
`alt.sport.foosball`	Table soccer
`alt.sport.lasertag`	Laser Tag
`alt.sport.officiating`	Officiating athletic contests
`alt.sport.paintball`	Paintball combat game
`alt.sport.photon`	Photon laser tag game
`alt.sport.pool`	Pool and billiards
`alt.sports.baseball.atlanta-braves`	Baseball: Atlanta Braves
`alt.sports.baseball.balt-orioles`	Baseball: Baltimore Orioles
`alt.sports.baseball.chicago-cubs`	Baseball: Chicago Cubs
`alt.sports.baseball.cinci-reds`	Baseball: Cincinnati Reds
`alt.sports.baseball.col-rockies`	Baseball: Colorado Rockies
`alt.sports.baseball.fla-marlins`	Baseball: Florida Marlins
`alt.sports.baseball.houston-astros`	Baseball: Houston Astros
`alt.sports.baseball.la-dodgers`	Baseball: Los Angeles Dodgers
`alt.sports.baseball.mke-brewers`	Baseball: Milwaukee Brewers
`alt.sports.baseball.mn-twins`	Baseball: Minnesota Twins
`alt.sports.baseball.montreal-expos`	Baseball: Montreal Expos
`alt.sports.baseball.ny-mets`	Baseball: New York Mets

Newsgroup	Description
`alt.sports.baseball.oakland-as`	Baseball: Oakland Athletics
`alt.sports.baseball.phila-phillies`	Baseball: Philadelphia Phillies
`alt.sports.baseball.pitt-pirates`	Baseball: Pittsburgh Pirates
`alt.sports.baseball.sd-padres`	Baseball: San Diego Padres
`alt.sports.baseball.sf-giants`	Baseball: San Francisco Giants
`alt.sports.baseball.stl-cardinals`	Baseball: St. Louis Cardinals
`alt.sports.baseball.tor-bluejays`	Baseball: Toronto Blue Jays
`alt.sports.darts`	Darts
`alt.sports.football.mn-vikings`	Football: Minnesota Vikings
`alt.sports.football.pro.wash-redskins`	Football: Washington Redskins
`alt.stagecraft`	Technical aspects of the theatre
`alt.startrek.creative`	Stories and parodies related to *Star Trek*
`alt.startrek.klingon`	Klingons and their language (from *Star Trek*)
`alt.stupidity`	Talk about stupid newsgroups
`alt.suburbs`	The suburbs
`alt.suicide.holiday`	Talk of why suicides increase at holidays
`alt.suit.att-bsdi`	Discussion of the AT&T v. BSDI lawsuit
`alt.super.nes`	Super Nintendo video game
`alt.supermodels`	Famous and beautiful models
`alt.support`	General support group
`alt.support.abuse-partners`	Partners of people who were abused
`alt.support.big-folks`	Support group for large people
`alt.support.cancer`	Support group for cancer patients
`alt.support.diet`	Support group for dieters
`alt.support.mult-sclerosis`	Multiple sclerosis
`alt.support.step-parents`	Support group for step parents
`alt.surfing`	Surfing
`alt.surrealism :surrealism`	Surrealism ideology, trancsending reality
`alt.sustainable.agriculture`	Ecologically-sound agriculture
`alt.sustainable.agriculture`	Politics and agriculture
`alt.swedish.chef.bork.bork.bork`	Talking with a Swedish accent like the Muppet
`alt.sys.amiga.demos`	Demo programs for Amiga computers
`alt.sys.amiga.uucp`	UUCP for the Amiga
`alt.sys.amiga.uucp.patches`	Corrections for Amiga UUCP software
`alt.sys.intergraph`	Intergraph computers
`alt.sys.pc-clone.gateway2000`	Gateway 2000 personal computers
`alt.sys.pdp8`	DEC PDP-8 computers
`alt.sys.perq`	Antique computers
`alt.sys.sun`	Sun computers
`alt.tasteless`	Talk about tasteless and disgusting topics
`alt.tasteless.jokes`	Tasteless jokes (offensive to everybody)
`alt.tasteless.pictures`	Pictures: tasteless
`alt.technology.obsolete`	Obsolete technology
`alt.test`	Place to send test articles
`alt.text.dwb`	AT&T Documenter's WorkBench
`alt.thrash`	Thrash music (an acquired taste...)
`alt.tla`	Palindromic fun, Three-Letter-Acronyms

`alt.toolkits.xview`	The X windows XView toolkit
`alt.toon-pics`	Pictures: cartoons
`alt.toys.hi-tech`	Toys: High-tech
`alt.toys.lego`	Toys: Lego
`alt.toys.transformers`	Toys: transformers
`alt.transgendered`	Changing one's sex
`alt.travel.road-trip`	Traveling by car
`alt.true-crime`	Famous crimes
`alt.tv.animaniacs`	*Animaniacs*, TV show
`alt.tv.antagonists`	*The Antagonists*, TV show
`alt.tv.babylon-5`	*Babylon 5*, TV show
`alt.tv.barney`	*Barney the Dinosaur*, TV show
`alt.tv.beakmans-world`	*Beakman's World*, TV show
`alt.tv.beavis-n-butthead`	*Beavis and Butt-head*, MTV cartoon
`alt.tv.bh90210`	*Beverly Hills 90210*, TV show
`alt.tv.dinosaur.barney.die.die.die`	Negative thoughts about Barney the Dinosaur
`alt.tv.dinosaurs`	Dinosaurs and television
`alt.tv.infomercials`	Infomercials
`alt.tv.la-law`	*L.A. Law*, TV show
`alt.tv.liquid-tv`	The BBC/MTV *Liquid TV* series (weird...)
`alt.tv.mash`	*M*A*S*H*, TV show
`alt.tv.melrose-place`	*Melrose Place*, TV show
`alt.tv.mst3k`	*Mystery Science Theatre 3000*, TV show
`alt.tv.muppets`	The Muppets
`alt.tv.mwc`	More TV shows
`alt.tv.northern-exp`	*Northern Exposure*, TV show
`alt.tv.prisoner`	*The Prisoner*, TV show
`alt.tv.red-dwarf`	*Red Dwarf* (British SciFi/comedy), TV show
`alt.tv.ren-n-stimpy`	*Ren and Stimpy*, TV show
`alt.tv.rockford-files`	*Rockford Files*, TV show
`alt.tv.saved-bell`	*Saved by the Bell*, TV Show
`alt.tv.seinfeld`	*Seinfeld*, TV show
`alt.tv.simpsons`	*The Simpsons*, TV show
`alt.tv.simpsons.itchy-scratchy`	*Itchy and Scratchy* (Bart Simpson's cartoon friends)
`alt.tv.snl`	*Saturday Night Live*, TV show
`alt.tv.talkshows.late`	Late night U.S. talk shows
`alt.tv.time-traxx`	*Time Traxx*, TV show
`alt.tv.tiny-toon`	*Tiny Toons*, TV Show
`alt.tv.twin-peaks`	*Twin Peaks*, TV show
`alt.usage.english`	English grammar, word usages, and related topics
`alt.usenet.offline-reader`	Reading the news off-line
`alt.usenet.recovery`	Support group for Usenet junkies
`alt.uu.announce`	Announcements of Usenet University (UU)
`alt.uu.comp.misc`	Computer department of Usenet University
`alt.uu.comp.os.linux.questions`	UU Linux learning group, questions and answers
`alt.uu.future`	Planning the future of Usenet University
`alt.uu.lang.esperanto.misc`	Usenet University Esperanto

`alt.uu.lang.misc`	Usenet University Language department
`alt.uu.lang.russian.misc`	Usenet University Russian
`alt.uu.math.misc`	Usenet University math
`alt.uu.misc.misc`	Usenet University miscellaneous departments
`alt.uu.tools`	Usenet University tools for education
`alt.uu.virtual-worlds.misc`	Usenet University study of virtual worlds
`alt.vampyres`	Vampires
`alt.video.laserdisc`	Laser disk movies and games
`alt.visa.us`	U.S. immigration visas
`alt.wais`	WAIS (Wide Area Information Service)
`alt.war`	War
`alt.war.civil.usa`	The United States Civil War
`alt.war.vietnam`	The Vietnam War
`alt.wedding`	First meetings, dates, romance, weddings, etc
`alt.whine`	Whining and complaining
`alt.windows.text`	Text-based (non-graphical) window systems
`alt.winsock`	Socket implementations for Microsoft Windows
`alt.wired`	Wired Magazine
`alt.wolves`	Wolves and wolf-mix dogs
`alt.world.taeis`	The shared-world project
`alt.zima`	Zima, a beer-like beverage
`alt.zines`	Small magazines, mostly noncommercial
`alt.znet.aeo`	*Atari Explorer Online*, electronic magazine
`alt.znet.pc`	PC-oriented electronic magazine

BIONET

`bionet.agroforestry`	Agroforestry
`bionet.announce`	Announcements for biologists (Moderated)
`bionet.biology.computational`	Computer and mathematical biology (Moderated)
`bionet.biology.tropical`	Tropical biology
`bionet.cellbiol`	Cell biology
`bionet.chlamydomonas`	Chlamydomonas, green alga
`bionet.drosophila`	Biology of Drosophila (fruit flies)
`bionet.general`	General forum for the biological sciences
`bionet.genome.arabidopsis`	The Arabidopsis project
`bionet.genome.chrom22`	Chromosome 22
`bionet.genome.chromosomes`	Mapping and sequencing of eucaryote chromosomes
`bionet.immunology`	Immunology
`bionet.info-theory`	Biological information theory
`bionet.jobs`	Job opportunities in biology
`bionet.journals.contents`	Contents of biology journals
`bionet.journals.note`	Advice on dealing with biology journals
`bionet.metabolic-reg`	Kinetics and thermodynamics at the celluar level
`bionet.molbio.ageing`	Cellular and organismal aging
`bionet.molbio.bio-matrix`	Computer applications to biological databases
`bionet.molbio.embldatabank`	The EMBL Nucleic acid database

`bionet.molbio.evolution`	Evolution of genes and proteins
`bionet.molbio.gdb`	Messages to and from the GDB database staff
`bionet.molbio.genbank`	The GenBank nucleic acid database
`bionet.molbio.genbank.updates`	News about GenBank (Moderated)
`bionet.molbio.gene-linkage`	Genetic linkage analysis
`bionet.molbio.gene-org`	How genes are organized on chromosomes
`bionet.molbio.genome-program`	The Human Genome Project
`bionet.molbio.hiv`	The molecular biology of HIV (AIDS virus)
`bionet.molbio.methds-reagnts`	Requests for information and lab reagents
`bionet.molbio.proteins`	Proteins and protein databases
`bionet.molbio.rapd`	Randomly Amplified Polymorphic DNA
`bionet.molbio.yeast`	The molecular biology and genetics of yeast
`bionet.mycology`	Fungi
`bionet.n2-fixation`	Nitrogen fixation
`bionet.neuroscience`	Neuroscience
`bionet.photosynthesis`	Photosynthesis
`bionet.plants`	All aspects of plant biology
`bionet.population-bio`	Population biology
`bionet.sci-resources`	Funding agencies, research grants, etc
`bionet.software`	Software for biology
`bionet.software.acedb`	Using ACEDB to access genome databases
`bionet.software.gcg`	GCG software
`bionet.software.sources`	Free programs relating to biology (Moderated)
`bionet.users.addresses`	Names and addresses in the world of biology
`bionet.virology`	Virology
`bionet.women-in-bio`	Women in biology
`bionet.xtallography`	Protein crystallography

BIT

`bit.admin`	Administrating Bitnet newsgroups
`bit.general`	General information on Bitnet and Usenet
`bit.lang.neder-l`	Dutch language and literature (Moderated)
`bit.listserv.3com-l`	3Com Products
`bit.listserv.9370-l`	IBM's 9370 and VM/IS operating system
`bit.listserv.ada-law`	ADA Law
`bit.listserv.advanc-l`	Geac Advanced Integrated Library System
`bit.listserv.advise-l`	User Services
`bit.listserv.aix-l`	IBM's AIX (Unix) operating system
`bit.listserv.allmusic`	All forms of music
`bit.listserv.appc-l`	IBM's APPC
`bit.listserv.apple2-l`	Apple II
`bit.listserv.applicat`	Applications under Bitnet
`bit.listserv.arie-l`	RLG Ariel Document Transmission Group
`bit.listserv.ashe-l`	Higher Education Policy and Research
`bit.listserv.asm370`	IBM 370 Assembly language programming
`bit.listserv.autism`	Autism and Developmental Disability List

`bit.listserv.axslib-l`	Library access for people with disabilities
`bit.listserv.banyan-l`	Banyan Vines Network Software
`bit.listserv.big-lan`	Campus-Size LAN Discussion Group (Moderated)
`bit.listserv.billing`	Chargeback of computer resources
`bit.listserv.biosph-l`	Biosphere, ecology
`bit.listserv.bitnews`	News about Bitnet
`bit.listserv.blindnws`	Blindness (Moderated)
`bit.listserv.buslib-l`	Business libraries
`bit.listserv.c+health`	Computer and health
`bit.listserv.c18-l`	18th Century interdisciplinary forum
`bit.listserv.c370-l`	IBM's C/370 programming language
`bit.listserv.candle-l`	Candle Products
`bit.listserv.catala`	Catalan: language of Catalonia, Andorra, Belearic Islands
`bit.listserv.catholic`	Free Catholics
`bit.listserv.cdromlan`	CD-ROM on Local Area Networks
`bit.listserv.cfs.newsletter`	Chronic Fatigue Syndrome Newsletter (Moderated)
`bit.listserv.christia`	Practical Christian Life
`bit.listserv.cics-l`	IBM's CICS (transaction processing)
`bit.listserv.cinema-l`	The cinema
`bit.listserv.circplus`	Circulation reserve and related library topics
`bit.listserv.cmspip-l`	IBM's VM/SP CMS Pipelines
`bit.listserv.commed`	Communication education
`bit.listserv.csg-l`	Control System Group Network
`bit.listserv.cumrec-l`	Computer use, college and university administration
`bit.listserv.cw-email`	Campus-wide electronic mail
`bit.listserv.cwis-l`	Campus-wide information systems
`bit.listserv.cyber-l`	CDC computers
`bit.listserv.dasig`	Database administration
`bit.listserv.db2-l`	IBM's DB2 (relational database)
`bit.listserv.dbase-l`	dBase IV (PC database)
`bit.listserv.deaf-l`	Deafness
`bit.listserv.decnews`	Digital Equipment Corporation news
`bit.listserv.dectei-l`	DECUS Education Software Library
`bit.listserv.devel-l`	Technology transfer in international development
`bit.listserv.dipl-l`	Diplomacy game
`bit.listserv.disarm-l`	Disarmament
`bit.listserv.domain-l`	Domain listings
`bit.listserv.down-syn`	Down syndrome
`bit.listserv.dsshe-l`	Disabled student services in higher education
`bit.listserv.earntech`	EARN technical group
`bit.listserv.ecolog-l`	Ecological Society of America
`bit.listserv.edi-l`	Electronic data interchange
`bit.listserv.edpolyan`	Professionals and students and education
`bit.listserv.edstat-l`	Statistics education
`bit.listserv.edtech`	Educational technology (Moderated)
`bit.listserv.edusig-l`	Education special interest group
`bit.listserv.emusic-l`	Electronic music

`bit.listserv.endnote`	Bibsoft Endnote
`bit.listserv.envbeh-1`	Environment and human behavior
`bit.listserv.erl-1`	Educational research
`bit.listserv.ethics-1`	Ethics in computing
`bit.listserv.ethology`	Ethology
`bit.listserv.euearn-1`	Eastern Europe
`bit.listserv.film-1`	Film making and reviews
`bit.listserv.fnord-1`	New ways of thinking
`bit.listserv.frac-1`	Fractals
`bit.listserv.free-1`	Father's rights
`bit.listserv.games-1`	Computer dames
`bit.listserv.gaynet`	GayNet List (Moderated)
`bit.listserv.gddm-1`	The GDDM
`bit.listserv.geodesic`	Buckminster Fuller
`bit.listserv.gguide`	Bitnic Gguide List
`bit.listserv.gophern`	"Let's Go Gopherin'", learning to use the Internet
`bit.listserv.govdoc-1`	Government Documents
`bit.listserv.gutnberg`	Project Gutenberg
`bit.listserv.hellas`	Hellenic topics (Moderated)
`bit.listserv.help-net`	Help on Bitnet and the Internet
`bit.listserv.hindu-d`	Hindu digest (Moderated)
`bit.listserv.history`	History
`bit.listserv.hp3000-1`	HP-3000 computers
`bit.listserv.hytel-1`	Hytelnet (Moderated)
`bit.listserv.i-amiga`	Amiga computers
`bit.listserv.ibm-hesc`	IBM higher education consortium
`bit.listserv.ibm-main`	IBM mainframe computers
`bit.listserv.ibm-nets`	IBM mainframes and networking
`bit.listserv.ibm7171`	IBM's 7171 Protocol Converter
`bit.listserv.ibmtcp-1`	IBM's TCP/IP products
`bit.listserv.india-d`	India (Moderated)
`bit.listserv.info-gcg`	GCG Genetics Software Discussion
`bit.listserv.infonets`	Redistribution from Infonets
`bit.listserv.ingrafx`	Information graphics
`bit.listserv.innopac`	Innovative Interfaces Online Public Access
`bit.listserv.ioob-1`	Industrial psychology
`bit.listserv.ipct-1`	Interpersonal computing and technology (Moderated)
`bit.listserv.isn`	ISN Data Switch
`bit.listserv.jes2-1`	IBM's JES2
`bit.listserv.jnet-1`	Jnet running under VMS
`bit.listserv.1-hcap`	Handicaps (Moderated)
`bit.listserv.1-vmctr`	VMCENTER Components
`bit.listserv.lawsch-1`	Law Schools
`bit.listserv.liaison`	Bitnic Liaison
`bit.listserv.libref-1`	Library Reference Issues (Moderated)
`bit.listserv.libres`	Library and Information Science Research
`bit.listserv.license`	Software Licensing

`bit.listserv.linkfail`	Link failure announcements
`bit.listserv.literary`	Literature
`bit.listserv.lstsrv-l`	Listserv
`bit.listserv.mail-l`	Mail
`bit.listserv.mailbook`	Mail/Mailbook
`bit.listserv.mba-l`	MBA student curriculums
`bit.listserv.mbu-l`	Megabyte University computers and writing
`bit.listserv.mdphd-l`	Dual degree programs
`bit.listserv.medforum`	Medical students (Moderated)
`bit.listserv.medlib-l`	Medical libraries
`bit.listserv.mednews`	Mednews Health Info-Com Network Newsletter
`bit.listserv.mideur-l`	Middle Europe
`bit.listserv.mla-l`	Music Library Association
`bit.listserv.netnws-l`	Netnews (Usenet)
`bit.listserv.nettrain`	Network trainers
`bit.listserv.new-list`	Announcements about new Bitnet lists (Moderated)
`bit.listserv.next-l`	Next computers
`bit.listserv.nodmgt-l`	Node management
`bit.listserv.notabene`	Nota Bene
`bit.listserv.notis-l`	Notis/Dobis
`bit.listserv.novell`	Novell LANs
`bit.listserv.omrscan`	OMR scanners
`bit.listserv.os2-l`	IBM's OS/2 operating system
`bit.listserv.ozone`	OZONE
`bit.listserv.pacs-l`	Public-Access Computer Systems (Moderated)
`bit.listserv.page-l`	IBM's 3812/3820 Tips and Problems
`bit.listserv.pagemakr`	PageMaker for Desktop Publishers
`bit.listserv.physhare`	Physics
`bit.listserv.pmdf-l`	PMDF
`bit.listserv.politics`	Politics
`bit.listserv.postcard`	Postcard collectors
`bit.listserv.power-l`	IBM's RS/6000 computers (the Power architecture)
`bit.listserv.powerh-l`	PowerHouse
`bit.listserv.psycgrad`	Psychology Grad Students
`bit.listserv.qualrs-l`	Qualitative Research of the Human Sciences
`bit.listserv.relusr-l`	Relay Users
`bit.listserv.rhetoric`	Rhetoric, social movements, persuasion
`bit.listserv.rra-l`	Romance Readers Anonymous (Moderated)
`bit.listserv.rscs-l`	IBM's VM/RSCS
`bit.listserv.rscsmods`	RSCS modifications
`bit.listserv.s-comput`	Supercomputers
`bit.listserv.sas-l`	SAS
`bit.listserv.scce-l`	Supercomputers for Central Europe
`bit.listserv.script-l`	IBM vs Waterloo SCRIPT
`bit.listserv.scuba-l`	Scuba diving
`bit.listserv.seasia-l`	Southeast Asia
`bit.listserv.seds-l`	Students for the Exploration and Development of Space

`bit.listserv.sedsnews`	Space news from SEDS
`bit.listserv.sfs-l`	IBM's VM Shared File System
`bit.listserv.sganet`	Student government global mail network
`bit.listserv.simula`	SIMULA programming (simulation) language
`bit.listserv.slart-l`	SLA Research and Teaching
`bit.listserv.slovak-l`	Slovaks
`bit.listserv.snamgt-l`	IBM's SNA Network Management
`bit.listserv.sos-data`	Social Science
`bit.listserv.spires-l`	Spires Conference
`bit.listserv.sportpsy`	Exercise and Sports Psychology
`bit.listserv.spssx-l`	SPSSX
`bit.listserv.sqlinfo`	IBM's SQL/DS (database language)
`bit.listserv.stat-l`	Statistical consulting
`bit.listserv.tech-l`	Bitnic TECH-L mailing list
`bit.listserv.techwr-l`	Technical writing
`bit.listserv.tecmat-l`	Technology in secondary mathematics
`bit.listserv.test`	Place to send test articles
`bit.listserv.tex-l`	The TeX typesetting system
`bit.listserv.tn3270-l`	tn3270 protocol
`bit.listserv.toolb-l`	Asymetrix Toolbook
`bit.listserv.trans-l`	Bitnic TRANS-L mailing list
`bit.listserv.travel-l`	Travel and tourism
`bit.listserv.tsorexx`	IBM's REXX langauge for TSO
`bit.listserv.ucp-l`	University Computing Project
`bit.listserv.ug-l`	Usage guidelines
`bit.listserv.uigis-l`	User interface for Geographical Info Systems
`bit.listserv.urep-l`	UREP software
`bit.listserv.usrdir-l`	User directory
`bit.listserv.uus-l`	Unitarian-Universalist church
`bit.listserv.valert-l`	Virus alerts
`bit.listserv.vfort-l`	IBM's VS-Fortran programming language
`bit.listserv.vm-util`	IBM's VM Utilities
`bit.listserv.vmesa-l`	IBM's VM/ESA operating system
`bit.listserv.vmslsv-l`	DEC's VAX/VMS operating system
`bit.listserv.vmxa-l`	IBM's VM/XA operating system
`bit.listserv.vnews-l`	VNEWS
`bit.listserv.vpiej-l`	Electronic publishing
`bit.listserv.wac-l`	Writing across the curriculum and writing centers
`bit.listserv.win3-l`	Microsoft Windows 3.x
`bit.listserv.words-l`	The English language
`bit.listserv.wpcorp-l`	WordPerfect products
`bit.listserv.wpwin-l`	WordPerfect for MS Windows
`bit.listserv.wx-talk`	The weather
`bit.listserv.x400-l`	The X.400 protocol
`bit.listserv.xcult-l`	International Intercultural Newsletter
`bit.listserv.xedit-l`	VM System Editor
`bit.listserv.xerox-l`	Xerox products

`bit.listserv.xmailer`	The Crosswell mailer
`bit.listserv.xtropy-l`	Extopian topics
`bit.mailserv.word-mac`	Word processing on the Macintosh
`bit.mailserv.word-pc`	Word processing on PCs
`bit.org.peace-corps`	Peace Corps and international volunteers
`bit.software.international`	International software (Moderated)

BIZ

`biz.americast`	The Americast company
`biz.americast.samples`	Americast samples
`biz.books.technical`	Selling and buying books
`biz.clarinet`	Announcements about Clarinet
`biz.clarinet.sample`	Free samples from Clarinet newsgroups
`biz.comp.hardware`	Generic commercial hardware
`biz.comp.services`	Generic commercial service
`biz.comp.software`	Generic commercial software
`biz.comp.telebit`	Telebit modems
`biz.comp.telebit.netblazer`	Telebit Netblazer
`biz.config`	Configuration and administration of biz newsgroups
`biz.control`	Usenet control information for biz newsgroups
`biz.dec`	DEC equipment and software
`biz.dec.decathena`	DEC Athena
`biz.dec.decnews`	DEC news releases and discussion
`biz.dec.ip`	IP networking on DEC machines
`biz.dec.workstations`	DEC workstations
`biz.digex.announce`	Digex
`biz.jobs.offered`	Jobs that are available
`biz.misc`	Miscellaneous postings of a commercial nature
`biz.next.newprod`	New products from the Next Company
`biz.oreilly.announce`	Announcements from O'Reilly & Associates (Moderated)
`biz.sco.announce`	Santa Cruz Operations (SCO) news (Moderated)
`biz.sco.binaries`	Programs for SCO Xenix, Unix, or ODT (Open Desktop)
`biz.sco.general`	General discussion about SCO products
`biz.sco.magazine`	The SCO magazine and its contents
`biz.sco.opendesktop`	Open Desktop
`biz.sco.sources`	Free programs to run under an SCO environment
`biz.sco.wserver`	SCO widget server
`biz.stolen`	Stolen items
`biz.tadpole.sparcbook`	The Sparcbook portable computer
`biz.test`	Place to send test articles
`biz.univel.misc`	Novell's Univel software
`biz.zeos.announce`	Announcements by Zeos International
`biz.zeos.general`	General discussion regarding Zeos

CLARI

clari.biz.commodity	Commodity news and price reports (Moderated)
clari.biz.courts	Lawsuits, business related legal matters (Moderated)
clari.biz.economy	Economic news and indicators (Moderated)
clari.biz.economy.world	Economy stories for non-US countries (Moderated)
clari.biz.features	Business feature stories (Moderated)
clari.biz.finance	Finance, currency, corporate finance (Moderated)
clari.biz.finance.earnings	Earnings and dividend reports (Moderated)
clari.biz.finance.personal	Personal investing and finance (Moderated)
clari.biz.finance.services	Banks and financial industries (Moderated)
clari.biz.invest	News for investors (Moderated)
clari.biz.labor	Strikes, unions and labor relations (Moderated)
clari.biz.market	General stock market news (Moderated)
clari.biz.market.amex	American Stock Exchange reports & news (Moderated)
clari.biz.market.dow	Dow Jones NYSE reports (Moderated)
clari.biz.market.ny	NYSE reports (Moderated)
clari.biz.market.otc	NASDAQ reports (Moderated)
clari.biz.market.report	General market reports, S&P, etc (Moderated)
clari.biz.mergers	Mergers and acquisitions (Moderated)
clari.biz.misc	Other business news (Moderated)
clari.biz.products	Important new products and services (Moderated)
clari.biz.top	Top business news (Moderated)
clari.biz.urgent	Breaking business news (Moderated)
clari.canada.biz	Canadian business summaries (Moderated)
clari.canada.briefs	Canadian news briefs (Moderated)
clari.canada.briefs.ont	Canadian news briefs (Ontario) (Moderated)
clari.canada.briefs.west	Canadian news briefs (Western) (Moderated)
clari.canada.features	Alamanac, Ottawa Special, Arts (Moderated)
clari.canada.general	Short items on Canadian news stories (Moderated)
clari.canada.gov	Government related news (all levels) (Moderated)
clari.canada.law	Crimes, the courts and the law (Moderated)
clari.canada.newscast	Regular newscast for Canadians (Moderated)
clari.canada.politics	Political and election items (Moderated)
clari.canada.trouble	Mishaps, accidents and serious problems (Moderated)
clari.feature.dave_barry	Columns of humorist Dave Barry (Moderated)
clari.feature.kinsey	Sex Q&A and advice from Kinsey Institute (Moderated)
clari.feature.lederer	Richard Lederer's "Looking at Language" (Moderated)
clari.feature.mike_royko	Chicago opinion columnist Mike Royko (Moderated)
clari.feature.miss_manners	Judith Martin's etiquette advice (Moderated)
clari.feature.movies	Discussion and reviews of feature movies
clari.local.alberta.briefs	Local news briefs (Moderated)
clari.local.arizona	Local news (Moderated)
clari.local.arizona.briefs	Local news briefs (Moderated)
clari.local.bc.briefs	Local news briefs (Moderated)
clari.local.california	Local news (Moderated)
clari.local.california.briefs	Local news briefs (Moderated)

clari.local.chicago	Local news (Moderated)
clari.local.chicago.briefs	Local news briefs (Moderated)
clari.local.florida	Local news (Moderated)
clari.local.florida.briefs	Local news briefs (Moderated)
clari.local.georgia	Local news (Moderated)
clari.local.georgia.briefs	Local news briefs (Moderated)
clari.local.headlines	Various local headline summaries (Moderated)
clari.local.illinois	Local news (Moderated)
clari.local.illinois.briefs	Local news briefs (Moderated)
clari.local.indiana	Local news (Moderated)
clari.local.indiana.briefs	Local news briefs (Moderated)
clari.local.iowa	Local news (Moderated)
clari.local.iowa.briefs	Local news briefs (Moderated)
clari.local.los_angeles	Local news (Moderated)
clari.local.los_angeles.briefs	Local news briefs (Moderated)
clari.local.louisiana	Local news (Moderated)
clari.local.manitoba.briefs	Local news briefs (Moderated)
clari.local.maritimes.briefs	Local news briefs (Moderated)
clari.local.maryland	Local news (Moderated)
clari.local.maryland.briefs	Local news briefs (Moderated)
clari.local.massachusetts	Local news (Moderated)
clari.local.massachusetts.briefs	Local news briefs (Moderated)
clari.local.michigan	Local news (Moderated)
clari.local.michigan.briefs	Local news briefs (Moderated)
clari.local.minnesota	Local news (Moderated)
clari.local.minnesota.briefs	Local news briefs (Moderated)
clari.local.missouri	Local news (Moderated)
clari.local.missouri.briefs	Local news briefs (Moderated)
clari.local.nebraska	Local news (Moderated)
clari.local.nebraska.briefs	Local news briefs (Moderated)
clari.local.nevada	Local news (Moderated)
clari.local.nevada.briefs	Local news briefs (Moderated)
clari.local.new_england	Local news (Moderated)
clari.local.new_hampshire	Local news (Moderated)
clari.local.new_jersey	Local news (Moderated)
clari.local.new_jersey.briefs	Local news briefs (Moderated)
clari.local.new_york	Local news (Moderated)
clari.local.new_york.briefs	Local news briefs (Moderated)
clari.local.nyc	Local news (New York City) (Moderated)
clari.local.nyc.briefs	Local news briefs (Moderated)
clari.local.ohio	Local news (Moderated)
clari.local.ohio.briefs	Local news briefs (Moderated)
clari.local.ontario.briefs	Local news briefs (Moderated)
clari.local.oregon	Local news (Moderated)
clari.local.oregon.briefs	Local news briefs (Moderated)
clari.local.pennsylvania	Local news (Moderated)
clari.local.pennsylvania.briefs	Local news briefs (Moderated)

`clari.local.saskatchewan.briefs`	Local news briefs (Moderated)
`clari.local.sfbay`	Stories datelined San Francisco Bay Area (Moderated)
`clari.local.texas`	Local news (Moderated)
`clari.local.texas.briefs`	Local news briefs (Moderated)
`clari.local.utah`	Local news (Moderated)
`clari.local.utah.briefs`	Local news briefs (Moderated)
`clari.local.virginia+dc`	Local news (Moderated)
`clari.local.virginia+dc.briefs`	Local news briefs (Moderated)
`clari.local.washington`	Local news (Moderated)
`clari.local.washington.briefs`	Local news briefs (Moderated)
`clari.local.wisconsin`	Local news (Moderated)
`clari.local.wisconsin.briefs`	Local news briefs (Moderated)
`clari.matrix_news`	Monthly journal about the Internet (Moderated)
`clari.nb.apple`	Newsbytes: Apple/Macintosh news (Moderated)
`clari.nb.business`	Newsbytes: business & industry news (Moderated)
`clari.nb.general`	Newsbytes: general computer news (Moderated)
`clari.nb.govt`	Newsbytes: legal and gov't computer news (Moderated)
`clari.nb.ibm`	Newsbytes: IBM news (Moderated)
`clari.nb.index`	Newsbytes: Index (Moderated)
`clari.nb.review`	Newsbytes: new product reviews (Moderated)
`clari.nb.telecom`	Newsbytes: telecom & online industry news (Moderated)
`clari.nb.top`	Newsbytes: top stories (crossposted) (Moderated)
`clari.nb.trends`	Newsbytes: new developments & trends (Moderated)
`clari.nb.unix`	Newsbytes: Unix news (Moderated)
`clari.net.admin`	Announcements for admins at Clarinet sites (Moderated)
`clari.net.announce`	Announcements for all Clarinet readers (Moderated)
`clari.net.newusers`	All about Clarinet (Moderated)
`clari.net.products`	New Clarinet products (Moderated)
`clari.net.talk`	Discussion of Clarinet only unmoderated group
`clari.news.almanac`	Daily almanac "This date in history" (Moderated)
`clari.news.arts`	Stage, drama and other fine arts (Moderated)
`clari.news.aviation`	Aviation industry and mishaps (Moderated)
`clari.news.books`	Books and publishing (Moderated)
`clari.news.briefs`	Regular news summaries (Moderated)
`clari.news.bulletin`	Major breaking stories of the week (Moderated)
`clari.news.canada`	News related to Canada (Moderated)
`clari.news.cast`	Regular U.S. news summary (Moderated)
`clari.news.children`	Children and parenting (Moderated)
`clari.news.consumer`	Consumer news, car reviews, etc (Moderated)
`clari.news.demonstration`	Demonstrations around the world (Moderated)
`clari.news.disaster`	Major problems, accidents, disasters (Moderated)
`clari.news.economy`	General economic news (Moderated)
`clari.news.election`	U.S. and international elections (Moderated)
`clari.news.entertain`	Entertainment industry news and features (Moderated)
`clari.news.europe`	News related to Europe (Moderated)
`clari.news.features`	Unclassified feature stories (Moderated)
`clari.news.fighting`	Clashes around the world (Moderated)

`clari.news.flash`	Ultra-important, once-a-year news flashes (Moderated)
`clari.news.goodnews`	Stories of success and survival (Moderated)
`clari.news.gov`	General Government related stories (Moderated)
`clari.news.gov.agency`	Government agencies, FBI, etc (Moderated)
`clari.news.gov.budget`	Budgets at all levels (Moderated)
`clari.news.gov.corrupt`	Government corruption, kickbacks, etc (Moderated)
`clari.news.gov.international`	International government-related stories (Moderated)
`clari.news.gov.officials`	Government officials and their problems (Moderated)
`clari.news.gov.state`	State gov't news of national importance (Moderated)
`clari.news.gov.taxes`	Tax laws, trials, etc (Moderated)
`clari.news.gov.usa`	US Federal government news [hgh volume] (Moderated)
`clari.news.group`	Special interest groups (Moderated)
`clari.news.group.blacks`	News of interest to black people (Moderated)
`clari.news.group.gays`	Homosexuality and gay rights (Moderated)
`clari.news.group.jews`	Jews and Jewish interests (Moderated)
`clari.news.group.women`	Women's issues and abortion (Moderated)
`clari.news.headlines`	Hourly list of top U.S./World headlines (Moderated)
`clari.news.hot.east_europe`	News from Eastern Europe (Moderated)
`clari.news.hot.iraq`	Persian Gulf Crisis news (Moderated)
`clari.news.hot.somalia`	News from Somalia (Moderated)
`clari.news.hot.ussr`	News from the Soviet Union (Moderated)
`clari.news.interest`	Human interest stories (Moderated)
`clari.news.interest.animals`	Animals in the news (Moderated)
`clari.news.interest.history`	Human interest/history in the making (Moderated)
`clari.news.interest.people`	Famous people in the news (Moderated)
`clari.news.interest.people.column`	Famous poeple in the news dailies (Moderated)
`clari.news.interest.quirks`	Unusual or funny news stories (Moderated)
`clari.news.issues`	Major issues not covered elsewhere (Moderated)
`clari.news.issues.civil_rights`	Freedom, racism, civil rights issues (Moderated)
`clari.news.issues.conflict`	Conflict between groups around the world (Moderated)
`clari.news.issues.family`	Family, child abuse, etc (Moderated)
`clari.news.labor`	Unions, strikes (Moderated)
`clari.news.labor.strike`	Strikes (Moderated)
`clari.news.law`	General group for law related issues (Moderated)
`clari.news.law.civil`	Civil trials and litigation (Moderated)
`clari.news.law.civil`	Civil trials and litigation (moderated)
`clari.news.law.crime`	Major crimes (Moderated)
`clari.news.law.crime.sex`	Sex crimes and trials (Moderated)
`clari.news.law.crime.trial`	Trials for criminal actions (Moderated)
`clari.news.law.crime.violent`	Violent crime and criminals (Moderated)
`clari.news.law.drugs`	Drug-related crimes and drug stories (Moderated)
`clari.news.law.investigation`	Investigation of crimes (Moderated)
`clari.news.law.police`	Police and law enforcement (Moderated)
`clari.news.law.prison`	Prisons, prisoners and escapes (Moderated)
`clari.news.law.profession`	Lawyers, judges, etc (Moderated)
`clari.news.law.supreme`	U.S. Supreme court rulings and news (Moderated)
`clari.news.lifestyle`	Fashion, leisure, etc (Moderated)

`clari.news.military`	Military equipment, people and issues (Moderated)
`clari.news.movies`	Reviews, news and stories on movie stars (Moderated)
`clari.news.music`	Reviews and issues concerning music (Moderated)
`clari.news.politics`	Politicians and politics. (Moderated)
`clari.news.politics.people`	Politicians and political personalities (Moderated)
`clari.news.religion`	Religion and religious leaders (Moderated)
`clari.news.sex`	Sexual issues and sex-related politics (Moderated)
`clari.news.terrorism`	Terrorist actions around the world (Moderated)
`clari.news.top`	Top US news stories (Moderated)
`clari.news.top.world`	Top international news stories (Moderated)
`clari.news.trends`	Surveys and trends. (Moderated)
`clari.news.trouble`	Major accidents, problems and mishaps (Moderated)
`clari.news.tv`	TV schedules, news, reviews and stars (Moderated)
`clari.news.urgent`	Major breaking stories of the day (Moderated)
`clari.news.weather`	Weather and temperature reports (Moderated)
`clari.sfbay.briefs`	S.F. Bay Area breaking news briefs (Moderated)
`clari.sfbay.entertain`	S.F. Bay Area entertainment and reviews (Moderated)
`clari.sfbay.fire`	S.F. Bay Area current fire information (Moderated)
`clari.sfbay.general`	S.F. Bay Area general announcements (Moderated)
`clari.sfbay.misc`	S.F. Bay Area miscellaneous information (Moderated)
`clari.sfbay.police`	S.F. Bay Area police activities/reports (Moderated)
`clari.sfbay.roads`	S.F. Bay Area road/traffic conditions (Moderated)
`clari.sfbay.short`	S.F. Bay Area headlines (Moderated)
`clari.sfbay.weather`	S.F. Bay Area weather reports/forecasts (Moderated)
`clari.sports.baseball`	Baseball scores, stories, games, stats (Moderated)
`clari.sports.baseball.games`	Info about specific baseball games (moderated)
`clari.sports.basketball`	Basketball coverage (Moderated)
`clari.sports.basketball.college`	College basketball coverage (Moderated)
`clari.sports.features`	Sports feature stories (Moderated)
`clari.sports.football`	Pro football coverage (Moderated)
`clari.sports.football.college`	College football coverage (Moderated)
`clari.sports.football.games`	Info about specific football games (Moderated)
`clari.sports.hockey`	NHL coverage (Moderated)
`clari.sports.misc`	Other sports, plus general sports news (Moderated)
`clari.sports.motor`	Racing, Motor Sports (Moderated)
`clari.sports.olympic`	The Olympic Games (Moderated)
`clari.sports.tennis`	Tennis news and scores (Moderated)
`clari.sports.top`	Top sports news (Moderated)
`clari.streetprice`	Direct buyer prices computer equipment (Moderated)
`clari.tw.aerospace`	Aerospace industry and companies (Moderated)
`clari.tw.computers`	Computer industry (Moderated)
`clari.tw.defense`	Defense industry issues (Moderated)
`clari.tw.education`	Universities and colleges (Moderated)
`clari.tw.electronics`	Electronics makers and sellers (Moderated)
`clari.tw.environment`	Environmental news, hazardous waste, etc (Moderated)
`clari.tw.health`	Health care and medicine (Moderated)
`clari.tw.health.aids`	AIDS stories, research, political issues (Moderated)

`clari.tw.misc`	General technical industry stories (Moderated)
`clari.tw.nuclear`	Nuclear power and waste (Moderated)
`clari.tw.science`	General science stories (Moderated)
`clari.tw.space`	NASA, astronomy and spaceflight (Moderated)
`clari.tw.stocks`	Computer and technology stock prices (Moderated)
`clari.tw.telecom`	Phones, satellites, media, telecom (Moderated)

COMP

`comp.admin.policy`	Discussions of site administration policies
`comp.ai`	Artificial intelligence discussions
`comp.ai.edu`	Applications of artificial intelligence to education
`comp.ai.fuzzy`	Fuzzy set theory, aka fuzzy logic
`comp.ai.genetic`	Using artificial intelligence for genetic research
`comp.ai.jair.announce`	Abstracts from the Journal of AI Research (Moderated)
`comp.ai.jair.papers`	Papers from the Journal of AI Research (Moderated)
`comp.ai.nat-lang`	Natural language processing by computers
`comp.ai.neural-nets`	All aspects of neural networks
`comp.ai.nlang-know-rep`	Natural lang/knowledge representation (Moderated)
`comp.ai.philosophy`	Philosophical aspects of artificial intelligence
`comp.ai.shells`	Artificial intelligence applied to shells
`comp.ai.vision`	Artificial intelligence vision research (Moderated)
`comp.answers`	Repository for periodic Usenet articles (Moderated)
`comp.apps.spreadsheets`	Spreadsheets on various platforms
`comp.arch`	Computer architecture
`comp.arch.bus.vmebus`	Hardware and software for VMEbus Systems
`comp.arch.storage`	Storage system issues, both hardware and software
`comp.archives`	Descriptions of public access archives (Moderated)
`comp.archives.admin`	Issues relating to computer archive administration
`comp.archives.msdos.announce`	Announcements about DOS archives (Moderated)
`comp.archives.msdos.d`	Discussion of materials available in DOS archives
`comp.bbs.misc`	All aspects of computer bulletin board systems
`comp.bbs.waffle`	The Waffle BBS and Usenet system on all platforms
`comp.benchmarks`	Discussion of benchmarking techniques and results
`comp.binaries.acorn`	Binary-only postings for Acorn machines (Moderated)
`comp.binaries.amiga`	Encoded public domain programs in binary (Moderated)
`comp.binaries.apple2`	Binary-only postings for the Apple II computer
`comp.binaries.atari.st`	Binary-only postings for the Atari ST (Moderated)
`comp.binaries.cbm`	Binary-only postings for 8-bit Commodore machines
`comp.binaries.ibm.pc`	Binary-only postings for IBM PC/MS-DOS (Moderated)
`comp.binaries.ibm.pc.archives`	PC archive sites
`comp.binaries.ibm.pc.d`	Discussions about IBM/PC binary postings
`comp.binaries.ibm.pc.wanted`	Requests for IBM PC and compatible programs
`comp.binaries.mac`	Encoded Macintosh programs in binary (Moderated)
`comp.binaries.ms-windows`	Binary programs for Microsoft Windows (Moderated)
`comp.binaries.os2`	Binaries for use under the OS/2 ABI (Moderated)
`comp.bugs.2bsd`	Reports of Unix version 2BSD related bugs

`comp.bugs.4bsd`	Reports of Unix version 4BSD related bugs
`comp.bugs.4bsd.ucb-fixes`	Bug reports/fixes for BSD Unix (Moderated)
`comp.bugs.misc`	General Unix bug reports and fixes (incl V7, uucp)
`comp.bugs.sys5`	Reports of USG (System III, V, etc) bugs
`comp.cad.cadence`	Users of Cadence Design Systems products
`comp.cad.compass`	Compass Design Automation EDA tools
`comp.cad.pro-engineer`	Parametric Technology's Pro/Engineer design package
`comp.cad.synthesis`	Logic synthesis
`comp.client-server`	Topics relating to client/server technology
`comp.cog-eng`	Cognitive engineering
`comp.compilers`	Compiler construction, theory, etc (Moderated)
`comp.compression`	Data compression algorithms and theory
`comp.compression.research`	Discussions about data compression research
`comp.databases`	Database and data management issues and theory
`comp.databases.informix`	Informix database management software discussions
`comp.databases.ingres`	Issues relating to Ingres products
`comp.databases.ms-access`	Microsoft Access, relational database
`comp.databases.object`	Object-oriented paradigms in databases systems
`comp.databases.oracle`	The SQL database products of the Oracle Corporation
`comp.databases.pick`	Pick-like, post-relational database systems
`comp.databases.sybase`	Implementations of the SQL Server
`comp.databases.theory`	Discussing advances in database technology
`comp.databases.xbase.fox`	Fox Software's xBase system
`comp.databases.xbase.misc`	xBase products
`comp.dcom.cell-relay`	Forum for discussion of cell relay-based products
`comp.dcom.fax`	Fax hardware, software, and protocols
`comp.dcom.isdn`	The Integrated Services Digital Network (ISDN)
`comp.dcom.lans.ethernet`	Discussions of the Ethernet/IEEE 802.3 protocols
`comp.dcom.lans.fddi`	Discussions of the FDDI protocol suite
`comp.dcom.lans.hyperchannel`	Hyperchannel networks within an IP network
`comp.dcom.lans.misc`	Local area network hardware and software
`comp.dcom.lans.token-ring`	Token-ring networks
`comp.dcom.modems`	Data communications hardware and software
`comp.dcom.servers`	Selecting and operating data communications servers
`comp.dcom.sys.cisco`	Info on Cisco routers and bridges
`comp.dcom.sys.wellfleet`	Wellfleet bridge and router systems
`comp.dcom.telecom`	Telecommunications digest (Moderated)
`comp.doc`	Archived public-domain documentation (Moderated)
`comp.doc.techreports`	Lists of technical reports (Moderated)
`comp.dsp`	Digital signal processing using computers
`comp.editors`	Topics related to computerized text editing
`comp.edu`	Computer science education
`comp.edu.composition`	Writing instruction in computer-based classrooms
`comp.emacs`	Emacs editors of different flavors
`comp.fonts`	Typefonts design, conversion, use, etc
`comp.graphics`	Computer graphics, art, animation, image processing
`comp.graphics.algorithms`	Algorithms used in producing computer graphics

`comp.graphics.animation`	Technical aspects of computer animation
`comp.graphics.avs`	The Application Visualization System
`comp.graphics.data-explorer`	IBM's Visualization Data Explorer, aka DX
`comp.graphics.explorer`	The Explorer Modular Visualisation Environment (MVE)
`comp.graphics.gnuplot`	The Gnuplot interactive function plotter
`comp.graphics.opengl`	The OpenGL 3D application programming interface
`comp.graphics.research`	Highly technical computer graphics (Moderated)
`comp.graphics.visualization`	Info on scientific visualization
`comp.groupware`	Shared interactive environments
`comp.human-factors`	Issues related to human-computer interaction (HCI)
`comp.infosystems`	Any discussion about information systems
`comp.infosystems.gis`	All aspects of Geographic Information Systems
`comp.infosystems.gopher`	Discussion of the Gopher information service
`comp.infosystems.wais`	The Z39.50-based Wais full-text search system
`comp.infosystems.www`	The World Wide Web
`comp.internet.library`	Discussing electronic libraries (Moderated)
`comp.ivideodisc`	Interactive videodiscs uses, potential, etc
`comp.lang.ada`	The Ada programming language
`comp.lang.apl`	The APL programming language
`comp.lang.asm370`	IBM System/370 assembly language
`comp.lang.c`	The C programming language
`comp.lang.c++`	The object-oriented C++ programming language
`comp.lang.clos`	Common Lisp Object System discussions
`comp.lang.clu`	The CLU language and related topics
`comp.lang.dylan`	The Dylan language
`comp.lang.eiffel`	The object-oriented Eiffel language
`comp.lang.forth`	The Forth programming language
`comp.lang.forth.mac`	The CSI MacForth programming environment
`comp.lang.fortran`	The Fortran programming language
`comp.lang.functional`	Discussion about functional programming languages
`comp.lang.hermes`	The Hermes language for distributed applications
`comp.lang.icon`	The ICON programming language
`comp.lang.idl`	IDL (the Interface Description Language)
`comp.lang.idl-pvwave`	IDL and PV-Wave language discussions
`comp.lang.lisp`	The Lisp programming language
`comp.lang.lisp.franz`	The Franz Lisp programming language
`comp.lang.lisp.mcl`	Apple's Macintosh Common Lisp
`comp.lang.lisp.x`	The XLISP language system
`comp.lang.logo`	The Logo teaching and learning language
`comp.lang.misc`	Different computer languages not specifically listed
`comp.lang.ml`	ML languages ML, CAML, Lazy ML, etc (Moderated)
`comp.lang.modula2`	The Modula-2 programming language
`comp.lang.modula3`	The Modula-3 programming language
`comp.lang.oberon`	The Oberon language and system
`comp.lang.objective-c`	The Objective-C language and environment
`comp.lang.pascal`	The Pascal programming language
`comp.lang.perl`	The Perl scripting language

`comp.lang.pop`	Pop11 and the Plug user group
`comp.lang.postscript`	The PostScript Page Description Language
`comp.lang.prolog`	The Prolog programming language
`comp.lang.rexx`	IBM's REXX command-scripting language
`comp.lang.sather`	Sather, object-oriented programming language
`comp.lang.scheme`	The Scheme programming language
`comp.lang.scheme.c`	The Scheme language environment
`comp.lang.sigplan`	Info and announcements from ACM SIGPLAN (Moderated)
`comp.lang.smalltalk`	The Smalltalk 80 programming language
`comp.lang.tcl`	The TCL programming language and related tools
`comp.lang.verilog`	The Verilog and PLI programming languages
`comp.lang.vhdl`	VHSIC Hardware Description Language, IEEE 1076/87
`comp.lang.visual`	Visual programming languages
`comp.laser-printers`	Laser printers, hardware and software (Moderated)
`comp.lsi`	Large scale integrated circuits
`comp.lsi.cad`	Computer Aided Design
`comp.lsi.testing`	Testing of electronic circuits
`comp.mail.elm`	Discussion and fixes for ELM mail system
`comp.mail.headers`	Gatewayed from the Internet header-people list
`comp.mail.maps`	Various maps, including UUCP maps (Moderated)
`comp.mail.mh`	The UCI version of the Rand Message Handling system
`comp.mail.mime`	Multipurpose Internet Mail Extensions of RFC 1341
`comp.mail.misc`	General discussions about computer mail
`comp.mail.multi-media`	Multimedia mail
`comp.mail.mush`	The Mail User's Shell (MUSH)
`comp.mail.sendmail`	Configuring and using the BSD sendmail agent
`comp.mail.uucp`	Mail in the UUCP network environment
`comp.misc`	General computer talk, not covered elsewhere
`comp.multimedia`	Interactive multimedia technologies of all kinds
`comp.music`	Applications of computers in music research
`comp.networks.noctools.announce`	Announcements about NOC tools (Moderated)
`comp.networks.noctools.bugs`	Bug reports and fixes for NOC tools
`comp.networks.noctools.d`	Discussion about NOC tools
`comp.networks.noctools.submissions`	New NOC tools submissions
`comp.networks.noctools.tools`	Descriptions of available NOC tools (Moderated)
`comp.networks.noctools.wanted`	Requests for NOC software
`comp.newprod`	Announcements of new products (Moderated)
`comp.object`	Object-oriented programming and languages
`comp.object.logic`	Integrating object-oriented and logic programming
`comp.org.acm`	Association for Computing Machinery
`comp.org.decus`	Digital Equipment Computer Users' Society
`comp.org.eff.news`	Electronic Frontiers Foundation (Moderated)
`comp.org.eff.talk`	Discussion of EFF goals, strategies, etc
`comp.org.fidonet`	Official digest of FidoNet Assoc (Moderated)
`comp.org.ieee`	Issues and announcements about the IEEE
`comp.org.isoc.interest`	The Internet Society
`comp.org.issnnet`	International Student Society for Neural Networks

comp.org.sug	The Sun User's Group
comp.org.usenix	Usenix Association events and announcements
comp.org.usenix.roomshare	Finding lodging during Usenix conferences
comp.os.386bsd.announce	The 386bsd operating system (Moderated)
comp.os.386bsd.apps	Applications which run under 386bsd OS
comp.os.386bsd.bugs	Bugs and fixes for the 386bsd OS and its clients
comp.os.386bsd.development	Working on 386bsd OS internals
comp.os.386bsd.misc	Aspects of 386bsd OS, not covered by other groups
comp.os.386bsd.questions	General questions about 386bsd
comp.os.aos	Data General's AOS/VS
comp.os.coherent	The Coherent operating system
comp.os.cpm	CP/M operating system
comp.os.cpm.amethyst	Amethyst, CP/M-80 software package
comp.os.geos	Geoworks' GEOS operating system
comp.os.linux	The free Unix clone for the 386/486, Linux
comp.os.linux.admin	Linux: installation and administration
comp.os.linux.announce	Announcements for the Linux community (Moderated)
comp.os.linux.development	Linux: development issues
comp.os.linux.help	Linux: questions and answers
comp.os.linux.misc	Linux: topics not covered by other newsgroups
comp.os.lynx	LynxOS and Lynx real-time systems
comp.os.mach	The Mach OS from CMU and other places
comp.os.minix	Discussion of Andy Tanenbaum's Minix system
comp.os.misc	OS-oriented discussion, not carried elsewhere
comp.os.ms-windows.advocacy	Debate about Microsoft Windows
comp.os.ms-windows.announce	Announcements relating to MS Windows (Moderated)
comp.os.ms-windows.apps	Applications in the MS Windows environment
comp.os.ms-windows.misc	General discussions about MS Windows issues
comp.os.ms-windows.nt.misc	Windows NT: general discussion
comp.os.ms-windows.nt.setup	Windows NT: confiuration and setup
comp.os.ms-windows.programmer.misc	Programming MS Windows
comp.os.ms-windows.programmer.tools	Development tools for MS Windows
comp.os.ms-windows.programmer.win32	32-bit MS Windows programming interfaces
comp.os.ms-windows.setup	Installing and configuring MS Windows
comp.os.msdos.4dos	The 4DOS command processor for DOS
comp.os.msdos.apps	DOS applications
comp.os.msdos.desqview	QuarterDeck's Desqview and related products
comp.os.msdos.mail-news	DOS mail and network news systems
comp.os.msdos.misc	Miscellaneous topics about DOS machines
comp.os.msdos.pcgeos	GeoWorks PC/GEOS and PC/GEOS-based packages
comp.os.msdos.programmer	DOS programming
comp.os.msdos.programmer.turbovision	Borland's text-based application libraries
comp.os.os2.advocacy	Debate about IBM's OS/2 operating system
comp.os.os2.announce	Announcements related to OS/2 (Moderated)
comp.os.os2.apps	OS/2 applications
comp.os.os2.beta	Beta releases of OS/2
comp.os.os2.bugs	Bug reports and fixes for OS/2

`comp.os.os2.misc`	Miscellaneous topics about OS/2 system
`comp.os.os2.multimedia`	Multimedia products and implementation on OS/2
`comp.os.os2.networking`	Networking in OS/2 environments
`comp.os.os2.programmer`	OS/2 programming
`comp.os.os2.programmer.misc`	More OS/2 programming
`comp.os.os2.programmer.porting`	Porting software to OS/2
`comp.os.os2.setup`	Setting up and configuring OS/2
`comp.os.os2.ver1x`	OS/2 versions 1.0 through 1.3
`comp.os.os9`	Discussions about the OS9 operating system
`comp.os.research`	Operating systems and related areas (Moderated)
`comp.os.rsts`	The PDP-11 RSTS/E operating system
`comp.os.v`	The V distributed operating system from Stanford
`comp.os.vms`	DEC's VAX line of computers and VMS operating system
`comp.os.vxworks`	The VxWorks real-time operating system
`comp.os.xinu`	The XINU operating system from Purdue (Doug Comer)
`comp.parallel`	Massively parallel hardware/software (Moderated)
`comp.parallel.pvm`	The PVM system of multicomputer parallelization
`comp.patents`	Patents of computer technology (Moderated)
`comp.periphs`	Peripheral devices
`comp.periphs.printers`	Printers
`comp.periphs.scsi`	SCSI-based peripheral devices
`comp.programming`	Programming issues that transcend languages and OSs
`comp.programming.literate`	Literate programming
`comp.protocols.appletalk`	Applebus hardware and software
`comp.protocols.dicom`	Digital imaging and communications in medicine
`comp.protocols.ibm`	Networking with IBM mainframes
`comp.protocols.iso`	The ISO protocol stack
`comp.protocols.iso.dev-environ`	ISO Development Environment
`comp.protocols.iso.x400`	X400 mail protocol
`comp.protocols.iso.x400.gateway`	X400 mail gateway (Moderated)
`comp.protocols.kerberos`	The Kerberos authentication server
`comp.protocols.kermit`	The Kermit communications package (Moderated)
`comp.protocols.misc`	General protocol discussions
`comp.protocols.nfs`	The Network File System protocol
`comp.protocols.pcnet`	PCNET (a personal computer network)
`comp.protocols.ppp`	The Point to Point Protocol
`comp.protocols.snmp`	The Simple Network Management Protocol
`comp.protocols.tcp-ip`	TCP and IP network protocols
`comp.protocols.tcp-ip.domains`	Domain-style names
`comp.protocols.tcp-ip.ibmpc`	TCP/IP for IBM-like personal computers
`comp.protocols.time.ntp`	The Network Time Protocol
`comp.publish.cdrom.hardware`	Hardware used in publishing with CD-ROM
`comp.publish.cdrom.multimedia`	Software for multimedia authoring and publishing
`comp.publish.cdrom.software`	Software used in publishing with CD-ROM
`comp.realtime`	Real-time computing
`comp.research.japan`	Research in Japan (Moderated)
`comp.risks`	Risks to public from computers and users (Moderated)

`comp.robotics`	Robots and their applications
`comp.security.announce`	Announcements from CERT about security (Moderated)
`comp.security.misc`	Security issues of computers and networks
`comp.security.unix`	Unix security
`comp.simulation`	Simulation methods, problems, uses (Moderated)
`comp.society`	The impact of technology on society (Moderated)
`comp.society.cu-digest`	The Computer Underground Digest (Moderated)
`comp.society.development`	Computer technology in developing countries
`comp.society.folklore`	Computer folklore, past and present (Moderated)
`comp.society.futures`	Events in technology affecting future computing
`comp.society.privacy`	Effects of technology on privacy (Moderated)
`comp.soft-sys.andrew`	Andrew file system from Carnegie Mellon University
`comp.soft-sys.khoros`	The Khoros X11 visualization system
`comp.soft-sys.matlab`	The MathWorks calculation and visualization package
`comp.soft-sys.nextstep`	The Nextstep computing environment
`comp.soft-sys.sas`	SAS statistics package
`comp.soft-sys.shazam`	Shazam software
`comp.soft-sys.spss`	SPSS statistics package
`comp.software-eng`	Software engineering and related topics
`comp.software.licensing`	Software licensing technology
`comp.software.testing`	Testing computer systems
`comp.sources.3b1`	Source code-only postings for AT&T 3b1 (Moderated)
`comp.sources.acorn`	Source code-only postings for Acorn (Moderated)
`comp.sources.amiga`	Source code-only postings for Amiga (Moderated)
`comp.sources.apple2`	Source code and discussion for Apple2 (Moderated)
`comp.sources.atari.st`	Source code-only postings for Atari ST (Moderated)
`comp.sources.bugs`	Bug reports, fixes, discussion for posted sources
`comp.sources.d`	For any discussion of source postings
`comp.sources.games`	Postings of recreational software (Moderated)
`comp.sources.games.bugs`	Bug reports and fixes for posted game software
`comp.sources.hp48`	Programs for HP48 and HP28 calculators (Moderated)
`comp.sources.mac`	Software for Apple Macintosh (Moderated)
`comp.sources.misc`	General postings of software (Moderated)
`comp.sources.postscript`	Source code for Postscript programs (Moderated)
`comp.sources.reviewed`	Source code evaluated by peer review (Moderated)
`comp.sources.sun`	Software for Sun workstations (Moderated)
`comp.sources.testers`	Finding people to test software
`comp.sources.unix`	Complete, Unix-oriented sources (Moderated)
`comp.sources.wanted`	Requests for software and fixes
`comp.sources.x`	Software for the X Window system (Moderated)
`comp.specification`	Languages and methodologies for formal specification
`comp.specification.z`	Discussion about formal specification notation Z
`comp.speech`	Research/applications in speech science
`comp.std.announce`	Announcements about standards activities (Moderated)
`comp.std.c`	C language standards
`comp.std.c++`	C++ language standards
`comp.std.internat`	International standards

USENET NEWSGROUPS

`comp.std.misc`	General discussion about standards
`comp.std.mumps`	The X11.1 committee on Mumps (Moderated)
`comp.std.unix`	The P1003 committee on Unix (Moderated)
`comp.std.wireless`	Wireless network technology standards (moderated)
`comp.sw.components`	Software components and related technology
`comp.sys.3b1`	The AT&T 7300/3B1/UnixPC
`comp.sys.acorn`	Acorn and ARM-based computers
`comp.sys.acorn.advocacy`	Debate about Acorn computers
`comp.sys.acorn.announce`	Announcements for Acorn and ARM users (Moderated)
`comp.sys.acorn.tech`	Technical aspects of Acorn and ARM products
`comp.sys.alliant`	Alliant computers
`comp.sys.amiga.advocacy`	Debate about Amiga computers
`comp.sys.amiga.announce`	Announcements about Amiga (Moderated)
`comp.sys.amiga.applications`	Miscellaneous applications
`comp.sys.amiga.audio`	Music, MIDI, speech synthesis, other sounds
`comp.sys.amiga.datacomm`	Methods of getting bytes in and out
`comp.sys.amiga.emulations`	Various hardware and software emulators
`comp.sys.amiga.games`	Games for the Commodore Amiga
`comp.sys.amiga.graphics`	Charts, graphs, pictures, etc
`comp.sys.amiga.hardware`	Amiga computer hardware
`comp.sys.amiga.introduction`	Newcomers to Amigas
`comp.sys.amiga.marketplace`	Buying and selling Amigas
`comp.sys.amiga.misc`	Discussions not in another Amiga group
`comp.sys.amiga.multimedia`	Animations, video, and multimedia
`comp.sys.amiga.programmer`	Developers and hobbyists
`comp.sys.amiga.reviews`	Reviews of software, hardware (Moderated)
`comp.sys.amiga.telecomm`	Amiga telecom
`comp.sys.amiga.unix`	Amiga Unix systems
`comp.sys.apollo`	Apollo computer systems
`comp.sys.apple2`	Apple II computers
`comp.sys.apple2.comm`	Apple II data communications
`comp.sys.apple2.gno`	The Apple IIgs GNO multitasking environment
`comp.sys.apple2.marketplace`	Buying and selling Apple II equipment
`comp.sys.apple2.programmer`	Programming the Apple II
`comp.sys.apple2.usergroups`	Apple II user groups
`comp.sys.atari.8bit`	8-bit Atari micros
`comp.sys.atari.advocacy`	Debate about Atari computers
`comp.sys.atari.st`	16-bit Atari micros
`comp.sys.atari.st.tech`	Technical discussions of Atari ST
`comp.sys.att`	AT&T microcomputers
`comp.sys.cbm`	Commodore computers
`comp.sys.cdc`	Control Data Corporation computers
`comp.sys.concurrent`	Concurrent/Masscomp computers (Moderated)
`comp.sys.convex`	Convex computers
`comp.sys.dec`	DEC computers
`comp.sys.dec.micro`	DEC micros (Rainbow, Professional 350/380)
`comp.sys.encore`	Encore's MultiMax computers

`comp.sys.handhelds`	Handheld computers and programmable calculators
`comp.sys.harris`	Harris computer systems, especially real-time systems
`comp.sys.hp`	Hewlett-Packard equipment
`comp.sys.hp.apps`	Software on all HP platforms
`comp.sys.hp.hardware`	HP hardware
`comp.sys.hp.hpux`	HP-UX and series 9000 computers
`comp.sys.hp.misc`	HP platforms general discussion
`comp.sys.hp.mpe`	HP MPE and series 3000 computers
`comp.sys.hp48`	Hewlett-Packard's HP48 and HP28 calculators
`comp.sys.ibm.pc.demos`	Demo programs for PCs
`comp.sys.ibm.pc.digest`	IBM-compatible PCs (Moderated)
`comp.sys.ibm.pc.games`	Games for PCs
`comp.sys.ibm.pc.games.action`	Action games
`comp.sys.ibm.pc.games.adventure`	Adventure games
`comp.sys.ibm.pc.games.announce`	Announcements relating to PC games (Moderated)
`comp.sys.ibm.pc.games.flight-sim`	PC flight simulators
`comp.sys.ibm.pc.games.misc`	Games that don't fall into another category
`comp.sys.ibm.pc.games.rpg`	Role-playing games on PCs
`comp.sys.ibm.pc.games.strategic`	Strategy games
`comp.sys.ibm.pc.hardware`	PC hardware, any vendor
`comp.sys.ibm.pc.misc`	General PC discussion
`comp.sys.ibm.pc.rt`	IBM's RT computer
`comp.sys.ibm.pc.soundcard`	Hardware and software aspects of PC sound cards
`comp.sys.ibm.pc.soundcard.GUS`	Gravis Ultrasound sound card
`comp.sys.ibm.ps2.hardware`	PS/2 and Microchannel hardware, any vendor
`comp.sys.intel`	Intel systems and parts
`comp.sys.intel.ipsc310`	The Intel 310
`comp.sys.isis`	The ISIS distributed system from Cornell
`comp.sys.laptops`	Laptop computers
`comp.sys.m6809`	6809 processors
`comp.sys.m68k`	68000 processors
`comp.sys.m68k.pc`	68000-based computers (Moderated)
`comp.sys.m88k`	88000-based computers
`comp.sys.mac.advocacy`	Debate about Macintosh computers
`comp.sys.mac.announce`	Important notices for Macintosh users (Moderated)
`comp.sys.mac.apps`	Macintosh applications
`comp.sys.mac.comm`	Macintosh communications
`comp.sys.mac.databases`	Macintosh database systems
`comp.sys.mac.digest`	Macintosh general talk, no programs (Moderated)
`comp.sys.mac.games`	Macintosh games
`comp.sys.mac.hardware`	Macintosh hardware
`comp.sys.mac.hypercard`	Macintosh Hypercard
`comp.sys.mac.misc`	General discussions about the Macintosh
`comp.sys.mac.oop.macapp3`	Version 3 of the MacApp object-oriented system
`comp.sys.mac.oop.misc`	Macintosh object-oriented programming
`comp.sys.mac.oop.tcl`	Programming the Macintosh with Think Class Libraries
`comp.sys.mac.portables`	Laptop Macintoshes

`comp.sys.mac.programmer`	Programming the Macintosh
`comp.sys.mac.scitech`	Macintosh for scientific and technological work
`comp.sys.mac.system`	Macintosh system software
`comp.sys.mac.wanted`	Requests for Macintosh-related software/hardware
`comp.sys.mentor`	Mentor Graphics products and Silicon Compiler System
`comp.sys.mips`	Systems based on MIPS chips
`comp.sys.misc`	General discussion about computers of all kinds
`comp.sys.ncr`	NCR computers
`comp.sys.newton.announce`	Newton announcements (Moderated)
`comp.sys.newton.misc`	Newton general discussion
`comp.sys.newton.programmer`	Newton software development
`comp.sys.next.advocacy`	Debate about Next computers
`comp.sys.next.announce`	Announcements about Next computer system (Moderated)
`comp.sys.next.bugs`	Discussion and solutions of known Next bugs
`comp.sys.next.hardware`	The physical aspects of Next computers
`comp.sys.next.marketplace`	Next hardware, software and jobs
`comp.sys.next.misc`	General discussion about the Next computer system
`comp.sys.next.programmer`	Next-related programming issues
`comp.sys.next.software`	Next computer programs
`comp.sys.next.sysadmin`	Next system administration
`comp.sys.northstar`	Northstar microcomputer users
`comp.sys.novell`	Novell Netware products
`comp.sys.nsc.32k`	National Semiconductor 32000 series chips
`comp.sys.palmtops`	Super-powered calculators for the palm of your hand
`comp.sys.pen`	Interacting with computers through pen gestures
`comp.sys.powerpc`	PowerPC architecture and products
`comp.sys.prime`	Prime Computer products
`comp.sys.proteon`	Proteon gateway products
`comp.sys.pyramid`	Pyramid 90x computers
`comp.sys.ridge`	Ridge 32 computers and ROS
`comp.sys.sequent`	Sequent systems (Balance and Symmetry)
`comp.sys.sgi`	Silicon Graphics' Iris workstations and software
`comp.sys.sgi.admin`	Silicon Graphics's Irises system administration
`comp.sys.sgi.announce`	Announcements for the SGI community (Moderated)
`comp.sys.sgi.apps`	Iris applications
`comp.sys.sgi.bugs`	Bugs in the IRIX operating system
`comp.sys.sgi.graphics`	Graphics packages on SGI machines
`comp.sys.sgi.hardware`	Base systems and peripherals for Iris computers
`comp.sys.sgi.misc`	General discussion about Silicon Graphics computers
`comp.sys.stratus`	Stratus products (System/88, CPS-32, VOS and FTX)
`comp.sys.sun.admin`	Sun system administration
`comp.sys.sun.announce`	Sun announcements and Sunergy mailings (Moderated)
`comp.sys.sun.apps`	Sun applications
`comp.sys.sun.hardware`	Sun hardware
`comp.sys.sun.misc`	Sun miscellaneous discussions
`comp.sys.sun.wanted`	Requests for Sun products and support
`comp.sys.super`	Supercomputers

`comp.sys.tahoe`	CCI 6/32, Harris HCX/7, and Sperry 7000 computers
`comp.sys.tandy`	Tandy computers new and old
`comp.sys.ti`	Texas Instruments products
`comp.sys.ti.explorer`	The Texas Instruments Explorer
`comp.sys.transputer`	The Transputer computer and OCCAM language
`comp.sys.unisys`	Sperry, Burroughs, Convergent and Unisys systems
`comp.sys.xerox`	Xerox 1100 workstations and protocols
`comp.sys.zenith`	Heath terminals and related Zenith products
`comp.sys.zenith.z100`	The Zenith Z-100 (Heath H-100) family of computers
`comp.terminals`	All sorts of terminals
`comp.terminals.bitgraph`	The BB&N BitGraph Terminal
`comp.terminals.tty5620`	AT&T Dot Mapped Display Terminals (5620 and BLIT)
`comp.text`	Text processing issues and methods
`comp.text.desktop`	Desktop publishing
`comp.text.frame`	Desktop publishing with FrameMaker
`comp.text.interleaf`	Interleaf software
`comp.text.sgml`	ISO 8879 SGML, structured documents, markup language
`comp.text.tex`	The TeX and LaTeX systems and macros
`comp.theory`	Theoretical computer science
`comp.theory.cell-automata`	Cellular automata
`comp.theory.dynamic-sys`	Ergodic Theory and dynamical Systems
`comp.theory.info-retrieval`	Information retrieval topics (Moderated)
`comp.theory.self-org-sys`	Self-organization topics
`comp.unix.admin`	Administering a Unix-based system
`comp.unix.aix`	IBM's version of Unix
`comp.unix.amiga`	Minix, SYSV4 and other Unix on an Amiga
`comp.unix.aux`	Unix for Macintosh computers
`comp.unix.bsd`	Berkeley Software Distribution Unix
`comp.unix.cray`	Cray computers and their operating systems
`comp.unix.dos-under-unix`	DOS running under Unix by whatever means
`comp.unix.internals`	Hacking Unix internals
`comp.unix.large`	Unix on mainframes and in large networks
`comp.unix.misc`	Various Unix topics that don't fit other groups
`comp.unix.osf.misc`	General talk about the Open Software Foundation
`comp.unix.osf.osf1`	Open Software Foundation's OSF/1 operating system
`comp.unix.pc-clone.16bit`	Unix on 16-bit PC architectures
`comp.unix.pc-clone.32bit`	Unix on 23-bit PC architectures
`comp.unix.programmer`	Questions regarding Unix programming
`comp.unix.questions`	Question and answer forum for Unix beginners
`comp.unix.shell`	Unix shells
`comp.unix.solaris`	The Solaris operating system
`comp.unix.sys3`	System III Unix
`comp.unix.sys5.misc`	Versions of System V which predate Release 3

comp.unix.sys5.r3	System V Release 3
comp.unix.sys5.r4	System V Release 4
comp.unix.sysv386	System V on the 386-based PCs
comp.unix.ultrix	DEC's Ultrix
comp.unix.user-friendly	Unix user friendliness
comp.unix.wizards	Questions for true Unix wizards only
comp.unix.xenix.misc	Non-SCO Xenix
comp.unix.xenix.sco	Santa Cruz Operation (SCO) Xenix
comp.virus	Computer viruses and security (Moderated)
comp.windows.garnet	Garnet user interface development environment
comp.windows.interviews	The InterViews object-oriented windowing system
comp.windows.misc	Various issues about windowing systems
comp.windows.news	Sun Microsystems' NeWS window system
comp.windows.open-look	Discussion about the Open Look GUI
comp.windows.suit	SUIT user interface toolkit
comp.windows.x	Discussion about the X Window System
comp.windows.x.announce	X Consortium announcements (Moderated)
comp.windows.x.apps	Getting and using (not programming) X applications
comp.windows.x.i386unix	The XFree86 window system and others
comp.windows.x.intrinsics	The X toolkit
comp.windows.x.motif	The Motif graphical user interface
comp.windows.x.pex	The PHIGS extension of the X Window System

DDN

ddn.mgt-bulletin	Defense Data Network Management Bulletin (Moderated)
ddn.newsletter	The DDN Newsletter (Moderated)

GNU

gnu.announce	News about the GNU project (Moderated)
gnu.bash.bug	Bugs and fixes Bash/Bourne Again shell (Moderated)
gnu.chess	The GNU Chess program
gnu.emacs.announce	GNU Emacs (Moderated)
gnu.emacs.bug	Bugs and fixes GNU Emacs (Moderated)
gnu.emacs.gnews	News reading under GNU Emacs using Weemba's Gnews
gnu.emacs.gnus	News reading under GNU Emacs using GNUS (in English)
gnu.emacs.help	Questions and answers about Emacs
gnu.emacs.sources	Free C and Lisp programs for GNU Emacs (no talk)
gnu.emacs.vm.bug	Bugs and fixes Emacs VM mail package
gnu.emacs.vm.info	The Emacs VM mail package
gnu.emacs.vms	Port of GNU Emacs to VMS
gnu.epoch.misc	The Epoch X11 extensions to Emacs
gnu.g++.announce	News about g++ (the GNU C++ compiler) (Moderated)
gnu.g++.bug	Bugs and fixes g++ (Moderated)
gnu.g++.help	Questions and answers about g++
gnu.g++.lib.bug	Bugs and fixes g++ library (Moderated)

`gnu.gcc.announce`	News about gcc (the GNU C compiler) (Moderated)
`gnu.gcc.bug`	Bugs and fixes gcc (Moderated)
`gnu.gcc.help`	GNU C Compiler (gcc) user queries and answers
`gnu.gdb.bug`	Bugs and fixes gcc/g++ debugger (Moderated)
`gnu.ghostscript.bug`	Bugs and fixes Ghostscript interpreter (Moderated)
`gnu.gnusenet.config`	GNU's Not Usenet administration and configuration
`gnu.gnusenet.test`	Place to send test articles
`gnu.groff.bug`	Bugs and fixes GNU roff programs (Moderated)
`gnu.misc.discuss`	General talk about the GNU (Gnu's Not Unix) project
`gnu.smalltalk.bug`	Bugs and fixes GNU Smalltalk (Moderated)
`gnu.utils.bug`	Bugs and fixes GNU utilities: gawk, etc (Moderated)

IEEE

`ieee.announce`	News for the IEEE community
`ieee.config`	Managing the `ieee.*` newsgroups
`ieee.general`	IEEE general discussion
`ieee.pcnfs`	Tips on PC-NFS
`ieee.rab.announce`	Regional Activities Board announcements
`ieee.rab.general`	Regional Activities Board general discussion
`ieee.region1`	Region 1 announcements
`ieee.tab.announce`	Technical Activities Board announcements
`ieee.tab.general`	Technical Activities Board general discussion
`ieee.tcos`	The TCOS newsletter and discussion (Moderated)
`ieee.usab.announce`	USAB Announcements
`ieee.usab.general`	USAB General discussion

INFO

`info.admin`	Managing the `info.*` newsgroups
`info.big-internet`	Issues facing a huge Internet
`info.bind`	The Berkeley BIND server (Moderated)
`info.brl-cad`	BRL's Solid modeling CAD system (Moderated)
`info.bsdi.users`	Users of BSDI's Unix operating system
`info.bytecounters`	NSstat network analysis
`info.convex`	Convex Company computers (Moderated)
`info.firearms`	Firearms non-political (Moderated)
`info.firearms.politics`	Firearms political
`info.gated`	Cornell's GATED program
`info.grass.programmer`	Programming GRASS geographic information system
`info.grass.user`	Using GRASS geographic information system
`info.ietf`	Internet Engineering Task Force (IETF)
`info.ietf.hosts`	IETF host requirements
`info.ietf.isoc`	The Internet society
`info.ietf.njm`	Joint Monitoring Access, Adjacent Nets (Moderated)
`info.ietf.smtp`	IETF SMTP extension
`info.isode`	The ISO Development Environment package

`info.jethro-tull`	Jethro Tull, (old) pop music group
`info.labmgr`	Computer lab managers (Moderated)
`info.mach`	The Mach operating system (Moderated)
`info.mh.workers`	MH development (Moderated)
`info.nets`	Inter-network connectivity
`info.nsf.grants`	NSF grants (Moderated)
`info.nsfnet.cert`	Computer Emergency Response Team
`info.nsfnet.status`	Status of NSFnet
`info.nupop`	Northwestern University's POP for PCs
`info.nysersnmp`	SNMP software distributed by PSI
`info.osf`	OSF's electronic bulletin (Moderated)
`info.pem-dev`	IETF privacy enhanced mail (Moderated)
`info.ph`	Qi, ph, sendmail/phquery
`info.rfc`	Announcements of newly released RFCs
`info.slug`	Symbolics Lisp machines
`info.snmp`	SNMP (Simple Gateway/Network Monitoring Protocol)
`info.solbourne`	Solbourne computers
`info.sun-managers`	Sun Managers digest (Moderated)
`info.sun-nets`	Sun Nets digest
`info.theorynt`	Theory (Moderated)
`info.unix-sw`	Unix software available by anonymous FTP
`info.wisenet`	Women In Science and Engineering NETwork

K12

`k12.chat.elementary`	Elementary students forum grades K-5
`k12.chat.junior`	Elementary students forum grades 6-8
`k12.chat.senior`	High school students forum
`k12.chat.teacher`	Teachers forum
`k12.ed.art`	Art curriculum
`k12.ed.business`	Business education curriculum
`k12.ed.comp.literacy`	Computer literacy
`k12.ed.health-pe`	Health and physical education
`k12.ed.life-skills`	Home economics and career education
`k12.ed.math`	Mathematics
`k12.ed.music`	Music and performing arts
`k12.ed.science`	Science
`k12.ed.soc-studies`	Social studies and history
`k12.ed.special`	Students with handicaps or special needs
`k12.ed.tag`	Talented and gifted students
`k12.ed.tech`	Industrial arts and vocational education
`k12.lang.art`	Language arts
`k12.lang.deutsch-eng`	German/English practice with native speakers
`k12.lang.esp-eng`	Spanish/English practice with native speakers
`k12.lang.francais`	French/English practice with native speakers
`k12.lang.russian`	Russian/English practice with native speakers
`k12.library`	Libraries and librarians

`k12.sys.channel0`	Forum for teachers
`k12.sys.channel1`	Forum for teachers
`k12.sys.channel10`	Forum for teachers
`k12.sys.channel11`	Forum for teachers
`k12.sys.channel112`	Forum for teachers
`k12.sys.channel2`	Forum for teachers
`k12.sys.channel3`	Forum for teachers
`k12.sys.channel4`	Forum for teachers
`k12.sys.channel5`	Forum for teachers
`k12.sys.channel6`	Forum for teachers
`k12.sys.channel7`	Forum for teachers
`k12.sys.channel8`	Forum for teachers
`k12.sys.channel9`	Forum for teachers
`k12.sys.projects`	Teaching projects

MISC

`misc.activism.progressive`	Progressive activism (Moderated)
`misc.answers`	FAQ lists and other periodic postings (Moderated)
`misc.books.technical`	Books about technical topics (including computers)
`misc.consumers`	Consumer interests, product reviews, etc
`misc.consumers.house`	Owning and maintaining a house
`misc.education`	The educational system
`misc.education.language.english`	Teaching the English language
`misc.emerg-services`	Paramedics and other first responders
`misc.entrepreneurs`	Operating your own business
`misc.fitness`	Physical fitness, exercise
`misc.forsale`	Short postings about items for sale
`misc.forsale.computers.d`	Discussion of `misc.forsale.computers.*`
`misc.forsale.computers.mac`	Macintosh-related computer items
`misc.forsale.computers.other`	Selling miscellaneous computer stuff
`misc.forsale.computers.pc-clone`	PC-related computer items
`misc.forsale.computers.workstation`	Workstation-related computer items
`misc.handicap`	Issues about the handicapped (Moderated)
`misc.headlines`	Current events
`misc.health.alternative`	Alternative health care
`misc.health.diabetes`	Diabetes
`misc.int-property`	Intellectual property rights
`misc.invest`	Investments and the handling of money
`misc.invest.canada`	Investing in Canadian financial markets
`misc.invest.real-estate`	Property investments
`misc.invest.technical`	Highly technical discussion of investment strategy
`misc.jobs.contract`	Contract labor
`misc.jobs.misc`	Employment, workplaces, careers
`misc.jobs.offered`	Announcements of positions available
`misc.jobs.offered.entry`	Job listings, entry-level positions only
`misc.jobs.resumes`	Postings of resumes and jobs wanted

`misc.kids`	Children, their behavior and activities
`misc.kids.computer`	The use of computers by children
`misc.legal`	Legalities and the ethics of law
`misc.legal.computing`	The legal climate of the computing world
`misc.misc`	Discussions not in any other group
`misc.news.east-europe.rferl`	Radio Free Europe/Radio Liberty (Moderated)
`misc.news.southasia`	News from Southeast Asia (Moderated)
`misc.rural`	Rural living
`misc.taxes`	Tax laws and advice
`misc.test`	Place to send test articles.
`misc.wanted`	Requests for things that are needed (NOT software)
`misc.writing`	Discussion of writing in all of its forms

NEWS

`news.admin.misc`	General network news administration
`news.admin.policy`	Policy issues of Usenet
`news.admin.technical`	Technical aspects of Usenet (Moderated)
`news.announce.conferences`	Calls for papers and conference notices (Moderated)
`news.announce.important`	General announcements of interest to all (Moderated)
`news.announce.newgroups`	Calls for new groups (Moderated)
`news.announce.newusers`	Explanatory postings for new users (Moderated)
`news.answers`	Repository for periodic Usenet articles (Moderated)
`news.config`	Postings of system down times and interruptions
`news.future`	The future technology of network news systems
`news.groups`	Discussions and lists of newsgroups
`news.lists`	Usenet statistics and lists (Moderated)
`news.lists.ps-maps`	Maps relating to Usenet traffic flows (Moderated)
`news.misc`	Discussions of Usenet itself
`news.newsites`	Postings of new site announcements
`news.newusers.questions`	Questions and answers for new Usenet users
`news.software.anu-news`	VMS B-news software from Australian National Univ
`news.software.b`	B-news-compatible software
`news.software.nn`	Discussion about the nn newsreader
`news.software.nntp`	The Network News Transfer Protocol
`news.software.notes`	Notesfile software from the University of Illinois
`news.software.readers`	Discussion of Usenet newsreader programs

REC

`rec.answers`	Repository for periodic Usenet articles (Moderated)
`rec.antiques`	Antiques and vintage items
`rec.aquaria`	Keeping fish and aquaria as a hobby
`rec.arts.animation`	Various kinds of animation
`rec.arts.anime`	Japanese animation
`rec.arts.anime.info`	The art of animation
`rec.arts.anime.marketplace`	Making money with animation

rec.arts.anime.stories	Animated stories
rec.arts.bodyart	Tattoos and body decoration
rec.arts.bonsai	Miniature trees and shrubbery
rec.arts.books	Books of all genres, and the publishing industry
rec.arts.books.tolkien	The works of J.R.R. Tolkien
rec.arts.cinema	The art of cinema (Moderated)
rec.arts.comics.info	Reviews, conventions and other news (Moderated)
rec.arts.comics.marketplace	The exchange of comics and related items
rec.arts.comics.misc	Comic books, graphic novels, sequential art
rec.arts.comics.strips	Comic strips
rec.arts.comics.xbooks	The Mutant Universe of Marvel Comics
rec.arts.dance	Aspects of dance not covered in another newsgroup
rec.arts.disney	Any Disney-related subjects
rec.arts.drwho	Dr Who
rec.arts.erotica	Erotic fiction and verse (Moderated)
rec.arts.fine	Fine arts and artists
rec.arts.int-fiction	Interactive fiction
rec.arts.manga	The Japanese storytelling art form
rec.arts.marching.drumcorps	Drum and bugle corps
rec.arts.marching.misc	Marching-related performance activities
rec.arts.misc	Discussions about the arts, not in other groups
rec.arts.movies	Movies and movie making
rec.arts.movies.reviews	Movie reviews (Moderated)
rec.arts.poems	For the posting of poems
rec.arts.prose	Short works of prose fiction and discussion
rec.arts.sf.announce	Major science fiction announcements (Moderated)
rec.arts.sf.fandom	Science fiction fan activities
rec.arts.sf.marketplace	Personal forsale notices of science fiction materials
rec.arts.sf.misc	General science fiction discussions
rec.arts.sf.movies	Science fiction movies
rec.arts.sf.reviews	Reviews of science fiction/fantasy/horror works (Moderated)
rec.arts.sf.science	Real and speculative aspects of science fiction science
rec.arts.sf.starwars	Discussion of the *Star Wars* universe
rec.arts.sf.tv	Science fiction on television
rec.arts.sf.written	Written science fiction and fantasy
rec.arts.startrek.current	New *Star Trek* shows, movies and books
rec.arts.startrek.fandom	*Star Trek* conventions and memorabilia
rec.arts.startrek.info	The universe of *Star Trek* (Moderated)
rec.arts.startrek.misc	General discussions of *Star Trek*
rec.arts.startrek.reviews	Reviews of *Star Trek* books, shows, films (Moderated)
rec.arts.startrek.tech	*Star Trek*'s depiction of future technologies
rec.arts.theatre	All aspects of stage work and theatre
rec.arts.tv	Television history, past and current shows
rec.arts.tv.soaps	Soap operas
rec.arts.tv.uk	Telly shows from the UK
rec.arts.wobegon	Literary and music esoterica
rec.audio	High fidelity audio

rec.audio.car	Automobile audio systems
rec.audio.high-end	High-end audio systems (Moderated)
rec.audio.pro	Professional audio recording and studio engineering
rec.autos	Automobiles, automotive products and laws
rec.autos.antique	Automobiles over 25 years old
rec.autos.driving	Driving automobiles
rec.autos.rod-n-custom	Souped-up and customized autos
rec.autos.sport	Organized, legal auto competitions
rec.autos.tech	Technical aspects of automobiles
rec.autos.vw	Volkswagen products
rec.aviation.announce	Events for the aviation community (Moderated)
rec.aviation.answers	Questions and answers about aviation (Moderated)
rec.aviation.homebuilt	Selecting, designing, building, restoring aircraft
rec.aviation.ifr	Flying under Instrument Flight Rules
rec.aviation.military	Military aircraft of the past, present and future
rec.aviation.misc	Miscellaneous topics in aviation
rec.aviation.owning	Owning airplanes
rec.aviation.piloting	General discussion for aviators
rec.aviation.products	Products useful to pilots
rec.aviation.simulators	Flight simulation on all levels
rec.aviation.soaring	Sailplanes and hang-gliders
rec.aviation.stories	Anecdotes of flight experiences (Moderated)
rec.aviation.student	Learning to fly
rec.backcountry	Outdoor activities
rec.bicycles.marketplace	Buying, selling and reviewing items for cycling
rec.bicycles.misc	General discussion of bicycling
rec.bicycles.racing	Bicycle racing techniques, rules and results
rec.bicycles.rides	Discussions of tours, training, commuting routes
rec.bicycles.soc	Societal issues of bicycling
rec.bicycles.tech	Cycling product design, construction, maintenance
rec.birds	Bird watching
rec.boats	Boating
rec.boats.paddle	Any boats with oars, paddles, etc
rec.climbing	Climbing techniques, announcements, etc
rec.collecting	Discussion among collectors of many things
rec.collecting.cards	Collecting sport and non-sport cards
rec.crafts.brewing	Making beers and meads
rec.crafts.metalworking	Working with metal
rec.crafts.misc	Handiwork arts not covered elsewhere
rec.crafts.quilting	Quilts and similar items
rec.crafts.textiles	Sewing, weaving, knitting and other fiber arts
rec.crafts.winemaking	Making wine
rec.equestrian	Discussion of horses and riding
rec.folk-dancing	Folk dances, dancers, and dancing
rec.food.cooking	Food, cooking, cookbooks, and recipes
rec.food.drink	Wines and spirits
rec.food.historic	The history of food making arts

rec.food.recipes	Recipes for interesting food and drink (Moderated)
rec.food.restaurants	Discussion of dining out
rec.food.sourdough	Making and baking with sourdough
rec.food.veg	Vegetarians
rec.gambling	Games of chance and betting
rec.games.abstract	Perfect information, pure strategy games
rec.games.backgammon	Backgammon
rec.games.board	Discussion and hints on board games
rec.games.board.ce	The Cosmic Encounter board game
rec.games.bridge	Bridge card game
rec.games.chess	Chess and computer chess
rec.games.corewar	The Core War computer game
rec.games.design	Game design-related issues
rec.games.diplomacy	The Diplomacy conquest game
rec.games.empire	The Empire game
rec.games.frp.advocacy	Debate about various role-playing systems
rec.games.frp.announce	Announcements in the role-playing world (Moderated)
rec.games.frp.archives	Archivable fantasy stories, etc (Moderated)
rec.games.frp.cyber	Cyberpunk related role-playing games
rec.games.frp.dnd	Fantasy role-playing with TSR's Dungeons and Dragons
rec.games.frp.marketplace	Role-playing game materials wanted and for sale
rec.games.frp.misc	General discussions of role-playing games
rec.games.go	The Go game
rec.games.hack	The Hack game
rec.games.int-fiction	Interactive fiction games
rec.games.mecha	Giant robot games
rec.games.miniatures	Tabletop wargaming
rec.games.misc	Games and computer games
rec.games.moria	The Moria game
rec.games.mud.admin	Admnistrative issues of multiuser dungeons
rec.games.mud.announce	Announcements about multiuser dungeons (Moderated)
rec.games.mud.diku	DikuMuds
rec.games.mud.lp	The LPMUD computer role-playing game
rec.games.mud.misc	Multiuser computer games
rec.games.mud.tiny	Tiny MUDs, like MUSH, MUSE and MOO
rec.games.netrek	The X window system game Netrek (XtrekII)
rec.games.pbm	Play by mail games
rec.games.pinball	Pinball-related games
rec.games.programmer	Adventure game programming
rec.games.rogue	The Rogue game
rec.games.roguelike.angband	Angband, rouge-like game
rec.games.roguelike.announce	Announcements about rogue-like games (Moderated)
rec.games.roguelike.misc	General discussion about rogue-like games
rec.games.trivia	Trivia
rec.games.vectrex	The Vectrex game system
rec.games.video	Video games
rec.games.video.arcade	Coin-operated video games

`rec.games.video.classic`	Older home video entertainment systems
`rec.games.video.marketplace`	Home video game stuff for sale or trade
`rec.games.video.misc`	General discussion about home video games
`rec.games.video.nintendo`	Nintendo video game systems and software
`rec.games.video.sega`	Sega video game systems and software
`rec.games.xtank.play`	Distributed game Xtank
`rec.games.xtank.programmer`	Coding the Xtank game and its robots
`rec.gardens`	Gardening, methods and results
`rec.guns`	Firearms (Moderated)
`rec.heraldry`	Coats of arms
`rec.humor`	Jokes (may be offensive)
`rec.humor.d`	Discussions on the content of `rec.humor` articles
`rec.humor.funny`	Jokes that a moderator thinks are funny (Moderated)
`rec.humor.oracle`	Sagacious advice from the Usenet Oracle (Moderated)
`rec.humor.oracle.d`	Comments about the Usenet Oracle's advice
`rec.hunting`	Hunting (Moderated)
`rec.juggling`	Juggling techniques, equipment and events
`rec.kites`	Kites and kiting
`rec.mag`	Magazine summaries, tables of contents, etc
`rec.mag.fsfnet`	A science fiction fanzine (Moderated)
`rec.martial-arts`	Martial arts
`rec.misc`	General topics about recreational activities
`rec.models.railroad`	Model railroads of all scales
`rec.models.rc`	Radio-controlled models
`rec.models.rockets`	Model rockets
`rec.models.scale`	Construction of models
`rec.motorcycles`	Motorcycles, related products and laws
`rec.motorcycles.dirt`	Motorcycles and ATVs off-road
`rec.motorcycles.harley`	Harley-Davidson motorcycles
`rec.motorcycles.racing`	Racing motorcycles
`rec.music.a-cappella`	A Cappella music, voice with no instruments
`rec.music.afro-latin`	Music with African and Latin influences
`rec.music.beatles`	The Beatles
`rec.music.bluenote`	Jazz, blues and related types of music
`rec.music.cd`	Music and CDs
`rec.music.celtic`	Celtic music, traditional and modern music
`rec.music.christian`	Christian music, both contemporary and traditional
`rec.music.classical`	Classical music
`rec.music.classical.guitar`	Classical guitar music
`rec.music.classical.performing`	Performing classical and early music
`rec.music.compose`	Creating musical and lyrical works
`rec.music.country.western`	Country and western music
`rec.music.dementia`	Comedy and novelty music
`rec.music.dylan`	Music of Bob Dylan
`rec.music.early`	Pre-classical European music
`rec.music.folk`	Folk music
`rec.music.funky`	Funk, rap, hip-hop, house, soul, R&B etc

rec.music.gaffa	Kate Bush and other alternative music (Moderated)
rec.music.gdead	Music of the Grateful Dead
rec.music.indian.classical	Hindustani and Carnatic Indian classical music
rec.music.indian.misc	Indian music in general
rec.music.industrial	Industrial-related music styles
rec.music.info	News on musical topics (Moderated)
rec.music.makers	Performers and their discussions
rec.music.makers.bass	Upright bass and bass guitar techniques, equipment
rec.music.makers.guitar	Electric and acoustic guitar techniques, equipment
rec.music.makers.guitar.acoustic	Acoustic guitar
rec.music.makers.guitar.tablature	Guitar tablature and chords
rec.music.makers.marketplace	Buying and selling music-making equipment
rec.music.makers.percussion	Drum, other percussion techniques and equipment
rec.music.makers.synth	Synthesizers and computer music
rec.music.marketplace	Records, tapes, and CDs wanted, for sale, etc
rec.music.misc	General music discussion
rec.music.newage	New Age music
rec.music.phish	The music of Phish
rec.music.reggae	Roots, Rockers, Dancehall Reggae
rec.music.reviews	Reviews of all types of music (Moderated)
rec.music.synth	Synthsizers and computer music
rec.music.video	Music videos and music video software
rec.nude	Naturist and nudist activities
rec.org.mensa	The Mensa high IQ society
rec.org.sca	The Society for Creative Anachronism
rec.outdoors.fishing	Sport and commercial fishing
rec.parks.theme	Theme parks
rec.pets	Pets, pet care, and household animals in general
rec.pets.birds	The culture and care of indoor birds
rec.pets.cats	Domestic cats
rec.pets.dogs	Dogs as pets
rec.pets.herp	Reptiles, amphibians and other exotic vivarium pets
rec.photo	Photography
rec.puzzles	Puzzles, problems, and quizzes
rec.puzzles.crosswords	Making and playing gridded word puzzles
rec.pyrotechnics	Fireworks, rocketry, safety, and other topics
rec.radio.amateur.antenna	Antennas, theory, techniques and construction
rec.radio.amateur.digital.misc	Packet radio and other digital radio modes
rec.radio.amateur.equipment	Amateur radio equipment
rec.radio.amateur.homebrew	Amateur radio construction and experimentation
rec.radio.amateur.misc	Amateur radio practices, contests, events, etc
rec.radio.amateur.packet	Packet radio setups
rec.radio.amateur.policy	Radio use and regulation policy
rec.radio.amateur.space	Amateur radio transmissions through space
rec.radio.broadcasting	Local area broadcast radio (Moderated)
rec.radio.cb	Citizen band radio
rec.radio.info	Informative postings related to radio (Moderated)

rec.radio.noncomm	Noncommercial radio
rec.radio.scanner	"Utility" broadcasting traffic above 30 MHz
rec.radio.shortwave	Shortwave radio
rec.radio.swap	Trading and swapping radio equipment
rec.railroad	Real and model trains
rec.roller-coaster	Roller coasters and other amusement park rides
rec.running	Running for enjoyment, sport, exercise, etc
rec.scouting	Scouting youth organizations worldwide
rec.scuba	Hobbyists interested in scuba diving
rec.skate	Ice skating and roller skating
rec.skiing	Snow skiing
rec.skydiving	Skydiving
rec.sport.baseball	Baseball
rec.sport.baseball.college	Baseball on the collegiate level
rec.sport.baseball.fantasy	Rotisserie (fantasy) baseball play
rec.sport.basketball.college	Basketball on the collegiate level
rec.sport.basketball.misc	General discussion about basketball
rec.sport.basketball.pro	Professional basketball
rec.sport.cricket	Cricket
rec.sport.cricket.scores	Scores from cricket matches (Moderated)
rec.sport.disc	Flying disc-based sports
rec.sport.fencing	All aspects of swordplay
rec.sport.football.australian	Australian (Rules) Football
rec.sport.football.canadian	Canadian football
rec.sport.football.college	American college football
rec.sport.football.misc	General discussion of American football
rec.sport.football.pro	American professional football
rec.sport.golf	Golf
rec.sport.hockey	Ice hockey
rec.sport.hockey.field	Field hockey
rec.sport.misc	Spectator sports
rec.sport.olympics	The Olympic Games
rec.sport.paintball	The survival game Paintball
rec.sport.pro-wrestling	Professional wrestling
rec.sport.rowing	Crew for competition or fitness
rec.sport.rugby	Rugby
rec.sport.soccer	Soccer (Association Football)
rec.sport.swimming	Training for and competing in swimming events
rec.sport.table-tennis	Ping Pong
rec.sport.tennis	Tennis
rec.sport.triathlon	Multi-event sports
rec.sport.volleyball	Volleyball
rec.sport.waterski	Waterskiing and related boat-towed activities
rec.travel	Traveling all over the world
rec.travel.air	Airline travel around the world
rec.travel.marketplace	Tickets and accommodations wanted and for sale
rec.video	Video and video components

rec.video.cable-tv	Technical and regulatory issues of cable television
rec.video.production	Making professional quality video productions
rec.video.releases	Prerecorded video releases, laserdisc and videotape
rec.video.satellite	Receiving video via satellite
rec.windsurfing	Wind surfing
rec.woodworking	Woodworking

SCI

sci.aeronautics	Aeronautics and related technology
sci.aeronautics.airliners	Airliner technology (Moderated)
sci.answers	Repository for periodic Usenet articles (Moderated)
sci.anthropology	All aspects of studying humankind
sci.aquaria	Scientifically oriented postings about aquaria
sci.archaeology	Studying antiquities of the world
sci.astro	Astronomy
sci.astro.fits	The Flexible Image Transport System
sci.astro.hubble	Hubble Space Telescope data (Moderated)
sci.astro.planetarium	Planetariums
sci.bio	Biology and related sciences
sci.bio.ecology	Ecological research
sci.bio.technology	Biotechnology
sci.chaos	Science of chaos
sci.chem	Chemistry and related sciences
sci.chem.organomet	Organometallic chemistry
sci.classics	Classical history, languages, art and more
sci.cognitive	Perception, memory, judgement and reasoning
sci.comp-aided	Computers as tools in scientific research
sci.cryonics	Biostasis, suspended animation, etc
sci.crypt	Data encryption and decryption
sci.data.formats	Modelling and storing scientific data
sci.econ	Economics
sci.econ.research	Economics research (Moderated)
sci.edu	Education
sci.electronics	Circuits, theory, electrons and discussions
sci.energy	Energy, science and technology
sci.energy.hydrogen	Hydrogen as an alternative fuel
sci.engr	Technical discussions about engineering tasks
sci.engr.advanced-tv	HDTV/DATV standards, formats, equipment, practices
sci.engr.biomed	Biomedical engineering
sci.engr.chem	Chemical engineering
sci.engr.civil	Civil engineering
sci.engr.control	The engineering of control systems
sci.engr.manufacturing	Manufacturing technology
sci.engr.mech	Mechanical engineering
sci.environment	Environment and ecology
sci.fractals	Objects of non-integral dimension and other chaos

sci.geo.fluids	Geophysical fluid dynamics
sci.geo.geology	Solid earth sciences
sci.geo.meteorology	Meteorology and related topics
sci.image.processing	Scientific image processing and analysis
sci.lang	Natural languages, communication, etc
sci.lang.japan	Japanese language, both spoken and written
sci.life-extension	Discussions about living longer
sci.logic	Mathematical logic, philosophical and computational aspects
sci.materials	Materials engineering
sci.math	Mathematics in general
sci.math.num-analysis	Numerical analysis
sci.math.research	Current mathematical research (Moderated)
sci.math.stat	Mathematics from a statistical viewpoint
sci.math.symbolic	Symbolic algebra
sci.med	Medicine, related products and regulations
sci.med.aids	AIDS and HIV Virus (Moderated)
sci.med.dentistry	Dentistry and teeth
sci.med.nutrition	Physiological aspects of diet and eating
sci.med.occupational	Occupational injuries
sci.med.pharmacy	Pharmacy
sci.med.physics	Physics in medical testing and care
sci.med.telemedicine	Clinical consulting through computer networks
sci.military	Science and the military (Moderated)
sci.misc	Short-lived discussions on subjects in the sciences
sci.nanotech	Self-reproducing molecular-size machines (Moderated)
sci.nonlinear	Chaotic and other nonlinear systems
sci.op-research	Operations research
sci.optics	Optics
sci.philosophy.meta	Metaphilosophy
sci.philosophy.tech	Technical philosophy math, science, logic, etc
sci.physics	Physics
sci.physics.accelerators	Particle accelerators
sci.physics.fusion	Fusion
sci.physics.research	Current physics research (Moderated)
sci.polymers	Polymer science
sci.psychology	Psychology
sci.psychology.digest	Psycoloquy Refereed Psychology Journal (Moderated)
sci.research	Research methods, funding, ethics, etc
sci.research.careers	Careers in scientific research
sci.skeptic	Skeptics discussing pseudo-science
sci.space	Space, space programs, space-related research, etc
sci.space.news	Space-related news items (Moderated)
sci.space.shuttle	Space shuttle and the STS program
sci.stat.consult	Statistical consulting
sci.stat.edu	Statistics education
sci.stat.math	Statistics from a mathematical viewpoint
sci.systems	Theory and application of systems science

sci.virtual-worlds	Modelling the universe (Moderated)
sci.virtual-worlds.apps	Virtual-worlds technology (Moderated)

SOC

soc.answers	Repository for periodic Usenet articles (Moderated)
soc.bi	Bisexuality
soc.college	College activities
soc.college.grad	Graduate schools
soc.college.gradinfo	Information about graduate schools
soc.college.teaching-asst	Teaching assistants in colleges and universities
soc.couples	Discussions for couples
soc.culture.afghanistan	Afghan society
soc.culture.african	Africa and things African
soc.culture.african.american	African-American issues
soc.culture.arabic	Technological and cultural issues (not politics)
soc.culture.argentina	Argentina
soc.culture.asean	Countries of the Association of S.E. Asian Nations
soc.culture.asian.american	Asian-Americans issues
soc.culture.australian	Australia
soc.culture.austria	Austria
soc.culture.baltics	The Baltic states
soc.culture.bangladesh	Bangladesh
soc.culture.bosna-herzgvna	Bosnia and Herzegovina
soc.culture.brazil	Brazil
soc.culture.british	Great Britain
soc.culture.bulgaria	Bulgaria
soc.culture.canada	Canada
soc.culture.caribbean	The Caribbean
soc.culture.celtic	Irish, Scottish, Breton, Cornish, Manx and Welsh
soc.culture.china	China and Chinese culture
soc.culture.croatia	Croatia
soc.culture.czecho-slovak	Bohemian, Slovak, Moravian and Silesian life
soc.culture.esperanto	The neutral international language Esperanto
soc.culture.europe	All-European society
soc.culture.filipino	The Filipino culture
soc.culture.french	France
soc.culture.german	Germany
soc.culture.greek	Greece
soc.culture.hongkong	Hong Kong
soc.culture.indian	India
soc.culture.indian.telugu	The Telugu people of India
soc.culture.indonesia	Indonesia
soc.culture.iranian	Iran and things Persian
soc.culture.italian	Italy
soc.culture.japan	Everything Japanese, except the Japanese language
soc.culture.jewish	Jewish culture and religion

`soc.culture.korean`	Korea
`soc.culture.laos`	Laos
`soc.culture.latin-america`	Latin America
`soc.culture.lebanon`	Lebanon
`soc.culture.maghreb`	Northwest Africa (Morrocco, Algeria, Tunis)
`soc.culture.magyar`	Hungary
`soc.culture.malaysia`	Malaysia
`soc.culture.mexican`	Mexico
`soc.culture.misc`	Discussion about other cultures
`soc.culture.native`	Aboriginal people around the world
`soc.culture.nepal`	Nepal
`soc.culture.netherlands`	The Netherlands and Belgium
`soc.culture.new-zealand`	New Zealand
`soc.culture.nordic`	Culture up north
`soc.culture.pakistan`	Pakistan
`soc.culture.peru`	Peru
`soc.culture.polish`	Poland
`soc.culture.portuguese`	Portugal
`soc.culture.romanian`	Romania and Moldavia people
`soc.culture.scientists`	Culture and scientists
`soc.culture.singapore`	Singapore
`soc.culture.soviet`	Russia and Soviet culture
`soc.culture.spain`	Spain
`soc.culture.sri-lanka`	Sri Lanka
`soc.culture.taiwan`	Taiwan
`soc.culture.tamil`	Tamil language, history and culture
`soc.culture.thai`	Thailand
`soc.culture.turkish`	Turkey
`soc.culture.ukrainian`	Ukrainian culture
`soc.culture.usa`	United States of America
`soc.culture.venezuela`	Venezuela
`soc.culture.vietnamese`	Vietnam
`soc.culture.yugoslavia`	The former Yugoslavia
`soc.feminism`	Feminism and feminist issues (Moderated)
`soc.history`	History
`soc.libraries.talk`	Libraries
`soc.men`	Men, their problems and relationships
`soc.misc`	Socially-oriented topics not in other groups
`soc.motss`	Homosexuality (members of the same sex)
`soc.net-people`	Announcements, requests, about people on the Net
`soc.penpals`	Penpals
`soc.politics`	Political problems, systems, solutions (Moderated)
`soc.politics.arms-d`	Arms discussion digest (Moderated)
`soc.religion.bahai`	The Baha'i Faith (Moderated)
`soc.religion.christian`	Christianity and related topics (Moderated)
`soc.religion.christian.bible-study`	The Holy Bible (Moderated)
`soc.religion.eastern`	Eastern religions (Moderated)

`soc.religion.islam`	The Islamic faith (Moderated)
`soc.religion.quaker`	The Religious Society of Friends (Quakers)
`soc.religion.shamanism`	Shamanism
`soc.rights.human`	Human rights and activism
`soc.roots`	Genealogy (tracing your roots)
`soc.singles`	Single people, their activities, etc
`soc.veterans`	Military veterans
`soc.women`	Women, their problems and relationships

TALK

`talk.abortion`	Discussions and arguments on abortion
`talk.answers`	Repository for periodic Usenet articles (Moderated)
`talk.bizarre`	The unusual, bizarre, curious and often stupid
`talk.environment`	The environment
`talk.origins`	Evolution versus creationism
`talk.philosophy.misc`	Philosophical musings on all topics
`talk.politics.animals`	The use and abuse of animals
`talk.politics.china`	Politics of China
`talk.politics.crypto`	Cryptography and government
`talk.politics.drugs`	Politics of drug issues
`talk.politics.guns`	Politics of firearm ownership
`talk.politics.medicine`	Politics of health care
`talk.politics.mideast`	Politics of the Middle East
`talk.politics.misc`	Political discussions and ravings of all kinds
`talk.politics.soviet`	Politics of the former Soviet Union
`talk.politics.space`	Non-technical issues affecting space exploration
`talk.politics.theory`	Theory of politics and political systems
`talk.rape`	Rape (not to be crossposted)
`talk.religion.misc`	Religious, ethical and moral discussions
`talk.religion.newage`	New Age religions and philosophies
`talk.rumors`	Rumors

U3B

`u3b.config`	3B distribution configuration
`u3b.misc`	AT&T 3B computers
`u3b.sources`	Free programs for AT&T 3B systems
`u3b.tech`	3B Technical discussions
`u3b.test`	Place to send test articles

VMSNET

`vmsnet.admin`	Managing VMS internals, MACRO-32, Bliss, etc
`vmsnet.alpha`	Alpha AXP architecture, systems, porting, etc
`vmsnet.announce`	General announcements of interest to all (Moderated)

vmsnet.announce.newusers	Orientation information for new users (Moderated)
vmsnet.databases.rdb	DEC's Rdb relational database
vmsnet.decus.journal	The DECUServe Journal (Moderated)
vmsnet.decus.lugs	DECUS Local User Groups and related issues
vmsnet.employment	Jobs sought and offered, employment related issues
vmsnet.infosystems.gopher	Gopher software for VMS
vmsnet.infosystems.misc	Infosystem software for VMS (Wais, WWW...)
vmsnet.internals	VMS internals, MACRO-32, Bliss, etc
vmsnet.mail.misc	Other electronic mail software
vmsnet.mail.mx	MX email system from RPI
vmsnet.mail.pmdf	PMDF email system
vmsnet.misc	General VMS topics not covered elsewhere
vmsnet.networks.desktop.misc	Other desktop integration software
vmsnet.networks.desktop.pathworks	DEC Pathworks desktop integration software
vmsnet.networks.management.decmcc	DECmcc and related software
vmsnet.networks.management.misc	Other network management software
vmsnet.networks.misc	General networking topics not covered elsewhere
vmsnet.networks.tcp-ip.cmu-tek	CMU-TEK TCP/IP package
vmsnet.networks.tcp-ip.misc	Other TCP/IP software for VMS
vmsnet.networks.tcp-ip.multinet	TGV's Multinet TCP/IP, gatewayed to info-multinet
vmsnet.networks.tcp-ip.tcpware	Process Software's TCPWARE TCP/IP software
vmsnet.networks.tcp-ip.ucx	DEC's VMS/Ultrix Connection, TCP/IP services for VMS
vmsnet.networks.tcp-ip.wintcp	The Wollongong Group's WIN-TCP TCP/IP software
vmsnet.pdp-11	PDP-11 hardware and software
vmsnet.sources	Free programs (no discussion) (Moderated)
vmsnet.sources.d	Discussion about and requests for free programs
vmsnet.sources.games	Recreational software
vmsnet.sysmgt	VMS system management
vmsnet.test	Place to send test articles
vmsnet.tpu	TPU language and applications
vmsnet.uucp	DECUS Uucp software
vmsnet.vms-posix	VMS Posix

Index

Main subject headings are shown in **bold**

*Main subject headings are shown in **bold***

*Main subject headings are shown in **bold***

*Main subject headings are shown in **bold***

*Main subject headings are shown in **bold***

*Main subject headings are shown in **bold***

*Main subject headings are shown in **bold***

*Main subject headings are shown in **bold***

*Main subject headings are shown in **bold***

*Main subject headings are shown in **bold***

*Main subject headings are shown in **bold***

*Main subject headings are shown in **bold***

*Main subject headings are shown in **bold***

*Main subject headings are shown in **bold***

*Main subject headings are shown in **bold***

*Main subject headings are shown in **bold***

*Main subject headings are shown in **bold***

*Main subject headings are shown in **bold***

*Main subject headings are shown in **bold***

*Main subject headings are shown in **bold***

Main subject headings are shown in **bold**

*Main subject headings are shown in **bold***

*Main subject headings are shown in **bold***

*Main subject headings are shown in **bold***

*Main subject headings are shown in **bold***

*Main subject headings are shown in **bold***